Robert Creeley, Edward Dorn, and Robert Duncan

a reference guide

A
Reference
Guide
to
Literature

Ronald Gottesman
Editor

Robert Creeley, Edward Dorn, and Robert Duncan

a reference guide

WILLARD FOX III

G.K.HALL&CO.
70 LINCOLN STREET, BOSTON, MASS.

Library of Congress Cataloging-in-Publication Data

Fox, Willard.
  Robert Creeley, Edward Dorn, and Robert Duncan.

  (A Reference guide to literature)
  Includes index.
  1. American poetry--20th century--History and
criticism--Bibliography. 2. Creeley, Robert, 1926-
--Bibliography. 3. Dorn, Edward--Bibliography.
4. Duncan, Robert Edward, 1919- --Bibliography.
I. Title. II. Series.
Z1231.P7F69 1988 [PS323.5] 016.811'54'09 88-24503
ISBN 0-8161-8604-9

This publication is printed on permanent/durable acid-free paper
MANUFACTURED IN THE UNITED STATES OF AMERICA

To the Memory of Robert Duncan

''I go gladly on into stages of pain, of aging,
of loss, of death, that belong to the passionate''

—*''What the Sonnet Means the Sonnet Means''*

Contents

Preface

This is a selective bibliography covering the period from 1944 to mid-1986.[1] The one hundred indexes, databases, bibliographies, catalogs, and other reference works consulted generated a source file of over 7,000 reviews, articles, books, theses, and dissertations. I examined nearly all of these items, rejecting material that did not mention the subject authors or that was inappropriate for a reference guide. This volume does not include:

1. Brief, nonsubstantive reviews. Such reviews, the largest category of rejected materials, are essential in charting the critical reception of a literary figure, but because this volume is intended as a reference guide, it includes only substantive reviews and reviews written by important literary figures.

2. Local items. Items from local newspapers are omitted because they usually have only a limited scholarly application. Substantive items from local publications that have a narrow scope, usually literary or artistic, and at least a regional readership, like San Francisco's <u>Poetry Flash</u>, are included.

3. Reviews of secondary works. Such reviews are excluded unless they provide new information or an original perspective on one of the subject authors.

4. Brief mentions. Books or articles that only briefly mention a subject author are excluded unless they provide information likely to be of interest to the scholar. In all cases, annotations for the latter begin with a statement as to their brevity.

5. Fiction and poetry. Creative material is excluded except when factual prose is intermixed with fictionalized material (as in

Creeley's <u>Presences</u>), in which case the factual portions are annotated.

6. Complete reprint information. The complete reprint history of every item is not charted in the bibliography.[2]

7. Blurbs. Because blurbs usually consist only of reprinted snippets from longer reviews, only substantive blurbs that reprint information from a difficult-to-locate source or that contain original material are included.[3]

8. Nonprint materials. Videotapes and audiotapes are not covered since most are not published and almost all are difficult to obtain.[4]

9. Instructors' guides. Instructor's guides are excluded because of their ephemeral nature.

The final volume contains annotations for approximately 1,700 reviews, review articles, articles, interviews, bibliographies, sections of books, books, dissertations, and theses from ten languages exclusive of English.[5] Besides theses, this volume includes the following types of items that are not typically covered in reference guides:

1. Articles and reviews in little magazines. Much of the history of modern and contemporary literature has been written in little magazines, noncommercial, literary periodicals with limited circulations and short runs. I have made a special effort to discover and include this material.[6]

2. Prefaces, reviews, articles, and books written by the subject authors as well as interviews with these authors. Such items are treated as secondary works when the subject author writes or speaks about his or her own life and work.[7] I recommend this approach to other writers of reference guides on the principle that what a writer says about his own life or work is at least as important as what others say.

3. Reprinted information. Since many items were originally published in obscure sources, the bibliography includes a great deal of selective reprint information. The original source and the most readily available reprint are always noted. In addition, I have attempted to collect all revisions as well as reprints of interest.[8]

If I have erred by any of the above criteria, I have tried to err on the side of inclusion.[9] Nine items, creating fourteen entries, were unavailable for annotation.[10] Asterisks precede their numbers, and their annotations note the situation and provide the sources for the citations. All items except one, RD1979.27, were annotated with the items in hand, not from abstracts. I have not attempted, however, to include the program notes and notes Duncan wrote for classes, workshops, and poetry readings (see D1 and D69-76 in RD1986.2).

After the introductory material, this volume contains four main sections, one for each of the poets (the running heads in these sections include the poets' initials), and an index. The annotated bibliography for each poet is preceded by a listing of that poet's book-length works. I have examined all listed works and have cited their titles in full.

The citations in the longer sections are given in the format of the University of Chicago Press's A Manual of Style,[11] with a few exceptions. I have placed quotation marks around Preface and Introduction if the sections are so titled. The language of non-English items is noted following the title of the cited item to avoid potential confusion. Citations of serials include full information on special issue.[12] The notation of passim, following the specific pagination dealing with the subject author, should be read "here and there elsewhere in the work," not "here and there within the pages given."[13]

I have tried to be extremely accurate in the citations, giving the fullest and most detailed information, because, due to the rarity of the sources, researchers may have to order many of the items through interlibrary loan. Citations provide full titles as well as subtitles, both of which occasionally change over the course of a few years. They list the information as it appears on the title page equivalent of the magazine unless fuller information was available elsewhere. When there is the possibility of confusion, the citation provides the city of origin in parentheses. Most of the magazines should be fairly well known to students of avant-garde contemporary American poetry, but if more information is needed, the researcher should check a reliable source on little magazines.[14]

I have occasionally added information in brackets to provide series information, to indicate transposed page numbers, to note conflicting information, to give "whole numbers" when a series varied between or gave two systems of notation, etc. Pagination of unpaginated material, provided in brackets, is calculated from the recto after the title page barring partial pagination. I have alphabetized Mac and Mc as a separate group prior to M and have included essays on a poet that are titled with his last name first prior to articles by that poet.

The length of the annotations is, generally, a reflection of the length and/or importance of the item annotated. Brief items begin with an announcement of their brevity. At the beginning of annotations, I have tried to include the date for items that are part of an occasion, such as interviews and discussions. In accordance with the publisher's guidelines, the unstated subject for all sentences is the document author's name.[15] Titles for the subject authors' creative works, where no confusion is possible, are given in a shortened form, usually omitting the subtitle. Titles and names for foreign works and authors, including transliterations,

are given in the form included in the <u>MLA International
Bibliography</u>. I have, however, distinguished between poems that are
treated as poems and poems treated as books.[16] I have tried to
allow the document authors to speak for themselves as much as
possible by relying upon quotations in the annotations. The
frequency of cross-referencing in the annotations is not meant to
distract but to aid the scholar who is trying to cover a certain
topic comprehensively,[17] to help the scholar find a reprinted item
whose original source is obscure, and to assist the scholar in
discovering the most recent or fullest version of a revised item.[18]

   The index is in four sections. There are three short indexes
covering the works of each of the primary authors, followed by a
lengthy author and subject index covering all three. These, like
the citations, are alphabetized in the letter-by-letter fashion, but
with <u>Mac</u> and <u>Mc</u> placed prior to <u>M</u>. In the three short indexes on
each poet's works, first lines used as titles or in addition to
titles are given within brackets. I have always used poem titles as
they appeared in the standard collections; variations are cross-
referenced. Occasionally a section of a poem is indexed when that
section could be read as a whole (as in Creeley's "Numbers" or
Duncan's "The Chimeras of Gérard de Nerval"); here, too, there is
adequate cross-referencing.

   It proved impossible, however, to list every poem that was
substantively discussed in annotations of lengthy works. Such
annotations will usually indicate that many poems from a given
volume were discussed. The scholar who wishes to see all of the
substantive treatments of a given poem, therefore, should check the
index under both the title of the poem and the title of the first
major volume in which it was collected.

   The last index, on document authors and subjects, is a
"projective index," containing a built-in thesaurus developed from
an awareness of the critical corpus. Since this index arises from
the terminology used by document authors,[19] it includes associated
terms to assure that a researcher will not miss related items.
Associated terms are also included to guide the scholar and,
perhaps, even stimulate research as interrelationships are
discovered and associations are followed. In addition there are a
number of "hub" terms (e.g., "animals," "artists," "the creative
process," "the female figure," "the media," "music," "mythological
figures," "techniques," etc.) that group associated terms and that
are cross-referenced with individual terms. The subject index does
not attempt to codify or categorize ideas or people, yet some
categorization is inevitable.[20] Although lengthy, the built-in
thesaurus is not intended to be comprehensive. I have deliberately
left out some possible associations,[21] and I am sure that I have
missed numerous others.

   I am certain that I have not found all the substantive items on
Creeley, Dorn, and Duncan. I solicit information on additional

Preface

material as well as information concerning the errors and failings in the present volume.

Notes

1. The volume also includes obvious and/or important items through the end of 1987

2. I especially ignored the Kraus and AMS reprints of little magazines, most of which are cataloged in libraries with regular serials. (I have, of course, examined these for original prefatory information.) I have also ignored Gale Research Co.'s Contemporary Literary Criticism and Dorothy Nyren Curley and Maurice Kramer's A Library of Literary Criticism, as well as Twentieth-Century American Literature, one of the hundreds of titles arising from Harold Bloom's frenetic "scholarly" activity. I found these sources undiscriminating in their choice of material and unselective in their excisions. In each case, the items included are readily available elsewhere, usually in more complete and exact form.

3   Scholars may have a difficult time finding blurbs since many libraries destroy dust jackets. They may need to visit or write a rare books room that would have the jacket sought. (I believe that the Poetry/Rare Books Collection at the State University of New York at Buffalo has every blurb listed here.)

4. Over the past twenty to thirty years, audio and video recorders have taped a wealth of important but uncollected information at public readings when writers, as they often do, talk about their lives and works. Libraries, audio-visual centers, and English and creative writing departments store the tapes, but there is no reference work that comprehensively accounts for them. Such a work, perhaps modeled upon American Literary Manuscripts, would greatly enhance the study of contemporary literature.

5. Dutch, French, German, Italian, Japanese, Norwegian, Polish, Portuguese, Rumanian, and Spanish. See index.

6. Scholars having difficulty locating these journals should consult New Serials Titles and the OCLC and RLIN library networks. My "The Archives: An Analysis of Little Magazine Collections in the United States and Canada," in American Literary Magazines: The Twentieth Century, ed. Edward Chielens (Westport, Conn.: Greenwood Press, forthcoming) and "Two Rooms: A History and Analysis of Little Magazine Collections at Buffalo, New York, and Madison, Wisconsin," Literary Research: A Journal of Scholarly Method and Technique 11, nos. 2-3 (Spring-Summer 1986):141-58, list collections and specify interlibrary loan and photocopying policies.

7. I have not covered items or annotated portions of included items that do not directly focus on the poets' lives or works. To gain a thorough knowledge of the poets' ideas about myth, education, or economics, for instance, the scholar must consult the relevant sources covered by primary bibliographies. Further, I have included information about the poets' personal reading only when the poets give this information in a biographical context.

8. Such as Aquila's unauthorized version of Duncan's "Towards an Open Universe" (RD1982.11) or Quixote's version of Dorn's "Nose from Newswhere" (ED1965.2).

9. One item, RD1984.26, makes no contribution to scholarship and was included only because of its length.

10. RC1970.2; 1974.3; 1975.2; 1981.26; ED1974.2; 1975,2; 1981.12; RD1968.8; 1969.24; 1974.27; 1975.10; 1978.31; 1979.27; 1981.19. Four of these, generating six entries (RC1975.2; ED1975.2; RD1968.8; 1969.24; 1975.10; 1978.31), were later published and are annotated without seeing the initial version. This, of course, is noted.

11. 12th ed. (Chicago and London: University of Chicago Press, 1969.)

12. Such information helps distinguish given issues, and occasionally isolated issues of journals are cataloged by special issue information in libraries. If the word issue was included in the special issue information, its initial letter will be capitalized; if not, it will begin in lower case.

13. A comma always precedes passim to indicate that it does not refer to the pagination noted.

14. The best recent information is contained in Peter Martin's "An Annotated Bibliography of Selected Little Magazines," in The Little Magazine in America: A Modern Documentary History, ed. Elliott Anderson and Mary Kinzie (Yonkers, N.Y.: Pushcart Press, 1978), pp. 666-750, and in Robert F. Roeming's Catalog of Little Magazines: A Collection in the Rare Book Room, Memorial Library, University of Wisconsin-Madison (Madison: University of Wisconsin Press, 1979), although the latter contains numerous errors. The databases accessed by OCLC and RLIN terminals will also help distinguish and locate magazines. American Literary Magazines: The Twentieth Century (Westport, Conn.: Greenwood Press), edited by Edward Chielens, is scheduled for publication in early 1989 and should contain useful information. Past issues of The International Directory of Little Magazines and Small Presses and Trace, a British little magazine, can be consulted with some profit, as can the standard indexes into little magazines (see section K in James L. Harner's Literary

Research Guide: A Guide to Reference Sources for the Study of Literatures in English and Related Topics [New York: Modern Language Association, forthcoming]).   For large collections of little magazines and their policies, see my two articles listed in note 6.

15. When the document author, however, is important to the annotation, his or her name is included as the subject.   This occurs frequently since many of the items are on Creeley, Dorn, or Duncan's relationship to or influence on a document author.

    In the case of unstated subjects, I have punctuated sentences as though the unstated subject were repeated.   Hence, there are commas prior to conjunctions between most predicates.

16. Thus, Dorn's "The North Atlantic Turbine" is The North Atlantic Turbine when the document author is treating it as a book.   This makes indexing more precise and aids the researcher who is only interested in a narrow treatment.

17. The annotation of Olson's "Against Wisdom as Such," for instance, is followed by references to Duncan's reactions to the essay and then by references to scholarly commentary on the essay and Duncan's response.   Although this clutters the annotation, it assures that the researcher will not miss important items dealing with this topic.

18. The interviews with Creeley by Lewis McAdams and Linda Welshimer Wagner (see RC1973.32, 47) are good examples of this.   I have tried to sort out such tangled webs for the scholar.

    The designation "Reprinted from" indicates that only a portion of the earlier item is reprinted.

19. The software used to create the raw index was BYU Concordance, Ver. 4.0 (Provo, Utah: Brigham Young University, 1986). Following item numbers (e.g., RC1984.3), keywords from the entire manuscript plus additional words (like "creative process") were typed onto an IBM compatible computer with WordPerfect Ver. 4.1 (Orem, Utah: Satellite Software International, 1985) software.   (Since two-word items would be broken apart by the program, names were included in hyphenated form, last name first; e.g. "abbott-keith.")   These files were converted to ASCII files and put through the several stages of BYU Concordance.   Added, unwanted punctuation had to be stripped from the finish files, and names and other terms had to be reestablished with correct capitalization and punctuation.   The thesaurus was keyed in by hand.

20. For example, "abstract expressionism" cross-references most of the individuals commonly referred to as abstract expressionists, but "New York poets" goes beyond the O'Hara-Berrigan-Ashbery school to include other poets who are to some extent associated with New York.

21. For example, even though some have referred to Irving Layton and Paul Carroll as Black Mountain poets, I have avoided such tenuous associations.

Acknowledgments

The debts one accumulates during the course of a lengthy research project become incalculable. One soon becomes aware, sadly, that they can never be truly repaid, but the realization that they can be acknowledged provides some consolation. Primarily, I am indebted to my teachers, fellow scholars, and colleagues. My largest debt is to Professor James L. Harner, now at Texas A & M University, who trained me, set me to this task, and thereafter offered encouragement and advice. The strengths of this work arise directly from his teaching and support, the faults from my wavering attention and impatience. Professors Frederick Eckman and Howard McCord brought my interest in these poets to an initial stage of maturity.

Professor Robert J. Bertholf, both personally and through his Robert Duncan: A Descriptive Bibliography (RD1986.2), has helped my work immeasurably. He has directed my attention to material I otherwise would have missed, allowed me to examine his personal books and magazines, responded to repeated and undoubtedly bothersome inquiries, and continually and generously provided advice. William McPheron, again both in person and through his fine bibliography, Charles Olson: The Critical Reception, 1941-1983: A Bibliographic Guide (New York and London: Garland Publishing, 1986), has also been an enormous help. The work of many other bibliographers, especially Mary Novik's work on Creeley (RC1973.37-38) supplemented with the work of Timothy D. Murray (RC1984.27) and George Butterick and David Streeter's work on Dorn (ED1973.1, 6), has greatly increased the comprehensiveness of this volume. (Butterick, who died 25 July 1988, has inspired scholarship on contemporary American poetry in many ways. He and his work will be missed.)

Curators, librarians, and their assistants, many of whom must remain anonymous, have greatly assisted my work. Robert Bertholf at the State University of New York at Buffalo, Deborah Reilly and

Acknowledgments

Barbara Richards at the University of Wisconsin at Madison, and Holly Hall, Timothy D. Murray, and Anne Posega at Washington University in St. Louis and their assistants (I remember especially Natalia Walter) have allowed me access to entire runs of journals; to boxes of manuscripts, letters, and catalogs; and to piles of rare small-press editions. They have also answered countless questions and informed me of additional data, often without my asking.

The reference librarians and graduate students in library science at Louisiana State University's Middleton Library deserve special thanks. I was pleasantly surprised to find that these librarians and students were some of the best-trained and knowledgeable professionals with whom I had ever worked. Much of my other reading for this volume took place at Dupré Library on the campus of the University of Southwestern Louisiana. I thank the entire staff, all of whom helped me at one time or another. I especially thank Anna Jane Marks for her herculean efforts in the interlibrary loan office. Beth Holly and Karen S. Bailey, both in acquisitions, cheerfully and tirelessly searched for and ordered rare and out-of-print small-press books on my behalf. Barbara Flynn helped answer some of my more difficult questions and efficiently ran data-base searches for me. Jeanie Gros in circulations, at her own initiation, went beyond the call of duty on my behalf. I also extend my gratitude to librarians around the country as well as in Canada, Great Britain, Australia, and Europe who responded to my direct appeals for material and information. Many have done far more than their jobs require.

I also wish to thank those who helped me with translations. I want to especially thank Mrs. Jacqueline Voorhies, wife of Dr. Vernon Voorhies, from New Iberia, Louisiana, who struggled the better part of a day translating Rumanian, a language she had not spoken since escaping from her native country as an adolescent. I also extend my gratitude to Professor Kohichi Sakaniwa who wrote out beautifully meticulous translations from the Japanese. Professor James Anderson, a colleague and friend, provided various translations cheerfully and immediately (but everyone is coming to expect this sort of thing from him). I also want to thank Brother Richard Arnandez, F.S.C., and Ines Lormand for their help and expertise.

I especially want to thank the chairman of the University of Southwestern Louisiana's English Department, Professor Albert W. Fields, who provided support during the initial, crucial, period of my research. This support was kindly continued by his successor, Professor Doris Meriwether. Joan L. Fields graciously provided special assistance to my project. Professor Carl Schaffer, now at the University of Scranton, attempted to look up material for me at New York Public Library and provided continual friendship, advice, and support. Professor Herb Fackler, another friend and colleague, generously allowed me access to his materials. Others in the department provided support and friendship, for which they have my

Acknowledgments

continuing gratitude. Two graduate students deserve mention. Anthony Fonseca cheerfully and capably assisted me in proofreading the text and in compiling the index, both thankless tasks. Mark Draper provided enormous help with the index, allowing me the use of his computer and tirelessly struggling to make an indexing program work on my material. The resultant index is the proof of his efforts.

I wish to also thank the many scholars and others who responded to my direct or published requests for assistance. Ms. Tandy Sturgeon evaluated some of my work on Dorn at an early stage and provided me with additional references. Both she and her husband, John Wolff, proved interesting and intelligent companions when I was on the road. The gracious assistance of many others was always gratifying. George Bowering, Pauline Butling, George Butterick, Hugh Fox, Stephen Fredman, Kevin Killian, Leverette T. Smith, Jr., and Harriet Zinnes come to mind immediately, but there were many others in the United States, Canada, and England who assisted me. My thanks to all.

A few bookstores, especially Talking Leaves in Buffalo, New York, provided help beyond financial compensation. I wish to also thank the members of Rochdale International Cooperative House in Madison, Wisconsin, for allowing me to share their home for an enlivening few weeks. The housing offices at Washington University, the University of Wisconsin at Madison, and the University of New York at Buffalo have also been helpful.

I thank the University of Southwestern Louisiana for providing me material assistance through a summer sabbatical for 1985, affording me the time for research on this and other projects by granting me release time, and providing me a graduate student for the Spring 1988 semester as a research assistant. It must be said that the University did this during a period of severe budgetary cutbacks. My gratitude, also, goes to the National Endowment for the Humanities for a Travel to Collections Grant (N.E.H. reference log no. RY-20528-84).

Last but not least, I must thank my wife, Cindi, my three children, Heather Ann, Bessie Lee, and Benjamin Ezra, and my parents, Dorothy and Bill, for their extraordinary patience and forbearance.

Introduction

Although Robert Creeley, Edward Dorn, and Robert Duncan are extremely diverse writers, they are brought together here because of their historical affiliations as well as their shared sources, critical audience and, to a certain extent, poetics. Historically they are associated with Black Mountain College. They are, in fact, the three most important poets who are accurately associated with the college after Charles Olson, on whom a bibliographic guide already exists.[1] Creeley has been almost exclusively associated with Black Mountain poetry, but Duncan has also been associated with the San Francisco Renaissance and Dorn with western writers. The Black Mountain label, however, has been the most enduring for each, which is in some ways appropriate, since each poet acknowledges the importance of Olson, rector of Black Mountain from 1951 or 1952 to 1956, to his life and work.

For Duncan, Olson's influence began after the younger poet had already made significant advances toward a personal poetic, a poetic that re-visions the romantic tradition in modern contexts. His introduction to Olson was nonetheless a revelation, an affirmation of his modernist inheritance charged with the energies and insights of the nascent postmodern poetics of Olson's "Projective Verse."[2] This essay helped redirect Duncan's attention to the emerging form of a poem realized through an alertness to its activities and a readiness to follow them. Further, when Duncan's romantic Neoplatonism, even as it became tempered with a sense of an evolving cosmos, met Olson's call in "Against Wisdom as Such" (RD1954.2) for an understanding-in-process that is not separable from a man or his activity, an ongoing dialectic was created that reverberated through and informed Duncan's poetry from the mid-1950s to the last.[3]

Although their correspondence demonstrates that Creeley was an important voice to Olson, continually realigning and reaffirming the older man's developing poetics and poetry, Olson was surely a guide for Creeley from nearly the beginning of the younger poet's artistic career. Later a symbol of inward energies and directions for his readers, Creeley was to Olson "the Figure of Outward,"[4] in part because of his objectification of the self that was "total[ly] IN" (RC1951.4) his work during the creative process. Olson nurtured and supported this artistic insistence, providing Creeley a theoretical and philosophical basis, one opposed to the separations that arise from the humanistic egotism of western philosophy as well as opposed to the staid and conservative liberalism of the prevailing literary establishment.

For Dorn, Olson was Maximus, the man, master to his pupil (ED1986.4). Olson surely influenced Dorn's views on power and economics as well as his "ideational discourse" (ED1975.7), or more accurately, gave permission, in Duncan's sense of the term, for Dorn's use of a discursive and analytic lyric. But Olson's real impact lies elsewhere: in his continual, if often implicit, emphasis on serious attention as a moral responsibility; in his disdain for the western sense of history as a set of temporal cause-and-effect progressions and isolated facts outside of personal context, the past as death or, worse, premise; in his belief that the activity of digging deeply down into a single locale, into the geography as lived,[5] is a significant undertaking in the work of one's own life; in his awareness that he who would come to the study of man with statistical methodology, begins at falsehood; and, as always, in his insistence that the field of knowledge is the man, his uses and activities.[6] All these continue to inform Dorn's poetic.

These three poets, then, share both the historical circumstance of Black Mountain College, stimulating the labeling frenzy of literary critics, and an important human connection, a source redirecting, challenging, supporting, opening. They have at least one more quality in common, one less exact and less prone to literary inquiry, but one that must be taken into account prior to any analysis that hopes to achieve a thorough and solid understanding of their work. Set into the critical foundation must be the realization that the work of these poets has a direct and intimate connection with their lives. For them, poetry is an activity, an experience, not a reflection upon experience. Although the terms may vary--and they certainly do shift during the course of a life's work--for Creeley, poetry is an act of definition and measure; for Dorn, an act of intellection; and for Duncan, an act of participation, often ritualistic.[7] To write what they already know, axiom for creative writing faculties, would be of no use to them and would belie their emphasis on the intensity and fullness of a life lived. Each of these poets seeks to explore, to discover, with the poem acting as an instrument of investigation or, better, as a territory in which the poetic activity becomes an act of self-creation in process as the self engages the energies and otherness of the world. Writing becomes an extension and continual reification of living, a part of experience itself. For the reader, the poem is not only the trail, the tracks left from the engagement, but an invitation and challenge to participate in the energies of the poem.

These are not easy poets. Their difficulty arises in part from the connection between their lives and works, their sense of poetry as an activity. Their work not only calls for the reader's involvement and active attention, but also demands a willingness to learn the languages of the poem. Understanding the lexicon of these languages goes beyond identifying a poem's theological, historical, mythological, literary, scientific, and/or personal allusions to an awareness of the poet's world of knowledge. The reader of these poets must attend to religion, including Christianity, the kabbalah, the Cao Dai Cult, etc.; social, cultural, and economic history, including the movement and displacement of populations and current political history; myth and the theories of myth, not limited to myth in the western tradition; cognitive theories and theories about the functions of the brain, including neurology, the evolution of mental functions, and information processing; linguistics; philosophy; science and scientific theory, including theories of biology and physics; architecture; literary tradition, including the work of Catullus, Mawlānā Jalāl al-Dīn Rūmī, Dante, Thomas Campion, George Herbert, Blake, Wordsworth, Whitman, Pound, W.C. Williams, D.H. Lawrence, H.D., Hart Crane, Zukofsky, Bunting, etc. Further, understanding the language requires an attention to the shifting semantics of the poem, often due to the active syntax of its attentions. This includes, but is not limited to, the lexical and syntactic ambiguities created by word choice, word play, and lineation, especially line breaks, that a number of critics have noted.[8] Since these poets are highly intelligent and inquisitive, and since the interests of their lives are those of their work, they bring multiple fields of engagement to their poetry. They believe in active possibilities and potential correspondences between these realms, between, for instance, the spiritual and the economic, the political and the intimate, the scientific and the religious, the mythic and the interpersonal. To understand the languages of their poetry, then, is also to follow as these possibilities and correspondences enter at many points, creating dynamic resonances within a poem and between poems and insisting upon an active poetic presence. At these points, ideas move, vectors jump toward other ideas, toward territories of thought and being, and toward further language acts and potential acts. These poets, especially Creeley and Duncan, rarely choose and follow a single possibility, letting the remainder dangle and atrophy; they maintain and often add to the possibilities as the poem progresses, until it concludes with the resonance of maximum possibility.[9]

These accumulations of multiple possibilities and correspondences are everywhere dynamic and do not cancel the linear temporality of their poems, as a few critics contend. To view these poets in their poetry as objects in a static, physical field is misguided. The poem should not be read in a different way than it was written: start to finish, temporally, often quite literally in the time that it physically took to write it--that is, spontaneously and with little or no substantive revision. These poets know that their medium is temporal and linear, if not progressive, as are their lives, and they are present in the poems as in their lives, actively and intensely. The poems need not resonate outside the field of their encounter in some time out of time or place beyond.

Not one of the three seeks to create the masterwork, the eternal and universal poem that, as a polished, finished creation, may seem beautiful, even stunning, but is not, ultimately, useful for either the poet or the audience. At least they feel that it is not worth sacrificing their lives, their multiple fields of engagement, for a cultural artifact, an egg worthy of an emperor. Therefore each, at different times and in somewhat different ways, seeks to disrupt the learned ways of the poem, especially what Creeley calls the "habits of articulation" (RC1968.5), facile, aesthetic ruts. They disturbed their own progress, arguing against success when success meant the endless replication of previously mastered performances. Dorn continually changed focus and methodology; Duncan often disrupted the poem at hand as he disrupted his development in the early 1950s;[10] and Creeley sought, after For Love, to bring the conditions of his life closer and closer to the creative process and to ignore "some final code of significance" (RC1968.5).

In spite of all of the above historical, theoretical, and personal similarities, and in spite of affiliations and areas of mutual admiration, each of these three poets is extremely different from the others. Each has his own intensities and maintains his own proper and improper confusions. From the typography alone, no one would mistake a Creeley poem for a Duncan poem, or a Duncan poem for a Dorn poem.[11]

Creeley's poem is, typically, one of definition and measure, focusing early on intimate relationships and/or internal spaces and lately on the sufficiencies of man's experience in the world and the means of existence within language, memory, and love. Throughout, Creeley has never lost sight of the requirement that his poetry and prose record and examine the slightest seismic registration of human emotional response, with himself as both observer and object. Although Duncan is surely right when he claims Creeley's poems have subjects (RC1978.37), Joe Sheffler is also correct when he writes "Creeley's poems do not engage subjects as exterior categories" (RC1971.21). The subject is as experienced, and as such it is on the page during the creative process. Thus, it seems the canonization of Creeley as an early saint of the nonreferential L=A=N=G=U=A=G=E school of poetry is overdrawn. Although Creeley has made numerous statements about certain poets and about signification that have given the L=A=N=G=U=A=G=E poets encouragement, and although the state to which Creeley refers in his poems does not necessarily exist prior to his writing, his poetry is expressionist, if creationist and presentational, in design and practice and, as such, closely allied to the abstract expressionism of the forties and fifties.

Such expression is both private in orientation and public by definition, but it rarely entertains overt political or social statement.[12] Creeley notes, however, that as a poet he has exercised his political responsibility by being true to what he "felt to be existent in the world and demonstrat[ing] its reality as best" as he was able (RC1965.24).

Dorn's poetry, at least his early work, does "engage subjects as exterior categories," and his subjects are much more explicitly social and political: the disposition and treatment of the poor and dispossessed, the nature of power, the removal of public responsibility, the displacement of populations, the interaction of man and the environment, the dislocations of mind and matter caused by mercantilism, the mutations of the public psyche and conscience, etc. But, like Creeley's, Dorn's emotional reaction is central in his early poems. The emotional response, in fact, not only brings these exteriors into the poem, but propels, focuses, and validates the poem's evolving statement.

During the publication of the Gunslinger books from 1968 to 1975, the emotional response dissipated as the subjective lyric ego was systematically disinherited.[13] By the time Slinger was published, the ego had been subsumed by a communal perspective--one without the traditional lyric emotional responses, but not without contempt, analysis, intelligence, and humor. Dorn even claims that in contemporary society "the ego is pretty obviously dead" and finds, only partially in jest, that "everybody's everybody else" (ED1974.8), probably in the sense that individual identity, at least as held by everyone save the individual, has been largely assimilated into the cultural collective, especially as driven by the mass media.[14]

As the explicitly individual perspective has dissipated and the traditional lyric response has been replaced, Dorn's audience has had to acquire new abilities. In his work of the late 1970s, beyond which few critics hazard, Dorn projects poetic statements in juxtaposed, sometimes intersecting, planes. But he is not engaged solely in juxtaposition.[15] The increasingly wide synapse between these statements, ideas, meditations, and pronouncements calls upon the reader to jump the gap, to actively discover the historical, cultural, logical, and/or comic connectives. In shorter poems, often of a single statement, the reader is called upon to create or re-create a social or intellectual context in which to locate the isolated language act.

The work of Duncan is the most difficult of the three in terms of its range of reference and in terms of its organic fusion of correspondences, allusions, and various musics. Believing in the inevitable and discernable harmony, or "rime," of all things within an evolving cosmos generated and continuously propelled by the forces of strife and Eros, Duncan allowed dynamic and often contending correspondences and contradictions to enter the kinetic field of his poetry as he followed the bipartite dictates of the poem: the language, including the syntax and the "tone-leading of vowels," and the sense, the associational, often playful, processes of the mind, the same trail of associations, based on eighteenth-century Scottish philosophy and psychology, feigned by Coleridge in his conversation poems and, in turn, by Wordsworth in "Lines Composed a Few Miles above Tintern Abbey." No other contemporary poet, in fact, has so placed his life and talents in the service of the art, in the service of that which Duncan referred to as "Poetry" or "the Grand Collage."

Further, no poet since Yeats has so brilliantly and continuously devoted himself to the life of the book. Duncan's five major collections since 1960 have reaffirmed and recast the lyric tradition that runs through the work of Baudelaire, Yeats, W.C. Williams, Olson, Creeley and, lately, Ashbery. This tradition, which might best be termed that of the "lyric volume," envisions the book as a whole, a body, not merely a retrospective collection of lyrics from a given period or even a collection with a common set of themes, figures, or motifs. Rather, a work within this tradition is created as a whole work of art, an entity with its own life, a volume embodied.[16] Duncan has successfully created and awaited the creation of individual poems toward such volumes for the past twenty-eight years and has probably written more lyric volumes than any other poet.[17] The challenge for Duncan's critics in terms of this tradition is to realize new notions of wholeness and structure that are not necessarily dependent upon narrative models but which do not lose sight of the linearity of Duncan's work.[18] At the same time, critics must attempt a reading of Duncan's work as an interlocking whole, at least since the advent of his serial, or sequence, poems in The Opening of the Field.

Despite the large number of reviews, articles, interviews, theses, dissertations, and books listed in this volume, the real work on Creeley, Dorn, and Duncan has barely begun. Thorough biographical work on the three poets either does not exist or is seriously outdated. The most complete biography of Creeley (contained in RC1973.38) is sketchy and covers his life only through the mid-1950s. Duncan's biography (RD1983.13), more thorough if occasionally inaccurate, covers his life only to 1950. No real biographical work has been done on Dorn.[19] Further, there is up-to-date bibliographical work only on Duncan. Robert Bertholf's bibliography (RD1986.2) and this volume should prove adequate for the near future, but new primary work is already underway in the form of a Collected Works and the secondary work seems to be expanding geometrically. The last primary bibliography of note on Creeley (RC1973.37) is seriously outdated, difficult to use, and not descriptive, and the Dorn bibliography (ED1973.6) only covers up until 1972.

New approaches need to be realized and attempted to do justice to the work of the three poets.[20] Each of them came of artistic age in a literary climate dominated by the New Criticism, and each found himself in direct opposition to this objectifying, conservative, academic stance that would surgically remove the poem from the poet's life, age, and audience. Their poetry, as maintained above, is too much a direct extension of their lives to expect a New Critical stance to be truly viable. Even hybrid versions of this stance that fall too close to the parent tree are likely to be of little real use.

Many critics included in his volume have realized this and have attempted to add a dimension of subjectivity to their inherited critical perspective. The spontaneous analysis and impressionism of Sherman Paul (see especially RC1978.61; 1981.24; ED1981.11; RD1981.18), giving rise to the less impressive "serial essay" of Carl Daniel Esbjorson (RD1985.25); the Heideggerian agenda and deconstructionism of William V. Spanos (see especially RC1978.67; 1980.32); the ta'wil or "visionary exegesis" of the poet George Quasha (RD1980.27); the "grammetrical reading" of Enikö Bollobás (RD1983.1; 1986.3); and the "hypocritical approach" of David Willbern (RD1983.37) are all attempts to include the subjectivity of the critic or to approach the work from a stance other than the New Critical. Although each is provoking, each fails to one extent or another. Occasionally this failure is because of the ardency or insularity of the perspective, but it is also occasionally because of the fact that the critic did not fully engage the poem at all points of him or herself, as Olson would do if he were a critic, or the fact that the critic did not, as Creeley might, objectify his or her subjectivity so that the personal reactions would not be self-indulgent but would be of ready use to his or her audience. Some of the most stimulating criticism has been heavily philosophical, aesthetic, or simply but thoughtfully negative. The work of Charles Altieri, Jerome Mazzaro, Eric Mottram, Cary Nelson, William V. Spanos, Geoffrey Thurley, and Andrew Kingsley Weatherhead, to name a few, should prove provoking to the fertile critical imagination. Comments by the poet himself, of course, as well as observations by fellow poets, often contain the seeds of new understandings and should not be dismissed with a paternalistic nod.

In terms of specific issues, much remains to be done. Besides the ideas imbedded in the preceding portions of the introduction,[21] ideas can be found and, with the aid of cross-referencing, followed throughout the index. Specifically, much more work need to be done on the techniques of each poet. Duncan's rhymes, spacing, and lineation, as well as his method of following vowel sounds and the mind's associational processes, deserve far greater attention. Creeley's simplistic surfaces and sudden dimensions, his use of rhyme,[22] and his reinvention of the poetic line have been briefly studied, but never systemically examined. Dorn's technical skill has been almost totally ignored.[23] Much more work needs done in the area of Creeley and Duncan's relationship to music and art.[24] Further, the role of intention in the work of Creeley and Duncan needs exploration in light of the emerging form of the poem.[25]

Work that should consider, but not be limited to, these poets includes work on the writing of the volume as a whole, what I have here termed the "lyric volume"; on the titling of poems; on the beginning of poems;[26] on the role of myth in contemporary poetry; on the spontaneity and revision of poetry; on the poet's awareness of his or her audience; etc. Again, it is hoped that the relative thoroughness of the index will both stimulate research and guarantee that Creeley, Dorn, and Duncan are considered for inclusion in general critical works, especially those covering the modern and contemporary period. They are, indeed, central figures of the period and deserve the highest level of attention, the same level that they have brought to their lives and work.

Notes

1. William McPheron, <u>Charles Oldon: The Critical Reception, 1941-1983: A Bibliographic Guide</u> (New York and London: Garland Publishing, 1986).

2. <u>Poetry New York</u> 3 (1950):13-22

3. But one cannot have, simply, a dialectic with Olson, and this arises from a simple but important fact, one that makes him attractive to all three poets in question. One must meet the man head-on, at all points, since his arguments are not separable, not single; each point exists within a body of arguments, ideas, and enthusiasms with relationships that will not suffer a single argument down an isolated draw. The attraction becomes obvious: the man is the argument, and meeting him head-on, the only way, an act of both criticism and creation.

4. In his dedication to <u>The Maximus Poems</u>, Jargon, 24 (New York: Jargon; Corinth Books, 1960).

5. By a native population, say, during or after its effectual exile or by those surrounded by the drone of the beautiful if vacuous daughter, the media, Medea, of a terrible culture.

6. Olson encapsuled most of the above ideas for Dorn in 1964.1.

7. To explore these ideas and others concerning art as an activity, an act of life, see the Author and Subject Index under "creative process."

8. Is Duncan's owl an only child in "An Owl Is an Only Bird of
    Poetry," or the only bird? Does the cross leave in the first
    line and, if so, like a tree or like a man from a room? Or are
    the leaves crossed? In "My Mother Would Be a Falconress," how
    would she be? In the imagination or through her will? Is the
    "treading" at her wrist in the second line sexual or the actual
    and regular pulse--a beginning of the blood motifs that resonate
    throughout the poem?
       What, in fact, is "hard going to the door" in Creeley's "The
    Door ['It is hard going to the door']"? And is it "hard going"
    or a difficult decision? What is the "it" that burdens the lady
    of "Lady Bird"? The desire for happiness, creating a past in
    the present with such a desire's implicit stasis? And what does
    the poem have to do with Charlie Parker, if anything?
       This idea may be less true for Dorn, but still the questions
    arise from the beginning of many of his poems. Is the air
    natural or a song in his "The Air of June Sings"? In his "From
    Gloucester Out," does "memory for me is nothing / there ever
    was" mean memory is nothing or that it cannot match reality?
    Or, as in "nothing there ever was," does it suggest the
    fragility of reality beyond man's interaction, in this case with
    memory, and thus, is the initial statement in the poem that
    memory and its magnifications are truer than the event itself?
    Or, better, another event of a higher order because magnified by
    more human interaction?

9. Dorn, more typically, makes a statement with an awareness of
    connections and then elaborates on the statement. In his
    earlier work, an emotional complex governed or generated the
    poem; in his later work an intellectual and/or linguistic
    context governs. His footnotes in his later work do tend,
    properly, to sheer off from the poem at hand, but they do not
    atrophy.

10. Duncan's refusals to publish a collection for over fifteen years
    from 1968 to 1984 might also arise form this will toward
    disruption.

11. And only rarely could a Creeley poem be mistaken for a Dorn
    poem.

12. As Creeley noted in RC1973.23, "America" and "The Sign Board"
    may be his only political poems. By stretching the definition,
    we might include the learned responses to women given dramatic
    enactment in "Mabel: A Story" as socially oriented.

13. Even in <u>Twenty-Four Love Songs</u> and <u>Manchester Square</u>, the ego
    has become increasingly displaced from the center.

14. Alan Golding's caution that "Dorn seeks to revise rather than
    destroy notions of person" (ED1987.2) deserves consideration.
    Although this does not necessarily preclude the above, it does

exist in apposition to it, an apposition which might generate a fruitful field for critical examination.

15. As he writes in "Correct usages of some words widely misused or abused in modern conversation & poetry," "<u>Juxtaposition</u> is ok if you can't do anything else."

16. The works I would, at this stage, list as central to the tradition include Baudelaire's <u>Les Fleurs du mal</u>; Yeats's <u>Responsibilities</u> and <u>The Tower</u>; W.C. Williams's <u>Spring and All</u>; Olson's <u>The Distances</u>; Creeley's <u>For Love</u>; Whitman's <u>Leaves of Grass</u>; and Ashbery's <u>The Tennis Court Oath</u> and <u>Rivers and Mountains</u>. Michael Palmer and Leslie Scalapino may be two younger American poets engaged in this activity at present. The collections by Duncan that I include are, of course, <u>The Opening of the Field</u>, <u>Roots and Branches</u>, <u>Bending the Bow</u>, <u>Ground Work: Before the War</u>, and <u>Ground Work II: In the Dark</u>.
     In fiction a parallel might be found in Joyce's <u>Dubliners</u>, Sherwood Anderson's <u>Winesburg, Ohio</u>, Jean Toomer's <u>Cane</u>, and Hemingway's <u>In Our Time</u>. In the case of the volumes of stories, the collections are held together by more than similar settings, recurring characters, and underlying narrative threads. In both the volumes of poetry and short stories, there is commonly a disruption of the text in practice if not by definition.
     Carl Schaffer, friend and colleague, was instrumental in developing this insight as regards the fiction writers. I also discussed this concept with Robert Bertholf, to my profit.

17. Unless we take Dickinson's fascicles to be lyric volumes in miniature. There is still, however, considerable critical debate about the nature and coherence of these fascicles.

18. Hazard Adams's recent "constitutive" reading of Yeats's <u>The Wind among the Reeds</u> as a "movement in the state of mind of the main character," a "fictive figure who eventually names himself Yeats," ("Constituting Yeats's Poems as a Book," in <u>Yeats: Annual of Critical and Textual Studies</u>, vol. 4, ed. Richard J. Finneran, Studies in Modern Literature, ed. A. Walton Litz, no. 61 [Ann Arbor: UMI Research Press, 1986], p. 1) is indicative of contemporary scholarship's unwillingness to posit ideas of wholeness and structure beyond the narrative.

19. This may be due to the fact that Dorn himself rarely speaks about his past. He is especially reticent concerning his childhood and adolescence.

20. This statement, of course, should not be limited to the work of Creeley, Dorn, and Duncan but applies to most experimental postmodern poets, especially David Antin, John Ashbery, Charles Bernstein, Ted Berrigan, Paul Blackburn, Clark Coolidge, Larry Eigner, Allen Ginsberg, Robert Kelly, Jackson Mac Low, Frank O'Hara, Charles Olson, Joel Oppenheimer, Jack Spicer, Michael

Palmer, Philip Whalen, and John Wieners. It may be appropriately extended to modern poets whose later work is often a direct outgrowth of their lives, such as W.C. Williams and Ezra Pound.

21. In this introduction, I have attempted to emphasize ideas that have been either neglected or understudied and that deserve detailed critical attention (e.g., the dialectic between Duncan's Neoplatonism and his reverent attention to Olson's "Against Wisdom as Such"; Creeley as both a subjective and objective poet; Dorn's sense of history; the fact that all three poets engage in poetry as an activity, an intimate part of their lives, and the impact that this realization has upon their technique, responsibility to the poem at hand, sense of the audience, etc.).

22. Creeley often expresses dismay over the inability of some in his audiences to hear rhyme (e.g., RC1974.5). Technically, his use of exact rhyme is extremely subtle and his use of off- and slant-rhyme matches the sophistication of Dickinson.

23. Dorn's early statement that he uses the line as a "clot of phrase" (ED1963.2) seems to have thrown critics off of his trail as concerns his technique. This might be desired by Dorn, but an attention to his verse reveals a considerable technical ability, especially as concerns lineation and rhyme.

24. Fortunately, Kevin Power has lain a firm foundation for the future study of Creeley and Duncan's artistic awareness. Unfortunately, no general work has yet been done on either poet's relationship to music, although the form and rhythm of isolated poems have been related to musical structures with some profit. (It is surprising that no critic has yet really sat down and listened to Charlie Parker prior to writing a thorough analysis of Creeley's work of the 1950s.)

25. And this probably also applies to the emerging form of the volume.

26. Why has there not yet been a <u>Poetic Inception: A Study of How Poems Begin</u>?

Robert Creeley

Major Works by Robert Creeley

1952   Le Fou. Columbus, Ohio: Golden Goose Press.

1953   The Immoral Proposition. Jargon, no. 8. Karlsruhe-Durlach, Germany and Highlands, N.C.: Jonathan Williams, Publisher.

        The Kind of Act Of. Palma de Mallorca, Spain: Divers Press.

1954   The Gold Diggers. Palma de Mallorca, Spain: Divers Press.

        A Snarling Garland of Xmas Verses. [Palma de Mallorca, Spain: Divers Press].

1955   All That is Lovely in Men. Jargon, no. 10. Asheville, N.C.: Jonathan Williams.

1956   If You. Poems and Pictures, no. 8. San Francisco: Porpoise Bookshop.

1957   The Whip. Worcester, Worcestershire, England: Migrant Books.

1959   A Form of Women: Poems by Robert Creeley. Jargon, no. 33. Highlands, N.C.: Jargon Books in association with Corinth Books.

        Four Poems from "A Form of Women." New York: Privately printed for the Friends of the Eighth Street Bookshop.

1962   For Love: Poems, 1950-1960. New York: Charles Scribner's Sons.

1963   The Island. New York: Charles Scribner's Sons.

1964   The Island. London: John Calder.

        Mister Blue: Sechzehn Geschichten. Translated by Klaus Reichert. Frankfurt: Insel Verlag.

1965   "The Gold Diggers" and Other Stories. New York: Charles Scribner's Sons; London: John Calder.

       Die Insel. Translated by Ernst Jandl. Frankfurt: Insel.

1966   About Women. Los Angeles: Gemini.

       "De Goudgravers" en andere Verhalen. Translated by Jan Donkers. Amsterdam: Polak & Van Gennep.

       Poems, 1950-1965. London: Calder & Boyars.

1967   "El Amante" y otros cuentos. Translated by Alfonso Esparza. Mexico City: Editoria Letras.

       The Charm: Robert Creeley, Early and Uncollected Poems. Mt. Horeb, Wis.: Perishable Press.

       Gedichte. Translated by Klaus Reichert. Frankfurt: Suhrkamp Verlag.

       Robert Creeley Reads. [Book & phonograph record.] London: Turret Books; Calder & Boyars.

       Words. New York: Charles Scribner's Sons.

1968   "Contexts of Poetry." Audit 5, no. 1 (Spring).

       "Divisions" and Other Early Poems. [Mt. Horeb, Wis.]: Perishable Press.

       The Finger. Los Angeles: Black Sparrow Press.

       5 Numbers. New York: Poets Press.

       Numbers. With Robert Indiana. Stuttgart: Edition Domberger; Düsseldorf: Galerie Schmela.

       Pieces. Los Angeles: Black Sparrow Press.

1969   The Charm: Early and Uncollected Poems. Writing, no. 23. San Francisco: Four Seasons Foundation.

       Mazatlan: Sea. [San Francisco]: Poets Press.

       Pieces. New York: Charles Scribner's Sons.

       A Wall. New York: Bouwerie Editions; Stuttgart: Edition Domberger.

1970   As Now It Would Be Snow: A Christmas Greeting from the Black Sparrow Press. Los Angeles: Black Sparrow Press.

Major Works by Robert Creeley

The Finger: Poems, 1966-1969. London: Calder & Boyars.

In London. Bolinas, Calif.: Angel Hair Books.

Mary's Fancy. New York: Bouwerie Editions.

A Quick Graph: Collected Notes and Essays. Edited by Donald
[Merriam] Allen. Writing Series, edited by Donald [Merriam]
Allen, no. 22. San Francisco: Four Seasons Foundation.

1971 The Charm: Early and Uncollected Poems. London: Calder &
Boyars.

1.2.3.4.5.6.7.8.9.0. Berkeley, Calif.: Shambala Publications;
San Francisco: Mudra.

St. Martin's. Los Angeles: Black Sparrow Press.

1972 A Day Book. New York: Charles Scribner's Sons.

Listen. Los Angeles: Black Sparrow Press.

Notebook. New York: Bouwerie Editions.

A Sense of Measure. Signature Series, no. 16. London: Calder
& Boyars.

1973 The Class of '47. With Joe Brainard. New York: Bouwerie
Editions.

Contexts of Poetry: Interviews, 1961-1971. Edited by Donald
[Merriam] Allen. Writing, no. 30. Bolinas, Calif.: Four
Seasons Foundation.

"The Creative." Sparrow, no. 6 (March).

For My Mother. Rushden, Northamptonshire, England: Sceptre
Press.

His Idea. Toronto: Coach House Press.

"Inside Out." Sparrow, no. 14 (November).

1974 Thirty Things. Los Angeles: Black Sparrow Press.

1975 Backwards. Knotting, Bedfordshire, England: Sceptre Press.

1976 Away. Santa Barbara, Calif.: Black Sparrow Press.

Hello. Christchurch, New Zealand: Hawk Press.

"Mabel: A Story" and Other Prose. London: Marion Boyars.

Major Works by Robert Creeley

Presences. With Marisol. New York: Charles Scribner's Sons.

Selected Poems. New York: Charles Scribner's Sons.

"Was That a Real Poem or Did You Just Make It Up Yourself." Sparrow, no. 40 (January).

1977 Myself. Knotting, Bedfordshire, England: Sceptre Press.

Thanks. Old Deerfield, Mass.: Deerfield Press; Dublin: Gallery Press.

1978 Desultory Days. Knotting, Bedfordshire, England: Sceptre Press.

Hello: A Journal. London: Marion Boyars.

Hello: A Journal, February 29–May 3, 1976. New York: New Directions Books.

Later. West Branch, Iowa: Toothpaste Press.

1979 Later. New York: New Directions Books.

"Was That a Real Poem" and Other Essays. Edited by Donald [Merriam] Allen. Writing, no. 39. Bolinas, Calif.: Four Seasons Foundation.

1980 Corn Close. Knotting, Bedfordshire, England: Sceptre Press.

1981 Mother's Voice. Santa Barbara, Calif.: Am Here Books, Immediate Editions.

1982 The Collected Poems of Robert Creeley, 1945–1975. Berkeley: University of California Press.

Echoes. West Branch, Iowa: Toothpaste Press.

Readings, May 1982. Durham, Durham, England: Pig Press.

1983 A Calendar: 1984. West Branch, Iowa: Toothpaste Press.

Lines on the Publication of "The Collected Poems of Robert Creeley, 1945–1975." [Buffalo, N.Y.]: Bolt Court Press.

Mirrors. New York: New Directions Books.

1984 A Calendar: Twelve Poems. Morning Coffee Chapbook, no. 5. West Branch, Iowa: [Coffee House Press].

The Collected Prose of Robert Creeley. New York and London: Marion Boyars.

<u>Memories</u>. Durham, Durham, England: Pig Press.

1986   <u>Memory Gardens</u>. New York: New Directions.

Writings about Robert Creeley

1   CREELEY, ROBERT. Concerning the Short Story. [In Japanese.]
    Translated by Kitasono Katsue. Vou: Revu de Vou Club, no. 35
    (August), p. 27.
        Creeley discusses his dislike of the emphasis on plot in the
    short story, compares the short story to the novel, and mentions
    Olson's advice to him on the role of memory in fiction. Notes his
    attempts to use the short story as a means of discovery, his lack
    of intentions, and his devotion to immediacy, as in "Mr. Blue,"
    hoping force will flow from the material. Mentions his sense of
    form as the extension of content and of the present in poetry.

2   . Letter to Kitasono Katsue. [In Japanese.] Translated
    by Kitasono Katsue. Vou: Revu de Vou Club, no. 35 (August),
    pp. 32-33.
        In this 6 April 1951 letter, Creeley gives biographical
    details about preparing to move to France, sends Kitasono ten
    dollars, and notes Corman's work with Origin.

3   . "Letters to Cid Corman." Origin: A Quarterly for the
    Creative, [1st ser.], no. 2 (Summer), pp. 71-75, 92, 104, 124.
        In these letters, Creeley provides a few biographical de-
    tails from September 1950 to February 1951 and discusses the role
    of form and content in poetry. Reprinted in part: 1975.8.

4   OLSON, CHARLES [given as OLSEN]. "Introduction to Robert
    Creeley." New Directions in Prose and Poetry, no. 13,
    pp. 92-93.
        In this introduction to five of Creeley's short shories,
    emphasizes Creeley's role as a presence within his own work, "mak-
    ing clear by way of his own person that life is preoccupation with
    itself." Reprinted: 1965.17; 1987.19.

1952

1   Blurb to <u>Le</u> <u>Fou</u>. Columbus, Ohio: Golden Goose Press, flap of
     rear cover.
         Reprint of 1952.3.

2   MARCUS, STEVEN. "Terrors of Yoknapatawpha and Fairfield: As
     Reflected in Their Regional Fiction." <u>Commentary</u> 14, no. 6
     (December):575–85.
         Feels Creeley's stories in <u>New</u> <u>Directions</u> <u>in</u> <u>Prose</u> <u>and</u>
     <u>Poetry</u>, no. 13 (1951), lose the sense of a "controlling intelli-
     gence" by eliminating the distance in narrational point of view.
     Finds this chaotic and disturbing.

3   Preface to "Anthology: Le Fou." <u>Golden</u> <u>Goose</u> 4, no. 5
     (October):20.
         Briefly mentions Creeley's craft and use of "the words &
     rhythms of spoken language." Reprinted: 1952.1.

1953

1   CORMAN, CID. "The Voice as the Instrument of Verse." <u>Origin:</u>
     <u>A</u> <u>Quarterly</u> <u>for</u> <u>the</u> <u>Creative</u>, 1st ser., no. 9 (Spring),
     pp. 1–6.
         Comments on Creeley's "expressive use of the open line," and
     discusses "The Crisis," finding "strict usage of language and a
     clear regard of the poet for the exact progressions of his voice."

1954

1   CORMAN, CID. "A Requisite Commitment." <u>Poetry</u> 83, no. 6
     (March):340–42.
         In a favorable review of <u>The</u> <u>Kind</u> <u>of</u> <u>Act</u> <u>Of</u>, explicates "The
     Kind of Act Of." Reprinted: 1987.19.

2   C[REELEY], R[OBERT]. "Comment." <u>Black</u> <u>Mountain</u> <u>Review</u> 1, no. 3
     (Fall):[64].
         Creeley stands by the publication of Martin Seymour-Smith's
     reviews of books by Theodore Roethke and Dylan Thomas in the first
     issue of the <u>Black</u> <u>Mountain</u> <u>Review</u>, even though Rexroth resigned
     as a contributing editor of the magazine in light of them.

3   CREELEY, ROBERT. "Preface" to <u>The</u> <u>Gold</u> <u>Diggers</u>. Palma de
     Mallorca, Spain: Divers Press, pp. 9–10.
         In this preface, Creeley comments on the lack of beginning
     and end in the stories in <u>The</u> <u>Gold</u> <u>Diggers</u>. Also mentions the
     role of intention in writing. Reprinted: 1959.3; 1963.7; 1965.9,

10; 1970.14; 1984.12. Translated into Dutch: 1966.6. Also translated into Spanish and German: see 1973.37, no. 915.

4   OLSON, CHARLES. <u>Mayan</u> <u>Letters</u>. Edited by Robert Creeley.
     Palma de Mallorca, Spain: Divers Press, 89 pp.
        Olson occasionally and briefly mentions the letters he re-
ceives from Creeley, including Creeley's information concerning
Slater Brown and Ann Creeley. Reprinted: 1966.22; 1968.19.
Expanded and included in 1983.30 and 1985.15.
        In his preface, Creeley very briefly mentions his corre-
spondence with Olson. Reprinted: 1968.7; 1970.14.

1955

1   CREELEY, ROBERT. Blurb to <u>All</u> <u>That</u> <u>Is</u> <u>Lovely</u> <u>in</u> <u>Men</u>. Jargon,
     no. 10. Asheville, N.C.: Jonathan Williams, front-rear flap
     of cover.
        In this lengthy blurb, Creeley writes of his line, noting
the parallel to jazz; answers charges that he is merely a domestic
poet; and comments on Dan Rice's drawings in <u>All</u> <u>That</u> <u>Is</u> <u>Lovely</u> <u>in</u>
<u>Men</u>. Reprinted: 1970.14.

1956

1   CREELEY, ROBERT. "On Love." <u>Black</u> <u>Mountain</u> <u>Review</u>, no. 6
     (Spring), pp. 217-22.
        Creeley writes of writing, love, and the pain of love, pro-
viding a few general biographical details. Reprinted: 1970.14.

2   ECKMAN, FREDERICK. "Six Poets, Young or Unknown." <u>Poetry</u> 89,
     no. 1 (October):52-63.
        In a favorable review of Creeley's <u>All</u> <u>That</u> <u>Is</u> <u>Lovely</u> <u>in</u>
<u>Men</u>, discusses the influence of W.C. Williams, and notes the
poetry's "constriction" and rhetorical appropriateness. Reprinted
in part: 1980.3.

1957

1   C[REELEY], R[OBERT]. "Preface" to <u>The</u> <u>Whip</u>. Worcester,
     Worcestershire, England: Migrant Books, [p. 3].
        In this preface, Creeley mentions why he writes poetry and
briefly characterizes the poems in <u>The</u> <u>Whip</u>. Reprinted: 1959.3;
1962.5; 1966.10; 1970.14; 1977.8; 1982.12.

2   CREELEY, ROBERT. Review of The Journals of Jean Cocteau, tran-
    scribed and edited by Wallace Fowlie. New Mexico Quarterly 26,
    no. 4 (Winter):397-400.
        In this review, Creeley provides some biographical details
    concerning his early reading of Cocteau and mentions seeing
    Cocteau's movies. Reprinted: 1970.14.

1958

1   ROSENTHAL, M[ACHA] L[EWIS]. "In Exquisite Chaos." Nation 187,
    no. 14 (1 November):324-27.
        In a brief, unfavorable comment, finds Creeley's poetry
    "almost inhibited" and "point[ing] to withdrawal rather than
    realization."

2   ZUKOFSKY, LOUIS. "'What I come to do is partial.'" Poetry 92,
    no. 2 (May):110-12.
        Favorably and very briefly reviews The Whip. Reprinted:
    1987.19.

1959

1   BLY, ROBERT [Crunk]. "The Work of Robert Creeley." Fifties,
    no. 2, pp. 10-21.
        Claims that Creeley, like other Black Mountain poets, does
    not work within the best traditions of avant-garde poetry. Finds
    his work modern only in its diction and honest expression of male-
    female relationships. Reprinted: 1987.19.

2   C[REELEY], R[OBERT]. "A Note to These Poems." In A Form of
    Women: Poems by Robert Creeley. Jargon, no. 33. Highlands,
    N.C.: Jargon Books in association with Corinth Books, [p. 1].
        In this introduction, Creeley provides a few generalized
    biographical details. Reprinted: 1970.14.

3   CREELEY, ROBERT. "Three Prefaces." Migrant, no. 3 (November),
    pp. 2-3.
        Reprint of 1954.3 and 1957.1.

4   H[ÖLLERER], W[ALTER]. "Junge amerikanische Literatur." [In
    German.] Akzente: Zeitschrift für Dichtung 6, no. 1
    (February):29-43.
        Discusses Creeley's use of everyday speech in his prose,
    using a section of "The Lover" as an example.

5   [WILLIAMS, JONATHAN?]. Blurb to <u>A Form of Women: Poems by</u>
     <u>Robert Creeley</u>. Jargon, no. 33. Highlands, N.C.: Jargon
     Books in association with Corinth Books, inside front cover.
         Mentions Creeley as an innovator of a "new poetics" and an
     heir to W.C. Williams and Pound.

6   YATES, PETER. "The Position of Poetry Today: Another Look."
     <u>Arts in Society: A Journal of the Arts in Adult Education</u> [1,
     no. 3] (Winter):51-62.
         Briefly notes the "instantaneous contemporaneity" of "I Know
     a Man," but finds its language dead.

1960

1   "Breathing Words into the Ear of an Unliterary Era." <u>Times</u>
     <u>Literary Supplement</u>, 9 September, p. xv.
         Discussing 1960.2, notes Creeley's line length in "I Know a
     Man," and comments on its meaning, finding a Christian theme (but
     see 1971.1). Compares the poem to Philip Larkin's "Days."

2   BROWNJOHN, ALAN. "Some Notes on Larkin and Creeley." <u>Migrant</u>,
     no. 6 (May), pp. 16-19.
         Contrasts the responses to "the brute fact of human mortal-
     ity" in Creeley's "I Know a Man" and Philip Larkin's "Days," find-
     ing Creeley's poem less resigned and abstract although more
     engaged, immediate, and violent. See also 1960.1.

3   CREELEY, ROBERT. "Olson and Others: Some Orts for the
     Sports." <u>Big Table</u> 1, no. 4 (Spring):119-23.
         Creeley discusses his initial contacts with Corman, Olson,
     Christopher Logue, and others. Reprinted: 1960.4; 1970.14.
     Reprinted in part: 1973.17.

4   ____. "Olson and Others: Some Orts for the Sports." In <u>The</u>
     <u>New American Poetry, 1945-1960</u>. Edited by Donald M[erriam]
     Allen. New York: Grove Press, pp. 408-11.
         Reprint of 1960.3.

5   FLES, JOHN, "The Root." <u>Kulchur</u>, no. 1 (Spring), pp. 39-42.
         Finds Creeley's work focusing on the side of human experi-
     ence that recognizes a "void."

1961

1   CREELEY, ROBERT. "'Statement' for Paterson Society." <u>Floating</u>
     <u>Bear: A Newsletter</u>, no. 6, [p. 12].

RC1961

In this statement, Creeley briefly claims that he is continually "saved" and "returned to possibility and hope" by writing.
Reprinted: 1970.14; 1973.20; 1982.14.

2 JONES, LeROI. Review of A Form of Women. Kulchur, no. 3
   (Spring-Summer), pp. 81-85.
      In this favorable review, finds affinities between A Form of
Women and Elizabethan poetry. Mentions its tortured syntax, and
finds "The Door ['It is hard going to the door']" and "The Hill"
fine poems.

3 WILLIAMS, JONATHAN. "Things Are Very Far Away." Nation 192,
   no. 21 (27 May):461-62.
      Quotes Creeley from a 1961 letter in which he comments on
working on The Island and mentions that he has not been writing
poetry recently. Revised: 1982.46.

4 WRIGHT, JAMES. "The Few Poets of England and America."
   Minnesota Review 1, no. 2 (January):248-56.
      In a review of The New American Poetry, 1945-1960, ed.
Donald M[erriam] Allen (New York: Grove Press, 1960), briefly
mentions Creeley's use of emotion and his small reading public.
Reprinted: 1983.36.

1962

1 CAMBON, GLAUCO. "Nuovi poeti americani." [In Italian.]
   Verri, n.s., no. 1 (February), pp. 59-72.
      Finding Creeley's a poetry of renunciation, mentions the
difficulty of his work due to its sparsity. Discusses "A Counterpoint," emphasizing its ambiguity; "The Warning," noting the counterpoint of violence and gentleness; and "The Innocence,"
commenting on Creeley's change of focus from reality to self-
contemplation as he realizes the partial nature of individual
action. Explains that "The Kind of Act Of" treats the scientific
view that sin is a psychological problem, noting the resultant
loss in the sense of responsibility and freedom. Mentions
Creeley's use of childish expressions, fables, and irony, commenting on a few poems, especially the ironical, nonsensical
development of "Just Friends" in which every human event is shown
to return to the nullity of its prehistory.

2 CARROLL, PAUL. "Country of Love." Nation 195, no. 4
   (25 August):77-78.
      In a favorable review of For Love, comments on Creeley's
distance from both the literary establishment and the avant-garde,
his "close-to-the-bone, fiercely personal poems," and his voice
that "delineate[s] complicated states of feeling in a bald style."

3   C[OLOMBO], J[OHN] R[OBERT]. Review of <u>For Love</u>. <u>Tamarack</u>
     <u>Review</u>, no. 24 (Summer), pp. 110–11.
          In this brief, favorable review, finds the poems "directly
     approachable, contemporary, colloquial, and idiomatic." Asso-
     ciates Creeley with "the beat movement."

4   CORMAN, CID. "<u>For Love</u> Of." <u>Kulchur</u> 2, no. 8 (Winter):49–64.
          In a favorable review of <u>For Love</u>, notes the influence of
     other poets, especially W.C. Williams, and charts the development
     in the volume toward a "tighter formal means" and from a tortured
     self-questioning to belief. Analyzes "The Innocence" and "The
     Crow." Compares Louis MacNeice's "The Wiper" with "I Know a Man,"
     W.C. Williams's "The Testament of Perpetual Change" with "Wait for
     Me," Duncan's "The Albigenses" with "The Rain ['All night the
     sound had']," and the beginning of Samuel Beckett's <u>Malloy</u> with
     "The Innocence." Reprinted: 1978.13; 1987.19.

5   C[REELEY], R[OBERT]. "Preface" to <u>For Love: Poems, 1950–1960</u>.
     New York: Charles Scribner's Sons, [p. 7].
          Reprint of 1957.1.

6   DAVISON, PETER. "The New Poetry." <u>Atlantic</u> 210, no. 5
     (November):85–88.
          In a brief, favorable review of <u>For Love</u>, comments on Creeley's
     rhyme and language, using "The Rain ['All night the sound had'],"
     as an example.

7   FITTS, DUDLEY. "Ear and Inner Eye of the Muse." <u>Saturday</u>
     <u>Review</u>, 4 August, pp. 22–24.
          In a brief, favorable review of <u>For Love</u>, finds "La Noche"
     an example of Creeley's ability to "contain eternity" in a "pas-
     sionate compression."

8   GUNN, THOM. "Things, Voices, Minds." <u>Yale Review</u> 52, no. 1
     (October):129–38.
          In a brief, moderately unfavorable review of <u>For Love</u>, feels
     Creeley's poetry is fragile and random, but notes a correspondence
     with Elizabethan poetry.

9   OLSON, CHARLES. Review of <u>For Love</u>. <u>Village Voice</u> 7, no. 47
     (13 September):4–5.
          In this favorable review, emphasizes the uniqueness, dis-
     tinctiveness, consistency, and range of Creeley's poetry. Re-
     printed: 1974.20.

10   OPPENHEIMER, JOEL [Tom White]. "Where It Is: <u>For Love:</u>
     <u>Poems, 1950–1960</u> by Robert Creeley." <u>Kulchur</u> 2, no. 5
     (Spring):96–99.

RC1962

In this favorable review, finds Creeley expanding from short poems with short lines in the first section to "uncharacteristic poetic structures" in the second, "most uneven," section. In the last section, finds a "sure handling of a variety of forms."

11   REXROTH, KENNETH. "Some Notes Are Borrowed." New York Times Book Review, 4 November, p. 38.
     In a generally favorable review of For Love, mentions the personal pain in Creeley's poetry. Criticizes America for not producing a "more 'major' poet" than Creeley. See 1963.21.

12   ROTHENBERG, JEROME, and CREELEY, ROBERT. "An Exchange: Deep Image and Mode." Kulchur 2, no. 6 (Summer):25-42.
     In this exchange of letters from 6 November 1960 to 10 January 1961, Creeley and Rothenberg argue about the "center of issue" of poetry. Rothenberg, supporting Robert Kelly's "Notes on the Poetry of Deep Image" (Trobar, no. 2 [1961], pp. 14-16), stresses pictorial elements, whereas Creeley emphasizes sound or prosody as central in the poetic process. Rothenberg occasionally uses Creeley's "The Door ['It is hard going to the door']" as an example of Creeley's use of the visual. Both discuss translation and the role of reference in poetry. In his introduction, Rothenberg provides the occasion of the exchange and mentions his relationship to Creeley. Reprinted in part: 1981.27.

13   SWARD, ROBERT. "Two New Books." Chelsea, no. 12 (September), pp. 146-51.
     In a review of For Love, finds the poetry occasionally moving but lacking the range of major work. Sees affinities with e.e. cummings in that both poets are "love-inspired" and both play with language.

14   TALLMAN, WARREN. "Robert Creeley's Portrait of an Artist." Tish, no. 7 (14 March), pp. 7-12.
     Using "3 Fate Tales," discusses the isolation of the self and the uniqueness of the self's knowledge and perception, both of which keep their own variable "measure." Points out the recurrences and the way "perceptions shift instantaneously" in the other pieces in The Gold Diggers. (See the response by Vincent Ferrini in his letter to the editor, Tish, no. 9 [14 May], p. 2.) Reprinted: 1964.14; 1973.46; 1977.20.

1963

1   BELL, MILLICENT. "The Jargon Idea." Books at Brown, no. 19 (May), pp. 1-12.
     Claims Creeley writes with a "studied incoherence." Likes such poems as "The Immoral Proposition" for their "moving and

coherent declaration." Lists Creeley's works published by Jargon
and provides some publication data. Reprinted: 1963.2.

2 _____. The Jargon Idea. Providence, R.I.: Brown University,
   pp. 7-9.
      Reprint of 1963.1.

3 BLACKBURN, PAUL. "The Grinding Down." Kulchur 3, no. 10
   (Summer):9-18.
      Blackburn mentions his early contacts with Creeley and dis-
   cusses Creeley's role in the Black Mountain Review. Lists
   Creeley's contributions to the magazine, identifying the initials
   and pseudonyms under which he wrote. See also 1965.20.

4 BROMIGE, DAVID. Part II of "Creeley's For Love: Two Responses." Northwest Review 6, no. 3 (Summer):110-22.
      In this favorable review, emphasizes Creeley's attraction to
   and repulsion by both the specific and momentary as well as the
   archetypal and eternal. Discusses the themes of "The Business"
   and "The Plan." Examines Creeley's use of female figures in "The
   Wife" and of the vernacular in "I Know a Man." Notes his use of
   understatement in "La Noche" and of rhyme in "The Interview."
   Believes poems like "The Name" are well "sustained."

5 CORRINGTON, JOHN WILLIAM. Part I of "Creeley's For Love: Two
   Responses." Northwest Review 6, no. 3 (Summer):106-10.
      In this unfavorable review, finds For Love "exorbitantly
   overrated" since the language, as in "Song ['What I took in my
   hand']," lacks imagination; the content, as in "Mind's Heart" and
   "The Eye ['Moon']," is epigrammatic; and the thought, as in "A
   Token," is banal. Reprinted: 1987.19.

6 "Creeley, Robert White." In Contemporary Authors: A Bio-
   Bibliographical Guide to Current Authors and Their Works. Vol.
   4. Edited by James M. Ethridge. Detroit: Gale Research Co.,
   p. 81.
      Provides a portion of a letter from Creeley in which he
   mentions his need for isolation and sense of audience. Expanded:
   1967.6; 1969.5.

7 CREELEY, ROBERT. "Preface to Gold Diggers." In The Moderns:
   An Anthology of New Writing in America. Edited by LeRoi Jones.
   New York: Corinth Books, p. 342.
      Reprint of 1954.3.

8 C[REELEY], R[OBERT]. Prefatory note to The Island. New York:
   Charles Scribner's Sons, [p. 5].
      In this note, Creeley briefly comments on the senses of the
   island in and the fictive world of The Island. Reprinted:
   1964.3; 1970.14; 1984.12. Translated: 1972.11.

9   D[AWSON], D[AVE], et al.   "Editorial: Olson/Creeley/Levertov/
    Duncan/Ginsberg/Whalen/Avison."   Tish: A Poetry Newsletter--
    Vancouver, no. 21 (September), pp. 1-8.
        In this series of notes on the July 1963 Vancouver Poetry
    Conference, provides impressions of Creeley's ideas on conscious-
    ness and immediacy.

10 DEANE, PETER.   Review of The Island.   Book Week 1, no. 5
    (13 October):16.
        In this unfavorable review, notes Lawrence's influence and
    compares the novel to Lawrence's work.

11 DICKEY, WILLIAM.   "Reticences of Pattern."   Poetry 101, no. 6
    (March):421-24.
        In a fairly unfavorable review of For Love, mentions
    Creeley's elusiveness, as in "The Rhyme," and his avoidance of
    pattern and imagery.   Finds the later work clearer.

12 DUNCAN, ROBERT.   "From The Day Book [The H.D. Book, Part II:
    prior to Chapter 1]."   Origin, 2d ser.:   Response, no. 10
    (July), pp. 1-47.
        Briefly mentions Creeley as the "fugitive hero" of Olson's
    O'Ryan.   Revised in part: 1968.11.   Reprinted in part: 1975.9.

13 _____.   Review of For Love.   New Mexico Quarterly 32, nos. 3-4
    (Autumn 1962-Winter):219-24.
        In this favorable review article, emphasizes Creeley's
    sources in Dante, the "cult of Amor," and the romance tradition in
    the work.   Also mentions the archetypal figure of the lady and the
    hero.   Comments on "The Wife," "The Whip," "Guido, i' vorrei che
    tu e Lapo ed io," and "The Door ['It is hard going to the door']."
    Notes the influence of W.C. Williams on Creeley's use of line,
    measure, and colloquial speech, using "For Love" as an example.
    Slightly revised: 1978.31; 1987.19.

14 FEDERMAN, DAVID.   "Creeley: Sabbath Notes."   Mother
    (Pittsburgh, Pa.), no. 2 [1963?], pp. 1-2.
        In this essay on modern disintegration, uses Creeley's
    poetry as an example of the "reduction seen in our literature."

15 FLINT, R.W.   "Upbeat."   New York Review of Books 1, no. 4
    (14 November):10.
        In a brief, favorable review of The Island, notes influences
    on and the role of men and women in the novel.

16 HARRIS, DANIEL A.   "An Introduction to Robert Creeley."   Yale
    Literary Magazine 131, nos. 3-4 (April):17-24.
        Discusses Creeley's compression and apparent simplicity,
    his use of language and choric repetition, and his sparing but

striking use of imagery. Comments on a number of poems, especially "A Form of Women," "Not Now," and "The Traveller." Finds
Creeley's compression allows for "poetic and philosophic
amplification."

17   OSSMAN, DAVID. The Sullen Art: Interviews by David Ossman.
     New York: Corinth Books, pp. 49, 56-64, passim.
        In this series of interviews for WBAI in New York, a number
of poets comment on Creeley. In his May 1961 interview, Creeley
mentions teaching at Black Mountain College and editing the Black
Mountain Review. He comments on other poets associated with Black
Mountain poetry, cultural changes from 1945 to 1960, and the
poetic atmosphere in the early 1950s. Also mentions his line
length and contacts with others, especially Olson and Corman. The
Creeley interview is reprinted: 1973.7.

18   ROSENTHAL, MACHA L[EWIS]. "Alienation of Sensibility and
     'Modernity.'" In Approaches to the Study of Twentieth-Century
     Literature. [Proceedings of the Conference in the Study of
     Twentieth-Century Literature, Third Session, Michigan State
     University, May 17-18, 1963.] East Lansing, Mich.: [Michigan
     State University?], pp. 49-59; with discussion, pp. 60-79.
        Briefly mentions that the poet is the center of Creeley's
poetry as a consciousness but not "as an artist." In the discussion, Roy Harvey Pearce finds Creeley a "dialogic poet," not an
alienated "monologic poet." Slightly revised: 1964.10.

19   SOUTHERN, TERRY. "Summer Retreat." New York Times Book
     Review, 22 September, p. 4.
        In a brief, favorable review of The Island, focuses on the
character of John.

20   [WEBB, JON EDGAR.] "The Editor's Bit." Outsider 1, no. 3
     (Spring):inside front cover, 103, 106, 130-32, 137-38.
        Responding to a letter by Creeley ("More on Kearns,"
Outsider 1, no. 3 [Spring]:20), takes exception to what is felt to
be the "digs" at the Outsider, and attacks Creeley as a "snob" who
promotes his own "clique" of "Black Mountaineers."

21   WEIL, JAMES L. "The Long and the Short of It." Elizabeth, no.
     6 (October), pp. 14-15.
        In a favorable review of For Love, refers to 1962.11, and
compares Creeley's reputation today with that of Theokritos in the
third century B.C. Claims both are seen as minor only because
their subject matter concerns the "trivia of daily life."

RC1964

1964

1   "All, All Alone." Times Literary Supplement, 3 September,
    p. 806.
        In a basically unfavorable review of The Island, emphasizes
    the "careful reproduction of . . . emotional movement" and percep-
    tions of the protagonist. Finds the writing "full of loose meta-
    physics and psychology, blurred thought, [and] wrong metaphor."
    Mentions Creeley's dislike of description. Reprinted: 1965.18.

2   BÉRGE, CAROL. The Vancouver Report. [New York: Fuck You
    Press], 17 pp.
        Details Creeley's participation in the 1963 Vancouver Poetry
    Conference, providing impressions, quotations, and biographical
    information. Finds Creeley never really critical or confronta-
    tional. Believes he is "going through a period of terrible doubt
    and negatively critical self-appraisal." Reprinted in small part:
    1976.4.

3   C[REELEY], R[OBERT]. Prefatory note to The Island. London:
    John Calder, [p. 5].
        Reprint of 1963.8.

4   CREELEY, ROBERT. "A Sense of Measure." Times Literary Supple-
    ment, 6 August, p. 699.
        Creeley discusses his sense of the creative process, includ-
    ing the role of subject, intention, and measure. Reprinted:
    1972.13; 1979.15.

5   EICHHORN, DOUG. "Robert Creeley: Love's Modern Poet." Trojan
    Horse (Ithaca, N.Y.: Cornell University) 5 [or 4?] (April):7-8.
        Notes Creeley's honesty and economy as in "The Warning."
    Also mentions his use of American speech, his sources in W.C.
    Williams, and his lack of description.

6   FRANKLYN, A. FREDRIC. "Toward Print (Excerpts from a Journal
    of the U. of British Columbia Seminar)." Trace, no. 51
    (Winter), pp. 277-84, 294.
        In this series of notes dated 24 July to 4 August 1963,
    provides details about Creeley's role at the Vancouver Poetry
    Conference. Records Creeley's comments on his work habits, music,
    poetry, criticism, emotions, and risks. Mentions Creeley's sense
    of craft.

7   HAMMOND, JOHN [GREER]. "The Island: An Explication." Corral:
    An Anthology of Student Writing (University of Texas at Austin),
    no. 4, pp. 50-57.

Discusses the characterization, relationships, and the
themes of isolation, communication, and sex in The Island.
Revised as part of 1973.29.

8   LEED, JACOB. Review of The Island. Penny Papers 1, no. 2
     (Fall-Winter):23-24.
        In this favorable review, finds the novel is about "life
becoming intolerable" as John reaches an impasse. Comments on
John's character and his relation to others.

9   [PERSKY, STAN?] Review of The Island. Open Space, no. 4 [the
     second no. 4; Taurus Issue] [(April), pp. 31, 33].
        In this unfavorable review, seems to believe that Creeley
became too involved with the mundane personal and marital problems
of his story rather than poetry or love.

10   ROSENTHAL, M[ACHA] L[EWIS]. "Alienation of Sensibility and
     'Modernity.'" Arts and Science [3, no. 1] (Spring):19-25.
        Slight reprint of 1963.18.

11   SAROYAN, ARAM. "'An extension of content.'" Poetry 104, no. 1
     (April):45-47.
        In a favorable review of The Island, comments on Creeley's
control of the words. Finds that Creeley's work is always personal and its content determines its form.

12   SIMON, ADELAIDE. Review of The Island. Free Lance: A Maga-
     zine of Poetry and Prose 8, no. 1:41-42.
        In this favorable review, notes Creeley's care and
sensitivity.

13   TALLMAN, WARREN. Review of The Island. Prose 1. Writing, no.
     2. San Francisco: Four Seasons Foundation, pp. 32-33.
        In this review, mentions Creeley's "rhythmic sense, from the
syllable on out to the paragraph." Reprinted: 1973.46.

14   _____. "Robert Creeley's Portrait of the Artist." Kulchur 4,
     no. 13 (Spring):15-26.
        Revision of 1962.14.

15   TOMLINSON, CHARLES. "Robert Creeley in Conversation with
     Charles Tomlinson." Review: A Magazine of Poetry and
     Criticism, no. 10 (January), pp. 24-35.
        In this Spring 1963 interview, Creeley discusses the con-
tinuity of American poetry. Comments on the differences between
the poets associated with Black Mountain and their affinities with
painters in the early fifties. Reprinted: 1965.23; 1973.7.

16   WAGNER, LINDA WELSHIMER. "The Poet as Novelist: Creeley's
      Novel." Critique: Studies in Modern Fiction 7, no. 1
      (Spring):119-22.
          In a favorable review of The Island, discusses Creeley's
      prose techniques, chiefly his use of phrasal units and of the
      "continuous present." Notes the final, ineffectual nature of
      human relationships as a theme. Occasionally compares the novel's
      style and themes to those of his poetry, and mentions his use of
      common speech. Reprinted: 1987.19.

                                 1965

1   ALLEN, GAY WILSON; RIDEOUT, WALTER B.; and ROBINSON, JAMES K.,
      eds. "Comments on Poems." In American Poetry. New York:
      Harper & Row, p. 1090.
          Provides notes for "Hart Crane ['He had been stuttering']."

2   BURLEIGH, ROBERT. "A Man to Forget: Robert Creely [sic]."
      Xenia, no. 1 (Fall), pp. 6-11.
          In an unfavorable review of For Love, finds little range in
      the subject matter, with some poems having no subject. Feels
      others that ostensively treat love, lack the erotic, a sense of
      commitment, or as "Somewhere," "psychological insight." Notes the
      "ultimate vagueness" in "Lady Bird," and finds a "flattened dic-
      tion" and lack of risk in the volume.

3   CREELEY, ROBERT. "Basil Bunting: An Appreciation." Granta 71
      (6 November):12.
          In an appreciation, Creeley discusses his relationship to
      Bunting from 1952 to 1964 and provides a reminiscence of the meet-
      ing and discussion he had with Bunting at Newcastle and Wylam in
      England in October 1964. Reprinted: 1969.6; 1970.14 (as "A Per-
      sonal Note").

4   _____. Letter to the Editor. El corno emplumado, no. 15
      (July), pp. 155-56.
          In this 22 April letter, Creeley discusses living and work-
      ing at a distance from cultural centers and friends. He also
      mentions the importance of his wife, Bobbie, and his children to
      him.

5   CREELEY, ROBERT, and POUND, EZRA. "A Note Followed by a Selec-
      tion of Letters from Ezra Pound." Agenda 4, no. 2 [Special
      Issue in Honor of Ezra Pound's Eightieth Birthday] (October-
      November):11-21.
          Creeley's note (pp. 11-14) discusses the influence of Pound
      on him and provides a few biographical details concerning their

correspondence. Translated: 1965.6. Creeley's note is reprinted (as "A Note on Ezra Pound"): 1970.14; 1973.1.

6   CREELEY, ROBERT. Note in "Lettres à Robert Creeley," by Ezra Pound. Translated by Michel Beaujour. L'Herme, [no. 6] [Ezra Pound, no. 1 issue], pp. 309-11.
    Translation of 1965.5.

7   ____. "A Note on The Black Mountain Review." Serif: Kent State University Quarterly 2, no. 2 (June):21-22.
    Creeley discusses his own role in the Black Mountain Review and provides a few biographical details from 1956.

8   ____. "A Note on Writing." In New American Story. Edited by Donald M[erriam] Allen and Robert Creeley. New York: Grove Press, pp. 263-64.
    Creeley describes how he feels when he writes short stories.

9   ____. "Preface to The Gold Diggers." In New American Story. Edited by Donald M[erriam] Allen and Robert Creeley. New York: Grove Press, pp. 262-63.
    Reprint of 1954.3.

10 C[REELEY], R[OBERT]. "Preface" to "The Gold Diggers" and Other Stories. New York: Charles Scribner's Sons; London: John Calder, pp. 7-8.
    Reprint of 1954.3.

11 DAVEY, FRANK[LAND WILMOT]. "Black Days on Black Mountain." Tamarack Review, no. 35 (Spring), pp. 62-71.
    Uses Creeley's "The Whip" as an example of Black Mountain poetry, "influenced and envisioned by Pound," which is written with a "care for the language." Reprinted: 1976.16. See also 1965.12.

12 DUDEK, LOUIS. "Lunchtime Reflections on Frank Davey's Defence of the Black Mountain Fort." Tamarack Review, no. 36 (Summer), pp. 58-63.
    In a response to 1965.11, believes few Canadian poets have been influenced by Creeley although many share W.C. Williams as a source. Claims the major influence on Olson, on the other hand, was Pound. Feels Creeley and Olson's styles are easily distinguished because of this difference in source. Reprinted: 1976.17; 1978.30.

13 ENRIGHT, D.J. "Manner over Matter." New Statesman 70 (6 August):187-88.
    In a brief, moderately unfavorable review of "The Gold Diggers" and Other Stories, notes the lack of subject matter.

14 HOROVITZ, MICHAEL. Review of The Island. Aylesford Review: A
    Literary Quarterly Sponsored by English Carmelites 7, no. 1
    (Spring):60-63.
        In this favorable review, believes the novel provides "a
    serious treatment of love & sex & friendship & loneliness." Feels
    The Island "defines the perimeters of human reality by means of an
    individual's perception of it." Discusses the main character's
    "marvellously probing, and unproductive, perception" which is
    unable to "opt for any categorical security." Finds jazz a source
    for the novel's rhythms with "each phrase probing its predecessor."

15 LEVERTOV, DENISE. "An Approach to Public Poetry Listenings."
    Virginia Quarterly Review 41, no. 3 (Summer):422-33.
        Briefly finds Creeley's stanza and line breaks indicate
    "thought- and feeling-patterns" as in "The Awakening." Reprinted:
    1981.19.

16 LINICK, ANTHONY. "A History of the American Literary Avant-
    Garde since World War II." Ph.D. dissertation, University of
    California, Los Angeles, pp. 76-77, 79-80, 306, 342, 382-84,
    passim.
        Occasionally mentions Creeley as a member of the avant-
    garde, detailing his role in little magazines during the period
    1951-64, including his role as editor of the Black Mountain Review
    and as contributor to other little magazines. Also occasionally
    comments on the publication of his books by small presses and his
    role in Divers Press. Provides the results of a poll of avant-
    garde writers ranking the importance and influence of Creeley and
    the Black Mountain Review. See Dissertation Abstracts Inter-
    ational 25 (1965):7226.

17 OLSON, CHARLES. "Introduction to Robert Creeley." In "Human
    Universe" and Other Essays. Edited by Donald [Merriam] Allen.
    San Francisco: Auerhahn Society, pp. 127-28.
        Reprint of 1951.4.

18 Review of The Island. T.L.S.: Essays and Reviews from the
    "Times Literary Supplement," 1964. Vol. 3. London: Oxford
    University Press, pp. 202-4.
        Reprint of 1964.1.

19 SHEPPARD, R.Z. "Passwords." Book Week 3, no. 5 (10 October):
    16.
        In a generally favorable review of "The Gold Diggers" and
    Other Stories, quotes from 1965.8 and "The Unsuccessful Husband."
    Emphasizes Creeley's "faith in the possibilities of words . . . to
    chart the flux of consciousness," and stresses his nontraditional
    approach.

20 SLEETH, IRENE LYNN. "An Index to The Black Mountain Review."
    Serif: Kent State University Library Quarterly 2, no. 2
    (June):22-28.
        Provides a list of Creeley's contributions to the Black
    Mountain Review, including those written under pseudonyms and
    different initials. See also 1963.3.

21 STEPANCHEV, STEPHEN. American Poetry since 1945: A Critical
    Survey. New York: Harper & Row, pp. 125, 151-57, passim.
        Mentions Creeley's "sparse, tight form," as in "I Know a
    Man," and his treatment of love and relationships, using a number
    of poems as examples. Comments on The Island.

22 TALLMAN, WARREN. "The Writing Life." In New American Story.
    Edited by Donald M[erriam] Allen and Robert Creeley. New York:
    Grove Press, pp. 1-12.
        In this introduction, stresses Creeley's attention to "the
    phenomenal world" and the "pacing" of his sentences. Reprinted:
    1977.22.

23 TOMLINSON, CHARLES. "Robert Creeley: In Conversation with
    Charles Tomlinson." Kulchur 4 [whole no. 16] (Winter):4-16.
        Reprint of 1964.15.

24 WAGNER, LINDA WELSHIMER. "An Interview with Robert Creeley."
    Minnesota Review, o.s. 5, nos. 3-4 (August-December):309-21.
        In this 1965 interview, Creeley provides biographical de-
    tails and remarks on his judgment of poetry and his sense of
    responsibility to the words in The Island. Also mentions reading
    Stendhal, seeing all of his work as a continuous whole, and using
    his own life in his work. Claims that he feels writing is a dis-
    covery and "the most intimate of all acts" for him. Examining the
    difference between writing poetry and prose, finds the former is
    intense and instantaneous, whereas the latter allows "a more ex-
    tended opportunity to think in."
        Refers to a novel he tried to write in the 1950s and indi-
    vidual short stories. Discusses his sense of form and content and
    his use of lines and stanzas to score rhythm. Examines his in-
    ability to write political poems, his use of quatrains, and his
    political commitments. Finds his teaching compatible with writ-
    ing, claims isolation is useful for him, and notes influences on
    his work, especially Olson, Zukofsky, Pound, and W.C. Williams.
        Reprinted: 1973.1. Revised, rearranged, and combined with
    MacAdams's interview in 1968.26, which is subsequently abridged
    and translated as 1971.22. Revised, rearranged, and expanded in
    1973.47, the fullest version.

25 WESLING, DONALD. "Berkeley: Free Speech and Free Verse."
    Nation 201, no. 15 (8 November):338-40.

RC1965

Notes Creeley's role, including his lecture, later published
as 1973.19, and his poetry reading, in the 1965 Berkeley Poetry
Conference. Comments on "Something."

26 WILLIAMS, JONATHAN. "Parsons Weems & Vachel Lindsay Rent a
Volkswagen and Go Looking for Lamedvovnit #37; or, Travails in
America Deserta." Arts in Society 3, no. 3:371-87.
     Williams mentions his correspondence with Creeley and an
unpublished Creeley poem. Also comments on publishing Creeley.

1966

1 ALDRICH, MICHAEL. Untitled. Incense (Buffalo, N.Y.) [Incense
Trace issue], [pp. 1-2].
     Provides details of Creeley's teaching, especially of W.C.
Williams's Paterson, at the State University of New York at
Buffalo. Also comments on his reading in a graduate class.

2 ALEXANDER, MICHAEL. "William Carlos Williams and Robert
Creeley." Agenda 4, nos. 3-4 (Summer):56-67.
     Commenting on For Love, notes the influence of W.C. Williams
and Zukofsky, Creeley's individuality, and the poetry's riddle-
like quality and seriousness.

3 "Am I Happy?" Times Literary Supplement, 1 December, p. 1128.
     In an unfavorable review of Poems, 1950-1965, finds the
poetry boring, with few images and a "numb repetition of colour-
less words," but notes a few good poems. Reprinted, omitting
another review: 1967.22.

4 CONSTABLE, JOHN. "The Poems of Robert Creeley." Cambridge
Review: A Journal of University Life and Thought 88 [mis-
numbered as 89], no. 2,130 (15 October):27-29.
     In a favorable review of Creeley's Poems, 1950-1965, finds
three types of poems. Poems of the first type are influenced by
W.C. Williams and "stay close to the visible appearances of
things." Those of the second type are totally subjective and
given to abstraction. Poems of the third, as "Kore," mediate
"between the inward and tangible worlds," and often explore the
tension between.

5 COOKSON, WILLIAM. Review of Creeley's Poems, 1950-1965.
Agenda 4, nos. 5-6 (Autumn):64-66.
     In this favorable review, emphasizes Creeley's ability to
write about "the frailest, finest qualities of the mind's
experience."

6   C[REELEY], R[OBERT]. "Inleiding" to "De Goudgravers" en andere
     Verhalen. [In Dutch.] Translated by Jan Donkers. Amsterdam:
     Polak & Van Gennep, pp. 7-8.
         Translation of 1954.3.

7   CREELEY, ROBERT, ed. "Introduction" to Selected Writings of
     Charles Olson. New York: New Directions, pp. 1-10.
         Creeley briefly mentions a letter he received from W.C.
     Williams and his feelings when facing the literary establishment's
     New Criticism, which dominated the poetic scene in the early
     1950s. Slightly revised: 1970.14.

8   CREELEY, ROBERT. Letter to Tom Raworth. Work (Detroit), no. 3
     (Winter), p. 32.
         In this 7 February 1964 letter, Creeley comments on trans-
     lating Rainer M. Gerhardt's "A Voice," and provides the text.

9   ____. "A Note." A Nosegay in Black 1, no. 1 (Autumn):
     [25-26].
         In this note, Creeley discusses his sense of music, of the
     origin of a poem, and of the creative process, including the role
     of emotion. Also comments on the nonreferential quality of po-
     etry. Reprinted: 1970.14 (as "'Poems are a complex'"); 1982.11.

10   C[REELEY], R[OBERT]. Preface to Poems, 1950-1965. London:
     Calder & Boyars, [p. 7].
         Reprint of 1957.1.

11   CREELEY, ROBERT. "Rainer Gerhardt: A Note." Work, no. 3
     (Winter 1965-66), pp. 4-5.
         Creeley comments on his relationship with Gerhardt and
     provides a few biographical details about meeting with him.
     Reprinted: 1970.14.

12   ____. "A Statement about 'The Name.'" In Poems for Young
     Readers: Selections from Their Own Writing by Poets Attending
     the Houston Festival of Contemporary Poetry. [Champaign, Il.]:
     National Council of Teachers of English, p. 9.
         In this statement, Creeley discusses the role of emotion in
     all of his poems as well as in "The Name." Also mentions the
     rhythms and rhymes in "The Name." Reprinted: 1970.14.

13   DONADIO, STEPHEN. "Some Younger Poets in America." In Modern
     Occasions. Edited by Philip Rahv. New York: Farrar, Straus,
     & Giroux, pp. 226-46.
         Claiming Creeley "is the most overrated poet of his genera-
     tion," finds his poems bland and lacking experience.

RC1966

14 DUNCAN, ROBERT. "Towards an Open Universe." In Poets on
    Poetry. Edited by Howard Nemerov. New York and London: Basic
    Books, pp. 133-46.
        Duncan briefly mentions that Creeley, influenced by Pound
    and W.C. Williams like himself, "derive[s] melody and story from
    impulse, not from plan." Reprinted: 1973.1; 1985.10. Revised:
    1973.24; 1974.10; 1982.18.

15 FRANKS, DAVID. "'The Goldiggers' [sic] and Other Takes:
    Robert Creeley, Charles Scribner's Sons: $1.65." Whe're 1,
    no. 1 (Summer):94-96.
        In this favorable review of "The Gold Diggers" and Other
    Stories, discusses Creeley's prose "measure" and his "immersion
    . . . in the medium."

16 GIRRI, ALBERTO. "Robert Creeley." [In Spanish.] In Quince
    poetas norteamericanos. America en letras. Buenos Aires,
    Argentina: Bibliografica Omeba, pp. 249-53.
        In a summary of Creeley's work, briefly mentions his use of
    language and of personal materials.

17 GNAROWSKI, MICHAEL. "Notes on the Background and History of
    Contact Magazine." In "Contact," 1952-1954. Montreal: Delta
    Canada, pp. 3-14.
        Discusses Creeley's influence on Contact through his cor-
    respondence with Raymond Souster, and provides the text for some
    of these letters.

18 JEROME, JUDSON. "The Lonely Orgy." Writer's Digest 46, no. 6
    (June):18, 20, 24.
        Finds Creeley's "The Mountains in the Desert" childish and
    self-absorbed when compared to Keats's "Ode to a Nightingale."

19 KENNEDY, X.J. An Introduction to Poetry. Boston and Toronto:
    Little, Brown, & Co., p. 29.
        Provides a brief explication of "Oh No." Slightly revised:
    1978.43. Slightly revised and expanded: 1982.26.

20 MASLOW, ELLEN. "A Discussion of Several of Creeley's Poems."
    Kulchur 5, no. 20 (Winter):66-71.
        Discusses the themes of fear and perception in "The Immoral
    Proposition" and social exclusion in "The Conspiracy." Examines
    the sense of arrival in "Oh No" and the "didactic purpose" of "The
    Warning." Finds ironic "false logic" common to these poems.

21 MOON, SAMUEL. "Creeley as Narrator." Poetry 108, no. 5
    (August):341-42.
        In a favorable review of "The Gold Diggers" and Other
    Stories, believes Creeley "has discarded conventional craft" for

"the kinesthetic rhythms of utterance." Finds the short stories
in a continuum "between the novel and the poems," and as does
1951.4, comments on Creeley's role in the stories.

22 OLSON, CHARLES. "Mayan Letters." In <u>Selected</u> <u>Writings</u> <u>of</u>
    <u>Charles Olson</u>. Edited by Robert Creeley. New York: New
    Directions, pp. 69-130.
        Reprint of 1954.4.

23 _____. <u>Reading at Berkeley</u>. Transcribed by [Ralph Maud].
    [Buffalo, N.Y.: privately printed], pp. 2-5, 8, 10, 12-15,
    22, 52, 60, passim.
        Another version of 1966.24. Revised: 1970.28.

24 _____. <u>Reading at Berkeley</u>. Transcribed by Zoe Brown.
    [Berkeley or San Francisco?]: Coyote, pp. 1-3, 6-8, 10-12,
    36-37, 44, passim.
        In this transcription of a 23 July 1965 reading and discus-
    sion at the Berkeley Poetry Conference, Olson occasionally addres-
    ses Creeley, mentions Creeley's reading the previous day, and
    notes Creeley's influence on him. Olson also comments on
    Creeley's work and provides biographical details concerning their
    relationship, especially at Black Mountain College and at the July
    1963 Vancouver Poetry Conference. See also 1966.23; 1970.28.
    (This, with 1970.28, forms the basis of 1978.59, the fullest, most
    accessible version.)

25 RODEFER, STEPHEN. "A Workable Bibliography of Robert Creeley."
    <u>Whe're</u> 1, no. 1 (Summer):58-60.
        Attempting to re-create Creeley's order of composition and
    publication of poems from 1962 to 1965, lists, in order of presen-
    tation, the fifty-four poems that Creeley read at the 1965
    Berkeley Poetry Conference and ten other poems, indicating the
    place of publication for all but seven.

26 SINCLAIR, JOHN, and EICHELE, ROBIN. "Interview: Robert
    Creeley." <u>Whe're</u> 1, no. 1 (Summer):47-59.
        In this interview, Creeley provides many biographical de-
    tails. Discusses the influence that jazz and working with fowl
    had on his work and on his "habits of . . . attention"; the early
    publication of his poetry and work with Divers Press; and the
    development of the <u>Black Mountain Review</u>. Also mentions his
    teaching at Black Mountain College, literary relationships of the
    1950s, and his relationships with Slater Brown, Martin Seymour-
    Smith, Corman, Olson, and Wieners. Reprinted: 1973.7.

27 TALLMAN, WARREN. "Robert Creeley's Rimethought." <u>A Nosegay in</u>
    <u>Black</u> 1, no. 1 (Autumn):[27-40].
        Reprinted from 1966.28.

28   . "Robert Creeley's Rimethought." <u>Tish: A Poetry</u>
<u>Newsletter--Vancouver</u>, no. 33 (4 January), pp. 2-10.
        Uses "Mr. Blue" as an example of Creeley's concentrated
engagement with his subject. Believes Creeley uses a form of
"rimethought" in which associated thoughts or images recur at
intervals as in "A Form of Women." Contrasts the "delicacy" of
the stresses, line breaks, and sound patterns of "A Token" with
Elizabethan songs, especially those of Ben Jonson. Finds "A
Wicker Basket" a "hyper-conscious" tour-de-force, and uses "The
House" to show how Creeley thinks with objects and their relationships. Reprinted: 1973.46; 1977.20. Reprinted in part: 1966.27.

29   WAGNER, LINDA [WELSHIMER]. Review of "<u>The Gold Diggers</u>" <u>and</u>
<u>Other Stories</u>. <u>Studies in Short Fiction</u> 3, no. 4 (Summer):
465-66.
        In this favorable review, notes the nature of the protago-
nists and the themes of isolation and loneliness. Reprinted:
1987.19.

30   WILLIAMS, JONATHAN. "A Preliminary Note." <u>Work</u> (Detroit), no.
3 (Winter 1965-66), pp. 3-4.
        Williams provides part of the text of a 23 September 1953
letter from Creeley concerning Creeley's correspondence with
Rainer M. Gerhardt.

1967

1   CALDER, JOHN. "Copyright." <u>Times Literary Supplement</u>, 1 June,
p. 487.
        In a response to 1967.18, Calder defends publishing
Creeley's <u>Poems, 1950-1965</u> three years after the American edition
of <u>For Love: Poems, 1950-1960</u>. Believes sales suffered due to
imports of the American edition. See also 1967.8, 24.

2   CAMERON, ALLEN BARRY. "'Love Comes Quietly': The Poetry of
Robert Creeley." <u>Chicago Review</u> 19, no. 2:92-103.
        Comments on Creeley's critical reception, the influence of
W.C. Williams, and his treatment of marriage and relationships.
Mentions his development as seen in <u>For Love</u>, and discusses his
subjectivity. Examines his principle that "Form is never more than
an extension of content," applying it to his own work, and his use
of the line as in "The Tunnel." Briefly explicates "The End," "The
Letter," "The Innocence," "Love Comes Quietly," "La Noche," and
"The Rain ['All night the sound had']."

3   [CARROLL, PAUL.] "The American Poets in Their Skins, 1950-
1967." <u>Choice: A Magazine of Poetry and Photography</u>, no. 5,
pp. 81-107.

Briefly praises Creeley as a love poet who follows the mind as it observes the heart. Expanded: 1968.1.

4   COMBS, MAXINE [SOLOW] GAUTHIER. "A Study of the Black Mountain Poets." Ph.D. dissertation, University of Oregon, pp. 1-4, 7-8, 96-133, 181-96.
     Focusing on poems from For Love and Words, discusses Creeley's treatment of poetry, movement and mutability, time, place, and order. Mentions the themes of marriage, love, sex, conflict, and constancy. Also examines his treatment of "the basic futility of experience," the inadequacy of language, the beauty of words, and the poetic process, including "the poet's sense of inadequacy." Focuses on "Le Fou," "The Rites," and "The Place ['What is the form is the gro-']," but also relates the themes to The Island. Finds the insights of a single poem by Creeley slight, but claims "each poem contributes to a larger view" that is "particular and unique."
     Also comments on Creeley's use of mythology and "water as an image for the impermanent," and notes parallels to Duncan's treatment of poetry. Mentions the influence of Olson on Creeley's poetics, but finds Creeley's own statements on poetry either expand Olson's or are unclear. Using "Enough," "Going," "The Riddle," and "The Gesture," notes Creeley's use of the short line to emphasize words, enforce the reader's participation in the activity of the ideas, and create lexical ambiguity. Also comments on his use of stanzaic patterns and stanza breaks. See Dissertation Abstracts International 28 (1968):3666A.

5   COOK, ALBERT [SPAULDING]. Prisms: Studies in Modern Literature. Bloomington and London: Indiana University Press, pp. 84-85, 151-52.
     Scans and discusses "For a Friend ['Who remembers him also, he thinks']," finding the poem's design "only hints at regularity, as the poem's statement only hints at identity." Feels the "transparency of the style allows the complexity to be more apparent."

6   "Creeley, Robert (White)." In Contemporary Authors: A Bio-Bibliographical Guide to Current Authors and Their Works. 1st revision. Vols. 1-4. Edited by James M. Ethridge and Barbara Kopala. Detroit: Gale Research Co., pp. 213-14.
     In an expanded version of 1963.6, provides an overview of Creeley's poetry and fiction, quoting from many on his work. Updated: 1969.5.

7   CREELEY, ROBERT. "Contemporary Voices in the Arts." Arts Magazine 41, no. 8 (Summer):18-20.
     Creeley provides a reminiscence about a tour he took with six other artists in 1967 as part of Contemporary Voices in the

RC1967

Arts, a program by the New York State Council on the Arts.
Reprinted (as "Feedback: 'Contemporary Voices in the Arts'"):
1970.14.

8   . "Copyright." Times Literary Supplement, 22 June,
p. 559.
       In this letter to the editor, partially in a response to
1967.18, Creeley discusses the publication and sale of his work in
England. See also 1967.1, 24.

9   . ["'Gedichte zu schreiben fällt mir zu.'"] [In German.]
Translated by Klaus Reichert. In Ein Gedicht und sein Autor:
Lyrik und Essay. Edited by Walter Höllerer. Berlin:
Literarisches Colloquium, pp. 242-55.
       German translation of 1967.12.

10   . Preface to The Charm: Robert Creeley, Early and Uncollected Poems. Mt. Horeb, Wis.: Perishable Press, [pp. 1-3].
       In this preface, Creeley discusses putting together the
poems in For Love, his early attempts at writing, withholding
poems from early volumes, and "The Charm." Reprinted: 1969.10;
1971.6; 1982.12.

11   . Preface to Words. New York: Charles Scribner's Sons,
p. 9.
       In this preface, Creeley states that his intentions in writ-
ing do not matter for his poems "will not say anything more than
they do." Reprinted: 1970.13-14; 1982.12.

12   . "Robert Creeley Talks about Poetry." Harper's Bazaar
101 (July):81, 120-21, 126.
       In this January 1967 lecture, Creeley discusses his sense of
writing as a "place" to be, comparing his concept to the "made
place" of Duncan and the "made poem" of W.C. Williams. Comments
on how he "came to be involved with poetry" in the 1940s and his
sense of intention, freedom, and limitation in writing. Discusses
what he learned from Duncan, W.C. Williams, Olson, and Pound.
Reprinted (as "'I'm given to write poems'"): 1970.14; 1972.13;
1973.1. Translated into German: 1967.9.

13 DAWSON, FIELDING. An Emotional Memoir of Franz Kline. New
York: Random House, Pantheon, pp. 67, 124-34.
       Provides a few reminiscences of Creeley in New York in
February 1967.

14 DUDEK, LOUIS. "The Everyday Self in Poetry." In The First
Person in Literature: Six Talks for CBC Radio. Toronto:
Canada Broadcasting Corporation Publications, pp. 57-68.

In a December 1966 radio talk, briefly finds Creeley's work "the extreme point of personal and intimate communication," and notes his influence on Canadian poets.

15   FALCK, COLIN. "Symbol-Shy." Encounter 28, no. 3 (March):68, 70-72.
       In this brief, unfavorable review of Poems: 1950-1960, comments on Creeley's lack of imagination.

16   FREEMAN, J.P. Review of "The Gold Diggers" and Other Stories. Cambridge Quarterly 2, no. 4 (Autumn):414-20.
       In this favorable review, finds a "moral substructure" in most of the stories in which the characters redefine themselves outside of social contexts. Commenting on the unnamed sister's "moral superiority," compares "A Death" to chapter 6 of The Island. Reprinted: 1987.19.

17   LUCIE-SMITH, EDWARD, interlocutor. "Notes on an Interview by Way of a Preface." Robert Creeley Reads. London: Turret Books; Calder & Boyars, pp. 3-4.
       In these excerpts from an interview, Creeley briefly comments on writing about relationships. Notes the new sense of relaxation that he has.

18   MUNDAY, MARGARET; KASHA, HUGO; MOSLEY, RICHARD; STONE, BERNARD; SANDERSON, HARRY; COBBING, BOB; KAVANAGH, TED; and MILES, [B.]. "Censorship Backlash Backlash." International Times, no. 13 (19 May-2 June), p. 12.
       Briefly complains that John Calder has "banned the sale of For Love . . . for three years" but that American imports have "created an interest and a demand" for this work. See 1967.1, 8, 24.

19   PERREAULT, JOHN. "Holding Back and Letting Go." New York Times Book Review, 19 November, p. 97.
       In an unfavorable review of Words, emphasizes W.C. Williams's influence, but finds a "thinness of vision" and "impoverishment of expression." See 1968.20, 28.

20   REICHERT, KLAUS. "Nachwort" [in German] to Gedichte, by Robert Creeley. Frankfurt: Suhrkamp Verlag, pp. 153-66.
       Compares Creeley to W.C. Williams in terms of their attention to the elemental and simple, as opposed to the European, and finds Williams's The Wedge influential on Creeley's development. Also notes the influence of Pound and action painting on Creeley, claiming Creeley's poetry might be considered action poetry. Mentions what makes translation of Creeley's poetry difficult, especially into German, including his broken speech and his semantics. Mentions Creeley's sense of the usefulness of poetry.

RC1967

21 _____. "Zur Technik des Übersetzens amerikanischer Gedichte."
    [In German.] Sprache im technischen Zeitalter, no. 21
    (January-March), pp. 1-16.
        Discusses the difficulties of translating Creeley's
    "Please": the title, the rhyme, and the punctuation that sepa-
    rates elements that retain a syntactical binding. Also discusses
    the difficulty of translating Creeley's use of rhyme for irony as
    in "Chanson," and discusses the rhythm in this poem. Defends his
    own German translations of the above poems.

22 Review of Poems, 1950-1965. In T.L.S.: Essays and Reviews
    from the "Times Literary Supplement," 1966. Vol. 5. London:
    Oxford University Press, pp. 146-50.
        Reprint of 1966.3.

23 ROSENTHAL, M[ACHA] L[EWIS]. The New Poets: American and
    British Poetry since World War II. New York: Oxford Univer-
    sity Press, pp. 14-15, 148-59, passim.
        Using "The Business" and "The Riddle," compares Creeley to
    W.C. Williams in terms of their tone of "casual introspection,"
    their treatment of love and sex, their wit and wry humor, and
    their minimalism. Discusses "The Riddle" in some detail, focusing
    on Creeley's reluctance to state a theme, and comments on "A Form
    of Women." Finds Creeley's work "demands a good deal of attentive
    sympathy and faith from the reader." Also comments on Creeley's
    "allegiance to the private sensibility at an ambiguously uncom-
    mitted stage," and occasionally mentions his subjectivity. See
    1975.18.

24 STONE, BERNARD; SANDERSON, HARRY; MILES, B.; WORSWICK, JEAN;
    MUNDAY, MARGARET; KAVANAGH, E.J.; and COBBING, BOB. "Copy-
    right." Times Literary Supplement, 8 June, p. 509.
        In a response to 1967.1, provides a different reason why
    Creeley's Poems, 1950-1965 did not sell well in Britain. See also
    1967.8, 18.

25 WAGNER, LINDA WELSHIMER. Denise Levertov. Twayne's United
    States Authors Series, edited by Sylvia E. Bowman, no. 113.
    New York: Twayne Publishers, pp. 22-23, 38, 51, passim.
        Occasionally and briefly compares Levertov's poetry to
    Creeley's. Speculates on Creeley's influence on her, and notes
    why they are often classified together.

26 The Washington University Libraries, the Friday Evening Reading
    Series, [and] the Student Assembly Present Robert Creeley [and]
    Robert Duncan Reading Their Works. St. Louis: Washington
    University Library, Friday Evening Reading Series, Student
    Assembly, 4 pp.

Announces Creeley's 28 April 1967 reading in St. Louis, and provides a biographical summary. Details the method by which Creeley was chosen as a poet whose books and manuscripts would be collected by the Rare Books Department of Olin Library.

27   WEATHERHEAD, A[NDREW] KINGSLEY. The Edge of the Image: Marianne Moore, William Carlos Williams, and Some Other Poets. Seattle and London: University of Washington Press, pp. 90-91, 202-3, passim.
Briefly notes the relationship of rhythm to phrasing in Creeley's poetry, and quotes from him on writing. Compares a section of "Anger" to Frost's "After Apple-Picking."

1968

1   CARROLL, PAUL. The Poem in Its Skin. Chicago: Follett Publishing Co., Big Table Book, pp. 31-38, 209-10, passim.
Provides a psychoanalytical explication of "A Wicker Basket," discussing its "complexity and ambiguity of feeling and attitude." Examines its treatment of marijuana, food, "infantile oral rage," and childish delight, and details its use of fantasy and irony. Also notes the tone of anger in the poem and its "hip attitude." Includes a slightly expanded version of 1968.3.

2   COLLINS, RAYMOND DOUGLAS, Jr. "Four Short Story Writers from Black Mountain College." M.A. thesis, University of North Carolina, pp. 17-43, passim.
In Creeley's "The Gold Diggers" and Other Stories, discusses the use of rooms as settings, the lack of symbolism and normal plots, and the role of the metaphysical and of generalization. Also examines the treatment of marriage, of male and female figures, and of song and music, and mentions the narrator as a participant, finding the stories reenact experience. Feels there is no easy way to "sum them up," but finds most of the stories are centered around an obsession. Claims the obsession of "Mr. Blue" is size and of "3 Fate Tales" is death, examining these tales as "portrait[s] of the artist." Comments on the role of place and the treatment of the characters' desire for stasis in "The Grace." Notes the treatment of walking, movement, and song in "The Book."

3   COLLINS, [RAYMOND] DOUGLAS, [Jr.]. "Notes on Robert Creeley." Lillabulero: Being a Periodical of Literature and the Arts 2, no. 1 (Winter):37-40.
In a favorable review of Words, comments upon how the mind perceives the mind and its "intense and insistent power . . . to insure itself measures of stability."

RC1968

4   CORMAN, CID. "A Note on the Founding of Origin." Serif:
     Kent State University Library Quarterly 5, no. 1 (March):29-30.
         Corman mentions his early contacts with Creeley, Creeley's
     aborted little magazine, and Creeley's role in Origin. Reprinted:
     1970.12.

5   CREELEY, ROBERT. "Contexts of Poetry." Transcribed by George
     F. Butterick. Audit 5, no. 1 (Spring):1-18.
         In this transcription of a 24 July 1963 tape made with
     Ginsberg at the Vancouver Poetry Conference, Creeley discusses his
     "particular habits of writing," including the use of the type-
     writer and certain types of paper, and maintaining an isolated and
     secure environment. Provides biographical information, and com-
     ments on composing The Island to certain types of music. Claims
     he feels "stuck with habits of articulation," in which "only cer-
     tain kinds of feeling can come."
         In a 14 April 1968 postscript (pp. 16-18), mentions trying to
     break his habits of composition by writing in longhand in note-
     books. Claims that this has allowed him to ignore "some final
     code of significance," and lists the poems in Words written in
     this way. Reprinted: 1970.16; 1973.7.

6   _____. Letter to Robert Bly. Sixties, no. 10 (Summer), p. 36.
         Creeley corrects Bly's errors in, under the pseudonym of
     Crunk, "The Work of Denise Levertov" (Sixties, no. 9 [Spring
     1967], pp. 48-65), about his own relationship to Levertov and
     Mitchell Goodman and provides a few biographical details.

7   _____, ed. "Preface" to Mayan Letters, by Charles Olson.
     London: Jonathan Cape, pp. 5-6.
         Reprint of 1954.4.

8   CREELEY, ROBERT. "The Province of the Poem." Cultural
     Affairs: A Quarterly Magazine of Associated Councils of the
     Arts, no. 3, p. 19.
         Creeley responds to the situation detailed in 1968.23 and
     briefly mentions his own teaching in secondary schools in
     Albuquerque, New Mexico.

9   _____. Statement. Quixote (Madison, Wis.) 3, "no. 9 or so"
     (May):83-85.
         In this transcription of statements made during a reading of
     his poetry, Creeley gives biographical details concerning teach-
     ing, taking LSD, and writing poetry. Discusses The Island, "The
     Dream" (probably "The Dream ['A lake in the head']"), "A Form of
     Women," and "For Love."

10   DAVEY, FRANKLAND WILMOT. "Theory and Practice in the Black
     Mountain Poets: Duncan, Olson, and Creeley." Ph.D.

dissertation, University of Southern California, pp. 1-7, 113-34, 262-303, passim.

Finds Creeley "has written no detailed defense of his own poetic theory" and is without a "developed view of the universe" because he is "unsure of the precise structure of the reality around him." Occasionally providing brief portions of unpublished tape-recorded lectures by Creeley from late August 1962, comments on Creeley's parallels to Olson and Duncan's poetic theories, especially in terms of the role of intention and of the ego in poetry as well as composition by field. Emphasizes his focus on a field of experience in which all is in a continual, confusing flux. Also finds slight differences between Creeley's theories and those of others in regard to the use of language as an action in the poem and the relationship between form and content. Mentions the lack of a dogmatism in Creeley's criticism, his use of poetry to momentarily define experience, and describes the creative process according to Creeley, noting the role of consciousness.

Using numerous poems as illustrations, discusses Creeley's poetry, especially its sense of desertion, "personal helplessness," and impending danger in a world of change. Also examines his treatment of love, objects, self-identity, relationships, and sex, and mentions his use of similes and surrealism. Finds the speaker in the poems insecure, confused, and short-sighted, unable to see a larger whole. Demonstrates the insecurity in "The Door ['It is hard going to the door']," and illustrates his use of field composition with one perception following another in "The Rain ['All night the sound had']." Finds Creeley uses poetry as a method of discovery, but feels his endings are occasionally contrived. See Dissertation Abstracts International 29 (1968):256A.

11 DUNCAN, ROBERT. "Nights and Days [The H.D. Book, Part II: Chapter 1]." Sumac 1, no. 1 (Fall):101-47.
Opening section is a revision of 1963.12. Duncan also notes a sense of belonging to a "constellation" of poets, including Creeley, who looked to W.C. Williams as a master.

12 FAUCHEREAU, SERGE. Lecture de la poésie américaine. [In French.] Critique. Paris: Editions de Minuit, pp. 220-21, 223, 228-34, passim.
Uses Creeley's "I Know a Man" to demonstrate Olson's theories of speech rhythms and kinetic energy in projective poetry. Discusses Creeley's use of line and stanza breaks, rhyme, and rhythm. Also comments on his evolving style and "The Name," comparing Creeley to Michel Deguy. Translated into Rumanian with a new introduction: 1974.11.

13 GLOVER, ALBERT GOULD, ed. "Introduction" and "Index" to "Charles Olson: Letters for Origin," by Olson. Ph.D.

dissertation, State University of New York at Buffalo, pp. i-xxxi, 338-95.

Mentions Creeley's relationship to Olson, his aborted little magazine, The Lititz Review, and his contacts with others. See Dissertation Abstracts International 29 (1968):1894-95A.

14   HONISCH, DIETER.   Preface to Numbers, by Robert Indiana and Robert Creeley.   [In English and German.]   Stuttgart: Edition Domberger; Düsseldorf: Galerie Schmela, [pp. 1, 3].

Compares Creeley's work with Indiana's, especially Creeley's Numbers with the work that influenced it, Number Paintings by Indiana.

15   HOWARD, RICHARD.   "Robert Creeley: 'I Begin Where I Can, and End When I See the Whole Thing Returning.'"   Minnesota Review 8, no. 2:143-50.

Does not believe Creeley has fallen into self-parody.   Finds the poetry truthfully recognizes and is a part of "momentary experience," and as such has no conclusion and avoids recurrences. Also finds it appears incomplete and attempts to forget the past and the mind's previous ways of dealing with experience.   Reprinted: 1969.13; 1980.20; 1987.19.

16   JUNKINS, DONALD.   "Creeley and Rexroth: No Simple Poets." Massachusetts Review: A Quarterly of Literature, the Arts, and Public Affairs 9, no. 3 (Summer):598-603.

In a favorable review of Words, finds the poetry mental, demonstrating "the complexity of the sensibility."   Mentions the treatment of love, measure, proportion, and relationships.   Comments on the deceptiveness of Creeley's ordinary language and a number of poems, notably "The Invitation."

17   KNIEF, WILLIAM.   "Robert Creeley: Interview."   Cottonwood Review [1, no. 4:1-8, 11-18].

In this interview, Creeley reviews his association with and his teaching at Black Mountain College as well as his initial contacts with Olson.   Mentions his similarities with other Black Mountain poets, his use of line breaks, the role of rhythm in his prose, and his inability to write drama.   Comments on first beginning to write both prose and poetry and going to college.   Claims that all of his writing "is the transcription of spoken possibility" and that he writes for himself as a "primary reader."

Mentions being arrested in San Francisco, and comments on being a poet in the 1950s.   Notes his sense of "entering into an activity which is called writing" and of being "called upon" to write, noting the role of reading.   Reviews many of his sources throughout, especially noting the influence of Lawrence, W.C. Williams, and Dostoevskiĭ.   Also mentions his sources for rhythm in jazz, and claims he writes in "spurts," using The Island to illustrate. Indicates projects he is currently contemplating.

18   OLSON, CHARLES. "Charles Olson: Letters for Origin." Edited by Albert Gould Glover. Ph.D. dissertation, State University of New York at Buffalo, pp. 64, 89-91, 98, 102-3, 118, 144-45, 148, 187, 189, 198, 231, 240-41, passim.
Olson continually refers to his relationship to Creeley as well as Creeley's relationship to Corman. Mentions Creeley's role in the Black Mountain Review and Origin, and comments on Creeley at Black Mountain College. Assesses Creeley's fiction, especially "In the Summer" and "The Party," and remarks on "Hart Crane 2 ['Answer: how old']."
Advises Corman concerning a "rupture" with Creeley in November 1951, commenting upon Creeley's seriousness. Reprinted in part: 1970.29; 1983.5, the latter containing some of Corman's letters to Olson. See Dissertation Abstracts International 29 (1968):1894-95A.

19   _____. Mayan Letters. Edited by Robert Creeley. London: Jonathan Cape, 91 pp.
Reprint of 1954.4.

20   PERREAULT, JOHN. "'A Void of Smug': Mr. Perreault Replies." New York Times Book Review, 7 January, p. 26.
In a response to 1968.28, argues the influence of Creeley is "negligible if not mildly pernicious," and claims his poetry is poor. See also 1967.19.

21   SOLT, MARY ELLEN. "A World Look at Concrete Poetry." Artes hispanicas/Hispanic Arts 1, nos. 3-4 (Winter-Spring):6-66.
Explicates "Le Fou," comparing it to a concrete poem in a few ways. Reprinted: 1970.21.

22   THOMPSON, JOHN. "An Alphabet of Poets." New York Review of Books 11, no. 2 (1 August):33-36.
In an unfavorable review of Words, finds Creeley's poetry vague and empty. Claims his readers participate in the ambiguous situations. Notes the lineation of "Joy." Reprinted in part: 1987.19.

23   VAS DIAS, ROBERT. "Memorandum to Monett." Cultural Affairs: A Quarterly Magazine of Associated Councils of the Arts, no. 3, pp. 15-19.
Details the objections parents in Monett, Missouri, had to his using Creeley's "I Know a Man" as an example of contemporary poetry in a junior and senior high school in January 1967. Explicates the poem and notes the comments made by students to sections of it. See 1968.8.

24   WAGGONER, HYATT H[OWE]. American Poets: From the Puritans to
      the Present. Boston: Houghton Mifflin Co., pp. 622–23,
      625–26.
           Quotes and briefly comments on the imagery in "The Mountains
      in the Desert." Suggests that Creeley is in the Emerson–Whitman
      tradition.

25   WAGNER, LINDA WELSHIMER. "Ancients and Moderns: Some Simi-
      larities." East–West Review: A Journal of Literary Criticism
      3, no. 3 (Winter):273–80.
           Claims that Creeley, like the Greek poets, uses his own
      "speech rhythm" to write as in "The Warning."

26   WAGNER, LINDA [WELSHIMER], and MacADAMS, LEWIS, [Jr.]. "The
      Art of Poetry, X: Robert Creeley." Paris Review 11, no. 44
      (Fall):155–87.
           In a series of interviews with Wagner from 1963 to 1965 and
      an interview in spring 1968 with MacAdams, Creeley provides fur-
      ther biographical information about his childhood, his contacts
      with Pound, his intensity and its effects on people, and his re-
      turn trip from England after World War II. Also mentions his stay
      in San Francisco in 1956; his fights, including one with Jackson
      Pollock; and his relationship to Duncan, Olson, Blackburn, René
      Laubiès, and a neighbor from New Hampshire, Ira Grant. Provides
      biographical information about living in Mallorca, teaching at
      Black Mountain College, smoking marijuana, and taking LSD, noting
      the latter's role in "The Finger."
           Creeley also mentions influences on him, especially Pound,
      and his influence on others. Comments on themes in his work, the
      creative process, his correspondence, and his writing habits.
      Also refers to writing what he does not know and not writing about
      subjects. Discusses his sense of place, locale, audience, commu-
      nication, and sincerity. When examining the differences between
      writing prose and poetry, finds prose is a way of working tenta-
      tively. Reminisces about planning to do another novel after The
      Island but dropping the plans. Mentions that he ends a poem when
      no "further activity is permitted."
           Wagner's interview is revised and rearranged from 1965.24.
      The entire is reprinted in 1972.13; abridged and translated as
      1971.22; a brief portion of MacAdams's interview is reprinted in
      1977.15. The fullest versions are in 1973.7 where both are re-
      vised, expanded, and separately published as 1973.32 and 1973.47.

27   WILL, FREDERIC. "To Take Place and to 'Take Heart.'" Poetry
      111, no. 4 (January):256–58.
           In a favorable review of Words, finds the poems narratives
      of "states of awareness, attention, and intention," mentioning a
      few poems, especially "Waiting." Reprinted: 1987.19.

28   WILLIAMS, JONATHAN. "'A Void of Smug': To the Editor." New
      York Times Book Review, 7 January, pp. 22, 26.
         In this letter to the editor, finds the tone of 1967.19
      smug, overly concerned with originality, and too ready to casti-
      gate Black Mountain poetry. See 1968.20.

                               1969

1   BAYES, RONALD H. Review of Pieces. Human Voice 5, nos. 1-4
      [whole nos. 18-21]:126-28.
         In this review, notes the sources of the poems, demonstrat-
      ing where Creeley "invokes" the voices of Zukofsky, Ginsberg,
      Eliot, Jonathan Williams, and Sam Miller. Especially praises
      "Numbers."

2   BRIEN, DOLORES ELISE. "A Study of the Poetry of Robert Creeley
      and Robert Duncan in Relation to the Emerson-Whitman Tradi-
      tion." Ph.D. dissertation, Brown University, pp. iv-viii, 1-
      67, 164-66.
         Links Creeley to the "empirical, skeptical, rebellious" side
      of the Emersonian tradition "which existed in polarity with the
      optimistic, idealistic, and mystical side." Compares Creeley's
      treatment of the self to Whitman's, noting that Creeley's "absorp-
      tion with the self" has roots in Emerson's emphasis on "the cen-
      trality of the individual." Compares Emerson's ideas on religion
      to Creeley's. In Creeley's poetry, discusses "the image of the
      'locked mind,' the mind as a prisoner of the psyche, powerless to
      know the truth or find meaning beyond an instant's occasion."
      Compares this image to the image of "the haunted mind" in
      Dickinson's poetry and to figures of self-imposed exile in
      Hawthorne's fiction. Discusses other recurring images in
      Creeley's work, especially that of "a placeless 'place'" and of
      the house, the latter often equated with the body and "connected
      with sexual and domestic conflict."
         Notes Coleridge and Emerson as sources for Creeley's state-
      ments on the organic nature of poetry. Comments on the sparsity
      of particulars in his poetry, noting another Emersonian parallel,
      and compares his work to Duncan's. Discusses Creeley's treatment
      of love, self-hatred, failure, and friendship. Also notes his
      themes of relationships, women, marriage, and sex, the latter
      "often associated with death and destruction." Comments on a
      number of Creeley's works, particularly "The Mountains in the
      Desert," "The Window ['Position is where you']," "A Sight,"
      "Anger," and The Island. See Dissertation Abstracts International
      35 (1975):5388-89A.

3   CHUNG, LING. "Predicaments in Robert Creeley's Words."
      Concerning Poetry 2, no. 2 (Fall):32-35.

RC1969

Uses "Walking," "The Circle ['Houses in']," "The Mountains
in the Desert," and "A Birthday" to argue that, in Words, Creeley
finds himself isolated, in a struggle with language, and unable to
communicate. Believes Creeley has "displaced the function of
physical and mental faculties" in his poetry, and notes walking
imagery.

4   COX, KENNETH. "Address and Posture in the Poetry of Robert
    Creeley." Cambridge Quarterly 4, no. 3 (Summer):237-43.
        Discusses the typical type of address, that of the "first
person [the poet] speaking to second (mute) with awareness of
unknown third [the reader]," and posture in Creeley's poetry.
Using a number of poems as examples, comments on Creeley's use of
language, rhyming words, silence, conclusions, and literary allusions. Finds that his poems provide an accurate measure of the
most minute of emotional and conscious states. Slightly revised:
1978.14; 1987.19.

5   "Creeley, Robert (White)." In 200 Contemporary Authors: Bio-
    Bibliographies of Selected Leading Writers of Today with Crit-
    ical and Personal Insights. Edited by Barbara Harte and
    Carolyn Riley. Detroit: Gale Research Co., pp. 83-85.
        Expansion of 1963.6; update of 1967.6.

6   CREELEY, ROBERT. "Basil Bunting: An Appreciation." Stony
    Brook, nos. 3-4 [America: A Prophecy issue], pp. 57-58.
        Reprint of 1965.3.

7   ____. "Introduction" to The Black Mountain Review. 3 vols.
    New York: AMS Press, 1:iii-xiii.
        Creeley provides the biographical and theoretical background
for his involvement as publisher of the Black Mountain Review and,
to a lesser extent, Divers Press. Mentions contacts with Jacob
Leed, W.C. Williams, Pound, Corman, Olson, Martin Seymour-Smith,
Irving Layton, Blackburn, Rexroth, Duncan, Levertov, and Alexander
Trocchi, who he identifies as Manus in The Island. Discusses his
early publications, especially in Origin and Golden Goose, and
comments on how these and other magazines of the early 1950s influenced Black Mountain Review. Mentions Olson's influence on
him, and provides biographical details from the spring of 1956.
Reprinted: 1978.21-22; 1979.15. Revised: 1971.5.

8   [CREELEY, ROBERT.] Note to A Wall. New York: Bouwerie Edi-
    tions; Stuttgart: Edition Domberger, [p. 5].
        Provides the specific occasion when "A Wall" was written.

9   CREELEY, ROBERT. "Notes Apropos 'Free Verse.'" In Naked
    Poetry: Recent American Poetry in Open Forms. Edited by

Stephen Berg and Robert Mezey. Indianapolis: Bobbs-Merrill
Co., pp. 185-87.
    In this 1966 essay, Creeley discusses his own writing,
describing how it is to work without forethought and drawing a
parallel to action painting. Also writes of how he senses a
rhythm in the poem at hand and draws parallels to the jazz of
Charlie Parker. Reprinted: 1970.14; 1972.13.

10   . "Preface" to The Charm: Early and Uncollected Poems.
    Writing, 23. San Francisco: Four Seasons Foundation, pp. xi-
    xii.
        Reprint of 1967.10.

11 DUDDY, THOMAS A[NTHONY]. "On Robert Creeley." Stony Brook,
    nos. 3-4 [America: A Prophecy issue], pp. 385-87.
        In a favorable review of Words, discusses Creeley's isola-
    tion, from which he describes a "limitless particularity of expe-
    rience." Comments on Creeley's poetry as an act, his imagery of
    the "existential void," and his themes of language and love.
    Discusses "A Piece."

12 [FLAHERTY, DOUGLAS, and BRADFORD, JAMES.] "An Interview with
    Robert Creeley." Road Apple Review 1, no. 1 (Winter):36-38;
    no. 2 (Spring):32-34; no. 3 (Fall):35-36.
        In this 1968 interview, Creeley comments on the type of
    experience that leads him to a poem. Reprinted: 1973.7.

13 HOWARD, RICHARD. "Robert Creeley: 'I Begin Where I Can, and
    End When I See the Whole Thing Returning.'" In Alone with
    America: Essays on the Art of Poetry in the United States
    since 1950. New York: Atheneum, pp. 65-74.
        Reprint of 1968.15.

14 JOHNSTON, RAND, ed. "An Interview with Robert Creeley." Opus
    (U.S. International University, California Western Campus),
    no. 7, pp. 46-48.
        In this interview, Creeley comments on his early attempts at
    writing, his inability to write political poetry or to revise, and
    his use of the quatrain. Mentions not questioning "formal real-
    ity" or the trivial in his recent poetry.

15 MARTZ, LOUIS L. "Recent Poetry: The End of an Era." Yale
    Review: A National Quarterly 59, no. 2 (December [Winter 1970
    on cover]):252-67.
        In a favorable review of Pieces, emphasizes Creeley's focus
    on "unstable, apparent forms" and his use of abstractions, noting
    "the process of creation and recreation" in the work. Reprinted
    in part: 1987.19.

RC1969

16   RABAN, JONATHAN. "Chance, Time, and Silence: The New American
      Verse." Journal of American Studies 3, no. 1 (July):89–101.
          Mentions Creeley's use of silence, immediacy, and "language
      as speech." In "Hello," finds "the formulaic language of the sex-
      and–violence thriller," but notes the phrases "are dislocated" to
      create new significance.

17   WHITTEMORE, REED. Review of Pieces. New Republic: A Journal
      of Politics and the Arts 161, no. 15 (11 October):25–26.
          In this unfavorable review, emphasizes the pedagogic quality
      of the poetry, claiming Creeley uses his work as a demonstration
      that, among other things, the poem need not be "an inviolable
      aesthetic and intellectual whole." Reprinted: 1987.19.

                                1970

1   AIKEN, WILLIAM [MINOR]. "'My mind to me a mangle is.'" Kayak,
      no. 23, pp. 63–67.
          In an unfavorable review of Pieces, finds "form understood
      purely as 'process,'" an "abstract solipsism," a haste in writing,
      and a "general insouciance," but finds a bit more imagery in the
      last few pages. Comparing many of the poems in For Love to those
      in Pieces, feels the poems in the former place more emphasis on
      the objective world. Notes variations in the published forms of
      some of the poems in Pieces, contradicting Creeley's stated
      "poetry as process" method. Revised as part of chapter 6, pp. 93–
      101, of 1977.1.

*2   BACON, REG. "An Interview with Robert Creeley." Cape Ann
      Summer Sun, 25 July, pp. 1–3.
          Unavailable for annotation. (Listed in 1984.27, p. 348.)

3   BANKS, RUSSELL. "Notes on Creeley's Pieces." Lillabulero: A
      Journal of Contemporary Writing, 2d ser., no. 8 (Winter),
      pp. 88–91.
          In this favorable review, discusses the thematic structure
      of Pieces which deals successively with "the unity of one"; the
      "duality of the monad"; motion; "the unity of the present"; the
      search for morality; the "transition from the self to Other"; and
      the "internalization of the past." Believes this sequence inte-
      grates the entire volume. Reprinted: 1987.19.

4   BERTHOLF, ROBERT J[OHN]. "The Key in the Window: Kent's Col-
      lection of Modern American Poetry." Serif: A Quarterly of
      the Kent State University Libraries 7, no. 3 (September):52–70.
          Mentions Creeley's relationship to other poets, especially
      Olson and Corman, comments on his role in Divers Press and the
      Black Mountain Review, and gives a few biographical details.

                                 44

Provides an overview of Creeley's publication history. Comments
on his focus on "the processes of his mind" and his more recent
relaxation.

5   BOWEN, C. [identified as CARL HARRISON-FORD in 1973.37, item
    B245]. "A Continuity, a Place: The Poetry of Robert Creeley."
    Poetry Magazine (Sydney) 18, no. 5 (October):3-9.
        Discusses the influence of Olson and projective poetics on
    Creeley. Compares "The Sentence" with "The Language," finding the
    latter more spontaneous, personal, and easier to locate in inci-
    dent. Discusses "The Riddle," "The Business," and "The End,"
    noting the moralism, stanza breaks, and rhymes.

6   BUCHOLTZ, MEL. "Dynamic Crystalization [sic]: Creeley's
    Pieces." Sumac 2, nos. 2-3 (Winter-Spring):237-39.
        In this favorable review, finds Pieces "a celebration of not
    having to grasp the world as a way of either knowing or appreciat-
    ing existence within/apart from it."

7   BUNKER, ROBERT. "Creeley's Hurts." New Mexico Review 2, nos.
    6-7 (June-July):27-29.
        In a favorable review of Pieces, notes the typography, use
    of fragments, and treatment of women figures, especially in "The
    Finger." Reminisces about Creeley's reading at New Mexico High-
    lands University.

8   BUTTERICK, GEORGE F. "An Annotated Guide to The Maximus Poems
    of Charles Olson." Ph.D. dissertation, State University of New
    York at Buffalo, pp. 1, 50, 103.
        Explains allusions to Creeley in Olson's The Maximus Poems.
    Revised and greatly expanded: 1978.8. See Dissertation Abstracts
    International 31 (1971):4756A.

9   CARRUTH, HAYDEN. "Creeley, Robert (White)." In Contemporary
    Poets of the English Language. Edited by Rosalie Murphy and
    James Vinson. Chicago and London: St. James Press,
    pp. 244-45.
        After a brief bibliography, notes Creeley's technical abil-
    ities and influence on others. Slightly revised with additional
    material in the bibliography: 1975.1.

10 CHARTERS, ANN. "Introduction" to The Special View of History,
    by Charles Olson. Berkeley: Oyez, pp. 1-12.
        Briefly mentions Creeley's role at Black Mountain College
    and quotes from a 7 July 1969 interview in which Creeley provides
    a few biographical details, especially on his first teaching at
    Black Mountain, his first meeting with Olson in 1954, and his
    contacts with Duncan in 1955. In a 5 June 1969 interview with
    Duncan, Duncan briefly mentions Creeley as a Black Mountain poet.

RC1970

11 COOLEY, PETER. Review of <u>Pieces</u>. <u>North American Review</u>, o.s.
    255, no. 2 [n.s. 7, no. 2--running concurrently] (Summer):
    74-76.
        In this unfavorable review, feels <u>Pieces</u> is self-conscious,
    too individual, and apparently overly concerned with language,
    unlike <u>For Love</u> and <u>Words</u>. Enjoys "Numbers," notes W.C.
    Williams's influence, and finds <u>Pieces</u> in the "American epic tra-
    dition." Reprinted: 1987.19.

12 CORMAN, CID. "Bibliographical Notes: A Note on the Founding
    of <u>Origin</u>." <u>Origin: A Quarterly for the Creative</u>, Ser. 1.
    Vol. 3. Nendeln, Liechtenstein: Kraus Reprint, [last 2 pp.].
    Reprint of 1968.4.

13 C[REELEY], R[OBERT]. Preface to <u>The Finger: Poems, 1966-1969</u>.
    London: Calder & Boyars, [p. 11].
    Reprint of 1967.11.

14 CREELEY, ROBERT. <u>A Quick Graph: Collected Notes and Essays</u>.
    Edited by Donald [Merriam] Allen. Writing, edited by Donald
    [Merriam] Allen, no. 22. San Francisco: Four Seasons Founda-
    tion, 365 pp.
        Includes reprints of 1954.3; 1955.1, 4; 1956.1; 1957.1-2;
    1959.2; 1960.3; 1961.1; 1963.8; 1965.3 (as "A Personal Note"), 5
    (as "A Note on Ezra Pound"); 1966.7, 9 (as "'Poems are a com-
    plex'"), 11-12; 1967.7 (as "Feedback: 'Contemporary Voices in the
    Arts'"), 11, 12 (as "'I'm given to write poems'"); 1969.9.

15 _____. Response in "The Writer's Situation, II." <u>New American
    Review</u>, no. 10, pp. 220-28.
        In this series of responses to six sets of questions,
    Creeley mentions his sense of intention in writing, his relation-
    ship to tradition, his past and present standards, and his inabil-
    ity to revise or write political poetry. Also comments on reviews
    of his work and on writing as a "reification, of <u>what is</u>."
    Reprinted (as "The Writer's Situation"): 1972.13; 1973.7.

16 _____. "Writing." In <u>Writers as Teachers/Teachers as Writers</u>.
    Edited by Jonathan Baumbach. New York: Holt, Rinehart, &
    Winston, pp. 26-41.
        Creeley provides a few biographical details about his teach-
    ing and includes a reprint of 1968.5.

17 DORN, EDWARD. Review of <u>Pieces</u>. <u>Caterpillar: "A Gathering of
    the Tribes</u>," no. 10 (January), pp. 248-50.
        In a favorable review, finds each poem or piece "a model of
    a social universe located by a very high degree of resolution,"
    each potentially defining the whole. See also 1971.18. Reprinted
    in part: 1980.15.

18   [EHRENPREIS, IRVIN.] "World of Sensible Particulars." Times
     Literary Supplement, 7 August, p. 871.
        In this lengthy, favorable review of The Charm (1969), dis-
     cusses Creeley's subjects, including the "complexities of rela-
     tionships," the "act of composition itself," and the "examination
     of selfhood." Discusses the sexual theme of "Two Times ['It takes
     so long to look down']." Examines the rhythm and shift in "Chas-
     ing the Bird," as well as "Not Again" and "Hélas." Less favorably
     reviews A Quick Graph. Reprinted: 1971.9; 1987.19.

19   "Falling Water and Fading Flames." Times Literary Supplement,
     11 December, p. 1436.
        In a moderately favorable review of The Finger: Poems,
     1966-1969 (1970), comments on the themes and on Creeley's "cryp-
     tic, offhand and disjointed" manner. Mentions "Here ['Past time--
     those']" and Creeley's continual "self-scrutiny."

20   FOX, HUGH. The Living Underground: A Critical Overview.
     Troy, N.Y.: Whitson Publishing Co., pp. 133, 139-40, 144.
        Although Richard Morris ridicules him in such poems as "The
     Conspiracy," finds Morris influenced by Creeley. Feels "Creelian
     reality" is "overly self involved" and divorced from the "new
     mystical socio-economic consciousness."

21   GOULDEN, ALBAN SHERMAN. "In Order to Continue the Tale over
     the Teller: Durrell, Creeley, Lawrence." M.A. thesis, Simon
     Fraser University, pp. 47-74, 115-16, passim.
        Discusses The Island, focusing on the characters and their
     relationships. Also examines the treatment of death, guilt, in-
     trusions, time, change, and the present. Comments on Creeley's
     use of narrative time, and notes the role of grace and of the
     characters' inaction. Also comments on "The Grace."

22   HAMBURGER, MICHAEL. The Truth of Poetry: Tensions in Modern
     Poetry from Baudelaire to the 1960s. New York: Harcourt,
     Brace, & World, pp. 122, 312, 284-86.
        Briefly mentions Pound's influence on Creeley and the impor-
     tance of hearing Creeley read his own work. Applies Creeley's
     "Introduction" to The New Writing in the USA, ed. Donald [Merriam]
     Allen and Robert Creeley (Harmondsworth, England: Penguin Books,
     1967), pp. 17-24, to his concept of the roles of ego, form, and
     place in poetry; the sense of the poem as a field; and writing as
     a process or an enactment. Also notes his perceptions of Pound
     and Olson.

23   HUGHES, DANIEL. "American Poetry, 1969: From B to Z."
     Massachusetts Review: A Quarterly of Literature, the Arts, and
     Public Affairs 11, no. 4 (Autumn):650-86.

RC1970

In a brief, unfavorable review of Pieces, compares Creeley's
emphasis on the present and spontaneity to D.H. Lawrence's, but
feels Creeley's poems "are all theory."

24   LEVERTOV, DENISE. "'What makes the shadows darker.'"
      Caterpillar: "A Gathering of the Tribes," no. 10 (January),
      pp. 246-48.
          In a favorable review of Pieces, finds the volume continuing
      the direction of "The Door ['It is hard going to the door']" into
      an openness and "immersion in what happens." Praises its "intui-
      tive basis" and sense of freedom. Reprinted: 1973.31; 1987.19.

25   LOCKE, JO ELLEN. "Robert Creeley: An Annotated Bibliography."
      M.L.S. thesis, Kent State University, 65 pp.
          Provides an annotated primary and secondary bibliography on
      Creeley, including his books; broadsides; works in anthologies and
      magazines; prefaces and introductions; essays, criticism, notes,
      reviews, published letters, and prose comments; and editorial
      work. Secondary work includes reviews and essays on Creeley as
      well as interviews with him.

26   McGANN, JEROME. "Poetry and Truth." Poetry 17, no. 3
      (December):195-203.
          Favorably reviewing Pieces, notes the sparsity of the
      poetry, and claims the pieces and the sequences are clearly seen.

27   MAZZARO, JEROME. "Integrites." Kenyon Review 32, no. 1 [whole
      no. 128] (Spring):163-68.
          In a favorable review of Pieces, notes the sense of stum-
      bling, the treatment of the woman figure, and the role of self-
      definition and the present in Creeley's poetry. Comments on "The
      Finger," For Love, and Words.

28   OLSON, CHARLES. The Berkeley Reading. Transcribed by Ralph
      Maud. [Burnaby, British Columbia: Ralph Maud, privately
      printed for classroom use], pp. 2-4, 8, 10, 12-15, 44, 55-56,
      64-65, 68, passim.
          Another version of 1966.23 with annotations, more attribu-
      tions of voices, transcription of intermission and peripheral
      conversation, and an index. Includes quotes from and comments on
      Creeley in annotations, mentioning that he "had broken down . . .
      the previous night [22 July 1965] 'from an excess of fatigue'
      after reading the poem 'To Bobbie.'" Relates the female figure in
      "The Door ['It is hard going to the door']" to feminine figures in
      his own and Ginsberg's poetry. (This, with 1966.24, forms the
      basis of 1978.57.)

29   _____. Letters for "Origin," 1950-1956. Edited by Albert
      [Gould] Glover. New York: Cape Goliard Press in association

with Grossman Publishers, pp. 59-60, 63, 66-67, 74, 87-88, 112, 133, 136-37, passim.
Reprinted from 1968.18, omitting letters and sections of letters. Reprinted in part: 1983.5, without later letters, adding portions of early ones, and including Corman's replies.

30 OPPENHEIMER, JOEL. "The Inner Tightrope: An Appreciation of Robert Creeley." Lillabulero: A Journal of Contemporary Writing, 2d ser., no. 8 (Winter), pp. 51-53.
In this appreciation, Oppenheimer discusses his relationship, beginning in 1951, to Creeley. Also mentions influences on Creeley, the tension in his poetry, and his "essential shyness."

31 SOLT, MARY ELLEN, ed. "A World Look at Concrete Poetry." In Concrete Poetry: A World View. Bloomington and London: Indiana University Press, pp. 6-66.
Reprint of 1968.21.

32 SORRENTINO, GILBERT. "Black Mountaineering." Poetry 116, no. 2 (May):110-20.
In a favorable review of Numbers, focuses on the volume as an extension of Words, but finds Robert Indiana's serigraphs unnecessary. Discusses Creeley as a successor of W.C. Williams and mentions his role as editor of the Black Mountain Review. Reprinted: 1984.36; reprinted in part: 1987.19.

33 TAGETT, RICHARD. Review of Pieces. Manroot, no. 2 (January): 61-64.
In this favorable review, focuses on the imperfection of the poems caused by the poet being a "very much In-The-World poet."

34 THURLEY, GEOFFREY. "The New Phenomenalist Poetry in the U.S.A." Southern Review (English Department, University of Adelaide, Australia) 4, no. 1:15-28.
Finding Creeley's sources in objectivism, claims he goes beyond "actual experience" to "metaphysical interpretation" in a poetry of "penetrating awareness."

35 [TOMLINSON, CHARLES.] "Working Their Way through College." Times Literary Supplement, 12 February, p. 178.
In a favorable review of the Black Mountain Review (3 vols. [New York: AMS Press, 1969]), briefly charts Creeley's role as editor.

1971

1 ANDRÉ, [KENNETH] MICHAEL. "Robert Creeley: An Interview." Unmuzzled Ox 1, no. 1 (November):23-45.

RC1971

In this June 1971 interview, continued in 1973.3, Creeley
discusses writing Listen, The Island, Pieces, "Numbers," and
"Canada," providing his intentions for Pieces and sources for the
latter two poems. Also discusses "The Dress," especially his use
of a cave in it, and "I Know a Man," commenting on his meaning and
the figure of John. Mentions other writers, especially those who
influenced him and who are friends such as Richard Brautigan; the
movie made from Jeremy Larner's Drive, He Said; and the lack of
political statement in his work. Also comments on some criticism
on his work, especially 1960.1, and his ideas of form. Discusses
trying to get to the essentials of an experience in his poetry,
dropping out of Harvard, and teaching in Vancouver. Provides a
number of biographical details. Reprinted: 1973.7; 1974.2.

2   BOWERING, GEORGE, and HOGG, ROBERT. Robert Duncan: An Inter-
    view. Toronto: [Coach House Press], Beaver Kosmos Folio, [pp.
    4-5, 11-12, 23-24, 26].
        In this 19 April 1969 interview, Duncan mentions first read-
ing and being puzzled by Creeley's poetry but being impressed by
his stories. Reminisces about visiting Creeley in Mallorca and
interesting him in Coleridge, Zukofsky, and H.D. Comments on "The
Door ['It is hard going to the door']," Creeley's sources in
Thomas Campion and Robert Graves, and the "sub-meaning levels" in
his poetry.

3   CHARTERS, SAMUEL. "Robert Creeley: 'Waiting,' 'The World,'
    'Water (2),' 'The Eye,' 'Fragments.'" In Some Poems/Poets:
    Studies in American Underground Poetry since 1945. Berkeley:
    Oyez, pp. 85-95.
        Analyzing "Waiting," "The World," "Water (2) ['Water
drips']," and "The Eye ['The eye I look out of']," discusses the
terseness and the "tension in poetic diction," the honesty and the
"intense emotional directness," and the theme of feared inadequacy.

4   COONEY, SEAMUS. A Checklist of the First One Hundred Publica-
    tions of the Black Sparrow Press. Los Angeles: Black Sparrow
    Press, pp. 18, 25-26, 37.
        Provides brief descriptive bibliographical information on
The Finger (1968), Pieces, and As Now It Would Be Snow. Also
notes statements contributed by Creeley to the works of others.
See 1981.21.

5   CREELEY, ROBERT. "The Black Mountain Review." Works: A
    Quarterly of Writing 2, no. 4 (Spring):45-54.
        Revision of 1969.7.

6   _____. "Preface" to The Charm: Early and Uncollected Poems.
    London: Calder & Boyars, pp. xi-xii.
        Reprint of 1967.10.

50

7 _____. Teenage Reading Habits. In Attacks of Taste. Edited
by Evelyn B. Byrne and Otto M. Penzler. New York: Gotham Book
Mart, pp. 15-16.
Creeley reminisces about his teenage reading, especially of
Tolstoÿ.

8 DUNN, STEVE; EMERSON, STEVE; and STOKES, HARRY. "An Interview
with Robert Creeley." Archive (Duke University) 83, no. 3
(Spring):63-73.
In this interview, Creeley mentions the lack of intention
and revision in his writing and his early shyness. Notes this
shyness might have made him "economical, wanting to say as little
as possible as often as possible," and wary "of overstatement and
any kind of excessive attributing of emotion." Comments on
Olson's influence, comparisons between himself and Ginsberg, and
his sense of projective verse. Provides biographical details
about learning to read in school and about "murmuring," articulat-
ing the sounds, when writing. Notes the "visual context" of some
of his early poems like "Hi There!," and claims that only recently
he has thought of himself as a poet. Mentions teaching, writing,
and learning how to teach at Black Mountain College, and teaching
at San Francisco State College. Remarks on the process of writing
A Day Book and the order, the coherence, of the work.

9 [EHRENPREIS, IRVIN.] "Poetry of 1970: Robert Creeley."
T.L.S.: Essays and Reviews from the "Times Literary
Supplement," 1970. Vol. 9. London: Oxford University Press,
pp. 79-83.
Reprint of 1970.18.

10 GRENIER, ROBERT. Review of Pieces. This, no. 1 (Winter),
[pp. 88-91].
In this favorable review, emphasizes Creeley's energetic use
of the language. Sees his poetry, in fact, as "the life of the
man in language."

11 _____. Review of A Quick Graph. This, no. 1 (Winter),
[pp. 82-85].
In this basically favorable review, finds the volume an
"introduction to twentieth century American poetry to date" and to
concepts "of crucial importance for anyone writing today," but
claims Creeley's groping with the language indicates the work's
referential, and thus expendable, nature.

12 JOHNSON, LEE ANN. "Robert Creeley: A Checklist, 1946-1970."
Twentieth Century Literature: A Scholarly and Critical Journal
17, no. 3 (July):181-98.
Provides a primary bibliography of Creeley's books, broadsides, contributions to books and periodicals, recordings,

RC1971

interviews, and poems, as well as a selected secondary bibliography of books, book reviews, dissertations, and essays on
Creeley's work.

13   KAUFMAN, ROBERT F. "The Poetry of Robert Creeley." Thoth:
      Syracuse University Graduate Studies in English 11 (Winter):
      28-36.
            Sees Creeley's work as highly projectivist, with "no real
      beginning and no real end," capturing the energy of the mind in
      flux. Finds parallels with Dickinson and a continual fear of loss
      and failure in the work. Explicates "The Riddle" and "The Rocks,"
      finding an integral connection between the love relationship and
      words.

14   KOSTELANETZ, RICHARD. "The Rule of Power, Corruption, and
      Repression." December: A Magazine of Arts and Opinion 13,
      nos. 1-2:11-39.
            Claims Creeley chose only Black Mountain and Beat Poets for
      inclusion in American Literary Anthology 1: The First Annual
      Collection of the Best from the Literary Magazines (New York:
      Farrar, Strauss, & Giroux, 1968). Finds A Quick Graph narrow in
      its sympathies. Reprinted: 1971.30.

15   LINK, FRANZ H. "Amerikanische Lyrik der Gegenwart." [In
      German.] In Amerikanische Literatur im 20. Jahrhundert/
      American Literature in the 20th Century. Edited by Alfred
      Weber and Dietmar Haack. Göttingen, West Germany: Vandenhoeck
      & Ruprecht, pp. 206-48.
            Comparing "I Know a Man" to Olson's "I, Maximus of
      Gloucester, to You," discusses Creeley's lineation, noting its
      breathlessness and staccato rhythms, and relineates the poem to
      clarify its meaning and to demonstrate its structure. Compares
      Creeley's use of darkness as fear in "I Know a Man" to William
      Stafford's in "Traveling through the Dark." Discusses his disap-
      pointment with the rhythm of Creeley's reading of "The Rhythm" on
      the record accompanying Robert Creeley Reads, and again suggests a
      relineation.

16   OLSON, CHARLES. Letter to Cid Corman. Origin, 3d ser.,
      Center, no. 20 (January), pp. 42-52.
            In this letter, probably from 30 May 1953, Olson occasion-
      ally notes his correspondence with Creeley and what he learned
      from Creeley's short stories. Slightly revised: 1975.16.

17   _____. Letter to Robert Creeley, 21 April 1950. Maps, no. 4
      [Charles Olson Issue], p. 8.
            Olson mentions W.C. Williams's recommendation that he write
      Creeley, and notes Creeley's reaction to the first poems that he
      submitted. Reprinted in 1973.4; 1979.21; 1980.26.

18   POTTS, CHARLES. "Pieces: The Decline of Creeley." West Coast
       Review: A Quarterly Magazine of the Arts 5, no. 4 (April):3-5.
         Arguing against 1970.17, finds Pieces to be "narrower in
    range than Creeley's earlier work" and lacking a "unified effect."
    Believes it contains poems written in self-emulation as well as a
    few good poems such as "The Finger." Classifies the poems into
    four types, notes Creeley's influence on others, and comments on
    his critical reception.

19   RABAN, JONATHAN. The Society of the Poem. London: George G.
       Harrap & Co., pp. 23-24, passim.
         Notes that "Hello" has the "cliché phrasing" of a thriller,
    briefly commenting on its lineation and syntax.

20   ROBINSON, WILLIAM R. "The Island." In Survey of Contemporary
       Literature. Edited by Frank N. Magill. Vol. 4. New York:
       Salem Press, pp. 2272-74.
         Places The Island in an American tradition that depicts the
    liberating value of art, but finds it more psychological and de-
    spondent than other work in the tradition. Characterizes John as
    an introvert unable to transcend his own painful existence. Re-
    printed: 1977.18.

21   SHEFFLER, RONALD ANTHONY. "The Development of Robert Creeley's
       Poetry." Ph.D. dissertation, University of Massachusetts,
       139 pp.
         Finds Creeley in the tradition of American poetry and
    aligned with Pound, W.C. Williams, Zukofsky, and Olson. Maintains
    that Creeley's work is not about a subject in the traditional
    sense and does not need the understanding of every reader, or
    "universal validity," to be viable. Notes that the reader must
    bring "his own awareness, his own intensities" to the poem. Em-
    phasizes his break with formalism and use of poetry as a means of
    spontaneous discovery, often of self-understanding. Provides
    brief but substantive readings for many of the poems in For Love,
    discussing "For Love" and "The Door ['It is hard going to the
    door']" at some length. Notes Creeley's use of repetition, humor,
    common language, myth, garden imagery, and rhythm. Discusses his
    treatment of isolation, loneliness, love, guilt, and torment.
    Also examines the themes of cruelty, thought, sex, and the woman
    figure as muse, wife, or mistress. Comments on his sense of form
    and content, his seriousness, and his attention to the simple and
    common.
         Discusses many of the poems in Words briefly but substan-
    tively, commenting on "Distance" and "Enough" at length as
    sequence-poems. Notes Creeley's "attentive passivity" in the
    creation of a poem, in the "open field of interest." Finds the
    phenomenology of Martin Heidegger "offers many parallels with
    Creeley's" work, especially noting the angst in a number of poems

as the mind loses "touch with the things-that-are." In Words, discusses Creeley's treatment of uncertainty, time, lack of fini- tude, disintegration, and place. Also mentions the themes of security, language, words, silence, and the natural rhythms of life in the volume, noting his use of the water metaphor. Also mentions the length of his lines and poems, discussing his use of the sequence.

   Claims Creeley uses the poetry in Pieces to reenact the thought processes and thereby make poetry, as Olson suggested, an active, kinetic force. Also mentions how the poems display a search for identity and how they entail "the immediate and sur- rounding circumstances" of Creeley's life. Notes the role of the present and of pieces within the whole, the treatment of words, actuality, and "here" and "there." Comments on many of the indi- vidual poems and especially discusses Creeley's atypical use of a subject, numbers, and his "destruction of simple progression" in "Numbers." Discusses "The Finger" in some detail, especially focusing on the role of LSD and the treatment of the poet and of the mythic woman figure or "Mother of All Living." Notes paral- lels to Robert Graves's The White Goddess. See Dissertation Abstracts International 32 (1971):2104A.

22   [WAGNER, LINDA WELSHIMER, and MacADAMS, LEWIS, Jr.] "Les Influences." [In French.] Lettres nouvelles [41 Poètes américains d'aujourd'hui issue], December 1970–January, pp. 213–17.
         Abridged and translated from 1968.26.

23   WESLING, DONALD. "The Prosodies of Free Verse." In Twentieth- Century Literature in Retrospect. Edited by Reuben A. Brower. Harvard English Studies, no. 2. Cambridge, Mass.: Harvard University Press, pp. 155–87.
         Uses "Le Fou" as an example of the use of a "dismembered" poetic line that is also continuous. Revised: 1985.25.

1972

1   ALPERT, BARRY. "Ed Dorn: An Interview." Vort, no. 1 [Ed Dorn/Tom Raworth Number] (Fall), pp. 2–20.
         In this 31 July 1972 interview, Dorn briefly mentions Creeley's role as the "outside examiner" of his written exam- inations at Black Mountain College. Reprinted: 1980.1.

2   ALTIERI, CHARLES. "The Unsure Egoist: Robert Creeley and the Theme of Nothingness." Contemporary Literature 13, no. 2 (Spring):162–85.
         Finds an opposition in Creeley's poetry between "action where self and world are united" and "description where subject

and object are disjoined," the self alienated. Finds the fear of
this void generates his best poetry (but see 1978.36), and notes
the sense of "dangling at the edge of an?abyss" in Creeley's use
of the short line. Examines his treatment of the failure of communication, his search for an adequate language, and his attempts
"to wrench the formulas of 'idle talk' into authentic speech"
using ambiguity and a limited vocabulary. Comments on the role of
speech in "I Know a Man" and the relationship of the object to
value and the inability to "rediscover the Ground of Being" in
"The Rhyme." Mentions the treatment of the self in "The Sign
Board," the role of puns in "The Kid ['If it falls flat']," and
the treatment of the "fragmented self" that desires unity in "The
Flower ['I think I grow tensions']." Charts the structure of For
Love from alienation, through the dissolution of his first marriage, and to the resolution of his new marriage.
    Discovers Creeley's "resolution has begun to crumble" in
Words since he sought a ground outside of time's flux; believes
the goal of Words is to discover the ideal ground that "can be
reconciled with the flux." Mentions the treatment of freedom,
desire, and fulfillment in "For W.C.W. ['The rhyme is after']."
Notes the themes of place and emptiness in "Joy" and of nothingness and love in "The Language." Feels Creeley finds the void
essential and that place "must be found within a series of shifting accommodations" in Words. Treats Creeley's use of "here" for
the "ideal of pure presence."
    In Pieces claims Creeley finds "'here' and 'there' must form
a kind of dialectic . . . in which permanence and flux, absence
and presence inform one another." Examines the resolution of "the
dualisms of man and nature, subject and object," as in "Numbers."
Finds an acceptance of "the absence needed to ground and generate
the form of relational system of numbers" in "Zero" from "Numbers." In this volume, also discusses Creeley's treatment of
possibility and limits, and discusses "They ['What could']."
Expanded and revised: 1979.1.

3   ANDRÉ, [KENNETH] MICHAEL. "Two Weeks with Creeley in Texas."
    Chicago Review 24, no. 2 [Voices, Faces: The War, the Rest--A
    Context issue]:81-86.
       Comments on Creeley's citation of others and his use of
    commas and "pet words" in his nonfiction prose, and on the charac-
    ter of the French painter in The Island. Also notes his use of
    line breaks, three-line stanzas, and word choice, claiming Creeley
    uses the "root meaning" of words in his poetry. Mentions the lack
    of both the "retrievable insights" and the "Great Issues" of
    "death and despair," as well as the tone of his poetry. Finds
    Pieces "skeptical" and dealing with the ego.

4   ARNOLD, EDMUND R., comp. "Robert Creeley: A Bibliography and
    Index of His Published Works and Criticism of Them to February

1, 1967." In Bibliographies in Contemporary Poetry. Collected
by Lewis Turco. Potsdam, N.Y.: Frederick W. Crumb Memorial
Library, pp. 9-16.
Provides a brief primary and secondary bibliography.

5   BLAZEK, DOUGLAS. "Two Reviews." Minnesota Review, NRP [New
Rivers Press—between the 1st and 2d ser.], no. 2 (Spring),
pp. 152-54.
In a negative review of St. Martin's, claims Creeley's
"sterile distance" is close to "existential indifference."

6   CALHOUN, DOUGLAS. "Robert Creeley: A Critical Checklist, Part
II: A Checklist." West Coast Review: A Quarterly Magazine of
the Arts 6, no. 3 (January):64-71.
Provides a single, alphabetical listing of "critical and
biographical" articles and reviews. In the introduction, provides
some biographical details and a list of interviews with and comments by Creeley.

7   CREELEY, ROBERT. Comments in "On the New Cultural Conserva-
tism." Partisan Review 39, no. 3 (Summer):415.
In this response to a set of questions, Creeley briefly
mentions that he artistically conservative.

8   _____. A Day Book. New York: Charles Scribner's Sons,
[163 pp.].
In the prose section, pp. [1-66], Creeley provides biographical details from 19 November 1968 to 27 February 1969, focusing
on his relationship to others, but also mentions his reading,
writing, and teaching. Comments on his trips, sexual encounters,
and poetry readings. Provides brief pieces of correspondence to
him from others, and reminisces about his mother and Aunt Bernice.
The prose section is reprinted with dates in 1976.5; 1984.12.

9   _____. "From 'Presences: A Text for Marisol.'" Big Sky, no.
4, [pp. 19-31].
Creeley provides biographical details about his childhood,
mentioning football, school, his glass eye, and friends. Reprinted in 1972.12; 1976.11-12.

10 _____. "A Note." Indian Journal of American Studies 2, no. 2
(December):15-16.
Creeley notes the first books by Pound that he had, the
influence of Pound on him, and Pound's importance to him.

11 _____. Prefatory note to L'Insulaire. Translated by Céline
Zins. Du monde entier. Paris: Gallimard, [p. 9].
Translation of 1963.8.

12 _____. "Presences." Io, no. 14 (Summer):183–226.
Includes reprints of 1972.9, 14. Reprinted: 1984.12.

13 _____. A Sense of Measure. Signature Series, no. 16. London:
Calder & Boyars, 120 pp.
Includes reprints of 1964.4; 1967.12 (as "'I'm Given to
Write Poems'"); 1968.26; 1969.9; 1970.15 (as "The Writer's
Situation").

14 _____. "The Stories Keep Coming." Fiction 1, no. 2 (Fall):
[24].
Creeley provides biographical details about living in New
Hampshire in the late 1940s and early 1950s, especially about
people who came by and visited with him and his wife Ann. Reprinted in 1972.12; 1976.11–12.

15 DEMBO, L[AWRENCE] S[ANFORD]. "An Interview with Paul
Blackburn." Contemporary Literature 13, no. 3 (Summer):133–43.
In this 25 May 1971 interview, Blackburn provides biographical details concerning his relationship to Creeley. Reprinted:
1983.8.

16 DUBERMAN, MARTIN. Black Mountain: An Exploration in Community. New York: E.P. Dutton & Co., pp. 378, 385–97, 400–
401, 490–92, passim.
Provides biographical material on Creeley, especially from
1950 to 1956, much of which came from a 3 October 1967 tape
Creeley made in response to a list of questions and from interviews and correspondence with others. Discusses Creeley's role in
the Black Mountain Review and his sense of similarity with others
classed as Black Mountain poets. Examines his teaching at Black
Mountain College and his relationship to others, especially Olson
and Dan Rice.

17 DUDDY, THOMAS A[NTHONY]. "Perception and Process: Studies in
the Poetry of Robert Creeley, Robert Duncan, Denise Levertov,
Charles Olson, and Louis Zukofsky." Ph.D. dissertation, State
University of New York at Buffalo, pp. 8–9, 80–106, passim.
Notes Creeley's use of line breaks or "stops," especially
when he reads his poetry. Finds his work an "enactment of the
mind," and discusses his treatment of time, thought, and reason.
Comments on his sense of measure and on "The Souvenir," noting its
imagery and dislocation. Discusses "Numbers" in detail, commenting on its circularity, and examines the treatment of isolation,
singularity and community, the child, and emptiness. Also mentions the figure of the fool and the role of sexuality, innocence,
and tension in the poem. See Dissertation Abstracts International
33 (1972):305–6A.

RC1972

18   GROSSINGER, RICHARD. "Interview with Stan Brakhage, 7 Jan.
      72." Io, no. 14 [Earth Geography Booklet, no. 3] (Summer),
      pp. 353-63.
           In this interview, Brakhage continually refers to a recent
      letter from Creeley which comments on recognition, Brakhage's
      work, and our culture's image of the moon.

19   LEWIS, PETER ELFED. "Robert Creeley and Gary Snyder: A
      British Assessment." Stand: Quarterly of the Arts 13, no.
      4:42-47.
           In a fairly unfavorable review of The Charm (1971), claims
      the poems "shed light on the evolution of Creeley's style," but
      finds many mediocre. Feels Creeley's poetry is limited and rari-
      fied but individual, not influenced by Black Mountain. Briefly
      compares Creeley to Snyder.

20   "'Little Mag/Small Presses and the Cultural Revolution.'"
      [Transcribed by Allen De Loach.] Intrepid, nos. 21-22 [Special
      COSMEP Conference Issue] (Winter-Spring), pp. 106-39.
           This transcript from the 13 June 1970 afternoon session,
      "Little Mags/Small Presses and the Cultural Revolution," of the
      COSMEP Conference in Buffalo, New York, provides the text of
      Creeley's talk in which he discusses his feelings toward pub-
      lishing his work, especially in little magazines, and mentions why
      he originally published his own work. Others discuss Creeley's
      audience.

21   MITCHELL, BEVERLEY JOAN. "A Critical Study of the Tish Group,
      1961-1963." M.A. thesis, University of Calgary, pp. 19-20, 22,
      passim.
           Notes Creeley's influence on the Vancouver poets associated
      with Tish, and uses his poetry as an example of the Black Mountain
      poets' desire for an immediacy of experience in poetry, as opposed
      to intellectualization. Also quotes Creeley on Olson's theories.

22   MITCHELL, BEVERLEY [JOAN]. "The Genealogy of Tish." Open
      Letter, 2d ser., no. 3 (Fall), pp. 32-51.
           Uses Creeley's "'I Keep to Myself Such Measures . . .'" and
      "A Place ['The wetness of that street, the light']" to demonstrate
      Olson's emphasis on experience, as opposed to its intellectualiza-
      tion, in his projective poetics. Reprinted: 1976.27.

23   NOVIK, [GERALDINE] MARY. "Robert Creeley: A Critical Check-
      list, Part I: Criticism, 1950-1970." West Coast Review: A
      Quarterly Magazine of the Arts 6, no. 3 (January):51-63.
           Provides a secondary bibliography of criticism on Creeley
      including reviews, essays, letters, prefaces, and sections of
      books and dissertations. Expanded: 1973.37-38.

24   OBERG, ARTHUR. "The Modern British and American Lyric: What
     Will Suffice." Papers on Language and Literature 8, no. 1
     (Winter):70-88.
        Finds Creeley experiments with the modern lyric in terms of
     what is adequate, mentioning his focus on form and treatment of
     love. Comments on a number of poems, notably "For W.C.W. ['The
     rhyme is after']," "The Gift," and "The Window ['There will be no
     simple']."

25   SIENICKA, MARTA. The Making of a New American Poem: Some
     Tendencies in the Post-World War II American Poetry. Seria
     filologia angielska, no. 5. Poznań, Poland: Wydawnictwo
     Naukowe Uniwersytetu im. Adama Mickiewicza w Poznañiu, pp. 36-
     38, 66-69, 78-80, 97-98, passim.
        Commenting on a few poems, especially "Poem for D.H.
     Lawrence," investigates the nature of the self in Creeley's poetry,
     Discusses the self in terms of projective poetics as "the observa-
     tion of processes in a human being" and a "self-conscious objec-
     tification" of the admittedly subjective. Also notes the increased
     self-knowledge and change in the self over the course of a poem.

1973

1   ALLEN, DONALD [MERRIAM], and TALLMAN, WARREN. Poetics of the
     New American Poetry. New York: Grove Press, 463 pp.
        Includes reprints of 1965.5, 24; 1966.14; 1967.12.

2   ALTIERI, CHARLES. "From Symbolist Thought to Immanence: The
     Ground of Postmodern American Poetics." Boundary 2: A Journal
     of Postmodern Literature 1, no. 3 [A Symposium 2] (Spring):
     605-41.
        Finds Creeley's insistence upon "the poem as event" a
     "desire for a union of creative subject and creative object."
     Notes the "strong autobiographical dimension in his work," and
     mentions that his "'decreation' of ordinary syntax" forces the
     reader "to try to recreate the dramatic exchange of energies
     driving the speech." Greatly abridged and revised: 1979.1.
     Abridged and translated into Italian: 1984.2.

3   ANDRÉ, [KENNETH] MICHAEL. "From an Interview with Robert
     Creeley." West End: A Volume of Poetry and Politics 1, no. 4
     (Spring):44-47.
        In this June 1971 interview, a continuation of 1971.1,
     Creeley provides a few biographical details, chiefly concerning
     teaching and moving to and living in Bolinas, California.

4   B[UTTERICK], G[EORGE] F.; CREELEY, ROBERT; and OLSON, CHARLES.
     "Olson and Creeley: The Beginning." Athanor, no. 4 (Spring),
     pp. 58-63.

RC1973

In his introduction, Butterick provides the context for and
mentions the nature of Creeley and Olson's correspondence. Reprints two letters from Creeley to Vincent Ferrini, Olson's first
letter to Creeley, and Creeley's response. Creeley's two letters
to Ferrini (29 March and 24 April 1950) discuss the projected
nature of the Lititz Review and the submissions, especially
Olson's which Creeley had received.
Olson's first letter to Creeley is reprinted from 1971.17.
Creeley's response (24 April 1950) mentions the help W.C. Williams
had provided, Olson's work, and plans for the Lititz Review.
Reprinted: 1978.10. Olson and Creeley's letters are also reprinted: 1980.26.

5   CORMAN, CID. "Projectile/Percussive/Prospective: The Making
     of a Voice." Prospice 1 (November):5-15.
     Comments on the influence of Olson's "Projective Verse" on
Creeley. Mentions the precision, "clarity, and trueness of
[Creeley's] scoring" as in "Time ['Moment to']," explicating por-
tions of the poem. Reprinted: 1982.8.

6   _____. Review of St. Martin's. Athanor, no. 4 (Spring),
     pp. 78-81.
     Comments on each poem in St. Martin's, especially "'Do You
Think . . .,'" "The Act of Love," and "The Birds ['I'll miss the
small birds that come']." Finds the poetry depicting the tension
of "trying to find something to hold to" while being uncertain of
"what it might be."

7   CREELEY, ROBERT. Contexts of Poetry: Interviews, 1961-1971.
     Edited by Donald [Merriam] Allen. Writing, no. 30. Bolinas,
     Calif.: Four Seasons Foundation, 214 pp.
     Includes reprints of 1963.17; 1964.14; 1966.26; 1968.5;
1969.12; 1970.15; 1971.1.

8   _____. "The Creative." Sparrow, no. 6 (March), 9 pp.
     In a 31 October 1972 lecture, Creeley claims his early sense
of creativity meant planning a poem when writing, comments on some
of his reading, and provides a few generalized biographical details. Reprinted: 1974.4; 1979.15.

9   _____. "Foreword" to "An Inventory, 1945-1970." In "Robert
     Creeley: A Writing Biography and Inventory," by Geraldine Mary
     Novik. Ph.D. dissertation, University of British Columbia,
     pp. 118-19.
     Creeley provides a few biographical details, focusing on his
acceptance and stay at Harvard. Reprinted: 1973.10. See Dissertation Abstracts International 34 (1974):7771-72A.

10   ____. "Foreword" to <u>Robert Creeley: An Inventory, 1945-1970</u>, by [Geraldine] Mary Novik. Serif Series: Bibliographies and Checklists, edited by William White, no. 28. Kent, Ohio: Kent State University Press; Montreal and London: McGill-Queen's University Press, pp. v-vi.
    Reprint of 1973.9.

11   ____. Foreword to <u>The Sterile Honeycomb</u>, by Arthur Axlerod. [Buffalo: Privately published], pp. i-iii.
    In this foreword, Creeley discusses his relationship to Axlerod from 1966 until Axlerod's death in the early 1970s.

12   ____. "Inside Out: Notes on the Autobiographical Mode." <u>Sparrow</u>, no. 14 (November), [pp. 1-11].
    In this 23 March 1973 lecture, Creeley briefly provides a few biographical details. Discusses his senses of the mind, auto-biography, thought, and the ego. Claims he is "very thick-skinned," and mentions talking with Olson. He also asserts that he lacks a sense of an audience for his work. Reprinted: 1979.15.

13   ____, ed. "Introduction" to <u>Whitman</u>. Poet to Poet. Harmondsworth, Middlesex, England: Penguin Books, pp. 7-20.
    In this introduction, Creeley charts his own varying atti-tudes toward Whitman from his college days in the early 1940s to the present and comments on the influence that Whitman has had on him. Also mentions writing a paper on Hart Crane at Harvard and what he has learned from Zukofsky, F.O. Matthiessen, and John Gerber about Whitman. Reprinted: 1979.15; 1981.8. Abridged: 1979.6.

14   CREELEY, ROBERT. "Letter to a Town Planner." <u>Beaulines: A Diary of Community Consciousness</u> (Bolinas, Calif.), no. 3 (March), pp. 3, 6-7, 11.
    In this letter, Creeley provides a few biographical details, especially commenting on his feeling of being local, or "at home," in a number of places he has lived. Mentions living in Bolinas, California, and Northeast Harbor, Maine.

15   ____. Letter to Cid Corman. <u>Athanor</u>, no. 4 (Spring), pp. 53-55.
    In a 14 December 1949 letter, Creeley notes having work rejected by <u>Poetry</u> and his lack of need for an audience.

16   ____. Letters. <u>Athanor</u>, no. 4 (Spring), pp. 59-60, 62-63.
    In these letters to Vincent Ferrini and Olson in March and April 1950, Creeley provides a few biographical details concerning the magazine (later titled <u>The Lititz Review</u>) that he is planning. Letters to and from Olson (see also 1973.4) are reprinted in 1980.26.

RC1973

17   _____. "Olson and Others: Some Orts for the Sports." In
Twentieth-Century Poetry and Poetics. Edited by Gary Geddes.
2d ed. Toronto: Oxford University Press, 467-70.
        Reprint of 1960.3.

18   C[REELEY], R[OBERT]. Preface to Contexts of Poetry: Interviews, 1961-1971. Edited by Donald [Merriam] Allen. Writing,
no. 30. Bolinas, Calif.: Four Seasons Foundation,
[pp. iii-iv].
        In this preface, Creeley briefly provides the occasions for
the interviews in Contexts of Poetry.

19   CREELEY, ROBERT; with DUNCAN, ROBERT; COLEMAN, VIC[TOR]; and
SNYDER, GARY. "A Sense of Measure: An Occasion at the Berkeley
Poetry Conference, July 23, 1965." Transcribed and edited by
Douglas Calhoun. Athanor, no. 4 (Spring), pp. 35-52.
        In this combination lecture and conversation on 23 July 1965
at the Berkeley Poetry Conference, Creeley discusses his sense of
measure as "the way verse may be reported to have rhythmic activity" compared to the conscious ordering of syllables or stresses.
Provides a few, brief biographical details. Comments on his sense
of numbers, of the responsibility of the poet, and of understanding poetry. Notes W.C. Williams and Olson's sense of measure and
Williams's influence on him. Also mentions his method of composing The Island.

20   CREELEY, ROBERT. "'Statement' for Paterson Society." In
Floating Bear: A Newsletter, Numbers 1-37, 1961-1969. Edited
by Diane di Prima and LeRoi Jones. La Jolla, Calif.: Laurence
McGilvery, p. 56.
        Reprint of 1961.1.

21   DAVIDSON, ROBERT MICHAEL. "'Disorders of the net': The Poetry
of Robert Duncan." Ph.D. dissertation, State University of New
York at Buffalo, pp. 54-58, 95.
        Comments on Creeley's treatment of identity in "A Form of
Women," noting Duncan's response in "A Dancing Concerning A Form
of Women." Also mentions his use of line breaks, illustrating
with a stanza from "The Finger." See Dissertation Abstracts
International 34 (1973):765A.

22   DAWSON, FIELDING. "On Creeley's Third Change." Athanor, no. 4
(Spring), pp. 57-58.
        Believes Creeley is on the brink of an artistic change in
which he will become "reborn in total humility . . . willing to
make art from the medium and him[self] . . . alone—beyond ego."

23   [DRAVES, CORNELIA P., and FORTUNATO, MARY JANE.] "Craft Interview with Robert Creeley." New York Quarterly, no. 13
(Winter), pp. 18-47.

In this interview, Creeley provides biographical details
about his scores on college boards, the reason he went to Harvard,
and his family life. Also mentions visits to psychiatrists;
teaching, especially at San Francisco State; and his relationship
to Duncan, Zukofsky, W.C. Williams, Ginsberg, Mitchell Goodman,
and Franz Kline. Comments on his first writing; influences, including Pound; and habits of writing, including the conditions,
the paper size, and the use of a typewriter or pen. Relates his
attempts to write in a continuity, reflected in the absence of
pagination in A Day Book, and his lack of interest in the visual
appearance of a poem. Notes his inability to write drama or to
revise, his early use of irony, and his use of free verse and the
colloquial. Claims he uses punctuation to "direct the reading of
the poem" and rhyme and other devices to end a poem.
     Mentions writing "The Finger," including his initial "false
start," and notes the role of his subconscious and drugs on its
composition. Discusses the female figure in "The Finger," "The
Cracks," "The Door ['It is hard going to the door']," and "The
Woman ['I have never']." Observes the lack of visual imagery in
his early poetry, finding himself more focused on thought.
Touches on "Four ['Before I die']," the occasion for and meaning
of "Change ['Turning']," and the ending of "For W.C.W. ['The
pleasure of the wit sustains']." Claims his use of the surreal
proceeds from "literal states of feeling" and that he does not
understand all of his own poems.
     Remarks on his present reading and writing and on titling
poems. Comments on his literal mindedness and his ideas on form
and content, finding sources in and correspondences with others.
Mentions his poetry readings and how he reads. Finds very few of
his poems directly political, noting he has not written "a poem of
direct political protest." The interviewers mention his use of
aphorisms. Slightly revised: 1974.8. Reprinted: 1987.5.

24   DUNCAN, ROBERT. "Towards an Open Universe." In Contemporary
     American Poetry. Edited by Howard Nemerov. Voice of America
     Forum Lectures. [Washington, D.C.: United States Information
     Agency, Voice of America], pp. 169–83.
         Revision of 1966.14.

25   ELLMANN, RICHARD, and O'CLAIR, ROBERT, eds. "Robert Creeley."
     In The Norton Anthology of Modern Poetry. New York: W.W.
     Norton & Co., pp. 1108–9.
         Provides an overview of Creeley's life and work, finding him
     "often opaque," and notes his use of form.

26   FRANK, ARMIN PAUL. "Robert Creeley." [In German.] In
     Amerikanische Literatur de Gegenwart. Edited by Martin
     Christadler. Kröners Taschenausgabe, vol. 412. Stuttgart,
     West Germany: Alfred Kröner Verlag, pp. 564–80.

RC1973

After a biographical summary, mentions Creeley's relationship to Olson. Discusses their correspondence and its role in
Creeley's poetics, especially field poetics, and the influence of
Olson on Creeley's criticism. Finds Creeley's poetry based on a
building block principle, and mentions the role of emotion and
musicality in his poetry. Comments on his use of plain diction,
caesurae, enjambment, syntax, and lineation, especially line
breaks. Also notes the importance of the articulation of the
entire poem to Creeley, and mentions the speech patterns in his
poetry and prose, remarking on the stuttering quality of his work.
Briefly compares his poetics and poetry to Pound's.

27   GERBER, PHILLIP L., and MAZZARO, JEROME. "From the Forest of
      Language: A Conversation with Robert Creeley." Edited by
      Philip L. Gerber. Athanor, no. 4 (Spring), pp. 9-15.
          In this transcription of a 1970 conversation, Creeley dis-
      cusses writing "The Three Ladies"; how he selects poems for a
      volume; and his work's relationship to that of Duncan, Ginsberg,
      and modern painters and musicians. Finds he is more aligned to
      Olson's poetic method of working with "what comes of the moment of
      possibility" rather than with Pound's "choice among possibilities."

28   GUILLORY, DANIEL [L.]. "Robert Creeley and the Surprise of
      Zen." Unicorn: A Miscellaneous Journal (Brooklyn, N.Y.) 2,
      no. 3 (Winter):18-20.
          Finds Creeley's poetry similar to Zen in that it is spon-
      taneous and it intends, as in "The Warning" and "Juggler's
      Thought," to surprise in order to halt thought and initiate
      experience. Recounts the surprise motif in poems like "The
      Invoice," finding that the world of recurrent surprises eventually
      empties the mind. Feels this emptiness frees the poet to accept
      "dynamic change," as in "Song ['The grit']," bringing him to a
      state of innocence, as in "The Innocence."

29   HAMMOND, JOHN GREER. "Robert Creeley's Art and Its Background."
      Ph.D. dissertation, Brandeis University, 131 pp.
          Discussing "Hart Crane ['He had been stuttering, by the
      edge']," "The Mountains in the Desert," "The Pool," "Numbers,"
      "The Finger," "'Do You Think . . .,'" and "The Door ['It is hard
      going to the door']," charts the theme "variously formulated as
      head vs. heart, language vs. experience, and mind vs. body."
      Finds love and, at times, imagination, poetry, or nature as an
      escape from the self in Creeley's poetry. Feels the mind-body
      theme "actually dominates [Pieces] and determines its organiza-
      tion," detailing its structure as "four meditative sequences," and
      locating individual poems or pieces within the "poetic environ-
      ment" of each. Also mentions Creeley's use of myth and dream.
          Discusses Creeley's distrust of language and his use of
      "inferential expression" in his treatment of emotions and the

inability to express emotions. Illustrating with a number of
poems, including "the Language," "The Riddle," "They Say," "Goodbye," "Was," "Love Comes Quietly," and "The Rocks," details his
use of counterpointed or "inner syntax"; rhythm; understatement;
awkwardness; punctuation; and direct, generalized, and abstract
description. Notes that his syntax shows a "distrust of the order
man imposes upon experience," and believes his "inferential style"
allows him to touch on "the most deep-seated human experience"
while avoiding "overt revelations."
    Provides Creeley's aesthetic background, finding a romantic
antirationalism with roots in Emerson's emphasis on impulse and in
a desire for "pure poetry," a poetry untainted with discursive,
rational, or denotative language. Also notes his grounding in the
Black Mountain poets' concept of poetic form as organic, kinetic,
and antirational. Unlike the romantics, however, finds that
Creeley desires "a projection of an emotion without description"
and without explicitly naming the emotion.
    Finds that Creeley's fiction concerns the failure of rela-
tionships, and notes his treatment of isolation, loneliness, and
love. Believes his characterization is often without psychological depth, although alluding to such depth. Demonstrates that
his characters' "need to escape from the individual solitude . . .
conflicts with the instinct to withdraw into a private world."
Notes his use of syntax and prose rhythms to portray emotions in
his fiction. Discusses "Mr. Blue," "The Boat," "The Dress," "The
Unsuccessful Husband," "A Death," "The Book," and in a revision of
1964.7, The Island. The last chapter is revised as 1975.12. See
Dissertation Abstracts International 34 (1974):4261A.

30 KOSTELANETZ, RICHARD. "The Rule of Corruption and Repression."
    In The End of Intelligent Writing: Literary Politics in
    America. New York: Universal Press Syndicate, Sheed & Ward,
    pp. 143-63.
        Reprint of 1971.14.

31 LEVERTOV, DENISE. "'What makes the shadows darker.'" In The
    Poet in the World. New York: New Directions, pp. 239-42.
        Reprint of 1970.24.

32 MacADAMS, LEWIS, [Jr.]. "Lewis MacAdams and Robert Creeley."
    In Contexts of Poetry: Interviews, 1961-1971, by Robert
    Creeley. Edited by Donald [Merriam] Allen. Writing, no. 30.
    Bolinas, Calif.: Four Seasons Foundation, pp. 137-70.
        In this revision of 1968.26 with previously unpublished
    material, Creeley provides biographical details about his child-
    hood, his mother and father's families, and his initial contacts
    with Olson. Also mentions his relationships to his family's
    friend, Theresa Turner, his neighbor, Ira Grant, his first wife,
    Ann, and Slater Brown. Recounts growing up around women, living

in West Acton, Massachusetts, and living in and leaving New
Hampshire. Also mentions living in France and attending college
at and leaving Harvard. Mentions a novel he tried to write prior
to The Island. Also discusses writing The Island, including the
influence of his second wife, Bobbie, the role of thought in it,
and the character of John. Provides its "point" and the circumstance of writing it, noting its structure is determined by dura-
tions. Comments on "For Love," "The Door ['It is hard going to
the door']," "The Finger," and the title of The Whip.

33   MALKOFF, KARL. "Creeley, Robert." In Crowell's Handbook of
      Contemporary American Poetry. New York: Thomas Y. Crowell
      Co., pp. 91-97.
          Discusses the influence of Olson on Creeley, the sense of
Creeley as a projectivist poet, and his use of the poem as an
almost Jamesian analytical instrument concentrating on the self.
Comments on his development from For Love and Words to Pieces,
finding the latter both the most abstract and subjective. Believes the form of his poetry, rather than its content, is that
which "engages the reader." Discusses "The Traveller," and comments on "The Mechanic," "A Piece," and "Numbers."

34   MAZZARO, JEROME. "Robert Creeley, the Domestic Muse, and Post-
      Modernism." Athanor, no. 4 (Spring), pp. 16-33.
          Mentioning many poems and essays by and interviews with
Creeley, including an unpublished interview in Brockport, New
York, examines the domesticity of his poetry, and lists early
influences. Points out that love in St. Martin's "commingles the
physical and the conceptual," compared to their separation in
earlier poetry. Remarks on Creeley's sense of the creative process and the givenness of poetry, finding he does not select a
subject prior to writing.
          Noting which poetry Creeley excludes from For Love, comments
on the intellection in The Charm: Early and Uncollected Poems
(1969). Relates the treatment of the self, separation, and unity
in two poems: "Poem for D.H. Lawrence," finding correspondences
with Marsilio Ficino, and "From Pico and the Women: A Life,"
noting the influence of Giovanni Pico della Mirandola. Mentions
his focus on emotion in For Love and his dislike of basing poetry
on content, including political content. Compares "Hart Crane 2
['Answer: how old']" to "Hart Crane ['He had been stuttering, by
the edge']" and the subjectivity in "The Wife" to "The Sentence"
and "For Martin."
          Contrasting his work to "the formal and psychological bents
of the forties," records Creeley's dislike of the literary establishment of that period, represented by Randall Jarrell. Compares
his ideas on the pragmatic value of poetry, subjectivity, and
objectivity to Jarrell's. Believes Creeley tries to make his
impact on the reader a personal one with magical, not rhetorical,

energies, and notes the role of puritanism in Creeley's thought.
Also compares Creeley to Jarrell in terms of literary politics.
   Using 1963.13, mentions Creeley's use of "'the Lady' of
Romance literature." Finds examples of this tradition in "A Gift
of Great Value," "The Hero ['Each voice which was asked']," "The
Door ['It is hard going to the door']," "The Three Ladies," and
"Kore," providing Creeley's unpublished comments on the latter two
from the Brockport interview. Examines Creeley's technique, remarking on his emphasis on the aural and his use of the line and
speech. Lists settings for the poems in For Love, notes his existentialism and treatment of nothingness, and comments on him as
a private poet who avoids "public utterances" and whose poems
provide "truths of the moment" only.

35   MOTTRAM, ERIC. "1924-1951: Politics and Form in Zukofsky."
     Maps, no. 5 [Louis Zukofsky issue], pp. 76-103.
        Concerning Creeley's "A Note" in Louis Zukofsky's "A" 1-12
     (Paris Review Editions [Garden City, N.Y.: Doubleday & Co.,
     1967], pp. vii-xvi), briefly mentions that Creeley only enjoyed
     the structural use of Marx in Zukofsky's "'A' 9" without realizing
     Zukofsky's purpose.

36   NOVIK, [GERALDINE] MARY. "A Creeley Chronology." Athanor,
     no. 4 (Spring), pp. 67-75.
        Provides biographical chronology from 1926 to 1972, empha-
     sizing 1943 to 1972. Focuses on Creeley's contacts with editors
     and other poets including Corman and Olson, as well as the dates
     he wrote and published his work. See 1973.38 for a much expanded
     version and 1979.26 for an updated version.

37   _____. Robert Creeley: An Inventory, 1945-1970. Serif
     Series: Bibliographies and Checklists, edited by William
     White, no. 28. Kent, Ohio: Kent State University Press;
     Montreal and London: McGill-Queen's University Press, 210 pp.
        A revision of "An Inventory, 1945-1970" of 1973.38 with a
     new introduction (pp. ix-xvii) that discusses Creeley's early
     writing and publications, his relationship to Olson and Corman,
     and his growing critical reception. The introduction also charts
     his publication history and comments on his development as seen in
     each of his books. The fullest bibliography of Creeley to date.

38   NOVIK, GERALDINE MARY. "Robert Creeley: A Writing Biography
     and Inventory." Ph.D. dissertation, University of British
     Columbia, 289 pp.
        In "A Writing Biography to 1957" (pp. 4-116), provides a
     lengthy biography of Creeley to 1957 relating his life to his
     work. Often notes the biographical background for poems, short
     stories, and The Island, including the sources for characters in
     the fiction. Gives details of his childhood, his role in the Dial

RC1973

and the Bull, magazines at Holderness School, and his time at
Harvard and role in the Wake, a Harvard literary magazine. Discusses his first marriage, his early attempts to write, his role
at Black Mountain College, and his life in New Hampshire, France,
and Mallorca. Examines his role in Divers Press and a number of
little magazines, especially Golden Goose, Origin, and the Black
Mountain Review, as well as his plans for the Lititz Review.
Refers to his initial attempts to write a novel and his development as a poet, comparing a few of his poems. Details his correspondence with and/or relationship to a number of people, including
Corman, W.C. Williams, Pound, Olson, Levertov, Blackburn, Duncan,
Mitchell Goodman, Richard Wirtz Emerson, and Jonathan Williams.
Also remarks on the early publication of his poems and stories;
the influence of jazz, Pound, and W.C. Williams on his work; and
the development of his poetics. Provides the publication history
and the critical reception of his work. Comments on a number of
Creeley's poems and stories, discussing The Island and "A Song ['I
had wanted a quiet testament']." Notes the revision of "The
Rhyme," and mentions his poetic techniques and Olson's comments on
his stories.
"A Writing Biography to 1957" also includes portions of
unpublished materials, especially of letters from Creeley to
others: a 16 October 1961 letter to Ian Hamilton Finlay on his
Scots heritage; a 28 February 1950 letter to Eugene Magner solic-
iting work for a magazine; a number of letters to Corman, notably
a 7 January 1951 letter on his short stories and a 13 May 1952
letter on his poetry, especially "The Innocence" and "The Crises";
two letters, 26 June 1950 and Fall 1950, to Emerson on poetry and
the rhythms of poetry and prose; and a number of letters to W.C.
Williams. Provides a portion of a 26 June 1966 autobiographical
sketch (later published as part of 1975.5) in which Creeley provides details about his childhood. Occasionally quotes from
Creeley's typescript journal covering 1 January to 18 October 1951
about Ann Creeley and writing fiction. Also quotes from a draft
of an introduction to the Lititz Review stating editorial policy
and from a transcription of a tape recorded reading on 3 May 1965
at Washington University in St. Louis, Missouri. Provides a portion of an introduction by Duncan on 16 July 1959 to a reading by
Creeley at San Francisco State College.
"An Inventory, 1945-1970" (pp. 117-289), lists, with occasional annotations, all Creeley publications: books, poems,
prose, translations, and interviews. Also lists unpublished materials: letters, proofs, unpublished work, recordings, films, and
manuscript collections. Provides a secondary bibliography expanded from 1972.23. In her introduction, pp. 122-27, mentions
Creeley's critical reception and publication history. The "Inventory," with a new introduction, is revised: 1973.37. See Dissertation Abstracts International 34 (1974):7771-72A.

39   O'REGAN, BRENDAN, and ALLAN, TONY. "An Interview with Robert
      Creeley." In Contexts of Poetry: Interviews, 1961-1971 by
      Robert Creeley. Edited by Donald [Merriam] Allen. Writing,
      no. 30. Bolinas, Calif.: Four Seasons Foundation, pp. 125-35.
         In this October 1967 interview, Creeley speaks of the novel
      he intended to write after The Island, noting the reasons he wrote
      The Island and its "emotional density." Comments on the differ-
      ences between writing poetry and novels, why he has not written a
      poem about the Vietnam War, and his ideas on form and content.
      Mentions his reading of and acquaintance with Buddhism and
      Japanese literature and his sense of literary tradition. Also
      claims he writes what he does not know and uses a poem to learn,
      to discover. Refers to taking LSD, reading British poets, and
      talking with a few of them.

40   PERLOFF, MARJORIE G. "Charles Olson and the 'Inferior Prede-
      cessors': 'Projective Verse' Revisited." ELH 40, no. 2
      (Summer):285-306.
         Occasionally notes Creeley's influence and lack of influence
      on Olson's "Projective Verse."

41   RICKS, CHRISTOPHER. Review of A Day Book. New York Times Book
      Review, 7 January, pp. 5, 22.
         In this brief, unfavorable review, finds the insistence upon
      "freedom of form" overly self-conscious, and believes it enslaves
      Creeley to his own conventions. See 1973.41.

42   ROSENTHAL, M[ACHA] L[EWIS]. "Problems of Robert Creeley."
      Parnassus: Poetry in Review 2, no. 1 (Fall-Winter):205-14.
         In an unfavorable review of A Day Book, comments on the
      natural speech and the "almost undifferentiated drift of con-
      sciousness," yet finds the "play of thought" occasionally inter-
      esting. Mentions the influence of W.C. Williams's "Love Song" on
      Creeley's "The Edge," but believes Creeley reduces Williams's
      "emotion to an abstraction." Notes parallels between Williams's A
      Dream of Love and Creeley's Listen. Claims Contexts of Poetry is
      interesting, but notes a few errors. See 1975.18. Reprinted:
      1987.19.

43   SHIVELY, CHARLES. "John Wieners: An Interview." Gay Sun-
      hine: A Newspaper of Gay Liberation, no. 17 (March-April),
      pp. 1-3.
         In this 8 February 1973 interview, Wieners provides some
      biographical information concerning his relationship to Creeley.
      Slightly revised and abridged with an added 27 March 1977 inter-
      view: 1982.41.

44   STANFORD, DEREK. Review of A Sense of Measure. Books and
      Bookmen 18, no. 9 [whole no. 213] (June):119-20.

RC1973

In this unfavorable review, finds Creeley self-indulgent in
his introspection and wrongheaded in his dislike of consciously
controlled poetry. Finds his prose style "stumbling" and his
language imprecise.

45   TALLMAN, WARREN. "Sunny Side Up: A Note on Robert Creeley."
      Athanor, no. 4 (Spring), pp. 64–66.
          Believes Creeley is an optimistic poet who is receptive to
      and perceptive of others and of his relationships with others.
      Feels the "black-mood" poems are the result of his contact with
      "null persons leading to void perceptions," not the result of his
      own despair.

46   _____. *Three Essays on Creeley*. A Beaver Kosmos Folio.
      Toronto: Coach House Press, [29 pp.].
          Reprint of 1962.14; 1964.13; 1966.28.

47   WAGNER, LINDA W[ELSHIMER]. "A Colloquy with Robert Creeley."
      In *Contexts of Poetry: Interviews, 1961–1971*, by Robert
      Creeley. Edited by Donald [Merriam] Allen. Writing, no. 30.
      Bolinas, Calif.: Four Seasons Foundation, pp. 71–124.
          A rearranged revision of 1965.24, with additional revised
      material from 1968.26 and previously unpublished material.
      Creeley remarks on his sense of a reader, his choice of prose or
      poetry on a given occasion, his critical writing, and his role at
      the Berkeley Poetry Conference and Buffalo Arts Festival. Con-
      siders the role of emotion in his work, as in "The Immoral Propo-
      sition," noting the self-destructiveness of the egoist in that
      poem. Comments more on not choosing subjects, on *The Island*, on
      learning from Pound's prose, and on his enjoyment of privacy.
      Mentions that writing *The Island* has given him the possibility of
      lengthening his poetry. Speaks of his influences and of the or-
      ganization of "For Love" and "The Door ['It is hard going to the
      door']."

48   WAGNER, LINDA [WELSHIMER]. "Stay Away from Our Door." *New
      York Times Book Review*, 18 February, p. 32.
          In a brief letter to the editor about 1973.48, claims a
      British reviewer cannot understand the American idiom.

49   WATTEN, BARRETT, and COOLIDGE, SUSAN. "Conversation with Clark
      Coolidge." *This*, no. 4 (Spring), [pp. 32–68].
          In this 6 November 1972 conversation, Coolidge comments on
      first trying to understand "The Gold Diggers" and Other Stories,
      Creeley's line length, and Creeley reading his own work. Watten
      briefly mentions the almost symbolic way Creeley uses the word
      "here."

1974

1   ALTIERI, CHARLES. "Olson's Poetics and the Tradition." Bound-
ary 2: A Journal of Postmodern Literature 2, nos. 1-2 [Charles
Olson: Essays, Reminiscences, Reviews issue] (Fall 1973-
Winter):173-88.
        In a note, claims Creeley's selection of texts as editor of
Selected Writings of Charles Olson (New York: New Directions,
1966) reflects his own interests, and mentions the influence of
Olson's earlier thought on Creeley.

2   ANDRÉ, KENNETH MICHAEL. "Levertov, Creeley, Wright, Auden,
Ginsberg, Corso, Dickey: Essays and Interviews with Contemporary American Poets." Ph.D. dissertation, Columbia University,
pp. 51-91, 155-56, 195, 306-7, 311-13, 321-22, passim.
        Includes a reprint of 1971.1 and a slight revision of
1972.3, dropping a brief section from the latter. André, in his
conclusion, argues with 1969.4, notes other commentaries on
Creeley, and mentions Creeley's feelings concerning criticism and
imitation. Ginsberg, in his interview (pp. 102-25), briefly mentions his relationship to Creeley. See Dissertation Abstracts
International 36 (1975):3681-82A.

*3   "Black Mountain: Olson, Dorn, Williams, Creeley, [and] Cage at
St. Andrews." Star-Web Paper, no. 4, pp. 52-68.
        Unavailable for annotation. (Listed in 1987.8, p. 288.)

4   CREELEY, ROBERT. "The Creative." MLN 89, no. 6 (December):
1029-40.
        Reprint of 1973.8.

5   _____. "On the Road: Notes on Artists and Poets, 1950-1965."
In Poets of the Cities New York and San Francisco, 1950-1965.
[Exhibition catalog.] [Edited by Neil A. Chassman.] New York:
E.P. Dutton & Co., pp. 56-63.
        Creeley provides a number of biographical details, espe-
cially concerning how he came to "the process of writing that made
both the thing said and the way of saying it an integral event,"
both before and while at Black Mountain College. Comments on his
relationship to Olson, Franz Kline, and Philip Guston, providing a
reminiscence about a meeting with Ann, his first wife, and Guston
in 1955. Mentions a reaction of the audience at a poetry reading
concerning rhyme, the occasion behind "After Mallarmé," and the
influence of W.C. Williams and Pound on his work. Slightly revised: 1979.15; 1982.10. Reprinted in part: 1978.16; 1980.8.

6   DAVIES, ALAN. Review of His Idea. World, no. 29 (April),
pp. 17-18.

RC1974

In this brief, favorable review, focuses on the nature and
relationship of the small poetic units.

7   DORFMAN, ELSA. Elsa's Housebook: A Woman's Photojournal.
     Boston: David R. Godine, pp. 9, 11–12, 36–38, 45, 55–56, 62.
     Dorfman discusses her relationship to Creeley, including
taking pictures of him and his visits with her in the Boston area
from 1969 on.

8   [DRAVES, CORNELIA P., and FORTUNATO, MARY JANE.] "Craft Inter-
     view with Robert Creeley." In The Craft of Poetry: Interviews
     from the "New York Quarterly." Edited by William Packard.
     Garden City, N.Y.: Doubleday, pp. 195–223.
     Slight revision of 1973.23.

9   DUNCAN, ROBERT. "Some Letters to Charles Olson." Maps, no. 6
     [Robert Duncan issue], pp. 56–67.
     In letters, 1955–1963, Duncan occasionally briefly mentions
Creeley and places him in a literary tradition.

10   ____. "Towards an Open Universe." Prospice 2 (1974),
     pp. 11–22.
     Revision of 1966.16.

11   FAUCHEREAU, SERGE. Introducere în poezia americană modernă.
     [In Rumanian.] Translated by C. Abăluță and Şt. Stoenescu.
     Biblioteca Pentru Toti, no. 810. Bucharest: Editura Minerva,
     pp. 265–66, 268, 275–82, passim.
     A translation of 1968.12 with a new introduction.

12   FELSON, LARRY. "Apraxia: The Local Swamp." Shocks, nos. 3–4
     [Poetry and Criticism: The Bay Area and Northern California
     issue] (March), pp. 11–15.
     Finds Creeley, as well as others, writing "to justify the
extreme isolation the poet feels at the time," and notes his
"anti-conceptual focus." Believes that such work, often "where
the act of composition becomes the actualization of reality itself," is "determined by the monopoly capitalist social formation." Also mentions Creeley's use of the local.

13   GLOTZER, DAVID. Review of A Day Book. Mulch 2, no. 2 [whole
     no. 4] (Winter):161–65.
     In this unfavorable review, stresses Creeley's despair,
believing he has, as in Pieces, "lost an idea of the poem qua
poem" as well as a sense of purpose other than a "desperate need
to locate the 'I.'" Finds his emphasis, unlike that of W.C.
Williams, is on "words as real objects." Feels he ignores "the
human situation" yet writes honestly and intensely, recording "the

struggle to maintain" dignity. Briefly notes Creeley's contributions to poetics, especially to Olson's theories, leading to the
concept of the poem as "an organic outgrowth of the poet's life."

14   KAFALENOS, EMMA MELLARD. "Possibilities of Isochrony: A Study
     of Rhythm in Modern Poetry." Ph.D. dissertation, Washington
     University, pp. 69-74.
        Discusses Creeley's use of the line as a breath-controlled,
     "isochronous unit," and scans "Saturday Afternoon" as an example,
     noting the use of line lengths and endings, punctuation, and
     stresses. See <u>Dissertation</u> <u>Abstracts</u> <u>International</u> 35 (1974):
     2273-74A.

15   KLINKOWITZ, JEROME. "Gilbert Sorrentino's Super-Fiction."
     <u>Chicago</u> <u>Review</u> 25, no. 4:77-89.
        In this set of taped sections of Sorrentino speaking with
     comments by the author, Sorrentino discusses Creeley's influence
     on his poetry from the late 1950s to the early 1960s but notes the
     differences in their poetry thereafter. Revised: 1974.16.

16   _____. "Gilbert Sorrentino's Super-Fiction." <u>Vort</u> 2, no. 3
     [whole no. 6] [Gilbert Sorrentino/Donald Phelps issue] (Fall):
     69-79.
        Revision of 1974.15 without changes to the Creeley
     discussion.

17   MANDEL, ANN. <u>Measures:</u> <u>Robert</u> <u>Creeley's</u> <u>Poetry</u>. Beaver
     Kosmos Folios, no. 6. Toronto: Coach House Press, [35 pp.].
        Using portions of numerous poems as examples, discusses the
     role of time, space, grace, care, and possibility in Creeley's
     poetry. Also notes his treatment of desire, guilt, the dance, the
     quest, and the present. Finds he uses poetry as a rite, for
     reification, and "'to come into the world,' to take its measure,
     and be measured thereby." Examines Creeley's treatment of place,
     and finds "a remarkably consistent and continuing world" in his
     work, commenting on his characters, landscapes, and objects, as
     well as his use of the female figure.

18   MOTTRAM, ERIC. "The Black Polar Night: The Poetry of Gilbert
     Sorrentino." <u>Vort</u> 2, no. 3 [whole no. 6] [Gilbert Sorrentino/
     Donald Phelps issue] (Fall):43-59.
        Mentions Creeley's influence on Sorrentino and compares
     their use of the first-person singular in poetry.

19   NAVERO, WILLIAM. "Duncan, Creely [<u>sic</u>], and Dorn." <u>Ethos</u>
     (State University of New York at Buffalo) 8, no. 14
     (12 December):27-28.
        Notes the lyricism and fracturing in <u>Thirty</u> <u>Things</u>.

20   OLSON, CHARLES. "Robert Creeley's <u>For Love</u>." In <u>Additional</u>
      <u>Prose</u>: "<u>A Bibliography</u> <u>on America</u>," "<u>Proprioception</u>," <u>and</u>
      <u>Other</u> <u>Notes</u> <u>and</u> <u>Essays</u>. Edited by George F. Butterick.
      Writing, edited by Donald [Merriam] Allen, no. 31. Bolinas,
      Calif.: Four Seasons Foundation, pp. 47-49.
          Reprint of 1962.9.

21   RICCIARDELLI, MICHELE. "Robert Creeley: Poeta della 'Black
      Mountain.'" [In Italian.] <u>Uomini</u> <u>e</u> <u>libri</u>, no. 47 (January-
      February), pp. 24-27.
          In this interview, Creeley mentions taking drugs and claims
      his work, as that of certain painters, is concerned with activity
      and with the discovery of what is not already known. He notes the
      lack of intention and revision of his work, and comments on his
      sense that writing is "given" to him to do. Notes his use of
      enjambment and the house motif, the continuity of the items in <u>A</u>
      <u>Day</u> <u>Book</u>, and his poetry's mission to point out a world with bet-
      ter possibilities and less personal isolation. Mentions a few
      poems including his variations from the poetry of Gaius Valerius
      Catullus in "Stomping with Catullus." Notes his treatment of love
      in "Guido, i' vorrei che tu e Lapo ed io" and his sense of
      Giovanni Pico della Mirandola on the existence of God in "From
      Pico & the Women: A Life."

22   SMITH, D[ONALD] NEWTON, [Jr.]. "The Influence of Music on the
      Black Mountain Poets, I." <u>St.</u> <u>Andrews</u> <u>Review:</u> <u>A</u> <u>Twice-Yearly</u>
      <u>Magazine</u> <u>of</u> <u>the</u> <u>Arts</u> <u>and</u> <u>Humanities</u> 3, no. 1 (Fall-Winter):
      99-115.
          Discusses the attraction jazz, especially the work of
      Charlie Parker, had on Creeley and the influence it had on his
      work: on his line breaks, as in "I Know a Man"; on his use of a
      "four-square" pattern and quatrain, as in "The Woman ['I called
      her across the room']"; on his use of rhythmic changes; and on his
      improvisational practice. Revised: 1974.23.

23   SMITH, DONALD NEWTON, [Jr.]. "The Origins of Black Mountain
      Poetry." Ph.D. dissertation, University of North Carolina, pp.
      21-24, 39, 61-69, 87-117, 181-88, 196-201, 206-7, 224-25, 246-
      57, 312-26, 351-53, 356-68, 377-82, 388-95, 399-401, 412-21,
      423-24, 426-27, passim.
          Half of chapter 6, "The Influence of Music on the Black
      Mountain Poets," pp. 243-69, is a revision of 1974.22. Comments
      on Creeley as one of the Black Mountain poets and on their antag-
      onistic relationship with academic poets and the New Critical
      stance that governed the literary climate of the 1940s and 1950s.
      Briefly comments on many of his poems throughout.
          Discusses influences on Creeley, finding that it was Pound's
      statements on prosody and poetics that influenced Creeley's sense
      of the inextricable nature of form and content, as well as his

sense of sincerity and of the role of speech in poetry. Also discusses W.C. Williams's parallels to and influence on Creeley in terms of Creeley's domestic focus, short lines and short poems, and his sense of the nature of poetry. Also notes W.C. Williams's influence on Creeley's use of line breaks, his use of the poem to think with, and his use of speech, especially the vernacular. Uses "The Dishonest Mailmen" as an example of Creeley's desire for a lack of intention in the creative process, paralleling Williams's, and notes the sense of place and the treatment of time in the poem. Also comments on his sense of the subjective and the objective and on his imitations of Williams.

Also notes Zukofsky's influence on Creeley in terms of his attention to "the minims of language" and his sense of the poem being independent from the world. Also mentions Zukofsky's influence on Creeley's sense of the continuity of all of his work and his ability to "trust words to find their own form in the poem" as in Pieces. Notes the possible influence of art, Hart Crane, and D.H. Lawrence on Creeley, especially as it is reflected in his concern with "the activity of art." Comments on his relationship to artists, including René Laubiès, Jackson Pollock, Philip Guston, Franz Kline, and other members of the New York school of painting, speculating on possible areas of influence.

Discusses Creeley's relationship to Olson and Duncan including his initial contacts and correspondence with them and others such as Blackburn and Jonathan Williams. Mentions Creeley and Olson's influence on one another and Creeley's publication in little magazines and by small presses. Notes Creeley's role in and life at Black Mountain College, occasionally quoting from an unpublished July 1970 tape by Creeley. Provides biographical details, and comments on Creeley's role in the Black Mountain Review. See Dissertation Abstracts International 35 (1974): 3771-72A.

24 STAUFFER, DONALD BARLOW. A Short History of American Poetry. New York: E.P. Dutton & Co., pp. 399, 417-19, 422.
Mentions Creeley's influence on W.S. Merwin and Levertov and his reading of his own work. Focuses on his sparse word use and his theme of love as in "The Way ['My love's manners in bed']."

25 TALLMAN, WARREN. "Wonder Merchants: Modernist Poetry in Vancouver during the 1960's." Boundary 2: A Journal of Postmodern Literature 3, no. 1 [A Canadian Issue] (Fall):57-89.
Discusses the response to Creeley's February 1962 reading in Vancouver and his influence on poets there. Reprinted: 1976.35; 1977.21.

26 TAYLOR, [L.] LORING. "Arta miniaturală la Robert Creeley." [In Rumanian.] Steaua 25, no. 1:45-46.

RC1974

Provides biographical details for Creeley including the
occasion for All That Is Lovely in Men. Noting that Creeley and
another man were both in love with the same woman, finds the volume sardonically treats the relationship between the two. Outlining influences on him, places Creeley in terms of literary
movements, especially his role in Black Mountain poetry, his reaction to different schools, and his sense of fighting the literary
establishment in the 1950s. Comments on Creeley's criticism, his
relationship to Canadian poets, and his use of the accidental.
Mentions his treatment of returning, his critical reception, his
sense of language, and his style. Remarks on the tension created
between his subtle observations or themes and his simplistic
vocabulary. Comparing his work to Richard Brautigan's, finds
Creeley does not need conclusions but allows forces within an
event to stand. Comments on "In an Act of Pity," comparing it to
the compressions and minimalism of "A Piece," and mentions the
treatment of the imagination in "Fancy."

27   V[OLD], J[AN] E[RIC]. "Creeley, Ginsberg, O'Hara, Bly: 4
     poeter født 1926." [In Norwegian.] Vinduet 28, no. 3:22-30.
          Comments on love as an interplay of spiritual and physical
     contact in Creeley's "The Warning." Comparing For Love to Pieces,
     finds the latter more fragmentary and less metaphysical. Praises
     A Day Book, and mentions meeting Creeley in Bolinas, California,
     and Buffalo, New York.

28   von HALLBERG, ROBERT. "Olson, Whitehead, and the
     Objectivists." Boundary 2: A Journal of Postmodern Literature
     2, nos. 1-2 [Charles Olson: Essays, Reminiscences, Reviews
     issue] (Fall 1973-Winter):85-111.
          Compares Creeley's sense of form and content to Olson's.
     Revised as chapter 3 of 1975.20; 1978.71

29   YIP, WAI-LIM. "Classical Chinese and Modern Anglo-American
     Poetry: Convergence of Languages and Poetry." Comparative
     Literature Studies 11, no. 1 (March):21-47.
          Compares Creeley to W.C. Williams, finding both promote "the
     physical presence of an experience," but believes Creeley is more
     subjective and less visual. Notes the "space breaks and stanza
     breaks" in "La Noche."

1975

1   CARRUTH, HAYDEN. "Creeley, Robert (White)." In Contemporary
     Poets. Edited by James Vinson and D.L. Kirkpatrick. 2d ed.
     London: St. James Press; New York: St. Martin's Press, pp.
     322-25.
          Reprint of 1970.9 with an expanded bibliography.

*2   CHRISTENSEN, PAUL NORMAN. "Charles Olson: Call Him Ishmael."
      Ph.D. dissertation, University of Pennsylvania, 392 pp.
          Dissertation was restricted, unavailable for annotation.
      See published version: 1979.2. See also Dissertation Abstracts
      International 36 (1976):8056A.

3   COOLIDGE, CLARK. "Notes Taken in Classes Conducted by Charles
      Olson at the University of British Columbia, Vancouver, August
      1963." Olson: The Journal of the Charles Olson Archives, no.
      4 (Fall), pp. 47-63.
          In these notes covering 12-16 August 1963, records Olson's
      comments on Creeley during classes at the Vancouver Poetry
      Conference.

4   CORMAN, CID, ed. "Introduction" to The Gist of "Origin," 1951-
      1971: An Anthology. New York: Viking Press, Grossman Pub-
      lishers, pp. xv-xxxvii.
          Corman mentions meeting Creeley and their relationship.
      Notes Creeley's role in the Lititz Review and Origin.

5   "Creeley, Robert (White)." In World Authors, 1950-1970.
      Edited by John Wakeman. New York: H.W. Wilson Co.,
      pp. 339-42.
          Providing biographical details, comments on Creeley's poetry
      and fiction as well as his critical reception. In an expansion of
      a biographical sketch included in 1973.38, Creeley mentions his
      beginnings as a writer and gives a few biographical details.

6   CREELEY, ROBERT. "From 'Mabel: A Story.'" TriQuarterly, no.
      34 (Fall), pp. 133-37.
          In a portion of this item, Creeley comments on his relation-
      ship to women, two in particular, providing a few biographical
      details. Reprinted in 1976.9.

7   _____. "Hier soir: Au hasard de mes souvenirs de San
      Francisco (Mars-Juin 1956)." [In French.] Translated by
      Etienne de Planchard. Entretiens, [no. 34] [Beat Generation
      issue], pp. 163-66.
          Creeley provides biographical details from March-June 1956
      concerning his immersion in the San Francisco poetry scene, espe-
      cially noting his contacts with Dorn, Kerouac, Ginsberg, and
      Marthe Rexroth. Lists poems he wrote during this period. In
      English: 1979.15.

8   _____. "Letter to Cid Corman." In The Gist of "Origin," 1951-
      1971: An Anthology. Edited by Cid Corman. New York: Viking
      Press, Grossman Publishers, pp. 11-14.
          Reprint of 1951.3.

RC1975

9   DUNCAN, ROBERT. "From The Day Book." In The Gist of "Origin,"
    1951-1971: An Anthology. Edited by Cid Corman. New York:
    Viking Press, Grossman Publishers, pp. 263-73.
        Reprinted from 1963.12.

10 GUIMOND, JAMES. "Poesia americana, 1913-1973: As duas
    revoluções." [In Portuguese.] Translated by Cecilia Inês
    Erthal. Revista letras, no. 24 (December), pp. 179-89.
        Briefly mentions that Creeley "scores" the poem on the page.
    Also notes his interiority and use of free verse.

11 GUSSIN, LENORE [JAY]. "The Crisis of Identity and Love:
    Themes in Twentieth-Century Poetry." Ph.D. dissertation,
    Columbia University, pp. 15, 113-17, 228-39, passim.
        Discusses the treatment of love in Creeley's poetry, noting
    "the fear of love' in "The Immoral Proposition"; the "attraction
    to, and repulsion of love" in "A Form of Women"; and sex and the
    lack of communication in "The Woman ['I have never']." Comments
    on the use of humor and the male's ego in "Ballad of the Despair-
    ing Husband." Also notes the treatment of sex, anger, women, and
    the failure of love in other poetry by Creeley. See Dissertation
    Abstracts International 36 (1975):3687A.

12 HAMMOND, JOHN G[REER]. "Solipsism and the Sexual Imagination
    in Robert Creeley's Fiction." Critique: Studies in Modern
    Fiction 16, no. 3:59-69.
        A revision of the last chapter of 1973.29.

13 KENNER, HUGH. A Homemade World: The American Modernist
    Writers. New York: Alfred A. Knopf, Borzoi Book, p. 184,
    passim.
        Briefly uses Creeley's "I Know a Man" as an example of
    poetry meant to look improvised.

14 LUCIE-SMITH, EDWARD. "An Interview with Frank O'Hara." In
    Standing Still and Walking in New York, by Frank O'Hara.
    Edited by Donald [Merriam] Allen. Bolinas, Calif.: Grey Fox
    Press, pp. 3-26.
        In this October 1965 interview (extensively expanded from
    Studio International: Journal of Modern Art 172, no. 881
    [September 1966]:112-13), O'Hara claims Creeley's emphasis on
    control and his use of a "pared down" diction draw attention away
    from the subject matter of the poem.

15 MOTTRAM, ERIC. "Sixties American Poetry, Poetics, and Poetic
    Movements." In American Literature since 1900. Edited by
    Marcus Cunliff. Vol. 9, History of Literature in the English
    Language. London: Barrie & Jenkins in association with Sphere
    Books, pp. 271-311.

Finding Creeley searches for stability, briefly compares him to Stevens and notes the influence of Ludwig Wittgenstein.

16   OLSON, CHARLES. "Letter to Cid Corman." In The Gist of "Origin," 1951-1971: An Anthology. Edited by Cid Corman. New York: Viking Press, Grossman Publishers, pp. 495-504.
      Slight revision of 1971.16.

17   OLSON, CHARLES; GINSBERG, ALLEN; CREELEY, ROBERT; DUNCAN, ROBERT; and WHALEN, PHILIP. "On 'History.'" Transcribed by Ralph Maud, edited by George F. Butterick. Olson: The Journal of the Charles Olson Archives, no. 4 (Fall), pp. 40-46.
      This discussion contains Creeley's participation in a 29 July 1963 symposium at the Vancouver Poetry Conference. The editor supplies a note on Creeley and quotes from 1964.2 on Creeley's appearance. An extended version: 1978.58.

18   PAUL, SHERMAN. "A Letter on Rosenthal's 'Problems of Robert Creeley.'" Boundary 2: A Journal of Postmodern Literature 3, no. 3 [The Oral Impulse in Contemporary American Poetry issue] (Spring):747-60.
      In a response to 1973.42 and often referring to 1967.23, questions Rosenthal's understanding of A Quick Graph and Contexts of Poetry, claiming Rosenthal's treatment of A Day Book reflects a lack of awareness of the emphasis Creeley places upon the poetic process. Discusses Pieces and A Day Book as part of a continuity reflecting Creeley's life, finding a movement in the latter "away from the self-reflection toward the external world." Sees W.C. Williams "recalled" in A Day Book as "a model of poetic activity and recovery," charting numerous allusions and correspondences. Notes the risk and exposure in Creeley's work, and mentions his treatment of stasis, death, and the wanderer in the two volumes. Comments on numerous works, especially "The Edge," Listen, and The Island.

19   PERLOFF, MARJORIE G. "The Corn-Porn Lyric: Poetry 1972-73." Contemporary Literature 16, no. 1 (Winter):84-125.
      In this essay containing an unfavorable review of A Day Book, claims the "central emotion is one of boredom and loss" despite the "brief bouts of violent sex." Believes Creeley as a character emerges as a chauvinist. See 1976.25.

20   von HALLBERG, ROBERT. "The Scholar's Art: The Poetics and Poetry of Charles Olson." Ph.D. dissertation, Stanford University, pp. 7-9, 60-63, 203-4, passim.
      Occasionally mentions Olson's influence on and relationship to Creeley, and compares Olson's rhetorical and Levertov's political poetics to Creeley's lyrical and personal poetic theory. Quotes from unpublished letters from Olson to Creeley. Chapter 3

is a revision of 1974.28. Revised: 1978.71. See <u>Dissertation</u>
<u>Abstracts</u> <u>International</u> 37 (1976):974-75A.

21 · WAGNER, LINDA W[ELSHIMER]. "The Latest Creeley." <u>American</u>
    <u>Poetry</u> <u>Review</u> 4, no. 5 (September-October):42-44.
        Compares Creeley's earlier work to <u>A</u> <u>Day</u> <u>Book</u> and <u>Pieces</u>.
    Finds many of the same concerns but fewer "aphoristic statements"
    and more wordplay and questioning of words in the later works.
    Notes his treatment of sex, and comments on his use of narration,
    various "breath units/sentences," humor, prose with his poetry,
    and the abstract, finding sources for the latter in Stevens.
    Comments on "For Benny and Sabina" and a few other poems.
    Reprinted: 1980.35.

22 WHITTEMORE, REED. <u>William</u> <u>Carlos</u> <u>Williams:</u> <u>Poet</u> <u>from</u> <u>Jersey</u>.
    Boston: Houghton Mifflin Co., pp. 321, 324-26.
        Mentions W.C. Williams's appreciation of Creeley's work.

<u>1976</u>

1 ADKINS, GEOFFREY. "The Poetry of Robert Creeley." <u>Limestone</u>
   (London), no. 4, pp. 32-36.
        Provides background on Creeley and comments on his short
   line and use of the "speaking voice." Finds the poems in <u>For</u> <u>Love</u>
   "superb" when the line directs the attention, but stale when
   Creeley "uses wit and archaic lyric forms." Finds better control
   in <u>Words</u>, but believes "the area of certainty has been diminish-
   ing" for Creeley until in <u>Pieces</u> "all knowledge which is not certain" has been eliminated.

2 AKEROYD, JOANNE VINSON, and BUTTERICK, GEORGE F. <u>Where</u> <u>Are</u>
   <u>Their</u> <u>Papers?</u> <u>A</u> <u>Union</u> <u>List</u> <u>Locating</u> <u>the</u> <u>Papers</u> <u>of</u> <u>Forty-Two</u>
   <u>Contemporary</u> <u>American</u> <u>Poets</u> <u>and</u> <u>Writers</u>. Bibliography Series,
   no. 9. Storrs, Conn.: University of Connecticut Library,
   pp. 20-21.
        Provides locations for specific manuscripts and papers of
   Creeley.

3 BACON, TERRY R. "How He Knows When to Stop: Creeley on
   Closure: A Conversation with the Poet." <u>American</u> <u>Poetry</u>
   <u>Review</u> 5, no. 6 (November-December):5-7.
        In this interview, Creeley discusses his sense of resolu-
   tion, termination, and closure in poetry. Mentions his desire for
   the speculative and his use of page lengths as an arbitrary unit
   of composition for such works as "<u>The</u> <u>Gold</u> <u>Diggers</u>" <u>and</u> <u>Other</u>
   <u>Stories</u> and <u>The</u> <u>Island</u>. Also comments on his elimination of the
   need to "wrap-up" or perfect poems in <u>Words</u> and <u>Pieces</u>, and notes
   his use of the couplet. Creeley remarks upon the composition of

Thirty Things and His Idea, the lack of interplay of prose and
poetry in A Day Book, and the role of silence in his work. He
provides some biographical details and finds himself "reductive in
impulse."

4   BERGÉ, CAROL. "The Vancouver Report." In The Writing Life:
    Historical and Critical Views of the "Tish" Movement. Edited
    by C[harles] H[enry] Gervais. Coatsworth, Ontario: Black
    Moss Press, pp. 143-49.
        Reprint of 1964.2. Only a small amount of the material on
Creeley is reprinted.

5   CREELEY, ROBERT. "A Day Book." In "Mabel: A Story" and Other
    Prose. London: Marion Boyars, pp. 7-58.
        Reprint of 1972.8, with dates.

6   _____. "From 'Mabel: A Story.'" Unmuzzled Ox 4, no. 1:84-88.
        Creeley provides biographical details concerning his rela-
tionship to women, notably relating a sexual encounter in Burma in
World War II. Describes himself at the age of eighteen. Reprinted in 1976.9; reprinted: 1980.7.

7   _____. "Introduction" to "Mabel: A Story" and Other Prose.
    London: Marion Boyars, [pp. 5-6].
        In this introduction, Creeley comments on the numerical
structure, the occasion, and the intent behind A Day Book,
Presences, and "Mabel: A Story." Also comments on the "scaf-
folding" he left in place in Pieces. Reprinted: 1984.12.

8   _____. "Lew." In ". . . where ring is what a bell does": An
    Appreciation of Lew Welch. Compiled by S. Fox. Stone Soup
    Chapbook Series, no. 10. Boston: Stone Soup Poetry,
    pp. 12-13.
        In this reminiscence, Creeley discusses first meeting Lew
Welch in 1956 and later in 1965 at the Berkeley Poetry Conference.

9   _____. "Mabel: A Story." In "Mabel: A Story" and Other
    Prose. London: Marion Boyars, pp. 115-70.
        Interspersed among fiction and fictionalized materials,
Creeley provides some family history on his mother's side and
biographical details from the mid to late-1950s in New Mexico and
Guadalajara (pp. 124-25, 139-47, 151-65, 166-69). Also mentions
his traveling during the period, obliquely refers to an affair
with Marthe Rexroth, and comments on his relationship to many
women. Includes reprints of 1975.6 and 1976.6. Reprinted in
1984.12.

10   _____. "A Note" in Hello. Christchurch, New Zealand: Hawk
    Press, [pp. 1-3].

RC1976

      In this note, Creeley mentions making a major change in his life in 1976 and provides a few biographical details from his visit to New Zealand in 1976.

11   _____. Presences. With Marisol. New York: Charles Scribner's Sons, 146 pp.
     Includes reprints of 1972.9, 14.

12   _____. "Presences: A Text for Marisol." In "Mabel: A Story" and Other Prose. London: Marion Boyars, pp. 59-113.
     Includes reprints of 1972.9, 14.

13   _____. "Was That a Real Poem or Did You Just Make It up Yourself?" In American Poets in 1976. Edited by William Heyen. Indianapolis: Bobbs-Merrill Educational Publishing, pp. 46-53.
     Reprint of 1976.15.

14   _____. "Was That a Real Poem or Did You Just Make It up Yourself." New Poetry: Magazine of the Poetry Society of Australia 24, no. 2:41-50.
     Reprint of 1976.15.

15   _____. "Was That a Real Poem or Did You Just Make It up Yourself." Sparrow, no. 40 (January), [13 pp.].
     In this lengthy essay, dated 31 July 1974, Creeley provides a number of generalized biographical details, primarily concerning his sense of the creative process. Mentions his first reasons for writing, his craftsmanship, and his occasional inability to write. Comments on his use of form, his tidinesses, and his reasons to change his poetry in the mid-1960s to reflect a sense of "continuance." Notes his pleasure in writing, his sense of writing as revelation, and his unwillingness to write for the same reasons and in the same manner as others.
     Also provides generalized details about his first marriage, his nature in the 1940s and 1950s, and his early reading. Mentions trying to teach a friend about rhythm in poetry and working on a collaborative poem. Comments on his loneliness and restlessness, his desire for his children to share his feelings, and his life in 1974. Refers to his and another's sense of love in "The Warning," and mentions affinities with W.C. Williams. Reprinted: 1976.13-14; 1979.15.

16 DAVEY, FRANK[LAND WILMOT]. "Black Days on Black Mountain." In The Writing Life: Historical and Critical Views of the "Tish" Movement. Edited by C[harles] H[enry] Gervais. Coatsworth, Ontario: Black Moss Press, pp. 117-27.
     Reprint of 1965.11.

17   DUDEK, LOUIS. "Lunchtime Reflections on Frank Davey's Defence
      of the Black Mountain Fort." In The Writing Life: Historical
      and Critical Views of the "Tish" Movement. Edited by C[harles]
      H[enry] Gervais. Coatsworth, Ontario: Black Moss Press,
      pp. 128-33.
         Reprint of 1965.12.

18   FAAS, EKBERT. "An Interview with Robert Bly." Boundary 2: A
      Journal of Postmodern Literature 4, no. 3 (Spring):677-700.
         In this interview, Bly criticizes Creeley's "Form is never
      more than an extension of content," finds him on "a weird path of
      his own," but claims to "feel very close to him."
         Faas mentions Creeley's method of revision and believes that
      "he is a poet fascinated by 'emptiness.'" Reprinted: 1980.16.

19   FRIEDMAN, ANDREA MARIAN. "'Driven by that density home':
      Herman Melville, Charles Olson, Robert Creeley, and the Problem
      of Knowledge in a World of Flux." Ph.D. dissertation, State
      University of New York at Buffalo, pp. 53-149, passim.
         Mainly provides a few Creeley quotations from 1970.14 to
      support Olson's theories on knowledge, language, man in nature,
      myth, and love. Also quotes Creeley on form, rhythm, the activity
      of writing, and the reality of poetry. Comments on "Apple Uppfle"
      and "A Form of Adaptation" as illustrations of emotional stages,
      and mentions the role of love in his poetry. Notes his use of
      end-stopped lines when reading his own work, finding this empha-
      sizes "the possibilities of each word." See Dissertation
      Abstracts International 37 (1976):2893-94A.

20   JACKRELL, TOM. Review of Presences. Contact II: A Bimonthly,
      "The Best of American Poetry" 1, no. 1 (November-December):back
      cover, pp. [28], 25.
         In this review, compares Creeley's text with Marisol's pic-
      tured sculptures, and comments on their relationships. Discusses
      the Baby Girl portion of the first section and the "mock-didactic
      style" of the last.

21   [JOHNSTON, ALASTAIR M.] A Bibliography of Auerhahn Press and
      Its Successor, Dave Haselwood Books. Berkeley: Poltroon
      Press, pp. 86-87.
         Provides bibliographical description of Creeley's broadside
      "Two Poems," correcting 1973.37 and 1973.38.

22   LEED, JACOB. "Robert Creeley and The Lititz Review: A Recol-
      lection with Letters." Journal of Modern Literature 5, no. 2
      (April):243-59.
         Leed gives biographical details about his relationship to
      Creeley, providing glimpses of Creeley at Harvard and in
      Littleton, New Hampshire. Also reminisces about trying to hand
      set and print the Lititz Review with Creeley, correcting Creeley's

memory of the event. Provides portions of letters from Creeley in
February to August 1950 about the Lititz Review, including his
contacts with writers to whom he wrote for contributions, such as
Pound and W.C. Williams. In the letters, Creeley also writes
about his relationship to Corman, his notion of an audience, his
own writing, and rejections of his work. Lists a few of the items
Creeley collected for the review, and includes letters to Creeley
from W.C. Williams and Marianne Moore, responding to his comments
and requests for material. Remembers printing an unpublished poem
by Creeley as an experiment, and provides portions of other unpublished poems by Creeley from the 1940s. See also 1987.10.

23 LEPPER, GARY M. "Robert Creeley." In A Bibliographical Intro-
 duction to Seventy-Five Modern American Authors. Berkeley:
 Serendipity Books, pp. 131-42.
 Provides a primary bibliography, with some description, of
Creeley's books and broadsides. See also 1983.29.

24 MacINTYRE, WENDY ELIZABETH. "Physics in the Poetics of Charles
 Olson." Ph.D. thesis, University of Edinburgh, pp. 2-3, 26,
 153-57, 168, passim.
 Briefly mentions Creeley's association with Olson and
Olson's influence on his work, noting Creeley's ideas on form and
content and the relation between writing and the "physiology of
the writer." Finds Creeley learned to follow "the poem's spontaneous lead" through following the play of syllables, noting this
"syllabic lead" in "Le Fou." Also comments on "The Finger," and
notes the "hesitant manner" in which Creeley reads his poetry.

25 MANHIRE, BILL. "Conversation with Robert Creeley." Islands:
 A New Zealand Quarterly of Arts and Letters 5, no. 1 [whole no.
 15] (September):32-49.
 In this 1976 interview, Creeley discusses giving readings
and using proper names and pronouns in poetry. Mentions the influence of Wallace Stevens on The Charm: Early and Uncollected
Poems (1969), the intention behind Pieces, and the erotic in A Day
Book (in response to 1975.19). Also comments on his fiction and
the composition of "For My Mother: Genevieve Jules Creeley."
Discusses his appreciation of or relationship to other poets,
especially Blackburn, Ginsberg, John Ashbery, Frank O'Hara, and
Robert Lowell. Remarks on Whitman's continuing influence on
poetry, and gives a few biographical details, mainly concerning
teaching at SUNY-Buffalo and his mother's death.

26 MILNER, PHILIP. "Life at All Its Points: An Interview with
 Robert Creeley." Antigonish Review, no. 26, pp. 37-47.
 In this 14 February 1976 interview in Halifax, Nova Scotia,
Creeley comments on his sense of rhyme and of physical and literal
language. Also mentions the influence of Pound on him and the

physical changes of his body due to aging. Provides biographical
information about his grandfather, about his sense of Canada as a
child, about living in Vancouver in 1962-63, and about leaving
Canada. Comments on his contacts with Canadian writers like
Irving Layton. In his preface, Milner notes the occasion for the
interview.

27　　MITCHELL, BEVERLEY [JOAN]. "The Genealogy of Tish." In The
　　　Writing Life: Historical and Critical Views of the "Tish"
　　　Movement. Edited by C[harles] H[enry] Gervais. Coatsworth,
　　　Ontario: Black Moss Press, pp. 70-93.
　　　　　Reprint of 1972.22.

28　　MORGAN, EDWIN. "One: Two: Three." Times Literary Supple-
　　　ment, 15 October, p. 1307.
　　　　　In a moderately favorable review of "Mabel: A Story" and
　　　Other Prose, briefly comments on Creeley's use of the triadic
　　　structure and the number three.

29　　OATES, JOYCE CAROL. Review of Selected Poems. New Republic:
　　　A Journal of Politics and the Arts 175, no. 25 (18 December):
　　　26-28.
　　　　　In this unfavorable review, feels "Creeley has not developed
　　　in any obvious way," mentions his spontaneity and minimalism, and
　　　notes the lack of emotion in his poetry. Praises "For My Mother:
　　　Genevieve Jules Creeley."

30　　PINSKY, ROBERT. The Situation of Poetry: Contemporary Poetry
　　　and Its Traditions. Princeton Essays in Literature.
　　　Princeton: Princeton University Press, pp. 9-12.
　　　　　Finds a "useful directness" in Creeley's "plain style," with
　　　its avoidance of descriptive rhetoric and metaphor as in such
　　　poems as "['Could write of fucking']." (But see 1980.32.)

31　　RICHARDSON, KEITH. Poetry and the Colonized Mind: "Tish."
　　　Oakville, Ottawa: Mosaic Press, Valley Editions, pp. 13-14,
　　　18-20, 38, 50, passim.
　　　　　Notes Creeley's relationship to Tish and his influence on
　　　poets associated with Tish.

32　　SAUNIER-OLLIER, JACQUELINE. "Contemporary Trends in American
　　　Poetry." Études anglo-américaines: Annales de la Faculté des
　　　Lettres et Sciences Humaines de Nice, no. 27, pp. 83-96.
　　　　　Notes the "self is reduced to the minimal" in Creeley's
　　　poetry and, using "Love ['Not enough. The question: what is'],"
　　　the "hesitations and unresolved conflicts."

33　　SEYMOUR-SMITH, MARTIN. "Creeley, Robert." In Who's Who in
　　　Twentieth Century Literature. New York: Holt, Rinehart, &
　　　Winston, pp. 88-89.

RC1976

Believes that Creeley's poems care for nothing "but the expression of his solipsist ego now," and finds his fiction "tortuous."

34   SILVANI, GIOVANNA. "L'isola di Robert Creeley." [In Italian.] Studi americani: Rivista annuale dedicata alle lettere e alle arti negli Stati Uniti d'America, nos. 21-22, pp. 475-94.
      Finds Creeley's prose style overly complex due to its blend of the poetic and prosaic. Comparing "The Gesture" with a section of The Island, demonstrates that Creeley's poetry is prosaic in syntax and diction and that his prose is poetic in rhythm. Feels his poetry often compares the sensory world of illusion to the world of being or truth.
      Discusses Creeley's prose style, and notes that the structure of his stories and his novel is erratic, often repetitious. In The Island, feels the minor episodes do not contribute to the growing tension of the work, finding that they tend to obstruct its continuity. Focusing on the character of John, discusses the immaturity in his flight from reality, his failure in relationships and in writing, and his egotism. Also mentions Creeley's treatment of sex, love, and marriage in The Island; his use of the epigraph from Parmenides; and the role of the sea and the island as symbols. Believes that the novel ends where it began, with nothing resolved. Also notes the autobiographical sense of the work and the lack of depth in the characterization of Marge and Artie.

35   TALLMAN, WARREN. "Wonder Merchants: Modernist Poetry in Vancouver during the 1960's." In The Writing Life: Historical and Critical Views of the "Tish" Movement. Edited by C[harles] H[enry] Gervais. Coatsworth, Ontario: Black Moss Press, pp. 27-69.
      Reprint of 1974.25.

36   ZVEREV, A[LEKSEI]. "Opening the Doors of Association: On Contemporary American Poetry." Translated by Ronald Vroon. In Twentieth Century American Literature: A Soviet View. Moscow: Progress Publishers, pp. 160-80.
      Feels Creeley struggles "against 'programmed poetry,'" but believes his overemphasizes individualism and the subjective while rejecting the communicative function that is essential to poetry.

1977

1   AIKEN, WILLIAM MINOR. "Charles Olson: The Uses of the Vatic." Ph.D. dissertation, Boston University, pp. 22, 81, 92-101, 104, 112, 191, 197, 200, 202-4, passim.
      Compares Creeley's poetry to Gary Snyder's and discusses the influence of Olson's projective poetics on Creeley's work, finding

that Olson's theories have increased Creeley's isolation and di-
minished his need to communicate. Briefly compares Zukofsky's
poetics to Creeley's, and discusses the energy in Creeley's use of
line length, using "Song ['I wouldn't']" as an example. Part of
chapter 6 is a revision of 1970.1. Chapter 10 is revised as
1978.1. See Dissertation Abstracts International 37 (1977):
7746A-47A.

2   BACON, TERRY R. "Closure in Robert Creeley's Poetry." Modern
    Poetry Studies 8, no. 3 (Winter):227-47.
        Notes the devices of continuation, closure, "non-closure,"
and "anti-closure" in "Le Fou"; "The Flower ['I think I grow tensions']"; "And"; "The Rain ['All night the sound had']"; "The
Language"; "Kid ['The kid left']"; His Idea; "Alice"; "A Loop";
Pieces, as "an integral whole"; and other poems. Explicates portions of the above and "Le Fou" in detail.
        Discusses Creeley's development from an emphasis upon the
poem as an "evolving form" to a focus on a single, isolated perception, but believes "the closure of the [latter] structure does
not imply the termination of the perceptions" since they continue
to provoke the reader.

3   BROMWICH, DAVID. "Verse Chronicle." Hudson Review 30, no. 2
    (Summer):279-92.
        In a review of Creeley's Away, finds the tone occasionally
charming, but feels Creeley often sounds like a "minor [W.C.]
Williams." Claims "Comfort" is a "pretty shocking theft" from
Williams's "To Elsie." Compares Creeley with Diane Wakoski.

4   CARRUTH, HAYDEN. "A Secular Lover." New York Times Book
    Review, 1 May, pp. 58-59.
        In a favorable review of Selected Poems, believes Creeley in
his later poems "has turned away . . . from what his talent does
most easily," writing love poems, to composing "a poetry of dissatisfaction."

5   COOPER, DENNIS. "An Interview with Gerard Malanga." Little
    Caesar Magazine, no. 4 (November), pp. 39-57.
        In this interview, Malanga discusses the influence of
Creeley's work upon his own.

6   CREELEY, ROBERT. Letter to the Editors. American Poetry
    Review 6, no. 1 (January-February):47.
        Creeley notes that Scribner's Sons', in Selected Poems,
dropped mention of Robert Grenier as editor and rearranged the
order of the poems. Announces that the volume does not have his
approval.

RC1977

7   C[REELEY], R[OBERT]. Note in Thanks. Old Deerfield, Mass.:
    Deerfield Press; Dublin: Gallery Press, [p. 2].
       In this note, Creeley comments on his relationship, as a
    child, with Theresa Turner.

8   CREELEY, ROBERT. "Preface." Purchase Poetry Review (State
    University of New York, College at Purchase) 1, no. 1
    (Autumn):i.
       Reprint of 1957.1.

9   DAVIDSON, [ROBERT] MICHAEL. "Incarnations of Jack Spicer:
    Heads of the Town up to the Aether." Boundary 2: A Journal of
    Postmodern Literature 6, no. 1 (Fall):103–34.
       Notes Spicer's treatment of Creeley in "Dash" from his
    Hommage to Creeley.

10 EDELBERG, CYNTHIA DUBIN. "The Poetry of Robert Creeley."
    Ph.D. dissertation, New York University, 222 pp.
       Provides a brief but substantive biographical sketch focus-
    ing on Creeley's childhood, his return after World War II, his
    marriage to Ann Creeley, and his relationship to Olson. Notes
    Creeley's critical reception, and finds Olson's influence on
    Creeley often overestimated. Examines the influence of the
    "Monsieur Teste pose" of the "dispassionate intelligence" and of
    the "mind in conversation with itself" from Valéry's Monsieur
    Teste.
       Notes this "detached posture" in For Love, discussing each
    of the sections in turn. Finds the first part deals with the
    "collapse of his first marriage," including his treatment of rela-
    tionships and women as well as influential poets and his own crea-
    tive experience. Claims the second section was "written in
    response to the dislocating separation and to the painful divorce
    in 1956," noting his treatment of emotional pain, women, and his
    wife. Also finds him "challenging the authority of established
    convention" in this section. Believes the third section shows
    Creeley "beginning to drop the mask [of the dispassionate self],
    beginning to express his hopes and fears about love in a more
    straightforward fashion." Also notes his treatment of poetry,
    marriage and thinking in this section. Discusses a number of
    poems from For Love, most substantively "A Song ['I had wanted a
    quiet testament']," "The Riddle," "The Business," "A Token," and
    "For Love."
       In Words, feels that Creeley reevaluates his "life-order
    suppositions concerning the intellect, love, and poetry," explor-
    ing the "possibilities of the non-intellectual orientation, the
    solitary existence, and the silent poetic voice." Discusses his
    treatment of the thinking mind, marriage, love, and communication,
    and examines the themes of the detachment of rational thought,
    "spontaneous impulse," and the creative process in a number of

poems, especially "The Mountains in the Desert," "A Piece,"
"Anger," "Enough," "The Language," and "Words."
    Finds Pieces, again, on "the nature of the thinking mind,
the poetic process, and the love relationship." Believes Creeley
attempts to balance the intuitive and the analytical, and feels he
focuses on the poet's role and his poetic achievement. Also comments on his search for the "philosophical significance of the
love relationship." Discusses the work as a romance with a journey including a series of descents, a confrontation, and a final
victory of discovery. Comments on many of the individual pieces,
especially "The Finger," "Numbers," and "Mazatlan: Sea." Notes
his allusions to Zukofsky and mythological figures. Points out
his treatment of the creative process, women, the goddess and hero
figures, the fool, the present, and numbers.
    Discusses Creeley's "aesthetic rationale" for the "effect of
untampered-with-immediacy" in In London, noting the influence of
Ginsberg, and comments on his use of projective poetics. Mentions
his treatment of death, love, loneliness, and of his wife, Bobbie
Creeley, in a number of pieces, especially "Dying" and "People ['I
knew where they were']," noting his occasional serenity.
    Provides a portion of a taped May 1975 conversation with
Creeley in which he both provides the biographical context for
"Return" and comments on "Hélas," especially his treatment of
Olson, Pound and W.C. Williams. Creeley also comments on his
feelings for Williams, on his early relationship to Olson, and on
his attraction to Válery's Monsieur Teste. Also includes an
August 1975 response by Creeley to a series of questions in which
he provides context for a number of poems, especially "Hélas,"
"The Innocence," "In an Act of Pity," "The Riddle," "The Flower
['I think I grow tensions']," "The Place ['What is the form is the
gro-']," "Ballad of the Despairing Husband," "The Figures," "After
Mallarmé," and "The Plan." He also mentions his feelings for
Thomas Campion and his lack of focus on theme. Creeley mentions
the emptiness and "sexual overtones" in Words and the patterns of
poems in his collections.
    Revised: 1978.33. Chapter 2, on Words, is slightly revised
as 1978.34. Chapter 4, on In London, is slightly revised in
1987.19. See Dissertation Abstracts International 38 (1978):
6131A.

11   FASS, EKBERT. "From 'Towards a New American Poetics.'"
     Sparrow, no. 60 (September), [22 pp.].
        Mentions the "almost pre-conceptual concreteness" of "The
Moon," and compares Creeley's development to that of Stéphane
Mallarmé. Finds Creeley goes beyond Mallarmé's discovery of the
void to a reawareness of the world. Also comments on Creeley's
idea of objectivity. Reprinted: 1978.38.

RC1977

12 GRAY, DARRELL. "Translations from Silence." In Essays and
    Dissolutions. Madison, Wis.: Abraxas Press, pp. 80–86.
        Gray mentions Creeley's influence on him and, using the
    first stanza of "The Cracks" as an example, notes the "interplay
    of vowels and consonants."

13 HUYBENSZ, JOANNE. "The Mind Dance ('wherein thot shows its
    pattern'): An Approach to the Poetry of Robert Duncan." Ph.D.
    dissertation, State University of New York at Stony Brook, pp.
    166–68, 213–15.
        Briefly summarizes Creeley's relationship to Duncan, noting
    Duncan's references to Creeley's poetry in his own. See Disserta-
    tion Abstracts International 38 (1977):1380A.

14 LEVITEN, DAVID. "The Starving Epistemologist and the Sound-
    Ripe Sonneteer." Parnassus: Poetry in Review 5, no. 2 [Fifth
    Anniversary Issue and a Tribute to Virgil Thomson on his 81st
    Birthday] (Spring–Summer):270–77.
        In unfavorable reviews of Selected Poems and Presences,
    comments on Creeley's solipsism and treatment of the self in the
    poetry, noting the entropy. Feels "The Act of Love" is less ab-
    stract than other poems, and brings "body and soul together."
    Finds Presences pretentious.

15 MacADAMS, LEWIS, [Jr.]. "From Robert Creeley's Contexts of
    Poetry: Interviews, 1961–1971, p. 161." Poetry Project News-
    letter, no. 47 (1 July), [pp. 7–8].
        Reprinted from 1968.26.

16 OBERG, ARTHUR. "Robert Creeley: 'And the power to tell / is
    glory.'" Ohio Review 18, no. 1 (Winter):79–97.
        Discusses "the unattractive poet, the attractive poet; the
    poet of glory, the poet of dark pain" as two of the selves in
    Creeley's work. Comments on a number of poems, especially "For
    W.C.W. ['The rhyme is after']," "The Window ['There will be no
    simple'']," and "The Rain ['All night the sound had']," and prose
    sections from A Day Book. Finds continual expressions of isola-
    tion, pain, insufficiency, and impending loss juxtaposed to "mo-
    ments of lyric ease." Claims "the riddle of a man and a woman is
    Creeley's major theme," and notes how he can "keep in motion . . .
    competing, even contradictory senses." Discusses W.C. Williams's
    influence on Creeley as well as their differences, and comments on
    John Berryman's treatment of him in "In & Out." Small portions
    extensively revised: 1978.56.

17 PERELMAN, ROBERT. Review of Selected Poems and Presences.
    American Book Review 1, no. 1 (December):15.
        In this basically favorable review, discusses Scribner's
    Sons' "stupid and dishonest misfocusing" of Selected Poems by

rearranging the order. Mentions Creeley's use of words as autonomous, and comments on a few poems, notably "A Piece." Favorably
reviews <u>Presences</u>, lising various narrative types.

18   ROBINSON, WILLIAM R.   "<u>The Island</u>." In <u>Survey of Contemporary</u>
      <u>Literature</u>. Edited by Frank N. Magill. Vol. 6. Englewood
      Cliffs, N.J.: Salem Press, pp. 3775-77.
          Reprint of 1971.20.

19   SCHUCHAT, SIMON. Review of <u>Selected Poems</u>. <u>Poetry Project</u>
      <u>Newsletter</u>, no. 42 (1 February), [pp. 1-3].
          In this favorable review, discusses the order of the poems
      and the relative roles of the various editors in the volume.
      Speculates on Charles Scribner's Sons' intentions, provides
      Creeley's reaction to the finished volume, and comments on his
      poetry's critical reception.

20   TALLMAN, WARREN. "Robert Creeley's Tales and Poems." <u>Open</u>
      <u>Letter</u>, 3d ser., no. 6 [Godawful Streets of Man: Essays by
      Warren Tallman issue] (Winter), pp. 93-118.
          Reprint of 1962.14 and 1966.28.

21   _____. "Wonder Merchants: Modernist Poetry in Vancouver dur-
      ing the 1960's." <u>Open Letter</u>, 3d ser., no. 6 [Godawful Streets
      of Man: Essays by Warren Tallman issue] (Winter), pp. 175-207.
          Reprint of 1974.25.

22   _____. "The Writing Life." <u>Open Letter</u>, 3d ser., no. 6
      [Godawful Streets of Man: Essays by Warren Tallman issue]
      (Winter), pp. 150-58.
          Reprint of 1965.22.

23   VINCENT, SYBIL KORFF. "'An old man called me darling': The
      Diction of the Love Poetry of Some Contemporary American Poets
      during the Period 1945 through 1975." Ph.D. dissertation,
      University of Toledo, pp. 66-67, 97-99, 175-78, 215-16, 293-
      301, 332-34, 336-37, 339, passim.
          Studies the diction of Creeley's love poetry, noting its
      changes from 1950 to 1975 by counting the frequency of word use in
      the categories of function words, verbs, modifiers, and nouns,
      including proper and abstract nouns. Also notes his use of slang
      and word coinages. Finds Creeley's language is plain and abstract
      in the early 1950s but "somewhat more explicit" in the late 1950s.
      Discovers the love poems of the late 1960s are "more abstract and
      enigmatic." Notes that there are fewer love poems in the early
      1970s, but feels the diction reflects Creeley's peace in accepting
      the separateness of "two people, of flesh and spirit, of desire
      and will," even though there has been an apparent "rejection of

the physical world" during this period. See <u>Dissertation</u>
<u>Abstracts</u> <u>International</u> 38 (1977):2797A.

1978

1   AIKEN, WILLIAM [MINOR]. "The Olson Poetics: Some Effects."
    <u>Contemporary</u> <u>Poetry:</u> <u>A</u> <u>Journal</u> <u>of</u> <u>Criticism</u> 3, no. 2
    (Summer):62–80.
       Revision of chapter 10 of 1977.1.

2   ALAPI, ZSOLT [ISTVÁN]; CAMPBELL, JAMES; and SNYDER, CARL.
    "Robert Creeley: An Interview." <u>Atropos</u> 1, no. 1 (Spring):
    24–30.
       In this 1976 interview, Creeley discusses the poem as an
    act, an event; the spontaneity of his writing; his lack of revi-
    sion; his use of himself as a subject, contrary to Olson's dictum;
    the self-revelation of his "psychic life" in such works as "<u>Mabel:</u>
    <u>A</u> <u>Story</u>" <u>and</u> <u>Other</u> <u>Prose</u> and <u>Away</u>; and the process of composing
    <u>Pieces</u> and <u>The</u> <u>Island</u>.

3   ALTIERI, CHARLES. "Motives in Metaphor: John Ashbery and the
    Modernist Long Poem." <u>Genre:</u> <u>A</u> <u>Quarterly</u> <u>Devoted</u> <u>to</u> <u>Generic</u>
    <u>Criticism</u> 11, no. 4 [The Long Poem in the Twentieth Century
    issue] (Winter):653–87.
       Briefly compares Ashbery's "version of poetry as an act of
    thinking" and as expression with Olson and Creeley's.

4   _____. "Placing Creeley's Recent Work: A Poetics of Conjec-
    ture." <u>Boundary</u> <u>2:</u> <u>A</u> <u>Journal</u> <u>of</u> <u>Postmodern</u> <u>Literature</u> 6, no.
    3–vol. 7, no. 1 [Robert Creeley: A Gathering] (Spring-Fall):
    513–39.
       Demonstrates that Creeley's "is a poetics of conjecture
    rather than closure, a poetics . . . whose aim is not so much to
    interpret experience as to extend it by making a situation simply
    the focus for overlapping reflective structures," a "set of multi-
    ple systems in continual play." Compares the philosophical and
    aesthetic bases behind modernism and postmodernism, especially as
    related to the lyric, and notes Creeley's place in the continuum.
    Demonstrates the influence of Olson's field poetics, W.C.
    Williams's poetry, especially his "rhetoric of casualness," and
    objectivism on Creeley's work. Explicates "Thinking ['Had not']"
    and portions of the paragraphs in <u>A</u> <u>Day</u> <u>Book</u>. Compares Creeley's
    poetry to abstract painting and John Ashbery's work, and details
    his use of "variations on a set of recurrent themes." Comments on
    "<u>Mabel:</u> <u>A</u> <u>Story</u>" <u>and</u> <u>Other</u> <u>Prose</u> and <u>Presences</u>.
       Also mentions his treatment of travel, place, desire, the
    self, relationships, systems, and sex. Treats his use of se-
    quences, serialogy, prose, tautology, solipsism, and self-parody;

and comments on the role of abstraction and particularity in his work. Revised: 1984.3.

5   BENSTON, KIMBERLY W. "Amiri Baraka: An Interview." Boundary 2: A Journal of Postmodern Literature 6, no. 2 (Winter): 303-16.
In this interview, Baraka occasionally mentions Creeley's influence on his work and comments on trying to go beyond that influence. Calls Creeley a "post-bourgeois/academic poet."

6   B[ERTHOLF], R[OBERT] J[OHN]. "Robert Creeley, 1926-." In First Printings of American Authors: Contributions toward Descriptive Checklists. Vol. 3. Edited by Matthew J. Bruccoli, C.E. Frazer Clark, Jr., Richard Layman, and Benjamin Franklin, V. A Bruccoli Clark Book. Detroit: Gale Research Co., pp. 53-69.
Provides an initial descriptive checklist for Creeley.

7   BINNI, FRANCESCO. Modernismo letterario anglo-americano: Permanenza e irrealtà di un'istituzione del progresso. [In Italian.] Biblioteca di cultura, no. 139. Rome: Bulzoni Editore, pp. 438, 440-41, passim.
Occasionally comments on Creeley's sense of form and content, and notes that his source of value is the world itself. Believes "After Mallarmé" concerns Creeley's inability to name or understand objects and names.

8   BRAKHAGE, STAN. "Poetry and Film, 22 March 1977." Transcribed by Robert J[ohn] Bertholf. Credences, [o.s.] 2, nos. 2-3 [whole nos. 5-6] (March):99-114.
In this talk, Brakhage mentions the occasion behind filming Two: Creeley McClure and provides impressions of Creeley. Reprinted: 1982.4.

9   BUTTERICK, GEORGE F. A Guide to "The Maximus Poems" of Charles Olson. Berkeley, Los Angeles, and London: University of California Press, pp. 3-4, 83, 634-35, 699, passim.
In a greatly expanded version of 1970.8, mentions Olson's sense of Creeley as "The Figure of Outward," and provides explanations of allusions to Creeley in The Maximus Poems. In the introduction and throughout, occasionally refers to and quotes from Creeley and Olson's correspondence, mostly letters from Olson to Creeley.

10 BUTTERICK, GEORGE F.; CREELEY, ROBERT; and OLSON, CHARLES. "Olson and Creeley: The Beginning." Boundary 2: A Journal of Postmodern Literature 6, no. 3-vol. 7, no. 1 [Robert Creeley: A Gathering] (Spring-Fall):129-34.
Reprint of 1973.4.

RC1978

11   CLARK, TOM. "'Desperate perhaps, and even foolish / but God
      knows useful': Creeley and the Experience of Space." Boundary
      2: A Journal of Postmodern Literature 6, no. 3-vol. 7, no. 1
      [Robert Creeley: A Gathering] (Spring-Fall):453-56.
         Provides a few anecdotal biographical details and briefly
      comments on Creeley's isolation, his treatment of intimacy and
      wetness, and his personal levity and puritanism. Briefly comments
      on a number of poems, especially "The Finger."

12   COOK, ALBERT [SPAULDING]. "Reflections on Creeley." Boundary
      2: A Journal of Postmodern Literature 6, no. 3-vol. 7, no. 1
      [Robert Creeley: A Gathering] (Spring-Fall):353-62.
         Discusses Creeley's use of "phrasal suspension," line
      length, three-line stanzas, and titles. Also comments on his use
      of images, rhythm, expectation of meaning, and associations.
      Examines these techniques in such works as "Here Again," "The
      Cracks," "She Went to Stay," "I Know a Man," "La Noche," "The
      Pattern," and Presences. Compares Creeley to W.C. Williams,
      Mallarmé, and surrealists. Comments on Creeley as a minimalist
      and an epigrammatist. Revised as part of 1985.6.

13   CORMAN, CID. "For Love Of." In Essays on the Arts of
      Language. Vol. 2, At Their Word. Santa Barbara, Calif.:
      Black Sparrow Press, pp. 72-90.
         Reprint of 1962.4.

14   COX, KENNETH. "Address and Posture in the Early Poetry of
      Robert Creeley." Boundary 2: A Journal of Postmodern Lit-
      erature 6, no. 3-vol. 7, no. 1 [Robert Creeley: A Gathering]
      (Spring-Fall):241-46.
         Slight revision of 1969.4.

15   CREELEY, ROBERT. "For L.Z." Paideuma: A Journal Devoted to
      Ezra Pound Scholarship 7, no. 3 [Louis Zukofsky, 1904-1978,
      issue] (Winter):383-85.
         Creeley provides biographical details and reminisces about
      his relationship with Zukofsky, especially his first and later
      visits with Zukofsky. Reprinted: 1979.5.

16   _____. "From 'On the Road: Notes on Artists and Poets, 1950-
      1965' in Poets of the Cities, 1974." Big Sky, nos. 11-12
      [Homage to Frank O'Hara issue], p. 68.
         Reprint of 1974.5.

17   _____. Letter to William Matheson. Boundary 2: A Journal of
      Postmodern Literature 6, no. 3-vol. 7, no. 1 [Robert Creeley:
      A Gathering] (Spring-Fall):488-90.
         In this 31 July 1964 letter, Creeley describes the methods
      and process of writing The Island and notes that revision serves

no purpose for him. Comments on the influence of Stendhal on
him, and provides the draft of the first page of The Island.

18   . "A Note." In Hello: A Journal, February 29-May 3,
     1976. New York: New Directions Books, p. 85.
          In this note, Creeley explains why he traveled to nine dif-
     ferent countries in 1976. Reprinted: 1978.20.

19   . "A Note: From 'Notebook, January 31-April 3, 1977.'"
     Boundary 2: A Journal of Postmodern Literature 6, no. 3-vol.
     7, no. 1 [Robert Creeley: A Gathering] (Spring-Fall):78-79.
          In this 22 March entry, Creeley mentions his reading of
     Turgenev, his sense of audience, and his use of three- and four-
     line stanzas. Also provides some general biographical details.

20   C[REELEY], R[OBERT]. "A Note to Hello: A Journal, February
     29-May 3, 1976." In Hello: A Journal. London: Marion Boyars,
     [p. v].
          Reprint of 1978.18.

21   CREELEY, ROBERT. "On Black Mountain Review." In The Little
     Magazine in America: A Modern Documentary History. Edited by
     Elliott Anderson and Mary Kinzie. Yonkers, N.Y.: Pushcart
     Press, pp. 248-61.
          Reprint of 1969.7.

22   . "On Black Mountain Review." TriQuarterly, no. 43
     (Fall), pp. 248-61.
          Reprint of 1969.7.

23   . Preface to "The Broken World of Robert Creeley," by
     Frederick Philip Hayes. Ph.D. dissertation, University of
     Denver, pp. v-vi.
          In this preface, Creeley comments on 1978.42, provides a few
     biographical details, and mentions his relationship to Hayes. See
     Dissertation Abstracts International 39 (1978):2273A.

24   . "Preface" to Nolo Contendere, by Judson Crews. Edited
     by J. Whitebird. Houston: Wings Press, pp. i-iii.
          In this preface, Creeley mentions his concepts of Texans
     when he was a child and his first meeting with Crews.

25   DALEY, JOHN. "The 1.2.3. of Presences." Intrepid, nos. 36-38,
     pp. 15-19.
          In Presences, mentions Creeley's use of time, associations,
     and words as "almost objective presence[s]." Also comments on the
     role of measure and spatial perspective in the volume, as well as
     its pattern. Notes the text's relationship to the sculpture of
     Marisol.

26   DANIELS, PATSY. "An Interview with Robert Creeley." <u>Davidson</u>
      <u>Miscellany</u> 14, no. 1 (Spring):53-59.
         In this March 1978 interview, Creeley provides a number of
      biographical details: his reasons for going to Harvard, his life
      in New Hampshire, and his first attempts at writing, including
      short stories. Also mentions his early influences and his first
      publications and rejections. Comments on the role of teaching in
      his life and his first wife's, Ann's, family.

27   DAVIDSON, [ROBERT] MICHAEL. "The Presence of the Present:
      Morality and the Problem of Value in Robert Creeley's Recent
      Prose." <u>Boundary 2: A Journal of Postmodern Literature</u> 6, no.
      3-vol. 7, no. 1 [Robert Creeley: A Gathering] (Spring-Fall):
      545-64.
         Finds much of Creeley's writing an "investigation of moral
      propositions." Commenting on "The Immoral Proposition" and "The
      Way ['My love's manners in bed']," finds the investigation cen-
      tered on "possible choices among alternatives" prior to <u>Pieces</u>.
      Comments on sections of <u>Pieces</u>, finding that "choice <u>per se</u> is the
      central value" in this volume. Believes it also interrogates "the
      limits of expression" and displays an "openness to immediate expe-
      rience." Mentions its treatment of the present, time, and
      language.
         Believes Creeley's "recent prose by its sheer openness pro-
      vides him with the opportunity to present a variety of individual
      situations and extend them into their problematic interrelation-
      ships" in order to investigate "the conditions under which moral
      decisions are made." Comments on portions of the prose section of
      <u>A Day Book</u>, identifying a Keats source and demonstrating that
      Creeley is searching for "a form that will be spontaneous and
      immediate to each occasion." Finds he is inquiring "into the
      limits of statement" in these portions of <u>A Day Book</u>. Discussing
      portions of <u>Presences</u>, notes Creeley's use of framing and his
      treatment of scale, place or location, size, and limit. Mentions
      his use of autobiographical materials in the book.

28   DeFANTI, CHARLES. <u>The Wages of Expectation: A Biography of</u>
      <u>Edward Dahlberg</u>. New York: New York University Press,
      pp. 173, 188-92.
         Quoting from an 11 August 1973 taped response from Creeley
      to a series of questions, provides a number of biographical de-
      tails concerning Creeley's relationship to Dahlberg, and to a
      lesser extent Robert Graves, in 1953.

29   DIEHL, PAUL. "The Literal Activity of Robert Creeley."
      <u>Boundary 2: A Journal of Postmodern Literature</u> 6, no. 3-vol.
      7, no. 1 [Robert Creeley: A Gathering] (Spring-Fall):335-46.
         Discusses Creeley's use of words as objects, commenting on
      their referential role. Also comments on his use of breath and

stanza and line breaks "to introduce new pauses into the flow of language" to create a literal emotion in his reader. Mentions his spontaneous method of composition. Uses the second and fourth sections of "Numbers" as examples, partially explicating the second.

30   DUDEK, LOUIS. "Lunchtime Reflections on Frank Davey's Defence of the Black Mountain Fort." In Selected Essays and Criticism. Tecumseh Working Texts Series. Ottawa: Tecumseh Press, pp. 211-16.
      Reprint of 1965.12 with appended corrections.

31   DUNCAN, ROBERT. "After For Love." Boundary 2: A Journal of Postmodern Literature 6, no. 3-vol. 7, no. 1 [Robert Creeley: A Gathering] (Spring-Fall):233-39.
      Slight revision of 1963.13.

32   _____. "A Reading of Thirty Things." Boundary 2: A Journal of Postmodern Literature 6, no. 3-vol. 7, no. 1 [Robert Creeley: A Gathering] (Spring-Fall):293-99.
      Discusses Thirty Things in detail, including the themes of time, old age, place, and music, including jazz. Also discusses the dedications, the ocean references, and the use of "silence around the event of the poem." Examines the sense of ending and the type of poetic field created, often comparing Creeley's poetry to Olson's. Reprinted: 1987.19.

33   EDELBERG, CYNTHIA DUBIN. Robert Creeley's Poetry: A Critical Introduction. Albuquerque: University of New Mexico Press, 186 pp.
      A slightly revised and abridged version of 1977.10 with an index. Chapter 4 is slightly revised: 1987.19.

34   _____. "Robert Creeley's Words: The Comedy of the Intellect." Boundary 2: A Journal of Postmodern Literature 6, no. 3-vol. 7, no. 1 [Robert Creeley: A Gathering] (Spring-Fall):265-91.
      Slight revision of chapter 2 of 1977.10.

35   FAAS, EKBERT. "Essay: Robert Creeley." In Towards a New American Poetics: Essays and Interviews. Santa Barbara, Calif.: Black Sparrow Press, pp. 147-64.
      Examining Creeley and Olson's relationship, points out Olson's influence on Creeley. Using "3 Fate Tales" as an example, compares Creeley's fiction to post-existential French fiction, especially that of Alain Robbe-Grillet, in terms of its nonreferential and self-contained character. Notes his use of ambiguity, the present, and the narrator.
      Considers Creeley's sense that his work is not about a subject, and refers to his affinity with minimal artists. Using a

number of poems as examples, discusses his emphasis on emptiness,
the void, as "the center of his experience" to which he tries to
return, as in "Waiting." Outlines "The Pool," noting an "aura of
total elusiveness," and the "speaker's yearning for a state of
quiet." Compares Creeley to Mallarmé in terms of their "vision of
emptiness" and to Gary Snyder in terms of their avoidance of egocentricity. Comments on his treatment of the female figure and
the feminine principle. After 1960, discovers more of a "yearning
for concrete reality and life" in Creeley's poetry, finding he now
"celebrates existence."

36   ____. "Interview: Robert Creeley." In Towards a New Amer-
        ican Poetics: Essays and Interviews. Santa Barbara, Calif.:
        Black Sparrow Press, pp. 165-98.
        In this interview, Creeley acknowledges the influence of
Joyce, Lawrence, and W.C. Williams on his fiction and refers to
early reactions to his short stories. Remarks on his correspondence with Pound about starting a magazine, and provides a few
biographical details. Reviews his reading of Arakawa Shusaku,
recording his infatuation with Arakawa's "zero set," and Beckett,
describing their meeting in some detail. Also mentions reading
French existential writers, Wittgenstein, W.C. Williams, and only
recently, Whitehead. Relates his inability to rewrite, his rest-
lessness, and his rejections of the known, contained, and familiar. Remarks on his awareness of "language as language," and his
affinities with and/or differences from Alain Robbe-Grillet,
Olson, Duncan, Wittgenstein, and Gertrude Stein. Recounts teaching Crane's The Bridge.
        Comments on writing "3 Fate Tales," The Island, and
Presences. Discusses the change in his writing in the 1960s,
especially as seen in Pieces, as an "easing" back "into the physical world." Notes Ginsberg's influence on his breaking out of
"modalities of saying things [that] had become ends in themselves."
Records the joy in writing "Mazatlan: Sea," and provides the
occasion of "For Walter Chappell" and "The Finger," mentioning the
treatment of the female figure in the latter. Registers his dissatisfaction with A Day Book, and notes that he had originally
thrown away "The Name." Explains Patrocinio Barela was the artist
referred to in "The Figures," and claims that the source for
"After Mallarmé" was actually Pierre-Jean Jouve.
        Briefly criticizes a statement in 1972.2 about his fear of
the void, and compares himself to Gary Snyder in terms of neuroses
and tensions, providing a few details concerning their relationship. Also points out his fascination with numbers, the influence
of the Metaphysical poets on his poetry, and his present general
dissatisfaction with writing poetry. Claims he writes "to recog-
nize and thus register states of consciousness," thereby to reify
"all the states of human consciousness." Relates that he graphs
the movements of his mind as he writes and that the poem ends for

him "when the energy drops," noting his lack of revision. Mentions his criteria for a good poem, for what he publishes.

37 _____. "Interview: Robert Duncan." In Towards a New American Poetics: Essays and Interviews. Santa Barbara, Calif.: Black Sparrow Press, pp. 55-85.
In his interview, Duncan mentions Creeley's initial reaction to his work, notes his relationship to Creeley, and claims that Creeley intentionally avoids reading Roland Barthes. Notes that Creeley's poetry has subjects and referential meaning.

38 _____. "Preamble" to Towards a New American Poetics: Essays and Interviews. Santa Barbara, Calif.: Black Sparrow Press, pp. 9-33.
Reprint of 1977.11 with notes.

39 FORD, ARTHUR L[EWIS]. Robert Creeley. Twayne's United States Authors Series, no. 310. Boston: G.K. Hall & Co., Twayne Publishers, 159 pp.
Provides biography of Creeley, discusses his critical reception and influences on him throughout, and emphasizes relationships between form and content in his poetry. Of Pieces, discusses the "obsession with the reality of the word" and of the poems, noting their nonreferential nature as "objects in themselves." Also examines the attempt to "isolate the moment," the process of "delineating the interior landscape," and the pattern of the total work. In Words, examines the search for the substantial, the themes of love and loneliness, and the concern with rendering the "precise moment of the poem's coming into creation." Discusses "the archetypal journey from darkness to light" in For Love. Finds the journey proceeds from the "double nature of human relationships" (love-hate) and the mocking of literary conventions to the easing of the conflict between love and domesticity and the increasing emphasis upon a "naturalness."
In "The Gold Diggers" and Other Stories and The Island examines plots, ironies, and conflicts. Also discusses the themes of love, loneliness, and the difficulty of relationships. Investigates the rhythms of language and images, and patterns of "alternate tensing and relaxing." Finds, in The Island, a failure of continuity. In A Day Book, discusses its idea of a "field" and its journalistic characteristics, especially its immediacy and its tendency to particularize a moment.
Feels Creeley is an uneasy classicist. Traces a conflict between external poetic form and the projective in the corpus ("a relaxation of the impression, if not always the line" in the later work), and finds the best work a combination of the "minimal art with the human element." Sees Creeley's work as both part of the American and New England traditions.
Chapter 3, on Words, is reprinted in 1987.19.

40   GINSBERG, ALLEN. "On Creeley's Ear Mind." Boundary 2: A
      Journal of Postmodern Literature 6, no. 3-vol. 7, no. 1 [Robert
      Creeley: A Gathering] (Spring-Fall):443-44.
          Recounts Creeley's summer 1976 reading at Naropa Institute,
      noting that his delivery gave an "awareness of the syllable as
      basic atom or brick of poetic mind."

41   GRENIER, ROBERT. "A Packet for Robert Creeley." Boundary 2:
      A Journal of Postmodern Literature 6, no. 3-vol. 7, no. 1
      [Robert Creeley: A Gathering] (Spring-Fall):421-41.
          Prior to his poetry on pp. 430-41, Grenier comments on his
      indebtedness to and appreciation of Creeley in a 5 February 1977
      letter to William V. Spanos. Provides his original, unpublished 6
      November 1975 introduction to Creeley's Selected Poems, and gives
      the original, intended order and pagination for the poems in
      Selected Poems.

42   HAYES, FREDERICK PHILIP. "The Broken World of Robert Creeley."
      Ph.D. dissertation, University of Denver, 209 pp.
          Notes the influence of Olson's theories of projective poetry
      and field composition and the theories of W.C. Williams, Pound,
      and Duncan on Creeley's poetics. Occasionally providing informa-
      tion from conversations with Creeley, discusses the work from For
      Love to Pieces as though it had a narrative structure, finding
      Creeley searches "for a 'place' where communication with Another
      is lasting."
          Discusses each section of For Love, commenting on many of
      the poems and focusing on a few. In the first section, charts
      Creeley's "quest for an Ideal Love," noting his treatment of
      courtly love, marriage, and a mythologized Lady or love goddess
      compared to normal women. Also refers to his themes of loneli-
      ness, isolation, and disillusionment with love. Mentions his
      treatment of Hart Crane in "Hart Crane ['He had been stuttering,
      by the edge']" and of relationships in "The Immoral Proposition."
      In the second section, focuses on Creeley's treatment of aliena-
      tion due to the breakup of his first marriage, also noting his
      treatment of divorce, despair, and futility. Comments on "Air:
      'Cat Bird Singing,'" noting its sources in Thomas Campion, and "The
      Door ['It is hard going to the door']," mentioning its treatment
      of sex. Finds Creeley reaches his "'place' of love," analyzing
      the naturalness of this "place," in the third section. Comments
      on his treatment of jealousy and love in "The Rose."
          Examining many of the poems in Words, finds Creeley still
      isolated and searching for communication. Uses Martin Heidegger's
      theories of being and language to shed light on Creeley's sense of
      "place," language, and silence. Discusses Creeley's treatment of
      desire, emptiness, sex, anger, movement, and change. Also refers
      to the themes of isolation within the mind and the world of flux.
      Comments on the "open field of experience" in "For W.C.W. ['The

rhyme is after']." Notes the use of water and rocks as symbols
and the treatment of desire in "The Rocks."

In Pieces, comments on the inseparability of parts and
Creeley's plan. Notes his use of dreams and the mirror image, and
points to his treatment of the eye, time, sex, others, and communication. Also investigates his themes of isolation, emptiness,
thinking, and "the dichotomy of mind (reason) and imagination
(intuition)." Especially discusses the treatment of the woman
figure and sex in "The Finger" and of the present in "'Follow the
drinking gourd. . . .'" Finds Creeley turns to numbers "in search
of a secure 'place'" in "Numbers," and compares him to Meursault
in Albert Camus's L'Étranger.

Believes Creeley's is a "Poetry of Implication," noting his
use of rhymes, rhythms, repetition, a "breath-formed" line length,
and "dislocated syntax." Discusses his field composition, his
sense of form and content, and his belief in the creative process
as a "mystic revelation" beyond the intention of the artist.
Notes his use of a question and statement structure and understatement, and finds his poetry is nondescriptive. Uses a number
of poems as examples, especially "I Know a Man" and "Goodbye."
See Dissertation Abstracts International 39 (1978):2273A.

43 KENNEDY, X.J. An Introduction to Poetry. 4th ed. Boston and
    Toronto: Little, Brown, & Co., p. 19.
    Slight revision of 1966.19.

44 KERN, ROBERT. "Composition as Recognition: Robert Creeley and
    Postmodern Poetics." Boundary 2: A Journal of Postmodern
    Literature 6, no. 3-vol. 7, no. 1 [Robert Creeley: A Gather-
    ing] (Spring-Fall):211-30.
    Quoting continually from 1970.14, investigates Creeley's
poetics, especially his emphasis on process and his sense of being
"given to write poetry," of being a recorder of the "immanent
order and value in external reality," rather than an "organizing
manipulator" of experience. Notes Creeley's "antipathy toward the
New Criticism" and discusses his statement, "Form is never more
than an extension of content." Discusses his formalism, but dis-
tinguishes it from the formalism of the modernists. Compares his
poetics to those of William Bronk, Gilbert Sorrentino, Levertov,
and Duncan, and notes his interest in Jackson Pollock. Applies
Gerald L. Bruns's theories of poetic language to Creeley's poetics.
    Mentions W.C. Williams's influence on Creeley and comments
on his use of the driving metaphor to describe the poetic process,
especially in "I Know a Man." Also interprets "The Immoral Proposition" and "For W.C.W. ['The rhyme is after']."
    Charts the development of Creeley's poetic practice, finding
that the poems up through For Love sought a "permanent peace outside of time" in which creation was an "act of will" and not, as

later, an "act of recognition" in which language is returned "to its place in experience."

45   LANSDOWN, ANDREW. "Poetry and Woetry: Some Pernicious Trends in Modern Poetry." Pacific Moana Quarterly: An International Review of Arts and Ideas [or Pacific Quarterly Moana] 3, no. 2 (April):149-58.
     Claims Creeley, as others, writes only for prestige and "is not concerned with communicating anything of value." Quotes a section of "Bits" as an example.

46   LAWRENCE, SEYMOUR. "Memoir of a 50-Year-Old Publisher on His Voyage to Outer Space." In The Little Magazine in America: A Modern Documentary History. Edited by Elliott Anderson and Mary Kinzie. Yonkers, N.Y.: Pushcart Press, pp. 143-63. Reprint of 1978.47.

47   _____. "Memoir of a 50-Year-Old Publisher on His Voyage to Outer Space." TriQuarterly, no. 43 (Fall), pp. 143-63.
     Lawrence reminisces about smoking ganjha with Creeley in the late 1940s and notes his role in Wake. Reprinted: 1978.46.

48   LIE, ULF. "The New Romantics." American Studies in Scandinavia 10, no. 1:15-64.
     Uses a portion of Creeley's "A Place ['The wetness of that street, the light']" as an example of poetry that "transfer[s] to the reader the reality which inspired the poem" and its energy without the poet's intellectualizing.

49   McNAUGHTON, DUNCAN. "Bullshitting about Creeley." Boundary 2: A Journal of Postmodern Literature 6, no. 3-vol. 7, no. 1 [Robert Creeley: A Gathering] (Spring-Fall):457-59.
     Briefly mentions a number of things about Creeley, chiefly his elusiveness and importance and the lack of the personal in his poetry.

50   MACKEY, NATHANIEL [ERNEST]. "'The Gold Diggers': Projective Prose." Boundary 2: A Journal of Postmodern Literature 6, no. 3-vol. 7, no. 1 [Robert Creeley: A Gathering] (Spring-Fall): 469-87.
     Demonstrates that Creeley's stories in "The Gold Diggers" and Other Stories are projective in nature since their "disavowal of 'subject' allows an indeterminacy to dictate what courses the tales may take." Details that indeterminacy in "A Death." Finds that the stories are "non-definitive," allowing the different events and objects in the field of the story to "maintain their proper confusions." Also notes that "Creeley's protagonists tend to deny themselves the comforts . . . of any presumed or ready-made coherence," using "The Gold Diggers" as an example of the

narrator withholding "interpretative comment." Finds that, contrary to 1951.4, Creeley goes beyond the "objective/subjective dichotomy" since he registers "the movement and contents of consciousness" but also never loses sight of conjecture as conjecture, as in "Mr. Blue." Also notes that others, such as Olson and Duncan, immediately accepted his stories but were hesitant concerning his poetry.

Compares Creeley's prose and poetry, notes his "practiced stumbling," and comments on his treatment of man as afflicted by a "ruminative lostness" and of woman as a muse. Comments on the lack of an objective correlative in the stories, and compares Creeley to Alain Robbe-Grillet.

51   MAKIN, PETER. "Bunting and Sound." Agenda 16, no. 1 [Basil Bunting Special Issue] (Spring):66-81.

Quotes from 1965.3 and, using "The Woman ['I have never']," comments on Creeley's use of line breaks, finding them somewhat unnatural but conveying a "general sense of grasping at thin fragments, of wistful (even in his reading, sobbing) awe in the face of life."

52   MARIANI, PAUL [LOUIS]. "'Fire of a very real order': Creeley and Williams." Boundary 2: A Journal of Postmodern Literature 6, no. 3-vol. 7, no. 1 [Robert Creeley: A Gathering] (Spring-Fall):173-90.

Discusses W.C. Williams's influence on Creeley's work throughout, especially the influence of "the altered rhythms as well as the syntactic strategies of Williams's late love lyrics." Charts this influence in such poems as "For Love," and notes the theme of love in both poets' work.

Details the relationship between Creeley and W.C. Williams, quoting extensively from their correspondence from 11 February 1950 to June 1962. In these letters, notes Williams's reaction to Creeley's short stories, prose style, reviews of Williams's own work, and poetic measure. In Creeley's letters, notes Creeley's love of Williams's prose and poetry, Williams's influence on his work, and his argument with Williams's sense of measure. Also quotes from Williams's letters to others and others' letters to Williams concerning Creeley.

Provides a few biographical details concerning Creeley, especially from 1944 to 1950, and the Lititz Review. Mentions his relationships with others, especially Olson and Pound. Notes Williams's role in his relationship with Olson. Reprinted: 1984.24.

53   MOON, SAMUEL. "The Springs of Action: A Psychological Portrait of Robert Creeley (Part I: The Whip)." Boundary 2: A Journal of Postmodern Literature 6, no. 3-vol. 7, no. 1 [Robert Creeley: A Gathering] (Spring-Fall):247-62.

RC1978

Provides a Freudian and Jungian analysis of the "process of
growth or individuation" of Creeley as seen in The Whip, explicating over half of the poems therein, especially "A Song ['I had
wanted a quiet testament']," "The Crow," and "I Know a Man."
Discusses the themes of marriage, friendship, writing, and language.

Finds Creeley "searching for simplicity, finding regression
unsatisfactory and advance impossibly blocked" and thwarted by
"unresolved guilt" arising from an Oedipal complex, his loss of an
eye, and his father's death. Provides biographical details concerning these events from a 3 October 1977 letter from Creeley.
Also discusses a section from The Island and Creeley's relationship to his first wife, Ann, his father and mother, and Olson.

54 MOORE, RICHARD. "Olson in Gloucester, 1966." Transcribed by
    George F. Butterick. In Muthologos: The Collected Lectures
    and Interviews, by Charles Olson. Edited by George F.
    Butterick. Vol. 1. Writing, no. 35. Bolinas, Calif.: Four
    Seasons Foundation, pp. 169-98 [pp. 175 and 176 are transposed].
        In a transcription "from the outtakes" of the 12 March 1966
    Olson N.E.T. film in the "USA: Poetry" series, Olson gives a few
    biographical details about his relationship to Creeley in the
    early 1950s, and provides a reminiscence concerning Creeley at
    Black Mountain College.

55 NAVERO, WILLIAM. "Robert Creeley: Close. In the Mind. Some
    Times. Some What." Boundary 2: A Journal of Postmodern Lit-
    erature 6, no. 3-vol. 7, no. 1 [Robert Creeley: A Gathering]
    (Spring-Fall):347-52.
        Discusses Creeley as a postmodern poet, comparing him to
    other avant-garde artists, composers, and musicians. Finds
    Creeley's work a "poesis of continual nascence." Notes its lack
    of referentiality, its collage methods, and its autobiographical
    nature.

56 OBERG, ARTHUR. "Robert Creeley: 'Locate I / love you'" and
    "Afterword." In Modern American Lyric: Lowell, Berryman,
    Creeley, and Plath. New Brunswick, N.J.: Rutgers University
    Press, pp. 93-125, 175-78.
        Discusses Creeley's preoccupation with returning language to
    where "language, thinking, and feeling could be pure and more
    exact." Examines his "unending examination . . . of every avail-
    able and existent idiom" and aspect of language including preposi-
    tions, articles, conjunctions, metaphors, and etymologies to
    create "a loving language for the finding of an adequate self."
    Discusses his varying treatment of love, writing, relationships,
    isolation, sex, and the location of or insistence upon the self in
    For Love, Words, Pieces, and A Day Book. Finds Creeley less con-
    cerned in A Day Book "with the lyric as a literary mode," and

comments on the epigraph as well as many poems and prose sections, especially "['I want to fuck you']." Small portions are greatly revised from 1977.16.

57   OLSON, CHARLES, and DORN, EDWARD. "Charles Olson and Edward Dorn." Transcribed by George F. Butterick. In <u>Muthologos:</u> <u>The Collected Lectures and Interviews</u>, by Charles Olson. Edited by George F. Butterick. Vol. 1. Writing, no. 35. Bolinas, Calif.: Four Seasons Foundation, pp. 157-68.
        In this transcription of a 24 July 1965 conversation between Dorn and Olson filmed at the Berkeley Poetry Conference (produced by Gordon Craig), Olson continually mentions Creeley, notably comparing Creeley's reading of his own work to Ginsberg's reading.

58   OLSON, CHARLES; CREELEY, ROBERT; DUNCAN, ROBERT; GINSBERG, ALLEN; and WHALEN, PHILIP. "On History." Transcribed by Ralph Maud, edited by George F. Butterick. In <u>Muthologos: The Collected Lectures and Interviews</u>, by Charles Olson. Edited by George F. Butterick. Vol. 1. Writing, no. 35. Bolinas, Calif.: Four Seasons Foundation, pp. 1-19.
        In an extended version of 1975.17, Creeley comments on the role of history in his schooling.

59   OLSON, CHARLES. "Reading at Berkeley." Transcribed by Zoe Brown and Ralph Maud, edited by George F. Butterick. In <u>Muthologos: The Collected Lectures and Interviews</u>, by Charles Olson. Edited by George F. Butterick. Vol. 1. Writing, no. 35. Bolinas, Calif.: Four Seasons Foundation, pp. 97-156.
        The fullest, most accessible version of Olson's lecture. Another version of 1966.24, corrected by 1970.28. Includes new annotations (pp. 210-24) that refer to Creeley as a publisher of Olson; and mention the theme of grace in his work, especially "A Song ['I had wanted a quiet testament']." Also provides Creeley's comments on "Song ['I wouldn't']" from a 22 July 1965 reading.

60   PAUL, SHERMAN. <u>Olson's Push: "Origin," Black Mountain, and Recent American Poetry</u>. Baton Rouge and London: Louisiana State University Press, pp. 59, passim.
        Occasionally refers to Creeley and Olson's correspondence, and quotes Creeley on Olson. Comments on "Hart Crane ['He had been stuttering']" and its appearance in <u>Origin</u>.

61   _____. "Rereading Creeley." <u>Boundary 2: A Journal of Post-modern Literature</u> 6, no. 3-vol. 7, no. 1 [Robert Creeley: A Gathering] (Spring-Fall):381-418.
        Discusses the autobiographical nature of Creeley's work. Treats each of his books in turn, especially <u>The Charm: Early and Uncollected Poems</u> (1969), <u>For Love</u>, <u>Pieces</u>, and <u>A Day Book</u>, commenting on many poems briefly and a few in more depth: "Poem for

RC1978

D.H. Lawrence," "The Finger," "Numbers," and "Mazatlan: Sea."
Meditates on Creeley's treatment of the female figure, place,
love, water, others, and form. Also mentions the themes of the
past, isolation, sex, and return or renewal. Comments on the role
of self-consciousness and rhythm in his work, and notes his use of
poetry as an activity. Discusses the influence of Whitman, Hart
Crane, W.C. Williams, and Olson on Creeley's work, and refers to
some of Creeley's prose, especially 1973.13. Revised and expanded: 1981.24.

62   PERLOFF, MARJORIE [G.]. "Four Times Five: Robert Creeley's
     The Island." Boundary 2: A Journal of Postmodern Literature
     6, no. 3-vol. 7, no. 1 [Robert Creeley: A Gathering] (Spring-
     Fall):491-507.
        Discusses the structure of The Island, including the role of
numbers in its composition. Focuses on recurrent motifs and in-
terrelations of parts, "recurrent manifestations" of Creeley's
style, and the internalized or subjective point of view. Finds
the novel an "embodiment of Olson's projectivist aesthetic," but
not an example of postmodern fiction since it retains causality,
coherent characterization, closure, and a theme comparable to one
found in D.H. Lawrence's novels. Finds it avoids total ambiguity,
and notes his treatment of memory, the past, and the sex act.
Comments on his use of syntax, repetition, qualification, and
discontinuities.

63   POWER, KEVIN. "Robert Creeley on Art and Poetry." Niagara
     Magazine, no. 9 (Fall), [37 pp.].
        In this 1976 interview, Creeley discusses his interest in
art and artists and mentions his relationship to such artists as
René Laubiès, Philip Guston, Franz Kline, Willem de Kooning, and
John Chamberlain, noting the latter's comments on Words. Compares
his work to that of contemporary artists, noting what he has
learned from them. Describes the literary scene of the 1950s,
provides biographical details, and notes some of his reading,
including Kafka. Mentions teaching at Black Mountain College, and
remembers his reaction to Robert Graves's poetic methods.
        Creeley also speaks of his sense of existentialism, the ego,
death, and language. Explains that he writes what he does not
know and becomes involved in writing as an event in an "energy
field." Remarks on the role of chance and of subjects in his
writing. Comments on the creative process and on A Day Book,
remarking on the ordering of the prose and poetry in the work.
Using "For Friendship," recounts his normal writing habits.
Records the occasion of "After Mallarmé" and "['We'll die']," and
provides some of the allusions in the latter. Observes his sense
of boundaries, as in Presences, commenting on its ordering and
structure. In his introduction (pp. [3-4]), Power compares

Creeley to contemporary painters, especially Marisol and R.B. Kitaj. Reprinted in part: 1978.19.

64   QUARTERMAIN, PETER. "Robert Creeley: What Counts." Boundary 2: A Journal of Postmodern Literature 6, no. 3-vol. 7, no. 1 [Robert Creeley: A Gathering] (Spring-Fall):329-34.
        Using "The Lover," discusses the role of naming in Creeley's poetry, noting that it has only provisional ability to "situate" the self or locate an experience. Finds that once the naming is complete, Creeley ends the poem since "the perceived moment acquires completion."

65   RUMAKER, MICHAEL. "Robert Creeley at Black Mountain." Boundary 2: A Journal of Postmodern Literature 6, no. 3-vol. 7, no. 1 [Robert Creeley: A Gathering] (Spring-Fall):137-70.
        In this lengthy reminiscence, Rumaker mentions first reading Creeley's short stories, emphasizing the inventiveness and the writer's "highly sensitized intelligence." Provides biographical details of Creeley in March 1954 when he first came to Black Mountain College, including first meeting him. Quoting from 1972.16, adds details concerning Creeley's first writing class and Creeley's encouragement of his, Rumaker's, work. Discusses Creeley's personal concerns in spring 1954 and his emotional state in the summer of 1955 due to the deterioration of his first marriage. Also outlines his relationship to Dan Rice, Cynthia Hormire, and himself, relates a car accident Creeley was involved in, and comments on his teaching. Mentions the composition of "A Wicker Basket."
        Provides texts of the 25 October 1954 and 12 March 1955 letters and part of a 25 February 1955 letter from Creeley to him. These detail Creeley's reaction to the work that Rumaker submitted to the Black Mountain Review and mention the planning of that magazine. Comments on "All That Is Lovely in Men" and "In the Summer." Discusses Creeley's writing as "a scrupulous and highly exact examination of conscious processes." Reprinted in part: 1987.19.

66   SPANOS, WILLIAM V. "'The fact of firstness': A Preface." Boundary 2: A Journal of Postmodern Literature 6, no. 3-vol. 7, no. 1 [Robert Creeley: A Gathering] (Spring-Fall):1-8.
        Spanos describes Creeley's 1965 reading at Knox College and its effect on him, leading him to question his New Critical orientation and move toward a postmodern stance. Using 1967.12 and Creeley's poetry, mentions Creeley's differences with the "hardened Western humanistic tradition" in his emphasis upon the aural over the visual and his intent to retrieve a "beginning," noting parallels with Heidegger's thought.

RC1978

67 _____. "Talking with Robert Creeley." Boundary 2: A Journal
of Postmodern Literature 6, no. 3-vol. 7, no. 1 [Robert
Creeley: A Gathering] (Spring-Fall):11-74.
    In this lengthy 12 July 1977 discussion, Spanos and Creeley
discuss Creeley's, and in some cases Olson's, sense of occasion,
care, measure, and the imagination. Also examines Creeley's ideas
on discovery, periplum, and writing as a participation in experience, rather than an objectified observation of experience. They
discuss Creeley's relative emphasis on the visual and aural, some
of the poems in Later (1979), and the idea of "content" in
Creeley's statement, "Form is never more than an extension of
content."
    Creeley comments on the lack of intention in his work, em-
phasizing the "activity" of poetry. Uses "['As real as thinking']"
as an illustration, and explains the central reference to Zukofsky
in the poem. Creeley also discusses poems in the beginning of
Pieces, demonstrating "an intention   to   write without over-
bearing decisions about the coherence," his and others' sense of
his development as a poet (see 1976.29), and comments on what he
wants to do in the future. Lists writers who were influential or
"crucial" to him such as Wordsworth, Dickinson, W.C. Williams, and
Zukofsky, as well as many books and authors he has recently read.
Discusses his sense of aging and provides many biographical details, including his relationship with Olson, other friends, and
wives; being a student, especially in an English class in his
junior year of high school; and his return to New Hampshire in
1954. Refers to a trip to Mexico and meeting a Lacandone Indian
in 1959 or 1960, living in Vancouver from 1962 to 1963, and his
1977 trip to England and Spain as well as other trips to Southeast
Asia. Mentions living with one eye and visiting friends, especially Olson in Gloucester and in the hospital.
    Spanos mentions "Beach," and applies many of Heidegger's
theories to Creeley's work, emphasizing Creeley's "sense   of
disintegration of the One," of dispersal. Also attempts to place
Creeley in an American tradition, grouping him with poets considered, by the New Critics, eccentric: Whitman, Pound, and W.C.
Williams, "poets who return   to the things themselves[,]   who
. . . insistently explore   in the dispersed world." Spanos also
comments on the titles of Creeley's work and the source of his
poetry "in the speech act."
    In his "Pre-face" and "Post-face" (pp. 13-14, 74), Spanos
provides details concerning the occasion of the discussion, the
form of the transcription, and Creeley. Notes Creeley's views on
the outcome of the discussion. A brief section is slightly revised: 1981.29.

68 SYLVESTER, WILLIAM. "Robert Creeley's Poetics: 'I know that I
hear you.'" Boundary 2: A Journal of Postmodern Literature 6,
no. 3-vol. 7, no. 1 [Robert Creeley: A Gathering] (Spring-
Fall):193-210.

Discusses how Creeley's "poems make our minds move and make us aware of the motion" by noting his use of tone, rhythm, line length, rhyme, punctuation, and words as objects. Also mentions some poems that "interrelate place, time and motion," and occasionally applies mathematical concepts to Creeley's work. Uses a number of poems as examples, especially "Stomping with Catullus," "['What is the / day of the']" from A Day Book, "A Piece," "The Rhythm," "The Time ['They walk in and fall into']," and "Citizen."
Discusses the continuity and sequencing of Pieces, and notes how words in one book connect with poems in earlier and later volumes.

69   TALLMAN, WARREN. "Haw: A Dream for Robert Creeley." Boundary 2: A Journal of Postmodern Literature 6, no. 3-vol. 7, no. 1 [Robert Creeley: A Gathering] (Spring-Fall):461-64.
Explicates "The Crow" to show Creeley's use of "the natural symbol," and mentions his improvisational method.

70   VERNON, JOHN. "'The cry of its own occasion': Robert Creeley," Boundary 2: A Journal of Postmodern Literature 6, no. 3-vol. 7, no. 1 [Robert Creeley: A Gathering] (Spring-Fall):309-27.
Discusses Creeley's use of words as actualities and of the poem as an enactment or "bodily gesture" within language rather than being necessarily representational. Also comments on Creeley's hesitancy and his provisional nature, his use of line breaks and rhythm as in "The Turn," and his treatment of pain, love, women, and language. Explicates "The Finger," finding a "self-reflexive language" which progressively allows existence to enter the poem. Also mentions "I Know a Man," "The Pattern," and "The Language." Revised (omitting the discussion of "The Finger"): 1979.29.

71   von HALLBERG, ROBERT. Charles Olson: The Scholar's Art. Cambridge, Mass. and London: Harvard University Press, pp. 113-14, passim.
Chapter 3 is a revision of 1974.28; the rest is a revision of 1975.20, dropping some of the substantive Creeley references.

72   _____. "Robert Creeley and the Pleasure of System." Boundary 2: A Journal of Postmodern Literature 6, no. 3-vol. 7, no. 1 [Robert Creeley: A Gathering] (Spring-Fall):365-79.
Demonstrates that Creeley is a "systematic poet" since he "discovers systematic behavior" in "commonly overlooked corners of experience" rather than inventing or declaring "his faith in . . . centralizing systems" like other important poets. Partially explicates "After Lorca," "The Lover," "The Business," "Something," "Midnight," and "Return" as examples. Also finds that his style "leans on the systemic symmetries of language," as in "Le Fou."

RC1978

Claims his use of both the "intimate and disembodied," as in "A Song ['I had wanted a quiet testament']" and "The Operation," is due to his shuttling "between the convention of sincerity and the discipline of systematic abstraction." Revised: 1985.23; reprinted: 1987.19.

73   WAGNER, LINDA W[ELSHIMER]. "Creeley's Late Poems: Contexts." Boundary 2: A Journal of Postmodern Literature 6, no. 3-vol. 7, no. 1 [Robert Creeley: A Gathering] (Spring-Fall):301-8.
      Comments on Creeley's use of immediate and intimate experience, language games, and words as "entities in themselves." Notes his "questioning of what seems to be self-knowledge," especially in The Island and A Day Book. Comments on a number of poems from Away. Reprinted: 1980.34; 1987.19.

                                  1979

1   ALTIERI, CHARLES. Enlarging the Temple: New Directions in American Poetry during the 1960s. Lewisburg, Pa.: Bucknell University Press; London: Associated University Presses, pp. 170-93, passim.
      In an enlarged revision of 1972.2, compares Creeley to W.S. Merwin, and comments more on Creeley's sense of absence and presence. Also includes a greatly abridged and revised version of 1973.2, dropping many of the references to Creeley.

2   CHRISTENSEN, PAUL [NORMAN]. Charles Olson: Call Him Ishmael. Austin and London: University of Texas Press, pp. 24-25, 71, 167-84, passim.
      An apparent revision of 1975.2. Summarizes Creeley's career and relationship to Olson. Compares him to Duncan, and notes the influence of Pound, W.C. Williams, Robert Graves, and Olson on him. Comments on his treatment of relationships, loneliness, love, and the despairing husband, and notes his sense of form and content. In A Form of Women, mentions Creeley's treatment of women and the male ego which desires both to submit to love and to remain solitary. Notes the treatment of two marriages in For Love and Words, and claims Pieces and A Day Book are unsuccessful long poems, commenting on the serial form of the latter. Discusses "Mr. Blue" and The Island as examples of a projectivist stance, treating the latter as a long poem. Finds the "verbal presence powerful, but almost too consciously achieved" in Presences.

3   _____. "Creeley, Robert (White)." In Poets. Edited by James Vinson and D.L. Kirkpatrick. Great Writers of the English Language. New York: St. Martin's Press, pp. 248-51.
      After an expanded bibliography of 1970.9, focuses on Creeley's treatment of identity and relationships, especially

marriage. Revised: 1980.9; 1983.3. Revised and expanded: 1985.5.

4 _____ . "Notes on Creeley's Tao." Little Caesar, no. 9 [Unprecedented Information issue], pp. 96-103.
Argues that Creeley emerges "selfless" in Pieces. Discusses his style, sense of mystery, and relationship to women. Examines his distrust of the referential or the capacity of poetic language and his use of words as materials in the activity of poetry, drawing parallels to the work of such painters as Jackson Pollock.

5 CREELEY, ROBERT. "For L.Z." Louis Zukofsky: Man and Poet. Edited by Carroll F. Terrell. Orono, Maine: University of Maine at Orono, National Poetry Foundation, pp. 75-77. Reprint of 1978.15.

6 _____ . "From the 'Introduction' to Penguin Leaves of Grass." Mickle Street Review, no. 1, pp. 33-38.
A highly abridged text of 1973.13.

7 _____ . "Holderness 100th Commencement Address." Holderness School Today 2, no. 3 (July):6-7.
Creeley provides biographical details about his life at Holderness School, especially concerning his role fabricating an interview for the Bull (the school newspaper).

8 _____ . List in "Non-Poetry." L=A=N=G=U=A=G=E 2, no. 1 [whole no. 7] (March):[19-20].
Creeley briefly lists books, excluding poetry, that he has recently read and that have had an effect on him.

9 _____ . "Notes on Film." Criss-Cross: Art Communications, nos. 7-9, pp. 68-70.
Creeley provides a few biographical details, especially about watching films as a youth and about betting on a horse race in college, and mentions his contacts with Duncan and Tim Lafarge. He also discusses his notion of correctness in writing and his sense of presence. Examines himself as a "personal writer," and comments on his "A Note on the Objective" (Goad, no. 1 [Summer 1951], pp. 20-21; reprinted in 1970.14). Reprinted (as "Three Films: Notes"): 1979.15.

10 _____ . "On 'Beat': 'Like flowers at a prom.'" Transcribed by Ed Vitelli. Read Street 1, no. 6 (Midsummer):19.
Creeley reminisces about his contacts with Beat writers in the late 1950s, especially Ginsberg and Kerouac.

11 C[REELEY], R[OBERT]. "Preface" to "Was That a Real Poem" and Other Essays. Edited by Donald [Merriam] Allen. Writing, no. 39. Bolinas, Calif.: Four Seasons Foundation, pp. 9-10.

RC1979

In this preface, Creeley comments on writing for payment and claims the essays in "Was That a Real Poem" and Other Essays "argue no progress," claiming the book has only himself as "the common denominator."

12   CREELEY, ROBERT. Statement on translation." In Petits pays, grandes littératures?/Small Countries, Great Literatures? Budapest: Hungarian Publishers' and Booksellers' Association, p. 18.
    In this response to a set of questions on translation, Creeley briefly mentions reading poetry in translation and meeting and listening to foreign writers.

13   _____. Statements in "The University and the Arts: Are They Compatible?" Works and Days: Essays in the Socio-Historical Dimensions of Literature and the Arts 1, no. 1 (Spring):69, 76–78, 81–84.
    Creeley very briefly mentions he is "wary about 'teaching' art," discusses the role teaching has had in his life, and provides a few biographical details.

14   _____. "The The." Wallace Stevens Journal 3, nos. 3–4 (Fall):121.
    Creeley notes reading and being influenced by Stevens and Valéry. Notes the source for "Divisions" was Stevens.

15   _____. "Was That a Real Poem" and Other Essays. Edited by Donald [Merriam] Allen. Writing, no. 39. Bolinas, Calif.: Four Seasons Foundation, 149 pp.
    Includes reprints of 1964.4; 1969.7; 1973.8, 12–13; 1976.15; 1979.9 (as "Three Films: Notes"); a slight revision of 1974.5; and the English version of 1975.7 (as "Last Night: Random Thoughts on San Francisco, March–June 1956").

16   "Creeley and Fixed Places." Two Hands News and Chicago Poetry Calendar, no. 19 (May), p. 1.
    Describes Creeley's 26 January Chicago poetry reading and the disturbance created by two poets in the audience. See also 1979.18.

17   EDELBERG, CYNTHIA [DUBIN]. "Senses of Self." Phantasm: Bi-Monthly Magazine 4, no. 5 [whole no. 23]:[30–31].
    Recounts Creeley's discussion of the self titled "Imagination Dead Imagine" during the special session "The Self in Postmodern Poetry" at the MLA Convention on 29 December 1979 in San Francisco. Relates Creeley claimed that American society does not provide the individual the sense of a "communal self."
    Reviewing Warren Tallman's discussion "The Romantic Self in Poetry" at the same session, recounts how Tallman used Creeley's

as an example of a poetry of inwardness, reflecting the workings
of the mind much as the romantic poets attempted to do.

18   ELLSWORTH, PETER. "Letter in Response to the Creeley Review in
      Issue 19." Two Hands News and Chicago Poetry Calendar, no. 20
      (July), p. 3.
         Responding to a description in 1979.16, briefly complains
      about the behavior of two poets at Creeley's 26 January 1979
      Chicago reading.

19   GÉFIN, LASZLO. "Ideogram: The History of a Poetic Method."
      Ph.D. dissertation, McGill University, pp. 255-56, 275-94,
      passim.
         Notes that Creeley's desire to write serially led him to
      compose the "takes" in The Island and, especially, Pieces. Finds
      each poem in Pieces, using "['Having to--']" and "['The car']" as
      examples, is an ideogram, "a miniature process." Feels each such
      "'take' of action" invites "imagination to bridge the gaps be-
      tween" poems and arrive at "universal truths." Demonstrates that
      Creeley's ideogrammic method is rooted in his fidelity to reality,
      compares his method to Duncan's, and notes the influence of Pound.
      Revised and abridged: 1982.21. See Dissertation Abstracts Inter-
      national 40 (1979):3299A.

20   GOLDING, ALAN. "The Olson Festival in Iowa." Two Hands News
      and Chicago Poetry Calendar, no. 20 (July), pp. 4-5.
         Describes Creeley's talk at the 5-11 November 1978 Charles
      Olson Festival.

21   HALDEN, JUDITH A. "The Temptation of the Mind: The Letters of
      Charles Olson." M.A. thesis, Pennsylvania State University,
      pp. 50-51, passim.
         Provides the text of Olson's 21 April 1950 letter to W.C.
      Williams in which Olson mentions his contact with Creeley and
      their relationship. Also includes a reprint of 1971.17.

22   HOFFMAN, DANIEL. "Poetry: Schools of Dissidents." In Harvard
      Guide to Contemporary American Writing. Edited by Daniel
      Hoffman. Cambridge, Mass. and London: Harvard University
      Press, Belknap Press, pp. 496-563.
         Briefly finds an "increasing fragmentation of experience" in
      Creeley's work. Comments on his renunciation of poetic conven-
      tions and "his commitment to the shapes and sounds of words and
      the truth of his own feelings."

23   HOLDEN, JONATHAN. "The 'Found' in Contemporary Poetry."
      Georgia Review 33, no. 2 (Summer):329-41.
         Explicates "I Know a Man" and uses it to support the idea
      that "framing" (asserting language to be poetic by placing it in

an artistic context) and closure, rather than traditional qualities, make the contemporary lyric poetic. Reprinted: 1980.19.

24   "Interview [with Charles Olson] in Gloucester, August 1968."
      Transcribed by George F. Butterick. In Muthologos: The Col-
      lected Lectures and Interviews, by Charles Olson. Edited by
      George F. Butterick. Vol. 2. Writing, no. 35. Bolinas,
      Calif.: Four Seasons Foundation, pp. 84-104.
          In this August 1968 interview, Olson mentions Creeley's
   orientation to the "printed word" but implies Creeley has changed
   his reading style to attract the audience's attention. Olson
   notes addressing Creeley at his own reading on 23 July 1965 at the
   Berkeley Poetry Conference (see 1966.23-24 or 1978.59).

25   MALANGA, GERARD. "From Through the Looking Glass/An Experiment
      in Autobiography." Little Caesar, no. 9 [Unprecedented Infor-
      mation issue], pp. 104-7.
          Discusses Creeley's use of personal concerns in his poetry
   and his employment of his own speaking voice.

26   NOVIK, [GERALDINE] MARY. A Creeley Chronology." In "Was That
      a Real Poem" and Other Essays, by Robert Creeley. Edited by
      Donald [Merriam] Allen. Writing, no. 39. Bolinas, Calif.:
      Four Seasons Foundation, pp. 133-49.
          Reprint and updated version of 1973.36.

27   PAUL, SHERMAN. "Clinging to the Advance: Some Remarks on
      'Projective Verse.'" North Dakota Quarterly 47, no. 1
      (Winter):7-14.
          Occasionally and briefly quotes from Creeley on Olson's
   ideas in "Projective Verse."

28   PETERS, ROBERT. "Robert Creeley's For Love Revisited." In The
      Great American Poetry Bake-Off. Metuchen, N.J. and London:
      Scarecrow Press, pp. 29-35.
          Favorably reassesses For Love. Comments on the projective
   verse, the use of the line, the role of the self, the sense of
   play, and the childlike viewpoint of such poems as "Le Fou," "The
   End," "The Innocence," and "Ballad of the Despairing Husband."
   Suggests the influence of Thomas Hardy on "Song ['Those rivers run
   from that land']," "Kore," and other poems. Reprinted in part:
   1987.19.

29   VERNON, JOHN. Poetry and the Body. Urbana, Chicago, and
      London: University of Illinois Press, pp. 38-39, 131-42, 145-
      46, passim.
          Includes a revision of 1978.70, omitting the discussion of
   "The Finger."

1980

1   ALPERT, BARRY. "An Interview with Barry Alpert." In <u>Inter-</u>
    <u>views</u>, by Edward Dorn. Edited by Donald [Merriam] Allen.
    Writing, no. 38. Bolinas, Calif.: Four Seasons Foundation,
    117 pp.
         Reprint of 1972.1.

2   BRESLIN, PAUL. "Black Mountain: A Critique of the Curriculum."
    <u>Poetry</u> 136, no. 4 (July):219–39.
         Finds Creeley a "lesser figure" than Olson or Duncan. Be-
    lieves Creeley always seems to be engaged "with some difficult
    problem," but feels he is evasive "about the specific nature of
    the problem." Mocks his "Preface" to Dorn's <u>Selected Poems</u>, ed.
    Donald [Merriam] Allen (Bolinas, Calif.: Grey Fox Press, 1978),
    pp. vii–viii.

3   BURNSTEEL, GERALD, and ANGST, BIM, eds. "Eckman on Poetics."
    In <u>The Continental Connection: Selected Writings of Fred</u>
    <u>Eckman</u>. Itinerary, no. 6: Poetry. [Bowling Green, Ohio:
    Itinerary], pp. 89–109.
         Includes portions of 1956.2 on Creeley.

4   BUTTERICK, GEORGE F., ed. "Editor's Introduction" to <u>Charles</u>
    <u>Olson and Robert Creeley: The Complete Correspondence</u>. Vol.
    1. Santa Barbara, Calif.: Black Sparrow Press, pp. ix–xv.
         Discusses the importance of Creeley and Olson's correspond-
    ence to both parties, including Olson's sense of Creeley as "The
    Figure of Outward." Notes the occasion of their first letters,
    and describes the correspondence. Provides a few biographical
    details from 1950, especially concerning their relationship, and
    comments on Creeley's use of punctuation.

5   CAPE, STEPHEN. <u>American Poetry, 1950–1980</u>. Bloomington:
    Indiana University, Lilly Library, pp. 9, 11–12.
         Describes the manuscripts, correspondence, and editions of
    Creeley in the Lilly Library and provides a photo of a page of a
    prose manuscript.

6   CHRISTENSEN, PAUL [NORMAN]. "Creeley, Robert (White)." In
    <u>Contemporary Poets</u>. Edited by James Vinson and D.L.
    Kirkpatrick. 3d ed. New York: St. Martin's Press,
    pp. 318–22.
         Revision of 1979.3. See also 1983.3; 1985.5.

7   CREELEY, ROBERT. "From 'Mabel: A Story.'" In <u>Editor's</u>
    <u>Choice: Literature and Graphics from the U.S. Small Press,</u>

RC1980

1965-1977. Edited by Morty Sklar and Jim Mulac. Iowa City: The Spirit That Moves Us Press, pp. 270-73.
Reprint of 1976.6.

8 _____. "From 'On the Road: Notes on Artists and Poets, 1950-1965' in Poets of the Cities, 1974." In Homage to Frank O'Hara. Edited by Bill Berkson and Joe LeSueur. Berkeley: Creative Arts Book Co., p. 68.
Reprinted from 1974.5.

9 _____. "'An Image of Man . . .': Working Notes on Charles Olson's Concept of Person." Iowa Review 11, no. 4 (Fall): 29-43.
Creeley discusses the influence that Olson's idea that the narrator must be totally in the story had on him. Also notes how long it took him to trust this information.

10 _____. Letter to the Editor. Poetry Comics, no. 6 (February), [p. 9].
In this letter, Creeley expresses delight for David Morice's illustration of "Oh No" in Poetry Comics (no. 5 [Contemporary Poets' Issue] [(January 1980), pp. 4-5]).

11 _____. "Preface" to Against the Silences, by Paul Blackburn. London and New York: Permanent Press, pp. 11-13.
In this preface, Creeley discusses his relationship to Blackburn from the late 1940s to 1971. Mentions Blackburn's suggestions on his early work.

12 _____. "Why Pound?" Agenda 17, nos. 3-4-vol. 18, no. 1 [Twenty-First Anniversary Ezra Pound Special Issue] (Autumn 1979-Winter-Spring):198-99.
Creeley mentions his reading Pound in Burma and later, as well as his initial contacts with Pound.

13 DAVIDSON, [ROBERT] MICHAEL. "Archeologist of Morning: Charles Olson, Edward Dorn, and Historical Method." ELH 47, no. 1 (Spring):158-79.
Notes that many critics of postmodernism appreciate Creeley's assertion of "personalist aspects" in his poetry which employs an "explorative, self-conscious voice."

14 DAY, FRANK. "Robert Creeley." In American Poets since World War II. Part 1, A-K. Edited by Donald J. Greiner. Dictionary of Literary Biography, vol. 5. Detroit: Gale Research Co., Bruccoli Clark Book, pp. 152-59.
Provides a sketch of Creeley's life and critical reception, and charts his development. Finds a suitably narrow range in For Love, commenting on the themes of love and relationships.

Believes many poems in Words have no meaning for the reader, and
finds this tendency "carried to extremes in Pieces." Believes
poems in The Charm: Early and Uncollected Poems (1969) are better, but finds A Day Book uneven and too much of an "existential
journal." Claims some of Creeley's most recent poems like those
in Boundary 2 (6, no. 3-vol. 7, no. 1 [Robert Creeley: A Gather-
ing] [Spring-Fall 1978]:63-71) are the best since For Love. Comments on "The Dishonest Mailmen."

15   DORN, EDWARD. "Robert Creeley's Pieces." In Views. Edited by
      Donald [Merriam] Allen. Writing, no. 40. San Francisco,
      Calif.: Four Seasons Foundation, pp. 118-21.
          Reprinted from 1970.17.

16   FAAS, EKBERT. "Infantilism and Adult Swiftness: An Interview
      with Ekbert Faas." In Talking All Morning, by Robert Bly.
      Poets on Poetry. Ann Arbor: University of Michigan Press,
      pp. 250-83.
          Reprint of 1976.18.

17   _____. "An Interview with Robert Duncan." Boundary 2: A
      Journal of Postmodern Literature 8, no. 2 (Winter):1-19.
          In this interview, Duncan comments on first reading Creeley,
      Creeley's reactions to his work, and their relationship, providing
      a number of biographical details.

18   FREDMAN, STEPHEN ALBERT. "Sentences: Three Works of American
      Prose Poetry." Ph.D. dissertation, Stanford University, pp.
      2-3, 90-163, 229-32, passim.
          Discusses Creeley's use of the "conjectural sentence," a
      sentence that explores "the relationship of language to being" and
      poses an "interrogation of language," in Presences. Finds sources
      for this type of sentence in the "generative sentence" of W.C.
      Williams that "proceeds by a process of discovery, trusting to a
      harmonious relationship between the forms of writing and the forms
      of nature" in Kora in Hell and in the work of Gertrude Stein.
      Compares Creeley's sense of conjecture with Olson's.
          Unlike W.C. Williams's "openness of a speech-generated
      wholeness responsible solely to the demands of the moment of writ-
      ing" in lieu of the completeness expected of sentences, demon-
      strates that Creeley "has never embraced wholeness to the
      exclusion of completeness." Notes Creeley's use of paratactic
      structures, and comments on the development of his prose. Expli-
      cates a few paragraphs of section one of Presences, and remarks on
      "The Letter."
          Mentions Creeley's sense of "repetition (interrogation of
      language) and appearance (listening to language)." Discusses his
      "desire to exist completely in the present" and his emphasis on
      the surface aspects of existence. Examines his exploration of

RC1980

"propositional language in order to see how grammar (the way words are used) and thinking are coextensive." Relates the above to the thought of Nietzsche, Heidegger, and Wittgenstein.

Discusses Presences as autobiographical. Notes the relationship of Creeley to Marisol and Creeley's use of Marisol and Lorca. Comments on the "narrative modes, or conjectural directions" in Presences: the transformational which "investigates grammar through puns, clichés, collage, rhymes, etc., rendering words as corporal presences"; the occasional which attempts to locate the self as a "human being in a present situation"; the memorial, in which Creeley locates "his present condition with reference to a distant or recent past"; and the fabulous which "presents mythical or magical situations" that "measure the literal present against a numinous realm." Also discusses Creeley's views of the body, morality, authenticity, and measure. Notes his commitment to process, his "ethic of presence," and his feeling toward the fictive. Revised: 1983.13. Revised in part: 1983.12. See Dissertation Abstracts International 41 (1981):3579.

19   HOLDEN, JONATHAN. "The 'Found' in Contemporary Poetry." In The Rhetoric of the Contemporary Lyric. Bloomington: Indiana University Press, pp. 22-37.
        Reprint of 1979.23.

20   HOWARD, RICHARD. "'I Begin Where I Can, and End When I See the Whole Thing Returning.'" In Alone with America: Essays on the Art of Poetry in the United States since 1950. Enlarged ed. New York: Antheneum, pp. 84-93.
        Reprint of 1968.15.

21   JORIS, PIERRE. "Reinventing Love." New Statesman 100 (21 November):20-21.
        In a brief, favorable review of Later (1979), focuses on Creeley's treatment of aging and death.

22   LEONG, LIEW GEOK. "Projectivism: Theory and Temperament in the Poetry of Charles Olson, Robert Duncan, and Robert Creeley." Ph.D. dissertation, George Washington University, pp. i-iii, 1-30, 134-96, 216-19, passim.
        Notes Creeley's attraction to Olson's "Projective Verse," and comments on his sense of open form poetry and composition by field, finding sources in organic poetry. Mentions Creeley's sense of the poem as a "field of force," the fragmentation in his work, and his use of the long poem. Finds his a "post-humanistic" world which is "no longer man-centered." Lists other influences as Pound, W.C. Williams, Zukofsky, and Stevens, and notes his similarities to and differences from Olson and Duncan.
        Finds that Creeley does not use myth like Olson and that in his work "Projectivism shrinks in scope." Discusses the

"Cartesian dichotomy between thought and being" in his poetry and his emphasis on the self and sincerity. Commenting on a few poems, notes Creeley's treatment of sex, the "primacy of feeling and intuition," and the "marriage of form and content, and love" in The Charm: Early and Uncollected Poems (1969). Mentions Creeley's objective treatment of the self and of feelings, especially in his love poetry. Remarks on the treatment of love, especially the "fragility and fallibility of sensibility," in the first section of For Love. Believes Creeley tries "to extend his scope and his lines" in the third section, noting his objectification. Comments on a number of poems from For Love, especially "The Crises" and the treatment of the ideal compared to the real woman in "The Wife."

Notes Creeley's "analytic focus" on particulars as a "means of objectification," his "microscopic approach to language," and his use of words in Words. Comments on a few of the poems from this volume, discussing "Anger" in some detail. Finds a reductive organicism in Pieces, noting Creeley's treatment of thought and his interest in process. Feels "America" and "The Puritan Ethos" are failures, and comments on "Numbers." Notes the use of myth in "The Finger." Briefly points out the freedom and objectivism in A Day Book. See Dissertation Abstracts International 41 (1981): 3582A.

23   LIKIS, KENNETH JAMES. "A Pardonable Wonder: Robert Creeley's Early Poetry." M.A. thesis, Auburn University, 73 pp.
        Proposes that the "elements of [Creeley's] poetry which some would construe as failings equally comprise its particular character and force." Especially remarks on his poetry's "awkwardnesses": "lapses in apparent stanza form, disrupted syntax, use of sing-song, sparsity of dramatic detail, sparsity of imagery, and abrupt shifts in rhythm, tone, and diction." Comments on Creeley's use of ambiguity, rhyme and rhyme schemes, and line lengths and breaks. Also mentions his use of inherited stanza forms and vernacular and colloquial language. Discusses his poetics, especially his emphasis on spontaneous composition and the poem as an agency of discovery. Also examines his distrust of intentions and inherited forms and his willingness to be awkward in "confronting experience." Comments on his critical reception.
        Discusses many poems, especially "Guido, i' vorrei che tu e Lapo ed io," "Stomping with Catullus," "The Rain ['All night the sound had']," "Song ['Were I myself more blithe']," "Ballad of the Despairing Husband," "A Wicker Basket," "The Way ['My love's manners in bed']," "If You," "A Counterpoint," "Please," and "The Whip."

24   MAZZARO, JEROME. "The Failure of Language: Theodore Roethke." In Postmodern American Poetry. Urbana: University of Illinois Press, pp. 59-84.

RC1980

In a revision of a previously published essay ("Theodore Roethke and the Failures of Language," Modern Poetry Studies 1, no. 1 [1970]:73-96) adds Creeley's negative views of Roethke.

25 NORRIS, KENNETH WAYNE. "The Role of the Little Magazine in the Development of Modernism and Post-Modernism in Canadian Poetry." Ph.D. dissertation, McGill University, pp. 186-87, 216-20, passim.
    Notes Creeley's influence on Canadian poetry, especially on the poets associated with Tish. Quotes from 1963.17 and 1964.15, and discusses Creeley's concept of a little magazine as in his "Why Bother?" (Tish, no. 13 (14 September), [pp. 1-2]). Revised: 1984.28. See Dissertation Abstracts International 41 (1981):3574A.

26 OLSON, CHARLES, and CREELEY, ROBERT. Charles Olson and Robert Creeley: The Complete Correspondence. Vol. 1. Edited by George F. Butterick. Santa Barbara, Calif.: Black Sparrow Press, 180 pp.
    In the correspondence between Creeley and Olson from 21 April to 24 July 1950, including a reprint of 1971.17 and reprints from 1973.4 and 1973.16, Creeley discusses plans for and troubles with his proposed the Lititz Review. Also comments on his sense of form and content, of the informal and the formal, and of sub-jectivity and objectivity. Mentions his relationship to, feelings for, and/or arguments with numerable people including Jacob Leed, Kitasono Katsue, Paul Goodman, Seymour Lawrence, Slater Brown, Richard Emerson, Ezra Pound, and W.C. Williams. He also remarks on his reading during the period, including Pound, W.C. Williams, Henry Miller, Melville, Stendahl, Miguel de Unamuno y Jugo, and Dostoevskiĭ. Continually relates that he is listening to jazz, and provides a number of biographical details from this period and earlier. Comments on his wife and child, his experiences during World War II, his living in Boston, and his use of drugs. He also provides material on his family, especially his grandmother.
    Creeley refers to his correspondence with others, especially Pound. At one time, finds himself in the middle of a dispute between Olson and Pound because he passed on some of Pound's com-ments on Olson. Also mentions having "The Unsuccessful Husband" accepted by Kenyon Review, and remarks on the story. Provides rejection slips and portions of one rejection letter he received.
    Creeley also refers to his writing and his style, noting his desire for a line that "throws back forward." Includes unpub-lished poems, earlier versions of published poems like "Still Life Or," and portions of an unpublished story. Creeley also gives an account of a number of his early short stories, some of which were later published, providing the dates of composition and his inten-tions. Comments on a number of his poems including "Littleton, N.H." and "Hart Crane ['He had been stuttering, by the edge']," as well as a few that were never published.

Olson considers and generally praises Creeley's poems and
prose, especially noting the cadence and rhythm of the poems, but
mentions some difficulties he has with them. Examines, particularly, "The Lover" and "Hart Crane ['He had been stuttering, by
the edge']."

The editor provides portions of Creeley's letters to Jacob
R. Leed from 1949 and photographs of two of Creeley's letters to
Olson. Portions of Olson's 8 June 1950 letter are reprinted:
1987.19.

27   . Charles Olson and Robert Creeley: The Complete Corre-
    spondence. Vol. 2. Edited by George F. Butterick. Santa
    Barbara, Calif.: Black Sparrow Press, 180 pp.

In the correspondence between Creeley and Olson from 24 June
to 21 September 1950, Creeley discusses plans for and frustrations
with the Lititz Review, his desire for a speech-centered prose
style, and his use of conjecture to "haul" the past into the present when writing about the past. Also comments on the objective
and subjective, the "single intelligence" in poetry and prose.
Mentions his relationship to and/or feelings for numerous people
including Jacob Leed, Pound, Robert Payne, Richard Wirtz
Emerson, Vincent Ferrini, Seymour Lawrence, Donald Berlin,
Mitchell Goodman, Levertov, Corman, Paul Goodman, and his mother,
Genevieve Jules Creeley. He also continually refers to his reading of the period, including Dostoevskiĭ, Lawrence, Hart Crane,
Melville, James M. Cain, Edward Dahlberg, and Stendahl, as well as
Olson's Call Me Ishmael. Provides a number of biographical
details, reporting on his neighbors and farm, his use of the
Dartmouth library, and his trip to Boston. Also relates his experiences during World War II and his reading on Corman's radio
program on WMEX in Boston. Creeley describes himself, emphasizing
his missing eye, and details his love of talk and desire to move.
In an unsent letter, Creeley reacts to Olson's picture and publishing. Relates his plans for a Guggenheim Fellowship, including
his hopes for references. Also notes his plans to continue working with the narrative.

Creeley mentions his correspondence with others, especially
Jacob Leed and Ferrini, and introduces Olson to Corman. Also
recounts submitting his work and trying to get into print, noting
acceptances and rejections. Remarks upon John Crowe Ransom's
rejection of "The Unsuccessful Husband" after it was paid for, and
worries about getting his stories back from other editors.

Creeley comments on published and unpublished poems that he
sent to Olson, and mentions revising "Littleton, N.H." in light of
Olson's comments. Also touches upon "Le Fou," providing an early
version, and sends Olson some poems that were never published.
Creeley also discusses writing prose and contemplates trying to
publish a book of short stories. In an unsent letter, Creeley

RC1980

comments on one of his stories and on his hopes in writing, reviewing the creative process.
Creeley occasionally criticizes Olson's work and Olson often
agrees. Also provides extensive comments and suggestions on "Projective Verse" and provides a portion of W.C. Williams's letter to
him about the essay. Creeley discusses prosody and the use of the
line, especially noting how Olson's thoughts on the line, previous
to the publication of "Projective Verse," have been of use to him.
He also notes the influence of Pound and Olson's sense of composition by field on him.
Olson examines "Le Fou," praising Creeley's awareness and
intelligence. Even though a number of Olson's letters are not
extant, his general reaction to Creeley's work is apparent given
Creeley's responses. The editor provides portions of two of
Creeley's 1950 letters to Leed about being on Corman's radio
program and about Kenyon Reviews's request for a rewrite of "The
Unsuccessful Husband." Also provides a photograph of a rejection
letter to Creeley from the Hopkins Review.

28 OSBORNE, JOHN, and EASY, PETER. "Robert Creeley and the Experimental Lyric Tradition." Poetry Information, nos. 20-21
(Winter), pp. 3-17.
Finds Creeley's predecessors in the use of the "experimental
lyric" to be Pound, Marianne Moore, e.e. cummings, and W.C.
Williams, indicating that the last was the largest influence.
Finds Creeley's poetry to be the "enactment of the mind's progress" during an "interior monologue." Deals with the nature of
time and the self and with the "existential dilemma" in the
poetry. Discusses "Something," "Love Comes Quietly," "The
Rescue," and "Like They Say." Provides a selective bibliography.

29 PERELMAN, BOB. "The First Person." Hills, nos. 6-7 [Talks
issue] (Spring), pp. 147-65.
Comments on Creeley's use of "I" in "The Pattern," and notes
the role of the third party in "Distance."

30 SARLES, DAVID GRIFFITH. "The Personae in Charles Olson's
Maximus Poems. Ph.D. dissertation, State University of New
York at Stony Brook, pp. 51-52, 58-60, 64, 68-69, 124-25, 151,
passim.
Discusses Olson's relationship to Creeley and his references
to Creeley in The Maximus Poems. See Dissertation Abstracts
International 40 (1980):5867A.

31 SEIDMAN, HUGH; GINSBERG, ALLEN; CREELEY ROBERT; and ZUKOFSKY,
CELIA. "A Commemorative Evening for Louis Zukofsky." American
Poetry Review 9, no. 1 (January-February):21-27.
In this 18 April 1979 series of short lectures and a dis-
cussion, Creeley comments on his first reading of Zukofsky,

reminisces about visiting Zukofsky, and discusses Zukofsky's
influence on him. Creeley also provides a number of biographical
details.
Celia Zukofsky comments on the friendship and rapport between Zukofsky and Creeley. Reprinted in part: 1987.19.

32 SPANOS, WILLIAM V. "The Destruction of Form in Postmodern
American Poetry: The Examples of Charles Olson and Robert
Creeley." Amerikastudien/American Studies 25, no. 1:375-404.
Applies Heidegger's phenomenology to characterize the "dis-
closure" and "'decreating' of received (fixed) forms" of postmodern poetry, of which Creeley's work is an example. Finds
Creeley's comment that poetry is "the measure of its occasion"
argues for a poetry of "being-in-the-world," and notes his immediacy and suspicion of the imagination. Arguing with 1976.30,
mentions that Creeley distrusts metaphors, as witnessed in
"['Could write of fucking']," not because of a puritanical bias
against ornamentation, but because metaphorical language removes
one from experience. Comments on Creeley's sense that he is
"given to write poems."

33 STORM, GARY. "The Michael McClure Interview." White Pine
Journal, nos. 24-25, pp. 75-88.
In this March 1980 interview, McClure briefly mentions
first recognizing the jazz origins he shared with Creeley.

34 WAGNER, LINDA W[ELSHIMER]. "Creeley's Late Poems: Contexts."
In American Modern: Essays in Fiction and Poetry. National
University Publications, Literary Criticism Series, edited by
John E. Becker. Port Washington, N.Y.: Kennikat Press,
pp. 178-86.
Reprint of 1978.73.

35 ____. "The Latest Creeley." In American Modern: Essays in
Fiction and Poetry. National University Publications, Literary
Criticism Series, edited by John E. Becker. Port Washington,
N.Y.: Kennikat Press, pp. 165-77.
Reprint of 1975.21.

36 WARREN, KENNETH. "On Creeley and Dorn." Cumberland Journal,
no. 9 (Winter), [pp. 51-57].
In a review of Hello: A Journal, February 29-May 3, 1976,
compares the volume with Dorn's Hello, La Jolla. Discusses the
role of aircraft and air and sky references in both, finding these
an extension of the American sense of place but opposed to the use
of automobile imagery and motifs in Beat poetry and prose.
Equates Creeley's references to air with abstraction, and comments
on the mixture of the "public and private reference" in his work.

RC1980

37   WHEATON, W[ALTER] BRUCE. "A Measure of Desire: Essays on
      Robert Duncan and Charles Olson." Ph.D. dissertation, Uni-
      versity of Iowa, pp. 141, 158–59, 240, passim.
           Briefly claims Creeley's work, with the exception of A Quick
      Graph, is often manneristic. Comments on a 6 November 1978 speech
      by Creeley at the Charles Olson Festival in Iowa City in which he
      objected to metaphorical or allegorical assessments of Olson and
      his own work. See Dissertation Abstracts International 42
      (1981):210A.

                                  1981

1   BERKE, ROBERTA [ELZEY]. Bounds Out of Bounds: A Compass for
      Recent American and British Poetry. New York: Oxford Univer-
      sity Press, pp. 32–34.
           Quoting from a number of poems, especially "The World,"
      discusses Creeley's focus on "the highly individual situation."
      Believes that from 1966 to 1977 his poetry has a "contrived con-
      descension and indifference to the reader" and its language was
      "non-specific." Finds that since 1977, Creeley has found new,
      worthwhile subjects: "growing old and dying."

2   BRABNER, WENDY. "'The act of seeing with one's own eyes':
      Stan Brakhage and Robert Creeley." Library Chronicle of the
      University of Texas 17:85–103.
           Compares Creeley's work to Brakhage's, noting their use of
      art to "confront the void" and reveal themselves. Comments on
      their control, treatment of women, emphasis on the process of
      thought, use of violent action to overcome fear, and need for
      sincerity. Also notes the influence of Olson on both and their
      use of silence. Briefly compares their lives, providing biograph-
      ical details. Quotes from an unpublished interview with Brakhage
      on their relationship and on Creeley's poetry. Compares Creeley's
      work to film.
           Finds Creeley's early view of women distorted due to the
      "concept of the Muse as female," noting poems of this type as well
      as ones that mock "the romantic tradition." Notes the hopeless-
      ness of romanticism in "The Mirror." Charts an awareness of the
      "'dishonesty' of his earlier poetry" and a "quest for the poem
      supreme" in "The Dishonest Mailmen." Mentions "The Operation" and
      "The Rhyme," his subjectivity, and his emphasis on the structure
      of poetry.
           Quotes from unpublished letters: in 1955 from Creeley to
      Edward Dahlberg on his desire for loneliness, and from 27 November
      1961 and 1966 from Creeley to Ian Hamilton Finlay on his second
      marriage and on his poetry. Reprinted in part: 1987.19.

3   BUTTERICK, GEORGE F., ed. "Editor's Introduction" to <u>Charles</u>
     <u>Olson</u> <u>and</u> <u>Robert</u> <u>Creeley:</u> <u>The</u> <u>Complete</u> <u>Correspondence</u>. Vol.
     3. Santa Barbara, Calif.: Black Sparrow Press, pp. vii-viii.
        Comments on Creeley and Olson's relationship, and provides
     biographical details from 1950, noting Creeley's efforts to secure
     a Guggenheim Fellowship.

4   CARAHER, BRIAN G. "'Gather the bits of road that were':
     Robert Creeley's <u>Later</u>." <u>Credences:</u> <u>A</u> <u>Journal</u> <u>of</u> <u>Twentieth-</u>
     <u>Century</u> <u>Poetry</u> <u>and</u> <u>Poetics</u>, n.s. 1, no. 1 pp. 196-202.
        In this favorable review, recounts the three sections of
     <u>Later</u> (1979): notebook-type entries on love and company; poems on
     friends; and poems countering wonder and companionship to the
     depression of "Desultory Days." Mentions a few poems, notably
     "Later ['Shan't be winding']" and "Prayer to Hermes."

5   CHILTON, H[ARRISON] RANDOLPH, [Jr.]. "The Object beyond the
     Image: A Study of Four Objectivist Poets." Ph.D. disserta-
     tion, University of Wisconsin-Madison, pp. 231-33.
        Summarizes an idea from Creeley's ". . . Paradise/Our/
     Speech . . ." (<u>Poetry</u> 107, no. 1 [October 1965]:52-55). See
     <u>Dissertation</u> <u>Abstracts</u> <u>International</u> 42 (1981):2127A.

6   CHRISTENSEN, PAUL [NORMAN]. "Introduction" to "The Letters of
     Edward Dahlberg and Charles Olson, Part II: An Unravelling
     Friendship, 1949-1950." <u>Sulfur:</u> <u>A</u> <u>Literary</u> <u>Tri-Quarterly</u> <u>of</u>
     <u>the</u> <u>Whole</u> <u>Art</u> 1, no. 2:65-71.
        Mentions the role Creeley played in Olson's "confused net-
     work of literary alliances," and notes Creeley's views of Dahlberg
     as given in 1980.27.

7   CREELEY, PENELOPE; CREELEY, ROBERT; De LOACH, ALLEN; GINSBERG,
     ALLEN; and ORLOVSKY, PETER. "Taped Conversation for <u>Niagara-</u>
     <u>Erie</u> <u>Writers</u> <u>Newsletter</u>." Transcribed by Ze've Keisch.
     <u>Niagara-Erie</u> <u>Writers</u> <u>Newsletter</u> 3, no. 7 (March):[7]; no. 8
     (April):[7-8]; no. 9 (May):[7].
        In this conversation, Creeley mentions his long relationship
     with Ginsberg and Orlovsky and his sense of quantity in speech
     and, as quantitative verse, in poetry. He also mentions not writ-
     ing much for two years since "whatever's coming" in the poem tends
     to dissipate. Ginsberg comments on the tension in Creeley's lines.

8   CREELEY, ROBERT. "Introduction to <u>Whitman</u> Selected by Robert
     Creeley." In <u>Walt</u> <u>Whitman:</u> <u>The</u> <u>Measure</u> <u>of</u> <u>His</u> <u>Song</u>. Edited
     by Jim Perlman, Ed Folsom, and Dan Campion. Minneapolis: Holy
     Cow! Press, 191-200.
        Reprint of 1973.13.

RC1981

9 _____. "Memories of John." New Mexico Studies in the Fine
Arts, no. 6, pp. 5-9.
    Focusing on his relationship to John Aloon from 1954 to
1969, Creeley also mentions his relationship to Julie Eastman and
provides biographical details about living in Mallorca.

10 DAVIDSON, [ROBERT] MICHAEL. "'By ear, he sd': Audio-Tapes and
Contemporary Criticism." Credences: A Journal of Twentieth-
Century Poetry and Poetics, n.s. 1, no. 1, pp. 105-20.
    Very briefly mentions Creeley reading his own poetry.

11 _____. Review of Charles Olson and Robert Creeley: The Complete Correspondence, vols. 1-2, edited by George F. Butterick.
Sulfur: A Literary Tri-Quarterly of the Whole Art no. 1,
pp. 226-29.
    In this favorable review, stresses the importance of the
correspondence to both Olson and Creeley, noting Creeley's emphasis on jazz and its relation to his poetry. Praises Butterick's
role as editor.

12 EGGINS, HEATHER. "A Place, a Habit, and a Heart: The Theme of
Place in the Poetry of Robert Creeley." Poetry Review 71, no.
4 (December):60-62.
    Briefly examines Creeley's treatment of place, especially in
the context of American rootlessness, and the relationship of
place to a sense of identity in his poetry.

13 JACKSON, RICHARD. "Projecting the Literal Word: An Interview
with Robert Creeley." Poetry Miscellany, no. 11, pp. 98-105.
    In this interview through the mail, Jackson comments on
Creeley's subverting the language, his prose, and place and presence in his poetry. Also mentions the role of the "I" in his work
and a number of his poems.
    Creeley comments on "['Could write of fucking']," metaphor
and simile, and words as acts. Also mentions criticism, reality,
the imagination, and his sense of time. Relates his use of the
typewriter and, since the mid-1960s, a notebook for his actual
writing. Reprinted: 1983.19.

14 JAMES, H[AREL] VANCE. "An Oral Interpretation Script Illustrating the Influence on Contemporary American Poetry of the
Three Black Mountain Poets: Charles Olson, Robert Creeley,
Robert Duncan." M.S. thesis, North Texas State University, pp.
3-4, 19-24, 33-34, 36-37, 39-42, 46-50, 52, 61, 64-65, 69-70,
72-73.
    Provides a biographical sketch of Creeley, notes influences
on his work, especially Olson, and comments on his role in the
Black Mountain Review and at Black Mountain College. For an oral
interpretative performance, comments on "The Conspiracy," "The
Door ['It is hard going to the door']," "The Awakening," "Words,"

and "Oh No," noting the poems' biographical context, themes, and personae. Speculates on Creeley's influence on others.

15   KELLER, R[OBERTA] LYNN. "Heirs of the Modernists: John Ashbery, Elizabeth Bishop, and Robert Creeley." Ph.D. dissertation, University of Chicago, pp. 207-315.
       Compares Creeley as a postmodernist poet to W.C. Williams, a modernist. From the early part of his career to the mid-1960s, discusses Creeley's reliance upon and imitation of Williams as an alternative to the literary establishment of the 1940s and 1950s. Also notes his "personal identifications" with Williams and his allusions to Williams in his poetry. Finds correspondences in the two poets' feelings toward inherited forms and techniques, the descriptive, and the role of emotion in poetry. Also compares their ideas of poetry as a means of thought, and finds "both men's poems arise from intimate, often sexual, energies." Discusses correspondences in their techniques. Finds parallels in their use of dialogue and the conversational with vernacular idioms, line breaks, "intra-phrasal junctures," syntactic deviations, ambiguity, rhythms, rhyme, repetition, assonance, and the short line. Also finds comparisons in their focus on the local and immediate. Demonstrates how both use syntax to create expectation and enact "dynamic tensions."
       Notes differences in Creeley and Williams, initially, in Creeley's more introverted, epistemological, and less sensual poetics. (Yet finds, in Words, a shifting to a "new physicality" corresponding to Williams's stance "against mind/body dualism.") Notes that even though Creeley incorporates "the low, the common, the trivial, the random, [and] the prerational," he does not attempt "to create larger structures in which these freshened perceptions might be meaningful," but allows the work to reflect the fragmentary nature of experience. Demonstrates his increasing distrust of "locating cohesive order," and remarks on his belief that "a coherence constitutes an evasion of the reality of imme- diate experience." Finds the result is a sensed lack of signifi- cance, of closure, and in Pieces through Later (1979), many tedious poems that are emotionally and "intellectually hollow."
       Notes Creeley's use of a more generalized terminology, and finds that "Creeley regards words as more independent of the ex- ternal world than Williams does." Claims Creeley believes words "occupy their own atemporal realm"; therefore, his work is less referential than Williams's. Also finds that Creeley, unlike Williams, has become wary of the imagination since it "may draw him away from immediate and elemental experience."
       Discusses a number of poems, especially "For Rainer Gerhardt," "I Know a Man," "A Form of Women," "Goodbye," "Out of Sight," "The Figures," "The Rose," "For W.C.W. ['The rhyme is after']," "Numbers," "'For Some Weeks . . .,'" and "Corn Close." Comments on each of Creeley's larger collections from The Charm:

RC1981

Early and Uncollected Poems (1969) to Later (1979). Notes that
Pieces and A Day Book emphasize the activity of writing itself and
rely on "unplanned process." Finds Thirty Things, Away, and Later
(1979) often slip into banalities and aphoristic statement. Believes "Creeley has extended the self-consciousness, reflexive
character of modernism to the point where meaningful statement or
intelligent evaluation of experience is no longer possible."
Finds "greater emotional complexity" in Later (1979) although the
replacement of the "demanding, perfect Lady" of his early poetry
with Hermes often allows him to make "simple-minded generaliza-
tions." Finds, however, his assertions more convincing than in
the preceeding three volumes.
        Comments on Creeley's "fascination with abstract man-made
systems" and arbitrary orders. Also mentions Creeley's contact
with Williams, quoting from a few unpublished letters written by
both poets. Notes the influence of Olson, the abstract expressionist painters, and Ludwig Wittgenstein on Creeley. Mentions
his treatment of sex, love, speech, language, and the past.
        A section, pp. 207-60, is revised as 1982.25 eliminating
some of the more technical correspondences between Creeley and
Williams.

16   KIBERD, DECLAN. Review of Later (1979). World Literature
      Today: A Literary Quarterly of the University of Oklahoma 55,
      no. 1 (Winter):104-5.
        In this brief, favorable review, finds Patrick Kavanagh an
influence, and mentions Creeley's treatment of aging. Notes his
new caution concerning spontaneity in composition.

17   LAMBERT, CHRISTOPHER. "Possibilities of Conclusion."
      Parnassus: Poetry in Review 9, no. 2 (Fall-Winter):255-67.
        In a favorable review of Later (1979), finds greater articu-
lation, acceptance, and conclusiveness but less ambiguity and
defiance in the use of language than in Creeley's earlier work.
Charts the use of language and the role of the self in For Love
through Words, Pieces, A Day Book and Thirty Things, finding "a
collision of the private with the public requirements of language
and audience." Finds the result is that the poems are often too
personal, minimal, elliptical, and fragmentary. Favorably mentions the Toothpaste Press edition of Later (1978) and, unfavor-
ably, "Was That a Real Poem" and Other Essays. Reprinted in part:
1987.19.

18   LANGE, ART. Review of Home, a recording with music by Steve
      Swallow, words by Robert Creeley. Down Beat: The Magazine of
      Contemporary Music 48, no. 4 (April):33-34.
        In this brief, favorable review, praises Swallow's music to
Creeley's poems, poems that would seem to resist such settings.

19 LEVERTOV, DENISE. "An Approach to Public Poetry Listenings."
    In Light Up the Cave. New York: New Directions, pp. 46-56.
    Reprint of 1965.15.

20 MARIANI, PAUL [LOUIS]. William Carlos Williams: A New World
    Naked. New York: McGraw-Hill Book Co., pp. 604, 669-70, 731,
    passim.
        Notes Creeley's correspondence with and reviews of Williams,
    and quotes from a 23 January 1957 unpublished letter from Williams
    to Levertov on Creeley's poetry.

21 MORROW, BRADFORD, and COONEY, SEAMUS. A Bibliography of the
    Black Sparrow Press, 1966-1978. Santa Barbara, Calif.: Black
    Sparrow Press, pp. 16-17, 44-45, 94-95, 102-3, 132-33, 140,
    159, 178-79, 214, 233-34, passim.
        Provides a descriptive bibliography for Creeley's The Finger
    (1968), Pieces (1968), As Now It Would Be Snow, St. Martin's,
    Listen, "The Creative," "Inside Out," Thirty Things, "Was That a
    Real Poem or Did You Just Make It Up Yourself," and Away. Also
    lists his other contributions to Black Sparrow publications,
    including introductions, blurbs, and statements on promotional
    fliers.

22 OLSON, CHARLES, and CREELEY, ROBERT. Charles Olson and Robert
    Creeley: The Complete Correspondence. Vol. 3. Edited by
    George F. Butterick. Santa Barbara, Calif.: Black Sparrow
    Press, 172 pp.
        In the correspondence between Creeley and Olson from 21
    September to 7 November 1950, Creeley recounts his relationship to
    Corman. Notes Corman's invitation to Olson and himself to be
    Origin's contributing editors. Details his assessment of and
    suggestions to Corman, and generally advises Olson not to accept
    editorial status. Provides a portion of a letter that he wrote to
    Corman on taste and how he had made selections for the Lititz
    Review.
        Creeley also discusses his relationship to, feelings for,
    and/or arguments with numerable others, including Slater Brown,
    Levertov, Richard Wirtz Emerson, Seymour Lawrence, Louis Simpson,
    and Rainer M. Gerhardt. Occasionally mentions his reading of the
    period including Lawrence, Stendhal, and Olson. Provides a number
    of biographical details, referring to his farm and financial situ-
    ation, his desire to move, his love of talk, and his neighbors and
    others in the area. Also comments on his trips, his wife, Ann,
    his son, David, and the approaching birth of a second child.
    Expresses doubts about his life, refers to listening to jazz,
    reminisces about visiting Black Mountain in 1944, and comments on
    teaching. Turns down the possibility of a position at Black Moun-
    tain College.

RC1981

Creeley continues to seek a Guggenheim Fellowship, discussing his plans and his choices for references. Provides a draft of his Guggenheim proposal that outlines his ideas on the short story and novel. Examines the role of conjecture, immediacy, and the past in fiction. Records what he has attempted to do with the short story. Uses "The Lover" as an example of how he keeps his "own present, that present defined, made, by the act of apprehension . . . as it can, does occur" in the story. (Olson reviews the proposal and Creeley's ideas.) Creeley provides a portion of a letter from Pound refusing to recommend Creeley for the Fellowship.

Creeley recounts his correspondence with others, including Jacob Leed, Richard Wirtz Emerson, Robert Payne, W.C. Williams, and Pound, including portions of letters from the latter two. Gives an account of first writing Pound and trying to reconcile him with Olson. Reports on preparing his stories for Emerson, and reacts to rejections of his work by Payne and others, providing a portion of a rejection note for "Mr. Blue" from Partisan Review. Includes the text of a letter from Random House expressing interest in his fiction, and relates John Crowe Ransom's final decision to publish "The Unsuccessful Husband." (The editor provides portions of Creeley's letters to Leed and photos of two postcards to Olson.)

Creeley emphasizes the role of conjecture in his work, especially in making the personal and the past relevant. Recounts his difficulty with "In the Summer" and his revision of unpublished stories as well as of "3 Fate Tales" and "Mr. Blue," often in accord with Olson's comments. Sends Olson revised versions of "3 Fate Tales," and explores their structure and purpose. Provides the biographical origin for and his intentions in "Mr. Blue," relates writing the story, and notes the role of each character. Comments on "Love ['The thing had']," and provides Slater Brown's observations on "Mr. Blue." Mentions a number of his short stories, providing his feelings for "The Unsuccessful Husband." Records trying to revise stories and write others from biographical materials, including a story of a car accident. Requests that Olson write an introduction to his short stories and, later, comments on an early version by Olson of 1951.4, which is included with Olson's queries about it.

23 PAUL, SHERMAN. "Gripping, Pushing, Moving." Parnassus: Poetry in Review 9, no. 2 (Fall-Winter):269-76.
    Reviewing 1980.26 and 1980.27, and finding theirs "one of the great correspondences of the twentieth century," emphasizes Creeley and Olson's relationship to each other. Also comments on their impatience with stasis. Notes "the impasse and impotence of thwarted hope and energy" when confronting the literary political scene of the early 1950s. Comments on the role Creeley and Olson's correspondence played in their poetics. Mentions

Creeley's plans for the Lititz Review, the need of Creeley's contacts with Pound and W.C. Williams, and a few poems, especially
"Le Fou." Reprinted: 1987.19.

24 _____. The Lost America of Love: Rereading Robert Creeley,
Edward Dorn, and Robert Duncan. Baton Rouge and London:
Louisiana State University Press, pp. 1-73, 240-41, passim.
   In this revision of 1978.61, includes more sections of
Creeley's poetry and prose for illustration, and adds a lengthy
explication of the ten sections of "Later ['Shan't be winding'],"
noting a few parallels to Hart Crane's work. Also occasionally
compares Dorn and Duncan's work to Creeley's, and mentions their
debt to him, especially noting echoes of Creeley in Duncan's Roots
and Branches.

25 POULIN, A[L], Jr., and CALHOUN, DOUGLAS. "Anarchy is Order:
An Interview with Michael McClure." Edited by Douglas Calhoun.
Credences: A Journal of Twentieth-Century Poetry and Poetics,
n.s. 1, no. 1:65-76.
   In this 3 March 1975 interview, McClure notes Creeley's
influence on him, notably on his use of end-stopped lines.

*26 POWER, KEVIN. "Post Modern Poetics: Four Views." Revista
canaria de estudios ingleses, no. 2 (March), pp. 51-69.
   Presumably uses Creeley's work as an example of post-
modernism. Unavailable for annotation; listed in 1981 MLA
International Bibliography I.7361.

27 ROTHENBERG, JEROME, and CREELEY, ROBERT. "From 'Deep Image and
Mode: An Exchange with Robert Creeley (1960).'" In Pre-Faces
and Other Writings, by Jerome Rothenberg. New York: New
Directions, pp. 52-64.
   Reprinted from 1962.12, dropping the last three letters and
abridging one, and adding a new introduction.

28 SOUSTER, RAYMOND. "Raymond Souster's Letters to Charles
Olson." Edited by Bruce Whitemen. Canadian Poetry: Studies,
Documents, Reviews, no. 9 (Fall-Winter), pp. 72-88.
   In these letters from 12 July 1952 to 3 October 1965,
Souster occasionally mentions his contacts with Creeley.

29 SPANOS, WILLIAM [V.]. "[Entirely There]." In Coherence.
Edited by Don Wellman, Irene Turner, Richard Waring, and Cola
Franzen. O.ARS, 1. Cambridge, Mass.: O.ARS, pp. 133-35.
   A brief, slightly revised section from 1978.67.

30 SUKENICK, RONALD. Review of "Was That a Real Poem" and Other
Essays. American Book Review 4, no. 1 (November-December)
[misnumbered as vol. 3, no. 6 (September-October 1981)]:2-3.

RC1981

In this lengthy, favorable review, believes the essays promote an "anti-systematic form . . . in which no pre-determined
procedure is desirable." Finds these essays indicate that writing
is "seen as agency, a process." Mentions "the kinship Creeley
feels with the action painters, who redefined the work of art in
terms of its continuity with experience," since Creeley believes
that poetry "is not 'about' experience, it is an extension of
experience." Slightly revised: 1985.22.

31   TRIPP, JOHN. Review of Later (1979). Poetry Wales 16, no. 3
     (Winter):102-4.
        In this brief, fairly unfavorable review, notes the fragmen-
     tation, simplicity, and mundane sentiments.

1982

1   BARTLETT, LEE. "Creeley's 'I Know a Man.'" Explicator 41, no.
    1 (Fall):53-54.
       Explicates "I Know a Man," claiming that, as "John" points
    out, "the central problem . . . is not an abstruse one but . . .
    simply attending fully to the present."

2   BERTSTEIN, CHARLES. "Hearing 'Here': Robert Creeley's Poetics
    of Duration." Sagetrieb: A Journal Devoted to Poets in the
    Pound-H.D.-Williams Tradition 1, no. 3 [Robert Creeley: Spe-
    cial Issue] (Winter):87-95.
       Quoting from Creeley's A Day Book, "Mabel: A Story," and
    "Was That a Real Poem" and Other Essays, discusses Creeley's use
    of poetry "to measure the contours and scales by which--in which--
    we, as humans, live." Also examines his use of the words "here"
    and "you," the latter referring to either the reader or "any point
    of spatial or temporal displacement." Comments on Creeley's sense
    of place as an occurrence in a sequence. Mentions his treatment
    of male sexuality in "Mabel: A Story" and of women as "the image
    of the 'other.'" Remarks on the heroic dimensions of Creeley's
    work in the context of the development of an alternative poetics
    in the 1950s, and compares his prose to Robert Grenier's, finding
    Creeley's relies on "a more time-based sequencing of events."
    Notes how Creeley attempts "to sound each articulation, to stop it
    short and let it be heard a second time." Reprinted: 1984.41;
    1986.3.

3   BERRY, ELEANOR von AUW. "Robert Creeley." In Critical Survey
    of Poetry, English Language Series. Vol. 2. Edited by Frank
    N. Magill. Englewood Cliffs, N.J.: Salem Press, pp. 675-91.
       Provides a skeleton biography and comments on each of
    Creeley's volumes of poetry from For Love to Later (1979),
    discussing a number of poems, especially "The Rain ['All night the

sound had'],""The Rose,""For Love,""Anger,""Enough," and
"Later ['Shan't be winding']." Notes a few of Creeley's poetic
techniques, especially his rhythm and lineation, and comments on
his treatment of relationships, language, and thought.

4   BRAKHAGE, STAN. "Poetry and Film." In Brakhage Scrapbook:
    Collected Writings, 1964-1980. Edited by Robert A. Haller.
    New Paltz, N.Y.: Documentext, pp. 218-30.
        Reprint of 1978.8.

5   BUTTERICK, GEORGE F., ed. "Editor's Introduction" to Charles
    Olson and Robert Creeley: The Complete Correspondence. Vol.
    4. Santa Barbara, Calif.: Black Sparrow Press, pp. vii-viii.
        Provides biographical details concerning Creeley, especially
    concerning his frustrations with publishing and his sense of iso-
    lation in 1950-1951.

6   BUTTERICK, GEORGE F. Robert Creeley and the Tradition."
    Sagetrieb: A Journal Devoted to Poets in the Pound-H.D.-
    Williams Tradition 1, no. 3 [Robert Creeley: Special Issue]
    (Winter):119-34.
        Explores the ways Creeley incorporates the literary tradi-
    tion into his poems, especially using "a purposeful variation of
    traditional beginnings" in "an effort to find an alternative to
    the dominant and oppressive forms of the day" and often parodying
    romantic attitudes. Notes his use of the tradition and allusions
    in a number of poems, including "Sanine to Leda," "The Three La-
    dies," "Ballad of the Despairing Husband," "Chasing the Bird,"
    "Just Friends," "The Bed," "Divisions," and "Hart Crane ['He had
    been stuttering, by the edge']," commenting on the revisions in
    the latter two poems. Notes the influence of D.H. Lawrence and
    discusses Creeley's use of poetry as definition, especially as
    seen in "The Kind of Act Of." Reprinted: 1984.41; 1987.19.

7   COOK, ALBERT [SPAULDING]. "The Construct of Image: Olson and
    Creeley." Sagetrieb: A Journal Devoted to Poets in the Pound-
    H.D.-Williams Tradition 1, no. 3 [Robert Creeley: Special
    Issue] (Winter):135-39.
        Discusses Creeley's use of images and the visual compared to
    that of Olson and W.C. Williams. Finds Creeley's poetry uses
    "syncopated rhythmic juxtaposition" to achieve a correspondence
    between rhythm, imagery, and knowing. Discusses "Blue Skies
    Motel" and "Morning ['Light's bright glimmer']." Reprinted:
    1984.41. Revised as part of 1985.6.

8   CORMAN, CID. Projectile/Percussive/Prospective: The Making of
    a Voice. Aquila Essays, no. 4. Portree, Isle of Skye,
    Scotland: J.C.R. Green Publishers, Aquila Publishing,
    [pp. 14-18].
        Reprint of 1973.5.

9   CREELEY, ROBERT. "My New Mexico." In In Place. Albuquerque,
    N.M.: Albuquerque Museum, [pp. 5-10].
       Creeley, commenting on New Mexican artists, mentions meeting
    with Bernard Plossu.

10 ____. "On the Road: Notes on Artists and Poets, 1950-1965."
    In Claims for Poetry. Edited by Donald Hall. Ann Arbor:
    University of Michigan Press, pp. 62-71.
       Slightly revised reprint of 1974.5.

11 ____. "Poems Are a Complex." In Claims for Poetry. Edited
    by Donald Hall. Ann Arbor: University of Michigan Press,
    pp. 76-77.
       Reprint of 1966.9.

12 [CREELEY, ROBERT.] Prefaces to The Charm, For Love, and Words.
    In The Collected Poems of Robert Creeley, 1945-1975. Berkeley:
    University of California Press, pp. 3-4, 105, 261.
       Reprints of 1967.10; 1957.1; 1967.11.

13 CREELEY, ROBERT. Prefatory Note to The Collected Poems of
    Robert Creeley, 1945-1975. Berkeley: University of California
    Press, pp. ix-x.
       In this prefatory note, Creeley mentions the decisions made
    in selecting poems for The Collected Poems of Robert Creeley,
    1945-1975, as well as his sense of them.

14 ____. "'Statement' for Paterson Society." In Claims for
    Poetry. Edited by Donald Hall. Ann Arbor: University of
    Michigan Press, p. 75.
       Reprint of 1961.1.

15 CROWDER, ASBY BLAND. "Modes of Marriage in Creeley and
    Levertov: A Note." South Central Bulletin 42, no. 4 [Studies
    by Members of SCMLA issue] (Winter):128.
       Compares Creeley's "The Wife" to Levertov's poem of the same
    title, finding love "represented as an imaginative act" and a
    "tension . . . between visible behavior and private images" in
    both. Discusses the theme of marriage.

16 CURNOW, ALLEN. "Olson as Oracle: 'Projective Verse' Thirty
    Years On." Turnbull Library Record 15, no. 1 (May):31-44.
       Occasionally argues with Creeley's statement, "Form is never
    more than an extension of content."

17 CURNOW, WYSTAN. "Post-Modernism in Poetry and the Visual
    Arts." Parallax: A Journal of Postmodern Literature and Art
    1, no. 1 (Spring):7-28.

Quotes Creeley a number of times in order to define post-
modernism, and briefly discusses his "['As real as thinking']"
from *Pieces*.

18   DUNCAN, ROBERT. *Towards an Open Universe*. Aquila Essays, no.
      17. Portree, Isle of Skye, Scotland: Johnston Green & Co.,
      Aquila Publishing, [p. 15].
      Revision of 1966.14.

19   EDELBERG, CYNTHIA DUBIN. "Creeley's Orphan Lines: The Rhyth-
      mic Character of the Sequences." *Sagetrieb: A Journal Devoted
      to Poets in the Pound-H.D.-Williams Tradition* 1, no. 3 [Robert
      Creeley: Special Issue] (Winter):143-62.
      Investigates the rhythmic character of *Pieces*, the "In
London" sequence from *A Day Book*, *Thirty Things*, and *Hello: A
Journal, February 29-May 3, 1976*. Finds rhythm gives context to
"orphan lines," lines that seem to break the sequences and make
little sense but which can be seen as "'tonal' comments on the
speaker's sensibility."
      Discovers "two dominant melodies" in *Pieces* and the "In
London" sequence. Notes a pattern of "lines winding around themselves" in a fluid and relaxed fashion when the speaker displays
his "love for the natural world" and for people. Counterpointed
to the fluid rhythm, finds a "tense rhythm" of "heavily stressed,
insistent" lines when the poet writes of his isolation from nature
and the community. Notes how the orphan lines are incorporated in
the sound system of *Thirty Things*, commenting on the "mellow mood"
of the volume and the references to drug use. Discusses Creeley's
"intense emotional struggle to come to terms with loneliness,"
occasioned by his separation from his wife, Bobbie, in *Hello*.
Notes how the "rhythm relaxes" toward the end of the book, signal-
ing a tentative catharsis, and finds the orphan lines "immediately
incorporated into the rhythmic character of the whole" due to the
narrative frame of the volume. Reprinted: 1984.41.

20   EIGNER, LARRY. Autobiographical Article. *Kaleidoscope:
      National Literary/Art Magazine for Disabled*, no. 5 (Spring),
      pp. 11-14.
      In this 2 October 1981 article, Eigner provides a number of
details concerning his relationship to Creeley and Creeley's work
as editor of his first book, *From the Sustaining Air* (Palma de
Mallorca, Spain: Divers Press, 1953).

21   GÉFIN, LASZLO. *Ideogram: History of a Poetic Method*. Austin:
      University of Texas Press; Stony Stratford, Milton Keynes,
      England: Open University Press, pp. 99, 108-16, passim. (Pub-
      lished in England as *Ideogram: Modern American Poetry*.)
      A revised and abridged version of 1979.19.

RC1982

22 GRENIER, ROBERT. "Robert Creeley's Later." L=A=N=G=U=A=G=E
    4/Open Letter, 5th ser., no. 1 (Winter), pp. 90–93.
        In this favorable review, quotes from and comments on many
    of the poems, especially "Speech," "Beach," "Prayer to Hermes,"
    "The Fact," and "This World." Finds that the poet, as an aging
    man, and the world are "densely scripted together," both closely
    associated and juxtaposed in terms of "inner/outer 'worlds.'"
    Notes the simplicity and "seeming transparency" of his use of
    language, especially his word choice. Finds an occasional "raspy,
    'growlery'" tone.

23 HALTER, PETER. "Dialogue of the Sister Arts: Number-Poems and
    Number-Paintings in America, 1920–1970." English Studies: A
    Journal of English Language and Literature 63, no. 3 (June):
    207–19.
        Discusses Creeley's Numbers, including the poetry's rela-
    tionship to the serigraphs by Robert Indiana. Focuses on "One
    ['What']," "Zero," and the use of Edward Waite's The Pictorial Key
    to the Tarot: Being Fragments of a Secret Tradition under the
    Veil of Divination (London: W. Rider, 1911) in "The Fool."

24 HELLER, MICHAEL. "A Note on Words: To Break with Insistence."
    Sagetrieb: A Journal Devoted to Poets in the Pound-H.D.-
    Williams Tradition 1, no. 3 [Robert Creeley: Special Issue]
    (Winter):171–74.
        Finds Words "a definite shift in Creeley's poetics" since it
    "acknowledges the force of the autonomous beyond the poem" allow-
    ing for a "more open and inclusive" poetry. Claims that this
    openness is unlike Creeley's earlier insistence on mastery or on
    form while "forcing through toward a direction." Comments espe-
    cially on "The Rhythm." Reprinted: 1984.41.

25 KELLER, [ROBERTA] LYNN. "Lessons from William Carlos Williams:
    Robert Creeley's Early Poetry." Modern Language Quarterly 43,
    no. 4 (December):369–94.
        In a revision of a section of 1981.15, eliminates the dis-
    cussion on some of the more technical correspondences between
    Creeley and Williams's poetry.

26 KENNEDY, X.J. An Introduction to Poetry. 5th ed. Boston and
    Toronto: Little, Brown, & Co., pp. 22, 456–57.
        Slight revision of 1966.19 with comments on the appropriate-
    ness of line breaks in "The Lover."

27 KOPCEWICZ, ANDREJ, and SIENICKA, MARTA. Historia literatury
    Stanów Zjednoczonych w zarysie: Wiek XX. [In Polish.]
    Warsaw: Państwowe Wydawnictwo Naukowe, pp. 190–91, passim.
        Briefly provides an overview of Creeley's work, noting the
    influence of Olson.

28 LITTLE, CARL. "On Robert Creeley's Prose." <u>Downtown</u> <u>Review</u> 3, nos. 1-2 (Fall 1981-Spring):43-45.
   Discusses Creeley's fiction, emphasizing his theme of relationships and his sense that language cannot fit experience. Finds <u>The</u> <u>Island</u> somewhat traditional, but notes the experimentalism in "Mabel: A Story."

29 McCLURE, MICHAEL. <u>Scratching the Beat Surface</u>. San Francisco: North Point Press, pp. 34, 85, passim.
   McClure mentions his own difficulty applying Creeley's comment on form and content. Finds Creeley's "Desultory Days" combines environment, time, and consciousness.

30 _____. "These Decades Are Echoes." <u>Sagetrieb: A Journal Devoted to Poets in the Pound-H.D.-Williams Tradition</u> 1, no. 3 [Robert Creeley: Special Issue] (Winter):15-18.
   McClure mentions first reading and meeting Creeley and trying to imitate him. Discusses the importance of Creeley for him, and provides a few biographical details. Believes Creeley's work is unique, using "The Whip" and "First Rain" as examples.

31 McGUIRE, JERRY. "No Boundaries: Robert Creeley as Post-Modern Man." <u>Sagetrieb: A Journal Devoted to Poets in the Pound-H.D.-Williams Tradition</u> 1, no. 3 [Robert Creeley: Special Issue] (Winter):97-118.
   Discusses the treatment of Creeley as a postmodern poet in <u>Boundary</u> 2 6, no. 3-vol. 7, no. 1 [Robert Creeley: A Gathering] (Spring/Fall 1978), especially 1978.12 and 1978.44. Using Jacques Derrida and Ferdinand de Saussure, finds Creeley "in essence conflictual," locating this sense of conflict in his "extraordinarily varied and powerful tension of line." Especially notes the "linguistic tensions from several perspectives--image, line, lyric genre, and dialogic form." Finds Creeley's use of image "leads by way of syntax to lineation, [and] lineation leads by way of its situation of linguistic convention to the literary focus of conventionality, genre."
   Notes that Creeley's poetry often acts both like a riddle, directing the reader to a given interpretation, and like a haiku, allowing "the centrifugal flight of free association" by the reader. Believes this dynamic provides a sense of both the presence and the absence of meaning and of the reader, the other who is posited in Creeley's poetry if not in his statements on poetic theory. Finds the "tension that has attracted so many readers to Creeley's work is that of a language act attempting to eradicate its otherness even as that otherness is felt and desired as a presence and absence." Discusses a number of Creeley's poems, especially "The Innocence." Reprinted: 1984.41.

32   MESCH, HARALD. "Robert Creeley's Epistemopathic Path."
     Sagetrieb: A Journal Devoted to Poets in the Pound-H.D.-
     Williams Tradition 1, no. 3 [Robert Creeley: Special Issue]
     (Winter):57-85.
          Finds Creeley avoids preconceptual thinking and "intention-
     ality of thought" by a "centrifugal orientation toward the world,"
     thinking of things. Feels he also manifests a reflexive orienta-
     tion, the "thinking the thinking of things." Discusses how his
     poetry realizes the self's "relational identity" to the world,
     reflected in a "relational act of language," which denies an
     identity "metaphysically fixed 'outside' of time" as "a self-
     alienating illusion." Feels, therefore, that the subject in the
     poem "can only 'take measure' of given things in relation to him-
     self" in the present instant as he rides "the crest of the tem-
     poral occasion." Believes Creeley's poetry promotes a "return of
     thought to the senses, to the body," which reflects Olson's orien-
     tation away from the subjective lyric ego to an awareness of the
     self as an object among objects in the world.
          Discusses Creeley's treatment of thought, intention, and the
     creative process. Also notes his themes of self-identity, objec-
     tivity, and the senses. Mentions the role of language and
     Creeley's use of the road metaphor, "line and word truncation,"
     and minimalism in his poetry. Discusses a number of prose pas-
     sages and poems, especially "'I Keep to Myself Such Meas-
     ures . . .,'" "The Dishonest Mailmen," "The Time ['They walk in
     and fall into']," "The Woman ['I called her across the room'],"
     and "The Measure." Reprinted: 1984.41. Translated and expanded:
     1984.25.

33   MURRAY, TIMOTHY. "The Robert Creeley Collection at Washington
     University, St. Louis, Missouri." Sagetrieb: A Journal
     Devoted to Poets in the Pound-H.D.-Williams Tradition 1, no. 3
     [Robert Creeley: Special Issue] (Winter):191-94.
          Describes the collection of materials related to Creeley at
     Washington University, including the collection of published mate-
     rials and, especially, the collection of Creeley's papers that
     includes manuscripts, notebooks, letters to and from Creeley, the
     files of the Black Mountain Review and Divers Press, and a "sub-
     stantial number of books and magazines" bought by or given to
     Creeley. See also 1985.14.

34   NICOSIA, GERALD. "'The closeness of mind': An Interview with
     Robert Duncan." Unspeakable Visions of the Individual, no. 12
     [Beat Angels issue], pp. 13-27 [pp. 17 and 18 are transposed].
          In this July 1978 interview, Duncan mentions his relation-
     ship to Creeley, providing a few biographical details. Duncan
     also notes Creeley's relationship to Marthe Rexroth and, espe-
     cially, Kerouac. Comments on Creeley's drinking.

35 OLSON, CHARLES, and CREELEY, ROBERT. <u>Charles Olson and Robert Creeley: The Complete Correspondence.</u> Vol. 4. Edited by George F. Butterick. Santa Barbara, Calif.: Black Sparrow Press, 152 pp.

In the correspondence between Creeley and Olson from 8 November 1950 to 11 February 1951, Creeley continues to recount his relationship to Corman concerning his and Olson's role in <u>Origin</u>. Details his varying assessments of and irritations with Corman related to their correspondence and visits. Includes portions of Corman's letters to him, and notes Corman's comments on his prose.

Creeley also notes his relationship to, feelings for, and/or correspondence with others, including Slater Brown, Kitasono Katsue, Louis Simpson, Richard Wirtz Emerson, Francis Parkman, Robert Payne, and Rainer M. Gerhardt. Includes a portion of a letter he wrote Gerhardt and of a letter he and Donald Berlin had written Seymour Lawrence. Also provides portions of letters from Jacob Leed, Emerson, Gerhardt, Kitasono, Norman Macleod, and his mother, Genevieve Jules Creeley, to him. Occasionally mentions his reading, including Lawrence, W.C. Williams, Pound, Freud, and Paul Klee.

Provides a number of biographical details about the birth of his second child, Thomas; his farm and financial situation; and his plans to move, variously to Mexico and France. Also mentions his travels during the war and, as a young man, to Florida and New York City, refers to his drinking and use of marijuana, and relates his dislike of present circumstances. Comments on flying his pigeons, skiing, learning French, and hearing a recording of Olson read. Refers to the weather and his difficulty in communicating with others. Creeley also writes of his dislike of being grouped with others in an anthology and W.C. Williams's recommendation of him for a Guggenheim Fellowship. Olson notes the difficulty in getting the Guggenheim committee to "awaken" to Creeley.

Creeley comments on the narrator in his short stories and his use of conjecture. Provides versions of translations and unpublished poems, examining the latter. Mentions revising "Mr. Blue" and "Hart Crane ['He had been stuttering, by the edge']" in light of Olson's observations, and reports on writing stories. Discusses his "An Alternative for Opposites," especially revising it as "From Type to Prototype" due to Olson's comments. Mentions sending his work to Gerhardt, Corman, Seymour Lawrence, and others, and notes Emerson's difficulty in printing his stories. The editor provides a photo of Creeley's drawing on the back of a letter and a line from a 1950 letter to Larry Eigner in which Creeley identifies the "he" in "Hart Crane ['He had been stuttering, by the edge']" as Picasso.

36 OSBORNE, JOHN. "The Black Mountain School." <u>Akros</u> 17, no. 49 [Special Number on American Poets] (April):75-86.

Comments on Creeley as a Black Mountain poet. Analyzes "Something" in terms of Olson's theories of projective verse, especially the use of pauses at the end of lines and the use of "quantitative or . . . syllabic intensities" instead of a qualitative prosody. Finds the syntax "bespeaks its author's struggle to bring sensitive matters to exact definition," and comments on Creeley's use of line breaks and lengths, especially on the seven-syllable line used as a base for this poem.

37   PAUL, SHERMAN. "Holding." North Dakota Quarterly 50, no. 3 (Summer):119–26.
Discussing 1981.22 and 1982.35, comments on Creeley and Olson's relationship and importance to each other, their desire to break free from a sense of stasis, and Creeley's treatment of Ann, his wife. Examines Creeley's theoretical ideas on fiction, and mentions his letters as revealing.

38   _____. So to Speak: Rereading David Antin. London: Binnacle Press, pp. 1, 37, 40, passim.
Occasionally very briefly mentions Creeley's ideas on storytelling and "the authenticity of the personal."

39   RASULA, JED. "Placing Pieces." Sagetrieb: A Journal Devoted to Poets in the Pound-H.D.-Williams Tradition 1, no. 3 [Robert Creeley: Special Issue] (Winter):163–69.
Notes the common sense and the sense of place in Pieces and, in terms of composition by field, shows Creeley's work to be part of a "communal practice" with other poets like Olson and Duncan who "bring themselves . . . to an articulate mutual locality." Comments on the breaking up of poems in Pieces and lists volumes of poetry influenced by it. Reprinted: 1984.41.

40   SHEPPARD, ROBERT. "Stories: Being an Information, an Interview." Sagetrieb: A Journal Devoted to Poets in the Pound-H.D.-Williams Tradition 1, no. 3 [Robert Creeley: Special Issue] (Winter):35–56.
In this 26 May 1982 interview, Creeley discusses his sources in jazz and relationships to jazz musicians, the inherent rhythm in his poetry, and a record he made with Olson in 1955. Also comments on his relationship to Olson, his feeling toward poets in the L=A=N=G=U=A=G=E school, especially Robert Grenier, and his reading of contemporary British poets. Mentions his two years of not writing, 1979–81, after Later (1979), and his marriage to Penelope. Notes that pain and despair are his conditions of writing. Discusses finding in 1963 "a mode that . . . would admit a far more open condition" for writing than before, resulting in Words with more casual patterns. Finds Later a drawing back from this openness to the use of form as a "constant" which allows him the freedom to be "variable in emotional feel" and content.

Also comments on 1980.26-27, 1981.22, and 1982.35, providing
the occasion behind their publication, agrees with an idea in
1970.3, and discusses the occasion behind Grenier's original
ordering of Selected Poems (see 1978.41). Mentions the narrative
sense of some of his poems, comments on his reading of John
Ashbery, and provides numerous biographical details.
In his introduction, Sheppard provides the occasion for the
interview and gives a few biographical details from the day of the
interview. Reprinted: 1984.41.

41   SHIVELY, CHARLEY [CHARLES]. "John Wieners." In "Gay Sunshine"
      Interviews. Vol. 2. Edited by Winston Leyland. San
      Francisco: Gay Sunshine Press, pp. 259-77.
          Slightly revised and abbreviated from 1973.43, with an added
      27 March 1977 interview.

42   SILLIMAN, RON. "For Charles Bernstein Has Such a Spirit. . . ."
      Difficulties 2, no. 1 [Charles Bernstein Issue] (Fall):98-114.
          Discusses the reference to Creeley's "The Warning" in
      Bernstein's "For Love Has Such a Spirit That If It Is Portrayed It
      Dies." Revised: 1987.14.

43   TREDELL, NICHOLAS. "Energy Discharge." PN Review 9, no. 3
      [whole no. 29], p. 52.
          In a favorable review of 1981.22, sees Creeley's letters as
      a portrait of the "struggling artist," finding them "vivid, frag-
      mented, oblique," and energetic.

44   TREMBLAY, BILL; ALEXANDER, FLOYCE; and SIMONS, PETER. "An
      Interview with Robert Creeley." Colorado State Review, n.s.
      10, no. 1 (Fall):4-9.
          In this 29 July 1982 interview, Creeley mentions his rela-
      tionship to Kerouac, providing a few biographical details about
      their encounters and about his participation in the Jack Kerouac
      Conference at Naropa Institute in July 1982. Also recounts some
      childhood memories, especially about his relationship to Harry
      Scribner, a friend. Notes his sense of estrangement from the
      "urbane, comfortable, upper middle class" English of Wallace
      Stevens and others, compared to his and Kerouac's more common
      language. Claims he always wanted a poetry "that could permit all
      that's happening to be there," not a poetry that anticipates the
      world. Claims when he reads, he hears "physical sounds and par-
      ticipates in them."

45   WAGNER, LINDA W[ELSHIMER]. "'Oh, Pioneers!': One Sense of
      Creeley's 'Place.'" Sagetrieb: A Journal Devoted to Poets in
      the Pound-H.D.-Williams Tradition 1, no. 3 [Robert Creeley:
      Special Issue] (Winter):175-81.

RC1982

Provides reminiscences of Creeley's talks at the 1963
Vancouver Poetry Conference, especially as he stressed the process
of poetry and lessons from Pound and W.C. Williams. Comments on
Creeley as an experimental poet who works intuitively within a
personal and open poetics, trying to achieve "emotional clarity."
Reprinted: 1984.41.

46   WILLIAMS, JONATHAN. "Mina Loy (An Old Essay and a New Note)."
     Sagetrieb: A Journal Devoted to Poets in the Pound-Williams
     Tradition 1, no. 1 (Spring):148-52.
         Revision of 1961.3.

47   WILSON, JOHN. "Modernism's Narrowing." Iowa Review 13, nos.
     3-4:233-45.
         In a fairly favorable review of The Collected Poems of
     Robert Creeley, 1945-1975, finds Creeley in a tradition which
     includes W.C. Williams, Zukofsky, Whitman, and Pound. Mentions
     his emphasis on "the act of perceiving and thinking" like action
     painting, his "reductive impulse," his experimentalism, and his
     intensity. Compares his work to W.C. Williams's, as well as to
     contemporary music and painting. Notes how "The Moon" avoids
     traditional approaches and how the poems in Words, compared to his
     earlier poetry, avoid closure. Discusses his treatment of emo-
     tion, especially love.

1983

1   BLACKBURN, PAUL. Review of Le Fou. Sulfur: A Literary Tri-
     Quarterly of the Whole Art 3, no. 1 [whole no. 7]:183-89.
         In this favorable review, published thirty years after it
     was written (see 1983.20), emphasizes that Creeley's poetry truth-
     fully documents the "negative side" of the "human equation." Also
     discusses the figure of women in the poetry and comments on many
     of the individual poems.

2   BUTTERICK, GEORGE F., ed. "Editor's Introduction" to Charles
     Olson and Robert Creeley: The Complete Correspondence. Vol.
     5. Santa Barbara, Calif.: Black Sparrow Press, pp. vii-x.
         Provides a few biographical details concerning Creeley in
     early 1951. Notes that a number of his letters to Olson were
     "bonded together" due to water damage, rendering their content
     unavailable at present.

3   CHRISTENSEN, PAUL [NORMAN]. "Creeley, Robert (White)." In
     American Writers since 1900. Edited by James Vinson and D.L.

Kirkpatrick. St. James Reference Guide to American Literature. Chicago: St. James Press, pp. 151-54.
Revision of 1979.3. See also 1985.5.

4   CLARK, TOM. Review of The Collected Poems of Robert Creeley, 1945-1975. Poetry Project Newsletter, no. 96 (February), p. 3.
In this brief, favorable review, focuses on how revolutionary Creeley's sense of form as an "extension of content" was in the 1950s; his sources, especially in the Renaissance; and his influence on younger poets.

5   CORMAN, CID, and OLSON, CHARLES. "A Selection from the Correspondence: Charles Olson and Cid Corman, 1950." Edited by George Evans. Origin, 5th ser., "the community of individuals," no. 1 (Fall), pp. 78-106.
In these 5 October to 20 November 1950 letters, Corman often mentions his contacts with Creeley, his plans to use Creeley's poetry and prose in Origin, and his differences with Creeley. Olson's letters to Corman are included in 1968.18 and, in part, 1970.29.

6   CREELEY, ROBERT. "Cowboys and Indians." Review of Contemporary Fiction 3, no. 1 (Spring):53-55.
Creeley mentions his correspondence with and relationship to William Eastlake, providing a number of reminiscences about his visits to Eastlake's house, especially in summer 1960.

7   [DAVIDSON, ROBERT MICHAEL?] Notes on Creeley. Archive Newsletter (San Diego, Calif.) (Winter), p. 2.
Announces Creeley's 23 February reading at the University of California at San Diego, and claims he helped change "the course of literature in the post-Pound/Williams generation."

8   DEMBO, L[AWRENCE] S[ANFORD]. "An Interview with Paul Blackburn." In Interviews with Contemporary Writers. 2d series, 1972-1982. Edited by L[awrence] S[anford] Dembo. Madison: University of Wisconsin Press, pp. 17-27.
Reprint of 1972.15.

9   DUNCAN, ROBERT. "Letters on Poetry and Poetics." Ironwood 11, no. 2 [whole no. 22] [Robert Duncan: A Special Issue] (Fall): 95-135.
Duncan occasionally mentions Creeley and claims that Creeley's work nourishes him.

10 EVANS, GEORGE, ed. Introduction to "A Selection from the Correspondence: Charles Olson and Cid Corman, 1950." Origin, 5th ser., "the community of individuals," no. 1 (Fall), p. 78.

RC1983

In an introduction to 1983.5, mentions Creeley's plans for a magazine and his initial contacts with Corman.

11 FAAS, EKBERT. "Robert Creeley." In The Beats: Literary Bohemians in Postwar America. Part 1, A–L. Edited by Ann Charters. Dictionary of Literary Biography, vol. 16. Detroit: Gale Research Co., Bruccoli Clark Book, pp. 141–48.
      Compares Creeley's background to Ginsberg's and discusses the relationship between the two, including their assessment of each other's work. Also provides biographical details, mentions the influence of W.C. Williams, and comments on Creeley as the editor of the Black Mountain Review.

12 FREDMAN, STEPHEN [ALBERT]. "American Poet's Prose and the Crisis of Verse." American Poetry 1, no. 1 (Fall):49–63.
      A revision of sections of 1980.18 or, more precisely, a revision of the first chapter and other, smaller sections of 1983.13.

13 _____. Poet's Prose: The Crisis in American Verse. Cambridge: Cambridge University Press, pp. 55–98, 117, 135, passim.
      In a revision of 1980.18, includes a discussion on the initiation of Presences, and mentions Creeley's correspondence with Marisol. Provides a number of sources for Presences: José Ramon Medina's Marisol (Caracas: Ediciones Armitano, 1968), a tape recording, a Buddhist fable, and a painting by Nicolas Poussin reproduced on a postcard. Also compares Presences to Duncan's "The Structure of Rime, I." Revised in part: 1983.12.

14 _____. "Why American Poets Write Prose." PN Review [Poetry Nation Review] 9, no. 6 [whole no. 32], pp. 10–11.
      Briefly comments on Creeley's prose, noting its "heroism of negation and receptivity."

15 GOLDING, ALAN. Review of The Collected Poems of Robert Creeley, 1945–1975. Magazine (Venice, Calif.) 13, no. 4 (Fall):14–15.
      In this generally favorable review, discusses, in turn, each book included in the volume. Mentions influences on The Charm: Early and Uncollected Poems (1969), commenting on "Poem for D.H. Lawrence" as typical of that volume. Emphasizes the "abstract diction" of For Love as well as the rhythm of its poems. Finds that "closure is even less frequent; the syntax becomes more twisted; and the mind becomes more and more of a trap" in Words, but also denotes a "healing" awareness of a world beyond the self. Focuses on the experimentation of Pieces, finding that the "short phrases and incomplete sentences probe the limits of minimalism and of the very term 'poem,'" but feels the cumulative effect

often "flattens emphasis." Believes the poetry in the later books denotes a relaxation as well as a "continued experimentation with sequence and with the boundaries of the 'poem.'"

16   GOLDONI, ANNALISA. "Olson, Creeley, ed il Black Mountain."
      [In Italian.] In I contemporanei: Novecento americano. Vol.
      2. Edited by Elémire Zolla. Rome: Lucarini Editore,
      pp. 459–83.
          Compares Creeley and Olson, finding Creeley's world exists
      only at the moment of writing without a need for history. Like
      the postmen in "The Dishonest Mailmen," finds Creeley destroying
      evidences of the world prior to composition so that he may begin
      with a tabula rasa. Also comments on his simplification and care.
          Discusses Creeley's self-imposed limitations such as his
      lack of metaphor, and mentions the control and tension in his
      reading of his own work. Also comments on Creeley's generalized
      word choice and lack of specifics.

17   GORSKI, HEDWIG. "Interview with Robert Creeley." Nit and Wit:
      Chicago's Art Magazine 5, no. 5 (September–October):46–49.
          In this interview, Creeley comments on lecturing at Naropa
      in July 1983 and working in mixed media in the 1960s. Mentions
      his sense of an audience, provides a few biographical details, and
      discusses his early reception as a poet.

18   GUNN, THOM. "'Small persistent difficulties.'" Times Literary
      Supplement, 4 November, p. 1226.
          In a favorable review of The Collected Poems of Robert
      Creeley, 1945–1975, mentions Creeley's use of language, his
      rhythm, and his lack of metaphor. Comments on "The World" and
      "For Friendship," and notes how he reads his work. Reprinted:
      1987.19.

19   JACKSON, RICHARD. "Projecting the Literal Word." In Acts of
      Mind: Conversations with Contemporary Poets. University:
      University of Alabama Press, pp. 164–71.
          Reprint of 1981.13.

20   JAROLIM, EDITH [BRENDA]. Introduction to a review of Le Fou,
      by Paul Blackburn. Sulfur: A Literary Tri-Quarterly of the
      Whole Art 3, no. 1 [whole no. 7]:183–85.
          Provides the occasion behind 1983.1, including biographical
      details concerning Creeley's relationship to and correspondence
      with Blackburn in 1953.

21   _____. "Paul Blackburn." In The Beats: Literary Bohemians in
      Post War America. Part 1, A–L. Edited by Ann Charters.

RC1983

Dictionary of Literary Biography, vol. 16. Detroit: Gale
Research Co., Bruccoli Clark Book, pp. 24-32.
Occasionally notes Blackburn's relationship to Creeley.

22   KELLER, EMILY. "An Interview by Emily Keller." American
     Poetry Review 12, no. 3 (May-June):24-28.
         In this lengthy interview with Creeley, Creeley discusses
     writing prose, especially The Island, and reading his poetry.
     Comments on Olson's advice to him not to imitate Stevens but to
     use his own speech patterns for his line length. Mentions writing
     "After Lorca" and "Time ['Out window roof's slope']," and notes
     Olson's editing of "Mr. Blue." Refers to the themes of relation-
     ships and isolation as well as the religious and political dimen-
     sions of his work. Also comments on the initiation of the
     creative process, the creative impulse, and revising during
     writing. Notes his enjoyment of writing and his use of syntax and
     speech patterns. Refers to "Beyond," "Then ['Don't go']," "The
     Women," and "The Awakening." Provides some biographical details,
     especially about meeting his third wife, Penelope, naming his
     children, the way he dresses, a few awards, and his political
     affiliations.
         Keller comments on a number of poems, especially "The Flower
     ['I think I grow tensions']" and "Love ['The thing comes']."

23   KENNER, HUGH. "Poetize or Bust." Harper's 267 (September):
     67-70.
         Briefly comments on "I Know a Man" and "The Answer," noting
     the importance Creeley achieves in minimal lines.

24   _____. "Robert Creeley's Continuum." New York Times Book
     Review, 7 August, p. 13.
         In a favorable review of The Collected Poems of Robert
     Creeley, 1945-1975, comments on "The Problem," and notes the
     Renaissance-like melody of "Air: 'The Love of a Woman.'" Feels
     Creeley's poems read best in a continuum. Reprinted: 1987.19.

25   MARLATT, DAPHNE; BOWERING, GEORGE; WAH, FRED[ERIC]; CREELEY,
     ROBERT; CULLEY, PETER; COLEMAN, VICTOR; McCAFFREY, STEVE;
     NICHOL, bp; OPPENHEIMER, JOEL; and BERTHOLF, ROBERT [JOHN].
     "The Roots of Present Writing." Credences: A Journal of
     Twentieth Century Poetry and Poetics, n.s. 2, nos. 2-3
     [Canadian Poetry Festival issue] (Fall-Winter):211-28.
         In this 20 October 1980 discussion, Creeley reminisces about
     writing a review of Arthur James Marshall Smith's Poems: New and
     Collected (Toronto: Oxford University Press, 1967) and about his
     role as editor of New Writing in the U.S.A. (also edited by Donald
     [Merriam] Allen [Harmondsworth, Middlesex, England: Penguin,
     1976]). Wah mentions Creeley's time in Vancouver and his writing
     for Tish, and Oppenheimer reminisces about an encounter with
     Creeley at Black Mountain College. Bowering mentions Creeley's

use of commas in prose, and Coleman comments on the risk in his writing.

26 MAZZARO, JEROME. "Witnessing: Robert Creeley's 'I.'" Crazy-
    horse, no. 24 (Spring), pp. 59-78.
    Examines the role of the self in Creeley's poetry, finding
his work, like Puritan autobiography, bears witness to his life.
Warning against closely identifying him with the Puritans, claims
he expresses a work ethic, desires accuracy and honesty, and
avoids ornamentation and rhetoric. Believes he uses poetry to
measure, define, yield truths, and seek a "wholeness," even as he
writes, until he achieves a sense of completion. Remarking on his
interior settings, feels Creeley favors the exterior, as in "The
Wife," and finds "materialization not sublimation is the direc-
tion" of poems like "For Love." Finds he treats the woman figure
as both inner and outer in "The Finger." Claims the "stumbling"
in For Love and Words is "a linear process toward something" but
becomes a circular movement in Pieces. Finds the exterior often
becomes the starting point in Hello: A Journal, February 29-May
3, 1976 and Later (1979). Notes his use of chance and spontaneity
when writing, and examines the sense "of the helplessness in the
face of determinism."
    Reports that Creeley, seeking definition "within or against
world views," often counters outside pressures, including language
and song, "with his own resilient expression." Comments on "The
Rain ['All night the sound had']" and "Intervals," finding "nature
provides the corollaries of the speaker's self" in both. Compares
the self as a participant ruled by chance in his early work to the
self as an onlooker in poems like "Myself." Notes the use of the
third person in "Self-Portrait."
    Mentions the influence of others on Creeley's use of the
"I," of Lawrence on his early sense of wholeness and "dynamic
consciousness," and of Valéry's Monsieur Teste on his "self-
conscious and ironic" early poetry. Believes Creeley found con-
firmations for his beliefs in terms of the intellect, art, the
subjective, and the objective in the theories of Bruno Snell and
Eric Havelock. Notes the influence of Whitehead on his objectification of the subjective, and speculates on the influence of
Lawrence on his use of religious terminology. Compares his to
Whitman's and Thoreau's transcendental use of autobiography.

27 NICOSIA, GERALD. Memory Babe: A Critical Biography of Jack
    Kerouac. New York: Grove Press, pp. 520-22, 524-26, 599.
    Details Creeley's meeting of and relationship to Kerouac in
1956, and notes his appreciation of Kerouac's work and improvisation. Also provides biographical details from 1956: fights
Creeley had with Dorn and a bartender, his arrest with Ron
Loewinsohn, his affair with Marthe Rexroth, and his relationship

to Neal Cassady. Comments on a letter Kerouac wrote Creeley in 1959.

28   NIEDECKER, LORINE. "Extracts from Letters to Kenneth Cox." In The Full Note: Lorine Niedecker. [Edited by Peter Dent?] Budleigh Salterton, Devon, England: Interim Press, pp. 36-42. Very briefly assesses Creeley's work.

29   Notes. Am Here Books, Catalogue 6. Santa Barbara, Calif.: Am Here Books, section 1 [pp. 52-56].
      Comments on many of Creeley's volumes of poetry, prose, and correspondence, including an item missed in 1976.23.

30   OLSON, CHARLES, and CREELEY, ROBERT. Charles Olson and Robert Creeley: The Complete Correspondence. Vol. 5. Edited by George F. Butterick. Santa Barbara, Calif.: Black Sparrow Press, 215 pp.
      Includes expanded versions of most of the letters in 1954.4, occasionally reordered, and other Olson letters not previously published. In the correspondence from 13 February 1951 to 26 April 1951, Creeley continues to relate his relationship to Corman concerning Origin, detailing his varying assessments of Corman and providing portions of Corman's letters. Creeley also discusses his correspondence with, relationship to, and/or feelings for a few others, including Slater Brown, Paul Blackburn, Richard Wirtz Emerson, James Laughlin, and Rainer M. Gerhardt.
      Creeley notes Emerson's unacknowledged use and misuse of his ideas in Frère Vital's Anthology: Being a Collection of the Principles of Vitalist Poetry from Divers Notes Gathered Together by Frère Vital (Columbus, Ohio: Golden Goose Press, 1951), and mentions reading Lawrence. Provides a few biographical details especially on his difficulties leaving the farm in Littleton, New Hampshire, and on his experiences during World War II.
      Olson mentions Creeley's comments on his own material and discusses "Hélas, suggesting possible revisions. He also encourages Creeley about the Guggenheim Fellowship and, when Creeley is turned down, speculates on the reasons. Comments on Corman's feeling for himself and Creeley, noting how they should treat Corman. The editor provides a photo of Creeley's comments and suggested revisions of Olson's "This."

31   PATERSON, ALISTAIR. "Creeley/Paterson: A Conversation." Buff, no. 3 1/2, pp. 44-51.
      In this 1982 conversation, Creeley occasionally reminisces about his 1976 trip to New Zealand and Australia and the Charles Olson Festival at the University of Iowa in November 1978. Also remembers beginning to write under the New Critical domination of the literary scene in the 1950s.

32   PAUL, SHERMAN. "Entering." North Dakota Quarterly 51, no. 2
      (Spring):144-51.
          Discussing 1983.30, mentions Creeley's letters to Olson and
      his role as editor of Olson's The Mayan Letters.

33   SILBERG, RICHARD. "Crow's Feet in the Snow." Poetry Flash:
      The Bay Area's Poetry Calendar and Review, no. 122 (May), pp.
      1, 7.
          In a favorable review of The Collected Poems of Robert
      Creeley, 1945-1975, emphasizes the power Creeley "generates" as a
      "miniaturist." Explicates "Love ['The thing comes']," discussing
      his use of line breaks and abstract words.

34   TERRELL, CARROLL F., ed. "A Visit to an Idol." In William
      Carlos Williams: Man and Poet. The Man and Poet Series,
      edited by Carroll F. Terrell. Orono, Maine: University of
      Maine at Orono, National Poetry Foundation, pp. 41-46.
          In this fall 1982 interview, Creeley provides biographical
      details concerning his visit with W.C. Williams in the spring of
      1954. Also briefly mentions his own work with the Black Mountain
      Review.

35   TILLINGHAST, RICHARD. "Yesterday's Avant Garde." Nation 237,
      no. 16 (19 November):501-4.
          In a fairly favorable review of The Collected Poems of
      Robert Creeley, 1945-1975, finds Creeley a "deliberately minor
      poet," notes the influence of W.C. Williams, and comments on "Hart
      Crane ['He had been stuttering, by the edge']."

36   WRIGHT, JAMES. "The Few Poets of England and America." In
      Collected Prose. Edited by Anne Wright. Ann Arbor: Univer-
      sity of Michigan Press, pp. 268-78.
          Reprint of 1961.4.

                              1984

1   ALAPI, ZSOLT ISTVÁN. "The Poetics of Postmodernism: Robert
      Creeley and Open Verse." Ph.D. thesis, McGill University,
      224 pp.
          Discusses Creeley's central "thematic concern, which is the
      integration of subjectivity and objectivity in a unified vision."
      Notes the influence of imagism, Pound, objectivism, Zukofsky, W.C.
      Williams, Olson, Wittgenstein, and D.H. Lawrence on Creeley's
      sense of language, measure, open verse, and proprioception. Also
      notes their influence on his ideas of objectivity and subjectiv-
      ity, man as both a subject and object, and writing as an activity,
      a dynamic process and energy exchange. Mentions the role of emo-
      tion, sincerity, discovery, the ideogram, and form and content in
      Creeley's poetry.

RC1984

Comments on the treatment of the mind in a number of poems, including "[Listless']," "The Name," "For Love," and "The Rhythm." Finds the intellect is often depicted as estranging man from and limiting his participation in the world. Mentions a number of other poems including "The Moon," "Enough," and "The Figures." Examines a number of poems in Words, noting the treatment of intentions, confusions, habits of the mind, and the validity of the world. In Pieces, feels Creeley "works toward the integration of the subjective-objective duality," and notes the sense of presence and the treatment of the mind, estrangement, and the woman figure. Examines the role of the mundane in "A Step"; the treatment of women and the mind in "The Finger"; and the unity and harmonies between the objective and subjective, the lover and the beloved, and "the singular and the All" in "Numbers." Also remarks on "Gemini" and "['Having to--']."

In Creeley's later poetry, discovers fewer abstractions and "a greater awareness and acceptance of his 'literal' condition in the world." Mentioning a number of separate pieces in A Day Book, discusses the volume's spontaneity and desired harmony between the mind and the body. Also examines the treatment of love, death, mortality, and relationships in A Day Book, noting Creeley's "desire to view and understand his actions objectively." Examining a number of poems in Hello: A Journal, February 29-May 3, 1976, especially "Window ['Aching sense']," discusses the "subjective-objective dichotomy" and the desire for relations. In Away, comments on the role of separation and the refusal to become sentimental in many poems like "For My Mother: Genevieve Jules Creeley," "The Plan Is the Body," and "Sitting Here." Examines the role of death, love, relationships, acceptance, unity, aging, youth, and memory in Later (1979), especially commenting on "Myself" and "For Pen." In Mirrors, notes a reconciliation of the subject and the object.

2   ALTIERI, CHARLES. "Dal pensiero simbolista all'immanenza: Il fondamento della poetica americana postmoderna." [In Italian.] Translated by Massimo Pesaresi. In Postmoderno e letteratura: Percorsi e visioni della critica in America. Edited by Peter Carravette and Paolo Spedicato. Studi Bompiani. Milan: Bompiani, pp. 123-60.
    Abridged translation of 1973.2.

3   _____. Self and Sensibility in Contemporary American Poetry. Cambridge Studies in American Literature and Culture, edited by Albert [J.] Gelpi. Cambridge: Cambridge University Press, pp. 18, 96-97, 101-31, passim.
    In a revision of 1978.4 with a brief added section on Later (1979), commentary on "The Rain ['All night the sound had']," and a further emphasis on Creeley's solipsism, finds "[John] Ashbery's

version of a poetics of thinking and [Adrienne] Rich's model of
selfhood more successful."

4   BALDWIN, NEIL. To All Gentleness: William Carlos Williams,
     the Doctor-Poet. New York: Atheneum, pp. xi, 184-86.
         From an interview with Creeley, provides a fairly detailed
     account of Creeley's first visit to W.C. Williams in the spring of
     1954.

5   BARBOUR, DOUGLAS. "Lyric/Anti-Lyric: Some Notes about a Con-
     cept." Line: A Journal of Contemporary Writing and Its
     Modernist Sources, no. 3 (Spring), pp. 45-63.
         Uses Creeley's "The Language" as an example of a type of
     "lyric/anti-lyric" that retrieves "the poet's self as poetic
     speaker [and] attack[s] the idea of a modernist lyric," which
     often depends upon a persona.

6   BASIL, ROBERT [G.]. "Creeley Teaches in Buffalo." In Robert
     Creeley: The Poet's Workshop. Edited by Carroll F. Terrell.
     The Poet's Workshop Series. Orono, Maine: University of Maine
     at Orono, National Poetry Foundation, pp. 301-9.
         Basil reminisces about Creeley as a teacher of a "Modern
     Poetry" class at SUNY-Buffalo and about his own and other stu-
     dents' relationships and reactions to Creeley. Found Creeley
     difficult to follow and rather formal in class. Mentions
     Creeley's role in Buffalo's cultural life and his affection for
     that city. Speculates on Creeley's relationship to Irving
     Feldman.

7   BAWER, BRUCE. Review of Mirrors. Poetry 144, no. 6
     (September):345-46.
         In this basically unfavorable review, stresses the theme of
     "the detachment of the Self," and notes the similarity in Creeley's
     poem titles. Praises "Memory, 1930."

8   BELLMAN, SAMUEL IRVING. Review of The Collected Poems of
     Robert Creeley, 1945-1975. Western American Literature 19, no.
     2 (Summer [August]):142-43.
         In this generally negative review, emphasizes Creeley's
     minimalism, labeling the poems in the volume "capers" and private
     "spastic responses."

9   CLARK, TOM. "Never Say Fiction." Rolling Stock, no. 7, p. 20.
         In a brief, favorable review of The Collected Prose of
     Robert Creeley, characterizes Creeley's voice, and finds a "unity
     and integrity in all of his work."

10   CONNIFF, BRIAN P. "The Lyric and Modern Poetry." Ph.D. dis-
      sertation, University of Notre Dame, pp. 15–16, 117–81, 190,
      266–68, passim.
           Finds Creeley "challenges the lyric conventions" because he
      attempts to bring "the actual world" into his poetry by way of
      whatever he "most immediately, intensely, and personally feels,"
      instead of seeking the "lyric paradise" of a timeless, changeless
      state removed from the present world.
           Discusses Creeley's sense of discovery in the poem, and
      examines his sense of the limitations on his art by history, eco-
      nomics, and politics, leading to the poem as an "act of recogni-
      tion" of "one's involvement in a finite condition and activity."
      Also analyzes his sense of "writing 'within' a world of objects
      rather than 'about' a subject." Mentions the influence of W.C.
      Williams and Olson, and comments on a number of Creeley's poems,
      especially "Mary's Fancy," "The Rites," "Alba," "For Rainer
      Gerhardt," and "Prayer to Hermes." Comments on Creeley's themes
      of the body and measure. See also 1984.11. See Dissertation
      Abstracts International 48 (1985):2522A.

11   CONNIFF, BRIAN [P.]. "The Lyricism of This World." In Robert
      Creeley: The Poet's Workshop. Edited by Carroll F. Terrell.
      The Poet's Workshop Series. Orono, Maine: University of Maine
      at Orono, National Poetry Foundation, pp. 289–300.
           Notes the influence of Olson on Creeley's poetics in his
      attempt "to break from the metaphysical tradition and its 'lyrical
      interference of the individual as ego.'" Finds Creeley's measure
      helps "to locate himself in the world at a particular time,"
      bringing "the lyrical voice . . . into the public world." Be-
      lieves this measure, however, provides only a provisional knowl-
      edge of "the common world," which often leads to "discomfort and
      the awareness of awkwardness." Discusses "This World" and
      Creeley's relationship to his audience as a lyric poet. See also
      1984.10.

12   CREELEY, ROBERT. The Collected Prose of Robert Creeley. New
      York and London: Marion Boyars, 432 pp.
           Includes reprints of 1954.3; 1963.8; 1972.8, 12; 1976.7, 9.

13   CREELEY, ROBERT, and OLSON, CHARLES. "Creeley/Olson: Letters."
      Edited by George F. Butterick. In Blast, 3. Edited by Seamus
      Cooney, Bradford Morrow, Bernard Lafourcade, and Hugh Kenner.
      Santa Barbara, Calif.: Black Sparrow Press, pp. 272–92.
           In these letters from 8 April to 19 July 1953, Creeley de-
      tails the influence of the work of Charlie Parker on his own sense
      of rhythm and rhythmic structure, using a section of "The Immoral
      Proposition" to illustrate. Olson briefly mentions Creeley's "The
      Operation."

14   CREELEY, ROBERT. "Introduction" to The Collected Prose of
     Robert Creeley. New York and London: Marion Boyars,
     pp. [5-6].
          In this introduction, Creeley comments that he had, when
     younger, wished to write more fiction and mentions a number of
     fiction writers that he has loved.

15   _____ . "A Visit with Dr. Williams." Sagetrieb: A Journal
     Devoted to Poets in the Pound-H.D.-Williams Tradition 3, no. 2
     (Fall):27-35.
          In an abbreviated transcription of a 24 August 1983 talk at
     the William Carlos Williams Commemorative Centennial Conference at
     the University of Maine at Orono, Creeley provides biographical
     details concerning his childhood, going to high school and
     Harvard, reading Pound and others during World War II, and
     listening to jazz. Notes his correspondence with Williams, and
     examines the influence of Pound, Williams, and others on him.
     Compares Williams's influence to that of Stevens and Yeats.

16   ESHLEMAN, CLAYTON. "With Love for the Muse in Charlie Parker
     Tempo." Los Angeles Times Book Review, 4 March, pp. 3, 7.
          In an unfavorable review of Mirrors, compares it to
     Creeley's early work, finding "an uninspired truthfulness" sub-
     stituted for his earlier "imaginative capability." Speculates
     that "Creeley's original dedication to a perceptive figure from
     without," a muse, might have precluded his development as a poet.
     Notes his treatment of love in his early work.

17   FAAS, EKBERT. "Layton and Creeley: Chronicle of a Literary
     Friendship." In Robert Creeley: The Poet's Workshop. Edited
     by Carroll F. Terrell. The Poet's Workshop Series. Orono,
     Maine: University of Maine at Orono, National Poetry Founda-
     tion, pp. 249-73.
          Quoting from the unpublished correspondence between Creeley
     and Irving Layton, discusses their relationship from 1953 to 1963,
     especially concerning Creeley's publication of Layton's In the
     Midst of My Fever (Palma de Mallorca, Spain: Divers Press, 1954)
     and their roles in the Black Mountain Review. Details their
     assessments of each other's work, especially Layton's assessment
     of Creeley's prose and Creeley's critical comments on Layton's
     poetry. Also mentions their relationships to and assessments of
     others, including Olson, Robert Graves, Edward Dahlberg, and Louis
     Dudek. Creeley's letters also mention his own writing block in
     the mid-1950s.

18   FELD, ROSS. "The Fate of Doing Nothing Right." Parnassas:
     Poetry in Review 12, no. 1 (Fall-Winter):95-122.
          Illustrating with a number of poems, traces Creeley's devel-
     opment or changes and continuities in his work. Discusses his

RC1984

treatment of doubt and monogamy, as well as his use of rhyme.
Examines the role of water, conceptualization, mirrors, sincerity,
uncertainty, and objectification in his work. Compares his poetry
to Lawrence's, and finds the influence of Zukofsky pervasive in
Pieces. Compares the poetry in Pieces to Boris Leonidovich
Pasternak's Sestra moia zhizn' (My Sister Life), finding both
poets sing "marginally not at the world but of and within the
beleagured categories that develop the world." Notes the treatment of age in Mirrors, and discusses "The Pool," "For W.C.W.
['The rhyme is after']," "['The car']," and the "male amity" in "I
Know a Man." Finds his poetry of the 1970s somewhat banal and
repetitive.

19   FREDMAN, STEPHEN [ALBERT]. Review of The Collected Poems of
     Robert Creeley, 1945-1975. American Poetry 1, no. 3 (Spring):
     93-95.
          In this fairly favorable review, finds a nakedness and "ego-
     lessness" in the work, but feels the volume raises the poems from
     the "flux of experience," their proper context.

20   HALL, DONALD. "Naming the Skin: Notes on the Erotics of Sound
     Form." Ironwood 12, no. 2 [whole no. 24] [Bearings:
     Approaches to Poetry and the Poem issue] (1984):58-70.
          Briefly uses "The Hill" to note how rhythm "mimics" the
     "mind's melody," finding Creeley an heir of Frost.

21   HASS, ROBERT. "Creeley, His Metric." Threepenny Review 4, no.
     4 [whole no. 16] (Winter):5-6.
          In a lengthy, favorable review of The Collected Poems of
     Robert Creeley, 1945-1975, finds Creeley's broad appeal in the
     1960s had to do with his sensitivity to language, his realization
     that it cannot be consciously controlled or merely used as a coun-
     ter. Also discusses "Again ['One more day gone']" and the influ-
     ence of W.C. Williams's line breaks on Creeley. Reprinted:
     1984.22; 1987.19.

22   _____. "Creeley, His Metric." In Twentieth Century Pleasures:
     Prose on Poetry. New York: Ecco Press, pp. 150-60.
          Reprint of 1984.21.

23   KING-EDWARDS, LUCILLE. Review of The Collected Poems of Robert
     Creeley, 1945-1975. Rubicon, no. 2 (Winter), pp. 116-20.
          In this favorable review, comments on Creeley's emphasis
     upon immediate presence and process as well as his dislike of
     metaphor and description. Comments on each of the books collected.

24   MARIANI, PAUL [LOUIS]. "Robert Creeley." In A Usable Past:
     Essays on Modern and Contemporary Poetry. Amherst: University
     of Massachusetts Press, 184-202.
          Reprint of 1978.52.

25   MESCH, HARALD. <u>Verweigerung</u> endgültiger Prädikation: <u>Ästhetische Formen</u> und <u>Denkstrukturen</u> der <u>amerikanischen</u> "Postmoderne," 1950-1970. [In German.] American Studies: A Monograph Series, vol. 58. Munich, West Germany: Wilhelm Fink Verlag, pp. 243-68, passim.
   Including a translation of 1982.32, occasionally also mentions Creeley's reversion of the Cartesian postulate: "I think; therefore I am not."

26   MOLESWORTH, CHARLES. Review of <u>Mirrors</u>. <u>Bluefish</u> 1, no. 2 (Spring):109-14.
   In this favorable review, mentions the role of process and the treatment of language, aging, love, acceptance, and self-consciousness. Notes Creeley's sources in Thomas Hardy and Robert Bresson and his "existential, improvisatory stance." Remarks on a few poems like "All the Way" and "Oh Love," comparing the latter to poems in <u>For Love</u>.

27   MURRAY, TIMOTHY, and BOARDWAY, STEPHEN. "Year by Year Bibliography of Robert Creeley." In <u>Robert Creeley: The Poet's Workshop</u>. Edited by Carroll F. Terrell. The Poet's Workshop Series. Orono, Maine: University of Maine at Orono, National Poetry Foundation, pp. 313-74.
   Provides a primary bibliography of Creeley, including individual poems, prose, books, letters to the editor, interviews, reviews, and prefatory matter from 1940 to 1983. Most of the section attributed to Boardway, 1940-70, is an inadequately attributed reordering of citations from sections of 1973.37.

28   NORRIS, KEN[NETH WAYNE]. <u>The Little Magazine in Canada, 1925-80: Its Role in the Development of Modernism and Post-Modernism in Canadian Poetry</u>. Toronto: ECW Press, pp. 101-2, 120, passim.
   Revision of 1980.25.

29   RADAVICH, DAVID A. Letter to the Editor. <u>American Book Review</u> 7, no. 1 (November-December):11.
   Claims 1984.32 lacks an "adequate critical assessment."

30   RAFFEL, BURTON. <u>How to Read a Poem</u>. New York: New American Library, Meridian Book, pp. 226-27.
   Briefly notes the sounds and form of "Like They Say."

31   RAJNATH. "Poetry, Language, and Reality: Some Notes on the Poetry of Robert Creeley." <u>Indian Journal of American Studies</u> 14, no. 1 (January):33-41.
   Notes Creeley's ideas on form and content, comments on his theory of poetry as a self-referential "linguistic activity," as seen in "A Piece" and, through the use of repetition, in "Four

RC1984

['Before I die']" and "The Flower ['I think I grow tensions']."
Finding "a conflict between verbal reality and its physical coun-
terpart" in "I Know a Man" and "The Language," believes Creeley is
best when he balances "musical and semantic properties" as in "The
Rhythm" and "The Finger." Discovers a dislocation of reality in
"For W.C.W. ['The rhyme is after']."

32   RASULA, JED. "Personal Weight." American Book Review 6, no. 4
     (May-June):21.
          In a favorable review of The Collected Poems of Robert
     Creeley, 1945-1975, emphasizes that the poetry is both personal
     and universal. See also 1984.29.

33   REYNOLDS, MICHAEL S. "The Collected Poems of Robert Creeley,
     1945-1975." In Magill's Literary Annual, 1984: Essay-Reviews
     of 200 Outstanding Books Published in the United States during
     1983. Edited by Frank N. Magill. Vol. 1. Englewood Cliffs,
     N.J.: Salem Press, pp. 189-93.
          In this favorable essay-review, finds the volume "Whitman-
     esque and existential." Notes the themes of love, isolation, and
     "the poet in the process of writing the poem." Provides biograph-
     ical details, notes Creeley's relationship to other writers and
     artists, and comments on the influence of Olson and W.C. Williams.

34   RICHEY, JOE. "Why Write." Naropa Magazine 1, no. 1
     (February):45.
          Provides information on Creeley's participation at Naropa
     Institute during the summer of 1983, including his views on poetry
     and contemporary culture.

35   SAVERY, PANCHO. "'The Character of the Speech': 56 Things for
     Robert Creeley." In Robert Creeley: The Poet's Workshop.
     Edited by Carroll F. Terrell. The Poet's Workshop Series.
     Orono, Maine: University of Maine at Orono, National Poetry
     Foundation, pp. 223-48.
          Discusses most poems in Echoes and Mother's Voice, espe-
     cially "First Rain," and compares Creeley to Thelonious Monk,
     Jean-Luc Goddard, Emily Dickinson, Ludwig Wittgenstein, Robert
     Bresson, and Thomas Hardy. Notes the jazz influence on Creeley's
     work, his treatment of time, and his "concentration on voice."
     Comments on his reading of his poetry and getting "to the root of
     experience."

36   SORRENTINO, GILBERT. "Black Mountaineering." In Something
     Said. San Francisco: North Point Press, pp. 242-51.
          Reprint of 1970.32.

37   STRATTON, DIRK. "If to Is: Robert Creeley's 'If You.'"
      Sagetrieb: A Journal Devoted to Poets in the Pound-H.D.-
      Williams Tradition 3, no. 1 (Spring):105-9.
          Explicates "If You," treating the poem as a narrative about
      writing the poem itself. Believes it begins as a "light exercise"
      that is "consumed by another darker purpose" as Creeley realizes
      innocence is a falsification of experience in a harsh, painful
      world. Also notes interruptions and shifts in metrical patterns.

38   SYLVESTER, WILLIAM. "Is That a Real Statue or Did Marisol Just
      Make It Up?: Affinities with Creeley's Presences." In Robert
      Creeley: The Poet's Workshop. Edited by Carroll F. Terrell.
      The Poet's Workshop Series. Orono, Maine: University of Maine
      at Orono, National Poetry Foundation, pp. 275-87.
          Largely discusses Marisol's sculptures, making implicit
      comparisons to Creeley's Presences. Notes the active nature of
      Marisol's work which involves the audience in a participation of
      continually changing ideas, and notes its comic and erotic quali-
      ties. Comments on "the patterns of numbers which permute before
      the sections of Presences and 'Mabel: A Story.'"

39   TERRELL, CARROLL F. "Dove Sta Memoria." In Robert Creeley:
      The Poet's Workshop. Edited by Carroll F. Terrell. The Poet's
      Workshop Series. Orono, Maine: University of Maine at Orono,
      National Poetry Foundation, pp. 199-222.
          In a 23 September 1983 interview, Creeley provides detailed
      biographical information concerning his childhood and adolescence,
      especially concerning the farm he lived on and the woods he played
      in. Also mentions his loss of an eye and his family.

40   _____. "Introduction" to Robert Creeley: The Poet's Workshop.
      Edited by Carroll F. Terrell. The Poet's Workshop Series.
      Orono, Maine: University of Maine at Orono, National Poetry
      Foundation, pp. 13-31.
          In the first section (pp. 13-14), provides his, Terrell's,
      introduction to a reading by Creeley in September 1982. In the
      remainder, discusses Creeley's statements on or treatment of emo-
      tion, suffering, his family, the present, sound in poetry, and the
      poet's reciprocal relationship to his place. Comments on the
      personal element in his poetry, "The Dress," and critical work
      done on and interviews with him, especially 1978.67. Compares
      Creeley to Dylan Thomas and provides biographical and genealogical
      information about Creeley, especially about his father and his
      loss of an eye.

41   _____, ed. Robert Creeley: The Poet's Workshop. The Poet's
      Workshop Series. Orono, Maine: University of Maine at Orono,
      National Poetry Foundation, pp. 35-181.
          Includes reprints of 1982.2, 6-7, 19, 24, 31-32, 39-40, 45.

42 TRAWICK, LEONARD; MILIC, LOUIS; FRIEDMAN, BARTON; and EDELBERG,
    CYNTHIA [DUBIN]. "Conversation with Robert Creeley." Gambut:
    A Journal of Ideas and Information, no. 12 (Spring-Summer),
    pp. 20-31.
        In this 30 June 1983 conversation, Creeley comments on writ-
    ing A Calendar, taking a creative writing class at Harvard under
    Delmore Schwartz, reading at poetry readings, and teaching crea-
    tive writing. Mentions his relationship to Scribner's and a num-
    ber of people such as John Hawkes and Donald Merriam Allen.
    Remarks on his own reading, and relates his sense of the creative
    process and of writing to be read aloud. The introductory note
    (p. 20) gives the occasion of the conversation and lists Creeley's
    activities at Cleveland State University in June 1983.

43 TURNER, ALBERTA [T.]. "The Same Skin, but Even More at Home in
    It." Field: Contemporary Poetry and Poetics, no. 30 (Spring),
    pp. 75-82.
        In this favorable review of Mirrors, maintains Creeley's
    development is discernible and that he no longer strains for
    effect. Feels the poems, unlike some earlier, do not present
    stylistic difficulties for the reader.

44 WILLIAMSON, ALAN. Introspection and Contemporary Poetry.
    Cambridge, Mass.: Harvard University Press, pp. 23-24, passim.
        Briefly uses Creeley's "A Form of Women" as an example of
    reflexive poetry.

1985

1   BERNSTEIN, MICHAEL ANDRÉ, and HATLEN, BURTON. "Interview with
    Robert Duncan." Sagetrieb: A Journal Devoted to Poets in the
    Pound-H.D.-Williams Tradition 4, nos. 2-3 [Robert Duncan
    Special Issue] (Fall-Winter):87-135.
        In this 7 January 1985 interview, Duncan occasionally men-
    tions Creeley's poetry and his relationship to Creeley.

2   BOWERING, GEORGE. Craft Slices. Ottawa: Oberon Press,
    pp. 24-25, 55-56.
        Briefly finds that St. Martin's details a healing process,
    mentions the source for the title of For Love, and acknowledges
    Creeley's influence on Vancouver poets.

3   BUCKEYE, ROBERT. "The Principle, the Demarkation Is Use:
    Selected Latters [sic] of Paul Blackburn in the Abernethy
    Library." Credences: A Journal of Twentieth Century Poetry
    and Poetics, n.s. 3, no. 2 (Spring):53-90.
        In these letters to Larry Bronfman from 21 May 1954 to 30
    October 1956, Blackburn provides a number of biographical details

concerning his relationship to Creeley, including their fight in
September 1954 in Mallorca. Blackburn also comments on Creeley's
character.

4   BUTTERICK, GEORGE F., ed. "Editor's Introduction" to Charles
     Olson and Robert Creeley: The Complete Correspondence. Vol.
     6. Santa Barbara, Calif.: Black Sparrow Press, pp. 7-11.
          Mentions Creeley's trip to France, and comments on his writ-
     ing and publishing in 1951.

5   CHRISTENSEN, PAUL [NORMAN]. "Creeley, Robert (White)." In
     Contemporary Poets. 4th ed. Edited by James Vinson and D.L.
     Kirkpatrick. New York: St. Martin's Press, 166-69.
          In an expansion and revision of 1979.3 with an updated bib-
     liography, comments on the role of the void in Creeley's work, and
     finds him a major poet.

6   COOK, ALBERT [SPAULDING]. "Maximizing Minimalism: The Con-
     struct of Image in Olson and Creeley." In Figural Choice in
     Poetry and Art. Hanover, N.H., and London: University Press
     of New England for Brown University, pp. 149-66, 244-45.
          Includes revisions of 1978.12 and 1982.7, and speculates on
     sources for Creeley's statement "Form is never more than an exten-
     sion of content."

7   CORMAN, CID. "Cid Corman." In Contemporary Authors: Auto-
     biography Series. Vol. 2. Edited by Adele Sarkissian.
     Detroit: Gale Research Co., pp. 129-47.
          Corman provides a few brief details about his relationship
     to Creeley and Creeley's to Blackburn.

8   CREELEY, ROBERT. Commentary on "For My Mother: Genevieve
     Jules Creeley, April 8, 1887-October 7, 1972." In 45 Contem-
     porary Poems: The Creative Process. Edited by Alberta T.
     Turner. New York and London: Longman, pp. 37-43.
          In a 7 May 1983 commentary in response to a series of
     comments and questions by Alberta Turner on "For My Mother:
     Genevieve Jules Creeley," Creeley discusses his intentions in the
     poem as they concern his mother and his emotions for her. Com-
     ments on the lineation and rhythm of the work as they delay any
     "pattern of statement" in order to avoid closure. Creeley also
     mentions his line endings, comparing them to those of W.C.
     Williams; his use of rhyme, especially half rhyme as well as
     assonance and consonance; and the influence of jazz on his use of
     monosyllabic words, short lines, and punctuation.

9   DAVIDSON, [ROBERT] MICHAEL. "Notes beyond the 'Notes':
     Wallace Stevens and Contemporary Poetics." In Wallace Stevens:
     The Poetics of Modernism. Edited by Albert [J.] Gelpi.

Cambridge Studies in American Literature and Culture, edited by Albert [J.] Gelpi. Cambridge: Cambridge University Press, pp. 141-60.
Briefly finds Creeley's statement that "form is never more than an extension of content" influenced by Stevens.

10   DUNCAN, ROBERT. "Towards an Open Universe." In *Fictive Certainties*. New York: New Directions, pp. 76-88.
Reprint of 1966.14.

11   HARRYMAN, CARLA. "The Middle." In *Writing/Talks*. Edited by Bob Perelman. Poetics of the New. Carbondale: Southern Illinois University Press, pp. 135-56.
Claims that for Creeley in *A Day Book*, the "daily proliferation [of language] arouses an argument to simplify," to reduce, unlike Larry Eigner who imitates the proliferation in "Blabbermouth."

12   KOSTELANETZ, RICHARD. "Poet's Prose." *American Book Review* 7, no. 3 (March-April):13-14.
In a review of *Claims for Poetry*, ed. Donald Hall (Ann Arbor: University of Michigan Press, 1982) finds Creeley's education is not, as he claims, "usual," and questions his agreement with Levertov's revision of his statement on the inseparability of form and content. See, especially, 1982.10-11.

13   LAWLOR, WILLIAM T. "Creeley's 'I Know a Man': A Metaphysical Conceit." *Iowa Review* 15, no. 2 (Spring-Summer):173-75.
Claiming the speaker of "I Know a Man" is both spiritually confused and drunk, explicates the poem with an emphasis on a religious Christian interpretation.

14   [MURRAY, TIMOTHY, et al.] *A Guide to the Modern Literary Manuscripts Collection in the Special Collections of the Washington University Libraries*. St. Louis: Washington University Libraries, pp. 28-33, passim.
Describes "The Robert Creeley Papers, the largest of Washington University's manuscript collections," basically listing all letters to and from a number of correspondents as well as manuscripts by these correspondents sent to Creeley. Also lists letters by Creeley in others' papers, his tapes, and proofs collected by the library. See also 1982.33.

15   OLSON, CHARLES, and CREELEY, ROBERT. *Charles Olson and Robert Creeley: The Complete Correspondence*. Vol. 6. Edited by George F. Butterick. Santa Barbara, Calif.: Black Sparrow Press, 244 pp.
Includes expanded versions of two letters in 1954.4 and other unpublished letters. In the correspondence between Creeley and Olson from 28 April to 27 July 1951, Creeley mentions his

correspondence with others, including Corman and Blackburn. Provides a portion of a letter from James Laughlin agreeing to publish his stories in New Directions in Prose and Poetry (no. 13
[1951]) and of Larry Eigner's letter reacting to Creeley's work in
Origin ([1st ser.], no. 2 [Summer 1951]). Creeley also refers to
his relationship to or feelings for Mitchell Goodman, Levertov,
and Rainer M. Gerhardt.
   Creeley comments on his sense of place, art, creativity, and
writing, especially writing as an act; and remarks on publishing
in Origin, Golden Goose, and elsewhere. Also discusses writing
and provides a chapter of an unpublished novel, an unpublished
short story "A Sort of a Song," and the essay "Notes on the Thea-
tre." He briefly mentions reading Ford Madox Ford, and provides a
number of biographical details including his impressions of France
and Europe and his financial situation. Also relates listening to
jazz and trying to find a place to live.
   Olson praises "Hart Crane ['He had been stuttering, by
the edge']," mentioning a few difficulties in the poem. Comments
on "The Honest Man," on an unpublished story, and on "Love ['Not
enough. The question: what is']," providing an early version of
this poem. Olson examines other prose pieces and short stories by
Creeley: notes the role of language and the use of sentences in
"Mr. Blue," suggesting a few more revisions; comments on "Notes
for a New Prose"; and surveys "3 Fate Tales," mentioning the
approval others at Black Mountain College gave the story. Creeley
also touches upon "3 Fate Tales" and notes Mitchell Goodman's
appraisal of the story. Olson occasionally mentions Creeley's
treatment of him and his work in Creeley's review of Y & X
(Montevallo Review 1, no. 2 [Summer 1951]:59-60). The editor
provides a photo of one of Creeley's letters to Olson.

16   PARKINSON, THOMAS. "The National Poetry Award." Sagetrieb:
     A Journal Devoted to Poets in the Pound-H.D.-Williams Tradition
     4, nos. 2-3 [Robert Duncan Special Issue] (Fall-Winter):309-21.
        In an included response to Duncan's receipt of The National
     Poetry Award (p. 312), Creeley briefly mentions Duncan's impor-
     tance to him.

17   PEARSON, TED. "Unit Structures." Poetics Journal, no. 5
     [Non/Narrative issue] (May), pp. 139-42.
        In a favorable review of "Mabel: A Story" and Other Prose,
     comments on Creeley's questioning of the "adequacy of narrative
     and . . . gender codes" and his "digressions and deferrals" in an
     attempt to retrieve narrative form.

18   PRUNTY, WYATT. "Emaciated Poetry." Sewanee Review 93, no. 1
     (January-March):78-94.
        Comments on Creeley's use of line breaks, a "halting pace,"
     enjambments, and diction in "I Know a Man" and "Quick-Step,"

RC1985

finding his reliance on such techniques gives a false sense of the
oracular to affectations and the whimsical. Relineates "Quick-
Step." See also 1985.21.

19   RUPPERT, JIM. "A More Mature Creeley." Contact II: A Poetry
     Review 7, nos. 36-37 (Fall):63-64.
          In a generally favorable review of Mirrors and Echoes, notes
     Creeley has always followed his perception and experience with
     precision. Finds he now distrusts the ability to know the natural
     world, and notes his treatment of age. Questions if memory can be
     a "path to experience" in a projectivist poetics.

20   SMITH, DAVE. Local Assays: On Contemporary American Poetry.
     Urbana: University of Illinois Press, p. 22.
          In an expanded version of a previous published essay, argues
     against Creeley's ideas on form and content.

21   STITT, PETER. "Tradition and the Innovative Godzilla."
     Georgia Review 39, no. 3 (Fall):635-48.
          In a brief, basically favorable review of The Collected
     Poems of Robert Creeley, 1945-1975, comments on "Swinging down
     Central," and finds the collection indiscriminate. Takes excep-
     tion with 1985.18.

22   SUKENICK, RONALD. "Writing on Writing; I. Robert Creeley."
     In In Form: Digressions on the Act of Fiction. Crosscurrents/
     Modern Critiques, edited by Jerome Klinkowitz, 3d ser.
     Carbondale: Southern Illinois University Press, pp. 226-31.
          Slight revision of 1981.30.

23   von HALLBERG, ROBERT. American Poetry and Culture, 1945-1980.
     Cambridge, Mass.: Harvard University Press, pp. 13, 38-53,
     passim.
          Mentions Creeley's publication history from 1952 to 1962 and
     includes a revision of 1978.72.

24   WATTEN, BARRETT. Total Syntax. Carbondale: Southern Illinois
     University Press, pp. 4-5, 98-99, 142-43, 175, 200.
          Compares Creeley to the symbolists in terms of his produc-
     tion of symbols and his emphasis on "the implicative character of
     illusions" over the "specificity of words."

25   WESLING, DONALD. "The Prosodies of Free Verse." In The New
     Poetries: Poetic Form since Coleridge and Wordsworth.
     Lewisberg, Pa.: Bucknell University Press; London, England,
     and Toronto, Ontario: Associated University Presses,
     pp. 145-71.
          Revision of 1971.23.

1986

1   ABBOTT, KEITH. "Brautigan in Bolinas." <u>Exquisite</u> <u>Corpse:</u> <u>A</u>
    <u>Monthly</u> <u>of</u> <u>Books</u> <u>and</u> <u>Ideas</u> 4, nos. 1–2 (January–February):
    12–13.
         Provides a reminiscence of Creeley at Richard Brautigan's
    house in Bolinas, California.

2   BARTLETT, LEE. <u>Talking</u> <u>Poetry:</u> <u>Conversations</u> <u>in</u> <u>the</u> <u>Workshop</u>
    <u>with</u> <u>Contemporary</u> <u>Poets</u>. Albuquerque: University of New
    Mexico Press, pp. 235–36, 245, 253, passim.
         A number of different poets briefly mention Creeley. Diane
    Wakoski, in her discussion, notes his development and his influ-
    ence on Dorn, and reminisces about Creeley reading at Buffalo in
    the early 1980s.

3   BERNSTEIN, CHARLES. "Hearing 'Here': Robert Creeley's Poetics
    of Duration." In <u>Content's</u> <u>Dream:</u> <u>Essays,</u> <u>1975–1984</u>. [<u>Sun</u>
    <u>and</u> <u>Moon:</u> <u>A</u> <u>Journal</u> <u>of</u> <u>Literature</u> <u>and</u> <u>Art</u>, nos. 17–18.] Los
    Angeles: Sun & Moon Press, pp. 292–304.
         Reprint of 1982.2.

4   CHARTERS, ANN. <u>Beats</u> <u>and</u> <u>Company:</u> <u>A</u> <u>Portrait</u> <u>of</u> <u>a</u> <u>Literary</u>
    <u>Generation</u>. Garden City, N.Y.: Doubleday & Co., Dolphin Book,
    pp. 130, 134, passim.
         Briefly mentions Creeley's relationship to Beat writers,
    especially Kerouac in 1956.

5   CREELEY, ROBERT. "Foreword" to <u>The</u> <u>Poet</u> <u>Exposed</u>, by
    Christopher Felver. New York: Alfred van der Marck Editions,
    pp. 8–9.
         In this foreword, Creeley provides some brief biographical
    information concerning his uncle.

6   _____. "The Girl Next Door." <u>Ironwood</u>, no. 28 [Listening for
    the Invisible: Emily Dickinson/Jack Spicer issue], pp. 38–50.
         In this 20 October 1985 lecture, Creeley mentions reading
    Dickinson and reading criticism on her. Notes some correspond-
    ences between his and her lives, providing a few biographical
    details about his friends and relatives.

7   _____. Note on "Après Anders." In <u>Memory</u> <u>Gardens</u>. New York:
    New Directions, p. ii.
         Very briefly notes that "Après Anders" is an improvisation
    on Richard Anders's poetry.

8   FINKELSTEIN, NORMAN [MARK]. "Pressing for the End." <u>Ironwood</u>
    14, no. 1 [whole no. 27] (Spring):59–70.

RC1986

Discusses Creeley's "devotion to personal revealed truth" instead of the historical, and finds he treats love as "eternal and pathetic." Believes he desires a finality in his poems but at the same time plays a "role of Love's servant . . . that never seems to rest." Comments on a number of poems, especially "Oh No."

9   KESSLER, JASCHA. Review of The Collected Poems of Robert Creeley, 1945-1975 in "Robert (White) Creeley." In Contemporary Literary Criticism: Excerpts from Criticism of the Works of Today's Novelists, Poets, Playwrights, Short Story Writers, Scriptwriters, and Other Creative Writers. Vol. 36. Edited by Daniel G. Marowski, Roger Matuz, and Jane E. Neidhardt. Detroit: Gale Research Co., p. 117.
In this text of a 23 March 1983 unfavorable review broadcast on KUSC-FM in Los Angeles, finds Creeley "has worked in a very narrow vein" with "only a few themes." Dislikes his "quirky obscurity" and solipsism. Believes his best work is on the theme of love, but finds that theme mostly in the poetry previous to 1960.

10 PAUL, SHERMAN. "Arriving." North Dakota Quarterly 54, no. 1 (Winter):51-58.
Discussing 1985.15, comments on Creeley and Olson's relationship and the biographical materials in the volume. Relates Creeley's letters to his fiction.

11 _____. In Search of the Primitive: Reading David Antin, Jerome Rothenberg, and Gary Snyder. Baton Rouge and London: Louisiana State University Press, pp. 83-84, passim.
Occasionally briefly compares Creeley to Antin, Snyder, and Rothenberg. Discusses Creeley's differences with Rothenberg in terms of deep image.

12 SILLIMAN, RON. "New Prose, New Prose Poetry." In Postmodern Fiction: A Bio-Bibliographical Guide. Edited by Larry McCaffery. Movements in the Arts, edited by Stanley Trachtenberg, no. 2. New York: Greenwood Press, pp. 157-74.
Notes that Creeley questions the notion of a unified self as a subject, and comments on his use of quantity as an "organizing principle" for his "intergeneric prose" sequences, especially Presences. Finds that "the poetic community" is the predominate audience for his fiction.

13 STEPHENS, MICHAEL [GREGORY]. The Dramaturgy of Style: Voice in Short Fiction. Crosscurrents/Modern Critiques, 3d ser. Carbondale: Southern Illinois University Press, pp. 68, 70, 72-74, 76-77, 92-93, passim.
Finds sources for Joel Oppenheimer's "voice-centered" and graceful poetry in Creeley and W.C. Williams's work, noting a few

differences, especially in the treatment of love. Also mentions
Creeley's influence on Gilbert Sorrentino.

1987

1   ASHLEY, PAUL. Review of <u>Memory</u> <u>Gardens</u>. <u>Another</u> <u>Chicago</u>
    <u>Magazine</u>, no. 17, pp. 191-97.
        In this favorable review, comments on the role of memory in
    the poems as well as the use of punctuation, word choice, and line
    breaks. Comments on a few poems, notably "Thanksgiving's Done"
    and "Echo ['Back in time']."

2   BUTTERICK, GEORGE F., ed. "Editor's Introduction" to <u>Charles</u>
    <u>Olson</u> and <u>Robert</u> <u>Creeley:</u> <u>The</u> <u>Complete</u> <u>Correspondence</u>. Vol.
    7. Santa Rosa, Calif.: Black Sparrow Press, pp. vii-xii.
        Provides biographical details of Creeley from July to
    October 1951, mentioning his writing and publishing, and char-
    acterizing his correspondence with Olson during this period.
    Notes Creeley's feelings for W.C. Williams.

3   _____. "Editor's Introduction" to <u>Charles</u> <u>Olson</u> <u>and</u> <u>Robert</u>
    <u>Creeley:</u> <u>The</u> <u>Complete</u> <u>Correspondence</u>. Vol. 8. Santa Rosa,
    Calif.: Black Sparrow Press, pp. vii-xii.
        Provides biographical details of Creeley from October to
    December 1951, mentioning his reading, his view of writing, his
    living conditions, and the importance of his correspondence with
    Olson for him.

4   CREELEY, ROBERT. On "The Whip." In <u>Ecstatic</u> <u>Occasions,</u> Expe-
    dient Forms: <u>65</u> <u>Leading</u> <u>Contemporary</u> <u>Poets</u> <u>Select</u> <u>and</u> <u>Comment</u>
    <u>on</u> <u>Their</u> <u>Poems</u>. Edited by David Lehman. New York: Macmillan
    Publishing Co.; London: Collier Macmillan Publishers,
    pp. 42-43.
        Creeley discusses form, listening to Charlie Parker, and the
    influence of Pound and W.C. Williams on his work. Notes the "im-
    plied narrative" of "The Whip" as in "The Musicians." Comments on
    the relationship of jazz to the poem's "rhythmic base" and its
    line length and duration.

5   [DRAVES, CORNELIA P., and FORTUNATO, MARY JANE.] "Robert
    Creeley." In <u>The</u> <u>Poet's</u> <u>Craft:</u> <u>Interviews</u> <u>from</u> <u>the</u> "<u>New</u> <u>York</u>
    <u>Quarterly</u>." [Rev. ed.] New York: Paragon House Publishers,
    pp. 153-77.
        Reprint of 1973.23.

6   FREDMAN, STEPHEN [ALBERT]. "Robert Creeley on the Ground."
    <u>North</u> <u>Dakota</u> <u>Quarterly</u> 55, no. 4 [Some Others: Contemporary
    American Poetry issue] (Fall):89-102.

RC1987

Finds Creeley, like many American poets who sense that their art lacks a "reality given by a unified tradition," attempts "to yoke nature and language together as a substitute for tradition," believing that words "reveal the truths and interconnection of nature and experience." Also notes his concern for a "picture-writing" is uniquely American, and mentions his "orientation toward words" as "objects with a right to stand on their own."

Claims that Creeley creates, as all projectivist poets, a limiting context for his work. Finds the projectivism of his poetry "uniquely dedicates itself to representing the activity of recognition" itself as it explores the ground of "experience in which the self finds itself," especially in his later poetry. Also notes the concentration on appearance and language as the ground of experience in the later poetry. Examines the treatment of words in "Corn Close" and the treatment of self-identity as well as the "self-enclosed mind engaged in reflection," the ground of present experience, in "This World." Also notes Creeley's use of "subtle modulations of sound" in "This World."

7   FRENCH, ROBERTS W. "Lawrence and American Poetry." In The Legend of D.H. Lawrence. Edited by Jeffrey Meyers. New York: St. Martin's Press, 109-34.
    Quoting an unpublished 12 April 1985 letter from Creeley, comments on the importance of Lawrence to him.

8   HARRIS, MARY EMMA. The Arts at Black Mountain College. Cambridge, Mass. and London: M.I.T. Press, pp. 178, 196, 200, 202, passim.
    Comments on Creeley's role at Black Mountain College and with the Black Mountain Review. Also mentions his correspondence with Olson, and provides a few biographical details, most significantly about the 1955 automobile accident that Creeley was involved in at Black Mountain.

9   MORAMARCO, FRED. "Pieces of a Mirror: Robert Creeley's Later Poetry." In Robert Creeley's Life and Work: A Sense of Increment. Edited by John Wilson. Under Discussion, edited by Donald Hall. Ann Arbor: University of Michigan Press, pp. 335-43.
    In a revised 29 December 1984 paper presented at the MLA Convention in Washington, D.C., finds a "sense of measure, which includes taking stock, assessing value, and discovering those things one values most, is what links Creeley's earlier and later work." Notes Creeley's early poetry broke from the modernist emphasis on memory, history, and tradition to a more spontaneous poetics emphasizing the present. Finds Later (1979) and Mirrors, however, emphasize the past, memory, aging, and the lack of surety. Mentions a few poems from these volumes, especially noting the treatment of weakness and the use of repetitions and rhythm in

"Prayer to Hermes." Also notes the role of memory in "Memory, 1930," and comments on the treatment of "the present incorporating the past" and the role of landscape in "Prospect." Compares Creeley's later poetry to that of Pound and W.C. Williams.

10   OLSON, CHARLES, and CREELEY, ROBERT. Charles Olson and Robert Creeley: The Complete Correspondence. Vol. 7. Edited by George F. Butterick. Santa Rosa, Calif.: Black Sparrow Press, 281 pp.

In the correspondence between Creeley and Olson from 25 July to 4 October 1951, Creeley mentions correspondence with others, including Kitasono Katsue, Mitchell Goodman, Caresse Crosby, Corman, and Pound. Also notes his relationship with Rainer M. Gerhardt, Ashley Bryan, Pound, and Richard Wirtz Emerson, including his plans to publish a booklet of his poems with Emerson. Emphasizes the importance for him to have Olson as a reader of his work. Includes portions of letters to him or about him and his stories from several people including Bryan and Vincent Ferrini. Creeley adds a letter to his mother from Alice A. Ainsworth, a former New Hampshire neighbor of his, providing biographical details. Ann Creeley occasionally adds to letters, providing biographical details and mentioning Creeley's sister, Helen. Creeley includes a 23 August 1951 letter from Adele Dogan, for William F. Morrow & Co., evaluating and rejecting his unpublished novel; Creeley includes his response in a 27 August 1951 letter to Dogan.

Provides biographical details about the births of his children, his lack of attachments to former homes, and Ann Creeley's upbringing and near marriage to another at Black Mountain College. Also comments on living in France, losing a child, and being jailed in Boston. Mentions his feelings for Corman and W.C. Williams.

Creeley occasionally refers to his writing of short stories and to his reading, including Hart Crane, Pound, Rimbaud, and Ernest Fenollosa. Discusses his unpublished novel, including its characters and its revisions. Comments on his short stories, especially "The Grace," "The Party," and "Mr. Blue," detailing his difficulties trying to revise the latter, and relates trying to write a new short story, probably "The Musicians." Sends an early version of "A Song ['I had wanted a quiet testament']," and comments on it. Mentions his use of the conjectural, his attempts "to move the base perception" in his work, and his publication in Origin, fragmente, and New Directions in Prose and Poetry.

Olson comments extensively on Creeley's unpublished novel, and discusses his short stories, including "Mr. Blue," "3 Fate Tales," "In the Summer," and "The Grace." Provides detailed comments and advice on Creeley's unpublished novel and "The Party," including suggested revisions for the latter. Mentions possibilities of getting Creeley's stories published. Reports on Vincent

RC1987

Ferrini's comments on his, Olson's, supposed influence on Creeley, adding how he corrected Ferrini.

In the notes, the editor includes portions of two letters: a September 1950 letter from Creeley to Jacob Leed not included in 1976.22 (n. 97) and a 2 August 1951 letter from W.C. Williams to Corman on Creeley (n. 64).

11 _____. Charles Olson and Robert Creeley: The Complete Correspondence. Vol. 8. Edited by George F. Butterick. Santa Rosa, Calif.: Black Sparrow Press, 280 pp.

In the correspondence between Creeley and Olson from 4 October to 28 December 1951, Creeley comments on his correspondence with Corman, Blackburn, Pound, Rainer M. Gerhardt, and René Laubiès. Mentions his relationship with Pound, Corman, Laubiès, Paul Goodman, W.C. Williams, Ira Grant, Richard Aldington, Donald Berlin, and Ashley Bryan, and his son David. Notes plans to meet Gerhardt, and includes portions of letters to him from Pound, Gerhardt, Laubiès, Corman, and Michell Goodman. Provides biographical details about an altercation with his French landlord and his life in France and New Hampshire. Also mentions past acquaintances, childhood memories, and hopes to leave France. Refers to a few dreams and his feelings about raising children.

Creeley also refers to his reading, including W.C. Williams, John Hawkes, Pound, Valéry, Stendhal, Shakespeare, Céline, Lawrence, and Coleridge. Comments on a number of his short stories, especially "3 Fate Tales," "The Party," and "Mr. Blue." Mentions writing "The Musicians" and "Jardou," reacting to Olson's comments on "Jardou." Notes the role of time and sequence in his short stories. Sends Olson unpublished early versions of poems, including "The Dead" and "Still Life Or," noting the intent of the latter. Mentions his plans to publish in Origin, New Mexico Quarterly, and fragmente, and to do a booklet with Richard Wirtz Emerson's (and Frederick Eckman's) Golden Goose Press. Discusses the selection and ordering of the poems to be published in Le Fou, noting his feelings for many of them.

Olson comments at length on an included early draft of "Jardou" (the editor provides a photo of the first page of the manuscript with Olson's notes). Olson also mentions "The Grace," Creeley's prose, and Creeley's relationship to Emerson. He advises Creeley on moving and requests his poems.

12 PERKINS, DAVID. A History of Modern Poetry: Modernism and After. Cambridge, Mass. and London: Harvard University Pres, Belknap Press, pp. 488, 505-7, passim.

Mentions the influence of W.C. Williams and Pound on Creeley, and notes his distinctive, nervous and minimal style. Comments on "The Business."

13 SAROYAN, ARAM. "Aram Saroyan." In Contemporary Authors: Autobiography Series. Vol. 5. Edited by Adele Sarkissian. Detroit: Gale Research Co., pp. 211-23.
Saroyan discusses Creeley's influence on him.

14 SILLIMAN, RON. "Controlling Interests." In The New Sentence. New York: Segue Foundation, Roof Books, pp. 171-84. Revision of 1982.42.

15 _____. "'My vocabulary did this to me.'" Acts: A Journal of New Writing, no. 6 [A Book of Correspondences for Jack Spicer issue, edited by David Levi Strauss and Benjamin Hollander], pp. 67-71.
Contrasts Spicer's sense of language to Creeley's.

16 WILLIAMS, WILLIAM CARLOS. "Excerpts from Letters to Robert Creeley." In Robert Creeley's Life and Work: A Sense of Increment. Edited by John Wilson. Under Discussion, edited by Donald Hall. Ann Arbor: University of Michigan Press, pp. 29-31.
In these portions from letters dated 8 November 1953 to 18 January 1960, Williams praises Creeley's work.

17 WILSON, JOHN, ed. "Bibliography." In Robert Creeley's Life and Work: A Sense of Increment. Under Discussion, edited by Donald Hall. Ann Arbor: University of Michigan Press, pp. 415-26.
Provides a primary bibliography of Creeley's works and a selected secondary bibliography on him.

18 _____. "Introduction" to Robert Creeley's Life and Work: A Sense of Increment. Under Discussion, edited by Donald Hall. Ann Arbor: University of Michigan Press, pp. 1-20.
Comments on Creeley's critical reception, use of the tradition, relationship to Olson, and treatment of love. Notes the source for "Versions" and the inversions, rhyme, and meter of "Kore." Mentions the influence of jazz and abstract expressionism on Words and Pieces, and refers to Creeley's minimalism as in "A Piece." Notes the reduction in "Mouths Nuzz" and the "pivoting in midclause" as in "['Down and']," a section of the 13 April entry in Hello: A Journal, February 29-May 3, 1976. Finds new concerns in Mirrors, noting his use of similes.

19 _____. Robert Creeley's Life and Work: A Sense of Increment. Under Discussion, edited by Donald Hall. Ann Arbor: University of Michigan Press, 426 pp.
As well as a few brief reviews, includes reprints of 1951.4; 1954.1; 1958.2; 1959.1; 1962.4; 1963.5; 1964.16; 1966.29;

RC1987

1967.16; 1968.15, 27; 1969.17; 1970.3, 11, 18, 24; 1973.42; 1978.32, 72–73; 1981.23; 1982.6; 1983.18, 24; 1984.21; reprints from 1968.22; 1969.15; 1970.32; 1978.63, 65; 1979.28; 1980.26, 31; 1981.2, 17; slight revisions of 1963.13; 1969.4; a reprint of chapter 3 from 1978.39; and a slight revision of chapter 4 from 1977.10 and 1978.33.

20   ZUKOFSKY, LOUIS. "A Letter to Robert Creeley." In Robert Creeley's Life and Work: A Sense of Increment. Edited by John Wilson. Under Discussion, edited by Donald Hall. Ann Arbor: University of Michigan Press, pp. 32–33.
        In this 11 October 1955 letter, Zukofsky comments on "The Gold Diggers" and Other Stories.

Edward Dorn

Major Works by Edward Dorn

1960   What I See in "The Maximus Poems." A Migrant Pamphlet.
Ventura, Calif.: Migrant.

1961   The Newly Fallen. New York: Totem Press in association with
the Paterson Society.

1964   From Gloucester Out. London: Matrix Press.

        Hands Up! New York: Totem Press in association with Corinth
Books.

1965   Geography. London: Fulcrum Press.

        Idaho Out. London: Fulcrum Press.

        The Rites of Passage: A Brief History. Buffalo, N.Y.:
Frontier Press. (Revised as By the Sound [1971].)

1966   The Shoshoneans: The People of the Basin-Plateau. Photographs
by Leroy Lucas. New York: William Morrow & Co.

1967   The North Atlantic Turbine. London: Fulcrum Press.

1968   Gunslinger, Book I. Los Angeles: Black Sparrow Press.

        Our Word: Guerrilla Poems from Latin America/Palabra de
guerrillero: Poesía guerrillera de Latinoamerica. Translated
by Edward Dorn and Gordon Brotherston. London: Cape Goliard
Press.

1969   Gunslinger, Book II. Los Angeles: Black Sparrow Press.
(Paperback version in 1970.)

        Pacheco, José Emilio. Arbol entre dos muros/Tree between Two
Walls. Translated by Edward Dorn and Gordon Brotherston. Los
Angeles: Black Sparrow Press.

Twenty-Four Love Songs. San Francisco: Frontier Press.

1970   *Gunslinger, 1 and 2*. London: Fulcrum Press.

Songs: Set Two: A Short Count. West Newbury, Mass.: Frontier Press.

1971   *By the Sound*. Mount Vernon, Wash.: Frontier Press. (Revision of *Rites of Passage* [1965].)

The Cycle. West Newbury, Mass.: Frontier Press.

Some Business Recently Transacted in the White World. West Newbury, Mass.: Frontier Press.

Spectrum Breakdown. A Microbook. N.p.: Athanor Books.

1972   *Gunslinger, Book III: The Winterbook, prologue to the great Book IIII: Kornerstone*. West Newbury, Mass.: Frontier Press.

1974   *Recollections of Gran Apachería*. San Francisco: Turtle Island Foundation.

1975   *The Collected Poems, 1956–1974*. Writing, edited by Donald [Merriam] Allen, no. 34. Bolinas, Calif.: Four Seasons Foundation.

Manchester Square. With Jennifer Dunbar. London and New York: Permanent Press.

Slinger. Berkeley, Calif.: Wingbow Press.

1976   *The Poet, the People, the Spirit*. Edited by Bob Rose. Transcribed by Derryll White. Vancouver, British Columbia: Talonbooks.

Vallejo, César. *Selected Poems*. Translated by Ed[ward] Dorn and Gordon Brotherston. Harmondsworth, Middlesex, England: Penguin Books.

1978   *Hello, La Jolla*. Berkeley, Calif.: Wingbow Press.

Selected Poems. Edited by Donald [Merriam] Allen. Bolinas, Calif.: Grey Fox Press.

1980   *Interviews*. Edited by Donald [Merriam] Allen. Writing, no. 38. Bolinas, Calif.: Four Seasons Foundation.

Views. Edited by Donald [Merriam] Allen. Writing, no. 40. San Francisco: Four Seasons Foundation.

1981   <u>Yellow Lola,</u> formerly titled <u>Japanese Neon</u> (<u>Hello La Jolla,</u>
        <u>Book II</u>). Santa Barbara, Calif.: Cadmus Editions.

1983   <u>Captain Jack's Chaps; or, Houston/MLA.</u> Madison, Wis.: Black
        Mesa Press.

        <u>The Collected Poems, 1956-1974.</u> Enlarged ed. Writing, edited
        by Donald [Merriam] Allen, no. 34. San Francisco: Four
        Seasons Foundation.

Writings about Edward Dorn

1959

1 DORN, EDWARD. "Ed Dorn in Santa Fe." <u>Migrant</u>, no. 3
   (November), pp. 17-22.
      In this third and last section of a longer work, Dorn pro-
   vides some biographical details concerning his stay in Santa Fe,
   New Mexico.

1960

1 DORN, EDWARD. Statement for the Paterson Society. [Cambridge,
   Mass.: Paterson Society], 1 p.
      In this statement, Dorn mentions his reason for writing
   poetry and reading his work publicly. Also comments on the types
   of things he writes about. Reprinted: 1980.6.

2 _____. What <u>I</u> See in "The <u>Maximus</u> Poems." A Migrant Pamphlet.
   Ventura, Calif.: Migrant, 17 pp.
      Dorn describes living in Santa Fe, New Mexico, and notes his
   sense of ego and place. Reprinted: 1961.3; 1973.4; 1980.6.

3 "What <u>I</u> See in 'The <u>Maximus</u> Poems.'" <u>Migrant</u>, no. 6
   (May), insert, 1 p.
      In this lengthy advertisement for What <u>I</u> See in <u>"The Maximus
   Poems,"</u> focuses on Dorn's idea of place.

1961

1 CREELEY, ROBERT. "Ed Dorn in the News." <u>Floating Bear: A
   Newsletter</u>, no. 6 [(April), p. 11].
      In a favorable review of <u>The Newly Fallen</u>, notes Dorn's
   use of the line, his anger, and his treatment of the topical.
   Reprinted: 1970.1; 1973.2.

ED1961

2   DORN, ED[WARD]. "New York, New York." <u>Floating</u> <u>Bear</u>: <u>A</u> <u>News</u>-
     <u>letter</u>, no. 8 [(May), pp. 10-12].
          Dorn provides a few biographical details about a trip to New
     York and a stopover in Chicago. Reprinted: 1973.3. Slightly
     revised: 1980.6.

3   _____. "What I See in <u>The</u> <u>Maximus</u> <u>Poems</u>." <u>Kulchur</u>, no. 4,
     pp. 31-44.
          Reprint of 1960.2.

4   OPPENHEIMER, JOEL. "Given Other Necessities: About <u>The</u> <u>Newly</u>
     <u>Fallen</u>, Ed Dorn, 1961." <u>Kulchur</u> 1, no. 4:102-4.
          In a sympathetic review of <u>The</u> <u>Newly</u> <u>Fallen</u>, discusses its
     "compression and weight," eclecticism, precision, and "domestic
     concerns."

                            1962

1   DORN, ED[WARD]. "Nose from Newswhere." <u>Floating</u> <u>Bear</u>: <u>A</u>
     <u>Newsletter</u>, no. 20 [(May), p. 10].
          Dorn provides a few biographical details from May 1961,
     especially concerning his trip to Salt Lake City, Utah, to pick up
     Ammon Hennacy. Reprinted: 1973.3; 1980.6. Slightly revised with
     errors: 1965.2.

2   HAZEL, ROBERT. "Embodied Knowledge." <u>Nation</u> 194, no. 3
     (20 January):64-65.
          In a favorable review of <u>The</u> <u>Newly</u> <u>Fallen</u>, notes Dorn's
     skill and accuracy in a number of poems. Comments on "Sousa" and
     "The Biggest Killing."

                            1963

1   DORN, EDWARD. "Clay." <u>Kulchur</u> 3, no. 12 (Winter):81-82.
          Dorn apparently provides the substance of a talk he gave to
     a class on James Joyce's "Clay."

2   OSSMAN, DAVID. "Ed Dorn." In <u>The</u> <u>Sullen</u> <u>Art</u>: <u>Interviews</u> <u>by</u>
     <u>David</u> <u>Ossman</u>. New York: Corinth Books, pp. 82-86.
          In this February 1961 interview for WBAI in New York, Dorn
     comments on going to Black Mountain College and the dissimilarity
     between Black Mountain poets. Also mentions his writing in terms
     of what he knows and his use of the line as a "clot of phrase."
     Notes writing in terms of political issues, writing a "fantasy of
     politics." Reprinted: 1980.5.

                            178

1964

1 OLSON, CHARLES. A Bibliography on America for Ed Dorn.
   Writing, no. 1. [San Francisco]: Four Seasons Foundation,
   16 pp.
      Provides Dorn with a list of readings. Reprinted with
   notes: 1974.9. See also 1980.7.

1965

1 DAVIE, DONALD. Review of Rites of Passage. Wivenhoe Park
   Review, no. 1 (Winter), pp. 112-18.
      In this lengthy, favorable review, discusses Dorn's style,
   comparing it to Mary Austin's in her The Land of Little Rain
   (Boston: Houghton Mifflin Co., 1903). Finds his style personal
   and lyric, and notes Dorn's ability to shift between levels of
   style. Examining the narrative voice, finds "the narrator does
   not exist as a voice in any way distinct from the author's."
   Reprinted: 1967.3.

2 DORN, ED[WARD]. "Nose from Nowhere [sic]." Quixote (Madison,
   Wis.) 1, no. 2 (December):21-23.
      Slight revision, with errors in title and dates, of 1962.1.

3 DORN, EDWARD. "Preface" to Idaho Out. London: Fulcrum Press,
   [p. 3].
      In this preface, Dorn implies that Idaho Out concerns an
   arbitrary place and is likewise arbitrary.

4 LINICK, ANTHONY. "A History of the American Literary Avant-
   Garde since World War II." Ph.D. dissertation, University of
   California, Los Angeles, pp. 106-7, 384, passim.
      Occasionally mentions Dorn as a member of the avant-garde,
   noting his contributions to little magazines. Provides a poll of
   avant-garde writers ranking the importance of Dorn. See
   Dissertation Abstracts International 25 (1965):7226.

5 WESLING, DONALD. "Berkeley: Free Speech and Free Verse."
   Nation 201, no. 15 (8 November):338-40.
      Notes Dorn's participation in the 1965 Berkeley Poetry Con-
   ference, commenting on his 21 July lecture (later published as
   1976.5).

1966

1 CREELEY, ROBERT. "Edward Dorn's Geography." Stand: Quarterly
   of the Arts 8, no. 2:74-76.

ED1966

In this favorable review, stresses Dorn's political poetry
and his literalness, disclosing "dry, tough, drawn, harsh,
unrelieved experience." Also notes his "careful thought and
weighted insight." Reprinted: 1970.1.

2   DORN, EDWARD. The Shoshoneans: The People of the Basin-
     Plateau. Photographs by Leroy Lucas. New York: William
     Morrow & Co., 96 pp.
         Dorn provides numerous biographical details from the summer
of 1965 as he traveled through the Basin-Plateau, focusing on his
relationship to Shoshoni Indians as well as the hostility of the
white culture to him and Leroy Lucas. See also 1976.5.

3   McGRATH, TOM. "Much More Than Protest." Peace News (London),
     25 February, p. 5.
         In a favorable review of Geography, notes the volume's re-
ception in England, and finds Dorn an intelligent Black Mountain
poet practicing a poetry more complex and concise than that of the
Beats. Finds "A Letter, in the Meantime, Not to Be Mailed,
Tonight" needlessly ambiguous.

4   NEWTON, J.M. "Two Men Who Matter?" Cambridge Quarterly 1, no.
     3 (Summer):284-98.
         In a favorable review of The Rites of Passage, finds a
truthfulness and freedom to the "meditative record," which appears
to be factual. Comments on the relaxed "transition from one feeling or mood to another."

5   PHELPS, DONALD. "Ed Dorn's Transients." For Now, no. 4,
     pp. 29-33.
         In a sympathetic review of The Rites of Passage as an exam-
ple of the "new journalism," emphasizes Dorn's theme of "the
struggle . . . of hard-driven people against the wastefulness
which engulfs them." Compares aspects of this "chronicle" to
earlier poems including "The Open Road." See 1974.6. Reprinted:
1969.2.

<u>1967</u>

1   CLARK, WALTER VAN TILBERG. "Red Men in a White World." New
     York Times Book Review 72, no. 11 (12 March):6-7, 37.
         In an unfavorable review of The Shoshoneans, finds Dorn's
text subjective, biased, and chaotic.

2   COMBS, MAXINE [SOLOW] GAUTHIER. "A Study of the Black Mountain
     Poets." Ph.D. dissertation, University of Oregon, pp. 1-2,
     146-59.

Commenting on a number of poems, especially "The Sparrow
Sky," "Goodbye to the Illinois" from "3 Farm Poems," and "Idaho
Out," notes Dorn's sense of location, of place, and his treatment
of American society and of nature as "a reflection of his own
attitudes . . . [and] a force which can . . . speak to him."
Discusses his social criticism. Comments on his style, including
his use of varying stanzaic patterns, shifting points of view, and
his method of intertwining different events and time frames, using
"Sousa" to illustrate. See Dissertation Abstracts International
28 (1968):3666A.

3   DAVIE, DONALD. "The Authority of Voice." Michigan Quarterly
     Review 6, no. 2 (Spring/April):133-36.
          Reprint of 1965.1.

4   Review of The Shoshoneans. Choice 4, no. 3 (November):1054,
     1056.
          In this very brief, adverse review, notes Dorn's errors.

5   WELLS, MERLE W. Review of The Shoshoneans. Pacific Northwest
     Quarterly 58, no. 4 (October):210.
          In this basically favorable review, finds Dorn lacks some
     sophistication and historical understanding, but believes the
     volume is "an effective presentation of the contemporary Indian
     scene."

1968

1   BANKS, RUSSELL. Review of Gunslinger, Book I. Lillabulero: A
     Journal of Contemporary Writing, 2d ser., no. 6 (Fall-Winter),
     pp. 68-71.
          In this favorable review, finds parallels to Olson's Maximus
     Poems, W.C. Williams's Paterson, and Pound's Cantos. Believes
     Dorn uses "uniquely American" materials to create a "horse opera"
     that "succeeds as epic." Focuses on the character of Slinger.

2   B[ROTHERSTON], G[ORDON], and D[ORN], E[DWARD], trans. Preface
     to Our Word: Guerrilla Poems from Latin America/Palabra de
     guerrillero: Poesía guerrillera de Latinoamerica. London:
     Cape Goliard Press, [pp. 2-3].
          In this preface in both Spanish and English, Brotherston and
     Dorn mention the intention of Our Word.

3   COLLINS, RAYMOND DOUGLAS, Jr. "Four Short Story Writers from
     Black Mountain College." M.A. thesis, University of North
     Carolina, pp. 44-69.
          Discusses the characterization, the treatment of place and
     loneliness, and the role of deficiency in "C.B. & Q.," finding

ED1968

fault with Dorn's attempt to "'dramatize' the idea that for most
men most places are non-places." Mentions the treatment of place
and of Beauty in "Beauty," and comments on the story as "a re-
enactment of Dorn's living in Albuquerque." In "1st Avenue,"
comments on the homelessness and loneliness. Calls Dorn a "for-
malist" and notes his preference for the lower classes and the
poor as characters in his short stories.

4   FAUCHEREAU, SERGE. Lecture de la poésie américaine. [In
    French.] Critique. Paris: Éditions de Minuit, pp. 240-42,
    passim.
       Briefly comments on the influence of Whitman on Dorn and
Dorn's use of geography. Translated into Rumanian with a new
introduction: 1974.5.

5   GOODER, R.D. "The Work of a Poet." Cambridge Quarterly 3, no.
    1 (Winter 1967-68):73-83.
       In a favorable review of The Shoshoneans, notes Leroy
Lucas's photographs, and discusses Dorn's knowledge of the Indians. Finds it a book of poetic discovery.

                                1969

1   DORN, EDWARD. "Driving across the Prairie." Evergreen Review
    13, no. 68 (July):33-37, 78.
       In this essay, Dorn reminisces about his home town, child-
hood, and adolescence. Reprinted: 1971.2.

2   PHELPS, DONALD. "Ed Dorn's Transients." In Covering Ground:
    Essays for Now. New York: Croton Press, pp. 122-27.
       Reprint of 1966.5.

3   RABAN, JONATHAN. "Chance, Time, and Silence: The New American
    Verse." Journal of American Studies 3, no. 1 (July):89-101.
       Noting that a "single syntactical activity controls both the
cowboy's eyes and the sky" in "Vaquero," finds Dorn's syntax and
tone "merges conceptually discrete elements into a single, unified
linguistic register." Feels such a register can synthesize "politics, styles, and manners" and combine the trivial with the momentous, using portions of "The North Atlantic Turbine" and "Oxford"
as examples. Comments on Dorn's humor, playfulness, and spontaneity as in "A Notation on the Evening of November 27, 1966."

4   SHARP, ROBIN. Review of Our Word. Agenda 7, no. 2 (Spring):
    88-89.
       In this unfavorable review, finds the translation poor.

                                182

1970

1   CREELEY, ROBERT. A Quick Graph: Collected Notes and Essays.
    Edited by Donald [Merriam] Allen. Writing, edited by Donald
    [Merriam] Allen, no. 22. San Francisco: Four Seasons Founda-
    tion, pp. 215-20.
      Includes reprints of 1961.1; 1966.1.

2   DAVIE, DONALD. "The Black Mountain Poets: Charles Olson and
    Edward Dorn." In Survival of Poetry: A Contemporary Survey.
    Edited by Martin Dodsworth. London: Faber & Faber,
    pp. 216-34.
      Discusses Dorn's emphasis "on the local terrain," on local-
    ity, and on locating in such poems as "Oxford." Also notes, as in
    "Idaho Out," his use of humor and the West. Comments on the humor
    in Gunslinger, 1 and 2. Reprinted: 1977.2 with an additional
    postscript.

3   _____. "John Ledyard: The American Traveler and His Senti-
    mental Journeys." Eighteenth-Century Studies: An Inter-
    disciplinary Journal 4, no. 1 (Fall):57-70.
      Very briefly notes Dorn's treatment of Ledyard in his
    "Ledyard: The Exhaustion of Sheer Distance."

4   DURGNAT, RAYMOND. "Bone Power and Black Mountain Blues."
    Poetry Review 61, no. 2 (Summer):162-65.
      In an unfavorable review of Gunslinger, 1 and 2, finds the
    work intellectualizing and "literary instead of mythical." Notes
    a few possible allegorical readings.

5   RAY, DAVID. "Dorn, Edward." In Contemporary Poets of the
    English Language. Edited by Rosalie Murphy and James Vinson.
    Chicago and London: St. James Press, pp. 302-4.
      Provides brief bibliography, and notes Dorn's exuberance and
    treatment of America. Reprinted with expanded bibliography:
    1975.6; 1980.12; 1985.6.

1971

1   COONEY, SEAMUS. A Checklist of the First One Hundred Publica-
    tions of the Black Sparrow Press. Los Angeles: Black Sparrow
    Press, pp. 22-23, 29.
      Provides brief descriptive bibliographical information on
    Gunslinger, Book I, Gunslinger, Book II, and Dorn and
    Brotherston's translation of Arbol entre dos muros/Tree between
    two Walls, by José Emilio Pacheco. (But see 1981.10.)

ED1971

2   DORN, EDWARD. "Driving across the Prairie." In Some Business
     Recently Transacted in the White World. West Newbury, Mass.:
     Frontier Press, pp. 54–65.
          Reprint of 1969.1.

3   _____. "A Narrative with Scattered Nouns." In Some Business
     Recently Transacted in the White World. West Newbury, Mass.:
     Frontier Press, pp. 1–9.
          Dorn provides a few biographical details about his "sojourn
     in New England."

4   MARTIEN, NORMAN. "I Hear America Singing." Partisan Review
     38, no. 1:122–27.
          In a favorable review of Gunslinger, Book I and Gunslinger,
     Book II, focuses on the comedy and the character of Slinger.

5   OLSON, CHARLES. Poetry and Truth: The Beloit Lectures and
     Poems. Transcribed and edited by George F. Butterick.
     Writing, edited by Donald [Merriam] Allen, no. 27. San
     Francisco: Four Seasons Foundation, pp. 48, 69.
          Olson briefly claims to have borrowed the word "orn" from
     Dorn. Butterick's note speculates on the borrowing. Reprinted:
     1979.8.

6   RABAN, JONATHAN. The Society of the Poem. London: George G.
     Harrap & Co., pp. 126–31, passim.
          Charts the development of Dorn's voice from a childish but
     "appealing whimsy, a studied simplese," to a "straight-talking
     monologue" in "A Theory of Truth," a section of "The North
     Atlantic Turbine." Notes the social criticism and the irony of
     the speaking voice in Gunslinger, 1 and 2.

7   WESLING, DONALD. "The Prosodies of Free Verse." In Twentieth-
     Century Literature in Retrospect. Edited by Reuben A. Brower.
     Harvard English Studies, no. 2. Cambridge, Mass.: Harvard
     University Press, pp. 155–87.
          Uses the opening of "Hemlocks" as an example of a "dis-
     membered" poetic line giving "an elegiac drone." Gives a section
     from Gunslinger, Book II as an example of the poet's voice resid-
     ing "just beneath the narrative line." Notes that "the public
     voice emerges from the private one" in this type of political
     poetry. Revised: 1985.11.

                              1972

1   ALBERT, BARRY. "Ed Dorn: An Interview." Vort, no. 1 [Ed
     Dorn/Tom Raworth Number] (Fall), pp. 2–20.

                              184

In this 31 July 1972 interview, Dorn comments on many of his books, especially the characterization of Carl Wyman and the use of autobiographical materials in By the Sound; the intimacy and fragmentary nature of Some Business Recently Transacted in the White World; and the nature of The Newly Fallen as a collection of poems. Mentions the song quality of the work in Twenty-Four Love Songs and Songs: Set Two. Notes the poet's presence, the voices, and different figures, especially the philosophers and the character I, in Slinger. Also discusses the nature of Robart and sources for the literate projector in "The Cycle." Remarks on the role of both The Cycle and Bean News in Slinger.

Dorn also provides biographical information about going to Black Mountain College and the University of Illinois, about his relationship to Olson, Creeley, and Ray Obermeyer, and about working in Santa Fe, New Mexico, and Pocatello, Idaho. Elaborates on his comparison, from 1960.2, of Santa Fe with Gloucester, Massachusetts, in terms of their fertility for the creation of art. Comments on his use of the long poem and of narrative poetry, especially "Idaho Out," and notes his interest in Carl Ortwin Sauer and entrepreneurs. Discusses the composition of "An Idle Visitation" and "The World Box-Score Cup of 1966," mentions the changes in tone and attention in his work, and briefly notes his treatment of the British in "Thesis." Reprinted: 1980.5.

2 _____. "The Inside Real and the Outsideral." Vort, no. 1 [Ed Dorn/Tom Raworth Number] (Fall), pp. 27-28.
    Briefly comments on Dorn's emphasis on experiential knowledge rather than codified knowledge, finding the former in a "state in which internal perceptions are balanced by external perceptions in time" in Gunslinger, Book III.

3 ANDREWS, DAVID G. "An Actual Earth of Value: The Development in the Concept of Landscape in The Maximus Poems of Charles Olson." M.A. thesis, Carleton University, pp. 6-9, passim.
    Briefly mentions Dorn's treatment of Gloucester, Massachusetts, and Olson in "From Gloucester Out."

4 DAVIE, DONALD. "Ed Dorn and the Treasures of Comedy." Vort, no. 1 [Ed Dorn/Tom Raworth Number] (Fall), pp. 24-25.
    Examines the "comic vision" of Slinger, finding the poem is not satirical, frivolous, reflexive, or social.

5 DORN, EDWARD. "September Entries." Tansy, no. 5 (Spring-Summer), pp. 58-79.
    Dorn provides a few biographical details from 1-22 September 1971, including his relationship to Donald Hall, and mentions some of his reading.

ED1972

6   DORN, JENNY [JENNIFER] DUNBAR.   "The Day Report."   Tansy, no. 5
     (Spring-Summer), pp. 58-79.
         Jennifer Dorn provides a few biographical details concerning
     Dorn from 1-22 September 1971.

7   WIATER, MICHAEL.   "The Terrific Actualism"   Toothpick, Lisbon,
     and the Orcas Islands 2, nos. 1-2 [whole no. 3] [The Wiater/
     Scott Issue] (Fall):[113-16].
         Briefly comments on Dorn and his work, and provides a por-
     tion of a letter from Dorn on working in the state of Washington.

1973

1   BUTTERICK, GEORGE F.   "Edward Dorn: A Checklist."   Athanor,
     no. 5 (Winter), pp. 51-68.
         Lists all books, pamphlets, broadsides, recordings, and
     appearances in anthologies by Dorn as well as interviews with,
     reviews of, and articles on Dorn.   See also 1973.6.

2   CREELEY, ROBERT.   "Edward Dorn in the News."   In The Floating
     Bear: A Newsletter.   Edited by Diane di Prima and LeRoi Jones.
     La Jolla, Calif.:   Laurence McGilvery, p. 55.
         Reprint of 1961.1.

3   DORN, EDWARD.   "New York, New York" and "Nose from Newswhere."
     In The Floating Bear: A Newsletter.   Edited by Diane di Prima
     and LeRoi Jones.   La Jolla, Calif.:   Laurence McGilvery, pp.
     78-80, 226, 568.
         Reprints of 1961.2; 1962.1 with note (no. 40).

4   _____ .   "What I See in The Maximus Poems."   In Poetics of the
     New American Poetry.   Edited by Donald [Merriam] Allen and
     Warren Tallman.   New York: Grove Press, pp. 293-307.
         Reprint of 1960.2.

5   ELLMANN, RICHARD, and O'CLAIR, ROBERT, eds.   "Edward Dorn."   In
     The Norton Anthology of Modern Poetry.   New York: W.W. Norton
     & Co., pp. 1210-11.
         Provides an overview of Dorn's life and work, noting the
     influence of Olson and commenting on Slinger.

6   STREETER, DAVID, comp.   A Bibliography of Ed Dorn.   New York:
     Phoenix Bookshop, 64 pp.
         Descriptively lists all primary Dorn publications, including
     books, broadsides, and recordings.   Lists secondary materials
     including reviews and biographical items.   See also 1973.1.

1974

1 BERTHOLF, ROBERT [JOHN]. "The Fictive Voice in the Poem: A First Statement." Io, no. 19 [Mind, Memory, and Psyche issue], pp. 7-15.
Finds Dorn one of the "current masters of the fictive voice of the poem" since he projects, in Slinger, "the geography of the American West," peopled with "personalities which cannot be fixed as the poet's." Reprinted: 1975.1.

*2 "Black Mountain: Olson, Dorn, Williams, Creeley, Cage at St. Andrews." Star-Web Paper, no. 4, pp. 52-68.
Unavailable for annotation. Listed in Mary Emma Harris's The Arts at Black Mountain College (Cambridge, Mass., and London: M.I.T. Press, 1987), p. 288.

3 DAWSON, FIELDING. Review of Some Business Recently Transacted in the White World. World, no. 29 (April), pp. 19-20.
In this favorable review, explicates a section of "The Terrifik Refinery in Biafra," and comments on Dorn's puns, his complexity and his ear. Claims Dorn "has his ego directly in the center of his consciousness, so that his moves are certain."

4 DORN, EDWARD. Introduction to To Max Douglas, by Kenneth Irby. [Tansy, no. 8.] [Lawrence, Kans.]: Tansy-Pegleg Press, [pp. 1-2].
In this introduction, Dorn mentions his mother, Louise Abercrombie Dorn, and himself as products of "the prairie sub-region" and provides reminiscences of being with Irby.

5 FAUCHEREAU, SERGE. Introducere în poezia americană modernă. [In Rumanian.] Translated by C. Abălută and Şt. Stoenescu. Biblioteca Pentru Toti, no. 810. Bucharest: Editura Minerva, pp. 289-91, passim.
A translation of 1968.4 with a new introduction.

6 MOTTRAM, ERIC. "The Performance of the Comedian under Law: The Criticism of Donald Phelps." Vort 2, no. 3 [whole no. 6] [Gilbert Sorrentino/Donald Phelps issue] (Fall):141-57.
Occasionally compares Dorn to Phelps, and discusses Phelps's criticism of Dorn, especially 1966.5.

7 NAVERO, WILLIAM. "Duncan, Creely [sic], and Dorn." Ethos (State University of New York at Buffalo) 8, no. 14 (12 December):27-28.
Notes the clarity, precision, and "multiple possibility of focus" of Recollections of Gran Apachería.

8   OKADA, ROY K. "An Interview with Edward Dorn." <u>Contemporary</u>
     <u>Literature</u> 15, no. 3 (Summer):297-314.
         In this 2 May 1973 interview, Dorn provides biographical
     details about wandering and working in the West, going to Black
     Mountain College, and teaching at Kent State. He comments on his
     relationship to Olson and mentions receiving Olson's <u>A Bibliog-</u>
     <u>raphy</u> <u>on</u> <u>America</u> <u>for</u> <u>Ed</u> <u>Dorn</u>. Discusses his sense of evil, the
     West, and England, and notes that his interest in geography cen-
     ters on "human movement." Feels he has "always been a narrative
     poet," even in the songs in <u>Geography</u>. Comments on the title of
     <u>Geography</u>, on the republication and titling of <u>By</u> <u>the</u> <u>Sound</u>, and
     on Idaho and Montana in "Idaho Out." Claims John Zachary Young's
     <u>Model</u> <u>of</u> <u>the</u> <u>Brain</u> (Oxford: Clarendon Press, 1964) is the source
     for "An Octupus Thinks with Its Arms."
         Recounts beginning <u>Slinger</u> as "An Idle Visitation," dis-
     cussing the former as a "psychological drama." In <u>Slinger</u> out-
     lines a "shift from geography to intensity," and comments on his
     use of language. Explains that reversals and backward spellings
     violate the "forwardness of the book." Discusses the Literate
     Projector and Sllab, the character of I, Lil, and Howard Hughes,
     and the use of the names of Heidegger, Parmenides, and Lévi-
     Strauss. Mentions writing <u>Slinger</u>, especially book 3, and the
     role and production of <u>Bean</u> <u>News</u>, providing attributions for dif-
     ferent sections. Describes a film script, <u>Abeline!</u> <u>Abeline!</u>, that
     he wrote for Stan Brakhage based on <u>Slinger</u>. Also mentions
     Michael Wiater's plan to make <u>Slinger</u> into a radio serial.
     Reprinted: 1980.5; 1983.5.

9   OLSON, CHARLES. "A Bibliography on America for Ed Dorn." In
     <u>Additional</u> <u>Prose:</u> <u>"A</u> <u>Bibliography</u> <u>on</u> <u>America,"</u> <u>"Propriocep-</u>
     <u>tion,"</u> <u>and</u> <u>Other</u> <u>Notes</u> <u>and</u> <u>Essays</u>, by Charles Olson. Edited by
     George F. Butterick. Writing, edited by Donald [Merriam] Allen,
     no. 31. Bolinas, Calif.: Four Seasons Foundation, pp. 1-14,
     81-84.
         Reprint of 1964.1 with notes by the editor.

10   SMITH, DONALD NEWTON, [Jr.]. "The Origins of Black Mountain
     Poetry." Ph.D. dissertation, University of North Carolina,
     pp. 406-8.
         Comments on Dorn's relationship to Olson, and notes his
     "obsession with space" and geography. See <u>Dissertation</u> <u>Abstracts</u>
     <u>International</u> 35 (1974):3771-72A.

1975

1   BERTHOLF, ROBERT [JOHN]. "The Fictive Voice in the Poem:
     Chapter I, Part I." <u>Credences</u>, [o.s.] 1, no. 1 [whole no. 1]
     (February):84-93.
         Reprint of 1974.1.

*2   CHRISTENSEN, PAUL NORMAN. "Charles Olson: Call Him Ishmael."
      Ph.D. dissertation, University of Pennsylvania, 392 pp.
          Dissertation was restricted, unavailable for annotation.
      See published version: 1979.2. See Dissertation Abstracts
      International 36 (1976):8056A.

3   CREELEY, ROBERT. "Hier soir: Au hasard de mes souvenirs de
      San Francisco (Mars-Juin 1956)." [In French.] Translated by
      Etienne de Planchard. Entretiens, [no. 34?] [Beat Generation
      issue], pp. 163-66.
          Creeley mentions his contacts with Dorn in March-June 1956
      in San Francisco, providing a few biographical details. In
      English: 1979.3.

4   "Dorn, Edward (Merton)." In World Authors, 1950-1970. Edited
      by John Wakeman. New York: H.W. Wilson Co., pp. 215-17.
          Provides a brief overview of Dorn's life and work, noting
      the critical reception.

5   DORN, EDWARD. "Preface" to The Collected Poems, 1956-1974.
      Writing, edited by Donald [Merriam] Allen, no. 34. Bolinas,
      Calif.: Four Seasons Foundation, p. v.
          In this preface, Dorn briefly mentions his publication
      habits, the structures of the volumes included in The Collected
      Poems, 1956-1974, and his relationship to his readers.

6   RAY, DAVID. "Dorn, Ed(ward Merton)." In Contemporary Poets.
      Edited by James Vinson and D.L. Kirkpatrick. 2d ed. London:
      St. James Press; New York: St. Martin's Press, pp. 387-89.
          Reprint of 1970.5 with an expanded bibliography. See also
      1980.12; 1985.6.

7   von HALLBERG, ROBERT. "The Scholar's Art: The Poetics and
      Poetry of Charles Olson." Ph.D. dissertation, Stanford Uni-
      versity, pp. 257-59, 385-59, 428, 484, passim.
          Notes that Olson's "ideational discourse," as that of Eliot
      and Marianne Moore, influenced Dorn. Briefly comments on Dorn's
      lack of interest in meter and lineation, and quotes from two 1962
      letters from Dorn to Amiri Baraka (then LeRoi Jones) on the par-
      ticular and on imagism. Revised: 1978.14. See Dissertation
      Abstracts International 37 (1976):974-75A.

                                   1976

1   AKEROYD, JOANNE VINSON, and BUTTERICK, GEORGE F. Where Are
      Their Papers? A Union List Locating the Papers of Forty-Two
      Contemporary American Poets and Writers. Bibliography Series,
      no. 9. Storrs: University of Connecticut Library, p. 23.

ED1976

Provides locations for specific manuscripts and papers of
Dorn.

2   BROMIGE, DAVID. "The Poetry of Edward Dorn." San Francisco
     Review of Books 1, no. 10 (February):21-22.
         In a favorable review of The Collected Poems, 1956-1974,
     Slinger, and Recollections of Gran Apachería, emphasizes the scorn
     of the satire in the first book and the accuracy and the "range of
     reference" in the second. Terms Recollections of Gran Apachería
     "a Romance of Resistance--even unto death."

3   BYRD, DON. "From 'The Barbaric Obedience: Desperate Medita-
     tions on the End of Kultural History.'" Io, no. 23 [An Olson-
     Melville Sourcebook, vol. 2, The Mediterranean, Eurasia],
     pp. 132-63.
         Notes "the appearance of space closed against its universal
     on-goingness" and the role of distance and Van Gogh's painting in
     Dorn's "Poem in Five Parts."

4   DORN, EDWARD. "Introduction" to The Poet, the People, the
     Spirit. Vancouver, British Columbia: Talonbooks, pp. 5-6.
         In a 30 September 1976 note, Dorn explains the occasion for
     1976.5 and comments on its unfinished nature.

5   _____. The Poet, the People, the Spirit. Transcribed by
     Derryll White. Edited by Bob Rose. Vancouver, British
     Columbia: Talonbooks, 29 pp.
         In this transcription of a 21 July 1965 lecture at the
     Berkeley Poetry Conference, Dorn provides biographical details
     concerning his contacts with Shoshoni Indians and his relationship
     to Leroy Lucas during the summer of 1965 while traveling about the
     Basin-Plateau. Reprinted: 1980.6. See also 1965.5; 1966.2;
     1976.5.

6   LEPPER, GARY M. "Edward Dorn." In A Bibliographical Introduc-
     tion to Seventy-Five Modern American Authors. Berkeley, Calif.:
     Serendipity Books, pp. 157-63.
         Provides a primary bibliography, with some description, of
     Dorn's books, broadsides, and translations. Updated: 1978.10.

7   PERLOFF, MARJORIE [G.]. Review of The Collected Poems, 1956-
     1974 and Slinger. New Republic: A Journal of Politics and the
     Arts 174, no. 17 (24 April):22-26.
         In this favorable review, emphasizes Dorn's use of geog-
     raphy. Discusses the wit, the role of I, and the use of the comic
     in Slinger, and comments on "The Rick of Green Wood" and "The
     First Note (From London" from "The North Atlantic Turbine."

8   RILEY, PETER. Review of Manchester Square. Poetry Informa-
    tion, no. 15 (Summer), p. 86.
        In this favorable review, emphasizes the political nature
    and the tension between the "facade of imposition, and the col-
    lapse of the human residue" in the book.

9   WARD, GEOFFREY. Review of Gunslinger, Book IIII. Perfect
    Bound, no. 1 (Spring), pp. 74-76.
        In this unfavorable review, finds too great a change in the
    characterization of Lil and Slinger. Feels this volume does not
    fit well with "The Cycle," but still recommends the entire
    Slinger. Revised in part: 1977.8.

10 ZAVATSKY, BILL. Review of The Collected Poems, 1956-1974. New
    York Times Book Review, 17 October, pp. 32-36.
        In this brief, fairly unfavorable review, finds "all of
    Dorn's work in inherently political."

1977

1   BERTHOLF, ROBERT [JOHN]. "Three Versions of the Poetic Line."
    Credences, [o.s.] 2, no. 1 [whole no. 4] (March):55-66.
        In this 1974 interview, Dorn discusses line length, multiple
    voices, and the female figure in Slinger. The section on Dorn is
    reprinted: 1980.5.

2   DAVIE, DONALD. "The Black Mountain Poets: Charles Olson and
    Edward Dorn." In The Poet in the Imaginary Museum, by Donald
    Davie. Edited by Barry Alpert. New York: Persea Books;
    Manchester, England: Carcanet New Press, pp. 117-90.
        Reprint of 1970.2 with appended postscript claiming Dorn has
    been ignored in England during the 1970s.

3   ESHLEMAN, CLAYTON. "A Note on the Malcolm Parr Review of the
    Dorn/Brotherston Vallejo Translation." Poetry Information, no.
    17 (Summer), pp. 84-87.
        In a response to 1977.7, finds "plenty wrong" with Dorn and
    Gordon Brotherston's translation of Selected Poems, by Cesar
    Vallejo, detailing sixteen errors in "[i]ntensity and height."

4   FREEMAN, JOHN. "Some Notes on Ed Dorn's Recollections of Gran
    Apachería." Palantir, no. 5 (March), pp. 29-35.
        In this favorable review of Recollections of Gran Apachería,
    stresses Dorn's "anti-idealizing" of the Indians, yet notes his
    portrayal of the "beauty and largeness" of their ideas. Finds
    Dorn attempting "to understand the historical roots of evil."

ED1977

5   HOWARD, BEN. "Four Voices." Poetry 130, no. 5 (August):
    285-92.
        In a moderately favorable review of The Collected Poems,
    1956-1974, believes Dorn's political and social concerns some-
    times detract from his work, but finds him also capable of "tran-
    scend[ing] the prejudices of his ideology." Finds the poems often
    document a "poet's painful confrontation with his American
    identity."

6   MAILLARD, PHIL. "Are We Still Here?" Poetry Information, no.
    16 (Winter), pp. 42-49.
        Discusses two of Dorn's concerns: the confrontation between
    whites and Indians and the account of "international economic and
    political realities." For the first, focuses on The Shoshoneans
    and Recollections of Gran Apachería, and for the second, The North
    Atlantic Turbine and Manchester Square. Comments on Slinger, and
    provides a selective bibliography.

7   PARR, MALCOLM. Review of Cesar Vallejo: Selected Poems,
    selected and translated by Edward Dorn and Gordon Brotherston.
    Poetry Information, no. 16 (Winter), pp. 76-77.
        In this brief, favorable review, mentions the high quality
    of the translations. (But see 1977.3.)

8   WARD, GEOFFREY. "Edward Dorn: Poetry and Illusion."
    Cambridge Quarterly 7, no. 3:267-73.
        In a favorable review of Slinger, comments on its theo-
    retical orientation, humor, and desire to disturb "perceptual
    bearings." Discussing "The Cycle," notes Dorn's treatment of
    Robart, "hidden source[s] of power," and injustice; finds this
    section points to "some being at the centre of meaning," but
    insists there is no "access to that centre." Notes Dorn's early
    belief that poetry could bring about social change, but finds a
    shift marked by the cynicism of The North Atlantic Turbine. A few
    sections are revised from 1976.9.

9   WESLING, DONALD. "A Bibliography on Edward Dorn for America."
    Parnassus: Poetry in Review 5, no. 2 (Spring-Summer):142-60.
        With a brief bibliography, surveys Dorn's work to date,
    noting it is theoretical, concerned with politics, social classes,
    economics, and "the hiddenness of contemporary power." Discusses
    Dorn as a political poet "writing for all the people," and com-
    ments on his treatment of the powerful economic leaders and
    "America's victims." Mentioning how Dorn reads Slinger, comments
    on its perspectives, allegories, and authorial presence. Also
    examines its treatment of cocaine, "ambiguities of language and
    selves," and the illustration ("g") on the cover as the barrel of
    a revolver. Discusses his treatment of the American Indian, as in
    Recollections of Gran Apachería, and his prosody, notably his use

of line length, "rhyme-effects," and punctuation. Revised:
1984.4.

1978

1   B[ERTHOLF], R[OBERT] J[OHN], and S[TREETER], D[AVID]. "Edward
     Dorn, 1929-." In First Printings of American Authors: Contri-
     butions toward Descriptive Checklists. Vol. 3. Edited by
     Matthew J. Bruccoli, C.E. Frazer Clark, Jr., Richard Layman,
     and Benjamin Franklin, V. A Bruccoli Clark Book. Detroit:
     Gale Research Co., pp. 79-86.
          Provides an initial descriptive checklist for Dorn.

2   BINNI, FRANCESCO. Modernismo letterario anglo-americano:
     Permanenza e irrealtà di un'istituzione del progresso. [In
     Italian.] Biblioteca di cultura, no. 139. Rome: Bulzoni
     Editore, pp. 397-98.
          Briefly notes Dorn's treatment of the I in Slinger and of
     the relationship of language to objects.

3   BUTTERICK, GEORGE F. A Guide to "The Maximus Poems" of Charles
     Olson. Berkeley, Los Angeles, and London: University of
     California Press, pp. 609, 670, 698, passim.
          Provides a small portion of a 18 July 1966 letter from Dorn
     to Olson, as well as explanations of allusions to Dorn in The
     Maximus Poems. Also mentions Olson's letters to Dorn and a con-
     versation between the two.

4   CREELEY, ROBERT. "Preface" to Selected Poems. Edited by Donald
     [Merriam] Allen. Bolinas, Calif.: Grey Fox Press,
     pp. vii-viii.
          Comments on Dorn's use of the sound of syllables, illustrat-
     ing from "The Rick of Green Wood." Discusses Dorn as a political
     poet who has not relinquished "that care, or humor, or anger, at
     what the world wants at times to do to itself." Provides a bio-
     graphical detail concerning Dorn's high school graduation dance in
     the late 1940s in Villa Grove, Illinois.

5   [DORN, EDWARD.] "Preface" to Hello, La Jolla. Berkeley,
     Calif.: Wingbow Press, [p. vii].
          Very briefly claims the poems in Hello, La Jolla should be
     seen as "light and essential."

6   DORN, EDWARD. "Strumming Language." In Talking Poetics from
     Naropa Institute: Annals of The Jack Kerouac School of Dis-
     embodied Poetics. Edited by Anne Waldman and Marilyn Webb.
     Vol. 1. Boulder, Colo., and London: Shambhala Publications,
     pp. 83-95.

ED1978

In this 8 June 1977 talk at Naropa Institute, Dorn discusses his sense of language, the poetic line, his attention to the media, and his methods of composing Hello, La Jolla. Reads unpublished sections from the notebooks from which Hello, La Jolla was gathered. Provides some background for "Here and Now."

7   DYKE, E.F. "P or Not-P? The Failure of Dichotomies."
    Boundary 2: A Journal of Postmodern Literature 6, no. 2
    (Winter):609-21.
    Providing a "structuralist review" of Slinger, finds it "a treatise on the breakdown of classical logic, in particular, on the inadequacy of the principle of the excluded third . . . for literature." Cites references to logic and reason throughout, including "the reality/fantasy dichotomy." Finds one of Dorn's theses is that "the phenomena of experience cannot be encompassed by a mentality based on the logic of negation" and another is that "the ego is neither alive or dead but conventional." Notes the role of language, I, and the horse in the poem.

8   FREDMAN, STEPHEN [ALBERT]. Roadtesting the Language: An
    Interview with Edward Dorn. Documents for New Poetry, edited
    by [Robert] Michael Davidson, no. 1. San Diego: University of
    California, San Diego, Archive for New Poetry, 48 pp.
    In an edited transcript of a 7 March and 10 August 1977 interview, Dorn provides biographical details about his work experiences, the places he has lived, and his childhood, mentioning the stories his mother, Louise Abercrombie Dorn, read or told to him. Also comments on his writing habits, claiming he is "not a working writer," his sense of himself as a poet, and the importance of translating for him. Notes the influence of popular culture on and the use of language in his writing.
    Focuses on his use of notebooks, the modes of speech and dramatic sense, and the form of Diamond Lil in Slinger. Also mentions the role of drugs, the nature of the voices, and the development of Sllab and its role in the poem. Provides sources for portions of Slinger, including Carlos Castaneda and, for the Cocaine Lil song, Sandburg. Comments on Hello, La Jolla, especially its formalism. Lists some of his current reading, including Samuel Johnson, and mentions going to movies, watching T.V., and listening to A.M. radio. In his introduction (p. 6), Fredman provides the occasion of the interview. Reprinted with abridged introduction: 1980.5.

9   GUGELBERGER, GEORG M. Review of Slinger. American Book Review
    1, no. 3 (Summer):2-4.
    In this lengthy, favorable review, finds that the "center of the book is language," discusses Slinger's apparent allegorical nature, and feels Dorn uses reality "to be de-realized." Provides a plot summary and charts the shift from the lyric and dramatic to

the epic within the work, focusing on Dorn's uses of the latter
mode. Discusses each character in turn, especially the quest and
dilemma of the character I. Also comments on Slinger as a
western.

10   LEPPER, GARY [M.], and FREDMAN, STEPHEN [ALBERT]. "A Checklist
     of Published Materials by Edward Dorn." In Roadtesting the
     Language: An Interview with Edward Dorn. Documents for New
     Poetry, edited by [Robert] Michael Davidson, no. 1. San Diego:
     University of California, San Diego, Archive for New Poetry,
     pp. 39-45.
          Provides a primary bibliography, updating 1976.6.

11   LOCKWOOD, WILLIAM J. "Ed Dorn's Mystique of the Real: His
     Poems for North America." Contemporary Literature 19, no. 1
     (Winter):58-79.
          Finding sources in Carl Ortwin Sauer and Olson, discusses
     Dorn's treatment of geography in relation to the human. Examines
     the treatment of place and human movement in Some Business
     Recently Transacted in the White World, finding the landscape both
     physical and "a conceptual field." Includes a discussion of the
     geological context of "A Narrative with Scattered Nouns"; the
     migration of populations in "Of Eastern Newfoundland, Its Inns &
     Outs"; and the humor and seriousness in "The Sheriff of McTooth
     County, Kansas." Examines "the nomadic pattern of American life"
     in "C.B. & Q.," noting a shift from the acquisitive patterns of
     East-West movement to a North-South movement representative of the
     "motion of the sun and erotic feelings." Mentions Dorn's sense of
     the poem as "an instrument of intellection" and his relation to
     his audience.
          Discusses the itinerary and the poet's shifts of attention
     from outward to inward in "Idaho Out." Also examines the treat-
     ment of social situations, women, evil, and Idaho. Finds his
     treatment of the Beauty of North Fork in "Idaho Out" is as "the
     principle of Eros" compared to the country's "crippled" conscious-
     ness. Also notes the reader's participatory role in the poem.
     Examines reasons for Dorn's recent focus on the American South-
     west, and comments on the journey in Slinger as "a vehicle for
     reflection on . . . the state of the American soul." Feels Dorn
     tries to alter "the reader's consciousness" in order to free his
     mind.

12   MOORE, RICHARD. "Olson in Gloucester, 1966." Transcribed by
     George F. Butterick. In Muthologos: The Collected Lectures
     and Interviews, by Charles Olson. Edited by George F.
     Butterick. Vol. 1. Writing, no. 35. Bolinas, Calif.: Four
     Seasons Foundation, pp. 169-98 [pp. 175 and 176 are transposed].
          In a transcription "from the outtakes" of the 12 March 1966
     Olson N.E.T. film in the "USA: Poetry" series, Olson comments on

ED1978

"The Sense Comes over Me, and the Waning Light of Man by the 1st
National Bank," and quotes from 1963.2.

13   OLSON, CHARLES, and DORN, EDWARD. "Charles Olson and Edward
      Dorn." Transcribed by George F. Butterick. In Muthologos:
      The Collected Lectures and Interviews, by Charles Olson.
      Edited by George F. Butterick. Vol. 1. Writing, no. 35.
      Bolinas, Calif.: Four Seasons Foundation, pp. 157-68.
          In a transcription of a 24 July 1965 filmed conversation
      between Dorn and Olson at the Berkeley Poetry Conference (produced
      by Gordon Craig), Dorn mentions writing what is "given" to him and
      printing a poem of Olson's at Black Mountain College. Dorn also
      comments on his travel among and study of the American Indian and
      the help Olson gave him when he began to write. Olson comments on
      Dorn's "C.B. & Q.," noting Dorn's treatment of the West. See also
      1981.9.

14   von HALLBERG, ROBERT. Charles Olson: The Scholar's Art.
      Cambridge, Mass., and London: Harvard University Press, pp.
      186, 223, 243, passim.
          Revision of 1975.7, dropping some of the substantive Dorn
      references.

                              1979

1   BUTTERICK, GEORGE [F.]. "A Fist in His Heart: Edward Dorn's
      Selected Poems." Chicago Review 30, no. 3 [Black Mountain and
      Since: Objectivist Writing in America] (Winter):157-62.
          In a favorable review of Selected Poems, mentions the sub-
      tleties in "The Rick of Green Wood," the enigmatic quality of "The
      Hide of My Mother," and the punctuation in "Are They Dancing."
      Also comments on "Idaho Out," Dorn's political poetry and social
      concerns, and his irony and satire. Provides the occasion for
      "From Gloucester Out."

2   CHRISTENSEN, PAUL [NORMAN]. Charles Olson: Call Him Ishmael.
      Austin and London: University of Texas Press, pp. 202-5,
      passim.
          In an apparent revision of 1975.2, finds Dorn "requires a
      large, loosely structured format," and notes the role of politics
      in his poetry as in The North Atlantic Turbine. Claims that al-
      though Slinger "disperses into rant," it points to popular culture
      as viable subject matter for the long poem.

3   CREELEY, ROBERT. "Last Night: Random Thoughts on San
      Francisco, March-June 1956." In "Was That a Real Poem" and

Other Essays. Edited by Donald [Merriam] Allen. Writing, no. 39. Bolinas, Calif.: Four Seasons Foundation, pp. 86–90. English version of 1975.3.

4   DAVIE, DONALD. "Steep Trajectories." Maxy's Journal, no. 2, pp. 11–14.
     In a generally favorable review of Hello, La Jolla, uses quotations from 1978.8 to demonstrate Dorn's ideas of using an interesting and descriptive, rather than a prescriptive, language in poetry. Notes the spelling errors, and finds Dorn's emphasis on the spoken language will not be appreciated by some. Reprinted: 1979.5.

5   _____. "Steep Trajectories." In Trying to Explain. Poets on Poetry. Ann Arbor: University of Michigan Press, pp. 13–17. Reprint of 1979.4.

6   FOX, HUGH. The Poetry of Charles Potts. American Dust Series, no. 12. Paradise, Calif.: Dustbooks, pp. 11–13, 19, 44.
     Quotes from The Shoshoneans on the Basin-Plateau, calls Dorn a "Beat," and details his influence on Potts.

7   GOLDING, ALAN. "The Olson Festival in Iowa." Two Hands News and Chicago Poetry Calendar, no. 20 (July), pp. 4–5.
     Describes Dorn's talk and his role at the 5–11 November 1978 Charles Olson Conference.

8   OLSON, CHARLES. "Poetry and Truth." Transcribed by George F. Butterick. In Muthologos: The Collected Lectures and Interviews, by Charles Olson. Edited by George F. Butterick. Vol. 2. Writing, no. 35. Bolinas, Calif.: Four Seasons Foundation, pp. 7–54.
     Reprint of 1971.5.

9   TUCKETT, HAROLD. "Filling the Empty Reservoirs: An Interview with Edward Dorn." Kwasind: A Literary Journal from the University of Michigan-Flint 1, no. 1 (Winter 1978–79):17–24.
     In this 8 November 1978 interview, Dorn mentions the role of the poet in society; comments on Buck and other characters in "C.B. & Q." as types; and discusses American society. Also mentions reading works on the eighteenth century, including histories.
     Tuckett notes the differences in Dorn's treatment of men and women, and in his introduction (p. 19), provides the occasion for the interview. Reprinted, without the introduction: 1980.5.

10   WHEALE, NIGEL. "Expense: J.H. Prynne's The White Stones." Grosseteste Review 12:103–18.

ED1979

In a review of The White Stones by J.H. Prynne (Lincoln,
England: Grosseteste Press, 1969), compares Dorn's figure of
Aklavik in the "Thesis" section of "The North Atlantic Turbine" to
Prynne's in "Aristeas, in Seven Years."

11 _____. "On the Air." Poetry Review 69, no. 2 (December):
43-47.
In a favorable review of Hello, La Jolla, emphasizes Dorn's
use of "the commonly damaged language."

1980

1 BRESLIN, PAUL. "Black Mountain: A Critique of the Curriculum."
Poetry 136, no. 4 (July):219-39.
In an unfavorable review of Selected Poems, claims "Dorn's
socially engaged poetry goes after all the easy targets and hits
them with a bludgeon," using "The Air of June Sings" as an example. Finds a few successful poems like "The Rick of Green Wood"
and "A Country Song." Believes the process orientation of Black
Mountain poetry keeps Dorn from personal investment in his subject.

2 CAPE, STEPHEN. American Poetry, 1950-1980. Bloomington:
Indiana University, Lilly Library, p. 12.
Describes the manuscripts, correspondence, and editions of
Dorn in the Lilly Library of Indiana University.

3 CLARK, TOM. "Ed Dorn's Views." In Views, by Edward Dorn.
Edited by Donald [Merriam] Allen. Writing, no. 40. San
Francisco: Four Seasons Foundation, pp. 9-24.
In this transcription of a February 1980 discussion, Dorn
comments on his essays, his style, and his treatment of and views
on the West and the cowboy figure. Also mentions his assignments
as a writer, and provides a few general biographical details.
In his introduction (p. 9), Clark comments on the essays
included in 1980.6.

4 DAVIDSON, [ROBERT] MICHAEL. "Archeologist of Morning: Charles
Olson, Edward Dorn, and Historical Method." ELH 47, no. 1
(Spring):158-79.
Comparing Olson and Dorn's use of history and treatment of
commercialism, examines Dorn's treatment of the "mediation of
landscape by commercial interests" including mercantilism's
"transformation of man from an independent consciousness to an
arbitrary classification" in "The North Atlantic Turbine." Finds
Dorn satirizes "structures which eliminate difference and distinc-
tion." In Slinger, mentions the role of the journey and
Parmenides. Also notes the characterization of Howard Hughes;
Slinger, "a time-traveller [and] a manipulator of codes"; and I, a

"selfconscious, ratiocinative ego." Comments on Slinger as an allegory, noting its "displacement of history," and mentions how its language gradually "breaks down" as it becomes "increasingly hermetic" and discontinuous, "refusing even the most generous paraphrase." Some of these ideas are included in 1981.5; 1985.1.

5   DORN, EDWARD. Interviews. Edited by Donald [Merriam] Allen. Writing, no. 38. Bolinas, Calif.: Four Seasons Foundation, 117 pp.
    Includes reprints from 1963.2; 1972.1; 1974.8; 1977.1; 1978.8; 1979.9, abridging the introductory material but not the interviews themselves.

6   _____. Views. Edited by Donald [Merriam] Allen. Writing, no. 40. San Francisco: Four Seasons Foundation, 142 pp.
    Includes reprints of 1960.1; 2; 1962.1; 1976.5 and a slight revision of 1961.2.

7   DRESMAN, PAUL CHARLES. "Between Here and Formerly: A Study of History in the Work of Edward Dorn." Ph.D. dissertation, University of California at San Diego, 239 pp.
    Charts Olson's influence on Dorn through A Bibliography on America for Ed Dorn (see 1964.1), noting the sources that Dorn accepted and his divergences in emphases and applications. Finding occasional precedents for Slinger, comments on a number of early poems in The Collected Poems, 1956-1974. As precedent, notes Dorn's humor, ability to combine the lyric with the narrative, and his treatment of farm life as in "On the Debt My Mother Owed to Sears Roebuck" and By the Sound. Mentions his use of historical figures and backgrounds, notably in "Ledyard: The Exhaustion of Sheer Distance" and "Los Mineros," and comments on his ability to combine personal experience with "public historic circumstances" as in "Trail Creek, Aug. 11: The Reason of Higher Powers."
    In Geography, discusses Dorn's political poetry, comparing him to Baraka, and mentions his use of historical events as in "Song: The Astronauts." Also examines the role of geography and history in "Idaho Out." Explores the dislocations caused by trade; the treatment of history, politics, and the railroad; and the use of humor in the poems in The North Atlantic Turbine, focusing on "A Theory of Truth: The North Atlantic Turbine." Also notes Dorn's use of a fictive voice in this latter poem. Discusses "Oxford" in detail, noting the treatment of sex, economics, geology, history, England, America, literacy, and Oxford University.
    Provides an extended discussion of Slinger, noting Dorn's treatment of the West, drugs, and society. Also comments on the role of and the nature of time, the hero, and the journey, in the work, as well as the role of icons and other works, including

ED1980

poems, within Slinger. Terms the work a dramatic narrative and a
comic epic, noting the types of humor used. Focuses on the characterization in Slinger (and in Abeline! Abeline!, an unpublished
screenplay), commenting on many of the individuals, finding them
archetypal and potentially having the coherence of a "singular
entity." Provides explanations for many allusions and esoteric
references in Slinger, and points out a number of sources, especially in Parmenides.

    Details Dorn's treatment of American Indians in a number of
works: the character of Ramona McCarty in By the Sound and the
treatment of geography and the cowboy in The Shoshoneans, commenting on the role of the photographs and their relationship to the
text in the latter work. Also examines the treatment of time,
Victoria and Geronimo's bands, and the difference between white
and Indian world views in Recollections of Gran Apachería, noting
the role of the illustrations in the work. Records Olson's influence on Dorn's interest in Indians, and lists a few of Dorn's
sources, especially in Álvar Núñez Cabeza de Vaca.

    The last chapter, on Dorn's treatment of the Indians, is
revised as 1985.2. See Dissertation Abstracts International 41
(1981):3104A.

8   FREDMAN, STEPHEN ALBERT. "Sentences: Three Works of American
    Prose Poetry." Ph.D. dissertation, Stanford University, pp.
    147-49, 158.

    Uses portions from Gunslinger, Book I to illustrate the
contemporary concern with knowledge as presence and the "attention
to appearances in the present." Notes Creeley's dislike of the
"fictional aspect of Slinger." Revised: 1983.4. See Dissertation Abstracts International 41 (1981):3579A.

9   LIKIS, KENNETH [JAMES]. "Edward Dorn." In American Poets
    since World War II. Part 1, A-K. Edited by Donald J. Greiner.
    Dictionary of Literary Biography, vol. 5. Detroit: Gale Re-
    search Co., Bruccoli Clark Book, pp. 205-10.

    Mentions Dorn's eloquence and lyricism, political poetry,
and use of "a wide range of poetic elements." Also examines his
treatment of the "debasement of language" and the chaos and clamor
in Slinger. Discusses the treatment of the individual in
Recollections of Gran Apachería and the social satire in Hello, La
Jolla. Comments on a number of individual poems, especially
"Sousa."

10   McPHILMEY, KATHLEEN. "Towards Open Form: A Study of Process
    Poetics in Relation to Four Long Poems: The Anathemata by
    David Jones, In Memoriam James Joyce by Hugh MacDiarmid,
    Passages by Robert Duncan, Gunslinger by Edward Dorn." Ph.D.
    dissertation, University of Edinburgh, pp. 351-89.

ED1980

Discusses <u>Slinger</u> as a long poem "with epic pretensions" in
which there is an "oscillation between the One and the Many, a
process which is the generating dynamic of the poem." Discusses
the treatment of process and language and the role of myth and
history in the work's "semi-autonomous world." Examines the role
of Howard Hughes, Robart, the Poet, <u>Bean</u> <u>News</u>, "The Cycle," Sllab,
the literate projector, and references to philosophes and others,
especially Parmenides, Heidegger, and Lévi-Strauss, in the poem.
Also discusses the role of the ego, drugs, and "[t]ime and
the nature of time," and notes the use of typographical devices,
mythologized materials, Universe City, and Lil as the female figure in <u>Slinger</u>. Mentioning Dorn's relationship to his audience,
comments on the occasional obscurity of his references, and examines the role of public and private allusions. Comments on the
role of the death of I as a potential destruction of the ego in
the poem.
Discusses "a basic opposition between 'we' and 'them'" in
the work, notes the revisions of the text from 1970 to 1975, comments on the role of synthesis and process in the poem, and attempts to explain portions of "The Cycle." Feels the different
characters or personalities in the poem may be seen as separate
components of a single psyche, and the journey as a quest for an
integration or synthesis of these components.
Finds Dorn's a "process or projective poetics" that derives
"very largely from an amalgam of Heidegger's thought and
Whitehead's <u>Process</u> and <u>Reality</u>, particularly as mediated by
Charles Olson." Uses Dorn's prefaces to his other works to shed
light on his poetics.

11   MIDDLETON, PETER. "From <u>Geography</u> to <u>Gunslinger</u>: The Poetry
      of Edward Dorn." <u>Poetry</u> <u>Information</u>, nos. 20-21 (Winter),
      pp. 18-30.
         Charts concerns central to <u>Slinger</u> which occur in Dorn's
      earlier work, especially the subject of geography and the role of
      imagination in reality. Sees Olson as an influence and notes a
      relationship to Creeley's poetics. Discusses "Oxford" and "The
      Land Below," as well as characterization, the "mythic aspect,"
      tone, and humor in <u>Slinger</u>.

12   RAY, DAVID. "Dorn, Ed(ward Merton)." In <u>Contemporary</u> <u>Poets</u>.
      Edited by James Vinson and D.L. Kirkpatrick. 3d ed. New York:
      St. Martin's Press, pp. 384-86.
         Revision of 1970.5 with an expanded bibliography. See also
      1975.6 and 1985.6.

13   SARLES, DAVID GRIFFITH. "The Personae in Charles Olson's
      <u>Maximus</u> <u>Poems</u>." Ph.D. dissertation, State University of New
      York at Stony Brook, pp. 65-68, 140-41, 149, 151.

ED1980

Comments on Olson's relationship to Dorn, providing a few
biographical details, and discusses his references to Dorn in The
Maximus Poems. See Dissertation Abstracts International 40
(1980):5867A.

14 WARREN, KENNETH. "On Creeley and Dorn." Cumberland Journal,
    no. 9 (Winter), [pp. 51-57].
        In a review of Hello, La Jolla, compares the volume to
    Creeley's Hello: A Journal, February 29-May 3, 1976. Discusses
    the role of the aircraft and air and sky references in both.
    Finds these references an extension of the American sense of place
    and opposed to the Beat use of automobile associations. Comments
    on Dorn's references to the radio and use of "public reference" in
    his poetry.

15 WESLING, DONALD. The Chances of Rhyme: Device and Modernity.
    Berkeley: University of California Press, pp. 92-94, passim.
        Notes Dorn's use of rhyme, consonance, and unmetered lines
    in Slinger.

16 WINKEL, MARTHA G., and ROSS, JEAN W. "Dorn, Edward (Merton)."
    In Contemporary Authors: A Bio-Bibliographical Guide to Cur-
    rent Writers in Fiction, General Nonfiction, Poetry, Journal-
    ism, Drama, Motion Pictures, Television, and Other Fields.
    Vols. 93-96. Edited by Francis C. Locher. Detroit: Gale
    Research Co., pp. 127-29.
        Winkel provides an overview of Dorn's work, quoting a number
    of critics. In a 4 May 1979 telephone interview with Ross (pp.
    128-29), Dorn mentions his current reading, his teaching of writ-
    ing, his statements in 1975.5 about publishing, and his classical
    allusions. Dorn also comments on his sense of Black Mountain as a
    school, the San Francisco poetry scene, and democracy. Notes
    Olson's influence on him.

1981

1 BERKE, ROBERTA [ELZEY]. Bounds Out of Bounds: A Compass for
   Recent American and British Poetry. New York: Oxford University Press, pp. 34-37.
       Quoting from "Wait by the Door Awhile Death, There Are
   Others," finds Dorn distinctly American but, unlike Olson, without
   a specific locality. Feels the West, as in Slinger, "compels his
   affection," and believes the "cowboy personifies Dorn's preoccupa-
   tion with movement." Comments on Dorn's political poems. Feels
   Manchester Square and Hello, La Jolla were failures.

2   CLARK, TOM. "Introduction" to Yellow Lola, formerly titled
     Japanese Neon (Hello La Jolla, Book II). Santa Barbara,
     Calif.: Cadmus Editions, p. 7.
         In this introduction, Clark mentions his own role in Yellow
     Lola.

3   C[LARK], T[OM], ed. Notes on Edward Dorn's Books. In Am Here
     Books, Catalogue Five, 1981-82: A Collection of Post-Modern
     Poetry: Books, Manuscripts, and Letters. Santa Barbara,
     Calif.: Am Here Books, pp. 35-38.
         Describes the content of Dorn's books, stressing his love
     for and knowledge of the land, his descriptions, and his focus on
     Indians and the figure of the stranger.

4   DAVIDSON, [ROBERT] MICHAEL. "'By ear, he sd': Audio-Tapes and
     Contemporary Criticism." Credences: A Journal of Twentieth-
     Century Poetry and Poetics, n.s. 1, no. 1, pp. 105-20.
         Very briefly mentions how Dorn reads Slinger.

5   _____. "'To eliminate the draw': Edward Dorn's Slinger."
     American Literature 53, no. 3 (November):443-64.
         Noting Olson's influence on Dorn's ideas of place, remarks
     on Dorn's choice of the American West and his sense of the local
     in Slinger, and compares the poem to Olson's Maximus Poems. Com-
     ments on Slinger as an allegory and notes its sources in popular
     culture. Examines its treatment of the economic West, time, West-
     ern metaphysics, being, thought, self-consciousness, Cartesian
     ontology, space, the subjective, the objective, Universe City,
     description, the Literate Projector, temporality, Sllab, industry,
     and warfare. Also comments on the use of Parmenides, jokes, puns,
     and narrative; the role of the journey, humor, and Bean News; and
     the characters of Slinger, I, Howard Hughes, Robart, and others,
     noting the shifting and merging of personalities. Studies the
     philosophical dimensions and the "mock trinitarian theology" in
     the poem. Attempts to summarize "The Cycle," and treats the opac-
     ity and the role of language in this section of the poem. Com-
     ments on the "breakdown in narrative continuity" in Slinger and
     the ways in which the poem seems incomplete, noting the "cosmolog-
     ical banter" and the "cartoon dialogues" in book 3, and the influ-
     ence of Olson on the end of the work. Finds Slinger an American
     poem. Draws from 1980.4. Expanded and revised: 1985.1.

6   DORN, EDWARD. "Introduction" to Yellow Lola, formerly titled
     Japanese Neon (Hello La Jolla, Book II). Santa Barbara,
     Calif.: Cadmus Editions, p. 7.
         In this introduction, Dorn comments on Tom Clark's role in
     the manuscript of Yellow Lola and its relationship to Hello, La
     Jolla.

ED1981

7 ____. "Introduction to Amiri Baraka's Reading, Valencia St.,
2 March 1977." Am Here Books, Catalogue Five, 1981–82: A
Collection of Post-Modern Poetry: Books, Manuscripts, and
Letters. Edited by Tom Clark. Santa Barbara, Calif.: Am Here
Books, p. 68.
    In this introduction, Dorn discusses his initial visits and
reactions to Chicago and New York as well as his relationship to
Baraka.

8 GERY, JOHN. "Edward Dorn, Community Poet." Occident 101, no.
1 (Fall):48–51.
    Discusses Dorn's "emphasis on plurality, rather than on the
singular voice" and his focus on man as a communal rather than an
individual being. Finds this focus in a number of works, especially The Rites of Passage and Slinger, noting the role of I's
ego in the latter. Finds Dorn occasionally treats "the singularity of . . . woman."

9 MAUD, RALPH. "Charles Olson: Posthumous Editions and
Studies." West Coast Review: A Quarterly Magazine of the Arts
14, no. 3 (January 1980):27–33; 15, no. 3 (Winter):37–42.
    Provides corrections to 1978.13.

10 MORROW, BRADFORD, and COONEY, SEAMUS. A Bibliography of the
Black Sparrow Press, 1966–1978. Santa Barbara, Calif.: Black
Sparrow Press, pp. 31–32, 53, 60–61, passim.
    Provides a descriptive bibliography for Dorn's Gunslinger,
Book I and Gunslinger, Book II as well as for his and Gordon
Brotherston's translation of Arbol entre dos muros/Tree between
Two Walls, by José Emilio Pacheco (see 1971.1).

11 PAUL, SHERMAN. The Lost America of Love: Rereading Robert
Creeley, Edward Dorn, and Robert Duncan. Baton Rouge, La., and
London: Louisiana State University Press, pp. 75–168, passim.
    Throughout Dorn's work, refers to his treatment of isola-
tion, Whitman, Indians, the wanderer or stranger, the meanness of
America, and acquisition. Occasionally mentions What I See in
"The Maximus Poems" as well as Dorn's relationship to Baraka and
sources in Carl Ortwin Sauer. Also compares Dorn's work to
Creeley's
    Examines The Newly Fallen, outlining the role of place and
the treatment of geography, politics, and America in the volume.
Comments on a number of poems, especially "The Rick of Green
Wood," "Geranium," and "Sousa." Considers the treatment of the
cowboy, love, the Indian, and the role of journeys and of inner
and outer spaces in Hands Up!, focusing on "Hemlocks" and "The
Land Below." In "From Gloucester Out," details the role of Olson
and the treatment of isolation and loneliness.

Mentioning the volume's cultural criticism and the treatment of women, discusses the poems of Geography. Outlines the relationship between women and landforms in "Idaho Out," and reviews the role of poverty in "The Sense Comes over Me, and the Waning Light of Man by the 1st National Bank." In By the Sound, comments on the characterization and the role of rites of passage and economic differences. Investigates the treatment of Indians, especially Willie Dorsey, and the role of Leroy Lucas in The Shoshoneans. Applies Olson's schema in 1964.1 to The Shoshoneans, finding it a travel book in which Dorn enters "the open field of experience."

Notes the treatment of England in The North Atlantic Turbine, focusing on "Wait by the Door Awhile Death, There Are Others." Finds Twenty-Four Love Songs a "journey of love," noting the role of Europa in the first, "['It is deep going from here']." In Recollections of Gran Apachería, examines the treatment of the Indian, the role of the railroad, and the use of history. Also notes the characterization of Captain Emmet Crawford in "A Period Portrait of Sympathy," and occasionally compares the volume to Slinger.

Terms Slinger a "postmodern epic," and discusses the role of Slinger, women, cocaine, and Robart. Provides a portion of a 24 October 1977 letter from Duncan comparing Slinger to Olson's The Maximus Poems. Finds Hello, La Jolla aphoristic and "closed," pointing to its political and investigative functions. Mentions the significance of the title of "A for Ism" and comments on the poem. Discovers sources for the volume in the eighteenth century, Olson, and W.C. Williams, and applies Dorn's comments from a lecture at Iowa on Ed Sanders's investigative poetry to the work.

*12 POWER, KEVIN. "Post Modern Poetics: Four Views." Revista canaria de estudios ingleses, no. 2 (March), pp. 51-69.
Presumably uses Dorn's work as an example of postmodernism. Unavailable for annotation; listed in 1981 MLA International Bibliography I.7361.

13 RODNEY, JANET. Review of Views. Montemora, no. 8, pp. 208-13.
In this favorable review, concentrates on "What I See in The Maximus Poems," and The Poet, the People, the Spirit, focusing on Dorn's views of creativity, place, ego, history, and Indians and how the latter essay illuminates Dorn's poetic treatment of the West, especially in Recollections of Gran Apachería. Explicates "La Máquina a Houston."

14 SHEVELOW, KATHRYN. Review of Yellow Lola. Chicago Review 33, no. 1 (Summer):101-4.
In this brief, favorable review, notes the satire and humor and the treatment of language and culture. Mentions the volume's relation to Hello, La Jolla.

ED1981

15   von HALLBERG, ROBERT. "Edward Dorn: 'This marvellous acci-
     dentalism.'" Boundary 2: A Journal of Postmodern Literature
     9, no. 2 [A Supplement on Contemporary Poetry] (Winter):51-80.
         Reviews changes in Dorn's poetry from 1958 to 1975, espe-
     cially in terms of politics and didacticism. Notes Olson's influ-
     ence on Dorn, especially on his discursiveness. Examines the role
     of sentimentality in "The Air of June Sings"; the treatment of
     exploration, loneliness, and the West in "Death while Journeying";
     and the casual style and the formal diction in "Los Mineros."
     Comments on the treatment of culture and suffering in "The Problem
     of the Poem for My Daughter, Left Unsolved" and the treatment of
     intellectuals and understanding in Dorn's prose. Quoting from
     unpublished September and October 1961 correspondence between Dorn
     and Amiri Baraka (then, LeRoi Jones) on "An Address for the First
     Woman to Face Death in Havana--Olga Herrara Marcos," here pub-
     lished for the first time, compares the obviousness of its polemic
     to "On the Debt My Mother Owed to Sears Roebuck." Comments on
     Dorn's "rudeness," and quotes from an unpublished 24 January 1968
     letter from Dorn.
         Noting possible sources for Slinger in nonsense literature,
     analyzes "the process of literalization, kept going by puns, meta-
     phors, live, dead, and merely implied." Also notes the use of
     language, pronouns, nonsense, allusions, repetitions, and word-
     play; the role of mutation and referentiality; and the lack of
     signification in the poem. Revised and expanded: 1985.8-9.

1982

1   KIMBALL, SUE L. "Edward Dorn." In Critical Survey of Poetry,
    English Language Series. Vol. 2. Edited by Frank N. Magill.
    Englewood Cliffs, N.J.: Salem Press, pp. 839-46.
        Providing sketchy biographical information, notes influences
    on Dorn and his use of popular culture and satire. Also mentions
    his treatment of the West, "the tension between man and landscape
    brought on by greed," and language. Comments on Slinger.

2   KOPCEWICZ, ANDREJ, and SIENICKA, MARTA. Historia literaury
    Stanów Zjednoczonych w zarysie: Wiek XX. [In Polish.]
    Warsaw: Państwowe Wydawnictwo Naukowe, pp. 191-92, passim.
        Providing an overview of Dorn's poetry, notes the role of
    geography in his work. Comments on The North Atlantic Turbine and
    Slinger.

3   PAUL, SHERMAN. So to Speak: Rereading David Antin. London:
    Binnacle Press, pp. 44, passim.
        Briefly comments on "the conflict of literal and oral cul-
    tures" in Recollections of Gran Apachería.

4   PERLOFF, MARJORIE [G.]. "From Image to Action: The Return of
    Story in Postmodern Poetry." Contemporary Literature 23, no. 4
    (Fall):411-27.
        Discusses Dorn's treatment of I in Slinger. Believes having
    I killed undercuts "the metaphysical tradition based on Being as
    presence" which, in turn, undercuts traditional story emphases.
    Finds that Dorn "foreground[s] the narrative codes themselves,"
    making language the "real hero." Reprinted: 1985.5.

5   von HALLBERG, ROBERT. "Poetry Chronicle: 1980." Contemporary
    Literature 23, no. 2 (Spring):225-38.
        In a favorable review of Yellow Lola, provides background
    for "In Defense of Pure Poetry" and "The Word (20 January 1977)."
    Finds Dorn tries to "goad his readers . . . into examining their
    pieties skeptically." Revised and expanded: 1985.8-9.

                              1983

1   COSTELLO, JAMES THOMAS. "Edward Dorn: The Range of Poetry."
    Ph.D. dissertation, State University of New York at Buffalo,
    207 pp.
        Prior to providing a close reading for a number of Dorn's
    poems, comments on his use of cowboy and drifter figures and his
    precision and irony, as in "The Encounter." Examining the polit-
    ical dimension of his work, notes Dorn's use of the personal and
    his focus on the individual while relating all to "the cultural
    matrix."
        Discusses the rhythms, assonance, and diction in "The Rick
    of Green Wood," comparing the hardships to those in By the Sound
    and noting parallels to work by Thoreau and Whitman. Examines the
    relationship of "Vaquero" to its source, a child's drawing, and
    notes its treatment of the child's perception of beauty. Empha-
    sizes the "tension between playfulness and seriousness," mention-
    ing Dorn's use of ambiguous language and humor, his treatment of
    his mother, Louise Abercrombie Dorn, and the role of aggression in
    "The Hide of My Mother." Also studies the treatment of loneliness
    and separation in "Are They Dancing" and the expropriation of land
    "for the profit of a few" in "The Air of June Sings."
        Details the use of dryness and the treatment of the economic
    system in "On the Debt My Mother Owed to Sears Roebuck." Comments
    on the role of associations and leaps between the present and the
    past; the use of history; and the treatment of economics, America,
    the common man in ancient time, and the Indian figure in "The Land
    Below." Mentions the treatment of his own self-consciousness,
    Olson's greatness and isolation in "From Gloucester Out," reading
    the poem as a testimony of Olson's influence.
        Notes the "private outlook" in the songs of Geography. Also
    discusses the treatment of contemporary culture, the field, sex,
    cultural entrophy, women, and the modern world as well as the use

of myth and female mythic figures in "The Problem of the Poem for
My Daughter, Left Unsolved." Comments on the treatment of the
economic oppression of the poor in both "Eugene Delacroix Says"
and "The Sense Comes over Me, and the Waning Light of Man by the
1st National Bank," noting the role of the Kafka reference in the
latter.

In The North Atlantic Turbine, details the treatment of
Aklavik and Western civilization and economics in "The North
Atlantic Turbine"; of death and homelessness in "Wait by the Door
Awhile Death, There Are Others"; of home in "A Notation on the
Evening of November 27, 1966"; and of Leroy Lucas and isolation in
America in "The Sundering U.P. Tracks." Discusses his treatment
of Indians, America, and Western man in The Shoshoneans and
Recollections of Gran Apachería. Emphasizes the treatment of
Willie Dorsey, the poverty of the Indians, the geography of the
Basin, and the Sun Dance in the former. Comments on "the absolute
dichotomy between world views of the white and Indian worlds" in
the latter.

Provides extended discussion of Slinger. In Gunslinger,
Book I, focuses on the characterization of Slinger, the use and
treatment of language, especially "verbal switching" and puns, and
the treatment of the eye, description, and meaning. In Gun-
Slinger, Book II, comments on the use of myth and of the journey
and the treatment of I's death. Notes the role of "The Cycle"
within the entire volume, and comments on its treatment of Slinger
compared to Robart, noting the latter's insulation and interiority. In Gunslinger, Book III, focuses on the role of language,
including puns, the treatment of the internal and the external,
and the role of the Parmenides figure and of process, noting
sources in Whitehead. Comments on the use of "the Heraclitian
image of the world as fire," the treatment of vision and the character I, and the role of Robart's arrival in the fourth book.

Examines the ways to read the poems in Hello, La Jolla and
Yellow Lola, and mentions the treatment of time, place, and the
role of the poet in society, the question of "authority in language," the ironic tone and word usage, and the eccentric positions on issues. Offers somewhat extended comments on
"Rauchenberg's Untitled (Early Egyptian Series" and "Del Mar."
See Dissertation Abstracts International 44 (1983):167A.

2   DOHERTY, THOMAS. "Poetry and History: Ed Dorn's Recollections
     of Gran Apachería." Southwestern American Literature 8, no. 2
     (Spring):12-20.
         Commenting on a number of individual pieces, discusses
Dorn's Recollections of Gran Apachería as a long poem in four
sections. Notes his use of source materials, principally Handbook
of American Indians North of Mexico, ed. Frederick Webb Hodge, 2
vols. ([Smithsonian Institution, Bureau of American Ethnology,

Bulletin, no. 30] Washington, D.C.: Government Printing Office,
1907-10), and emphasizes Dorn's treatment of "the political force
of the Western Mind." Finds that Dorn insists that "Americans are
still living this history" as evidenced by the Vietnam War. Discusses the illustrations, as well as Dorn's treatment of "the
nature of perception and language," and of "the Apache's relation
to his land."

3   DORN, JENNIFER [as JENNIFER DUNBAR]. "Excerpt from a Letter:
     Jenny to Her Parents." In Captain Jack's Chaps; or, Houston/
     MLA. Madison, Wis.: Black Mesa Press, [p. 3].
         In this letter, Jennifer Dorn provides a number of biograph-
     ical details of Dorn from December 1980, focusing on his relation-
     ship with Dobro Dick Dillof.

4   FREDMAN, STEPHEN [ALBERT]. Poet's Prose: The Crisis in
     American Verse. Cambridge: Cambridge University Press,
     pp. 88-89, 94.
         Revision of 1980.8.

5   OKADA, ROY K. "An Interview with Edward Dorn." In Interviews
     with Contemporary Writers, 2d ser., 1972-1982. Edited by
     L[awrence] S[anford] Dembo. Madison: University of Wisconsin
     Press, pp. 130-47.
         Reprint of 1974.8.

6   POWER, KEVIN. "Ed Dorn's Gunslinger: A Postmodern Comic Epic."
     In Literary and Linguistic Aspects of Humor. VI AEDEAN Con-
     ference Proceedings. Barcelona: Departamento de Lengua y
     Literatura Inglesa de la Universidad de Barcelona, pp. 191-98.
         Notes the role of Nietzschean humor in Slinger forcing the
     culture to "think back on itself," and believes Dorn's "comedy is
     vindictive, never ameliorative." Finds Slinger an "epic of con-
     sciousness," notes Dorn's use of language and its relationship to
     landscape, and mentions the role of Howard Hughes. Also comments
     on Lil and I, as well as the characterization of Slinger as an
     archetype.

7   RICOU, LAURIE. "Prairie Poetry and Metaphors of Plain/s
     Space." Great Plains Quarterly 3, no. 2 (Spring):109-19.
         Discusses Dorn's treatment of space, the Midwest, and lan-
     guage, as well as his use of the word "areal" and of metaphor in
     "Idaho Out." Finds sources for the poem in Carl Ortwin Sauer's
     The Morphology of Landscape (Berkeley: University of California
     Press, 1925), and compares the poem to Robert Kroetsch's "Seed
     Catalogue."

8   SELERIE, GAVIN R. The Riverside Interviews. Vol. 6, Tom
     McGrath. London: Binnacle Press, pp. 90-91, passim.

ED1983

In the October 1980 interview, McGrath reminisces about first reading and meeting Dorn, and comments on Dorn's reaction to the Naropa Institute.

9   SHEVELOW, KATHRYN. "Reading Edward Dorn's Hello, La Jolla and Yellow Lola." Sagetrieb: A Journal Devoted to Poets in the Pound-H.D.-Williams Tradition 2, no. 2 (Summer-Fall):99-109.
        Comparing Dorn to the Augustan satirists, notes his rhetorical and didactic strategies in Hello, La Jolla and Yellow Lola. Finds he directly addresses his audience, disarming them, and then undermines their sense of "insider's complacency" by revealing their "complicity in the matter under attack." Also comments on the epigrammatic quality of the poems, noting their innerrelatedness within the books. Mentions Dorn's use of satire and social criticism, his sense that the "composed poem . . . consists of details selected out of the mass of poetry which is everywhere being written," and his relation to his audience.

10   STURGEON, TANDY. "Weighing the Shorter Dorn." Exquisite Corpse 1, no. 12 (December):4.
        In a review of Captain Jack's Chaps, stresses Dorn's satiric perception of place and event and his ability to write with "adroit concision." Argues against critics who believe Dorn's short poems are not durable.

1984

1   TROTTER, DAVID [W.]. The Making of the Reader: Language and Subjectivity in Modern American, English, and Irish Poetry. New York: St. Martin's Press, pp. 165-76, passim.
        Finds the "play between subjectivity . . . and its opposite" central to Dorn's poetry. Demonstrates that subjectivity, which discovers and states a thesis, is central to "Idaho Out," The North Atlantic Turbine, Hello, La Jolla, and Geography. Finds such a thesis is an "argument, decision, [and/or] loyality" locating the self to a "determinate identity" in a social context. Sees Dorn also exploring "the possibilities of undogmatic statement" in the skepticism of "On the Debt My Mother Owed to Sears Roebuck" and Slinger, demonstrating that the latter "announces its revision of American foundation-myths" through its "social skepticism and . . . discontinuous spread of idioms."

2   WAKOSKI, DIANE. "Diane Wakoski." In Contemporary Authors: Autobiography Series. Vol. 1. Edited by Dedria Bryforski. Detroit: Gale Research Co., pp. 353-72.
        Wakoski provides a few biographical details of Dorn in the summer of 1964. Claims her interest in the West, her poem "Follow

That Stagecoach," and Mac Hammond's poem "Horse Opera" influenced the inception of Slinger.

3 WEINBERGER, ELIOT. "A Case of AIDS Hysteria." Sulfur: A Literary Tri-Quarterly of the Whole Art 3, no. 3 [whole no. 9]:170-72.
   Negatively discusses "The 1983 AIDS Awards for Poetry: In Recognition of the Current Epidemic of Idiocy on the Poetry Scene" (Rolling Stock, no. 5 [1983], p. 13), which he attributes to Dorn and Tom Clark, finding them "unlikely mouthpieces for Reagan America."

4 WESLING, DONALD. "The Poetry of Edward Dorn." In Modern American Poetry. Edited by R.W. (Herbie) Butterfield. London: Vision Press; Totowa, N.J.: Barnes & Noble Books, pp. 218-33.
   In a revision of 1977.9, drops the section on American Indians, adds a brief commentary on Hello, La Jolla and Yellow Lola, and abbreviates the section on prosody.

1985

1 DAVIDSON, [ROBERT] MICHAEL. "'To eliminate the draw': Narrative and Language in Slinger." In Internal Resistances: The Poetry of Edward Dorn. Edited by Donald Wesling. Berkeley: University of California Press, pp. 113-49.
   In an expansion and revision of 1981.5, claims the characters in Slinger "speak as various aspects of the poet's mind or as figures in a dream allegory." Comments on the power plant and the role of the Vietnam War and drugs in the poem. Adds more on "The Cycle," the ego of I, the treatment of temporality, and the role of paradoxes and Deweyan epistemology in the poem. Also mentions Dorn's sources in Carl Ortwin Sauer and his "commentary on technological and industrial life."

2 DRESMAN, PAUL CHARLES. "Internal Resistances: Edward Dorn on the American Indian." In Internal Resistances: The Poetry of Edward Dorn. Edited by Donald Wesling. Berkeley: University of California Press, pp. 87-112.
   A revision of the last chapter of 1980.7, emphasizing the cultural resistance of the American Indian to the white culture.

3 GOLDING, ALAN. "Edward Dorn's 'Pontificatory use of the art': Hello, La Jolla and Yellow Lola." In Internal Resistances: The Poetry of Edward Dorn. Edited by Donald Wesling. Berkeley: University of California Press, pp. 208-34.
   Comments on many of the poems, and examines the didacticism in Hello, La Jolla and Yellow Lola. Explores Dorn's attempt to provide society the means "for self-appraisal and self-evaluation"

by providing a new language for cultural diagnosis, isolating and
analyzing words and cleaning the language by "debunking it."
Points out that he offers propositions in his poetry and focuses
on content, function, the intellect, and judgment rather than
style, emotion, and expression. Quotes from an unpublished 21
October 1961 letter to Amiri Baraka (then LeRoi Jones), and mentions the role of language in Slinger. Comments on the treatment
of language and cultural and intellectual stasis in earlier work.
In terms of his rhetoric and discursiveness, notes how his didacticism has changed.

Discusses the poems in Hello, La Jolla and Yellow Lola as
epigrams, comparing Dorn's work to that of the eighteenth century,
Byron, and J.V. Cunningham. Finds sources in Pound and Olson, but
notes that Dorn uses humor instead of "earnest persuasion." Mentions Dorn's "capacity to adopt a surprising position that throws
new light on a situation." Comments on his use of irony, free
verse, closure, syntax, the line, the insult, the secondary
source, vulgarity, quotation, contention, abstraction, and diction. Also refers to his movement from detail to generalization
as well as his treatment of the future and society, including the
intellectual failings of society and its tendency to categorize
and its "habit[s] of discrimination." Notes his refusal "to posit
any new order that simply defines itself as a 'negative' of the
old one." Observes that some of the poems "sound facile or trivial" in isolation, but claims they build on each other in sequence.

4   LOCKWOOD, WILLIAM J. "Art Rising to Clarity: Edward Dorn's
     Compleat Slinger." In Internal Resistances: The Poetry of
     Edward Dorn. Edited by Donald Wesling. Berkeley: University
     of California Press, pp. 150-207.
         Noting the inability of wit to sustain Slinger, finds the
poem "predominantly grounded in the mode of song . . . [which] is
grounded in Dorn's sense of the 'intensity'" of place, and comments on Dorn's use of song as celebration. Especially charts
"the way in which the stylized mode of Book I yields to the alle-
goricalized mode of Book II as the poem initiates its arching
trajectory." Records how the "trajectory gets interrupted in 'The
Cycle,' reaches its zenith at the close of Book III, and then
splits off into two motions, toward the sun (the Slinger's home)
and toward the earth (ours)," in book 4.
         In book 1, examines "Dorn's stylized treatment of the West-
erner," centering on the figure of Slinger. Claims when the styl-
ization became familiar, Dorn turned "Slinger into . . . an ab-
stracted version of the drifting Western hero." Illustrates the
growing allegorical nature of the work by comparing settings,
songs, and characterizations, especially of Slinger and the horse,
from books 1 and 2. Also notes the sources in Parmenides, the
treatment of smell, and the role of the hero.

Finds the journey in book 2 allegorically both an "actual trip by a horse-drawn coach and an intellective journey." Discusses the role of humor in the songs. Analyzes "The Cycle" as a "field of disturbance in the poem's journey," noting its "twisted iconographic style." Also mentions the role of language; the treatment of Howard Hughes, Rupert, corporate technology, Atlantes, and negativity; and the sources in Thoreau in this section. Comments on the drawings in "The Cycle" and Dorn's attempt, with this section, to "create a cognizance in the society of itself."

In book 3, provides a few references, especially literary allusions. Reviews the creative disorder, the role of burlesque and parody, and the treatment of the biplane pilot and of external versus indigenous "forms of authority." Also notes the use of multiple voices in a chorus "receiving and transmitting information." In book 4, discusses the "beneficial mutation of consciousness," the "rapid succession of scene shifts," and the "continuous arrival onstage of colorful characters possessed of diverse language acts." Also notes the treatment of Slinger, the moon, and Cocaine Lil and the role of song.

5   PERLOFF, MARJORIE [G.]. "From Image to Action: The Return of Story in Postmodern Poetry." In The Dance of the Intellect: Studies in the Poetry of the Pound Tradition. Cambridge Studies in American Literature and Culture. Cambridge: Cambridge University Press, pp. 155-71.
     Reprint of 1982.4.

6   RAY, DAVID. "Dorn, Ed(ward Merton)." In Contemporary Poets. 4th ed. Edited by James Vinson and D.L. Kirkpatrick. New York: St. Martin's Press, pp. 203-4.
     Reprint of 1970.5 with an updated bibliography. See also 1975.6 and 1980.12.

7   SIMMONS, KENITH L[EVICOFF]. "The Floating Bear and the Poetry Wars of the 1960s." Concerning Poetry 18, nos. 1-2:1-20.
     Notes Dorn's role in The Floating Bear and in its debate with academia and academic poets, especially noting his "The Poet Lectures Famous Potatoes."

8   von HALLBERG, ROBERT. American Poetry and Culture, 1945-1980. Cambridge, Mass.: Harvard University Press, pp. 15-16, 197-227, passim.
     Revision of 1981.15 with a revision of 1982.5, adding brief discussions on Dorn's type of political poetry and the quality of his ideas. Revision of 1985.9, slightly abridging the central essay, but adding comments on Dorn's audience and the critical reception of Slinger.

213

ED1985

9   . "'This marvellous accidentalism.'" In <u>Internal</u>
<u>Resistances: The Poetry of Edward Dorn</u>. Edited by Donald
Wesling. Berkeley: University of California Press, pp. 45-86.
        Revision of 1981.15 with a revision of 1982.5, adding brief
discussions on Dorn's type of political poetry and the quality of
his ideas. Revised in 1985.8.

10   [WESLING, DONALD; DRESMAN, PAUL CHARLES; DAVIDSON, ROBERT
MICHAEL; and GOLDING, ALAN.] "Introduction" to <u>Internal</u>
<u>Resistances: The Poetry of Edward Dorn</u>. Edited by Donald
Wesling. Berkeley: University of California Press, pp. 1-12.
        Finding him important, mentions Dorn's originality and re-
sistance to the literary establishment. Comments on him as a
"writer on the margin," and a political and moral poet.

11   WESLING, DONALD. "The Prosodies of Free Verse." In <u>The New</u>
<u>Poetries: Poetic Form since Coleridge and Wordsworth</u>.
Lewisburg, Pa.: Bucknell University Press; London and Toronto:
Associated University Presses, pp. 145-71.
        Revision of 1971.7.

12   . "'To fire we give everything': Dorn's Shorter Poems."
In <u>Internal Resistances: The Poetry of Edward Dorn</u>. Edited by
Donald Wesling. Berkeley: University of California Press,
pp. 13-44.
        Mentions Dorn's contempt for and treatment of society, espe-
cially the American public. Comments on his relationship to his
audience, comparing him to Jonathan Swift and the Augustans.
Treats him as a political poet, a classicist, and a satirist;
comments on his treatment of attention; and notes his use of
irony, humor, and lyricism. Finds his "Comedic Center" attempts
an integration of song, wit, and pronuncimento, and provides examples of different predominate types: the lyricism of "Vaquero"
and "Song ['my wife is lovely'],", and the wit of "Oxford." Outlines Dorn's differences from conventional lyricism and his dislike of lyric expansiveness. Comments on "The Rick of Green
Wood," "If It Should Ever Come," "The Deer's Eye the Hunter's
Nose," and a couple of the "Love Songs."

1986

1   BARTLETT, LEE. <u>Talking Poetry: Conversations in the Workshop</u>
<u>with Contemporary Poets</u>. Albuquerque: University of New
Mexico Press, pp. 109, 112, 191-93, 245, passim.
        A number of poets briefly mention Dorn. In their discus-
sions, Kenneth Irby mentions the books Dorn recommended to him,
Stephen Rodefer mentions Dorn's role at the Berkeley Poetry Conference in 1965, and Diane Wakoski mentions the originality of
<u>Slinger</u> and how Dorn came to write it.

2   BOLLOBÁS, ENIKÖ. "Versions of the Whole Earth Catalog: On the
     Poetry of Robert Duncan and Edward Dorn." In High and Low in
     American Culture. Edited by Charlotte Kretzoi. Budapest: L.
     Eötvös University, Department of English, pp. 39-53.
          Mentions Dorn's sense of poetry's "moral commitment," pro-
     viding a corrective to society by forcing the reader to conscious-
     ness. Notes his emphasis on attention and alertness as in "An
     Opinion on a Matter of Public Safety."

3   PAUL, SHERMAN. In Search of the Primitive: Reading David
     Antin, Jerome Rothenberg, and Gary Snyder. Baton Rouge, La.,
     and London: Louisiana State University Press, pp. 60, 147,
     231, passim.
          Occasionally briefly compares Dorn to Antin, Rothenberg, and
     Snyder.

4   STURGEON, TANDY. "An Interview with Edward Dorn." Contempo-
     rary Literature 27, no. 1 (Spring):1-16.
          In this 19 November 1984 interview, Dorn refers to Black
     Mountain College, political poetry, and "the struggle of a life to
     write." Also mentions his teaching, his relationship to Olson and
     what he learned from Olson, and publishing his books with individ-
     uals. Comments on Hello, La Jolla and Yellow Lola, especially
     "Sirius in January," "The song of the vulgar boatmen," "['Time
     definitely']," "['one must not be guilty']," and "['"one must not
     be unkind"']." Compares his work to Tom Raworth's. Mentions
     writers he values, Abhorrences, and the difference in his treat-
     ment of men and women. Notes his current feeling for The
     Shoshoneans and a few poems like "The Biggest Killing."
          Sturgeon describes Dorn's 17 November talk at the University
     of Wisconsin at Madison and his pragmatic political nature. Also
     notes his treatment of women.

                              1987

1   DORN, ED. "El Elko: Almost the Big Time: Notes on the 3rd
     Annual Cowboy Poetry Gathering, January 29-31, 1987." Rolling
     Stock, no. 12 [actually no. 13], pp. 4-6.
          Dorn provides biographical details about his trip, with
     Anselm Hollo, to the Cowboy Poetry Gathering in January 1987.
     Provides his observations and conversations with a number of peo-
     ple there, especially Dobro Dick Dillof.

2   GOLDING, ALAN. "History, Mutation, and the Mutation of History
     in Edward Dorn's Slinger." Sagetrieb: A Journal Devoted to
     Poets in the Imagist/Objectivist Tradition 6, no. 1 (Spring):
     7-20.

ED1987

    Comparing <u>Slinger</u> to long poems by other American twentieth-
century poets, finds a lack of the biographical and a separation
from history in Dorn's poem. Comments on the role of language and
the treatment of history and the self in <u>Slinger</u>. Also notes the
treatment of the character I, Howard Hughes, and "immense wealth
and power," including its "control over people's lives" in the
poem. Claims "Dorn seeks to revise rather than destroy notions of
personhood or the subject," and discusses his "interest in mind-
forms." Notes lack of external time and place as well as traditional characterization in the poem. Also points out genetic
references; the role of mutations in logic and language; rever-
sals, including reverse spellings and the "reversal of 'I'"; and
the death of I in the work. Notes the lack of personality, even
in the style which resists identification with "an individual
poetic sensibility." Mentions Dorn's treatment of power and
wealth as well as genetic references in earlier poems.

3   PERKINS, DAVID. <u>A</u> <u>History</u> <u>of</u> <u>Modern</u> <u>Poetry</u>: <u>Modernism</u> <u>and</u>
    <u>After</u>. Cambridge, Mass., and London: Harvard University
    Press, Belknap Press, pp. 494, 512-14, passim.
        Comments on Dorn's diction, the economic and historical
context of "On the Debt My Mother Owed to Sears Roebuck," and the
treatment of meaning and language in <u>Slinger</u>.

Robert Duncan

Major Works by Robert Duncan

1947   Heavenly City, Earthly City. Berkeley, Calif.: Bern Porter.

1949   Poems, 1948-49. [Berkeley, Calif.]: Berkeley Miscellany Editions.

1950   Medieval Scenes. San Francisco: Centaur Press.

1952   Fragments of a Disorderd Devotion. [San Francisco]: n.p.

1953   Faust Foutu: Act One. [San Francisco]: n.p.

       "Pages from a Notebook: None of Us Are/Is? Entirely Pleasant." Artist's View (San Francisco), no. 5 (July, [4 pp.]

1955   Caesar's Gate: Poems, 1949-1950. With collages by Jess Collins. Palma de Mallorca, Spain: Divers Press.

1958   Faust Foutu: A Comic Mask, Act One of Four Acts. [Santa Barbara, Calif.]: White Rabbit Press.

       Letters: Poems, 1953-1956. Jargon, no. 14. Highlands, N.C.: Jonathan Williams.

1959   Faust Foutu: An Entertainment in Four Parts. Stinson Beach, Calif.: Enkidu Surrogate.

       Selected Poems. Pocket Poets Series, no. 10. San Francisco: City Lights Books.

1960   The Opening of the Field. New York: Grove Press, Evergreen Books.

1963   From the Mabinogion. [Chapel Hill, N.C.]: Quarterly Review of Literature.

1964   As Testimony: The Poem and the Scene. San Francisco: White Rabbit Press.

Roots and Branches. New York: Charles Scribner's Sons.

Writing Writing: A Composition Book for Madison, 1953: Stein Imitations. Albuquerque, N.M.: Sumbooks.

1965   Medea at Kolchis: The Maiden Head. Berkeley, Calif.: Oyez.

The Sweetness and Greatness of Dante's "Divine Comedy": Lecture Given October 27th, 1965, at the Dominican College of San Rafael. San Francisco: Open Space.

1966   A Book of Resemblances: Poems, 1950-1953. New Haven, Conn.: Henry Wenning.

Fragments of a Disorderd Devotion. San Francisco: Gnomon Press; Toronto: Island Press.

Of the War: "Passages," 22-27. Berkeley, Calif.: Oyez.

Six Prose Pieces. [Madison, Wis.]: Perishable Press.

The Years as Catches: First Poems, 1939-1946. Berkeley, Calif.: Oyez.

1967   The Cat and the Blackbird. San Francisco: White Rabbit Press.

Epilogos. [Los Angeles]: Black Sparrow Press.

1968   Bending the Bow. New York: New Directions Books.

Names of People. Illustrated by Jess. Los Angeles: Black Sparrow Press.

The Truth and Life of Myth: An Essay in Essential Autobiography. Crown Octavos, no. 16. New York: House of Books.

1969   Achilles' Song. New York: Phoenix Book Shop.

Derivations: Selected Poems, 1950-1956. London: Fulcrum Press.

The First Decade: Selected Poems, 1940-1950. London: Fulcrum Press.

The Opening of the Field. London: Jonathan Cape.

Play Time, Pseudo Stein: From the Laboratory Records: Notebook, 1953. [San Francisco]: Tenth Muse.

1970   A Selection of 65 Drawings from One Drawing-Book, 1952-1956. Los Angeles: Black Sparrow Press.

Tribunals: <u>"Passages,"</u> <u>31-35</u>. Los Angeles: Black Sparrow Press.

1971   <u>Bending the Bow</u>. London: Jonathan Cape.

<u>Writing Writing</u>: <u>A Composition Book for Madison, 1953</u>: <u>Stein Imitations</u>. Portland, Oreg.: Trask House.

1972   <u>Caesar's Gate</u>: <u>Poems, 1949-50</u>. With Paste-Ups by Jess. Sand Dollar, no. 8. [Berkeley, Calif.]: Sand Dollar.

1973   <u>The Opening of the Field</u>. New York: New Directions Books.

<u>A Seventeenth Century Suite in Homage to the Metaphysical Genius in English Poetry, 1590-1690</u>: <u>Being Imitations, Derivations, and Variations upon Certain Conceits and Findings Made among Strong Lines, c. Nov. 5, 1971-Decm. 16, 1971, Aug. 5-18 and Oct. 22, 1973</u>. San Francisco: n.p.

<u>The Truth and Life of Myth</u>: <u>An Essay in Essential Autobiography</u>. Fremont, Mich.: Sumac Press in cooperation with SOMA Books.

1974   <u>Dante</u>. A Curriculum of the Soul, no. 8. Canton, N.Y.: Institute of Further Studies.

<u>An Ode and Arcadia</u>. With Jack Spicer. Berkeley, Calif.: Ark Press.

1975   <u>The Venice Poem</u>. [Sydney, Australia]: Prism.

1977   <u>Passages et structures</u>. Translated by Serge Fauchereau. Paris: Christian Bourgois Editeur.

1978   <u>Medieval Scenes, 1950 and 1959</u>. Kent, Ohio: Kent State University Libraries.

1979   <u>Veil, Turbine, Cord, and Bird</u>. [Sets of Syllables, Sets of Words, Sets of Lines, Sets of Poems Addressing: Veil, Turbine, Cord, and Bird.] Brooklyn, N.Y.: Jordan Davis.

1981   <u>The Five Songs</u>. La Jolla, Calif.: Friends of the UCSD Library and Archive for New Poetry, [University of California at San Diego].

1982   <u>Towards an Open Universe</u>. Aquila Essays, no. 17. Portree, Isle of Skye, Scotland: Johnston Green & Co. Publishers, Aquila Publishing.

1984   <u>Ground Work</u>: <u>Before the War</u>. New York: New Directions Books.

1985   Faust Foutu: A Comic Masque. Barrytown, N.Y.: Station Hill
        Press. (A reprint of Faust Foutu: An Entertainment in Four
        Parts [1959].)

        Fictive Certainties. New York: New Directions.

1987   Ground Work II: In the Dark. New York: New Directions.

Writings about Robert Duncan

1944

1   DUNCAN, ROBERT. "The Homosexual in Society." Politics: A
     Monthly Review 1, no. 7 (August):209-11.
        In this article, Duncan claims that in the past he partially
     denied his full participation in the human because he, as a homo-
     sexual, joined with some who exaggerated their differences from
     others in an almost demonic fashion and who formed a cult that
     "rejected any struggle toward recognition in social equality."
     Believes such cult groupings to be forces of inhumanity, and im-
     plicitly vows to hold "only one devotion . . . to human freedom,
     toward the liberation of human love, human conflicts, human aspir-
     ations." Also claims to have misrepresented "direct emotions and
     realizations" as "conflicts rising from mystical sources. Re-
     printed: 1973.9; reprinted in 1983.13; slightly revised with an
     introduction, postscript, and footnotes, all written in 1959:
     1985.20. See also 1979.1, 22, 27; 1980.5; 1983.13.

1945

1   KUENNING, WILLIAM. "A Reply." Direct Action, Summer,
     pp. 39-42.
        Argues with Duncan's suggestion in "What to Do Now" (Direct
     Action, Summer 1945, pp. 35-39) that people should steal excess
     food supplies.

1947

1   "About Robert Duncan," blurb to Heavenly City, Earthly City.
     Berkeley, Calif.: Bern Porter, inside front flap of jacket.
        Briefly quotes Duncan on the composition of "Treesbank
     Poems" and on influences on him.

1948

1   BERRYMAN, JOHN. "Waiting for the End, Boys." Partisan Review
     15, no. 2:254-67.
         In an unfavorable review of Heavenly City, Earthly City,
     quotes from 1947.1, and feels Duncan has not profited from those
     he lists as influences.

2   MILES, JOSEPHINE. "Pacific Coast Poetry: 1947." Pacific
     Spectator: A Journal of Interpretation 2, no. 2 (Spring):
     134-50.
         Briefly mentions the cadence in "An Apollonian Elegy."

3   RUKEYSER, MURIEL. "Myth and Torment." Poetry 72, no. 1
     (April):48-51.
         In a favorable review of Heavenly City, Earthly City,
     mentions influences on Duncan, and notes reactions against his
     homosexuality.

1949

1   DUNCAN, ROBERT. Statement in "The Poet and Poetry: A Sym-
     posium." Occident, Fall, pp. 39-40.
         In his section, Duncan discusses the "interesting problems"
     of writing poetry for him: the way "to increase the complexity of
     interpenetration of parts" of the poem while making it "go on as
     long as possible," so that the "final performance . . . will keep
     [him] intrigued intellectually and emotionally." Also notes the
     influences of Kenneth Rexroth and Josephine Miles and the idea of
     poetry as a projection of the poet's life into the world, a rit-
     ual. Reprinted in 1983.13.

1953

1   DUNCAN, ROBERT. "Pages from a Notebook: None of Us Are/Is?
     Entirely Pleasant." Artist's View (San Francisco), no. 5
     (July), [4 pp.].
         Duncan comments on his concept of revision and discusses his
     sense of the creative process as play, as violence, as confusion,
     as intoxication, and as controlled although beyond design. See
     1954.2 and 1955.1. Reprinted in part: 1960.5.

1954

1   DUNCAN, ROBERT. "near-far Mister Olson." Origin: A Quarterly
     for the Creative, 1st ser., no. 12 (Spring):210-11.

In this January 1954 letter to Olson, Duncan mentions what he is learning from Olson and compares their poetry. Provides a few biographical details.

2   OLSON, CHARLES. "Against Wisdom as Such." Black Mountain Review 1, no. 1 (Spring):35-39.
    In a response to 1953.1, discusses Duncan's sense of wisdom, arguing that it is not universal or extricable from one's self. Claims Duncan exercises his wisdom every time he writes. (Duncan often refers to this; see 1955.1; 1969.5; 1976.22; 1978.15; 1981.8. See also 1972.16; 1977.4, 7, 11; 1979.8; 1980.16-17, 21, 30; 1983.6.) Reprinted: 1964.16. Reprinted in part: 1965.11; 1967.10; 1968.21.

1955

1   DUNCAN, ROBERT. "From a Notebook, 11/1/54." Black Mountain Review, no. 5 (Summer), pp. 209-12.
    Duncan comments on Olson's quarrel with him concerning wisdom (see 1953.1 and 1954.2). Finds himself indebted to the romantics, especially Stevens, Mallarmé, and Poe. Comments on his sense of his own mortality and his lack of concern about the opinions of others and "writing the great poem." Mentions his awareness of his joy in the very process of creation aided through his use of mescaline. Reprinted: 1973.1; 1985.17.

2   _____. "Preface for Caesar's Gate." Caesar's Gate: Poems, 1949-1950. Palma de Mallorca, Spain: Divers Press, [pp. 11-15].
    Duncan discusses the hell-like state of misery he came to while writing the poems in Caesar's Gate. Reprinted: 1972.9.

1956

1   CREELEY, ROBERT. "On Love." Black Mountain Review, no. 6 (Spring), pp. 217-22.
    Creeley provides a portion of a letter from Duncan on love. Reprinted: 1970.4.

2   DUNCAN, ROBERT. "Notes." Black Mountain Review, no. 6 (Spring), pp. 5-14.
    Duncan writes of the "closeness of Cocteau's journal to [his, Duncan's] own designs" and his "abilities at imitation" which the culture does not value. Also comments on his reaction to moral or emotional proscriptions, his love of art and literature, and his belief in "Love." Quotes from "The Human Communion Traces" when discussing his love of others. Claims a condemnation

RD1956

to extinction for "being a confirmed Sodomite, as written in the Zohar," will "give . . . an enduring pathos to [his] writing."

3   _____. "Notes on Poetics Regarding Olson's Maximus." Black Mountain Review, no. 6 (Spring), pp. 201–11.
     In this essay on Pound, Joyce, and especially Olson, Duncan mentions his own debts to American painters and to "Zukofsky's work on Shakespeare." Reprinted: 1964.11; 1973.1; 1985.17.

4   ECKMAN, FREDERICK. "Six Poets, Young or Unknown." Poetry 89, no. 1 (October):52–63.
     In an unfavorable review of Caesar's Gate (1955), finds much of Duncan's poetry manneristic, "quasi-daemonic," and overly rhetorical.

1957

1   CREELEY, ROBERT. Review of The Journals of Jean Cocteau, transcribed and edited by Wallace Fowlie. New Mexico Quarterly 26, no. 4 (Winter):397–400.
     Quotes from an unpublished notebook of Duncan's on Cocteau's Journal d'un inconnu. Reprinted: 1970.4.

2   REXROTH, KENNETH. "San Francisco Letter." Evergreen Review 1, no. 2:5–14.
     Briefly finds Duncan is a "member of the international avant garde" but not a modernist; notes his affiliations with other writers. Reprinted in part: 1960.6. See also 1982.19.

1958

1   DUNCAN, ROBERT. Letter to the Editor. Poetry 92, no. 3 (June):196–97.
     In this letter, Duncan briefly discusses his debt to Pound and his interest in Coleridge.

2   _____. Preface to Letters. Highlands, N.C.: Jonathan Williams, pp. i–vi.
     In this preface written in 1956, Duncan discusses writing the poems and prose pieces in Letters. Mentions the "process of re-vision and disorganization," and comments on his service to the language and his use of myth and the past. Reprinted: 1968.11.

1959

1   ROSENTHAL, M[ACHA] L[EWIS]. "Notes from the Future: Two
    Poets." Nation 189, no. 13 (24 October):257-58.
        In brief, fairly favorable reviews of Selected Poems and
    Letters, finds Duncan a derivative, mystical poet.

1960

1   AMMONS, A[RCHIE] R[ANDOLPH]. "Three Poets." Poetry 96, no. 1
    (April):52-55.
        In a relatively unfavorable review of Duncan's Selected
    Poems, believes the "poems are illustrations, objectifications of
    the interchange between order and disorder." Finds they contain
    too much "comment and explanation" although they occasionally "say
    something wonderful." Lists influences on Duncan.

2   CREELEY, ROBERT. "'A light, a glory, a fair luminous cloud.'"
    Poetry 96, no. 1 (April):55-57.
        In a favorable review of Duncan's Letters, frequently quotes
    from the work, and focuses on the creative process itself, espe-
    cially noting the risk for the poet. Finds the creation shapes
    the creator. Reprinted: 1970.4.

3   DUNCAN, ROBERT. Biographical Note. In The New American
    Poetry, 1945-1960. Edited by Donald M[erriam] Allen. New
    York: Grove Press, pp. 432-36.
        In this lengthy note, Duncan mentions what he learned from
    and/or his relationship to Edna Keough, Ernst Kantorowicz, Mary
    Fabilli, Sanders Russell, Spicer, Creeley, Levertov, Whitehead,
    Olson, Jess, Helen Adam, and others.

4   ____. Note to "Come, Let Me Free Myself." Migrant, no. 8
    (September), p. 33.
        Duncan briefly provides background material concerning the
    inception and creation of "Come, Let Me Free Myself."

5   ____. "Pages from a Notebook." In The New American Poetry,
    1945-1960. Edited by Donald M[erriam] Allen. New York: Grove
    Press, pp. 400-407.
        Reprinted from 1953.1.

6   REXROTH, KENNETH. Blurb to The Opening of the Field. New
    York: Grove Press, Evergreen Books, rear cover.
        Reprint only of the Duncan section of 1957.2.

7   SNODGRASS, W[ILLIAM] D[EWITT]. "Four Gentlemen, Two Ladies."
    Hudson Review 13, no. 1 (Spring):120-31.

RD1960

In a brief, favorable review of Selected Poems, comments on Duncan's use of language and on his struggle "to merge the mythic with . . . immediate experience."

1961

1 DUNCAN, ROBERT. "Ideas of the Meaning of Form." Kulchur, no. 4 (Winter), pp. 61-74.
    In this essay on rationality and "the concept of form as the imposing of rules" in the tradition of literature, Duncan briefly comments on his need for "free association" and "inspirational chaos." Revised: 1973.10; 1982.9; 1985.17.

2 REXROTH, KENNETH. "The Belated Discovery." Nation 192, no. 2 (14 January):35-36.
    In a favorable review of The Opening of the Field, briefly finds Duncan in a tradition of postwar poets "of experimentation and revolt."

3 _____. "Poets, Old and New." In Assays. New York: New Directions, pp. 206-39.
    Mentions the literary establishment has ignored Duncan. Finds his work tries both to communicate and to reflect an "inner life attitude of immense seriousness and devotion."

4 WRIGHT, JAMES. "The Few Poets of England and America." Minnesota Review 1, no. 2 (January):248-56.
    In a review of The New American Poetry, 1945-1960, ed. Donald Merriam Allen (New York: Grove Press, 1960), briefly mentions the rhetorical quality and musicality of Duncan's poetry. Reprinted: 1983.38.

1962

1 CAMBON, GLAUCO. "Nuovi poeti americani." [In Italian.] Verri, n.s., no. 1 (February), pp. 59-72.
    Mentions Duncan's favorable foreign reception and his use of open form poetics, noting his lack of intention as he follows the unforeseen arc of the poem. Comments on his treatment of language as magic and the fact that he, like Blake, throws himself into the consuming fire of the poem. Notes his understanding of the possible in "The Structure of Rime, II," believing the female figure, lion, serpent, male figure, and human forest in the first five The Structure of Rime poems arise from the same sense of the formless. Notes the ecstasy in "Apprehensions" and the rhythmic-visionary thought in a few other poems.

2   DICKEY, JAMES. "The Stillness at the Center of the Target."
    Sewanee Review 70, no. 3 (Summer/July-September):484-503.
        In a somewhat favorable review of The Opening of the Field,
    dislikes Duncan's pretentious mysticism. Enjoys his original mind
    and sense of poetry as "a divine form of speech." Comments on
    "The Structure of Rime, XI." Reprinted in part, with slight revi-
    sions: 1968.3a; 1973.8.

3   DUNCAN, ROBERT. "For the Novices of Vancouver, August 25-28,
    1962." Tish: A Poetry Newsletter--Vancouver, no. 13
    (14 September), pp. 3-5.
        In this letter, Duncan mentions a section from Hart Crane's
    Voyages that he applies to his own homosexuality and poetry.

4   GILBERT, JACK. "Between Verses: Report on a West Coast Poetry
    Festival." New York Times Book Review, 9 September, pp. 5, 34.
        Briefly notes Duncan's refusal to participate in the San
    Francisco Poetry Festival in the summer of 1962.

5   SORRENTINO, GILBERT. Review of The Opening of the Field.
    Yugen, no. 8, pp. 11-15.
        In this favorable review, emphasizes Duncan's life within
    the life of his poetry, his sincerity, his beliefs, his "freshness
    of language, [and his] mastery of the line."

                                1963

1   ARONSON, S.M.L. "Robert Duncan." Yale Literary Magazine 131,
    nos. 3-4 [New Poetry issue] (April):15-16.
        Briefly finds many poems in The Opening of the Field rely on
    an authoritative vision and craftsmanship. Dislikes occasional
    "hysterical passages" and the overuse of imagery.

2   BRAKHAGE, STAN. "Metaphors on Vision." Film Culture, no. 30
    (Fall), [pp. 23-86].
        Briefly mentions Faust Foutu, "Adam's Way," and The Opening
    of the Field, and quotes from Duncan on "'depth' and 'complexity.'"
    Also provides Olson's reminiscence of a conversation with Duncan
    about starting a college and Olson's comments concerning Duncan's
    thoughts on magic and the Adam myth. The last section revised:
    1970.2; 1971.2.

3   D[AWSON], D[AVE], et al. "Editorial: Olson/Creeley/Levertov/
    Duncan/Ginsberg/Whalen/Avison." Tish: A Poetry Newsletter--
    Vancouver, no. 21 (September), pp. 1-8.
        In this series of notes on the July 1963 Vancouver Poetry
    Conference, provides impressions of Duncan's ideas on the uncon-
    scious, the language, and the use of performance. Briefly

RD1963

compares Ginsberg's "Howl" with Duncan's "A Poem Beginning with a Line by Pindar."

4   DUNCAN, ROBERT. "From The Day Book [The H.D. Book, Part II: prior to Chapter 1]." Origin, 2d ser., Response, no. 10 (July), pp. 1-47.
        Duncan lists some of his reading, notes his sense of poems as "occasions of Poetry," and mentions that his idea of poetry was changed by Olson's work. Reminisces about Olson reading O'Ryan in 1955 at Black Mountain College. In part revised in 1968.9. Reprinted in part: 1975.15.

5   _____. Notes to "Two Messages." Quarterly Review of Literature 12, no. 3:190-91.
        Duncan provides notes to "Two Messages," later titled "Two Presentations." Reprinted: 1974.16; 1975.18. Revised and slightly expanded: 1964.12; 1972.8.

6   SCHAFF, DAVID [S.S.]. "Some Statements on Projective Verse." Yale Literary Magazine 131, nos. 3-4 (April):5-14.
        Praises Duncan's imagination and "grand voice." Faults his treatment of writing and poetry as well as his opulence.

1964

1   BERGÉ, CAROL. The Vancouver Report. [New York: Fuck You Press], 17 pp.
        Details Duncan's participation in the 1963 Vancouver Poetry Conference, providing impressions, quotations, and biographical information. Does not find Duncan a good poet, but can accept him as "jolly, clever, . . . a performer to the end." Claims he dominated some of the sessions, and quotes him on being open to experence and on the use of drugs. Briefly quotes Duncan on Medieval Scenes and "A Poem Beginning with a Line by Pindar." Reprinted in part: 1964.2; 1976.6.

2   _____. "The Vancouver Report; or, How I Fell in Love with Robert Duncan." Open Space, no. 7 [(July), p. 39].
        Reprints a small portion of 1964.1 on Duncan.

3   BOWERING, GEORGE. "The New American Prosody: A Look at the Problem of Notating 'Free' Verse." Kulchur 4, no. 15 (Autumn):3-15.
        Briefly quotes from 1961.1 on poetic form and control.

4   CARRUTH, HAYDEN. "Scales of the Marvelous." Nation 199, no. 18 (7 December):442-44.

In a favorable review of Roots and Branches, mentions the
tension in Duncan's work and his use of traditional forms in modern ways, illustrating with a section of "Four Songs the Night
Nurse Sang." Slightly revised: 1982.4.

5   DUNCAN, ROBERT. As Testimony: The Poem and the Scene. San
    Francisco: White Rabbit Press, 20 pp.
    In this essay, begun as a 24 February 1958 letter to George
Stanley, Duncan comments on an argument with Stanley at a 23
February reading of poetry. Continues to argue for his sense of
meaningfulness in poetry, illustrating with poems read by Harold
Dull and Joanne Kyger. Mentions his current reading and a past
argument with Donald Thayer Bliss. Notes the source for a line of
"A Poem Beginning with a Line by Pindar" in a novel by Charles
Williams. Adds a few biographical details from 25-26 February
about his contacts with others, including Spicer. See also
1984.12, 31.

6   _____. "At Lammas Tide: Presentation Note to Pat and Helen
    Adam." Open Space, no. 8 [(August), p. 12].
    Provides occasion for "My Mother Would Be a Falconress,"
giving biographical details from 1946 and 1 August 1964. Revised:
1966.7; 1968.7; 1971.12.

7   _____. "The H.D. Book: Chapter 5." Aion: A Journal of Tra-
    ditionary Science, no. 1 (December), [pp. 5-29].
    Duncan provides some reminiscences from his childhood con-
cerning fairy tales; his early understanding and exposure to the
occult; and his dreams. Comments on his relatives, including his
Aunt Fay, his maternal grandmother, and his adopted parents. Also
mentions his early and later reading and his early imaginings of
and play concerning Atlantis and the destruction of the world.
Reprinted in part and slightly revised: 1968.4. Reprinted:
1983.8.

8   _____. Letters to Kenneth Irby. Sum: A Newsletter of Current
    Workings, no. 2 (February), p. 28.
    In these excerpts from May 1963 letters, Duncan describes
how he feels during the creative process.

9   _____. "Nights and Days." Sumac 1, no. 1 (Fall):101-46.
    In this section from The H.D. Book, Duncan provides a few
biographical details concerning his relationship with Olson and
mentions Olson's influence on him.

10 _____. "A Note for Open Space 7." Open Space, no. 7 [(July),
    pp. 7-9].

RD1964

Comments on the poems in the Passages sequence, especially
how they are being written and their numbering and titling. Provides revisions for the portions already published, especially
nos. 2-9.

11   . "Notes on Poetics: Regarding Olson's Maximus."
Review: A Magazine of Poetry and Criticism, no. 10 (January),
pp. 36-42.
        Reprint of 1956.3.

12   . Notes to "Two Presentations." In Roots and Branches.
New York: Charles Scribner's Sons, pp. 73, 74.
        A revision and slight expansion of 1963.5.

13   . "Novices: October 27, 3-4 AM, 1963." Matter, no. 3,
[pp. 1-3].
        Duncan mentions the reactions of Olson and Olson's students
at the State University of New York at Buffalo to his creative
etymology and use of the word "hallucination" to describe vision.
Also mentions two visions he had, and discusses the imagination.

14   FRANKLYN, A. FREDRIC. Letter. El corno emplumado, no. 9
(January), pp. 151-52.
        In this August 1963 letter, quotes from Duncan, and mentions
his participation in the Vancouver Poetry Conference.

15   . "Toward Print (Excerpts from a Journal of the U. of
British Columbia Seminar)." Trace, no. 51 (Winter), pp. 277-
84, 294.
        In this series of notes dated 24 July to 4 August 1963 taken
at the Vancouver Poetry Conference, provides details about
Duncan's role at the conference. Records a number of Duncan's
comments, especially those on a poet's relationship to events.
Notes Ginsberg's reaction to Duncan.

16   OLSON, CHARLES. "Against Wisdom as Such." Open Space, no. 8
[(August), pp. 16-19].
        Reprint of 1954.2.

17   VANCE, EUGENE, and SCHAFF, DAVID [S.S.]. "On Poetry." Yale
Reports (WTIC-Hartford, radio programs), no. 328 (31 May),
9 pp.
        In a transcript of a 31 May 1964 radio discussion, Duncan
comments on various poetry scenes in San Francisco and his attraction to medieval and Renaissance periods and figures. Also notes
his feeling for Zukofsky, Olson, and Pound as mentors and the role
of intention in his work. Discusses in detail his sense of the
creative process including achieving a "readiness" to write; following the "integrity of the process" while discovering a form;

and interrupting himself and otherwise avoiding his usual themes such as the "dancing motif" so that the writing will be a continual discovery.

18   WILLIAMS, JONATHAN. "Zou-cough's Key's Nest of Poultry." Kulchur 4, no. 14 (Summer):4-13.
        Quotes letters Duncan wrote concerning his relationship to and appreciation of Zukofsky.

1965

1   DAVEY, FRANK[LAND WILMOT]. "Rime: A Scholarly Piece Written Whilst Pursuing an Academical Education." Evidence, no. 9, pp. 98-103.
        Discusses Duncan's theory of rhyme as "the measurable distance between two corresponding elements" including "themes, images, syntactic units," and phonetic echoes. Mentions Lionel Kearns's limited application of Duncan's theory. Reprinted: 1967.4; 1976.9.

2   DONOGHUE, DENIS. Connoisseurs of Chaos: Ideas of Order in Modern American Poetry. New York: Macmillan Co., pp. 49-50.
        Believes Duncan's The Opening of the Field is influenced by and extends Whitman's Leaves of Grass. Reprinted: 1984.6.

3   DORN, EDWARD. "The Outcasts of Foker Plat: News from the States." Wivenhoe Park Review, no. 1 (Winter), pp. 51-62.
        Briefly praises Duncan's "The Multiversity: Passages, 21," but questions if Clark Kerr or Chancellor Edward William Strong are worth derision. Reprinted: 1980.9.

4   DUNCAN, ROBERT. "Another Preface, 1963/1965," in Medea at Kolchis: The Maiden Head. Berkeley, Calif.: Oyez, [pp. vii-x].
        In this preface, Duncan provides the creative development of Medea at Kolchis. Discusses each chapter in turn, and comments on a few of the scenes. Describes the settings used at the 29-30 August 1956 performances at Black Mountain College, and mentions the acting at those performances.
        Also remembers some childhood and later imaginings.

5   _____. "The Lasting Contribution of Ezra Pound." Agenda 4, no. 2 [Special Issue in Honor of Ezra Pound's Eightieth Birthday] (October-November):23-26.
        Duncan details the importance of Pound for his poetry insofar as Pound dealt with tradition, order, and rhythm.

6 _____. "Notes from a Reading at the Poetry Center, San
Francisco, March 1, 1959." Floating Bear, no. 31 [(June),
pp. 8–9].
Duncan discusses his sense of the spiritual world, of his
mortality, and of himself as a poet in the service of Poetry.
Reprinted with a note: 1973.13.

7 _____. The Sweetness and Greatness of Dante's "Divine Comedy."
San Francisco: Open Space, [26 pp.].
In this 27 October 1965 lecture, Duncan discusses reading
and rereading Dante. Reprinted: 1985.17.

8 EICHELE, ROBIN. "A Personal Re-cognizance." Work (Detroit),
no. 2 (Fall), pp. 73–79.
Provides a summary and impressions of Duncan's 12–16 July
1965 seminar at the Berkeley Poetry Conference. Discusses the
sense of chaos and spontaneity in Duncan's poetics.

9 LINICK, ANTHONY. "A History of the American Literary Avant-
Garde since World War II." Ph.D. dissertation, University of
California, Los Angeles, pp. 27, 45, 57–58, 383–84, passim.
Continually mentions Duncan as a member of the avant-garde,
detailing his roles as editor of and contributor to little magazines and commenting on his political ideas. Also occasionally
mentions the publication of his books by small presses. Provides
the results of a poll of avant-garde writers ranking the importance and influence of Duncan. See Dissertation Abstracts
International 25 (1965):7226.

10 MAZZOCCO, ROBERT. "A Philosophical Poet." New York Review of
Books 4, no. 9 (3 June):20–23.
In a fairly unfavorable review of Roots and Branches, finds
Duncan unusual, and mentions parallels to Whitehead. Notes the
role of continuities and homosexuality in his work, and comments
on "Sonnet 1" and "The Law."

11 OLSON, CHARLES. "Against Wisdom as Such." In "Human Universe"
and Other Essays. Edited by Donald [Merriam] Allen. San
Francisco: Auerhahn Society, pp. 67–71.
Reprint of 1954.2.

12 STEPANCHEV, STEPHEN. American Poetry since 1945: A Critical
Survey. New York: Harper & Row, Publishers, pp. 145–56,
passim.
Notes Duncan's use of projective verse and treatment of
evil, suffering, the poet, imagination, and love as God.

13 WAGNER, LINDA WELSHIMER. "An Interview with Robert Creeley."
Minnesota Review, o.s. 5, nos. 3–4 (August–December):309–21.

In this 1965 interview, Creeley notes his envy of Duncan's long poems and praises Duncan's political poems. Revised, rearranged, and combined with Lewis MacAdams's interview in 1968.29 which, in turn, is revised, rearranged, and expanded as 1973.29, the fullest version of Wagner's interview.

14   WILL, FREDERICK. "Notes on Robert Duncan." Poetry 106, no. 6 (September):427-28.
       In a fairly favorable review of Roots and Branches, notes the reader's sense of being "under the influence of a higher power," Duncan, as "both master and mountebank."

1966

1   CLARK, THOMAS. "The Exchange: A Concern." Kulchur 5, no. 20 (Winter):96-100.
      Discusses Duncan's "physical basis" for poetry as seen in "A Poem Beginning with a Line by Pindar" and "Notes on Poetics Regarding Olson's Maximus," and notes his views on Pound and Harold Dull in As Testimony (see 1964.5). Finds Duncan calls for an exchange between the subjective, human world and the objective, nonhuman.

2   CREELEY, ROBERT. "'To disclose that vision particular to dreams.'" Humanist 26, no. 1 (January-February):28.
      In a favorable review of Roots and Branches, finds Duncan "informed by a 'voice'" beyond his intention. Notes his commitment, treatment of Eve and the Great Mother figure, and use of a "vision particular to dreams" in his poetry. Reprinted: 1970.4.

3   DEMBO, L[AWRENCE] S[ANFORD]. "Postscript: Charles Olson and Robert Duncan: The Mystique of Speech and Rhythm." In Conceptions of Reality in Modern American Poetry. Berkeley: University of California Press, pp. 208-19.
      Illustrating with several poems, notes Duncan's "speech mysticism," sense of language, and obedience to language and life. Mentions the treatment of speech in "Doves" and of "sex, music, and cosmos" in "A Set of Romantic Hymns."

4   DUNCAN, ROBERT. "Beginnings: Chapter 1 of the The H.D. Book, Part 1." Coyote's Journal, nos. 5-6, pp. 8-31.
      In this section from The H.D. Book, Duncan provides a reminiscence concerning his relationship to his high school English teacher, Edna Keough, and, through her, his development of a love for certain writers, including H.D. Also explains why he chose to follow the "authority of the poem" over that of the state or university by relating an incident in 1937 about reading Joyce

RD1966

aloud to Cecily Kramer and Lillian Fabilli while attending the
University of California at Berkeley.

5   [DUNCAN, ROBERT?] "Bibliography of Work Written 1937-1946."
     In The Years as Catches: First Poems, 1939-1946. Berkeley,
     Calif.: Oyez, [pp. 95-99].
        Provides a bibliography of Duncan's work from 1937 to 1946,
     including his comments on the "Treesbank Poems."

6   DUNCAN, ROBERT. "Introduction" to The Years as Catches: First
     Poems, 1939-1946. Berkeley, Calif.: Oyez, pp. i-xi.
        In this introduction, Duncan provides biographical details
     from 1937 to 1946, discussing his awareness of his homosexuality,
     the title of The Years as Catches, his poetry as a "source of
     feeling and thought," his sense of the state's power, and his
     relationship to Sanders Russell. Notes the influence of Milton,
     Blake, Sanders Russell, George Baker, Auden, Pound, and Saint-John
     Perse on his work. Also comments about Lorca's influence on "An
     African Elegy" and Laura Riding's influence on "King Haydn of
     Miami Beach." Provides a model of his life work, and comments on
     his present reaction to his early work.

7   _____. Note to "Lammas Dream Poem." Paris Review 9, no. 36
     (Winter):74.
        A revision of 1964.6, omitting some of the material and
     adding information about the bells in "My Mother Would Be a
     Falconress."

8   _____. Preface to A Book of Resemblances: Poems, 1950-1953.
     New Haven, Conn.: Henry Wenning, pp. vii-x.
        In this lengthy preface, Duncan discusses his intention in
     such poems as "An Imaginary War Elegy," "An Essay at War," and "A
     Book of Resemblances"; his sense of writing as a natural process;
     and his reading of books on myth and hermetic poetry. Discusses
     the influence of Hans Arp, Gertrude Stein, and W.C. Williams on
     his work, including A Book of Resemblances, and comments on his
     relationship to Jess and Jess's illustrations for the book.
     Claims that painting and the work of Jess were the influence on
     other work such as Fragments of a Disorderd Devotion and Caesar's
     Gate. Also provides a few biographical details from 1950 to 1954,
     and mentions the composition of Faust Foutu and Writing Writing.

9   _____. "A Statement about 'The Law.'" In Poems for Young
     Readers: Selections from Their Own Writings by Poets Attending
     the Houston Festival of Contemporary Poetry. [Champaign,
     Ill.]: National Council of Teachers of English, p. 48.
        In this preface, Duncan mentions his own "passionate life
     experience" and searchings in his late teens. Comments on the

rhythms, tones, and content of "The Law" and the idea of law in the poem.

10 _____ . "Towards an Open Universe." In Poets on Poetry.
Edited by Howard Nemerov. New York and London: Basic Books, pp. 133–46.
In this essay, Duncan discusses "the birth of life itself" in the last section of "Apprehensions," as well as "Atlantis" and "A Storm of White," finding in that "poetry enacts in its order the order of first things." Also provides the occasion behind "Food for Fire, Food for Thought" and "A Poem Beginning with a Line by Pindar," discussing the figure of Hermes in the latter. Provides his sense of the creative process as a moment-by-moment discovery of the "divine order or natural order" in his immediate surroundings. Influenced by the later work of Pound and W.C. Williams, feels that he and others learned to "derive melody and story from impulse not from plan" and that this has "opened out upon a new art." Reprinted: 1973.1; 1985.17. Revised: 1973.15; 1974.20; 1982.11.

11 KASOWITZ, DAN. "A Description of 'Apprehensions': The Tantamounce." Tish: A Poetry Newsletter--Vancouver, no. 37 (18 June), pp. 3–4.
Discusses "Apprehensions" in terms of its structure, involv- ing the interplay of motifs from archaeology and architecture. Details its theme: the "generations of the living world" and the "formation . . . of man's mind." (But see 1966.14.)

12 OLSON, CHARLES. Reading at Berkeley. Transcribed by [Ralph Maud]. [Buffalo, N.Y.: privately printed], pp. 22, 24, 38– 40, 45, 59, passim.
Another version of 1966.13. See also 1970.15; 1978.33.

13 _____ . Reading at Berkeley. Transcribed by Zoe Brown.
[Berkeley or San Francisco], Calif.: Coyote, pp. 17, 19, 25– 26, 43, passim.
In this transcription of a 23 July 1965 reading and discus- sion at the Berkeley Poetry Conference, Olson occasionally addres- ses Duncan and mentions Duncan's introduction of him. Also mentions The H.D. Book and a dream Duncan had of him. Provides a few biographical details concerning Duncan at the Vancouver Poetry Conference. See also 1966.12; 1970.15. The fullest, most acces- sible version is 1978.33.

14 PERSKY, STAN. Letter to the Editor. Tish: A Poetry Newsletter--Vancouver, no. 38 (13 November), p. 2.
Claims 1966.11 is self-indulgent and does a disservice to the "poetic experience" of "Apprehensions."

15 WAH, PAULINE [later Pauline Butling]. "Robert Duncan: The
   Poem as Process." M.A. thesis, University of British Columbia,
   85 pp.
       Providing material from an unpublished 1963 application by
   Duncan for a Guggenheim Fellowship, focuses on Duncan's poetry as
   a multiphasic process lacking imposed form. From 1942 to 1950,
   finds it "centered on a subject (love), while language and process
   are the focus of attention in the later work." Notes the use of
   free association in "An African Elegy" and the sense of evoking
   magic in Medieval Scenes. Finds these works, as "The Venice Poem,"
   are enactments of experiences, commenting on the role of music in
   the latter. Mentions Duncan's sense of the artist, of obedience
   during the creative process, of rhyme as recurrence, and of the
   role of limits and guides such as mythological figures. Finds
   sources in Dante, Blake, and W.C. Williams.
       In Letters, comments on Duncan's treatment of poetry and the
   role of language. Finds the "field is in language," and notes the
   treatment of the communal in "Often I Am Permitted to Return to a
   Meadow." Discusses the creative process, charting the poet's
   shifting attentions, the role of the poet, and the treatment of
   process in "A Poem Beginning with a Line by Pindar." Comments on
   the recurrences and variations of themes in "Apprehensions."
   Discusses the intricate phonological patterning, including consonance, assonance, and rhyme, and the rhythms, stresses, and use
   of a "melodic line" in Duncan's poetry, illustrating with "Roots
   and Branches" and "A Poem Beginning with a Line by Pindar."

1967

1 COMBS, MAXINE [SOLOW] GAUTHIER. "A Study of the Black Mountain
   Poets." Ph.D. dissertation, University of Oregon, pp. 1-2, 4,
   6-8, 59-95, 115-18, 196-204.
       Discusses the role of dualistic thought, "akin to a medieval
   dualism," in Duncan's earlier poetry, especially the contrasts of
   body and spirit, sensuality and love, physical desire and spiritual yearning, wrath and pity, and "the darkness of human experience and the light of inward vision" in such works as "Heavenly
   City, Earthly City," Medieval Scenes, and Caesar's Gate. Notes
   that he drops the dualism to treat other themes--poetry as imita-
   tive, as a method of discovery, as a natural and free form of
   expression, and as a field--in "The Venice Poem" and in much of
   his work since the mid-1950s, including Letters and poems in The
   Structure of Rime sequence.
       Comments on his desire to participate in "the rhythmic im-
   pulses of natural occurrences" with his poetry, on his use of myth
   and the image of a fir tree, and on his treatment of dream and
   women. Notes parallels to Creeley's treatment of poetry and,
   using "Keeping the Rhyme" and "A Poem Beginning with a Line by

Pindar," discusses Duncan's poetic techniques, especially "his
handling of the line and the juxtaposition of sounds." Also notes
his care for structure. See <u>Dissertation</u> <u>Abstracts</u> <u>International</u>
28 (1968):3666A.

2   CREELEY, ROBERT. "['Gedichte zu schreiben fällt mir zu']."
    [In German.] Translated by Klaus Reichert. In <u>Ein</u> <u>Gedicht</u> <u>und</u>
    <u>sein</u> <u>Autor</u>: <u>Lyrik</u> <u>und</u> <u>Essay</u>. Edited by Walter Höllerer.
    Berlin: Literarisches Colloquium, pp. 242-55.
        German translation of 1967.3.

3   _____. "Robert Creeley Talks about Poetry." <u>Harper's</u> <u>Bazaar</u>
    101 (July):81, 120-21, 126.
        In this January 1967 lecture, Creeley quotes from "Often I
    Am Permitted to Return to a Meadow" to explain his own sense of
    writing as a "made place" in which to be. Also mentions a conver-
    sation in which Duncan qualified Olson's "sense of 'choice' as
    being 'recognition.'" Reprinted (as "'I'm given to write poems'"):
    1970.4; 1972.1; 1973.1. Translated into German: 1967.2.

4   DAVEY, FRANK[LAND WILMOT]. "Rime: A Scholarly Piece." In <u>The</u>
    <u>Making</u> <u>of</u> <u>Modern</u> <u>Poetry</u> <u>in</u> <u>Canada</u>: <u>Essential</u> <u>Articles</u> <u>on</u>
    <u>Contemporary</u> <u>Canadian</u> <u>Poetry</u> <u>in</u> <u>English</u>. Edited by Louis Dudek
    and Michael Gnarowski. Toronto: Ryerson Press, pp. 295-300.
        Reprint of 1965.1.

5   DUNCAN, ROBERT. Comments. <u>Audit</u> 4, no. 3 [Poetry/<u>Audit</u>
    issue]:62-64.
        Including versions of "<u>Passages</u>, 26: The Soldiers" provides
    notes on its composition. Five lines from "Shadows: <u>Passages</u>,
    11" with notes, following 1967.6, implicitly provide sources to
    allusions in that poem.

6   _____. "Returning to <u>Les</u> <u>Chimères</u> of Gérard de Nerval." <u>Audit</u>
    4, no. 3 [Poetry/<u>Audit</u> issue]:42-61.
        Duncan mentions reading Nerval in the early 1960s and find-
    ing correspondences with his own beliefs and his other readings.
    Comments on his translations of Nerval in "The Chimeras of Gérard
    de Nerval," especially "El Desdichado (The Disinherited)," which
    he began because of Robin Blaser's poor translations. Provides
    portions of the correspondence with Blaser from 1965 to 1966. In
    his 18 November 1966 letter, Duncan notes he found himself in "a
    confluence of traditions" while translating, mentions his sense of
    the communal, and compares his translations to Blaser's. Also
    provides biographical details concerning his relationship to
    Blaser, and gives the source for the star image in "Variations on
    Two Dicta of William Blake." (Duncan occasionally comments on
    this; see 1968.13; 1969.13. See also 1977.6; 1982.2; 1983.12.)

RD1967

7   GELPI, ALBERT J. "The Uses of Language." <u>Southern</u> <u>Review</u>,
    n.s. 3, no. 4 (October):1024-35.
        In a favorable review of <u>Roots and Branches</u>, mentions
    Duncan's treatment of unity in the face of dualities and of
    poetry, especially as the unity denotes "the triumph of Love over
    Death." Also comments on Duncan's use of myth.

8   HOFFMAN, FREDERICK J. "Contemporary American Poetry." In <u>Pat-</u>
    <u>terns</u> <u>of</u> <u>Commitment</u> <u>in</u> <u>American</u> <u>Literature</u>. Edited by Marston
    LaFrance. Toronto: University of Toronto Press in association
    with Carleton University, pp. 193-207.
        Quoting from "For a Muse Meant," finds Duncan very different
    from Creeley. Feels Duncan is, at times, much like Olson, but at
    other times, "stand[s] quite entirely free of him." Believes
    Duncan is "perhaps one of the most accomplished of our poets."

9   KOCH, KENNETH. "Performance without a Net." <u>Nation</u> 204, no.
    17 (24 April):524-26.
        Praises Duncan's work for its rhetoric and religious empha-
    sis, among other things, but also finds an irrelevance. Comments
    on the first seven lines of "<u>The</u> <u>Structure</u> <u>of</u> <u>Rime</u>, III."

10 OLSON, CHARLES. "Against Wisdom as Such." <u>Georgia</u> <u>Straight:</u>
    <u>Vancouver</u> <u>Free</u> <u>Press</u> 1, no. 8 (24 November-8 December):5.
    Reprinted from 1954.2.

11 PERREAULT, JOHN. "Holding Back and Letting Go." <u>New</u> <u>York</u>
    <u>Times</u> <u>Book</u> <u>Review</u>, 19 November, p. 97.
        In an unfavorable review of <u>The</u> <u>Years</u> <u>as</u> <u>Catches</u>, feels the
    volume "is only of interest because of the light it throws" on
    Duncan's subsequent work. See also 1968.25, 30.

12 ROSENTHAL, M[ACHA] L[EWIS]. <u>The</u> <u>New</u> <u>Poets:</u> <u>American</u> <u>and</u>
    <u>British</u> <u>Poetry</u> <u>since</u> <u>World</u> <u>War</u> <u>II</u>. New York: Oxford Uni-
    versity Press, pp. 23-24, 147, 174-84, passim.
        Noting Duncan's "emotional range," claims his virtuosity
    "enables him to encompass opposite states of awareness and feeling
    through the interplay of both traditional and highly personal
    modes of expression." Discusses "Often I Am Permitted to Return
    to a Meadow," charting the "curve of feeling" in the work, and "A
    Poem Beginning with a Line by Pindar," commenting on its "pattern
    of soaring movement, depressive scattering of energies, and rein-
    tegration." Also comments on Duncan's mysticism, his treatment of
    homosexuality, and his use of "intrusions" and autobiographical
    materials.
        Finds a "sentimental philosophizing" and a shift from the
    literal to a "girlish outcry" in the "Dream Data" section of "A
    Sequence of Poems for H.D.'s Birthday." See also 1972.10.

13   TURNBULL, GAEL. "Some Notes on the Poetry of Robert Duncan."
      New Measure: A Magazine of Poetry, no. 6 (Summer), pp. 40-45.
          Comments on Duncan's use of language, especially the multi-
      dimensional role of the word in his work, and his concept of the
      creative process.

14   WAGNER, LINDA WELSHIMER. Denise Levertov. Twayne's United
      States Authors Series, edited by Sylvia E. Bowman, no. 113.
      New York: Twayne Publishers, pp. 22-23, 138, passim.
          Briefly speculates on Duncan's influence on Levertov, and
      notes why they are often classified together.

15   The Washington University Libraries, the Friday Evening Reading
      Series, [and] the Student Assembly Present Robert Creeley [and]
      Robert Duncan Reading Their Works. St. Louis: Washington
      University Library, Friday Evening Reading Series, Student
      Assembly, 4 pp.
          Announces Duncan's 28 April 1967 reading in St. Louis, pro-
      vides a biographical summary, and details the method by which
      Duncan was chosen as a poet to be collected by the Rare Books
      Department of Olin Library at Washington University.

16   WEATHERHEAD, A[NDREW] KINGSLEY. The Edge of the Image:
      Marianne Moore, William Carlos Williams, and Some Other Poets.
      Seattle, Wash., and London: University of Washington Press,
      pp. 232-44, passim.
          Mentions Duncan's treatment of Christ and children; his
      feelings about Christianity and childhood's "spontaneous intuitive
      perception"; and his dislike of wisdom, "fixed, formal, unmagical
      knowledge and old orders." Mentions his use of the recurring
      image of "crossed or double vision" as a "duality which looks both
      to wisdom and intuition." Comments on a number of poems, espe-
      cially "Crosses of Harmony and Disharmony." Compares Duncan's
      poetry to Marianne Moore's, noting her influence on him. Also
      compares his work to W.C. Williams's, finding similarities in the
      value they place on fancy; their sense of words as things, illus-
      trating with "The Dance"; and their treatment of the "creativity
      of destruction" as in "Food for Fire, Food for Thought." Notes
      the lack of vivid imagery in Duncan's poetry.

1968

1   CARRUTH, HAYDEN. "Making It New." Hudson Review 21, no. 2
      (Summer):399-412.
          In a favorable review of Bending the Bow, discusses the
      political nature of the poetry, and compares the Passages sequence
      to Pound's Cantos. Comments on the unity and inclusiveness of
      Passages.

RD1968

2 DAVEY, FRANKLAND WILMOT. "Theory and Practice in the Black
Mountain Poets: Duncan, Olson, and Creeley." Ph.D. dissertation, University of Southern California, pp. 1-60, 136-203,
299-303, passim.

Quotes important sections from unpublished lectures by
Duncan from the early 1960s in Vancouver (especially 5 August 1963
at the Vancouver Poetry Conference and July and August 1961 at
Warren Tallman's house) and Berkeley (on 13 July 1965 at the
Berkeley Poetry Conference). Discusses Duncan's sense "that the
divine or numinous informs . . . all natural objects, including
man." Also examines Duncan's sense that it is the role of the
poet, by attending to the divine in the actual and in language, to
make others aware that "everything is dependent on the divine for
its origin and sustenance" and is "participant in immeasurable and
purposive cosmic processes." Mentions Duncan's belief that each
man needs to obey "the orders of life" to fulfill his own destiny
and each man needs to avoid that which would keep him in ignorance
of the numinous, such as an emphasis on discipline or reason,
noting America's and Protestantism's fear of the divine. Notes
Duncan's sense that the poet cannot impose a form on poetry and
that the poet must "lose his identity during the process of composition" in order to be in the service of the poem, aiding it to
achieve its own form. Occasionally comments on his use of Christ,
Dionysus, and the dance to explain Duncan's concept of the process
of the universe and of the poem.

Using numerous poems as examples, discusses Duncan's treatment of the Law; the divine as a part of this world; "man as an
integral part of the universe"; mother figures; poetry and the
role of the poet; art; language; and the Vietnam War. Also refers
to his "sense of a shared identity with the universe," noting his
search for resemblances. Mentions his use of the tree metaphor
and sources in the Kabbalah. Comments on his sense of rhyme, of
following the orders of a poem, of the divine, and of the poet as
a prophet. Notes how Duncan appears to be following the language
in "For a Muse Meant," and examines his treatment of the creative
process in "Light Song." Provides, from unpublished sources, the
biographical context for Medieval Scenes, including Duncan's explanation of allusions in the poem and a description of its composition. Charts the movement of Duncan's mind as it follows
"images, thoughts, and associations" in "A Poem Beginning with a
Line by Pindar." See Dissertation Abstracts International 29
(1968):256A.

3a DICKEY, JAMES. "Robert Duncan." In Babel to Byzantium: Poets
and Poetry Now. New York: Farrar, Straus, & Giroux,
pp. 173-77.

A reprint of the Duncan section from 1962.2, slightly revised, with a section from an unannotated review.

3b DUNCAN, ROBERT. Blurb to The First Decade: Selected Poems, 1940-1950. London: Fulcrum Press, front-rear flap of jacket.
    In this lengthy blurb, Duncan comments on the selection of poems in The First Decade and claims that he "seek[s] a consonance . . . with the particular experience that arises in the process of a poem." Describes the creative process when he wrote these poems, and discusses the "crises of truth and permission" in the work, especially as stated in Medieval Scenes and "The Venice Poem."

4   . "From The H.D. Book: Part I: Beginnings; Chapter 5: Occult Matters." Stony Brook, nos. 1-2 (Post-Fall), pp. 4-19.
    An abridged and slightly revised text of 1964.7.

5   . "The H.D. Book, Part I: Chapter 2." Coyote's Journal, no. 8, pp. 27-35.
    Duncan discusses finding his "life in poetry through the agency of certain women," noting the importance of women poets, especially H.D., as well as women he read to and who read to him, especially Edna Keough, his high school teacher. Discusses his love for and relationship to Keough, who gave him both "heroic resolve" and made Eros his master in art. Also lists what she had him read in school. Notes his lack of affiliations, the reading directions Louise Antoinette Krause gave to him, his awareness that his work should "reveal inner forces," his "conversion to Poetry," and his sense of setting out on an adventure, preparing a ground between love and "Eros and Form." Finds himself a romantic and a formalist.

6   . "Introduction" to Bending the Bow. New York: New Directions Books, pp. i-x.
    In this introduction, Duncan discusses Bending the Bow in general, especially its political emphasis, its metrical notations, its sonnets, and the Passages sequence. Provides biographical details from the 21-22 October 1967 March on the Pentagon, a demonstration against the Vietnam War at which he was to speak, and comments on his sense of inspiration, of being the voice of a larger power. Reprinted: 1971.12. Abridged: 1976.11.

7   . "A Lammas Tiding." In Bending the Bow. New York: New Directions Books, p. 51.
    Revision and slight expansion of 1964.6 with additional information about the bells in "My Mother Would Be a Falconress." Reprinted: 1971.12.

*8   . "Man's Fulfillment in Order and Strife." In Language and World Order: Prospectus, 1963 Symposium. [Ellensburg: Central Washington State College], pp. 7-8.
    Excerpt of a lecture. (Unavailable for annotation. See 1969.9 for full text.)

RD1968

9 _____. "Nights and Days [The H.D. Book, Part II: Chapter 1]."
Sumac 1, no. 1 (Fall):101–47.
Opening section is a revision of 1963.4. Duncan discusses
H.D., Pound, W.C. Williams, and others as his masters. Mentions
first reading H.D.'s work and belonging to a "constellation" of
poets, including Olson, who influenced him. Briefly mentions his
contacts with Olson.

10 _____. "Notes" to Bending the Bow. New York: New Directions
Books, [pp. 139–40].
Provides notes to the poems in Bending the Bow. Reprinted:
1971.12.

11 _____. "Preface" to Letters. In Derivations: Selected Poems,
1950–1956. London: Fulcrum Press, pp. 89–93.
Reprint of 1958.2.

12 _____. The Truth and Life of Myth: An Essay in Essential
Autobiography. New York: House of Books, 78 pp.
In a greatly expanded version of 1968.13, Duncan comments
more on his emotional reactions to the idea of a fountain, and
discusses "the workings of myth" in his life. Provides biographical details about reading and being read to as a child, commenting on stories, poetry, books, and illustrations. Notes that some
of these works—especially Plato; myths, including those of Cupid
and Psyche; a Bashō poem; and Katharine Sturges's illustrations—
influenced his mythopoetic imagination. Describes his parents'
and grandmother's hermeticism and world view. Commenting on the
"modern demythologizing mind," discusses the role of myth, pattern, and free association in his poetry and writing poetry as
"wrestling with Form to liberate Form."
Mentions the process of writing the essay at hand and of
composing "A Poem Beginning with a Line by Pindar," describing the
creative process in some detail. Claims that in writing he goes
"deeper and deeper into the experience of the process of the poem
itself," and notes the role of inspiration in his work. Comments
on a number of other poems briefly, especially "The Venice Poem."
Also notes the role of association and childhood memories in "The
Fire: Passages, 13" and "Chords: Passages, 14." Discusses his
early use of mythological figures as part of his psychological
reality until Helen Adam, reading Blake, awoke him to "the mythological reality in the actual." (See also 1974.1; 1976.22;
1979.11; 1980.24; 1981.18.) Reprinted: 1973.16; 1985.17.

13 _____. "The Truth and Life of Myth in Poetry." In Parable,
Myth, and Language. Edited by Tony Stoneburner. Cambridge,
Mass.: Church Society for College Work, pp. 37–44.
Duncan, in a paper presented at a meeting of poets and theo-
logians at the College of Preachers, Washington, D.C., held 13–15

October 1967 (see 1968.28), discusses poetry and myth, including
his sense of the poem as an "active presence" obeying its own
orders, and his sense of Eros, Psyche, and the numen. Relates a
fountain in his childhood to weeping, as George Herbert's theme of
weeping, and to the fountain in "Four Poems as a Night Song."
Mentions his sense of himself as a bard and of achieving "universal authenticity" for his poetry by relying on language as a
"store of human experience." Notes how the poem "has its motive
beyond the conscious and personal intent" of the poet. Comments
on 1967.6, and notes the role of error and his treatment of the
creative process in his poetry. Claims to follow the "tone-
leading of vowels," and mentions his poetry as cunning. Reprinted
and greatly expanded: 1968.12.

14   . "Two Chapters from H.D. [Part I: Chapters 3 and 4]."
     TriQuarterly, no. 12 (Spring), pp. 67–98.
     Duncan mentions first hearing the Psyche and Eros myth and
what it has meant to him since, implicitly shedding light on "A
Poem Beginning with a Line by Pindar." Notes the importance of
myth to him and its role in his work. Briefly comments on his
first attempts at writing poetry.

15   FAIRCHILD, HOXIE NEALE. Valley of Dry Bones, 1920–1965. Vol.
     6, Religious Trends in English Literature. New York: Columbia
     University Press, pp. 222, 224–25, 403, passim.
     Quoting from a few poems, briefly mentions Duncan's treat-
ment of God, imagination, and creation. Notes his use of the
field as an image.

16   FAUCHEREAU, SERGE. Lecture de la poésie américaine. [In
     French.] Critique. Paris: Éditions de Minuit, pp. 234–40,
     passim.
     Mentions Duncan's relationship to Spicer, his complexity,
his use of the poem as a magic incantation, and his treatment of
political issues. Comments on the influence of the occult and
fin-de-siècle sensibility on his work. Also discusses his use of
apocalyptic imagery and Bergman's Trämålning in "Ingmar Bergman's
Seventh Seal." Translated into Rumanian with a new introduction:
1974.21.

17   GLOVER, ALBERT GOULD, ed. "Introduction" and "Index" to
     "Charles Olson: Letters for Origin." Ph.D. dissertation,
     State University of New York at Buffalo, pp. i–xxxi, 338–95.
     Quotes from an unpublished July 1961 lecture by Duncan
largely concerning Olson and his relationship to Olson. See
Dissertation Abstracts International 29 (1969):1894–95A.

18   HARRISON, JIM. "Pure Poetry." New York Times Book Review, 29
     September, pp. 66–67.

RD1968

    In a favorable review of Bending the Bow, notes its
"aggressive syncretism," difficulties for the reader, and nonlinear nature, especially the Passages sequence.

19   KNIEF, WILLIAM. "Robert Creeley: Interview." Cottonwood
      Review [1, no. 4:1-8, 11-18].
          In this interview, Creeley occasionally mentions his admira-
      tion of Duncan, Duncan's use of Whitman, and the correspondence
      between reading and writing for Duncan.

20   LEVERTOV, DENISE; DUNCAN, ROBERT; WILDER, AMOS N.; LAEUCHLI,
      SAMUEL; CRITES, STEPHEN D.; ROBINSON, JAMES M.; FUNK, ROBERT
      W.; ZABRISKIE, PHILIP T.; and SUMMERS, HOLLIS. "Discussion,"
      "Discussion," "Another Discussion," and "Final Discussion." In
      Parable, Myth, and Language. Edited by Tony Stoneburner.
      Cambridge, Mass.: Church Society for College Work, pp. 14-18,
      26, 31-36, 53-56.
          In a series of discussions at a meeting of poets and theolo-
      gians at the College of Preachers, Washington, D.C., held 13-15
      October 1967, Duncan mentions his sense of myth, poetry, language,
      Christianity, and the future, and briefly comments on his belief
      in science. Robinson argues that Duncan has "demythologized
      Christianity" and "pietized mythology." Laeuchli and others argue
      with Duncan's sense of Christ, Christianity, and myth, and
      Laeuchli claims to find a difference between Duncan's poetry and
      presentation (see 1968.13). A few of the others imply Duncan's
      apprehension of a mythical world is a "pseudo-experience." Funk
      comments on Duncan's lack of logic in arguments but notes his
      forceful language.

21   OLSON, CHARLES. "Against Wisdom as Such." Quixote (Madison,
      Wis.) 3, "no. 9 or so" (May):42-44.
          Reprinted from 1954.2, omitting two paragraphs.

22   _____. "Charles Olson: Letters for Origin." Edited by Albert
      Gould Glover. Ph.D. dissertation, State University of New York
      at Buffalo, pp. 127, 147-48, passim.
          In these letters to Corman, Olson occasionally mentions
      Duncan, provides his appraisals of Duncan and his work, and urges
      Corman to publish Duncan in Origin. (These letters are not
      included in Olson's Letters for Origin, 1950-1956, ed. Albert
      [Gould] Glover [New York: Cape Goliard Press in association with
      Grossman Publishers, 1970].) See Dissertation Abstracts Inter-
      national 29 (1969):1894-95A.

23   PACK, ROBERT. "To Be Loved for Its Voice." Saturday Review
      51, no. 34 (24 August):39-40.

In a brief review of Bending the Bow, finds Duncan's political poetry dogmatic with "pretentious language, dull rhythms,
glib phrasing," and meaningless accusations.

24   PEARCE, ROY HARVEY. "Whitman and Our Hope for Poetry." In The
      Poetic Tradition: Essays on Greek, Latin, and English Poetry.
      Edited by Don Cameron Allen and Henry T. Rowell. The Percy
      Graeme Turnbull Memorial Lectures on Poetry. Baltimore: Johns
      Hopkins Press, pp. 123-40.
          Extensively quoting from "A Poem Beginning with a Line by
      Pindar," discusses the figure of Whitman in the work. Finds
      Duncan, like other contemporary poets, looks to Whitman as a
      humanizing spirit of renewal whose political poetry and sense of
      authentic culture might be a guide to bring a "productive order"
      to the nation. Slightly revised with added notes: 1969.20.

25   PERREAULT, JOHN. "'A Void of Smug': Mr. Perreault Replies."
      New York Times Book Review, 7 January, p. 26.
          In a response to 1968.30, argues the influence of Duncan is
      "negligible if not mildly pernicious," and believes his poetry is
      poor. See also 1967.11.

26   SEIDMAN, HUGH. Review of Bending the Bow. Caterpillar: "A
      Gathering of the Tribes," no. 5 (October), pp. 142-44.
          In this sympathetic review, discusses the confrontation of
      "Eros and Death" in the poems on the Vietnam War.

27   SKELTON, ROBIN. "The Poet as Guru." Kayak, no. 16, pp. 59-62.
          In a basically unfavorable review of Bending the Bow, notes
      Duncan's fondness for "magniloquence of sentiment" and, as Pound,
      for pedantry. Notes mixed metaphors, and finds the poetry "ar-
      tistically unbalanced," but believes Duncan to be in the true
      service of art and, as a "guru" rather than as a craftsman, de-
      serving some admiration.

28   STONEBURNER, TONY, ed. "Introduction" to Parable, Myth, and
      Language. Cambridge, Mass.: Church Society for College Work,
      pp. 4-6.
          Provides the occasion for and summarizes 1968.13, mentioning
      his own, Stoneburner's, role in cutting it.

29   WAGNER, LINDA [WELSHIMER], and MacADAMS, LEWIS, [Jr.]. "The
      Art of Poetry, X: Robert Creeley." Paris Review 11, no. 44
      (Fall):155-87.
          In these interviews, Creeley mentions Duncan a number of
      times, especially noting their first meeting in Mallorca, Spain.
      Wagner's interview is revised and rearranged from 1965.13. The
      entire is reprinted in 1972.24. The fullest versions are in
      Creeley's Contexts of Poetry: Interviews, 1961-1971, ed. Donald

RD1968

[Merriam] Allen, Writing, no. 30 (Bolinas, Calif.: Four Seasons
Foundation, 1973), where both are revised, expanded, and sepa-
rately published as 1973.21 and 29.

30   WILLIAMS, JONATHAN. "'A Void of Smug': To the Editor." New
     York Times Book Review, 7 January, pp. 22, 26.
          In this letter to the editor, finds 1967.11 smug, overly
     concerned with the lack of innovation, and too ready to castigate
     Black Mountain poetry. See also 1968.25.

31   ZWEIG, PAUL. "Robert Duncan's World." Poetry 111, no. 6
     (March):402-5.
          In fairly unfavorable reviews of The Years as Catches, The
     Sweetness and Greatness of Dante's "Divine Comedy," and Medea at
     Kolchis, finds the "intelligence and the vision separated" and the
     poetry overly rhetorical. Favorably comments on "Up Rising:
     Passages, 25" and "An African Elegy."

1969

1   BRIEN, DOLORES ELISE. "A Study of the Poetry of Robert Creeley
     and Robert Duncan in Relation to the Emerson-Whitman Tradition."
     Ph.D. dissertation, Brown University, pp. iv-viii, 66-166.
          Finds Duncan's "syncretic world view," assimilation of
     others' work, and identification with all others in a Neoplatonic
     unity, acknowledging the "centrality of the individual in the
     universe of relations," corresponds to the beliefs of Whitman and
     Emerson. Claims all three of these poets are in the occult tradi-
     tion, and traces and compares a number of hermetic themes in their
     prose and poetry, including their treatment of the self; God; the
     body; love; animals; grass; Christ; the role of poetry in society;
     and the creative process. Also charts their treatment of the
     correspondences between masculinity and femininity; man's separa-
     tion from the divine; the rational as opposed to the intuitional;
     the organic nature of poetry; poetry as a means to the "primordial
     union with the divine"; and the poet as, variously, an innocent,
     childlike Adam, a lightbearing Lucifer, and a shaman "receptive to
     the divine afflatus." Notes Duncan's use of myth and the erotic
     as well as his allusions to Whitman. Also comments on his use of
     the image of the "World Tree," the "central axis by which heaven,
     earth, and the underworld are linked together." A section prior
     to the discussion of the hermetic themes, pp. 66-80, is revised as
     1975.8. See Dissertation Abstracts International 35 (1975):
     5388-89A.

2   CREELEY, ROBERT. "Introduction" to Black Mountain Review.
     3 vols. New York: AMS Press, 1:iii-xiii.

Creeley mentions Duncan's contributions to the Black Mountain Review, noting Levertov's reactions to "For a Muse Meant,"
originally published as "Letters for Denise Levertov: An a Muse
Ment." Reprinted: 1979.13.

3   "Duncan, Robert." In 200 Contemporary Authors: Bio-
     Bibliographies of Selected Leading Writers of Today with
     Critical and Personal Insights. Edited by Barbara Harte and
     Carolyn Riley. Detroit: Gale Research Co., pp. 94-95.
        Provides an overview of Duncan's poetry, quoting from Duncan
and others on his work. Expanded: 1974.9.

4   DUNCAN, ROBERT. "A Critical Difference of View." Stony Brook,
     nos. 3-4 [America: A Prophecy issue], pp. 360-63.
        Arguing against reviews by Hayden Carruth and Adrienne Rich,
Duncan briefly notes his desire that other times and "the words of
other men" enter his work. Finds his poetry "other and less" than
what Rich desires.

5   _____. "The H.D. Book, Part II: Night and Days, Chapter 2."
     Caterpillar: A Gathering of the Tribes, no. 6 (January),
     pp. 16-38.
        Duncan mentions reading works in "the German romantic tradi-
tion," including translations of Ludwig Tieck and E.T.A. Hoffmann.
Describes a 5 April 1963 dream involving H.D. Mentions the role
of the syllable in his poetry and his beginnings as a writer,
noting the importance of the owl to him. Provides a number of
biographical details, commenting on his birth and the death of his
mother. Also reminisces about learning the alphabet and going
with his mother to visit Mrs. Richards, her spiritual advisor.
Against Olson's assessment of him in 1954.2, claims he is not "an
occultist or a mystic but a poet."

6   _____. "The H.D. Book, Part 2: Chapter 3." Io, no. 6
     [Ethnoastronomy Issue] (Summer), pp. 117-40.
        Duncan briefly provides a childhood memory and a 1961 dream.
Comments on the role of associations in his work, and his sense
and use of others' poetry and painting as events in "a field of
meanings." Notes reading Pound since 1938, mentioning the sense
of art he gained from Pound and others as the composition of content, as "a thing in itself," and as a "personal achievement of
form." Mentions poetry "in terms of a narrative and emblematic
tapestry."

7   _____. "The H.D. Book, Part II: Chapter 4." Caterpillar: "A
     Gathering of the Tribes," 2, no. 2 [whole no. 7] (April):27-60.
        Duncan notes his original intentions for The H.D. Book, and
comments on composing the book.

RD1969

8 _____ . Introduction to Charles Olson and Comments in <u>Causal</u>
<u>Mythology</u>, by Charles Olson. Transcribed by Donald [Merriam]
Allen. Writing, edited by Donald [Merriam] Allen, no. 16. San
Francisco: Four Seasons Foundation, pp. 1, 36–37.
     In an introduction to and comments within this 20 July 1965
lecture by Olson at the Berkeley Poetry Conference, Duncan mentions his use of material from other cultures and claims he feels
compelled to study Pound, Zukofsky, Olson, Creeley, and Levertov.
Reprinted: 1978.13. See also 1981.13.

9 _____ . "Man's Fulfillment in Order and Strife." <u>Caterpillar:</u>
<u>A Gathering of the Tribes</u>, nos. 8–9 (October), pp. 229–49.
     In this transcript of a 20 April 1968 lecture, Duncan pro-
vides biographical details. Claims his first decision to become a
poet "was a disordering of the world," a reaction against social
expectations, noting the influence of Robert Browning on this
decision. Mentions his sense of process, of the world as a drama,
of multiplicity, and of participating in a Poetry that gives him
orders, in which the language takes over. Comments on the writing
of <u>The Structure of Rime</u> sequence and his sense of "letting the
poem speak for itself," the reasons for his pacifism, and his
delight in Poe when young. Discusses "Up Rising: <u>Passages</u>, 25"
as a political poem belonging "to the imagination of Man," mentioning its "demonic voice" and detailing the influence of poems
by Blake, Lawrence, and James Dickey on it. Also comments on the
role of the hydra and eagle and the treatment of Johnson in this
poem. Expanded version of 1968.8; reprinted: 1985.17.

10 _____ . "Preface" to <u>Play Time, Pseudo Stein: From the</u>
<u>Laboratory Records: Notebook, 1953</u>. [San Francisco]: Tenth
Muse, [pp. 1–4].
     In this preface, Duncan provides the publication history of
<u>Play Time, Pseudo Stein</u>, including the printed edition published
by Diane di Prima for Poet's Press.

11 _____ . Statement in "An <u>Occident</u> Symposium." <u>Occident</u>, n.s. 3
(Spring–Summer):101–13.
     Duncan discusses his reading of many types of authors from
all times, writers who have provided "deep-life-experiences" for
him and/or who have given "primary revelation of the spiritual
world." Also mentions a number of contemporary writers that he
reads with profit.

12 _____ . "<u>Structure of Rime</u>, XXVII: Jess's Paste-Ups."
<u>Quarterly Review of Literature</u> 16, nos. 1–2, pp. 33–34.
     Duncan comments on his aesthetic and spiritual relationship
to Jess. Slightly revised: 1984.11.

13 _____ . "Text from 'The Chimeras of Gérard de Nerval' to Follow
Page 91 in the First Edition of Bending the Bow (New Directions, 1968)." Caterpillar: "A Gathering of the Tribes" 2,
no. 2 [whole no. 7] (April):89–91.
Duncan reconstructs how material was lost from "The Christ
in the Olive Grove" of "The Chimeras of Gérard de Nerval" and how
pages were renumbered by Graham Mackintosh to hide the error.
Mentions checking figures in the page proofs and galleys; provides
revisions for "The Christ in the Olive Grove," noting their ra-
tionale; and takes exception with Blaser's translation (see
1967.6).

14 JOHNSTON, RAND, ed. "An Interview with Robert Creeley." Opus
[U.S. International University, California Western Campus], no.
7, pp. 46–48.
Creeley briefly mentions that writing political poems about
the Vietnam War has become part of Duncan's nature.

15 LANSING, GERRIT. "Test of Translation, IX: Nerval's 'Horus.'"
Caterpillar: "A Gathering of the Tribes," 2, no. 2 [whole no.
7] (April), pp. 77–88, inside back cover.
Comparing Duncan's translation of Gérard de Nerval's "Horus"
to other contemporary translations, discusses Duncan's accuracy
and subtlety. Reprinted: 1971.13.

16 LIEBERMAN, LAURENCE. "Critic of the Month, VII: A Confluence
of Poets." Poetry 114, no. 1 (April):40–58.
In a favorable review of Bending the Bow, finds Duncan rids
his poetry of the "monologue of private reverie and myth" which it
had become since The Opening of the Field's "mysticism, visionary
terror, . . . [and] high romance." Notes his use of emblems and
treatment of the Vietnam War. Reprinted in part: 1977.13.

17 NELSON, RUDOLPH L[ORENS]. "Edge of the Transcendent: The
Poetry of Levertov and Duncan." Southwest Review 54, no. 2
(Spring):188–202.
Compares Duncan to Levertov in terms of their theory of
organic form and their treatment of transcendence. Finds they
both use poetry as "a dynamic means of exploration beyond what we
already know into a realm of wonder or eternity." Claims their
senses of a transcendent realm differ, illustrating with a few
poems. Also finds Duncan's poetry esoteric, obscure, and complex
in comparison to Levertov's focus on "common life." Notes their
estimate of each other's poetry, and comments on Duncan's treatment of boundaries and thresholds. Revised and expanded:
1971.15.

18 NIN, ANAÏS. The Diary of Anaïs Nin. [Vol. 3], 1939–1944.
Edited by Gunther Stuhlmann. New York: Harcourt Brace

RD1969

Jovanovich, pp. 16, 18-19, 75-76, 81-87, 89-100, 111-12, 114-15, 125, 159-60, 163, 166-71, 182-83, 187, passim.
In her diary, Nin provides details of her relationship to Duncan from the winter of 1939 to January 1942, focusing on their intimacy and gradual disaffection. She provides numerous biographical details and comments on and provides portions of Duncan's diary of the period in which he discusses writing, Patchen, sex, and God. Also describes his homosexual relationships of the period, especially with her cousin, known only as Paul. See also 1972.10; 1978.21; 1983.13.

19   PARKINSON, THOMAS. "Perspective: 'Yes, beautiful rare wilderness.'" New Orleans Review 1, no. 4 (Summer):381-87.
Finds "A Poem Beginning with a Line by Pindar" an "emblem for much beyond itself," including man's potential harmony with nature. Comments on the "dream world" it "occupies."

20   PEARCE, ROY HARVEY. "Whitman and Our Hope for Poetry." In Historicism Once More: Problems and Occasions for the American Scholar. Princeton: Princeton University Press, pp. 327-50.
Slight revision of 1968.24 with added notes.

21   PORTER, PETER. "Huts of Words." London Magazine, n.s. 9, nos. 4-5 [whole no. 100] (July-August):194-200.
In a mildly favorable review of The First Decade and Derivations, emphasizes the poetry's romantic qualities, and comments on Duncan's experimental imitations of Stein.

22   RABAN, JONATHAN. "Chance, Time, and Silence: The New American Verse." Journal of American Studies 3, no. 1 (July):89-101.
Briefly finds that Duncan's poetry illustrates the theory of "language as speech." Notes his use of immediacy and silence.

23   "Read or Written?" Times Literary Supplement, 1 May, p. 467.
In an unfavorable review of The First Decade and Derivations, finds Duncan's demands upon his readers excessive, especially in terms of his use of "private or eccentric" references and allusions. Reprinted: 1970.16.

*24   TALLMAN, WARREN. "Robert Duncan: Poet of Passion." Montreal Star, 13 September, p. 6.
In a favorable review of The First Decade and Derivations, comments on the musicality and treatment of the child in "Strawberries under the Snow" from "Homage to The Brothers Grimm," and mentions influences on Duncan, especially Pound. Notes Duncan's attention to the "act of writing," and finds Letters an homage and devotion to language. (Unavailable for annotation; annotated from reprint. Listed in 1986.2; item J86.) Reprinted: 1977.23.

25 ZINNES, HARRIET. "Duncan's One Poem." Prairie Schooner 43
    [misnumbered as 44], no. 3 (Fall):317-20.
       In a basically unfavorable review of Bending the Bow,
    objects to Duncan's reliance on Rudolf Steiner and Eastern
    mysticism in his poetry about the Vietnam War, and finds the work
    often too "self-involved." Notes Duncan's "all-encompassing aes-
    thetic which insists . . . on the . . . centrality of art in a
    confused world," and comments on "Passages, 26: The Soldiers."

1970

1 BERTHOLF, ROBERT J[OHN]. "The Key in the Window: Kent's Collection of Modern American Poetry." Serif: Quarterly of the
   Kent State University Libraries 7, no. 3 (September):52-70.
      Comments on Duncan as a mystical poet who uses myth, and
   mentions his publication history with small presses. Provides a
   few biographical details.

2 BRAKHAGE, STAN. "Respond Dance." In "Film Culture" Reader.
   Edited by P. Adams Sitney. New York: Praeger Publishers, pp.
   234-57. (British publication: 1971.2.)
      Revision of the last section of 1963.2.

3 CHARTERS, ANN. "Introduction" to The Special View of History,
   by Charles Olson. Berkeley, Calif.: Oyez, pp. 1-12.
      In a section from a 7 July 1969 interview with Creeley,
   Creeley mentions his contacts with Duncan in 1955 and Duncan's
   lack of interest in history. Also quotes from a 5 July 1969
   interview with Duncan in which Duncan provides biographical details on his stay at Black Mountain College in 1956, including the
   performances of his plays, his teaching, his living conditions,
   and his relationship with Olson. Duncan also mentions listening
   to Olson in 1957 in San Francisco and comments on himself as a
   Black Mountain poet.

4 CREELEY, ROBERT. A Quick Graph: Collected Notes and Essays.
   Edited by Donald [Merriam] Allen. Writing, edited by Donald
   [Merriam] Allen, no. 22. San Francisco: Four Seasons Foundation, pp. 61-72, 195-201, 305-13.
      Includes reprints of 1956.1; 1957.1; 1960.2; 1966.2; 1967.3
   (as "I'm Given to Write Poems").

5 DAVEY, FRANK[LAND WILMOT]. Five Readings of Olson's "Maximus."
   [Montreal: Beaver Kosmos], pp. 17-20, passim.
      Occasionally quotes from Duncan's taped 23 July 1961 lecture
   at Warren Tallman's house in Vancouver on Olson's The Maximus
   Poems. Revised and expanded: 1974.8.

6   DONOGHUE, DENIS. "Oasis Poetry." New York Review of Books 14,
    no. 9 (7 May):35-38.
        In a favorable review of Derivations, notes Duncan's desire
    to achieve self-creation through poetry and to find a natural
    order as he writes. Notes his "discontinuity of detail" and the
    influence of Gertrude Stein.

7   DUNCAN, ROBERT. "Changing Perspectives in Reading Whitman."
    In The Artistic Legacy of Walt Whitman: A Tribute to Gay
    Wilson Allen. Edited by Edwin Haviland Miller. New York: New
    York University Press, pp. 73-102.
        Claiming that Leaves of Grass has been in his "own creative
    life an incarnation of that Presence of a Poetry," Duncan dis-
    cusses the influence of Whitman on his work, noting Whitman's use
    of the vernacular and his treatment of love, sex, the poet, order,
    possibility, democracy, the individual, law, and potentiality.
    Mentions writing poetry with lines of Whitman in mind, calls him-
    self an "ensemblist" after Whitman, but finds himself impatient
    with "Whitman's themes of improvement and progress." Also men-
    tions the influence of Dante, Pound, and W.C. Williams. Re-
    printed: 1985.17.

8   _____. Note on "The Feast: Passages, 34: Facsimile of the
    Holograph Notebook and of Final Typescript." In Tribunals:
    "Passages," 31-35. Los Angeles: Black Sparrow Press, [p. 1 of
    16-p. pamphlet included in hardbound edition].
        In this preface to a facsimile of "Passages, 34: The Feast
    (Tribunals)," Duncan comments on his various phases of composi-
    tion, from handwriting to typewriter, especially in the Passages
    sequence. Also mentions how the final printed version should
    look. Reprinted in 1974.17.

9   _____. "Notes on Grossinger's Solar Journal: Oecological
    Sections." In Solar Journal: (Oecological Sections), by
    Richard Grossinger. Los Angeles: Black Sparrow Press, foldout
    insert, [6 pp.].
        Duncan briefly mentions Pound's comment in a letter about
    the lack of plan in "The Venice Poem."

10 _____. "Preface to a Reading of Passages, 1-22: March 6,
    1970." Berkeley, Calif.: mimeographed for a reading sponsored
    by Cody's Books, [2 pp.].
        In this preface to a 6 March 1970 reading of the Passages
    sequence, Duncan discusses the inspiration of the work and ex-
    plains a few references. Reprinted: 1974.18.

11 [FAUCHEREAU, SERGE]. "Black Mountain." [In French.] Lettres
    nouvelles [41 poètes américains d'aujourd'hui issue], December
    1970-January, pp. 69-73.

Fauchereau quotes from correspondence he had with Duncan
after he translated "Passages, 32: [Ancient Reveries and
Declamations] (Tribunals)" without recognizing Duncan's adaptation
from Gérard de Nerval's "Isis" in the last eleven lines. Also
comments on Duncan as a visionary poet and quotes from "Up Rising:
Passages, 25."

12   HAMBURGER, MICHAEL. The Truth of Poetry: Tensions in Modern
      Poetry from Baudelaire to the 1960s. New York: Harcourt,
      Brace, & World, pp. 122, 247, 284-87.
           Discusses Duncan's thoughts on form in poetry; his principle
      of "discovering, not imposing, order"; and his view of science and
      technology. Mentions his use of the personal in poetry to reveal
      "general truths of a meaningful kind."

13   HARRISON-FORD, CARL. "'The Jungle Leaps In': Obscurity in
      Recent US Verse." Poetry Magazine (Sydney) 18, no. 2 (April):
      3-12.
           Uses Duncan's "A Poem Beginning with a Line by Pindar" as an
      example of poetry that seems obscure but that allows for associa-
      tions and mental wanderings in order to be more open than formal
      poetry.

14   HAYMAN, RONALD. "The City and the House." Encounter 34, no. 2
      (February):84-91.
           In a basically favorable review of The First Decade and
      Derivations, comments especially on "The Venice Poem" and "An
      Essay at War," noting Olson's influence.

15   OLSON, CHARLES. The Berkeley Reading. Transcribed by Ralph
      Maud. [Burnaby, British Columbia: Ralph Maud, privately
      printed for classroom use], pp. 1, 26-27, 36, 42-44, 63,
      passim.
           Another version of 1966.12 with annotations, more attribu-
      tions of voices, and an index. Includes a transcription of more
      peripheral voices and of the conversation during the intermission.
      Includes mention of Duncan in annotations, and provides the text
      of his introduction of Olson (p. 1). See also 1966.13; 1978.33.

16   "Poetry of 1969: Robert Duncan." T.L.S.: Essays and Reviews
      from the "Times Literary Supplement," 1969. Vol. 8. London:
      Oxford University Press, pp. 152-54.
           Reprint of 1969.23.

17   ROSENTHAL, M[ACHA] L[EWIS]. "Dynamics of Form and Motive in
      Some Representative Twentieth-Century Lyric Poems." ELH 37,
      no. 1 (March):136-51.
           Explicates "Strains of Sight" as a "'field' of association
      around . . . motifs" and notes how the "poem as a whole moves

RD1970

forward, while disparate elements are placed in relation to one
another in a momentary spatial relationship as in a moble [sic]."
Also notes Duncan's use of traditional form and "less predictable
and stable elements." Comments on his "dialogue with the tradition" in such poems as "Shelley's 'Arethusa' Set to New Measures,"
and mentions Pound's influence.

18   SORRENTINO, GILBERT. "Black Mountaineering." Poetry 116, no.
      2 (May):110-20.
         In a favorable review of The First Decade, Derivations, and
Roots and Branches, finds Duncan an important and powerful writer
who places himself "in service and bondage to The Art of Poetry."
Believes Duncan emphasizes the reality of the imagination and of
the poem to such an extent that for him "there is no understanding
or recognition of the real unless it can be so seen in the language of the poem." Reprinted: 1984.28.

19   SPICER, JACK. "From the Vancouver Lectures." Caterpillar: "A
      Gathering of the Tribes," no. 12 (July), pp. 175-212.
         In a transcript from a 1965 lecture and question-and-answer
session in Vancouver, continually refers to Duncan as a "medium"
or conduit for poetry. Reprinted in part: 1973.1.

20   _____. "Letters to Jim Alexander." Caterpillar: "A Gathering
      of the Tribes," no. 12 (July), pp. 162-74.
         In one letter, Spicer mentions reading his own work in prog-
ress to Duncan, and notes Duncan's reaction. Reprinted: 1971.20.

21   TAYLOR, NEILL. "Duncan, Robert Edward." In Contemporary Poets
      of the English Language. Edited by Rosalie Murphy and James
      Vinson. Chicago and London: St. James Press, pp. 312-14.
         After a brief bibliography, provides an overview of Duncan's
work, focusing on his occultism and language. Expanded, without
acknowledgment, including an updated bibliography: 1975.23. See
also 1979.37 and 1980.10.

22   TOMLINSON, CHARLES. "Poetry and Possibility: The Work of
      Robert Duncan." Agenda 8, nos. 3-4 [Special Issue in Honour of
      Ezra Pound's Eighty-Fifth Birthday] (Autumn-Winter):159-70.
         Quoting from a number of poems and prose works, mentions
Duncan's use of Freud, Pound, and W.C. Williams, as well as of
myth, Gnosticism, and discord. Comments on sections of failure in
"The Venice Poem" and "A Poem Beginning with a Line by Pindar,"
and notes the role of the body in and the muscularity of his
poetics.

1971

1 BOWERING, GEORGE, and HOGG, ROBERT. Robert Duncan: An Interview. Toronto: [Coach House Press], Beaver Kosmos Folio, [29 pp.].

In this 19 April 1969 interview, Duncan discusses his various reactions to and senses of Olson's "Projective Verse" and his ideas on Whitman, Freud, Marx, Zukofsky, language, form, individuality, science, time, space, and particle physics. Also mentions his use of rhetoric in his poems, his sense of writing by field composition, and his attention to the syllable or to the phrase at different periods of his writing. Providing biographical details, Duncan reminisces about his first and later reactions to reading Creeley, his visit to Creeley in Mallorca, Spain, his relationship to Spicer, and his first and later meetings with W.C. Williams and Olson. He also mentions his drawing, the reaction of W.C. Williams to the language in his work, and the influence of Olson, Eliot, and Rilke on his poetry. Briefly comments on a few poems, especially "Heavenly City, Earthly City," and compares himself to Olson in terms of dogma and heresy.

2 BRAKHAGE, STAN. "Respond Dance." In "Film Culture": An Anthology. Edited by P. Adams Sitney. London: Secker & Warburg, pp. 234-57. (American publication: 1970.2.)

Revision of the last section of 1963.2.

3 CHARTERS, SAMUEL. "Robert Duncan: 'Lammas Dream Poem.'" In Some Poems/Poets: Studies in American Underground Poetry since 1945. Berkeley, Calif.: Oyez, pp. 47-55.

Explicates "My Mother Would Be a Falconress," emphasizing the child's struggle for freedom from the mother, and notes homosexual interpretations. Also discusses variety in the Passages sequence, and examines Duncan's eclecticism, correspondences with the Pre-Raphaelites, and "sense of the medieval."

4 COLLINS, BECKY GOOKINS. "Form and Structure in Robert Duncan's Passages Poems." M.A. thesis, Kent State University, 137 pp.

Characterizing Duncan's poetry as projective and open, comments on many poems, but concentrates on the Passages sequence, finding it a serial poem. Noting the relationship to process poetics and to Duncan's emphasis on the "process of becoming," comments on his use of myth to return to origins that "will permit the move forward to the present." Discusses the role of myth in Duncan's poetry, especially noting the treatment of origins, creation, and memory in "Tribal Memories: Passages, 1"; of Achilles in "At the Loom: Passages, 2"; and of the "creation-destruction-recreation process," as well as of Dionysus, Christ, love, alienation, and music in a number of poems.

RD1971

Demonstrates Duncan's alteration of the myths by extending
them to "include the realm of [the] creative process," and finds
"in the retelling, the myths become connected in new ways." Discusses Duncan's treatment of Athena, Cybele, Orpheus, and Ahriman
in a number of poems, as well as creation and creation figures
related to the "generative center of the universe" in "Wine:
Passages, 12" and "Chords: Passages, 14." Also examines mythic
evil and oppressive figures in "Passages, 26: The Soldiers."
  Charts archetypal images and patterns in Passages, noting
mother and Mother Earth images in many poems. Finds Duncan treats
good as a "release to the archetypal nature of man" and evil as
the "destruction of the natural attunement to the cosmos." Discusses the role of the dance to discover cosmic identity and to
aid the poet's return to a world of myth as in "Often I Am Permitted to Return to a Meadow." Notes the cyclic pattern and the
repetition in Duncan's work as indicative of his journey back to a
center, to origins. Also comments on Duncan's use of contraries.

5   COOK, BRUCE. The Beat Generation. New York: Charles
    Scribner's Sons, pp. 56, 60, 126–32, 215–16, passim.
    Mentions Duncan's relationship to Beat poets, role in the
San Francisco Renaissance and Black Mountain poetry, and detach-
ment from the literary scene. Also quotes from Rexroth and
McClure on their early relationship with Duncan, and describes
Duncan's house.
    Quotes from an interview in which Duncan discusses his
poetry as "indwelling" and "the imagination of what a man is" and
comments on his politics and on his relationship to other poets.
Duncan also mentions academic poets, provides biographical de-
tails, and classifies himself and others in The New American
Poetry, 1945–1960, ed. Donald M[erriam] Allen (New York: Grove
Press, 1960).

6   COOLEY, DENNIS [ORIN].   "Keeping the Green: The Vegetative
    Myth of Renewal in Robert Duncan's Poetry."   Ph.D. disserta-
    tion, University of Rochester, 317 pp.
    Explores the "informing myth of seasonal renewal" in
Duncan's poetry using an archetypal and formalistic approach as
well as biographical material and Duncan's prose to help explicate
the poetry.
    In the first chapter, details Duncan's use of W.C. Williams,
Pindar, Whitman, Goya, and Pound, as well as myth and legend including that of Psyche, Cupid, Eros, Jason, and Isis in "A Poem
Beginning with a Line by Pindar." Also discusses Duncan's treatment of the mythic fall of man into knowledge, American political
leadership, man's search to "achieve a balance of reflective and
instinctual faculties," and the poet's role in society in "A Poem
Beginning with a Line by Pindar." Notes his associative method of
composition and his verbal play, and mentions his treatment of

American Indians, light and dark, dancing children, redemption, and art in the poem.

In the second chapter, discusses motifs, imagery, and figures of "regenerative powers" in various works by Duncan: childhood compared to age, illustrated in "The Structure of Rime, VI"; the meadow or "pastoral green world" in "Often I Am Permitted to Return to a Meadow"; the vegetative and vegetable myths, especially Kore, in "Evocation"; peasants or "common people" in "A Song of the Old Order"; the imaginative in "Nel Mezzo del Cammin di Nostra Vita"; Adam in "Adam's Way"; the poet and poetry in "Poetry, a Natural Thing"; the "primitive dark world" and the unconscious in "Nor Is the Past Pure"; the poet as a gardener and roots and branches for "many rooted" and "many-branched" man in "Returning to the Rhetoric of an Early Mode"; man as a plant "issuing forth" or as a baby being born in "As in the Old Days: Passages, 8"; and the sexual act and Eros in "At Christmas." Also mentions Duncan's treatment of vision, the poet as priest, and dreams.

In the third chapter, explicates "The Fire: Passages, 13," focusing on forces opposing the regenerative powers of the "green world" in Duncan's poetry. In this poem, discusses Duncan's treatment of language; artists, especially Piero di Cosimo; public officials; scientists; politics; war; plague; dreams; fire; nature; and the city. Comments on his use of Christ and Satan figures and of Whitman, and notes the polemical nature of the work. Also mentions war and fire imagery in "Passages, 26: The Soldiers," and the treatment of animals and nature in "Golden Lines," translated from Gérard de Nerval as a part of "The Chimeras of Gérard de Nerval."

Discusses a number of poems in the forth chapter, especially "The Law," "God-Spell," "Tribal Memories: Passages, 1," "Now the Record Now Record," and "Earth's Winter Song," and notes the influence of Heraclitus. Describes the "comic resolution" of the struggle of the regenerative and the destructive or repressive powers in Duncan's poetry. Also comments on his treatment of Spring, seeds, sparks, Christ, and the poet as a "fiery soul" in these poems.

Chapter 2 is abridged and revised as 1976.7; a portion of chapter 3 and a small section of chapter 4 are revised as 1980.7. See Dissertation Abstracts International 33 (1972):302-3A.

7   COONEY, SEAMUS. A Checklist of the First One Hundred Publications of the Black Sparrow Press. Los Angeles: Black Sparrow Press, pp. 16-17, 25, 35, 37.
   Provides brief descriptive bibliographical information on Epilogos; Christmas Present, Christmas Presence!; Names of People; A Selection of 65 Drawings from One Drawing Book, 1952-1956; and Tribunals: "Passages," 31-35. Also notes Duncan's contributions

to the works of others. See 1981.15 and, the fullest bibliography on Duncan, 1986.2.

8   DULL, HAROLD. "In Prose." Georgia Straight Writing Supplement
     (Vancouver), no. 7 (May), pp. 7-9.
         Reminiscing about Sunday meetings with Spicer and Duncan in
San Francisco in 1958, Dull discusses his own relationship to both
poets and their influence upon him. Reprinted: 1975.13.

9   DUNCAN, ROBERT. "Glimpses of the Last Day: From Chapter 11 of
     The H.D. Book." Io, no. 10, pp. 212-15.
         Duncan describes a 1961 dream. Reprinted and greatly
expanded: 1981.8.

10   _____. Ground Work. San Francisco: n.p., 12 pp.
         In these "passages from notebooks" dated 20 December to 22
January [1971], Duncan comments on titling Ground Work, his plans
to send friends early versions of his work, and the role of the
Zohar and Kabbalah in Letters and in his later work and thought.
Also mentions reading Gershom Gerhard Scholem's Major Trends in
Jewish Mysticism (Jerusalem: Schocken Publishing House, 1941) and
Norman O. Brown's work, commenting on Freudianism and the relationship of sex, language, and poetry. Mentions being attacked
for his poetry's concern "with the experience of poetry and language." Supplies a few biographical details about being invited
to teach at the University of California at Santa Cruz by Brown
and learning to play the piano. Provides an early version of a
portion of "Santa Cruz Propositions," commenting on the occasion
behind the poem. Notes that "events in Santa Cruz"--his teaching
and reading W.C. Williams's Paterson, Joyce's Finnegans Wake and
the work of Levertov and Brown, as well as Brown's History of the
Consciousness program--"belong" to "Santa Cruz Propositions." In
"A Prospectus" (p. i), Duncan comments on his plans to publish
Ground Work without using printers.

11   _____. "Iconographical Extensions," in Translations, by Jess
     [Collins]. Los Angeles: Black Sparrow Press; New York:
     Odyssia Gallery, pp. i-xiv.
         In this introduction, Duncan comments on the possible influ-
ence his relationship to Jess and contact with Jess's paintings
and paste-ups had on his poetry. Mentions that the stars in
"Passages, 31: The Concert (Tribunals)" may refer to colors in
Jess's paintings.

12   _____. "Introduction," "A Lammas Tiding," and "Notes" to
     Bending the Bow. London: Jonathan Cape, pp. i-x, 51, 139-40.
         Reprints of 1968.6-7, 10.

13 LANSING, GERRIT. "Test of Translation, IX: Nerval's 'Horus.'"
    A "Caterpillar" Anthology: A Selection of Poetry and Prose
    from "Caterpillar" Magazine. Edited by Clayton Eshleman.
    Garden City, N.Y.: Doubleday & Co., Anchor Books, pp. 237-51.
    Reprint of 1969.15.

14 MELTZER, DAVID, ed. The San Francisco Poets. New York:
    Ballantine Books, pp. 91-92, 94, 221, 245-46, passim.
        In his fall 1969 interview, William Everson mentions his
    initial contacts with Duncan and provides a few biographical
    details. In his summer 1969 interview, Lew Welch comments on
    Duncan's poetry. In his fall 1969 interview, Michael McClure
    mentions taking Duncan's 1954 poetry workshop and Duncan as a
    teacher. (Meltzer and occasionally Jack Shoemaker are the
    interviewers.) Revised: 1976.21.

15 NELSON, RUDOLPH LORENS. "Denise Levertov and Robert Duncan:
    'The world is not with us enough.'" In "The Search for Tran-
    scendence in Contemporary American Poetry." Ph.D. disserta-
    tion, Brown University, pp. 155-93.
        Revised and expanded version of 1969.17 with an added dis-
    cussion of Duncan's treatment of the Vietnam War in a few poems
    from the Passages sequence, noting his use of concrete images and
    the quotidian world. Terms Duncan's transcendence "ontological"
    in comparison to Levertov's more secular variety. See Disserta-
    tion Abstracts International 32 (1972):5240A.

16 Note in "Notes and Comments." New Poetry: Magazine of the
    Poetry Society of Australia 19, no. 1 (February):52-53.
        Argues against Duncan's classification with the projectivist
    poets because The Years as Catches predates his association with
    Olson yet prefigures his later work.

17 OLSON, CHARLES. "On Black Mountain." Transcribed by George F.
    Butterick. Maps, no. 4, pp. 16-41.
        In this 26 March 1968 discussion at Beliot College, Olson
    claims Duncan is becoming a major American poet. Reprinted:
    1979.35.

18 QUARTERMAIN, PETER. "Body Politic." Tuatara, no. 6
    (November), pp. 62-63.
        In a review of Tribunals: "Passages," 31-35, discusses
    Duncan's "courtship of chaos without dogma" and his sense of
    empire and language compared to the cellular or the word.

19 SAUNDERS, JOHN. "New Poetry." Stand: Quarterly of the Arts
    12, no. 4 (1971):63-67.
        In an unfavorable review of Bending the Bow, notes Duncan's
    mysticism and use of a collage method.

20   SPICER, JACK. "Letters to Jim Alexander." A "Caterpillar"
      Anthology: A Selection of Poetry and Prose from "Caterpillar"
      Magazine. Edited by Clayton Eshleman. Garden City, N.Y.:
      Doubleday & Co., Anchor Books, pp. 477–89.
          Reprint of 1970.20.

21   WESLING, DONALD. "The Prosodies of Free Verse." In Twentieth-
      Century Literature in Retrospect. Edited by Reuben A. Brower.
      Harvard English Studies, no. 2. Cambridge, Mass.: Harvard
      University Press, pp. 155–87.
          Briefly uses a portion from section 2 of "A Poem Beginning
      with a Line by Pindar" as an example of a "dismembered" poetic
      line used by the poet to indicate the "contrast between the his-
      torical moment and an imagined or lost moment of innocence."
      Revised: 1985.55.

1972

1   CREELEY, ROBERT. "'I'm Given to Write Poems.'" In A Sense of
      Measure. Signature Series, no. 16. London: Calder & Boyars,
      pp. 54–67.
          Reprint of 1967.3.

2   DUBERMAN, MARTIN. Black Mountain: An Exploration in Community.
      New York: E.P. Dutton & Co., pp. 391–92, 405–6, 411–12, passim.
          Provides a few biographical details concerning Duncan at
      Black Mountain College, including his relationship to Olson, his
      writing of Medea at Kolchis, and his leaving for San Francisco.
      Mentions the reaction of Levertov and Olson to Duncan's "For a
      Muse Meant."

3   DUDDY, THOMAS A[NTHONY]. "Perception and Process: Studies in
      the Poetry of Robert Creeley, Robert Duncan, Denise Levertov,
      Charles Olson, and Louis Zukofsky." Ph.D. dissertation, State
      University of New York at Buffalo, pp. 9–10, 62–79, passim.
          Notes Duncan's use of silence and of the dance as both love
      and a "principle of order," as well as biographical material in
      his work. Discusses "Doves" in detail, noting the "pre-occupation
      with language as a form of dynamic becoming," the use of images
      and myth, the role of the primordial, and the treatment of si-
      lence. Mentions Duncan's typical themes and the structural pat-
      terns in "A Poem Beginning with a Line by Pindar." In a few other
      poems, comments on his treatment of language's role in naming. See
      Dissertation Abstracts International 33 (1972):305–6A.

4   DUNCAN, ROBERT. "Epilogue" to Caesar's Gate: Poems, 1949–50.
      Sand Dollar, no. 8. [Berkeley, Calif.]: Sand Dollar,
      pp. 59–71.

In recounting a group session, presumably on 11 July 1972, of a "structured phantasy," Duncan provides information on the role of the bee and bee imagery in his poetry, claiming he has "pursued [the] lore of the bee world from [his] own earliest memories." Implicitly relates this to "What Is It You Have Come to Tell Me, García Lorca?"

5 _____. "A Glooming Peace." Transcribed by Cynthia Kellogg. Grape Writing Supplement [formerly Georgia Straight Writing Supplement] (Vancouver, British Columbia), no. 11 (15 March), pp. 1–3.
    In this introduction to a 29 February 1972 lecture on Shakespeare's Romeo and Juliet, Duncan discusses the "complexity" that others seem to sense in his poetry. Mentions his relationship with Olson and Olson's early perceptions of him.

6 _____. "The Museum." Beyond Poetry, [no. 1, pp. 1–3].
    Reprint of 1972.7.

7 _____. "The Museum." New Poetry: Magazine of the Poetry Society of Australia 20, nos. 5–6 (October–December):8–10.
    Duncan explains how "a womanly grace," a muse, comes to him when in the presence of myth and art, and leads him to further poetry. Reprinted: 1972.6; 1973.11; 1984.7.

8 _____. Notes to "Two Presentations." In An Introduction to Poetry. Edited by Louis Simpson. 2d ed. New York: St. Martin's Press, pp. 344–45.
    A revision and slight expansion of 1963.5.

9 _____. "Preface for Caesar's Gate." Caesar's Gate: Poems, 1949–50. Sand Dollar, no. 8. [Berkeley, Calif.]: Sand Dollar, pp. xlv–xlix.
    Reprint of 1955.2.

10 _____. "Preface (1972)" to Caesar's Gate: Poems, 1949–50. Sand Dollar, no. 8. [Berkeley, Calif.]: Sand Dollar, pp. i–xli.
    Duncan provides the biographical background for the period when Caesar's Gate was written, focusing on his writing and homosexuality, as well as giving a few other biographical details, some of which provide context for the blood imagery in "The Venice Poem." Comments on his sources for the title of the volume and on his ideal reader. Notes the title of "H.M.S. Bearskin," and discusses the figure of Bearskin as a part of himself. Examines the figure of Alexander the Great and his use of Asia in "The Second Night in the Week," and by extension in "Despair in Being Tedious." Comments on the title of and elements in "Four Poems as a Night Song," especially the figure of Federico García Lorca. Also discusses in detail how García Lorca's Poeta en Nueva York provides

context to Caesar's Gate. Details the imagery, the mannered sense,
and the sources for "Processionals I." Notes his use of continents
and empires as a realm of poetics in Caesar's Gate, A Book of
Resemblances, and Letters, discussing the "structural imperative"
he followed in "The Venice Poem" but which was lost to him until
the poetry in The Opening of the Field. Mentions his attraction
to surrealism.
    Claims Rosenthal's understanding, in 1967.12, of the senti-
mental in the "Dream Data" section of "A Sequence of Poems for
H.D.'s Birthday" is limited, discussing this section of the poem
in some detail and commenting on the next section, "['I must wake
up into the morning world']." Mentions his relationship to Anaïs
Nin, and discusses how both her reaction to his homosexuality in
1969.18 and García Lorca's reaction to homosexuality in general
"inform the personae of Caesar's Gate." Notes why he added poems
to this 1972 edition of the work from his notebooks, and discusses
his own reactions at both reading over Caesar's Gate and writing
about it. Reprinted in part: 1978.12.

11   . "Shakespeare's Romeo and Juliet as It Appears in the
    Mysteries of a Late Twentieth Century Poetics." Fathar,
    [no. 4] [Fathar For] (June), [pp. 53–57].
        Discusses the composition of "Over There," noting the role
of music in the poem. Comments on the creative process, development, and the role of inspiration in his poetry. Notes his sense
of music in language. Also comments on his "fear of naming" and
of being overly conscious of the creative process. Relates these
concerns to Jack Spicer's poetics.

12   . Statement in Caesar's Gate: Poems, 1949–50. Sand
    Dollar, no. 8. [Berkeley, Calif.]: Sand Dollar, verso of page
    preceding half-title.
        In this statement, Duncan claims that he will not "issue
another collection of [his] work . . . until 1983."

13 HARRISON, LOU. "Notes to "Peace Piece Two: 'Passages, 25' by
    Robert Duncan." Soundings, nos. 3–4 (July–October), [p. 129].
        Harrison provides brief notes for the performance of his
musical version of "Up Rising: Passages, 25," titled "Peace Piece
Two: 'Passages, 25' by Robert Duncan."

14 McINNES, CRAIG. "Wednesday, February 15." Grape Writing Sup-
    plement [formerly Georgia Straight Writing Supplement]
    (Vancouver, British Columbia), no. 11 (15 March), p. 5.
        Describes meeting Duncan on 15 February 1972, and provides
impressions of him.

15 MacINTYRE, WENDY ELIZABETH. "The Open Universe of Robert
    Duncan." M.A. thesis, Carleton University, 145 pp.

Discusses Duncan as a religious poet whose poetry is a "re-enactment of the invisible orders of the Cosmos, the ongoing evolution of forms." Finding that Duncan's sense of the Logos comes from Christian and Gnostic traditions, studies his "mystical background," especially Gnosticism. Also explores his sense of the "Divine Utterance" and the "self-determinism of the Word." Discovers Duncan believes that "the human word has volition and is a force with which the poet must co-operate." Finds he also feels the power of language can "determine the growth of poetic structure."

Examines Duncan's notion of the poem as a "'biological reality,' a life form enacting in its own orders the orders of the Cosmos," noting that the word can both give "witness to an invisible spiritual reality" and "possess an independent energy enabling it to determine its own place in the sentence and to regulate the growth of the poetic form." Delineates the sources of his sense of the power and mystery of language in the Zohar and Neoplatonism, especially in Marsilio Ficino.

Discusses Duncan's sources in Pound, H.D., and W.C. Williams, finding all three influenced his sense of the image and of the "spirituality of language." Also finds that Pound influenced his use of montage; H.D., his sense of the hidden power of words and the image as a "conjunction of the material and the divine"; and W.C. Williams, his desire for a "poetic form comprehending all things." Examines the influence of Whitehead and Olson on Duncan's sense of "the poem's internal development," his "poetics of organism" and field composition, and his use of melodic form, musical phrase, and the syllable, including the "tone leading of vowels." Examines his servitude and resistance to the language and his "correlation of poetic and cosmic life," noting sources in Jakob Böhme, Ficino, and the Zohar. Treats Duncan's sense of rhyme, return, and recurrence.

Investigates Duncan's use of a Master of Rime figure and an "incorporal 'Other.'" Explores his belief in the "spiritual aspect of the Word, the cumulative soul of the poem," by investigating his sense of myth. Notes sources in Ernst Cassirer and Jane Harrison's ideas on wonder, the daimon, myth, and the relationship between myth and language. Studies his sense of mythic persona and plot and the poem as a rite, as well as his treatment of myth: of Orpheus, the Orphic World Egg, Adam, Psyche, Eros, the Christ figure, and Kore, noting that his syncretism often combines these. Examines his identification of language, order, the world, and the poem. Notes his ideas of the orders of the poem, of freedom, and of the Law.

Notes the parable of two types of poetics in "The Structure of Rime, VI"; his treatment of the Master of Rime figure in The Structure of Rime sequence; the tapestry theme in "At the Loom: Passages, 2"; and the treatment of the spiritual in "Passages, 35: Before the Judgment (Tribunals)." Comments on the use of Orphic

myth in "Tribal Memories: Passages, 1"; Duncan's syncretism and
his treatment of Christ in "At Christmas"; and his use of myth and
the treatment of the mother figure and sadism in "My Mother Would
Be a Falconress." Notes his use of myth and the treatment of the
meadow, imagination, and childhood in "Often I Am Permitted to
Return to a Meadow"; and his treatment of the Law in "The Law."
Throughout, briefly uses a number of other works for examples;
especially notes the use of puns as in "The Dance"; the aperiodic
development of his poetry as in "Keeping the Rhyme"; the incorpor-
ation of "inattentions" or errors as in "Two Presentations"; and
the "incremental process of organic growth" as in "The Fire:
Passages, 13," noting how "the words are the sole progenitors of
the poem's form."
    A portion of chapter 1, pp. 5–34, revised as 1974.23; a
portion of chapter 3, pp. 100–124, slightly revised as 1973.22.

16   MAGNANI, PETER S. "Spenser's 'House of Temperance,' Yeats'
      'Supernatural Songs,' on Olson 'On Duncan on the Pantokrator.'"
      M.A. thesis, Simon Fraser University, pp. vii–viii, 143–76.
      Discussing 1953.1 and 1954.2, comments on the differences
between Duncan and Olson's sense of wisdom. Quotes from correspondence between them in 1955, especially Duncan's letter describing the Tahill Christ Pantokrator during his trip to Spain
(see also 1974.19), and notes Olson's use of Duncan's letter in
"On Duncan on the Pantokrator." Comments on a drawing in A Selection of 65 Drawings from One Drawing-Book, 1952–1956 as an example
of the influence of Olson's "reductive process" on Duncan.

17   MARLATT, DAPHNE. "Thoughts on a Sunday Morning, February 27,
      Paradise Valley." Grape Writing Supplement [formerly Georgia
      Straight Writing Supplement] (Vancouver, British Columbia),
      no. 11 (15 March), p. 6.
      Describes a conversation on 27 February 1972 during which
Duncan discussed the poet's role in society.

18   MERSMANN, JAMES F. "Out of the Vortex: A Study of Poets and
      Poetry against the Vietnam War." Ph.D. dissertation, Univer-
      sity of Kansas, pp. 119, 142–43, 209–70, 286, 329–30, passim.
      Quotes from Duncan on Levertov's "repressed obsession with
sexual violence." Notes the figures of Psyche and Cupid in
Duncan's poetry, especially "A Poem Beginning with a Line by
Pindar," discussing his belief in love as a force to submit one-
self to and, in his poetry, as a conduit for the reader to "Divine
Eros." Discusses the motifs of "the plant, the dance, and the
irrational" in Duncan's work. Finds them integral to his organic
theory of poetry and his sense of the interplay of order and chaos
in a cosmos which is constantly growing and in which the poet must
surrender himself to the order of the poem and the divine, rather
than impose his reason and will on experience.

Uses "An Essay at War" and "Passages, 26: The Soldiers" to examine Duncan's theme that modern war is anti-poetic since it depends upon coercion in the service of a plan that is antithetical to "individual volition," to the "medley of voices and words operating in free harmony." Feels Duncan finds such a harmony necessary for both true community and poetry and finds defeat in war preferable since then there will be a "giving-in of the ego." Examines his use of Parmenides and Pythagoras's thoughts on number and limit as applied to the motifs of darkness, fire, the infinite, and war in such works as "Moira's Cathedral." Discusses his sense of evil and emptiness as well as the hydra figure, especially in "Up Rising: Passages, 25." Notes the optimism in some poems from Bending the Bow, especially "Earth's Winter Song." Also comments on "The Multiversity: Passages, 21" (but see 1985.11).

Believes Duncan, unlike Levertov, often fails "to convincingly ground the transcendental within the proximate and actual" and lacks an "intense visceral experience of war's suffering." Feels his "mythic imagination" gives his work a "remoteness and grandeur" since it helps place the war in "a large spiritual perspective." Revised: 1974.24. See Dissertation Abstracts International 33 (1972):2944A.

19 MITCHELL, BEVERLY JOAN. "A Critical Study of the Tish Group, 1961-1963." M.A. thesis, University of Calgary, pp. 5-6, 19-20, 23-24, 27, 70-71, passim.
     Charts Duncan's influence on the Vancouver poets associated with Tish. Uses Duncan's poetry as an example of Black Mountain poetry based on Olson's theories: the poem's form should arise from its content, the perceptions in the poem should not be dictated by the intellect, and these perceptions should move naturally and swiftly.

20 MITCHELL, BEVERLY [JOAN]. "The Genealogy of Tish." Open Letter, 2d ser., no. 3 (Fall), pp. 32-51.
     Uses Duncan's "Keeping the Rhyme" to show that Black Mountain poets are interested in form and "Poetry, a Natural Thing," to demonstrate Olson's concepts of perceptions and sound in projective poetics. Reprinted: 1976.23.

21 MOTTRAM, ERIC. "The Triumph of the Mobile: The Structure of Information, the Language of Computers, and Contemporary Poetry." Intrepid, nos. 23-24 (Summer-Fall), pp. 7-21.
     Uses a number of sections of 1968.6 on Pound, on form and the poem as a field, and on the "political implications" of poetic form. Mentions the potential for confusion that exists in poetry like Duncan's

RD1972

22   SIENICKA, MARTA. The Making of a New American Poem: Some
     Tendencies in the Post-World War II American Poetry.   Seria
     Filologia Angielska, no. 5.   Poznań, Poland: Wydawnictwo
     Naukowe Uniwersytetu im. Adama Mickiewicza w Poznañiu, pp. 40-
     43, 68-69, 82-83, 95-97, 106-14, 116-17, 123-24, 136-38, 148-
     59, passim.
          Discusses Duncan's work and poetic theories in terms of a
     projective poetics, continually comparing his poetry and ideas to
     those of Whitman, Olson, W.C. Williams, and Freud. Analyzes the
     nature of the self, "the speaking voice and the place of the poet"
     in Duncan's poetry, finding he "attempts at objective reconstruc-
     tion of his personal states," and notes his identification with
     cosmic processes and "a wider facet of human universe." Uses
     "Passages, 31:   The Concert (Tribunals)" to illustrate Duncan's
     treatment of the "multiplicity of oneness" of all life.   Notes his
     preference for the subconscious, especially over the rational, in
     order to create a poetry "organically linked with the structure of
     the outside world," yet also notes the role of conscious decision
     in Duncan's poetic creation.
          Discusses "The Dance" and "Often I Am Permitted to Return
     to a Meadow" in some detail, comparing the latter to Duncan's
     Atlantis dream given in 1964.7, examining his treatment of
     children and dream.   Also notes his treatment of the dance as the
     poet's consciousness during creation and the meadow as "a state in
     which the poet loses his selfconscious 'artistic' intentions" to
     surrender "to the 'dance's initiative.'"   (See also 1972.23.)
     Continually emphasizes the "organic link between the poet's actual
     life and his art," and mentions Duncan's treatment of language,
     his emphasis on the role of breath for the poetic line, and his
     use of grass and flower imagery.

23   _____ . "William Carlos Williams and Some Younger Poets."
     Studia Anglica Posnaniensia: An International Review of
     English Studies 4, nos. 1-2:183-93.
          Analyzes W.C. Williams's influence on projective poetics.
     Employs Duncan's "The Dance," his use of dance imagery, and his
     statements on poetics to show his sense of the poem's "inner spon-
     taneity resulting from its organic nature." See also 1972.22.

24   WAGNER, LINDA, and MacADAMS, LEWIS, Jr.   "The Art of Poetry."
     In A Sense of Measure, by Robert Creeley.   Signature Series,
     no. 16.   London: Calder & Boyars, pp. 68-107.
          Reprint of 1968.29.

25   WEBER, ROBERT CHARLES.   "Roots of Language: The Major Poetry
     of Robert Duncan."   Ph.D. dissertation, University of
     Wisconsin, 344 pp.
          Focusing on Duncan's use of myth in poetry, notes his
     sources in Heraclitus, Olson, W.C. Williams, Pound, and Denis

Saurat's <u>Gods of the People</u> (London: J. Westhouse, 1947). Occasionally quotes from unpublished correspondence with Duncan in 1971-72 and from a 23 March 1967 interview with Duncan by Lawrence Dembo, also unpublished.

Provides a detailed reading of <u>The Structure of Rime</u> sequence as an "'inward' epic" depicting the "growth of the poet as hero." Discusses his treatment of the Lasting Sentence, "the Law of the ordered universe," the "transcendental reality," the goal of permanence for poetry, his own early writing, language, rhyme, measure, and syntax. Notes Duncan's use of male and female voices and figures, especially the female temptress, the Master of Rime, and Black King Glêlê. Also comments on his use of open form and caves, grass, and animal images, especially the lion, snake, and fish.

Comments on the role of dream and the female figure in "Often I Am Permitted to Return to a Meadow" and of cross-eyed vision and time in "Crosses of Harmony and Disharmony." Discusses the poet's quest for and engagement in a transcendent or "primordial reality" through the "recognition of divine Law," "primal and instinctive forces," and "the permanence of myth" in <u>The Opening of the Field</u>. Focuses on the above themes in a number of poems, especially noting the treatment of sex, the past, corruption, and seeds in "Nor Is the Past Pure," and death and immortality in "Under Ground." Notes the treatment of Kore and the dance in "Evocation"; love in "A Poem Slow Beginning"; and myth and love in "A Poem Beginning with a Line by Pindar." Discusses his treatment of futility in "Ingmar Bergman's <u>Seventh Seal</u>"; poetry in the second "Yes, As a Look Springs to <u>Its</u> Face"; and poetry and language in both "The Natural Doctrine" and "Food for Fire, Food for Thought." Also significantly discusses "Atlantis" and the poems in "The inbinding mirrors a process returning to roots of first feeling."

Notes the ways in which "mythic consciousness receives expression" through "poems on poetry," through the "idea of a divine Law," through primal, often instinctual, forces, and through "personal poems . . . utiliz[ing] the myth of the Great Mother" in <u>Roots and Branches</u>. Comments on these and other themes in a number of poems, especially the treatment of the reality of the "unseen world" in "Roots and Branches"; of "actual earth" in "Returning to the Rhetoric of an Early Mode"; and of poetry and the shadowy figure in "A New Poem (for Jack Spicer)." Notes Duncan's treatment of divine Law compared to man's laws in "The Law"; of the Kabbalah in "What Do I Know of the Old Lore?"; and of the Albigensian and Erik Satie in "Sonneries of the Rose Cross." Comments on his treatment of the progress toward mythic unity in "Osiris and Set," "The Continent," "Nel Mezzo del Cammin di Nostra Vita," and, especially, "Apprehensions." Examines his treatment of H.D., his mother, language, the Great Mother figure, and bees in "A Sequence of Poems for H.D.'s Birthday," "Two Presentations,"

"After Reading H.D.'s Hermetic Definitions," and "Doves." Also
notes the sources for a few of the above poems.
     Focusing on two movements in the Passages sequence, dis-
cusses "the individual's connections with the past" in "Tribal
Memories: Passages, 1," "At the Loom: Passages, 2," "As in the
Old Days: Passages, 8," and "The Architecture: Passages, 9."
Examines "the emergence of a social voice, the beginnings of a
political involvement, and the role of the poet-spokesman" in "The
Fire: Passages, 13," "Chords: Passages, 14," "The Multiversity:
Passages, 21," "In the Place of a Passage 22," "Orders: Passages,
24," "Up Rising: Passages, 25," "Passages, 26: The Soldiers,"
"Eye of God: Passages, 29," and "Passages, 30: Stage Directions." Providing sources and a historical context, also notes
the use of the collage, open form, and the poem as a field. Mentions the treatment of myth, language, Heraclitean "dynamic
strife," "human nature," power, protest, community, American armed
forces, the Vietnam War, and the Cao Dai cult in a number of the
above works.
     A section of the last chapter on "The Fire: Passages, 13"
is revised: 1978.43. See Dissertation Abstracts International 33
(1973):4437-38A.

1973

1   ALLEN, DONALD [MERRIAM], and TALLMAN, WARREN. Poetics of the
      New American Poetry. New York: Grove Press, 463 pp.
           Includes reprints of 1955.1; 1956.3; 1966.10; 1967.3 (as
      "'I'm Given to Write Poems'"); and a reprint from 1970.19.

2   ALPERT, BARRY. "David Bromige: An Interview." Vort 1, no. 3
      [David Bromige/Ken Irby Number] (Summer):2-23.
           In this 1972 interview, Bromige mentions his relationship to
      and impressions of Duncan from 1961 on. Comments on the publica-
      tion of Writing Writing.

3   ALTIERI, CHARLES. "From Symbolist Thought to Immanence: The
      Ground of Postmodern American Poetics." Boundary 2: A Journal
      of Postmodern Literature 1, no. 3 [A Symposium 2] (Spring):
      605-41.
           Briefly notes Duncan's antipathy to the idea "that value and
      order depend on man's creative imagination." Also mentions his
      belief in "the ordering force in nature" and the mythopoetic.
      Greatly abridged and revised: 1979.3. Translated and abridged:
      1984.2.

4   Comments. In A Selection of Robert Duncan's Poetry and Prose
      with Some Tentative Responses to the Context within Which His

Work Lies. [Aberystwyth, Wales: University of Wales], pp. 3, 5, [17, 19-20], passim.
Briefly comments on Duncan's poetry and understanding of H.D. Lists the publication history of The H.D. Book.

5   CREELEY, ROBERT, ed. "Introduction" to Whitman. Poet to Poet. Harmondsworth, Middlesex, England: Penguin Books, pp. 7-20.
Briefly compares the role of the poet in Whitman's 1855 preface to Leaves of Grass to that of 1966.10. Comments on Whitman's presence in "A Poem Beginning with a Line by Pindar," and mentions Duncan's observation on W.C. Williams's attitude toward Whitman's work. Reprinted: 1979.13; 1981.4.

6   CREELEY, ROBERT; with DUNCAN, ROBERT; COLEMAN, VIC[TOR]; and SNYDER, GARY. "A Sense of Measure: An Occasion at the Berkeley Poetry Conference, July 23, 1965." Transcribed and edited by Douglas Calhoun. Athanor, no. 4 (Spring), pp. 35-52.
In this combination of lecture and conversation at the Berkeley Poetry Conference, Duncan comments on his sense of measure and of rhythm in poetry as opposed to the conscious counting of syllables. He also provides a few biographical details and briefly mentions the measured lines in "The Dance."

7   DAVIDSON, ROBERT MICHAEL. "'Disorders of the net': The Poetry of Robert Duncan." Ph.D. dissertation, State University of New York at Buffalo, 253 pp.
Provides an introductory biography of Duncan with an illustrative section of poems. Using Heidegger's terminology and noting romantic correspondences, discusses the "crises of recognition which takes place between a fictive I and the poet" when Duncan recognizes a "'thereness' or 'otherness' to being" during composition. Comments on the dissociation of personality, the role of the reader, the problem of presence and absence, and the unclear boundaries of poetry as well as Duncan's treatment of wastage and identity in a number of poems, especially "The Fire: Passages, 13," "Over There," "Variations on Two Dicta of William Blake," and "A Dancing Concerning A Form of Women." Notes his use of ambiguity, imagery, and pronouns in the above poems.
Discusses Duncan's poetics, noting his sources in and parallels to Pound, W.C. Williams, Olson, and Stein. Mentions his use of syntax and phrasal units; his "patterning of sounds"; and his use of assonance, alliteration, and rhyme. Also comments on his use of spaces, caesurae, and word and line breaks that create "internal and terminal juncture" and project "doubled meanings," illustrating with a section from "The Torso: Passages, 18." Discusses his use of "'[p]olysemous' or 'multiphasic' ordering" as "a method of composition by which multiple images coexist and sounds are filled with a variety of rhythmic and syntactic roles." Notes the repetition and changing sense of words in sections of

RD1973

Medieval Scenes and the rhymes, repetitions, and assonance in "The Venice Poem." Mentions the puns, which "allow for a variety of semantic groupings," and the syncopation of sounds in "Eluard's Death"; the form of The Structure of Rime sequence; and the line breaks, stresses, and rhythmic tensions in "First Invention on the Theme of the Adam."

The last chapter provides a detailed "poem by poem account" of The Opening of the Field, discussing Duncan's treatment of and/or sources in Whitman, Olson, Whitehead, Rimbaud, Blake, Pound, Zukofsky, W.C. Williams, and Pindar. Quotes unpublished sections from Duncan's notebooks, and identifies many of the other sources, including those from the Kabbalah, the Bible, mythology, and art. Occasionally comments on the style of the poetry, including Duncan's use of puns, rhythm, multiphasic meanings, alliteration and other sound correspondences, and rhyme. Identifies images, figures, and allusions. Provides biographical background for a few poems, and comments on his use of female and king figures. Details Duncan's themes, including his treatment of language, poetry, origins, music, history, boundaries, beauty, love, sex, sight, gold, death, and memory. Notes his use of field, cave, dance, bear, fire, rose, and Christ images. This last chapter is extensively condensed and revised as 1979.14. (See also 1982.22.) Includes a checklist of primary works (pp. 247-53). See Dissertation Abstracts International 34 (1973):765A.

8   DICKEY, JAMES. "Robert Duncan." In Babel to Byzantium: Poets and Poetry Now. New York: Farrar, Straus, & Giroux, Octagon Books, pp. 173-77.
A reprint of the Duncan section from 1962.2, slightly revised, with a section from an unannotated review.

9   DUNCAN, ROBERT. "The Homosexual in Society." Fag Rag, no. 5 [Fag Rag Five] (Summer), pp. 3, 20.
Reprint of of 1944.1.

10   _____. "Ideas on the Meaning of Form." Poetics of the New American Poetry. Edited by Donald [Merriam] Allen and Warren Tallman. New York: Grove Press, pp. 195-211.
Revision of 1961.1.

11   _____. "The Museum." New Directions in Prose and Poetry, no. 26, pp. 35-38.
Reprint of 1972.7.

12   _____. "A Note" to A Seventeenth Century Suite in Homage to the Metaphysical Genius in English Poetry, 1590-1690: Being Imitations, Derivations, and Variations upon Certain Conceits and Findings Made among Strong Lines, c. Nov. 5, 1971-Decm. 16, 1971, Aug. 5-18 and Oct. 22, 1973. N.p., [p. 25].

Provides the history of the composition of A Seventeenth
Century Suite.

13 _____ . "Notes from a Reading at the Poetry Center, San
Francisco, March 1, 1959." In The Floating Bear: A News-
letter. Edited by Diane di Prima and LeRoi Jones. La Jolla,
Calif.: Laurence McGilvery, pp. 398-99, 571.
Reprint of 1965.6 with a note (no. 103).

14 _____ . A Selection of Robert Duncan's Poetry and Prose with
Some Tentative Responses to the Context within Which His Work
Lies. [Aberystwyth, Wales: University of Wales], 26 pp.
In preparation for a 11 May 1973 reading at the University
of Wales at Aberystwyth, reprints previous published comments by
Duncan on his work (especially from 1966.6; 1969.8; 1972.10) with
a selection of his poetry.

15 _____ . "Towards an Open Universe." In Contemporary American
Poetry. Edited by Howard Nemerov. Voice of America Forum
Lectures. [Washington, D.C.: United States Information
Agency, Voice of America], pp. 169-83.
Revision of 1966.10.

16 _____ . The Truth and Life of Myth: An Essay in Essential
Autobiography. Fremont, Mich.: Sumac Press in cooperation
with SOMA Books.
Reprint of 1968.12.

17 ELLMANN, RICHARD, and O'CLAIR, ROBERT, eds. "Robert Duncan."
In The Norton Anthology of Modern Poetry. New York: W.W.
Norton & Co., pp. 962-64.
Provides an overview of Duncan's life and work, noting in-
fluences on him and his mysticism.

18 GALASSI, JONATHAN. "An Open Idiom." Poetry 121, no. 6
(March):343-48.
In a brief, favorable review of Tribunals, emphasizes
Duncan's difficulty for the reader. Also notes his treatment of
contemporary events and use of language.

19 HAMMOND, JOHN GREER. "Robert Creeley's Art and Its Background." Ph.D. dissertation, Brandeis University, pp. 83-87.
Demonstrates that Duncan, like other Black Mountain poets,
saw poetic form as antirational and as an embodiment of experience. See Dissertation Abstracts International 34 (1974):4261A.

20 HUDSON, LEE. "Beat Generation Poetics and the Oral Tradition
of Literature." Ph.D. dissertation, University of Texas at
Austin, pp. 114, 120-21, 129-30, passim.

RD1973

Occasionally comments on Duncan's poetics, and quotes from
Duncan. See Dissertation Abstracts International 34 (1973):2800A.

21   MacADAMS, LEWIS, [Jr.]. "Lewis MacAdams and Robert Creeley."
     In Contexts of Poetry: Interviews, 1961-1971, by Robert
     Creeley. Edited by Donald [Merriam] Allen. Writing, no. 30.
     Bolinas, Calif.: Four Seasons Foundation, pp. 137-70.
        In this revision of 1968.29 with previously unpublished
     material, Creeley occasionally mentions Duncan, and provides
     secondhand details about Duncan and Olson's first meeting.

22   MacINTYRE, WENDY [ELIZABETH]. "Robert Duncan: The Activity of
     Myth." Open Letter, 2d ser., no. 4 (Spring), pp. 38-54.
        A slight revision of 1972.15, pp. 100-24, discussing the
     role and treatment of myth and a number of poems.

23   MALKOFF, KARL. Crowell's Handbook of Contemporary American
     Poetry. New York: Thomas Y. Crowell Co., pp. 11-13, 111-17,
     passim.
        Comments on Duncan's sense of a "muscular" poetry. Notes
     his treatment of the field and of poetry in "Often I Am Permitted
     to Return to a Meadow" and the energy of "A Poem Beginning with a
     Line by Pindar." Mentions the influences, especially Dante, on
     Roots and Branches, and refers to the political concerns of
     Bending the Bow.

24   NOVIK, GERALDINE MARY. "Robert Creeley: A Writing Biography
     and Inventory." Ph.D. dissertation, University of British
     Columbia, pp. 71, 81, 99, 103.
        Mentions Creeley's appreciation of Duncan's work and his
     role in publishing Caesar's Gate: Poems, 1949-1950 (1955). See
     Dissertation Abstracts International 34 (1974):7771-72A.

25   REID, IAN [W.]. "'Toward a Possible Music': The Poetry of
     Robert Duncan." New Poetry: Magazine of the Poetry Society of
     Australia 21, no. 2 (April):17-27.
        Finds sources of Duncan's work in that of Olson, W.C.
     Williams, and Whitman, and compares it to the poetry of Levertov
     and Creeley. Concentrates on Duncan's idea of open field composi-
     tion, finding him interested in self-creation through the process
     of writing. Sees his use of the theme of nakedness and the motifs
     of the dance and trees as indicative of his romanticism.

26   "Robert Duncan." In Modern American Poetry Conference.
     [London: Polytechnic of Central London], pp. 37-39.
        In these notes for the 25-27 May 1973 Modern American Poetry
     Conference at Polytechnic of Central London, provides a sketchy
     but full bibliography. See 1986.2 for the fullest bibliography on
     Duncan.

27 SHIVELY, CHARLES. "John Wieners: An Interview." Gay Sun-
    shine: A Newspaper of Gay Liberation, no. 17 (March-April),
    pp. 1-3.
        In this 8 February 1973 interview, Wieners provides some
    biographical information about his relationship to Duncan. In-
    cludes a small section of a letter that he received 7 February
    1973 from Duncan on homosexuality and language. Slightly revised
    and abridged with an added 27 March 1977 interview: 1982.25.

28 SUTTON, WALTER. American Free Verse: The Modern Revolution in
    Poetry. New York: New Directions, pp. 180-81.
        Briefly notes Duncan's influences, notably Eliot, Pound,
    Whitman, and Olson.

29 WAGNER, LINDA W[ELSHIMER]. "A Colloquy with Robert Creeley."
    In Contexts of Poetry: Interviews, 1961-1971, by Robert
    Creeley. Edited by Donald [Merriam] Allen. Writing, no. 30.
    Bolinas, Calif.: Four Seasons Foundation, pp. 71-124.
        Rearranged revision of 1965.13, with additional revised
    material from 1968.29 and previously unpublished material.
    Creeley notes Duncan's use of the "rhetorical mode" and his role
    at the Berkeley Poetry Conference. Also mentions Duncan's
    response to his own The Island.

                              1974

1   AIKEN, WILLIAM [MINOR]. "Charles Olson and the Vatic."
    Boundary 2: A Journal of Postmodern Literature 2, nos. 1-2
    [Charles Olson: Essays, Reminiscences, Reviews issue] (Fall
    1973-Winter):26-37.
        Quotes from Duncan on Olson's views of poetry and education
    from 1970.3 and on the poet as a prophet from 1968.12. Expanded
    and revised as chapter 2 of 1977.1.

2   ALPERT, BARRY. "Robert Kelly: An Interview." Vort 2, no. 2
    [whole no. 5] [Robert Kelly issue] (Summer):5-43.
        In this interview, Kelly contrasts his and Duncan's use of
    the circle or "round dance" as an image and comments on the quan-
    tity of Duncan's personal reading.

3   BERG, WILLIAM. "Introduction" and "Idylls" in Early Virgil, by
    Virgil. Translated by William Berg. London: Athlone Press,
    University of London, pp. 1-6, 7-25.
        Finds the garden or field, as in Duncan's "Often I Am Per-
    mitted to Return to a Meadow," a recurrent image in the history of
    poetry, and sees Duncan's poem as "a record of the poet's reflec-
    tion upon his art." Also discusses the pastoral conventions in
    the poem.

RD1974

4   BERTHOLF, ROBERT [JOHN]. "The Fictive Voice in the Poem: A
    First Statement." Io, no. 19 [Mind, Memory, and Psyche issue],
    pp. 7-15.
        Finds Duncan one of "the current masters" of the fictive
    voice in poetry since he projects himself as the poet "writing out
    of a mystical presence of first forms," represented by the meadow,
    a "primordial realm," in "Often I Am Permitted to Return to a
    Meadow." Reprinted: 1975.2.

5   BLEVINS, RICHARD. "First Things." Io, no. 19 [Mind, Memory,
    and Psyche issue], pp. 17-27.
        Blevins continually refers to Duncan's poetry, demonstrating
    what it has meant to him and his own work. Also briefly mentions
    the influence of Heidegger on Duncan and Duncan's use of Federico
    García Lorca.

6   CEBULSKI, F.J. "Introduction" to An Ode and Arcadia, by Robert
    Duncan and Jack Spicer. Berkeley, Calif.: Ark Press,
    [pp. 1-6].
        Discusses Duncan's relationship to Spicer, Dick Brown, and
    Kenneth Rexroth. Also comments on his role in the post-World War
    II San Francisco literary scene and his "Ode for Dick Brown,"
    including its occasion. Provides some biographical details from
    1945 to 1947.

7   CREELEY, ROBERT. "On the Road: Notes on Artists and Poets,
    1950-1965." In Poets of the Cities New York and San Francisco,
    1950-1965. [Exhibition catalog.] Edited by [Neil A. Chassman].
    New York: E.P. Dutton & Co., pp. 56-63.
        Quotes Duncan, from conversation, on American literature,
    language in poetry, the energies shaping "The Venice Poem," style,
    perception, action painters, Frank O'Hara, and professionalism.
    Also provides a quotation from Duncan addressed to Olson on the
    latter's deathbed concerning history in poetry and poetry as an
    adventure. Slightly revised: 1979.13; 1982.7. Reprinted in
    part: 1978.9; 1980.8.

8   DAVEY, FRANK[LAND WILMOT]. "Six Readings of Olson's Maximus."
    Boundary 2: A Journal of Postmodern Literature 2, nos. 1-2
    [Charles Olson: Essays, Reminiscences, Reviews issue] (Fall
    1973-Winter):291-321.
        Revision and expansion of 1970.5.

9   "Duncan, Robert." In Contemporary Authors: A Bio-
    Bibliographical Guide to Current Authors and Their Works. 1st
    revision. Vols. 9-12. Edited by Clare D. Kinsman and Mary
    Ann Tennenhouse. Detroit: Gale Research Co., pp. 225-52.
        An expanded version of 1969.3.

10   DUNCAN, ROBERT. "Dante Études" in <u>Dante</u>. Curriculum of the
     Soul, no. 8. Canton, N.Y.: Institute of Further Studies,
     [p. 1].
         In this preface, Duncan discusses the intention and sources
     of "Dante Etudes" and what Dante's work means to him. Reprinted:
     1984.8.

11   DUNCAN, ROBERT, and GINSBERG, ALLEN. "Early Poetic Community
     (with Robert Duncan)." In <u>Allen Verbatim: Lectures on Poetry,
     Politics, Consciousness</u>, by Allen Ginsberg. Edited by Gordon
     Ball. New York: McGraw-Hill Book Co., pp. 131-50.
         Reprint of 1974.12.

12   _____ . "Early Poetic Community (with Robert Duncan)." <u>Amer-
     ican Poetry Review</u> 3, no. 3 (May-June):54-58.
         In this talk from the Arts Festival at Kent State University
     on 7 April 1971, Duncan discusses his first meetings with Olson
     and what Olson has meant to him as a poet. Also mentions his
     contact with Frank O'Hara and the sense that <u>The New American
     Poetry, 1945-1960</u>, ed. Donald M[erriam] Allen (New York: Grove
     Press, 1960), gave him of "poetic community." Comments on his
     relationship to Jack Spicer.
         Ginsberg and Duncan provide details about a meeting between
     them in the early 1950s, and Ginsberg recalls what Duncan told him
     about writing without revision. Reprinted: 1974.11. Reprinted
     in part: 1978.11; 1980.12.

13   DUNCAN, ROBERT. "From Notes on <u>The Structure of Rime</u> Done for
     Warren Tallman, Spring 1961." <u>Maps</u>, no. 6 [Robert Duncan
     issue], pp. 42-52.
         In this 1961 commentary with appended notes and a section
     from 1973, Duncan discusses his concept of rime and form; the
     influences on and his plans for <u>The Structure of Rime</u> sequence;
     and the importance of Pound's <u>Cantos</u>, Sir Charles Scott
     Sherrington's <u>Man on His Nature</u> (Cambridge: Cambridge University
     Press, 1940), and Robert Thomas Rundle Clark's <u>Myth and Symbol in
     Ancient Egypt</u> (London: Thomas & Hudson, 1959) to his work. Also
     provides some biographical details from his childhood concerning
     the telling of stories.

14   _____ . "Letter to Jess after His Last Visit to Olson in New
     York Hospital, 1970." <u>Olson: The Journal of the Charles Olson
     Archives</u>, no. 1 (Spring), pp. 4-6.
         In this 4 January 1970 letter, Duncan provides a reminis-
     cence of visiting Olson on his deathbed in New York Hospital in
     January.

RD1974

15   _____. Letter to Kenneth Rexroth. In An Ode and Arcadia, by
     Robert Duncan and Jack Spicer. Berkeley, Calif.: Ark Press,
     [pp. 21-22].
        In this 1947 letter, Duncan speaks of the "elegiac tone"
     that he shares with William Everson and other San Francisco poets
     and provides a few biographical details from 1947. Briefly men-
     tions his other current work.

16   _____. Notes to "Two Messages." Quarterly Review of Litera-
     ture 19, nos. 1-2 [30th Anniversary Poetry Retrospective]:
     235-36.
        Reprint of 1963.5.

17   _____. "A Preface Prepared for Maps #6: The Issue." Maps,
     no. 6 [Robert Duncan issue], pp. 1-16.
        Including a reprint of 1970.8, Duncan recounts his relation-
     ship with John Martin at Black Sparrow Press, especially detailing
     their arguments over the publication of Tribunals. Provides a
     portion of an October 1970 letter to Martin that comments on the
     difficulties he has had with printers such as Graham Mackintosh,
     who dropped twenty-four lines from "The Christ in the Olive Grove"
     of "The Chimeras of Gérard de Nerval" (see 1969.13), and notes his
     decision to publish his own work. Reconstructs much of their
     argument on spacing, and provides examples of the instructions he
     sent the printer, Saul Marks. Also gives examples of his notes
     after reading the page proofs and a portion of Martin's reply on
     the costs of the suggested changes.
        Comments on "scoring" his poetry on a typewriter for this
     issue of Maps, and mentions his arguments with John Taggart about
     printing the typescript, providing details on their relationship.
     Discusses his sense of responsibility toward his poetry, its pre-
     sentation, and "means of production." Claims he has often felt
     rushed into print, and notes the freedom his decision to use a
     typewriter has given him.

18   _____. "Preface to a Reading of Passages, 1-22, March 6,
     1970." Maps, no. 6 [Robert Duncan issue], pp. 53-55.
        Reprint of 1970.10.

19   _____. "Some Letters to Charles Olson." Maps, no. 6 [Robert
     Duncan issue], pp. 56-67.
        In these letters from 14 August 1955 to 9 March 1963 with
     added notes, Duncan provides a few biographical details, and men-
     tions his current work, reading, and correspondence with others.
     In August 1955, he comments on his work on Letters, and questions
     his role as an examiner of Michael Rumaker. In June of 1960, he
     notes reading Whitehead, explains the role of the stars in "The
     Structure of Rime, XIII," and mentions where "the order of the
     poem arises from" when he writes. In March 1963, claims he did

not know what he was doing until he wrote <u>Medieval Scenes</u>, and places himself in a tradition.

20 _____. "Towards an Open Universe." <u>Prospice</u> 2 (1974):11-22.
Revision of 1966.10.

21 FAUCHEREAU, SERGE. <u>Introducere în poezia americană modernă</u>.
[In Rumanian.] Translated by C. Abăluță and Şt. Stoenescu.
Biblioteca Pentru Toti, no. 810. Bucharest: Editura Minerva,
pp. 282-89, passim.
A translation of 1968.16 with a new introduction.

22 GINSBERG, ALLEN, and DUNCAN, ROBERT. "Advice to Youth (with
Robert Duncan)." In <u>Allen Verbatim: Lectures on Poetry,
Politics, Consciousness</u>, by Allen Ginsberg. Edited by Gordon
Ball. New York: McGraw-Hill Book Co., pp. 103-30.
In this 5 April 1971 talk at the Kent State Arts Festival,
Duncan touches upon his artistic background, especially concerning
his family and his attempts at writing poetry in his early ado-
lescence. Comments on the inspiration that finally came with
writing "The Venice Poem" and his artistic models. Mentions
teaching in school and his continuing "problems with poetry."

23 MacINTYRE, WENDY [ELIZABETH]. "The Logos of Robert Duncan."
<u>Maps</u>, no. 6 [Robert Duncan issue], pp. 81-98.
Revision of 1972.15, pp. 5-34, on the <u>Zohar</u>, "orders of the
Cosmos," Neoplatonism, Pound, W.C. Williams, and H.D.

24 MERSMANN, JAMES F. <u>Out of the Vietnam Vortex: A Study of
Poets and Poetry against the War</u>. Lawrence: University Press
of Kansas, pp. 93-94, 159-204, 219, 249-50, passim.
Revision of 1972.18.

25 MOTTRAM, ERIC. "Performance: Charles Olson's Rebirth between
Power and Love." <u>Sixpack</u>, no. 6 (Winter), pp. 95-114.
Mentions Duncan's perceptions of Olson, and gives his re-
sponses to Olson's 1965 lecture at the Berkeley Poetry Conference.

26 NAVERO, WILLIAM. "Duncan, Creely [sic], and Dorn." <u>Ethos</u>
(State University of New York at Buffalo) 8, no. 14
(12 December):27-28.
Finds Duncan's writing an event, "an enacted poetics," as
in his "Dante Études."

*27 PIGNARD, SIMONE RASOARILALAO. "Influence de William Blake sur
quatre poètes américains contemporains: Kenneth Patchen,
Theodore Roethke, Robert Duncan, Allen Ginsberg." Ph.D. dissertation, Paris III.

Presumably discusses Blake's influence on Duncan. Not available for annotation. Listed as J273 in 1986.2.

28   SILLIMAN, RON. "Opening." Maps, no. 6 [Robert Duncan issue], pp. 72-80.
Explicates "Often I Am Permitted to Return to a Meadow," "The Dance," and "The Law I Love Is Major Mover" to demonstrate a conflict central to The Opening of the Field: a desire for cohesion or synthesis opposed to a desire for "opening," for the possibility that anything might enter the poem. Sees this volume as preparatory for Duncan's later poetry.

29   SMITH, D[ONALD] NEWTON, [Jr.]. "The Influence of Music on the Black Mountain Poets, I." St. Andrews Review: A Twice-Yearly Magazine of the Arts and Humanities 3, no. 1 (Fall-Winter): 99-115.
Discusses Duncan's attraction to romantic and avant-garde music by such composers as Erik Satie and Igor Stravinsky, its influence on his poetry, and his continual use of music as a metaphor. Examines the "symphonic form" of "The Venice Poem," noting the themes of music and sound in the work. Revised as part of 1974.30.

30   SMITH, DONALD NEWTON, [Jr.]. "The Origins of Black Mountain Poetry." Ph.D. dissertation, University of North Carolina, pp. 23-24, 39, 69-80, 87-90, 117-138, 188-92, 201-3, 207-8, 220-21, 223, 226-31, 257-67, 326-39, 351-52, 354-56, 368-79, 388-89, 411, 419-20, 422-23, 428-29, passim.
Half of chapter 6, "The Influence of Music on the Black Mountain Poets," pp. 243-69, is a revision of 1974.29. Comments on Duncan as one of the Black Mountain poets, noting their antagonistic relationship with academic poets and the New Critical stance than governed the literary climate of the 1940s and 1950s.
Discusses influences on Duncan. Notes the influence of Pound and imagism, finding Pound a guide for Duncan's interest in Eros, hermeticism, and emphasis on emotion, and comments on his use of Pound in "A Poem Beginning with a Line by Pindar." Discusses W.C. Williams's influence on and parallels to Duncan in terms of Duncan's sense of preestablished forms and of meaning arising from the world. Also notes Duncan's relationship to Williams, and compares their sense of struggle, discontinuity, and opposition. Examines Williams's potential influence on Duncan's sense of the poem's occurrences as opposed to the poet's intentions and the treatment and role of destruction. Also notes Williams's possible influence on Duncan's use of free association when writing, as in "Food for Fire, Food for Thought." Comments on the role of images in this poem.
Mentions Zukofsky's influence on Duncan, especially by directing Duncan's attention to the minims of the poem: "the

words, the juncture, the line." Notes Duncan's sense of Hart
Crane and the potential influence of D.H. Lawrence and others.
Also discusses Gertrude Stein's influence in terms of Duncan's
playfulness and treatment of children, as well as his sense of the
poet as an instrument who "must attend to the forms that reveal
themselves" and not worry about meaning. Mentions the influence
of art, especially dadaism, on Duncan, and notes his "parallel
development" with Jess. Comments on Duncan's drawing and role of
painting in "The Venice Poem" and drawing in "An Owl Is an Only
Bird of Poetry."
    Discusses Duncan's relationship to Olson and Creeley, in-
cluding his initial contacts with them. Surveys his relationship
to others such as Levertov, commenting on his poem-letters, collected in Letters, to her and others. Mentions Duncan's publication in little magazines, including Origin and the Black
Mountain Review. Includes biographical details, especially concerning his role at Black Mountain College. John Wieners, in a 24
March 1970 unpublished letter, describes Duncan's courses at Black
Mountain. See Dissertation Abstracts International 35 (1974):
3771-72A.

31   STAUFFER, DONALD BARLOW. A Short History of American Poetry.
      New York: E.P. Dutton & Co., pp. 266, 278, 419-22.
          Mentions the influence of Pound, H.D., Olson, and Stevens on
    Duncan as well as Duncan's influence on Levertov. Focuses on
    Duncan's virtuosity, his desire "to return to wholeness and full-
    ness of feeling," and his sense of the "vital connection between
    life and poetry" as witnessed in "Tribal Memories: Passages, 1."

32   TALLMAN, WARREN. "Wonder Merchants: Modernist Poetry in
      Vancouver during the 1960's." Boundary 2: A Journal of
      Postmodern Literature 3, no. 1 (Fall):57-89.
          Discusses Duncan's influence on Vancouver poets through his
    modernism; his sense of proprioception, derived from Olson; and
    his knowledge. Provides details of Duncan's visits to Vancouver
    in 1961. Reprinted: 1976.29; 1977.24.

33   TAYLOR, [L.] LORING. "Pietre în cîmpul lui Robert Duncan."
      [In Rumanian.] Translated by Ion Bitea and N. Harsanyi.
      Steaua 25, no. 3:45-48.
          Places Duncan in terms of literary movements, refers to his
    relationship with Black Mountain poetry, and provides biographical
    details on him. Compares his work to Robert Browning's and de-
    tails influences on him, especially Eliot's and Pound's, noting
    differences between his work and theirs. Discusses Duncan as an
    imitative and derivative poet, pointing out that he writes in the
    style of poets he admires. Remarks on Duncan's attraction to
    medieval and later periods, noting his experimentation with tradi-
    tional and other forms. Comments on "Homage and Lament for Ezra

RD1974

Pound in Captivity, May 12, 1944." Mentions the treatment of
destiny and identity in "A Country Wife's Song" and the sources of
"The Ballad of the Forfar Witches' Sing."
    Outlines Duncan's use of Shakespeare, puns, parody, and the
collage technique, claiming he desires to demythify with lucidity.
In terms of the elemental functions of language, an understanding
of the absurd, and an ability to deconstruct the clichés embedded
in expressions, reviews the role of his imitations of Gertrude
Stein in his development. Compares "A Language for Poetry" to the
poems of "Domestic Scenes," considering the role of divinity,
elegance, and nobility in "Electric Iron." Reviews the treatment
of sexual awakening, femininity, and the duality between the male
and the female in "The Maiden" and the treatment of communication
in "Thank You For Love." Mentions the use of wordplay in "For a
Muse Meant." Examines "Heavenly City, Earthly City" as the product of Duncan's first ten years of writing, and notes the role of
imagination and the perceptions of reality, ongoing themes of
Duncan, in the poem. Also notes Shelley's stylistic influence,
an influence that has persisted in terms of both style and ideas.
Often compares Duncan's work to Blake's and Wordsworth's. Finds
Duncan's Passages sequence and The Structure of Rime sequence fuse
to form one poem comparable to Wordsworth's Prelude.
    Contrasts Duncan's emphasis on synthesis with Pound's juxta-
position. Comments on Duncan's decomposition and reassembly of
language to achieve new syntheses in the 1950s. Discusses his
multidimensional use of the field as a symbol throughout The Open-
ng of the Field, noting its relationship to relativistic physics,
field composition, linguistic fields, fields of the self and poetry, experiential fields, and the field of memory, especially
childhood memory. In "Often I Am Permitted to Return to a
Meadow," notes the role of the imagination, fantasy, beginnings,
evasion, and freedom and acceptance.

34   von HALLBERG, ROBERT. "Olson's Relation to Pound and Williams."
     Contemporary Literature 15, no. 1 (Winter):15-48.
        Briefly quotes from a 20 June 1956 letter from Olson to
Eigner on Duncan's "playfulness concerning etymology." Enlarged
and revised as chapter 2 of 1975.25 and 1978.42.

1975

1   ALPERT, BARRY. "David Antin: An Interview." Vort 3, no. 1
    [whole no. 7] [David Antin/Jerome Rothenberg issue]:3-33.
        In this 3 November 1973 interview, Antin comments on his
ambivalent feelings toward Duncan, claiming Duncan's use of myth
as well as the way he "embraces everything that is not reason"
makes him a "fraudulent poet." Notes some redeeming features to

this fraudulence, and finds him a poet of the "preposterously beautiful."

2   BERTHOLF, ROBERT [JOHN]. "The Fictive Voice in the Poem: Chapter I, Part I." <u>Credences</u>, [o.s.] 1, no. 1 [whole no. 1] (February):84-93.
     Reprint of 1974.4.

3   BERTHOLF, ROBERT J[OHN], and NURMI, RUTH. "'Scales of the marvelous': Robert Duncan's 'The Venice Poem.'" <u>New Poetry: Magazine of the Poetry Society of Australia</u> 23, no. 2:22-32.
     Discusses in detail the structure of Duncan's "The Venice Poem" as it is modeled on Igor Stravinsky's <u>Symphony in Three Movements</u> with "three main sections, each presenting variations on the two major themes of jealousy and the joy of love." Delineates "the exposition, development, and recapitulation of the sonata form" with an "interlude or bridge between the second and third sections." Also details the ideas, allusions, repetitions, and imagery in the poem. Mentions Duncan's use of associations and his treatment of himself as a "fictive form." Comments on his use of work by Pound, Proust, and Henri Rousseau.

4   BERTHOLF, ROBERT J[OHN]. "Shelley, Stevens, and Robert Duncan: The Poetry of Approximations." In <u>Artful Thunder: Versions of the Romantic Tradition in American Literature in Honor of Howard P. Vincent</u>. Edited by Robert J. DeMott and Sanford E. Marovitz. Kent, Ohio: Kent State University Press, pp. 269-99.
     In a poetry of "self-creation," finds Duncan's work, like that of Shelley and Stevens, employs "approximate images and statements" to describe the "numinous experience" in which the poet is "allowed entrance into the sacred presence of the creating processes themselves." Claims Duncan's poetry leads him, via "musical rhythms," into the "presence of primal creation," where he attempts "to recreate himself by illustrating the dance of the phonemes in the cadences and processes of language as it engages itself in the music of genesis," as in the <u>Passages</u> sequence.
     Explains that Duncan, like Shelley and Stevens, creates "a fictive habitation" for this "fictive self" to occupy, a "field of poetic action" where he might participate with other visionary poets in the larger Poem of which his poetry is but a part. Finds the <u>Passages</u> sequence "presents its form as the morphology of the musical and mystical energy which excites it," and describes the "evolving design" of the poem as a collage and a tapestry, noting its incompletion and lack of closure and convention. Also mentions Duncan's use of myth, quoting from a number of individual works, and comments on the internal tensions in his work.

RD1975

5   BLASER, ROBIN; DUNCAN, ROBERT; and SPICER, JACK. "A Backward
    Glance." In The Collected Books of Jack Spicer. Edited by
    Robin Blaser. Los Angeles: Black Sparrow Press, pp. 361-67.
        Blaser comments on Duncan and Spicer's relationship and
    correspondence. Includes two 1951 letters from Duncan to Spicer
    in which Duncan provides a few biographical details and comments
    on the creative process and on a previous discussion he had with
    Spicer on myth. Duncan also notes the relationship of myth to
    poetry and compares himself as a poet to Spicer. Includes a let-
    ter from Spicer to Duncan that reacts to Duncan's first letter,
    and notes Duncan's relationship to Landis Everson.

6   BLASER, ROBIN. "The Practice of Outside: An Essay." In
    The Collected Books of Jack Spicer. Edited by Robin Blaser.
    Los Angeles: Black Sparrow Press, pp. 269-329.
        Blaser occasionally reminisces about the relationship be-
    tween himself, Duncan, and Spicer.

7   BLUFORD, KEN. Review of Tribunals: "Passages," 31-35 and A
    Seventeenth Century Suite. Painted Bride Quarterly 2, no. 2
    (Spring):32-36.
        In this favorable review, observes the influences of Emerson
    and Whitman, the role of the Vietnam War, and Duncan's view of "a
    historical dissociation of sensibility."

8   BRIEN, DOLORES ELISE. "Robert Duncan: A Poet in the Emerson-
    Whitman Tradition." Centennial Review 19, no. 4 (Fall):308-16.
        A revision of an abridged portion of 1969.1.

9   BROMIGE, DAVID. "Beyond Prediction." Credences, [o.s.] 1, no.
    2 [whole no. 2] (July):101-13.
        Reacts to and comments on Duncan reading "Moving the Moving
    Image: Passages, 17," noting the music, the treatment of love,
    the use of language, and the role of Hermes and Hermes's chant in
    the poem.

*10 CHRISTENSEN, PAUL NORMAN. "Charles Olson: Call Him Ishmael."
    Ph.D. dissertation, University of Pennsylvania, 392 pp.
        Dissertation was restricted, unavailable for annotation.
    See published version: 1979.10. See Dissertation Abstracts
    International 36 (1976):8056A.

11 COOLIDGE, CLARK. "Notes Taken in Classes Conducted by Charles
    Olson at the University of British Columbia, Vancouver, August
    1963." Olson: The Journal of Charles Olson Archives, no. 4
    (Fall), pp. 47-63.
        In these notes covering 12-16 August 1963, records Olson's
    comments on Duncan and Duncan's interjections during classes at
    the Vancouver Poetry Conference.

12 DAVEY, FRANK[LAND WILMOT], ed. "Introduction" to Tish, No. 1-
    19. Vancouver, British Columbia: Talonbooks, pp. 7-11.
        Reminisces about Duncan's 1961 trip to Vancouver and his
    role in the inception of and philosophy behind Tish. Provides a
    partial transcript of a lecture given by Duncan on 23 July 1961.
    Reprinted: 1976.8.

13 DULL, HAROLD. "In Prose." Manroot, no. 10 [The Jack Spicer
    Issue] (Fall 1974-Winter), pp. 22-25.
        Reprint of 1971.8.

14 "Duncan, Robert." In World Authors, 1950-1970. Edited by John
    Wakeman. New York: H.W. Wilson Co., pp. 412-13.
        Provides a brief overview of Duncan's work, noting the crit-
    ical reaction.

15 DUNCAN, ROBERT. "From The Day Book." In The Gist of "Origin,"
    1951-1971: An Anthology. Edited by Cid Corman. New York:
    Viking Press, Grossman Publishers; Toronto: Macmillan Co. of
    Canada, pp. 263-73.
        Reprinted from 1963.4.

16 _____. "[From The H.D. Book] Chapter 7, Part Two."
    Credences, [o.s.] 1, no. 2 [whole no. 2] (July):53-67.
        Duncan mentions his intentions in revising parts of The H.D.
    Book and the composition of the work. Provides the details of a
    dream and a few biographical details from March 1961, and mentions
    his sense of the romantic spirit of poetry, finding it opposed by
    the literary establishment. Comments on his sense of Pound and
    others as masters and his correspondence with Norman Holmes
    Pearson, including Pearson's role in The H.D. Book.

17 _____. "[From The H.D. Book] Chapter 8, Part Two."
    Credences, [o.s.] 1, no. 2 [whole no. 2] (July):68-94.
        Mentions a 1961 dream, some of his reading, and a conversa-
    tion with Spicer on the etymology of "verse."

18 _____. Notes to "Two Messages." In Contemporary Poetry: A
    Retrospective from the "Quarterly Review of Literature."
    Edited by T[heodore] Weiss and Reneé Weiss. Princeton:
    Princeton University Press, pp. 235-36.
        Reprint of 1963.5.

19 EVANS, P[AUL] J.D. "Robert Duncan and American Poetry since
    the First World War." M.Phil. thesis, Kings College, Univer-
    sity of London, 98 pp.
        Notes Duncan's imitation of other writers, finding echoes of
    Auden in "Passage over Water," George Baker in "From 'Toward the
    Shaman,'" and Sanders Russell in "A Spring Memorandum: Fort Knox."

RD1975

Mentions the treatment of death in "An African Elegy" and of his
"psyche-life" in "The Venice Poem," finding the latter a transi-
tional poem to a process poetics. Comments on Platonism and the
treatment of the dance and invention in "Often I Am Permitted to
Return to a Meadow"; the sources in Teutonic myth and the Kabbalah,
and the role of the world-tree in "The Structure of Rime, V"; and
the treatment of Adam and light in "Apprehensions." Discusses the
treatment of politics, the role of myth, and the conflict between
order and open form in "A Poem Beginning with a Line by Pindar."
Finds a possible source in George Fox for the title of The Opening
of the Field, and mentions "Food for Fire, Food for Thought," "The
Dance," The Structure of Rime sequence, and "Three Pages from a
Birthday Book."
   Discusses the Passages sequence, comparing it to the work of
Pound, Blake, and Stevens, noting the role of the ego and the
treatment of war. Comments on the mother figure in Duncan's
poems, especially in "Two Presentations" and "Passages, 23:
Benefice"; the sources in Emperor Julian (Flavius Claudius
Julianus) for "Tribal Memories: Passages, 1"; and the treatment
of authority and law in "The Multiversity: Passages, 21." Compares Duncan's Heraclitean to his Platonic stance, noting the role
of discontinuity in his work. Comments on his use of language,
the esoteric, free verse, and words in the sequence. Notes the
role of hidden meanings and the treatment of Christ, childhood,
Adam, and light. Also comments on the sense of permission; the
influence of W.C. Williams, Pound, and Olson; Platonism; and
sources in the Kabbalah. Compares his religious sense to that of
modern poets.

20   LENFEST, DAVID S. "Notes toward a Study of Nathaniel Tarn's
     The Beautiful Contradictions: The Poetry of Material Trans-
     migration." Boundary 2: A Journal of Postmodern Literature 4,
     no. 1 (Fall):77-95.
          Comments on Duncan's use of the "archetypal mother figure"
     as the muse, comparing the Queen figure in "Often I Am Permitted
     to Return to a Meadow" to Tarn's feminine figure in The Beautiful
     Contradictions (London: Cape Goliard Press, 1969; New York:
     Random House, 1970). Also, using 1973.3, mentions the relation of
     "materiality and spirituality" in Duncan's work.

21   MACKEY, NATHANIEL ERNEST. "Call Me Tantra: Open Field Poetics
     as Muse." Ph.D. dissertation, Stanford University, pp. 6-9,
     43-48, 53-54, 88-90, 100-172, 174-91, 193-96, 201-12, 216-22,
     passim.
          Discusses Duncan's sense of form, including open form; the
     muse; obscurity; "the poet as a kind of imperialist"; and poetry
     as dissonance or as a dance, noting the need for conflicts, dis-
     turbances, and opposites. Also discusses his sense of or sources
     in Pound, H.D., W.C. Williams, and Olson, noting his differences

as well as similarities with them. Notes the "connection between
. . . disturbance and an erotic intention" in his work as in "The
Venice Poem."
Examines "The Continent" in detail, commenting on Duncan's
use of assonance, consonance, and word association. Details his
treatment of the mythic female figure; America and the value of
the American locale for the artist; serpents and beasts; the
Orient; unity and wholeness; separation; continental drift;
poetry; and the horizon. Identifies the artist figure in the poem
as W.C. Williams, and notes references to Williams here and in
"Apprehensions," occasionally commenting on and finding sources
for the latter. Also finds sources for "The Continent" in science, myth, ritual, and in the work of Olson and H.D., as well as
in Géza Róheim's The Eternal Ones of the Dream: A Psychoanalytic
Interpretation of Australian Myth and Ritual (New York: International University Presses, 1945). Provides some biographical
context for "The Continent," and comments on its title. Mentions
the role of metallurgy, the unicorn, Christ, and Osiris here and
elsewhere, and notes the importance of Duncan's sense of kinship
with other poets.
In Bending the Bow and Tribunals, especially the war poems
in the Passages sequence from number 24 to 35, speculates on
Duncan's sources, especially in H.D. Comments on his treatment of
love, wrath, doom, the communal, Kronos, America, America's western expansionism, poetry, war, time, nationalism, and politics in
these poems. Also mentions the role of doom and hope, dreams, the
Child figure, and Egypt. Comments on "Duncan's Dantean reading of
Darwin" and its role in his sense of poetry's relationship to the
cosmos. Part 2, on "The Continent," is abridged and extensively
revised as 1980.22. See Dissertation Abstracts International 35
(1975):7913-14A.

22 OLSON, CHARLES; GINSBERG, ALLEN; CREELEY, ROBERT; DUNCAN,
   ROBERT; and WHALEN, PHILIP. "On 'History.'" Transcribed by
   Ralph Maud, edited by George F. Butterick. Olson: The Journal
   of the Charles Olson Archive, no. 4 (Fall), pp. 40-46.
   This discussion contains Duncan's participation in a 29 July
1963 symposium at the Vancouver Poetry Conference. The editor
supplies the text of a 18 December 1961 letter from Duncan to
Olson on history, and Olson comments on this letter. An extended
version: 1978.32.

23 RAY, DAVID. "Duncan, Robert (White)." In Contemporary Poets.
   Edited by James Vinson and D.L. Kirkpatrick. 2d ed. London:
   St. James Press; New York: St. Martin's Press, pp. 397-400.
   Unacknowledged reprint of 1970.21, expanded with an updated
bibliography. See also 1979.37 and 1980.10.

RD1975

24   SWEENEY, MICHAEL J.   "Robert Duncan: An Annotated Bibliog-
      raphy." M.L.S. thesis, Kent State University, 74 pp.
          Provides an annotated primary and secondary bibliography on
      Duncan including his books, broadsides, and poetry and prose con-
      tributions to periodicals and anthologies. Secondary work in-
      cludes reviews, essays, sections of books, and dissertations. See
      1986.2 for the fullest bibliography on Duncan.

25   von HALLBERG, ROBERT. "The Scholar's Art: The Poetics and
      Poetry of Charles Olson." Ph.D. dissertation, Stanford Univer-
      sity, pp. 142, passim.
          Chapter 2, which contains the only substantive mention of
      Duncan, is an expansion and revision of 1974.34. Revised:
      1978.42. See Dissertation Abstracts International 37 (1976):
      974-75A.

26   VORDTRIEDE, WERNER. Das verlassene Haus: Tagebuch aus dem
      amerikanischen Exil, 1938-1947. [In German.] Munich, West
      Germany: Carl Hanser Verlag, pp. 334-36, 368, passim.
          Vortriede provides a description of a 18 September 1945
      reading by Duncan in Woodstock, N.Y., and gives details about his
      contacts with and relationship to Duncan.

27   WEATHERHEAD, A[NDREW] K[INGSLEY]. "Robert Duncan and the
      Lyric." Contemporary Literature 16, no. 2 (Spring):163-74.
          Noting Pound, Eliot, and W.C. Williams's influence, dis-
      cusses Duncan's sense "of poems as spatial objects" defying tempo-
      rality, and his use of the collage as a method of composition.
      Also examines his emphasis on process and his references to the
      spatial and temporal in a number of poems, including the bow and
      lyre in "Bending the Bow" and architecture in "The Architecture:
      Passages, 9." Finds Duncan avoids "the single meaning," claiming
      his poetry often becomes a "heterogeneous assemblage" of elements.
      Believes he, because of his belief in a divine order and a "Grand
      Symphony" of which his poetry is but a part, allows his poetry to
      be fragmentary. Feels that his allegiance to an open poetry that
      will allow anything to enter, in part due to his political and
      social conscience, keeps him from the practice of the "exclusive
      kind of action that is demanded in the creation of a lyric."

1976

1   AKEROYD, JOANNE VINSON, and BUTTERICK, GEORGE F. Where Are
      Their Papers? A Union List Locating the Papers of Forty-Two
      Contemporary American Poets and Writers. Bibliography Series,
      no. 9. Storrs, Conn.: University of Connecticut Library,
      pp. 24-25.
          Provides locations for specific manuscripts and papers of
      Duncan.

2   ALPERT, BARRY. "Ronald Johnson: An Interview." <u>Vort</u> 3, no. 3
    [Guy Davenport/Ronald Johnson number]:77-85.
         In this 13 August 1974 interview, Johnson mentions the in-
    fluence of Duncan's "The Fire: <u>Passages</u>, 13" on his "The Dif-
    ferent Music."

3   ALTIERI, CHARLES. "The Book of the World: Robert Duncan's
    Poetics of Presence." <u>Sun and Moon</u>: <u>A Quarterly of Literature</u>
    <u>and Art</u>, no. 1 (Winter), pp. 66-94.
         Analyzes Duncan's use of the romantic myth of the world as
    "the book of God." Unlike the traditional version, finds Duncan's
    God is "not a static Logos but a force in the process of realizing
    himself." Also claims his poet in this myth "is not simply one
    who reads the book but one who must . . . decreate the established
    ways of reading the book in order that it can continually be re-
    created" and his poem is "a reflection of larger synthesizing
    powers of the cosmos" reconciling contradictions. Finds that
    Duncan uses language to make "interconnections between natural
    energy, the force of consciousness, and the traces of cosmic de-
    sign." Mentions the role of Logos, Christian and Greek mythology,
    and Whitehead's cosmology in Duncan's poetics.
         Examines Duncan's sense of the sentence and of poetic lan-
    guage, which must be violent to "decreate what is understood [so]
    that presence might stand" yet obedient to serve "a Law whose
    principle is creative evolution towards a Form of Forms." Men-
    tions Duncan's use of the allegorical and of myth to provide "co-
    herent speculative visions not just of single experiences but of
    the very ontological grounds for imaginative activity and for the
    values the poet professes." Comments on the role of metaphor in
    "Roots and Branches," noting how the poem reflects Duncan's sense
    of passages. Details the treatment of the dance, the use of re-
    currences and puns, and the "six modes of consciousness" in "The
    Dance." Discusses his use of the Eros and Psyche myth in "A Poem
    Beginning with a Line by Pindar," and briefly compares Duncan's
    work to Ashbery's. Revised: 1979.3.

4   BEHM, RICHARD H. "A Study of the Function of Myth in the Work
    of Four Contemporary Poets: Charles Simic, Galway Kinnell,
    Gary Snyder, and Robert Duncan." Ph.D. dissertation, Bowling
    Green State University, pp. ii-iii, 4, 6, 13, 173-219.
         Counters the critical objections to Duncan's work, chiefly
    concerning his use of literary allusions, and traces the influence
    of Olson, Pound, and Gertrude Stein on his poetry. Concentrates
    on the "role that myth plays with [Duncan's] poetic theory."
    Finds that "the notion of poetry as a dance of words . . . is the
    means by which Duncan attempts to enter into the sacred time of
    the mythological present"; therefore "his poems take on aspects of
    chant, of litany, of ritual drama, of improvisational dance."
    Mentions his treatment of the past, the primitive, and poetry, as

RD1976

well as his use of an "associational process," rhythm, and typography, including spacing. Discusses a number of poems, especially "5th Sonnet," "The Dance," "The Structure of Rime, XV," "The Structure of Rime, XVI," and "Chords: Passages, 14." See Dissertation Abstracts International 37 (1977):5118A.

5   BERGÉ, CAROL. "The Vancouver Report." In The Writing Life: Historical and Critical Views of the "Tish" Movement. Edited by C[harles] H[enry] Gervais. Coatsworth, Ontario: Black Moss Press, pp. 143-49.
        Reprinted from 1964.1.

6   BOWERING, GEORGE [F.]. "Robert Duncan in Canada." Essays on Canadian Writing, no. 4 (Spring), pp. 16-18.
        Describes Duncan's influence on Canadian poetry, especially through his visits to Vancouver in the early 1960s and his role in the inception of Tish.

7   COOLEY, DENNIS [ORIN]. "Keeping the Green: Robert Duncan's Pastoral Vision." Capilano Review, nos. 8-9 (Fall-Spring), pp. 368-86.
        Abridged and revised from chapter 2, of 1971.6.

8   DAVEY, FRANK[LAND WILMOT]. "Introducing Tish." In The Writing Life: Historical and Critical Views of the "Tish" Movement. Edited by C[harles] H[enry] Gervais. Coatsworth, Ontario: Black Moss Press, pp. 150-61.
        Reprint of 1975.12 combined with another essay.

9   _____. "Rime: A Scholarly Piece." In The Writing Life: Historical and Critical Views of the "Tish" Movement. Edited by C[harles] H[enry] Gervais. Coatsworth, Ontario: Black Moss Press, pp. 165-71.
        Reprint of 1965.1.

10 DAVIDSON, [ROBERT] MICHAEL. "Organic Poetry." Reader: San Diego's Weekly 5, no. 15 (15-22 April):4.
        In this article on a 1976 reading by Duncan, discusses his use of literary and foreign allusions, private reference, "multi-layered" language, and consonance. Uses "Sonnet 1," "These Past Years: Passages, 10," and "A Poem Beginning with a Line by Pindar" to illustrate.

11 DUNCAN, ROBERT. "Articulations." In The New Naked Poetry: Recent American Poetry in Open Form. Edited by Stephen Berg and Robert Mezey. Indianapolis: Bobbs-Merrill Educational Publishing, pp. 46-47.
        An abridged text of 1968.6.

12   . "Partisan View." In "Contemporary American and
Australian Poetry: A Symposium," by John Tranter et al.
Meanjin Quarterly 35, no. 4 [Summer Issue] (December):368-69.
    Duncan explains why he allowed Thomas W. Shapcott to include
his work in Contemporary American and Australian Poetry, ed.
Thomas Shapcott ([St. Lucia, Queensland, Australia]: University
of Queensland Press, 1976) and why he wishes he had not. See
1977.20.

13   FAAS, EKBERT. "An Interview with Robert Bly." Boundary 2: A
Journal of Postmodern Literature 4, no. 3 (Spring):677-700.
    In this interview, Faas quotes from Duncan on the image as
an archetype and on romances in the Western tradition as aligned
to "heretical movements." Also mentions his assessment of
imagism. Reprinted: 1980.15.

14   GOLDONI, ANNALISA. "Robert Duncan o la poesia come religione."
[In Italian.] Studi americani: Revista annuale dedicata alle
lettere e alle arti negli Stati Uniti d'America, nos. 21-22,
pp. 445-73.
    Comparing him to a priest, discusses Duncan as a religious
poet who seeks to discover the links between the forms of creation. Focuses on the role of dualisms in his work, especially
between the real, the spiritual, and the actual, or sensual,
world. Comments on a number of his works, noting the treatment of
salvation in "Heavenly City, Earthly City" and of the poet's role
in society in "A Poem Beginning with a Line by Pindar." Mentions
the use of dreams, surrealism, and Freudian allusions; the sources
in Federico García Lorca; and the role of homosexuality in
Caesar's Gate. Finds The Opening of the Field often rhetorical,
but notes an indissoluble link of poetry and language in the work.
Mentions a few sources for Duncan's work, especially Olson, noting
Duncan's sense that all poets are engaged in a single poetic en-
deavor. Also comments on the role of his homosexuality and music,
and his treatment of the irrational, love, war, and American
political leaders in individual poems, especially in the Passages
sequence. Comments on Duncan's political or "civil" poetry, and
charts the development of his civil awareness.

15   JONHSON, RONALD. "A Fairy Tale for Robert Duncan." Parnassus:
Poetry in Review 5, no. 1 (Fall-Winter):260-62.
    Retells Duncan's life impressionistically and sketchily, as
though it were a fairy tale, providing biographical details, and
mentions Duncan's search for "the anima, The White Goddess."

16   [JOHNSTON, ALASTAIR M.] A Bibliography of Auerhahn Press and
Its Successor, David Haselwood Books. Berkeley, Calif.:
Poltroon Press, pp. 46, 48-49, 55, 84, 86-87.

Provides a copy and bibliographical description of Auerhahn Press's announcement for the aborted first volume of Duncan's A Book of Resemblances and a copy of an announcement of its cancellation, commenting on the circumstances. Also includes a bibliographical description of Duncan's "Wine," a broadside.

Quotes from a 22 March 1964 letter from Jonathan Williams that briefly mentions Duncan's view of Andrew Hoyem, the printer.

17 JONES, STEPHEN JEFFREY. "The Poetry of Robert Duncan." M.A. thesis, University of North Carolina at Greensboro, 148 pp.

Comments on Duncan's identification as a Black Mountain poet. Discusses his treatment of society, sex, failing love, and a return to an Edenic state of origins, and examines his use of Freud, surrealism, and images of destruction in The Years as Catches, focusing on "From 'Toward the Shaman.'"

Studies "Heavenly City, Earthly City" as an introspective poem dealing with loss, love, and the creative will. Also comments on the role of the redeemer figure, the sun, myth, and voices; the sources in John Donne; and the use of the resolution. Mentions the use of the city metaphor for the self in the poem, and finds that the Orpheus, Eurydice, and Icarus figures are "portions of the persona's inner self." Remarks on the "abandonment of the 'static' concept of the self" in "Processionals II."

Recounts the influence of W.C. Williams, Federico García Lorca, H.D., Pound, and Olson on Duncan, and comments on Duncan as a derivative poet. Examines introspection, the role of process and language, and the use of myth in his poetry. Outlines the influence of Olson's "Projective Verse" on Duncan in terms of field composition, proprioception, and immediacy, but notes Duncan's misunderstandings of and deviations from Olson's theories. Claims Duncan managed to avoid the literal sense of Olson's "breath line" by interpreting it to include notions of inspiration, rhythm, dance, and language. Also remarks on Duncan's use of the dance metaphor, his treatment of the creative process, and his sense of creation, the "division of the One into many."

In The Opening of the Field, comments on Duncan's treatment of the Great Mother and female figures, the creative process, poetry, and the poet. In Roots and Branches, notes the use of the collage method, the sources in Blake and others, the role of myth and Osiris. Finds the conflict of the "forces of reason, totalitarian rule, bureaucratic codes . . . against the Law of life itself, Love, and the way of the imagination" in the book. Comments on the law in "The Law." In the Passages sequence, outlines the role of Eros and love and the use of the World-Egg as a creation myth. Comments on the role of the poet-persona and the treatment of history in Bending the Bow.

18 LAFON, MARIANNE, and NORRIS, KEN[NETH WAYNE]. "Curiouser and Curiouser." CrossCountry: A Magazine of Canadian-U.S. Poetry, no. 5, pp. 12-19.
   In this 17 February 1976 interview with George Bowering, Bowering recounts Duncan's influence on Vancouver poetry and his role in Tish. Also relates Duncan's first impression of Olson's "Projective Verse." Reprinted: 1977.12.

19 LEPPER, GARY M. "Robert Duncan." In A Bibliographical Introduction to Seventy-Five Modern American Authors. Berkeley, Calif.: Serendipity Books, pp. 165-74.
   Provides a primary bibliography, with some description, of Duncan's books and broadsides. See 1986.2 for the fullest bibliography on Duncan.

20 MacINTYRE, WENDY ELIZABETH. "Physics in the Poetics of Charles Olson." Ph.D. thesis, University of Edinburgh, pp. 2-3, 57-58, 149-50, 154, 157-60, 168-69, 171-72, 174, 312, passim.
   Briefly mentions Duncan's association with Olson and Olson's influence on him. Occasionally quotes from Duncan on poetry, once from an unpublished 25 November 1974 letter. Comments on Duncan's use of field composition, and finds he achieves an "obedient stance" in relation to "the orders" of the poem. Clarifies how he interpreted Olson's ideas of poetry's "syllabic lead," including Duncan's sense of the poet following the "spontaneous excitations of the syllables." Charts his "play on verbal constellation" in "These Past Years: Passages, 10," including his use of assonance and alliteration. Refers to his concept of Logos and the role of "syllabic harmony" in his work, quoting from a number of poems. Notes his treatment of "the idiosyncrasy of authorship" in "Passages, 31: The Concert (Tribunals)."

21 MELTZER, DAVID, ed. Golden Gate: Interviews with 5 San Francisco Poets. Redtail Reprint Series. [Berkeley, Calif.]: Wingbow Press, pp. 85-86, 88, 186-87, 197-98, passim.
   Revision of 1971.14.

22 MESCH, HOWARD. "Robert Duncan's Interview." Edited by [Kenneth] Michael André. Unmuzzled Ox 4, no. 2 [whole no. 14], pp. 79-96.
   In this 1974 interview, Duncan comments on his earliest poetry, his lack of development and style, the title of Letters, and intention in his poetry. Notes Medieval Scenes and "The Venice Poem" are based on musical forms, not the process development of "An Essay at War" and Letters, comparing the latter to The Opening of the Field. Discusses the Passages sequence at length, including its openness in time and place, its limitation in terms of its "particular tone," its nonsequential quality, and its images of weaving. Also comments on it as a tapestry, and mentions

his correspondence with Levertov on the sequence. Notes differences in The Structure of Rime and the Passages sequences and why
they are not in books of their own since they are integrated into
the volumes of which they are a part.
   Duncan notes he is not a mythical or a religious poet, but a
theosophist fascinated with systems of thought and belief. Mentions his use of myths, and explains a few statements from
1968.12. Also claims he is "not a symbolist" but will "play with
symbols," and comments on the creative process, his sense of language, "Against Wisdom as Such" (see 1954.2), and his relationship
to Olson. Mentions Arnold Schönberg's observation about harmony
in "The Structure of Rime, I."

23   MITCHELL, BEVERLEY [JOAN]. "The Genealogy of Tish." In The
     Writing Life: Historical and Critical Views of the "Tish"
     Movement. Edited by C[harles] H[enry] Gervais. Coatsworth,
     Ontario: Black Moss Press, pp. 70-93.
        Reprint of 1972.20.

24   MORGAN, STUART. "Linearity and Passionate Dispersion: Notes
     on Robert Duncan's '[A] Poem Beginning with a Line by Pindar'
     (The Opening of the Field 1959)." New Lugano Review, nos. 11-
     12, pp. 34-39, 60.
        Finding openness, not closure, "provides the key to both
     the technique and themes of Robert Duncan's The Opening of the
     Field," discusses "A Poem Beginning with a Line by Pindar" as a
     poem "about experiencing the creation of a work of art." Claims
     Duncan values "the state of mind created by entering" the work
     over "the object before the reader," and notes the poem's disper-
     sion and "technique of constantly allowing access to new mate-
     rial." Feels all parts of the poem, especially the first line,
     are present in most other parts, yet finds it retains a linearity.
     Mentions the focus on God, the sources in Pindar, the role of
     ants, the "typographic play," and the sets of old men, matters,
     and politicians in the poem. Also comments on the dichotomies,
     the various tones, and the use of the Cupid and Psyche myth,
     notably Psyche's "moment of vision." Mentions the treatment of
     W.C. Williams, Pound, politics, Psyche, Cupid, and love's contra-
     dictions, and details how Francisco Goya y Lucientes's painting,
     which undermines expectations, fits into the poem.

25   MOTTRAM, ERIC. "No Centre to Hold: A Commentary on Derrida."
     Curtains, nos. 14-17 [Le Prochain Step issue], pp. 38-57.
        Demonstrating Jacques Derrida's ideas in contemporary po-
     etry, discusses the sense of a center or platonic form for struc-
     ture and its creation in The Opening of the Field and in The H.D.
     Book. Recounts Duncan's discussions concerning the "return of the
     gods" in the work of Eliot, Pound, and H.D. Finds Duncan's work
     often questions the nature of "a free man . . . within the history

of culture he inherits," finding this concern present in "The
Venice Poem" and in the sections of the Passages sequence including in Bending the Bow. Believes Duncan's poetry "emerges from a
consistent pattern of contemporary thinking" and "is an attempt to
express an integrated experience," as Duncan implies in 1966.10.

26   RICHARDSON, KEITH. Poetry and the Colonized Mind: "Tish."
     Oakville and Ottawa, Ontario: Mosaic Press, Valley Editions,
     pp. 14, 19-25, 34-41, 59-61, passim.
        Charts Duncan's role in Tish, notes his influence on the
     poets associated with Tish, and occasionally mentions his poetics.

27   SAUNIER-OLLIER, JACQUELINE. "Contemporary Trends in American
     Poetry." Études anglo-américaines: Annales de la Faculté des
     lettres et sciences humaines de Nice, no. 27, pp. 83-96.
        Mentions Duncan's range and use of field composition.

28   SHARPLESS, JACK. "Interview: Jonathan Williams and Tom Meyer,
     Part II." Gay Sunshine: A Journal of Gay Liberation, no. 28
     (Spring), pp. 3-6.
        In this 1975 interview, Williams briefly mentions his rela-
     tionship to Duncan and provides an evaluation of Duncan's work.

29   TALLMAN, WARREN. "Wonder Merchants: Modernist Poetry in
     Vancouver during the 1960's." In The Writing Life: Historical
     and Critical Views of the "Tish" Movement. Edited by C[harles]
     H[enry] Gervais. Coatsworth, Ontario: Black Moss Press,
     pp. 27-69.
        Reprint of 1974.32.

30   THORNE, TIM. "Confronting the Mid-20th Century." Australian,
     5 June, p. 29 [or p. 820W].
        In a favorable review of The Venice Poem, focuses on
     Duncan's treatment of "the role, attitudes, and experience of the
     artist in the post-war world." Comments on his use of diverse
     cultural materials.

31   ZVEREV, A[LEKSEI]. "Opening the Doors of Association: On
     Contemporary American Poetry." Translated by Ronald Vroom. In
     Twentieth Century American literature: A Soviet View. Moscow:
     Progress Publishers, pp. 160-80.
        Finds Duncan attempts a rapport "without abandoning complex-
     ity [or] expressiveness." Quotes from "Night Scenes" to demon-
     strate that "poets perceive Whitman's poetics through [W.C.]
     Williams' experience."

1977

1   AIKEN, WILLIAM MINOR. "Charles Olson: The Uses of the Vatic."
    Ph.D. dissertation, Boston University, pp. 22, 117-19, 128-45,
    151-57, 191-92, 198, passim.
        Finds Duncan's usual focus is "on his own sufferings."
Comments on the unfinished or "flawed" quality of his poems, yet
discusses the careful arrangement of each volume, with many pieces
acting as preparation, building to the performance of a "concert
poem." Finds "longing to return to [an] . . . unified paradise"
and "to achieve both personal identity and poetic 'performance'"
central to Duncan's work. Also discusses the theme of speech and
the "clusters of meaning . . . according to similarity of sounds"
in "Doves" and "Epilogos."
        Comments on the respect between Duncan and Levertov despite
the vast differences in their work, and discusses the influence
each had upon the other, finding that Levertov helped Duncan to
make his poetry "more responsive to the particulars of the outside
world." Uses "Passages, 26: The Soldiers" and "Transgressing the
Real: Passages, 27" as examples of this influence, but feels that
both poems fail since they are still "so removed from particulars
that any assertion of their transformation strikes one as hollow."
        Occasionally mentions the influence of Olson's projectivism
on Duncan but finds it has increased Duncan's isolation, diminish-
ing his need to communicate. Explains a few biographical references in the poetry, especially in Roots and Branches.
        Chapter 2 is a revision of 1974.1. Chapters 7 and 8 are
revised as 1981.1. Chapter 10 is revised as 1978.1. See Dissertation Abstracts International 37 (1977):7746-47A.

2a COOPER, MADELEINE J. "Centres and Boundaries: The Presenta-
    tion of Self in the Work of William Burroughs, Thomas Pynchon,
    Charles Olson, and Robert Duncan." Ph.D. thesis, University of
    Nottingham, pp. 32-33, 294-362.
        In Duncan's poetry, finds "an oscillation between open and
closed verse, between the discovery of boundaries and centres,"
both a centripetal and a centrifugal force. Feels the former due
to a "self-conscious and . . . self-reflexive attention on the
process of evolving poetic form" as well as to "ideas of hidden
[Platonic] centres, original pulses of energy." Finds the
"'outward' centrifugal movement" in Duncan's experimentations and
discoveries through the "tone-leading [of vowels], the discontinuities, and the dislocated syntax." Compares him to Olson in terms
of self-discovery and to Stevens in terms of his abstraction and
belief in the imagination. Finds Duncan's a search for "numinous
or eternal 'forms' that underpin the reality of transient forms."
        Discusses the role of experimentation in Derivations, noting
the wordplay, rhythms, and half-rhymes as well as the "complica-
tion of syntax, to expand the sonic and semantic possibilities of

language in a field of overlapping energies suggestive of complex interwoven nets between the self and the reality his language creates." Comments on a number of individual works in the "Imitations of Gertrude Stein, 1953-1955" section, discussing "Orchards" at length, especially noting its rhythms, sounds, and syntax as well as its organic imagery. Noting Duncan's ideas on writing's relationship to organic growth, feels his use of animal and organic imagery in other poems from Derivations and elsewhere testify to his "view of art as self-generating," an activity that can discover "realities through its movement."

Commenting on the role of flux and boundaries, the self and the other, discusses a number of works from The Opening of the Field, especially "The Propositions" and "A Storm of White." Also discusses the role of the woman figure and the law in Duncan's work. Finds his a "poetry of shape-shifting, but paradoxically maintaining a constant flux."

Mentions a number of poems from Roots and Branches and Bending the Bow. Especially discusses the role of continuity and discontinuity, concord and discord, the past and the present, and the treatment of language, meaning, and the self in "Apprehensions," finding sources in Olson. Feels the Passages sequence "explores the reciprocity between self and other" and notes the images of weaving.

2b CRISP, PETER [BRUCE LANDON]. "Tailfeather: Robert Duncan in Auckland." Islands: A New Zealand Quarterly of Arts and Letters 5, no. 3 [whole no. 17] (March):326-28.
    Provides a description of Duncan's reading and talk at the University of Auckland in New Zealand in late September of 1976. Comments on Duncan's delivery when reading and the flow of his intelligence when talking.

3 EVERSON, WILLIAM. "Dionysus & the Beat: Four Letters on the Archetype." Sparrow, no. 63 (December), [14 pp.].
    In the 8 August 1975 letter to Lee Bartlett, briefly mentions that Duncan was the "dionysian aesthetic" in Rexroth's plan for the poetry scene in the late 1940s until he fell "under Olson's spell."

4 FAAS, EKBERT. "From 'Towards a New American Poetics.'" Sparrow, no. 60 (September), [22 pp.].
    Mentions Duncan's inclusion in anthologies and his sense of a tradition. Discusses his romanticism; his use of the heretical; the role of the occult in his childhood; and the influence of Whitman and Blake on his work. Comments on 1954.2, and believes Duncan is not a follower of Olson. Reprinted: 1978.25.

5 [FAUCHEREAU, SERGE.] Notes to Passages et structures, by Robert Duncan. [In French.] Paris: Christian Bourgois Éditeur, pp. 103-7.

RD1977

Provides notes to a few poems in the Passages and The
Structure of Rime sequences.

6   FAUCHEREAU, SERGE. Preface to Passages et structures, by
     Robert Duncan. [In French.] Paris: Christian Bourgois
     Éditeur, pp. 7-15.
         Notes the range of Duncan's audience and influences on him.
     Mentions ambiguities in his work, provides a biographical sketch,
     and comments on Duncan as an imitative poet. Mentions his argu-
     ment with Blaser (see 1967.6) on the translation of Gérard de
     Nerval. Discusses "Passages, 32: [Ancient Reveries and Declama-
     tions] (Tribunals)," especially Duncan's use of source materials.
     Provides a portion of a 21 May 1970 letter from Duncan in which he
     comments on this poem, especially on his use of Nerval's "Isis."
     Examines Duncan's word use and treatment of war, as in "Passages,
     26: The Soldiers," and use of word correspondences and sounds in
     a section from "Passages, 34: The Feast (Tribunals)."

7   FAWCETT, BRIAN. "Poetry and the 1970s." Capilano Review, no.
     12, pp. 146-49.
         Agrees with Olson's criticism of 1954.2 that "personal
     orders" based on the subjective alone create only chaos and an
     "asocial phenomenology."

8   HASKELL, DENNIS. "Thoughts on Some Recent Poetry." Australian
     Literary Studies 8, no. 2 [New Writing in Australia--Special
     Issue] (October):136-48.
         Briefly mentions Duncan's influence on Robert Adamson.

9   HAVEN, RICHARD. "Some Perspectives in Three Poems by Gray,
     Wordsworth, and Duncan." In Romantic and Modern: Revaluations
     of Literary Tradition. Edited by George Bornstein. Pittsburgh:
     University of Pittsburgh Press, pp. 69-88.
         Comparing "The Fire: Passages, 13" to Thomas Gray's "Elegy
     Written in a Country Churchyard" and Wordsworth's "Lines Composed
     a Few Miles above Tinturn Abbey," finds it a "circular poem," with
     a similar beginning and end. Discusses the word choice and the
     rhythm of the first and last sections, and the structure of the
     poem, which begins and ends with the "suggestion of a peaceful and
     rural scene" but with "a vision of an order . . . and of the dis-
     order that threatens it" in the middle. Applying 1968.6, mentions
     Duncan's treatment of "the world of natural and magical harmony,"
     an Eden, and his use of Hieronymus Bosch and Piero di Cosimo.
     Comments on the poem's political background, including the Vietnam
     War.

10   HELLER, MICHAEL. "Duncan's Concert." Montemora, no. 3
     (Spring), pp. 190-94.

In a highly favorable review of the Passages sequence, claims it speaks to "the very grounds of our being" and addresses the question of "human limitation." Discusses its empathetic and, in comparison to Pound's prescriptive use of the past in the early Cantos, imaginative and vulnerable nature as the poet allows himself to be inhabited by voices of the past. Also compares Duncan's experimentalism with that of W.C. Williams.

11   HUYBENSZ, JOANNE. "The Mind Dance ('wherein thot shows its pattern'): An Approach to the Poetry of Robert Duncan." Ph.D. dissertation, State University of New York at Stony Brook, 785 pp.
    Finding Duncan's oeuvre is best seen as a synchronic field incorporating mythologized personal fact as well as world myth, provides a structural approach to his poetry focusing on six categories of myth or "levels of interest." Occasionally briefly quotes from a personal conversation with Duncan.
    In the first level, the poetry of retrospect, provides biographical context for some of Duncan's poetry, and discusses, in a number of poems, Duncan's use and/or treatment of the "Wynken, Blynken, and Nod boat," the cross-eyed persona, animal-ark images. Also discusses the bear figure and its relationship to his homosexuality, the lion figure, rooms, the family, and a "mother-matrix" of associations, especially Freudian and Jungian. Notes Duncan's use and/or treatment of the "nurse-voice" and fairy tales in "Four Songs the Night Nurse Sang," Greek myth and birth in Medea at Kolchis, and bee myths and nursery animals in The Cat and the Blackbird. Also examines fairy tales in "Homage to The Brothers Grimm"; nursery rhymes, parents, guilt, and homosexual love in "Sleeping All Night"; and the figure of Faust in Faust Foutu. Comments on ancestor figures in "Apprehensions," women and sexuality in "Berkeley Poems," and the father figure and homosexuality in "Random Lines: A Discourse on Love." Also investigates Kipling and the mother figure in "The Earth: Passages, 19," and the mother figure in "A Sequence of Poems for H.D.'s Birthday," "Two Presentations," and "My Mother Would Be a Falconress." Notes the influence of nursery rhymes on his style, the importance of Federico García Lorca to him, and his sources in Laura Riding's nursery rhymes.
    Categorizes the second type of poetry as that of "personal involvement, which includes the influence of his contemporaries in poetry and the arts." Provides biographical context, including his reading and the "personal experiences and emotional states" for a number of these poems. Notes his own changing evaluation of his early work; the influence of Edna Keough, his high school teacher, on him and his reading; his relationship to other students at the University of California at Berkeley; and his changing views of his homosexuality. Discusses Nin's treatment of his homosexuality in 1969.18, noting Duncan's reaction in 1972.10, and

claims "Nin influences two distinctly different poetic depictions
of Duncan's early sexuality, the one erotic and exotic [in The
Years as Catches], the other perverse and sordid [in Caesar's
Gate]." Discusses "Duncan's personal relationships as they appear
in his poetry" including his relationship to Blaser, Spicer, W.C.
Williams, and Jess. Treating individual poems in some detail,
notes Duncan's use of sounds and rhymes, his sources in Stein, and
his treatment of Spicer and Jess, among others, in Names of People.
In his poetry, notes the role of painting, especially in "A Poem
Beginning with a Line by Pindar" and "The Fire: Passages, 13."
Also notes his use of music, as order and harmony, and film, especially in "Ingmar Bergman's Seventh Seal." Discusses the role of
other poets, such as Zukofsky, Levertov, Creeley, and Olson,
"their pronouncements, their personalities, and their works" as
"presences" in Duncan's poetry. Details the influence of Olson's
"Projective Verse" on him (contrary to 1975.3), and notes references to Olson in his work as well as his reactions to Olson's
1954.2. Also comments on his use of French poets, especially
Rimbaud.
    The third category, Duncan's "poetry of reaction," charts
the treatment of love and war in the poetry, finding him "cojoin-
ing" these two themes as a "war with himself over his sexuality"
and noting the "war-sex correlations." Discusses his treatment of
World War II, sexuality, and "love as an inner strife," and mentions his use of wasteland imagery, myth, classical ideas, and
political commentary in a number of poems, especially "Persephone,"
"A Spring Memorandum: Fort Knox," and "Ode for Dick Brown," noting Duncan's relative use of imaginary and personal experience.
Focuses on his treatment of the Korean War, fire, love, and sex;
his use of Asian images; and his concern with poetics in "An Imaginary War Elegy," "The Song of the Borderguard," and "An Essay at
War." With the Vietnam War, notes Duncan's use of the hydra myth
and the religious-war myth as well as his use of fire and underworld images. Also examines his treatment of renewal in his
Vietnam War poetry, finding the typical protest poem "centers on
current issues; . . . then singles out individuals and institu-
tions at fault; [alludes to] earlier poetic images and poets;
. . . [and] finally [presents] the idea of community . . . as a
potential ideal. . . ." Comments on many of Duncan's poems from
the Passages sequence from 21–36 as well as other poems, spending
a bit more time on "Up Rising: Passages, 25" and "Passages, 31:
The Concert (Tribunals)."
    Surveying Duncan's treatment of love and homosexuality,
notes his use of the "image of the lyre of the body" and of Christianity and Greek mythology, especially the figures of Orpheus and
Apollo. Also comments on his use of the domestic scene, images of
femininity, especially the siren image, and images of renewal in a
number of poems, especially "An Apollonian Elegy" and "Heavenly
City, Earthly City." Notes the treatment of the mundane and the

tawdry compared to the magical and sexual in "Domestic Scenes," and compares a few of these poems to drawings from A Selection of 65 Drawings from One Drawing Book, 1952-1956, noting mage, hero, fairy, and grotesque figures, as well as Duncan's "twinning motif" in the drawings. Comments on the treatment of youth and love in "Goodbye to Youth," the sexuality and empire in Fragments of a Disorderd Devotion, and the treatment of love in The Opening of the Field, especially the reciprocal love depicted in "The Propositions," as well as its use of legend. Examines the treatment of homosexuality and the use of the erotic, musical images, Shakespeare, and the city as both feminine and masculine in "Night Scenes." Mentions the treatment of the lyre as the body in "Cyparissus." Notes Duncan's treatment of love and his use of Dante and domestic scenes in the sonnet sequence contained in both Roots and Branches and Bending the Bow. Discusses other love poems in the latter volume, especially "These Past Years: Passages, 10," noting his use of sounds, the pathetic fallacy, and Christianity as well as his treatment of marriages. Also mentions "The Torso: Passages, 18," concentrating on his treatment of the body and homosexual love and his use of religious allusions, especially to Christ. Notes his use of Parmenides in "A Shrine to Ameinias."

In the fourth category, details the importance of earlier writers to Duncan. Finding "Whitman's direct effect on Duncan fairly minimal," traces allusions to Whitman in a few poems and Duncan's use of Whitman's political thinking and ideas on individuality. Notes Duncan's allusions to Eliot and his use of a wasteland motif in "Heavenly City, Earthly City." Also briefly compares his cadences to Eliot's and comments on his and W.C. Williams's treatment of Eliot. Comments on W.C. Williams's influence on Duncan, noting Duncan's refusal to restrict himself to Williams's sense of an American language. Noting H.D.'s personal importance to him, discusses Duncan's sources in and treatment of H.D. Focuses on The H.D. Book and a few poems, notes her influence on the interweaving of material in Medieval Scenes, and comments on the role of dream, animal imagery, sex, women, and Christ allusions in these poems. Also compares Duncan to H.D., including their use of images, their multiphasic structures, their theosophical backgrounds, and their attraction to a Freudian interpretation of dreams. Discusses Duncan's treatment of and allusions to Pound in a number of poems, especially "Homage and Lament for Ezra Pound in Captivity, May 12, 1944." Notes his emulations of Pound's style, especially Pound's "musically luminous lines" and Pound's diction, as in the Passages sequence. Also notes Duncan's reaction to Pound's need for order and interest in the romance tradition. Comments on the influence of Stein on Duncan, including her approach to syntax and content and her use of repetition, illustrating with poems from Names of People and A Book of

RD1977

Resemblances. Believes Stein helped free Duncan from surreal-
istic, inward poetry.

   Discusses Duncan's use of Christian imagery and religious
myth in the poetry influenced by Milton and Dante. Notes the
influence of Milton's religious idealism in a number of poems,
especially "Variations upon Phrases from Milton's The Reason of
Church Government." Noting Duncan's discussion of Dante in
1965.7, comments on Dante's influence on Duncan, especially on the
latter's treatment of love in his sonnets and on his depiction of
hell and paradise. Notes Duncan's treatment of Dante and others,
including friends, in "Dante Études," and comments on his use of
Sir Walter Raleigh, Robert Southwell, George Herbert, and Ben
Jonson in A Seventeenth Century Suite. Notes the treatment of
love, poetics, and religion, including Christ images, and comments
on the use of language in A Seventeenth Century Suite.

   In the fifth category, the poetry of myth, focuses on the
"mythic figures and situations Duncan himself creates," often out
of existent world myth, and finds a general progress outward and
upward in his use of myth: from Kore in hell to the city of God,
from the id to the ego. Concentrates on Duncan's continual use of
the Persephone, Orpheus, green, and vegetative myths, as well as
his treatment of the underground and the field. In Caesar's Gate,
concentrates on worm-egg images and Duncan's treatment of hell
paralleling Buddhism's Bardo state. Comments on Christian imagery
in "The Green Lady," noting the role of Adam here and in Derivations, especially Letters. Discussing a number of poems, especially "Often I Am Permitted to Return to a Meadow" and "A Poem
Beginning with a Line by Pindar," notes the changes in the
Persephone myth in The Opening of the Field. Also mentions
Duncan's use of the meadow or field, the dance, and the cavern as
a "constellation of images" in this volume. In Roots and
Branches, concentrates on Duncan's use of "tree-field symbolism of
the self" and the self's "firmly founded ego." Discusses the role
of Adam, Atlantis, and Eden in "Adam's Way," and Duncan's use of
the city myth in a number of poems, especially "Variations upon
Phrases from Milton's The Reason of Church Government," "Heavenly
City, Earthly City," and "Dante Études." Compares this treatment
to the ideal city or community in Saint Augustine, Pound, and
Dante. Also notes his treatment of order, the Law, and its relationship to the individual and to poetry. Comments on the relationship of Duncan's use of myth to religion.

   In the sixth section, discusses Duncan's poetic myth and its
four major elements: the "other place" or Cosmos; the poet; some
"means of mediation between the two"; and poetry representing the
"relation between the Self and the Other Place." Comments on
Duncan's Aristotelian orientation and his treatment of poetry's
relationship to the body as a poetry of irregularity. Notes his
treatment of poetry in The First Decade, especially "The Venice
Poem." Discusses Duncan's use of bees as mediators, noting their

relationship to his use of the bear totem and the moon, and comments on a number of works, especially The Cat and the Blackbird. Mentions his treatment of language and writing in Derivations, noting the role of birds. Providing a close reading of the poems in The Structure of Rime sequence, discusses the Master of Rime figure as well as other figures associated with the Thoth figure and female figures. Also examines, in the sequence, the treatment of Syntax, the "diabolical spirit," and the world of vision, noting the role of language, ladders, birds, the real and the unreal, Christianity, memories, and the field in the individual poems. Also mentions "Another Animadversion" and "Apprehensions." Discusses the treatment of poetry in "Reflections" and the "Dante Études," as well as in the Passages sequence, spending a bit more time on "At the Loom: Passages, 2," "The Collage: Passages, 6," and "Spelling: Passages, 15."
   Applies Claude Lévi-Strauss's structural approach to myth to Duncan's poetry, illustrating with a detailed reading of "In the Place of a Passage 22." See Dissertation Abstracts International 38 (1977):1380A.

12   LAFTON, MARIANNE, and NORRIS, KEN[NETH WAYNE]. "Curiouser and Curiouser." In Western Windows: A Comparative Anthology of Poetry in British Columbia. Edited by Patricia M. Ellis. Vancouver, British Columbia: CommCept Publishing, pp. 198-205.
      Reprint of 1976.18.

13   LIEBERMAN, LAURENCE. "Robert Duncan." In Unassigned Frequences: American Poetry in Review, 1964-77. Urbana: University of Illinois Press, pp. 196-97.
      Reprinted from 1969.16.

14   LOUPPE, LAURENCE. "Robert Duncan." Bulletin Centre National d'Art et Culture George Pompidou, no. 3 (June-September), pp. 16-18.
      In this brief interview, Duncan comments on the resonances he believes exist in the world and on his interest in Gnosticism and the occult. Also mentions his sense of passage and conflict and the image of war in his work.

15   MALKOFF, KARL. Escape from the Self: A Study in Contemporary American Poetry and Poetics. New York: Columbia University Press, pp. 40, 90-91, 157.
      Quotes from 1956.3 on applying the organic metaphor to poetry, emphasizing the body as a response to the universe.

16   MOTTRAM, ERIC. "Open Field Poetry." Poetry Information, no. 17 (Summer), pp. 3-23.
      Discusses Duncan's concept of open field composition and its relation to myth. Finds sources in W.C. Williams, Pound, and Olson.

17 MURDOCK, ROBERT M. "Introduction" to Translations, Salvages, Paste-Ups: An Exhibition Organized by the Dallas Museum of Fine Arts, April 6 through May 15, 1977 with the Participation of University Art Museum, Berkeley, June 7 through July 24, 1977 [and] Des Moines Art Center October 26 through December 4, 1977, by Jess [Collins]. Dallas: Dallas Museum of Fine Arts, [pp. 2-3].
    Comments on the relationship between Jess and Duncan's work.

18 POTTS, CHARLES. "The Grass Prophet Review." In Valga Krusa. Salt Lake City, Utah: Litmus, pp. 73-86.
    Potts mentions a few meetings he had with Duncan.

19 SCHIFFER, REINHOLD. "Antike Mythologie und moderne amerikanische Lyrik: Bemerkungen zu einigen Rezeptionsweisen." [In German.] In Die amerikanische Literatur der Gegenwart: Aspekt und Tendenzen. Edited by Hans Bungert. Stuttgart: Philipp Reclam, pp. 112-27.
    Briefly notes Duncan's use of classical mythology.

20 SHAPCOTT, THOMAS [W.]. "Placing the Inheritors." Meanjin Quarterly 36, no. 1 (May):63-66.
    Responding in part to 1976.12, both argues and agrees with Duncan's sense of tradition and importance.

21 STEPHEN, SID. "Securing the Historical Beach Head." CV/II: Contemporary Verse Two: A Quarterly of Canadian Poetry Criticism 3, no. 1 (Spring):6-7.
    In a review article on Tish, 1-19, ed. Frank[land Wilmot] Davey (Vancouver, British Columbia: Talonbooks, 1975), mentions the role that Duncan played in the development of Tish.

22 STUART, COLIN CHRISTOPHER, and SCOGGAN, JOHN. "The Orientation of the Parasols: Saussure, Derrida, and Spicer." Boundary 2: A Journal of Postmodern Literature 6, no. 1 (Fall):191-257.
    Occasionally mentions Duncan's relationship to Spicer, noting their quarrels as seen in Spicer's work.

23 TALLMAN, WARREN. "The Eternal Mood: Robert Duncan's Devotion to Language." Open Letter, 3d ser., no. 6 [Godawful Streets of Man: Essays by Warren Tallman issue] (Winter), pp. 70-74.
    Reprint of 1969.24.

24 _____. "Wonder Merchants: Modernist Poetry in Vancouver during the 1960's." Open Letter, 3d ser., no. 6 [Godawful Streets of Man: Essays by Warren Tallman issue] (Winter), pp. 175-207.
    Reprint of 1974.32.

25 THURLEY, GEOFFREY. The American Moment: American Poetry in
    the Mid-Century. New York: St. Martin's Press; London: Edward
    Arnold, pp. 139-55, 218, passim.
        Believes Duncan to be highly talented, noting his emotional
    control. Feels, however, the theories of projective verse,
    Duncan's attraction to pseudoscience, and his sources in Pound,
    Whitehead, Gérard de Nerval, George Barker, and hermetic lore mar
    his work, noting a "lack of intellectual and moral rigor." Finds
    his lack of true complexity, of a "problematic," distinctly Amer-
    ican and limiting. Notes an "ontological vagueness" in the poetry
    and, when treating religion, an "emotional sense of significance"
    but "a confused intellectual understanding." Comments on "Mother
    to Whom I Have Come Home"; the rhythm, structure, and Miltonic
    allusion in "Bending the Bow"; and the structure and emotion in
    "Such Is the Sickness of Many a Good Thing." Finds the second
    line of "My Mother Would Be a Falconress" diffuse, and discusses
    "A Poem Beginning with a Line by Pindar," noting a "rhapsodic
    tone" mingled with banalities, and charting sources in Eliot and
    Yeats.

26 V[ARELA], W[ILLIE]. "Excerpts from a Conversation with Stan
    Brakhage." Cinemanews [formerly Canyon Cinemanews] 77
    [listed as vol. 77, but inaccurate], no. 1:4-8.
        In this interview, Brakhage reminisces about his relation-
    ship with Duncan.

1978

1   AIKEN, WILLIAM [MINOR]. "The Olson Poetics: Some Effects."
    Contemporary Poetry: A Journal of Criticism 3, no. 2 (Summer):
    62-80.
        Revision of chapter 10 of 1977.1.

2   BAYARD, CAROLINE, and DAVID, JACK. Out-Posts/Avant-Posts.
    Three Solitudes: Contemporary Literary Criticism in Canada,
    vol. 4. Erin, Ontario: Press Porcepic, pp. [in English sec-
    tion] 9, 66, 84, passim.
        Briefly notes Duncan's influence on Canadian poets as does
    Bill Bissett. In a 4 March 1976 interview, Bowering tries to
    remember Duncan's term for the poets in Tish.

3   BERTHOLF, ROBERT [JOHN]. "An Afterword" to Medieval Scenes,
    1950 and 1959. Kent, Ohio: Kent State University Libraries,
    [pp. 45-47].
        Provides a few biographical details of Duncan from 1936 to
    1947, describing the occasion and the creative processes of
    Medieval Scenes. Discusses manuscripts, drafts, revisions, and
    the two versions of the poem, as well as its original printing.

RD1978

4   B[ERTHOLF], R[OBERT] J[OHN]. "Robert Duncan, 1919-." In <u>First</u>
     <u>Printings</u> of <u>American</u> <u>Authors</u>: <u>Contributions</u> <u>toward</u> <u>Descrip-</u>
     <u>tive</u> <u>Checklists</u>. Vol. 3. Edited by Matthew J. Bruccoli, C.E.
     Frazer Clark, Jr., Richard Layman, and Benjamin Franklin, V. A
     Bruccoli Clark Book. Detroit: Gale Research Co., pp. 87-99.
          Provides an initial descriptive checklist for Duncan. See
     1986.2.

5   BINNI, FRANCESCO. <u>Modernismo</u> <u>letterario</u> <u>anglo-americano</u>:
     <u>Permanenza</u> <u>e</u> <u>irrealtà</u> <u>di</u> <u>un'istituzione</u> <u>del</u> <u>progresso</u>. [In
     Italian.] Biblioteca di cultura, no. 139. Rome: Bulzoni
     Editore, pp. 424, 427-28, passim.
          Comments on Duncan's sense of the world as a poem and his
     ideas on the relationship between language and reality, form and
     content, and art and life. Notes his belief that the poet does
     not imitate but discovers a divine order and an objective form in
     reality.

6   BUTTERICK, GEORGE F. <u>A</u> <u>Guide</u> <u>to</u> "<u>The</u> <u>Maximus</u> <u>Poems</u>" <u>of</u> <u>Charles</u>
     <u>Olson</u>. Berkeley and London: University of California Press,
     pp. 295-96, 421, passim.
          Provides explanations of allusions to Duncan in <u>The</u> <u>Maximus</u>
     <u>Poems</u>, discusses Olson and Duncan's initial contacts, and includes
     a small portion of a letter Duncan wrote to Olson early in 1961.
     See also 1981.13.

7   BYRD, DON. Review of <u>Medieval</u> <u>Scenes</u>. <u>Back</u> <u>Door</u>, nos. 11-12
     (Fall), pp. 76-79.
          In this favorable review, notes Duncan's sense of unity and
     "discordant parts." Mentions his development, finding early works
     like <u>The</u> <u>Years</u> <u>as</u> <u>Catches</u> closer to <u>Bending</u> <u>the</u> <u>Bow</u> than <u>Medieval</u>
     <u>Scenes</u> or the works of the 1950s which are not autobiographical.
     Comments on Duncan's use of musical form, paradox, and the auto-
     biographical in <u>Medieval</u> <u>Scenes</u> and <u>Bending</u> <u>the</u> <u>Bow</u>. Also men-
     tions his treatment of the tree in these two volumes.

8   CORBETT, WILLIAM. "Notes on Michael Palmer's <u>Without</u> <u>Music</u>."
     <u>L=A=N=G=U=A=G=E</u> 1, no. 2 (April):[13-15].
          Very briefly notes the echo of Duncan's "Often I Am Per-
     mitted to Return to a Meadow" in Palmer's "The Meadow."

9   CREELEY, ROBERT. "From 'On the Road: Notes on Artists and
     Poets, 1950-1965' in <u>Poets</u> <u>of</u> <u>the</u> <u>Cities</u>, 1974." <u>Big</u> <u>Sky</u>, nos.
     11-12 [Homage to Frank O'Hara issue], p. 68.
          Reprinted from 1974.7.

10   DUNCAN, ROBERT. "As Testimony: Reading Zukofsky These Forty
     Years." <u>Paideuma</u>: <u>A</u> <u>Journal</u> <u>Devoted</u> <u>to</u> <u>Ezra</u> <u>Pound</u> <u>Scholarship</u>
     7, no. 3 (Winter):421-27.

Duncan attests to the influence of modernism, Pound, W.C. Williams, Olson, and especially Zukofsky on his poetry. Also provides some biographical information, chiefly concerning how culture of the late 1930s, both aesthetic and popular, affected him. See also 1979.10.

11   DUNCAN, ROBERT, and GINSBERG, ALLEN. "From 'Early Poetic Community' Discussion at Kent State April 7, 1971, in Allen Verbatim." Big Sky, nos. 11-12 [Homage to Frank O'Hara issue], p. 63.
Reprinted from 1974.12.

12   DUNCAN, ROBERT. From "Preface (1972)" to Caesar's Gate: Poems, 1949-50. Firehouse, no. 21 [Special Blaser Duncan Issue] (19 February), [pp. 3-4].
Reprinted from 1972.10.

13   _____. Introduction to Charles Olson and Comments in "Causal Mythology," by Charles Olson, transcribed by Donald [Merriam] Allen. In Muthologos: The Collected Lectures and Interviews, by Charles Olson. Edited by George F. Butterick. Vol. 1. Writing, no. 35. Bolinas, Calif.: Four Seasons Foundation, pp. 63-96.
Reprint of 1969.8.

14   _____. "Preface" to Medieval Scenes, 1950 and 1959. Kent, Ohio: Kent State University Libraries, [pp. 1-2].
In this preface, Duncan discusses the creative processes engaged in when writing the original Medieval Scenes in 1950. Also mentions Spicer's role in the process and the differences between the versions of the book.

15   _____. "A Reading of Thirty Things." Boundary 2: A Journal of Postmodern Literature 6, no. 3-vol. 7, no. 1 [Robert Creeley: A Gathering] (Spring-Fall):293-99.
In this 1974 essay on Creeley's Thirty Things, Duncan mentions 1954.2, his current readings, and his sense of aging.
Reprinted: 1987.7.

16   _____. "Son écrit d'un text parlé." [In French.] In Le Récit et sa représentation: Colloque de Saint-Hubert, 5-8 mai 1977. Traces, edited by Roger Dadoun. Paris: Éditions Payot, pp. 65-69.
Commenting on sound, myth, evolution, the muse, memory, and Eros, Duncan notes the role of Necessity as a figure in "Santa Cruz Propositions."

17   _____. "Wallace Berman: The Fashioning Spirit." In Wallace Berman Retrospective, October 24 to November 26, 1978: An

Exhibition Initiated and Sponsored by Fellows of Contemporary Art in Cooperation with the Otis Art Institute Gallery. Los Angeles:, Fellows of Contemporary Art, pp. 19-21, 23-24.

In this essay, Duncan discusses his relationship to Berman from 1954 on and his association with Kenneth Anger. Comments on his sense of artistic "alliance with the critical breakthru [sic] of Dada and Surrealism" as well as romanticism and the importance of Artaud to himself and others. Also mentions his disagreements with Jung and his sense of his generation beginning its work before World War II "by the descent into the underground of the city" and by the use of drugs.

18 _____. "Warp and Woof: Notes from a Talk." In Talking Poetics from Naropa Institute: Annals of the Jack Kerouac School of Disembodied Poetics. Edited by Anne Waldman and Marilyn Webb. Vol. 1. Boulder, Colo., and London: Shambhala Publications, pp. 1-10.

In a March 1978 statement, Duncan comments on his talk at Naropa and his dislike concerning its publication. In the 10 June 1976 talk itself, he comments on his sense of making, of fabricating, a poem. Mentions his lack of planning in his writing, and notes the influence of Pound and Robert Browning on his work.

19 ESHLEMAN, CLAYTON. "Doing Caterpillar." In The Little Magazine in America: A Modern Documentary History. Edited by Elliott Anderson and Mary Kinzie. Yonkers, N.Y.: Pushcart Press, pp. 450-71.
Reprint of 1978.20.

20 _____. "Doing Caterpillar." TriQuarterly, no. 43 (Fall), pp. 450-71.

Eshleman reminisces about an incident in which he did not return the manuscript for the second half of "Rites of Participation" to Duncan as requested which was, reportedly, resented by Duncan. Reprinted: 1978.19.

21 FAAS, EKBERT. "'The barbaric friendship with Robert': A Biographical Palimpsest." Mosaic: A Journal for the Comparative Study of Literature and Ideas 11, no. 2 [The World of Anaïs Nin: Critical and Cultural Perspectives issue] (Winter): 141-52.

Quoting from Duncan's journals and Nin's unpublished letters to Duncan and her treatment of him in 1969.18, as well as Duncan's reaction to that treatment in 1972.10, discusses the relationship between Duncan and Nin in the early 1940s. Also quotes from an unpublished 26 December 1940 letter from Henry Miller to Duncan. Mentions Nin's influence on "From 'Toward the Shaman,'" Duncan's contributions to Nin's collection of erotica, and Duncan's psychoanalysis in the early 1940s. Believing Duncan anticipated open

form aesthetics in his notebooks, compares his use of the note-
books to Rilke's use of <u>Die</u> <u>Aufzeichnungen</u> <u>des</u> <u>Malte</u> <u>Laurids</u>
<u>Brigge</u> as "shamanistic quest for a new self," noting Duncan's
plans to use the journals as a base for a novel.

22 _____. "Interview: Gary Snyder." In <u>Towards a New American</u>
<u>Poetics</u>: <u>Essays</u> <u>and</u> <u>Interviews</u>. Santa Barbara, Calif.: Black
Sparrow Press, pp. 105-42.
In this interview, Snyder mentions Duncan's role as a guru
in San Francisco in the 1950s, responds to comments that Duncan
made about his work, describes a dream he had about Duncan, and
claims that Duncan is his favorite poet.

23 _____. "Interview: Robert Creeley." In <u>Towards a New Amer-</u>
<u>ican Poetics</u>: <u>Essays</u> <u>and</u> <u>Interviews</u>. Santa Barbara, Calif.:
Black Sparrow Press, pp. 165-98.
In this interview, Creeley mentions that he sends his work
to Duncan for an appraisal and compares his sense of language to
Duncan's. Notes Duncan's "ability to realize an incredible compass of reality" in his poetry, and comments on Duncan's reaction
to Gary Snyder's work.

24 _____. "Interview: Robert Duncan." In <u>Towards a New American</u>
<u>Poetics</u>: <u>Essays</u> <u>and</u> <u>Interviews</u>. Santa Barbara, Calif.: Black
Sparrow Press, pp. 55-85.
In this interview, Duncan recounts his contacts with Olson,
especially his visit to Olson's deathbed in 1972, and outlines
details of their last conversations, especially about death and
field composition. Relates Olson's initial reaction to his work,
reads an inscription Olson wrote to him in a copy of <u>Letters to</u>
"<u>Origin</u>," and remarks on Creeley's initial reactions to him and
his relationship to Creeley. Noting his sense of being in a poetic movement, relates his first contacts with Black Mountain
poets. Recounts his correspondence with and relationship to
Levertov, including their disaffection. Relates his correspondence with James Dickey, noting his use of Dickey's "The Firebomb-
ing" for "Up Rising: <u>Passages</u>, 25." Mentions reading Maurice
Merleau-Ponty, Whitman, Whitehead, Wittgenstein, and Rimbaud.
Compares his work to Snyder's, and notes teaching at Black Mountain College.
Comments on his sense of field poetry, Jung, the unconsciousness, and poetry as "dream-work." Mentions his ideas on
chance in composition; language, especially language as reification; and law, providing the occasion for "The Law I Love Is Major
Mover." Also mentions writing "A Derivation from Rimbaud," and
observes his sense of receiving writing from outside and of ending
a poem. Comments on the importance of melody and rhetoric for
him; the writing he began at Black Mountain College; the influence
of Spanish surrealism on him; his crossed eyes; and his brief

RD1978

correspondence with Bly. Provides biographical details about
taking drugs like mescalin in 1952, describing the vision he had,
which included the "world tree." Claims he usually does not rewrite, but notes the revisions of Medieval Scenes. Claims he sees
himself as a romantic, and comments on the truthfulness of presences in his poetry.

25 _____. "Preamble" to Towards a New American Poetics: Essays
and Interviews. Santa Barbara, Calif.: Black Sparrow Press,
pp. 9-33.
Reprint of 1977.4 with notes.

26 FREDMAN, STEPHEN [ALBERT]. Roadtesting the Language: An
Interview with Edward Dorn. Documents for New Poetry, edited
by [Robert] Michael Davidson, no. 1. San Diego: University of
California, San Diego, Archive for New Poetry, 48 pp.
In this 1977 interview, Dorn briefly mentions that only
Duncan dealt directly with the Vietnam War, finding it "just
flowed into his work." Reprinted in part: 1980.18.

27 HAYES, FREDERICK PHILIP. "The Broken World of Robert Creeley."
Ph.D. dissertation, University of Denver, pp. 16-19, passim.
Comments on Duncan's theories of poetry and their influence
on Creeley's. See Dissertation Abstracts International 39
(1978):2273A.

28 KERN, ROBERT. "Composition as Recognition: Robert Creeley and
Postmodern Poetics." Boundary 2: A Journal of Postmodern
Literature 6, no. 3-vol. 7, no. 1 [Robert Creeley: A Gather-
ing] (Spring-Fall):211-30.
Quoting from 1966.10, briefly claims Duncan has helped to
establish a "postmodern literary imagination" by emphasizing the
poet as a recorder of the "immanent order and value in external
reality."

29 McCLURE, MICHAEL; GINSBERG, ALLEN; and DUNCAN, ROBERT. Comments. In Jack's Book: An Oral Biography of Jack Kerouac, by
Barry Gifford and Lawrence Lee. New York: St. Martin's Press,
pp. 195-200, 220-24.
McClure and Ginsberg mention their relationship to Duncan
and Duncan's role in the San Francisco literary scene. Duncan
provides a reminiscence of his meetings with Ginsberg and other
Beat writers in the mid-1950s.

30 MACKEY, NATHANIEL [ERNEST]. "'The Gold Diggers': Projective
Prose." Boundary 2: A Journal of Postmodern Literature 6, no.
3-vol. 7, no. 1 [Robert Creeley: A Gathering] (Spring-Fall):
469-87.

Notes Duncan's immediate appreciation of Creeley's stories
and his initial hesitations concerning Creeley's poetry.

*31   MARTIN, ROBERT KESSLER. "The 'Half-Hid Warp': Whitman, Crane,
and the Tradition of Adhesiveness in American Poetry." Ph.D.
dissertation, Brown University.
     Dissertation was restricted, unavailable for annotation.
According to the author, the section on Duncan is identical to
1979.33. See Dissertation Abstracts International 46 (1986):
2693-94A.

32   OLSON, CHARLES; CREELEY, ROBERT; DUNCAN, ROBERT; GINSBERG,
ALLEN; and WHALEN, PHILIP. "On History." Transcribed by Ralph
Maud, edited by George F. Butterick. In Muthologos: The Col-
lected Lectures and Interviews, by Charles Olson. Edited by
George F. Butterick. Vol. 1. Writing, no. 35. Bolinas,
Calif.: Four Seasons Foundation, pp. 1-19.
     In an extended version of 1975.22, Duncan provides a few
biographical details, and Creeley briefly mentions a letter Duncan
received from W.C. Williams.

33   OLSON, CHARLES. "Reading at Berkeley." Transcribed by Zoe
Brown and Ralph Maud, edited by George F. Butterick. In
Muthologos: The Collected Lectures and Interviews, by Charles
Olson. Edited by George F. Butterick. Vol. 1. Writing, no.
35. Bolinas, Calif.: Four Seasons Foundation, pp. 97-156.
     The fullest, most accessible version of Olson's lecture.
Another version of 1966.13, corrected by 1970.15, but with new
annotations (pp. 210-24).

34   PAUL, SHERMAN. "Rereading Creeley." Boundary 2: A Journal of
Postmodern Literature 6, no. 3-vol. 7, no. 1 [Robert Creeley:
A Gathering] (Spring-Fall):381-418.
     Occasionally briefly relates "Often I Am Permitted to Return
to a Meadow" to Creeley's poetry, and praises Duncan's review of
Creeley's For Love: Poems, 1950-1960 (New Mexico Quarterly 32,
nos. 3-4 [Autumn 1963-Winter 1963]:219-24). Revised in 1981.18.

35   PEIGNOT, JÉRÔME; LEWINTER, ROGER; SOJCHER, JACQUES; FAYE,
MARIE-ODILE; DUNCAN, ROBERT; FAUCHEREAU, SERGE; NOËL, BERNARD;
VERHEGGEN, JEAN-PIERRE; and LEMAIR, GÉRARD-GEORGES. "Débats:
Vendredi après midi." [In French.] In Le Récit et sa
représentation: Colloque de Saint-Hubert, 5-8 mai 1977.
Traces, edited by Roger Dadoun. Paris: Éditions Payot,
pp. 87-92.
     In a 6 May 1977 discussion, Duncan mentions his double vi-
sion, the poem as an experience, the creative process, and the
relation of the poem's tone and sound to his body. Fauchereau
briefly compares Duncan to Bernard Noël.

RD1978

36   PORTER, BERN. "Berkeley and How It Was." Credences, [o.s.] 2,
     nos. 2-3 [whole nos. 5-6] (March):57-59.
        Reminisces about Duncan as a writer in Berkeley and about
     publication of Heavenly City, Earthly City in 1947.

37   ROSENMEIER, HENRIK. "The Sense of Public Responsibility and
     American History in Some Poetry of the Fifties." In America in
     the Fifties: A Collection of Introductory Lectures. Edited by
     Anne R. Clauss. Anglica et Americana, no. 5. Copenhagen:
     University of Copenhagen, pp. 57-68.
        Mentions that "A Poem Beginning with a Line by Pindar" com-
     bines nostalgia for the past with "criticism of [the present's]
     monumental public dullness and stupidity."

38   RUMAKER, MICHAEL. "Robert Duncan in San Francisco."
     Credences, [o.s.] 2, nos. 2-3 [whole nos. 5-6] (March):12-55.
        In this lengthy reminiscence covering 1954 to 1958, espe-
     cially 1956-57 in San Francisco, focuses on Duncan's homosexuality
     and his relationship with Jess within the context of San
     Francisco's homosexual scene, which was in conflict with the
     social and legal structures of the time. Rumaker also discusses
     Duncan's relationship to Spicer, Olson, Helen Adam, and himself.

39   SAROTTE, GEORGES-MICHEL. "La Poésie de Robert Duncan." [In
     French.] Quinzaine littéraire, no. 276 (15 April), p. 12.
        In a favorable review of Passages et structures, notes
     Duncan's word use and treatment of desire and love.

40   SIMMONS, KENITH LEVICOFF. "Old Maids and the Domination of the
     Sea: Robert Duncan, Stan Brakhage, and Robert Kelly on the
     Self in Context." Ph.D. dissertation, University of Wisconsin
     at Madison, pp. 25-67, passim.
        Finds Olson and Duncan both argue against distinctions be-
     tween the subject and object and both see the universe as "an
     organic, inexorably interdependent unity to which man is joined as
     a participant, but from which he excludes himself if he insists
     upon functioning as an ultimate controlling 'subject,'" noting
     sources in Alfred North Whitehead's philosophy of organism. Com-
     ments on a number of poems by Duncan, especially from Roots and
     Branches, noting his treatment of freewill, nature, language, and
     the past and present. Also mentions his sense of similarity, of
     the "contemporaneousness of all events," and of relatedness.
     Notes his use of myth and his dislike of fixed conventions in
     poems from this volume.
        Discusses the need for laws to change in accord with chang-
     ing nature in "The Law." Examines the unifying repetitions of
     sound patterns and/or words in "Roots and Branches" and "Night
     Scenes." Comments on astrology, erotic and spiritual love, the
     "ingression of the eternal into time," and the unity of diverse

elements in "A Sequence of Poems for H.D.'s Birthday." In "Apprehensions," details the "process by which history shapes the present moment," and notes Duncan's use of his reading, chiefly about
Giordano Bruno. Finds "Apprehensions" "subjectivist history," and
comments on "Nel Mezzo del Cammin di Nostra Vita." See Dissertation Abstracts International 40 (1979):1461-62A.

41   SPANOS, WILLIAM V. "Talking with Robert Creeley." Boundary 2:
     A Journal of Postmodern Literature 6, no. 3-vol. 7, no. 1
     [Robert Creeley: A Gathering] (Spring-Fall):11-74.
        In this 12 July 1977 discussion, Creeley occasionally men-
     tions Duncan, especially his own parallels with him, feeling that
     both of them are "given to write poems as opposed to casting
     about for various possible themes or subjects."

42   von HALLBERG, ROBERT. Charles Olson: The Scholar's Art.
     Cambridge, Mass., and London: Harvard University Press, pp.
     78, passim.
        The second chapter, which contains the only substantive
     mention of Duncan, is an expansion and revision of 1974.34; the
     rest is a revision of 1975.25.

43   WEBER, ROBERT C[HARLES]. "Robert Duncan and the Poem of
     Resonance." Concerning Poetry 11, no. 1 (Spring):67-73.
        In an expansion and revision of the discussion of "The Fire:
     Passages, 13" from the fourth chapter of 1972.25, emphasizes
     Duncan's use of collage form in which each element in a poem reso-
     nates with all other elements.

1979

1   ABBOTT, STEVE, and SHURIN, AARON. "Interview: Robert Duncan."
    Gay Sunshine, nos. 40-41 (Summer-Fall), pp. 1-8.
       In this lengthy interview from December 1978 and January
    1979, Duncan provides a great deal of both general and specific
    biographical information concentrating on his "sexual nature in
    its development" from early adolescence to the present. Discusses
    his love relationships to Gerald Ackerman and Jess and the role
    these relationships and his sexual life have played in his poetry,
    including the use of "darkness and blood" imagery in such work as
    "The Venice Poem." Also discusses in detail his beating at the
    age of seventeen by a homosexual and his own homosexuality, in-
    cluding one-night stands and the enticement of men in a number of
    ways. Provides the biographical, often the sexual, background for
    the poems in Caesar's Gate. Comments on the role of hermeticism,
    Gnosticism, and myth, especially Greek myth, in his poetry and
    life, including his upbringing. Mentions he has often been in
    love, and discusses his sense of his own manhood.

RD1979

Duncan also comments on writing 1944.1, on his ideal reader, on the role of myth and the mask in his work, and on a number of specific poems, especially "An African Elegy" and "H.M.S. Bearskin." Discusses poetry as revelation, notes his sense of writing as fearful, and comments on the role of rhetoric, melody, and romance in his writing. Mentions his sense of creation and the role that domestication has had on his work. Revised and greatly abridged: 1982.26. See 1980.1 for the remainder of this interview.

2   ADAM, HELEN. "A Few Notes on Robert Duncan." In Robert Duncan: Scales of the Marvelous. Edited by Robert J[ohn] Bertholf and Ian W. Reid. Insights: Working Papers in Contemporary Criticism. New York: New Directions Books; Toronto: George J. McLeod, pp. 36-37.
       In this reminiscence about Duncan covering the 1950s on, Adam identifies the "god mother" of "My Mother Would Be a Falconress" as herself.

3   ALTIERI, CHARLES. Enlarging the Temple: New Directions in American Poetry during the 1960s. Lewisburg, Pa.: Bucknell University Press; London: Associated University Presses, pp. 128-30, 150-69, passim.
       In a revision of 1976.3, omits the discussion of "A Poem Beginning with a Line by Pindar," and occasionally compares Duncan to Snyder. Also includes a greatly abridged and revised version of 1973.3, dropping many of the Duncan references.

4   _____. "The Objectivist Tradition." Chicago Review 30, no. 3 [Black Mountain and Since: Objectivist Writing in America issue] (Winter):5-22.
       Discusses The H.D. Book, especially 1979.16, in light of Duncan's projective or field poetics and romanticism as well as his relationship to Olson, W.C. Williams, and Pound.

5   BERTHOLF, ROBERT J[OHN]. "A Conversation with Joanna and Michael McClure." In Robert Duncan: Scales of the Marvelous. Edited by Robert J[ohn] Bertholf and Ian W. Reid. Insights: Working Papers in Contemporary Criticism. New York: New Directions Books; Toronto: George J. McLeod, pp. 14-21.
       In this interview, the McClures reminisce about Duncan from 1954 through the 1960s, emphasizing Duncan as a teacher, an influence on Michael McClure, and as a poet in the San Francisco tradition. Also discusses Duncan's poetics, including line length, in Letters.

6   _____. Introduction to Robert Duncan: Scales of the Marvelous. Edited by Robert J[ohn] Bertholf and Ian W. Reid.

Insights: Working Papers in Contemporary Criticism. New York: New Directions Books; Toronto: George J. McLeod, pp. vi-x.
In a short, critical biography, focuses on 1936 to 1974 and Duncan's relationship to Olson.

7 [BERTHOLF, ROBERT JOHN.] "Robert Duncan: A Selected Check-list." In Robert Duncan: Scales of the Marvelous. Edited by Robert J[ohn] Bertholf and Ian W. Reid. Insights: Working Papers in Contemporary Criticism. New York: New Directions Books; Toronto: George J. McLeod, pp. 241-43.
Provides a bibliography, primarily of books by Duncan but also listing the appearances of The H.D. Book to date. See also 1986.2.

8 BYRD, DON. "The Question of Wisdom as Such." In Robert Duncan: Scales of the Marvelous. Edited by Robert J[ohn] Bertholf and Ian W. Reid. Insights: Working Papers in Contemporary Criticism. New York: New Directions Books; Toronto: George J. McLeod, pp. 38-55.
Analyzes Duncan's relationship to Olson, contrasting their reactions to Pound's cultural elitism and sense of literary tradition. Also contrasts Olson's objectivism, totalitarianism, and fact orientation to the physical world to Duncan's subjectivism, anarchism, and imaginative orientation to the fictive world, as seen in such documents as 1954.2 and Duncan's reaction to it. Also comments on their use of Whitehead and Jung and their view of the body or the "physiological as the condition of the poem."

9 CALLAHAN, BOB. "The World of Jaime de Angulo." Netzahualcoyotl News 1, no. 1 (Summer):1-5, 14-16.
In this transcription of a radio conversation, Duncan discusses his relationship as a typist and a friend of Jaime de Angulo in 1949 and 1950, and mentions his relationship with Spicer and Pound during the same period.

10 CHRISTENSEN, PAUL [NORMAN]. Charles Olson: Call Him Ishmael. Austin and London: University of Texas Press, pp. 183-90, passim.
In an apparent revision of 1975.10, mentions Duncan's use of myth, treatment of the imagists and war in The H.D. Book, and sources in romanticism and Olson, noting his use of projective poetry. Compares his work to Creeley and Olson's, noting Duncan's emphasis on the individual ego as a source of lyricism. Outlines The Structure of Rime and the Passages sequences.

11 CLAUSEN, CHRISTOPHER. "Poetry as Revelation: A Nineteenth-Century Mirage." Georgia Review 33, no. 1 (Spring):89-107.
Finds that Duncan's The Truth and Life of Myth (see 1968.12) argues passionately for "poetry as revelation." Feels its use of

myth is important in the understanding of a world that "remains
genuinely mysterious" despite modern science. Discusses Duncan's
belief that the poet and the reader must be possessed by poetry,
and notes his "wrath" against poets and critics who have domes-
ticated poetry. Reprinted in part: 1981.3.

12   CREELEY, ROBERT. "Notes on Film." Criss-Cross: Art
     Communications, nos. 7-9, pp. 68-70.
        Creeley briefly notes that Duncan once identified for him
all "the ways in which rhyme might occur in poetry." Reprinted:
1979.15 (as "Three Films: Notes").

13   _____. "Was That a Real Poem" and Other Essays. Edited by
     Donald [Merriam] Allen. Writing, no. 39. Bolinas, Calif.:
     Four Seasons Foundation, 149 pp.
        Includes reprints of 1969.2, 1973.4, and 1979.12 (as "Three
Films: Notes") as well as a slight revision of 1974.7.

14   DAVIDSON, [ROBERT] MICHAEL. "A Book of First Things: The
     Opening of the Field." In Robert Duncan: Scales of the Mar-
     velous. Edited by Robert J[ohn] Bertholf and Ian W. Reid.
     Insights: Working Papers in Contemporary Criticism. New York:
     New Directions Books; Toronto: George J. McLeod, pp. 56-84.
        In an extensive revision and condensation of 1973.7, quoting
further from unpublished notebooks, discusses a number of poems
from The Opening of the Field, especially "Often I Am Permitted to
Return to a Meadow" and "A Poem Beginning with a Line by Pindar."
Emphasizes Duncan's treatment of creation, beginnings, language,
the field, and Logos. Also examines his treatment of emergent
poetic form, renewal, and the divine, especially the forms of
Christ and Eros. Comments on Duncan's sense of field poetics and
his use of rhythm, language, a "new prosody," and the metaphor of
the hearth. See also 1982.22.

15   DUNCAN, ROBERT. "At Cambridge: An Address to Young Poets
     Native to the Land of my Mothertongue." Periodics: A Magazine
     Devoted to Prose, no. 5 (Spring), pp. 35-36.
        Duncan provides an impressionistic remembrance of childhood
at three years old and discusses his sense of language. Reprinted:
1987.4.

16a _____. "The H.D. Book, Part Two: Nights and Days, Chapter 9."
     Chicago Review 30, no. 3 [Black Mountain and Since: Objec-
     tivist Writing in America issue] (Winter):37-88.
        Claiming he reads "not to find what art is" but "what life
might be," mentions some of his reading, including Baudelaire,
Dorothy Richardson, and Laura Riding. Notes his sense of "cosmic
extension" to others.

16b [DUNCAN, ROBERT.] "What the Sonnet Means the Sonnet Means."
     In Veil, Turbine, Cord, and Bird. [Sets of Syllables, Sets of
     Words, Sets of Lines, Sets of Poems Addressing: Veil, Turbine,
     Cord, and Bird.] Brooklyn, N.Y.: Jordan Davis, [p. 12].
         Duncan mentions that he has always followed "the Way of
     Romance" and gladly goes through stages of life and death.
     Reprinted: 1987.4.

17   FRANKLIN, BENJAMIN, V, and SCHNEIDER, DUANE. Anaïs Nin: An
     Introduction. Athens: Ohio University Press, pp. 212–14,
     passim.
         Relying on 1969.18, sketches Duncan's relationship to Nin.

18   FURTH, PAULINE. "Remembering Robert Symmes." Follies: A
     Journal of the Arts and Opinion 4, no. 11 (August):11.
         In this reminiscence, Furth describes Duncan as a college
     student from 1936 to 1939, and provides details of him at a party
     in Berkeley.

19   GÉFIN, LASZLO. "Ideogram: The History of a Poetic Method."
     Ph.D. dissertation, McGill University, pp. 255–75, 290–92,
     passim.
         Finds Duncan an "ideogrammic artist" whose collage technique
     extends from a view of the poem as an "enactment of the process
     and structure of . . . universal juxtaposition" in all things, of
     the "grand collage" of "language and of the world." Uses The
     Structure of Rime sequence, especially "The Structure of Rime,
     III," as well as "The Collage: Passages, 6," as examples.
         Mentions the influence of Pound's "isomorphic ideograms,"
     and notes the parallel to Jess's collages. Discusses Duncan's
     sense of field and projective poetics, his use of aperiodic
     form, and his belief that the structure of a poem should be
     "achieved as an extension of the perception and not simply imposed
     beforehand" by the will and reason of the poet. Revised:
     1982.13. See Dissertation Abstracts International 40
     (1979):3299A.

20   GOLDEN, SÉAN V. "Duncan's Celtic Mode." In Robert Duncan:
     Scales of the Marvelous. Edited by Robert J[ohn] Bertholf and
     Ian W. Reid. Insights: Working Papers in Contemporary Criti-
     cism. New York: New Directions Books; Toronto: George J.
     McLeod, pp. 208–24.
         Claims the Celtic mode of enchantment, of "the casting of
     spells by the weaving of words," is "integral to Duncan's poetry,
     and to his view of Poetry." Reviews his associations with Celtic
     thought and life, including his references to fairies and casting
     spells in his poetry. Includes biographical details that "may
     have provided the inclination and the base from which Duncan began

RD1979

his exploration of the Celtic world," and reviews his reading of modern writers who wrote of this world, such as Joyce.
Examines Duncan's use of sound play and the intricacy of sound, including "puns and rhymes [that] interweave with the images to create a multiphasic portrait," following "the spirit of . . . [a Celtic] bardic attention to sound," as in Faust Foutu and elsewhere. Notes his allusions to illuminated manuscripts as in "The Continent," and mentions his prose on Celtic art, poetry, and magic. Outlines "specific Celtic devices, allusions, and key plots [that] structure particular poems," including Medieval Scenes, and briefly identifies Duncan's use of Irish tales in "Poetry, a Natural Thing" and "Apprehensions." Records his use of Mabinogi in "From The Mabinogion."

21 GOLDING, ALAN. "The Olson Festival in Iowa." Two Hands News and Chicago Poetry Calendar, no. 20 (July), pp. 4-5.
Describes Duncan's talk and role at the 5-11 November 1978 Charles Olson Festival.

22 GUNN, THOM. "Homosexuality in Robert Duncan's Poetry." In Robert Duncan: Scales of the Marvelous. Edited by Robert J[ohn] Bertholf and Ian W. Reid. Insights: Working Papers in Contemporary Criticism. New York: New Directions Books; Toronto: George J. McLeod, pp. 143-60.
Noting the difficulty of publicly admitting one's homosexuality in the 1940s, comments on 1944.1. Charts the treatment of love, defiance, narcissism, separation, and homosexuality throughout his work, mentioning his development as a poet. Finds Duncan's early poetry treats homosexuality as irregular even though "love is already starting to be his central theme." Suggests Caesar's Gate "focuses on sexual fury," outlining its treatment of hell and its sources in earlier poets. Compares Duncan's apparent desire to disown his homosexuality in "H.M.S. Bearskin" with his acceptance of it in "This Place Rumored to Have Been Sodom," but finds the muse female, noting the fertility, in the rest of The Opening of the Field.
Discusses the figures of the searcher, often a sexually restless adolescent on a quest; the mother, including real and ideal mothers; and the lover in Duncan's work. Examines the mother figure in "My Mother Would Be a Falconress," also noting the role of dream and sleep. Treats the lover figure as the "male dream image" in "A New Poem (for Jack Spicer)," and notes its permutation in his sonnets. Also remarks on the "dream basis" of much of Duncan's poetry. Slightly revised: 1982.14; 1985.29.

23 HARRISON, LOU. "A Note about Robert Duncan and Music." In Robert Duncan: Scales of the Marvelous. Edited by Robert J[ohn] Bertholf and Ian W. Reid. Insights: Working Papers in

Contemporary Criticism. New York: New Directions Books;
Toronto: George J. McLeod, pp. 200-202.
Harrison comments on setting Duncan's poetry to music. Also
mentions the musicality of his poetry and his "knowledge of the
whole art of music," noting his use of musical references.
Describes Duncan singing his poems at readings.

24   HATLEN, BURTON. "Stalin and/or Zukofsky: A Note." Paideuma:
A Journal Devoted to Ezra Pound Scholarship 8, no. 1 (Spring):
149-51.
Argues against Duncan's claim, in 1978.10, that Zukofsky
praised Stalin.

25   "Interview [with Charles Olson] in Gloucester, August 1968."
Transcribed by George F. Butterick. In Muthologos: The
Collected Lectures and Interviews, by Charles Olson. Edited
by George F. Butterick. Vol. 2. Writing, no. 35. Bolinas,
Calif.: Four Seasons Foundation, pp. 84-104.
In this August 1968 interview, Olson mentions Duncan's role
at his, Olson's, reading on 23 July 1965 at the Berkeley Poetry
Conference. See also 1966.13 and 1978.33.

26   JOHNSON, MARK [ANDREW], and DeMOTT, ROBERT [J.]. "'An Inheritance of Spirit': Robert Duncan and Walt Whitman." In Robert
Duncan: Scales of the Marvelous. Edited by Robert J[ohn]
Bertholf and Ian W. Reid. Insights: Working Papers in Contemporary Criticism. New York: New Directions Books; Toronto:
George J. McLeod, pp. 225-40.
Outlines Duncan's allusions to and sources in Whitman, and
examines parallels between the two poets, including their use of
common language and unpoetic materials and their concern with a
number of subjects: "the meaning of America" and "the individual
and his place in the world," especially the "multiple self" and
the creative individual in society. Also notes their interest in
egalitarianism, the incompleteness of a single man's work, and the
primal, including beginnings and mythic origins. Comments on
Duncan's treatment of evil and his generally greater pessimism.
Discusses his treatment of Whitman and political systems and the
role of the poet in "A Poem Beginning with a Line by Pindar."
Relates Duncan's use of an organic, open form, his "adoption of
the poem as a field of composition," and his use of the collage as
a technique to Whitman's "expansive form."

*27   JOHNSTONE, HEATHER KAY. "Robert Duncan as Homosexual and Love
Poet." M.A. thesis, York University, 131 pp.
Focusing on Duncan's homosexuality, discusses how he wrote
of love and sexuality in his poetry from 1938 to 1951. Finds the
years 1940-46, the period of Duncan's apprenticeship, filled with
"experimentation both sexual and literary." Also comments on

Duncan's treatment of women, and examines 1944.1, noting Duncan's subsequent correspondence with John Crowe Ransom. (Not available for annotation; annotated from abstract.)

28   KITAJ, R.B. Reminiscences of Duncan. In Robert Duncan: Scales of the Marvelous. Edited by Robert J[ohn] Bertholf and Ian W. Reid. Insights: Working Papers in Contemporary Criticism. New York: New Directions Books; Toronto: George J. McLeod, pp. 203-7.
     Kitaj reminisces about his relationship to Duncan, notes Duncan's effect on him as a painter, and briefly describes Duncan and Jess's house.

29   LANSING, GERRIT. "Robert Duncan and the Power to Cohere." In Robert Duncan: Scales of the Marvelous. Edited by Robert J[ohn] Bertholf and Ian W. Reid. Insights: Working Papers in Contemporary Criticism. New York: New Directions Books; Toronto: George J. McLeod, pp. 198-99.
     Notes Duncan's care, and comments on his poetry's coherence and open form, finding it a "mill of dreams."

30   LEVERTOV, DENISE. "Some Duncan Letters: A Memoir and a Critical Tribute." In Robert Duncan: Scales of the Marvelous. Edited by Robert J[ohn] Bertholf and Ian W. Reid. Insights: Working Papers in Contemporary Criticism. New York: New Directions Books; Toronto: George J. McLeod, pp. 85-115.
     Within her own text, Levertov provides selected portions of her correspondence with Duncan from 1952 to 1968. In these letters, Duncan compares some of Levertov's poetry to his own; refers to what Levertov meant to him as a poet; and discusses revision, detailing some of his revisions of "A Poem Beginning with a Line by Pindar," "Risk," and "The Structure of Rime, XXI." Duncan also describes writing and revising poems in The Opening of the Field, provides biographical details about living in Mallorca, Spain, and comments on the Vietnam War and his reaction to it.
     Levertov provides the occasion for "Bending the Bow," recounts her own initial and subsequent reaction to Duncan's poetry, and touches upon his wit and self-criticism. Relates his sense of serving Poetry, of imitation, and of the mystery of poetry; and comments on his writing poetry about poetry. Throughout, she details her relationship to Duncan, noting their early correspondence and meetings. Levertov also mentions her first understanding of "For a Muse Meant" and provides a portion of her letter in reaction to it, noting Duncan's reply.
     Levertov focuses on Duncan's role in "the development of [her] consciousness as a poet" as a mentor in "aesthetic ethics," noting his criticism and suggested revisions of her work. Mentions how his comments helped her, but also details some of Duncan's "misreadings" of her poems, one dealing with a question

of imagination and fancy. She also chronicles their quarrel, beginning with their arguments centering on the role of preconception, honesty, and conviction compared to the unintentional and the accidental in poetry. She provides a portion of his letter criticizing some of her poetry on the Vietnam War, and claims he felt she "was acting coercively toward herself and--possibly-- toward others." Notes his protest against the Vietnam War, but implicitly faults Duncan for not being more actively engaged against it, finding his political awareness "static," still somewhat anarchist. Slightly revised: 1981.12. Reprinted: 1986.11.

31   MACKEY, NATHANIEL [ERNEST]. "Uroboros: 'Dante' and A Seventeenth Century Suite." In Robert Duncan: Scales of the Marvelous. Edited by Robert J[ohn] Bertholf and Ian W. Reid. Insights: Working Papers in Contemporary Criticism. New York: New Directions Books; Toronto: George J. McLeod, pp. 181-97.
        Treats both "Dante Études" and A Seventeenth Century Suite as derivative and preoccupied with community, especially "the commune of Poetry," which Duncan believes is "Creation--the World or Cosmos--itself." Denotes a sense of exhaustion, a desire for an escape from closure and limitation through the "commune of Poetry," using language as a "communal, or communalizing, act." Quotes from an unpublished 1967 interview on the relationship between sound and meaning, finding the former related to the perceptions of children and animals and thus a gate to the "world at large," a passage out of the self to the limitless.
        Also sees Duncan's act of communion with earlier poets as an attempt at boundlessness. Discusses the works as both derivative and confessional, the latter as a "mix of the autobiographic and the mediumistic" in which Duncan seems to merge with others. Believes that although the "poems attest to a marriage . . . between the present and the past," they are haunted with the possibility that the communion sought is "not with others but with an Other which is simply a trope for the self." Mentions the potential narcissism of Duncan's poetry and his treatment of death as another desired realm of the infinite.

32   MALANGA, GERARD; LANSING, GERRIT; and BROWN, HARVEY. "Paris Review Interview [with Charles Olson]." Transcribed by Ralph Maud, edited by George F. Butterick. In Muthologos: The Collected Lectures and Interviews, by Charles Olson. Edited by George F. Butterick. Vol. 2. Writing, no. 35. Bolinas, Calif.: Four Seasons Foundation, pp. 105-53.
        In a revised version of a 16 April 1969 interview (previously published as "The Art of Poetry, XII: Charles Olson," Paris Review 13, no. 49 [Summer 1970]:177-204), Olson briefly mentions Duncan as a "progressive compositionist," especially in his Passages sequence.

33 MARTIN, ROBERT K[ESSLER]. "Some Contemporary Poets: Robert
    Duncan." In The Homosexual Tradition in American Poetry.
    Austin and London: University of Texas Press, pp. 170-79.
        Treats Duncan as a homosexual poet "firmly in the tradition
    of body mysticism established by Whitman and continued by Crane."
    Discusses "The Torso: Passages, 18," "An Encounter," "Dance Early
    Spring Weather Magic," "An Apollonian Elegy," and part 2 of "Night
    Scenes," finding correspondences with Whitman's Song of Myself,
    Hart Crane's The Bridge, and the work of Eliot, Freud, and
    Nietzsche.
        According to the author, this is identical to his treatment
    of Duncan in 1978.31.

34 MOTTRAM, ERIC. "Heroic Survival through Ecstatic Form: Robert
    Duncan's Roots and Branches." In Robert Duncan: Scales of the
    Marvelous. Edited by Robert J[ohn] Bertholf and Ian W. Reid.
    Insights: Working Papers in Contemporary Criticism. New York:
    New Directions Books; Toronto: George J. McLeod, pp. 116-42.
        Notes the influence of Carlyle's "The Hero as Poet" on
    Duncan's thought in the early 1960s. Claims this influence led to
    Duncan's desire "for poetic power," for vatic poetry with the poet
    as a hero making "Song the structure of the seer and . . . melody
    the vesture of 'inward harmony of coherence,'" resulting in Roots
    and Branches. Points out the obsession "with mastery and author-
    ity" and the attraction with magic, the occult, and night in the
    book. Also examines the treatment of home, form, risk, nature,
    art, homosexual love, love, freedom, resurrection, and obedience,
    and comments on the role of melos, of derivation, and of the poet
    as prophet and/or hero. Notes the use of tree, garden, and sexual
    imagery in the volume, dealing with most of the individual poems
    in turn.
        Provides somewhat extended treatment of homosexuality, sex-
    ual love, and authority in "Night Scenes," and of birth, inspira-
    tion, the feminine, and the mother figure in "A Sequence of Poems
    for H.D.'s Birthday." Comments on the mother figure in "Two Pre-
    sentations" and Osiris and inspiration in "What Happened: Prel-
    ude." Notes the treatment of Eros, Orpheus, and order in "A Set
    of Romantic Hymns" and of Adam, Eden, creation, and love in
    "Adam's Way," also mentioning the use of myth and garden imagery
    in the latter. Finds "Apprehensions" deals with "distinctions to
    be made out of nature and culture," including the treatment
    of love and order. Also notes the role of myth and the musical
    structure in the poem.

35 OLSON, CHARLES. "On Black Mountain." Transcribed by George F.
    Butterick. In Muthologos: The Collected Lectures and Inter-
    views, by Charles Olson. Edited by George F. Butterick. Vol.

2. Writing, no. 35. Bolinas, Calif.: Four Seasons Foundation, pp. 55-79.
 Reprint of 1971.17.

36 PRUITT, JOHN. "Robert Duncan at the 92nd Street Y, April 16,
1979." Downtown Review 1, nos. 3-4 (May-June):46-47.
 Reviews a reading by Duncan, and surveys his life and work,
focusing on his perception of earlier writers and movements such
as modernism.

37 QUARTERMAIN, PETER. "Duncan, Robert (Edward)." In Poets.
Edited by James Vinson and D.L. Kirkpatrick. Great Writers of
the English Language. New York: St. Martin's Press,
pp. 339-41.
 After an expanded bibliography of 1970.21, focuses on
Duncan's mysticism, and comments on "A Poem Beginning with a Line
by Pindar." Reprinted: 1983.27. See also 1975.23 and 1980.10.

38 RASULA, JED. "Charles Olson and Robert Duncan: Muthologist-
ical Grounding." Spring: An Annual of Archetypal Psychology
and Jungian Thought, pp. 102-17.
 Examines Duncan's use of myth in his poetry. Notes he
treats history mythically, giving a "mythic resonance" to current
events as in the Passages sequence. Discusses his reliance upon
an "animal intelligence," an unconsciousness, and examines his use
of the accidental and mistakes to create a "pluralization of
sense." Claims that Duncan feels a primary "verbal event" is the
"grounding" for his poetry. Mentions Duncan's sense of himself as
derivative, his use of Freud, and his romanticism. Comments on
the role of Psyche and Eros in his work and the visual shape of
his poetry.

39 REID, IAN W. "The Plural Text: Passages." In Robert Duncan:
Scales of the Marvelous. Edited by Robert J[ohn] Bertholf and
Ian W. Reid. Insights: Working Papers in Contemporary Criticism. New York: New Directions Books; Toronto: George J.
McLeod, pp. 161-80.
 Finds "Passages conjures forth an active field of myth for
which Memory is the informing muse, in which Love, War, and Music
are presiding figures, and through which creativity itself, multi-
farious, is the fertile ground." Claims the "myth-making activity, for Duncan, is predominantly retrospective, a return to first
things, beginnings," origins. Outlines his treatment of Eros in
various mutations, especially in "Chords: Passages, 14," as well
as his treatment of strife and evil and the role of Mnemosyne in
his work. Finds Passages 22 through 27 transcend their contemporary context, examining them not as "anti-war poems but as war
poems, studies in struggle," in which Duncan attempts to "discover

the creative essence of the antagonism . . . endemic in man and
the universe."
     Relates the story of Gassire in "Orders: Passages, 24" to
the destruction in the poem, noting the relationship between
strife and music. Discusses Duncan's poetics as a poetry of
process, and finds the form of the Passages sequence regenerative,
noting his treatment of birth and rebirth. Also finds his work
reflexive, commenting on the self-referentiality of the language
and the poetry; participatory, claiming the poet becomes a "reader
at our side"; and playful, mentioning Duncan's "openness to 'meanings at play.'" Illustrates with many of the poems from the
Passages sequence, and occasionally quotes from an unpublished
28 January 1976 letter from Duncan.

40   TYLER, HAMILTON, and TYLER, MARY. "In the Beginning; or, Re-
     catching The Years as Catches with Robert Duncan, in the Years
     1942 and 1945-46." In Robert Duncan: Scales of the Marvelous.
     Edited by Robert J[ohn] Bertholf and Ian W. Reid. Insights:
     Working Papers in Contemporary Criticism. New York: New
     Directions Books; Toronto: George J. McLeod, pp. 1-13.
          In this reminiscence covering periods in 1942, 1945, and
     1946, provides occasions behind or contexts of "The Years as
     Catches," "The End of the Year," "My Mother Would Be a Falconress,"
     and "An Apollonian Elegy." Discusses Duncan's thematic use of
     polarities, including those between light and dark and between
     "Being and chaos." Also notes the importance of Christ, Apollo,
     Milton, and Freud to Duncan's early work.

41   WALKER, JAYNE L. "Exercises in Disorder: Duncan's Imitations
     of Gertrude Stein." In Robert Duncan: Scales of the Marvel-
     ous. Edited by Robert J[ohn] Bertholf and Ian W. Reid. In-
     sights: Working Papers in Contemporary Criticism. New York:
     New Directions Books; Toronto: George J. McLeod, pp. 22-35.
          Traces Duncan's study and imitation of Stein through his
     "Imitations of Gertrude Stein, 1953-1955," collected in Deriva-
     tions, and Writing Writing. Shows how Duncan abandoned the "dis-
     cursive function of language" in order to give himself to its
     "substantial qualities," but later "experimented with Stein's idea
     of language as rigorously denotative."
          Finds Duncan abandoned Stein's "theoretical presuppositions"
     and accepted the multiple associations that words had from "their
     prior uses in the literary tradition." Believes, however, that
     Duncan's apprenticeship remains evident in his techniques and in
     his attention to words and "their sound associations."

42   ZWICKY, FAY. "An Interview with Denise Levertov." Westerly:
     A Quarterly Review 24, no. 2 (July):119-26.
          In this interview, Levertov mentions her friendship with
     Duncan and his offense to her. Comments on 1979.30.

1980

1   ABBOTT, STEVE, and SHURIN, AARON. "Interview/Workshop with
     Robert Duncan." Soup, no. 1, pp. 30-57, 79.
          A continuation, with a few reprinted sections, of 1979.1,
     containing mainly a day-long interview from January 1979. In this
     interview, Duncan basically discusses his sense of homosexuality,
     war, love, ideals, romance, and rhetoric. Provides a few bio-
     graphical details, especially concerning his relationship to Jess
     and his love of others and its expression in his poetry. He also
     discusses "My Mother Would Be a Falconress," providing its bio-
     graphical background and mentioning its bird and sexual imagery,
     and a few other poems such as Medieval Scenes and "H.M.S.
     Bearskin." Finds language terrifying in some ways, and believes
     his work to be romantic. He also comments on his coming into his
     own voice and notes his use of rhetoric and fountain imagery, the
     latter especially in "The Waste, The Room, The Discarded Timbers"
     from "Four Poems as a Night Song."

2   BROMIGE, DAVID, et al. "Intention and Poetry." Hills, nos. 6-
     7 [Talks issue] (Spring), pp. 25-49.
          In a conversation, Bromige and Barrett Watten briefly men-
     tion Duncan's use of etymology and note his sense of inspiration,
     of receiving poetry from beyond.

3   BROUGHTON, JAMES. "Homage to the Great Bear." Credences,
     [o.s.] 3, nos. 2-3 [whole nos. 8-9] (March):140-45.
          Broughton reminisces about his relationship to Duncan from
     1950 to 1973. Provides portions of unpublished poems by Duncan
     including "A Pre Preface for James on his Sixtieth Birthday, 10
     Nov. 1973" and a poem Duncan wrote for the 15 May 1966 christening
     of Broughton's son, Orion. Comments on Duncan's influence on him
     and the importance of "An Owl Is an Only Bird of Poetry" to him,
     and provides portions of poems he wrote to Duncan. Mentions
     Duncan's devotion to poetry and relationship to Jess. Describes
     Duncan's spontaneity when writing and notes a few poems in The
     Opening of the Field "were written as gifts" for the "ritual
     feasts for the Devotees of The Maiden," especially "Three Pages
     from a Birthday Book."

4   BUTTERICK, GEORGE F. "Robert Duncan." In American Poets since
     World War II. Part 1, A-K. Edited by Donald J. Greiner.
     Dictionary of Literary Biography, vol. 5. Detroit: Gale
     Research Co., Bruccoli Clark Book, pp. 217-29.
          After a brief bibliographical and biographical summary,
     charts Duncan's development and relationship to others. Claims
     Ground Work: Before the War was completed but for "four lines in
     a single poem." Comments on a number of his poems, especially
     "The Song of the Borderguard," "An Owl Is an Only Bird of Poetry,"

RD1980

The Structure of Rime sequence, "My Mother Would Be a Falconress,"
and "Apprehensions." Mentions the setting for "The Venice Poem"
and the treatment of war in "An Essay at War," his first poem of
exploration which was "constantly seeking a plan." Provides the
occasion and original title for The Opening of the Field, and
notes the influence of process poetics on Letters. Examines the
treatment of the dance in "The Dance" and the treatment of the
dance, the meadow, poetry, and the female figure, as well as the
use of repetition in "Often I Am Permitted to Return to a Meadow."
Follows the associations in "A Poem Beginning with a Line by
Pindar," providing a few allusions, and noting the role of the
dance. Notes process in the Passages sequence, and discusses it
as a long poem. Finds sources for "Passages, 37: O" in Olson's
notes, and notes sources for "At the Loom: Passages, 2." Comments on Duncan's sense of rhyme and a few of his recurrent themes.
Includes a photo of the first manuscript page of "Passages, 23:
Benefice."

5 COHN, JACK R., and O'DONNELL, THOMAS J. "An Interview with
   Robert Duncan." Contemporary Literature 21, no. 4 (Autumn):
   513-48.
        In this lengthy February and July 1976 interview, Duncan
   claims that he is not part of the current literary scene but that
   he was when Olson was alive. Recounts his first conversations
   with Olson and his relationship to Olson and Spicer, claiming he
   "played heretic" to their positions. Mentions his and Spicer's
   attraction to the Stefan George Circle. Reviews the importance of
   the Black Mountain movement for him and his sense of being a Black
   Mountain poet. Mentions the influence of "Projective Verse" and
   Pound's ideogram on his work, and comments on his sense of poetry
   as a quest and his early realization that he would have only the
   profession of poet. Provides biographical details about his homosexuality, his relationship to Ernst Kantorowicz, and his affair
   with Werner Vordtriede. Also relates séances in the 1930s and
   mentions writing 1944.1, noting John Crowe Ransom's rejection of
   "An African Elegy" because of its publication. Duncan claims he
   often refused to take drugs because it was "too easy for [him] to
   let go."
        Relates a few of his visitations and dreams, including his
   dream of light in "The Light: Passages, 28" and/or of pillars in
   "Orders: Passages 24," as well as the visitation of the Carpenter
   figure in "A Letter." Also refers to the lion in "The Structure
   of Rime, III" and recurring words like "sentence" in poems. Notes
   the role of Freud, Darwin, and Whitehead on his thought, especially on his sense of purpose and process, and mentions trying to
   lose a sense of purpose in Letters and The Opening of the Field.
   Also comments on the titling of the latter poem.
        Examines "Often I Am Permitted to Return to a Meadow" as
   "nuclear," as a "thematic center," to The Opening of the Field,

326

comments on writing the poem, and details the sense of permission
in the work, especially permission to be free from "angels" of
propositions in poetry. Remarks on its revisions and its union of
the Celtic and the Judaic. Also touches on the role of the meadow
and dream in and sources for the poem, focusing on sources for the
"folded field."

Remarks on his work habits, using his manuscripts and notebooks for "'Eidolon of the Aion'" as an example, and mentions he
is not thinking of finishing The H.D. Book by a deadline. Notes
the impulses for beginning a poem, how he feels compelled to
write, and how he senses he is "making buildings and architec-
tures." Discusses his art as a process of "bringing out qualities" in the language, using "The Dance" to illustrate his
attention to words, especially their polysemous nature. Comments
on poetry's relationship to performance, on reading his own poetry, on his difficulty for readers, on his multiple sources, and
on his use of Milton. Mentions that his use of the collage is a
way to contain "the conglomerate," and finds language and poetry
perilous and promising.

In their introduction, Cohn and O'Donnell comment on
Duncan's energy and his teaching at the University of Kansas, note
the occasions for the interview, and describe his house in San
Francisco. Reprinted: 1983.5. See also 1985.11.

6   COOLEY, DENNIS [ORIN]. "The Poetics of Robert Duncan."
     Boundary 2: A Journal of Postmodern Literature 8, no. 2
     (Winter):45-73.
         Quoting often from Duncan's prose, provides his ideas on
     conventional forms compared to organic poetry and on the role of
     conclusion, gaps, errors, and the poet's personality in poetry.
     Mentions his ideas on craft as a readiness to faithfully follow
     the orders of the poem and on the role of poetry in society.
     Notes Duncan's use of the dance motif, line length, and of prose
     with poetry, and emphasizes the Heraclitean struggle of elements
     in his work. Finds "he becomes a participant, not a personality,
     in the poem," provides reasons for his allusions to and quotations
     from others, and realizes he "fails to root his poetry deeply in
     the material world" at times. Mentions his revision and editing
     practices as well as the poems he has kept from publication.

7   _____. "Robert Duncan's Green Wor[l]ds" [Cooley's brackets].
     Credences, [o.s.] 3, nos. 2-3 [whole nos. 8-9] (March):152-60.
         Abridged and revised sections of chapters 3 and 4 of 1971.6.

8   CREELEY, ROBERT. "From 'On the Road: Notes on Artists and
     Poets, 1950-1965' in Poets of the Cities, 1974." In Homage to
     Frank O'Hara. Edited by Bill Berkson and Joe LeSueur.
     Berkeley, Calif.: Creative Arts Book Co., p. 68.
         Reprinted from 1974.7.

RD1980

9   DORN, EDWARD. "The Outcasts of Foker Plat: News from the
      States." In Views. Edited by Donald [Merriam] Allen. Writing,
      no. 40. San Francisco: Four Seasons Foundation, pp. 79-92.
      Reprint of 1965.3.

10   DOYLE, CHARLES. "Duncan, Robert (Edward)." In Contemporary
      Poets. Edited by James Vinson and D.L. Kirkpatrick. 3d ed.
      New York: St. Martin's Press, pp. 396-99.
            After an expanded bibliography of 1970.21, comments on
      Duncan's musical sense, privacy, and use of open form and poetry
      as magic or ritual. Notes influences on Duncan. Reprinted:
      1985.15 with an updated bibliography. See also 1975.23 and
      1979.37.

11   DUNCAN, ROBERT. Communication and Debat in "Premier jour:
      Première séance plénière." [In French.] Liberté [Montreal,
      Quebec] 22, no. 4 [whole no. 130] [Et la poésie? Actes de la
      huitième recontre québécoise internationale des écrivains
      issue] (July-August):12-13, 32.
            In his 1 October 1979 address and comment, Duncan mentions
      being possessed by and following the intention or spirit of the
      poem itself during the creative process. States that he is not a
      Platonist, but a Freudian.

12   DUNCAN, ROBERT, and GINSBERG, ALLEN. "From 'Early Poetic Com-
      munity' Discussion at Kent State April 7, 1971, in Allen
      Verbatim." In Homage to Frank O'Hara. Edited by Bill Berkson
      and Joe LeSueur. Berkeley, Calif.: Creative Arts Book Co.,
      p. 63.
            Reprinted from 1974.12.

13   DUNCAN, ROBERT. "Preface" to "One Night Stand" and Other
      Poems, by Jack Spicer. San Francisco, Calif.: Grey Fox Press,
      pp. ix-xxvii.
            Duncan discusses the influence of "Heavenly City, Earthly
      City" on Spicer and provides a number of biographical details
      concerning their relationship between 1946 and 1950.

14   EVERSON, WILLIAM. "Of Robert Duncan." Credences, [o.s.] 3,
      nos. 2-3 [whole nos. 8-9] (March):147-51.
            In this reminiscence, Everson discusses Duncan's readings
      and soirees and his relationship to Rexroth. Comments on the
      sexual energy in his poetry and his homosexuality's influence upon
      his "celebration of Imagination as an entity or domain itself."

15   FAAS, EKBERT. "Infantilism and Adult Swiftness: An Interview
      with Ekbert Faas." In Talking All Morning, by Robert Bly.
      Poets on Poetry. Ann Arbor: University of Michigan Press, pp.
      250-83.
            Reprint of 1976.13.

16 _____. "An Interview with Robert Duncan." Boundary 2: A
Journal of Postmodern Literature 8, no. 2 (Winter):1-19.
In this interview, Duncan discusses the importance of other
poets and thinkers to him, especially Stein, Pound, Lawrence,
Whitman, and H.D.; comments on his relationship to Creeley, Olson,
and Spicer; and provides his ideas of a poem and of open form and
field poetry. He also finds reading poetry a "ritualistic performance" and mentions his love of enigma. Provides biographical
details, and discusses the occasion and/or composition of Medieval
Scenes, "Domestic Scenes," and Play Time, Pseudo Stein. Comments
on the composition and meanings of "The Venice Poem" and The H.D.
Book, providing the structure of and plans for the latter. Comments on his decision not to write a book for fifteen years, and
explains the image of a "folded field" in "Often I Am Permitted to
Return to a Meadow." Also comments on 1961.1 and 1954.2.

17 FINKELSTEIN, NORMAN MARK. "The Utopian Invariant: Interiority
and Exteriority in the Twentieth-Century Poetic Consciousness."
Ph.D. dissertation, Emory University, pp. 230-61, 264-65,
passim.
Finds Duncan's poetry a synthesis of interiority, personal
reactions, and mythic understandings with exteriority, material,
political and historical events, claiming his work "is the first
real synthesis of Romantic and Modernist modes." Notes his ability to break down the "rigid subject/object dichotomy imposed by
certain advances of Modernism." Discusses the development of
Duncan's poetry in terms of its focus on exterior events and/or
interior responses, finding early poems, such as "An African
Elegy" and "Berkeley Poems," vacillating between the two, and
later poems, using The Structure of Rime sequence and the Passages
sequence as examples, achieving a conscious synthesis.
Finds "Duncan's mature work polarizes around the notion of
lawfulness" in terms of cosmic orders reflected in the structure
of language, the laws of syntax. Also mentions Duncan's treatment
of politics, love, sex, language, and desire, his lyricism, and
his romantic precursors and identifications. Comments on 1954.2
and 1955.1. Discusses his use of open form and field poetics and
the role of myth in his work. Revised: 1983.14. See Dissertation Abstracts International 41 (1981):3104-5A.

18 FREDMAN, STEPHEN [ALBERT]. "Roadtesting the Language." In
Interviews, by Edward Dorn. Edited by Donald [Merriam] Allen.
Writing, no. 38. Bolinas, Calif.: Four Seasons Foundation,
pp. 64-106.
Reprinted from 1978.26.

19 JONES, PETER. "Robert Duncan." In A Reader's Guide to Fifty
American Poets. Reader's Guide Series. London: Heinemann;
Totowa, N.J.: Barnes & Noble, pp. 299-304.

RD1980

In an introduction to Duncan, provides a biographical
sketch, notes influences on him, and mentions associations he
makes. Notes his use of metaphor and allusions.

20   KIKEL, RUDY. "After Whitman and Auden: Gay Male Sensibility
      in Poetry since 1945." Gay Sunshine, nos. 44-45 [10th Anni-
      versary Issue] (Autumn-Winter), sec. 2, pp. 34-39.
         Mentions Duncan's treatment of love and homosexuality, even
      his criticism of homosexuality in 1944.1.

21   LEONG, LIEW GEOK. "Projectivism: Theory and Temperament
      in the Poetry of Charles Olson, Robert Duncan, and Robert
      Creeley." Ph.D. dissertation, George Washington University,
      pp. i-iii, 1-30, 90-133, 194-96, 208-16, passim.
         Noting Duncan's attraction to Olson's "Projective Verse,"
      comments on his sense of open form poetry and composition by
      field, finding sources in theories of organic poetry. Comments on
      Duncan's expansiveness, "embracing cosmology," and use of myth.
      Lists other influences as Pound, W.C. Williams, Eliot, and
      Zukofsky, and mentions his belief in a "post-humanistic" world
      that is "no longer man-centered." Notes Duncan's emphasis on
      physiology in the writing of poetry and his similarities to and
      differences from Olson and Creeley.
         Mentions Duncan as a Platonist and a romantic poet, noting
      his sense that the poet is a synthesizer of opposites in search of
      "eternal poetic truths." Discusses his treatment of love and
      death in "An Apollonian Elegy" and of poetry in "Heavenly City,
      Earthly City," noting his use of myth in the latter poem. Finding
      The Opening of the Field a "Platonic Quest" for an "ideal aes-
      thetic," comments on a few of the poems, focusing on the treatment
      of the past and the expansiveness of "A Poem Beginning with a Line
      by Pindar." Also mentions the serial nature of The Structure of
      Rime sequence, finding the sequence a quest for "eternal forms of
      poetry."
         Comments on Duncan's search for wisdom, noting Olson's ob-
      jection in 1954.2 and Duncan's reaction to it. Finds Duncan occa-
      sionally "engaged in self-indulgent rapture." In Roots and
      Branches, focuses on Duncan's use of the long poem, distinguishing
      between the sequence poem and the serial poem. Notes the collage
      structure of the latter. Comments on a number of poems, focusing
      on Duncan's treatment of law, poetry, and the oneness of all,
      spending a bit more time on "Variations on Two Dicta of William
      Blake" and "A Set of Romantic Hymns."
         Comparing it to Olson's Maximus Poems, discusses Duncan's
      use of the collage structure in the Passages sequence, commenting
      how it "accords well with Duncan's belief in the oneness of all
      ages" and how it exhibits the "projective influence at work."
      Notes his use of discontinuity and disorder in the sequence and

the range of themes and the shifting of themes, especially commenting on Duncan's treatment of the Vietnam War. See Dissertation Abstracts International 41 (1981):3582A.

22   MACKEY, NATHANIEL [ERNEST]. "The World Poem in Microcosm:
     Robert Duncan's 'The Continent.'" ELH 47, no. 3 (Fall):
     595-618.
        Abridged and extensively revised from 1975.21 with an added
     discussion of Duncan as a derivative poet. Also mentions Duncan's
     differences from poets with whom he is usually associated and his
     attempt to lessen his rhetorical approach in "The Continent."

23   McPHILMEY, KATHLEEN. "Towards Open Form: A Study of Process
     Poetics in Relation to Four Long Poems: The Anathemata by
     David Jones, In Memoriam James Joyce by Hugh MacDiarmid,
     Passages by Robert Duncan, Gunslinger by Edward Dorn." Ph.D.
     dissertation, University of Edinburgh, pp. 302-50.
        Comments on Duncan as a derivative poet, a shaman or bard in
     the service of Poetry, and a "preserver of the tradition of the
     race." Notes the influence of Whitehead, Whitman, and Gnosticism,
     especially through Hans Jonas's The Gnostic Religion: The Message
     of the Alien God and the Beginnings of Christianity (Boston,
     Mass.: Beacon Press, 1958), on his thought. Discusses the impor-
     tance of process, myth, open form, the interconnectedness of all
     poetry, and "the reality of the present instant" to his poetics.
     Mentions the role of revision and error in his work, notes his
     sense of language, and compares Duncan's poetics to Heidegger's
     thought.
        Discusses the Passages sequence as a long poem in open form,
     examining the role of opposites—Eros and Thanatos, poetry as
     process and poetry as product, order and strife or disorder—in
     the poem. Also investigates the role of dynamic imagery, war, the
     city, the household, the sexual and erotic, the community, Gnostic
     cosmology, language, dualism, and the harmony of discordant ele-
     ments, as well as the treatment of Logos, love, homosexuality, and
     poetry in the sequence.
        Mentions many of the specific poems in Passages, especially
     noting the role of mythology and the treatment of the city, dis-
     order, and unity in "Tribal Memories: Passages, 1"; the role of
     politics and the erotic in "The Fire: Passages, 13"; and the
     treatment of order and the city and the role of the story of
     Gassire's lute in "Orders: Passages, 24." Discusses Duncan's use
     of Gustave Stickley's Craftsman Homes (New York: Craftsman Pub-
     lishing Co., 1909; more recently, Craftsman Homes: Architecture
     and Furnishing of the American Arts and Crafts Movement [New York:
     Dover, 1979]) in "The Architecture: Passages, 9." In the later
     Passages, discusses the role of politics, the Vietnam War, the
     domestic, and order and disorder, as well as the treatment of the
     American society, often as the "swollen city."

RD1980

Also comments on "Passages 32: [Ancient Reveries and
Declamations] (Tribunals)," and "The Torso: Passages, 18," and
often refers to The Truth and Life of Myth (1968.12), to explain
Duncan's ideas. Especially examined his idea of the word as a
cellular individual, drawn from Sir Charles Scott Sherrington's
Man on His Nature (Cambridge: Cambridge University Press, 1940).

24 MICHELSON, PETER. "A Materialist Critique of Duncan's Grand
   Collage." Boundary 2: A Journal of Postmodern Literature 8,
   no. 2 (Winter):21-43.
      Compares Marx's dialectical materialism to Duncan's dialec-
   tic of belief and unbelief, the devotional and the critical, religion and science. Finds both men attempt to change the quality of
   life and both attend to the "suffering spirit." Details the role
   of poetry, mythopoetic religion, and the notion of the "Grand
   Collage" in Duncan's dialectic as seen in The Truth and Life of
   Myth (1968.12), "Passages, 26: The Soldiers," and "Eye of God:
   Passages, 29," finding a "weave of religious myth and critical
   analysis," not a denial of the latter.
      Finds, however, that "Transgressing the Real: Passages,
   27," "Up Rising: Passages, 25," and "At the Loom: Passages, 2"
   display an "aggressive idealist imperative" that ignores the critical spirit and places too much faith in the "Grand Collage."
   Feels this faith allows evil to be too easily transcended and
   makes these poems "ethically meaningless at any literal or sensual
   level."

25 NORRIS, KENNETH WAYNE. "The Role of the Little Magazine in the
   Development of Modernism and Post-Modernism in Canadian Poetry." Ph.D. dissertation, McGill University, pp. 197-200,
   219-20, passim.
      Recounts Duncan's influence on Canadian poetry in Vancouver
   and his role in the founding of Tish, relying on 1974.32 and
   1976.8 and commenting on 1962.3. Revised: 1984.21. See Dissertation Abstracts International 41 (1981):3574A.

26 PETERS, ROBERT. "'Where the Bee sucks': A Meditation on
   Robert Duncan's 'Night Scenes.'" Little Caesar, no. 11,
   pp. 225-28.
      Explicates Duncan's "Night Scenes," describing the three
   movements as "strategic improvisations on a young homosexual's
   maturity" from fear, to psychologically disguising his love of
   males, and finally to an acceptance of homosexuality without
   fantasy. Reprinted: 1982.21.

27 QUASHA, GEORGE. "Duncan's Reading." Credences, [o.s.] 3,
   nos. 2-3 [whole nos. 8-9] (March):162-75.
      Examines Duncan's ideas on and treatment of reading, in-
   cluding reading the world as a text, "self-reading," and his

audience's reading. Finds a heretical multiplicity in his "reflexive reading," an intentional "self-heresy" and "self dialectic" in his work. Noting that an objective criticism would violate Duncan's poetics, feels a "visionary exegesis," or ta'wil more appropriate, believing Duncan's reader should have a "dialectic of attraction and resistance" to the text. Mentions the role of myth in his work and his self-reading, psychological "self-exegesis," and discovery. Mentions his instructions to his readers, his relationship to modernism, and his belief that reading will renew the consciousness of his readers.

Believes Duncan's challenge of dualisms based on the subjective-objective dichotomy creates a torsion that prepares the ground for a broad, polysemous discourse. Claims his poetry after Letters is created "in close relation to the act of reading." Considers the "invented reader" in The Opening of the Field and the "ways of readership" in Roots and Branches, commenting on the "dream's demand" in "Apprehensions." Notes the increased demands on the reader in the Passages sequence with themes concerning the reader and reading, and remarks on his desire for an "aroused" readership. Mentions the influence of Pound, especially on "Passages, 23: Benefice," noting its ideogrammatic construction and "intertextual complexity."

28   SARLES, DAVID GRIFFITH. "The Personae in Charles Olson's Maximus Poems." Ph.D. dissertation, State University of New York at Stony Brook, pp. 60–63.
     Discusses Olson's references to Duncan in The Maximus Poems. See Dissertation Abstracts International 40 (1980):5867A.

29   SCHIFFER, REINHOLD. "Robert Duncan: The Poetics and Poetry of Syncretic Hermeticism." In Poetic Knowledge: Circumference and Centre: Papers from the Wuppertal Symposium, 1978. Edited by Roland Hagenbüchle and Joseph T. Swann. Schriftenreihe Literaturwissenschaft, edited by Thomas Koebner et al., vol. 18. Bonn, West Germany: Bouvier Verlag Herbert Grundmann, pp. 160–65.
     Believes Eros and hermetic love is the syncretic principle through which Duncan "recreates meaning," noting his treatment of community, cosmic unity, and the numinous. Notes his use of mythic and Christian figures and of the collage as an apprehension of unity. Comments on his sense that divine messengers and the poets of the past speak to the poet, and notes his belief in the correspondence of all things. Finds Duncan a "secularized mythologist" and a romantic, and mentions the role of emotion in his writing. Translated into Italian and expanded: 1983.29.

30   SITNEY, P. ADAMS. "Figures of the Present Dance: Maurice Blanchot and Charles Olson." Ph.D. dissertation, Yale University, pp. 112–36, 149–51, passim.

RD1980

Discusses Olson's respect for and relationship to Duncan,
especially in terms of 1954.2 and as witnessed in their correspondence in the early 1950s. Examines the themes of poetic inspiration and continuity, love, and time in "The Years as Catches"
and, especially, "The Venice Poem," and notes Duncan's allusions
to Milton, Hart Crane, Whitman, Stevens, Pound, Shakespeare, and
Igor Stravinsky. See <u>Dissertation</u> <u>Abstracts</u> <u>International</u> 41
(1980):2099A.

31   WELCH, LEW, et al. <u>I</u> <u>Remain:</u> <u>The</u> <u>Letters</u> <u>of</u> <u>Lew</u> <u>Welch</u> <u>and</u> <u>the</u>
      <u>Correspondence</u> <u>of</u> <u>His</u> <u>Friends</u>. Edited by Donald [Merriam]
      Allen. 2 vols. Bolinas, Calif.: Grey Fox Press, 2:51-56,
      106, passim.
          Welch reveals a variety of feelings toward Duncan, from
      respect to dislike, over a period from August 1960 to July 1968,
      and notices Rilke's apparent influence on him. In a July 1962
      draft of an unsent letter to Duncan, Welch speaks of Duncan's gift
      to be open to the "flow" of poetry, having gone through periods as
      "black" as he, Welch, has recently gone through.

32   WHEATON, W[ALTER] BRUCE. "A Measure of Desire: Essays on
      Robert Duncan and Charles Olson." Ph.D. dissertation, Uni-
      versity of Iowa, pp. 32-34, 65-108, passim.
          Discusses Duncan's sense of memory and the poem, as the
      universe, always moving toward a fullness without ending or formal
      closure, and uses "The Inbinding" from "Another Animadversion" as
      an example, noting the treatment of sound and memory. Comments on
      the role of imagined space in his work and his treatment of the
      tree as the universe and as the "communal Self," noting sources in
      the Kabbalah. Mentions his treatment of the matrix as memory in
      "In the Place of a <u>Passage</u> 22," commenting on his use of imagery
      and "ideogrammatic superimposition" as a method. Comments on his,
      like Whitman's, treatment of both the "particular and expansive
      selves." Also mentions his treatment of the meadow and dance in
      poems in <u>The</u> <u>Opening</u> <u>of</u> <u>the</u> <u>Field</u>.
          Discusses the role of the dance, memory, and myth, espe-
      cially of Psyche, Cupid, and Eros, in "A Poem Beginning with a
      Line by Pindar." Notes Duncan's use of his sources in Goya and
      Pindar, his ability to see "the past at once with the present,"
      and his treatment of Pound and W.C. Williams in the poem. See
      <u>Dissertation</u> <u>Abstracts</u> <u>International</u> 42 (1981):210A.

33   WILSON, ROBERT A[LFRED JUMP]. <u>Modern</u> <u>Book</u> <u>Collecting</u>. New
      York: Alfred A. Knopf, p. 173.
          Provides a photo of the first page of Duncan's corrections
      of his author's galleys of <u>Veil,</u> <u>Turbine,</u> <u>Cord,</u> <u>and</u> <u>Bird</u>, indi-
      cating his attention to spacing.

1981

1 AIKEN, WILLIAM [MINOR]. "Denise Levertov, Robert Duncan, and Allen Ginsberg: Modes of the Self in Projective Poetry." Modern Poetry Studies 10, nos. 2-3:200-240.
   Revision of chapters 7 and 8 of 1977.1.

2 BERKE, ROBERTA [ELZEY]. Bounds Out of Bounds: A Compass for Recent American and British Poetry. New York: Oxford University Press, pp. 40-44.
   Discusses Duncan's obscurity, providing explanations for some of the alchemical symbols in The Structure of Rime sequence. Comments on Duncan's sources, including Olson, and discusses his collage method and use of "the poem as a simultaneous 'field.'" Quotes from "Revival" as a love poem that transcends its homosexual context as well as "The Dance" and "Poetry, a Natural Thing."

3 CLAUSEN, CHRISTOPHER. "Poetry as Revelation." In The Place of Poetry: Two Centuries of an Art in Crises. Lexington: University Press of Kentucky, pp. 28-47.
   Reprinted from 1979.11.

4 CREELEY, ROBERT. "Introduction to Whitman Selected by Robert Creeley." In Walt Whitman: The Measure of His Song. Edited by Jim Perlman, Ed Folsom, and Dan Campion. Minneapolis: Holy Cow! Press, pp. 191-200.
   Reprint of 1973.5.

5 DARRAS, JACQUES. "Deux poètes américains face à William Carlos Williams." [In French.] In' Hui 14 [William Carlos Williams issue] (Winter 1980-81), pp. 319-30.
   In this 28 July 1980 interview with Michael Palmer and Duncan, Duncan mentions his romanticism and his initial contacts with the work of Pound and W.C. Williams.

6 DAVIDSON, [ROBERT] MICHAEL. "'By ear, he sd': Audio-Tapes and Contemporary Criticism." Credences: A Journal of Twentieth-Century Poetry and Poetics, n.s. 1, no. 1:105-20.
   Very briefly comments on Duncan reading his own poetry and his typographical notation.

7 _____. "The Five Songs" in The Five Songs. La Jolla, Calif.: Friends of the UCSD Library and Archive for New Poetry, [University of California at San Diego], 1 p. insert.
   Discusses Duncan's source for The Five Songs, the poetry of Mawlānā Jalāl al-Dīn Rūmī (1207-73), and mentions how this source and Persian Sufism coincides with Duncan's "abiding care for music and dance." Comments on Duncan within the tradition of Western poetry.

RD1981

8   DUNCAN, ROBERT. "From The H.D. Book, Part Two: Nights and
    Days, Chapter 11." Montemora, no. 8, pp. 77-113.
        In a reprinted and greatly expanded version of 1971.9,
    Duncan mentions his early contacts with Olson, including a 1947
    meeting, and Olson's injunctions to him in 1954.2.

9   _____. "[Structure of Rime] of The Five Songs" [Duncan's
    brackets]. In The Five Songs. La Jolla, Calif.: Friends of
    the UCSD Library and Archive for New Poetry, [University of
    California at San Diego, p. 2].
        Discusses the use of the number 5 in The Five Songs.
    Reprinted: 1987.4.

10 GUILLORY, DANIEL L. "Leaving the Atocha Station: Contempo-
    rary Poetry and Technology." TriQuarterly, no. 52 [Freedom in
    American Art and Culture issue] (Fall), pp. 165-81.
        Very briefly notes that Duncan's sense of field in field
    composition "describes a structure of knowledge."

11 JAMES H[AREL] VANCE. "An Oral Interpretation Script Illustrat-
    ing the Influence on Contemporary American Poetry of the Three
    Black Mountain Poets: Charles Olson, Robert Creeley, Robert
    Duncan." M.S. thesis, North Texas State University, pp. 4, 25-
    28, 34-35, 38-39, 46-47, 49-50, 52, 61-62, 72-73.
        Provides a biographical sketch of Duncan, comments on his
    role in the San Francisco literary scene and at Black Mountain
    College, and notes influences on his work, especially Olson. With
    an eye to an oral interpretive performance, comments on "Come, Let
    Me Free Myself," "Thank You For Love," and "The Dance," noting the
    poems' biographical context, themes and images, and personae.
    Briefly speculates on Duncan's influence on others.

12 LEVERTOV, DENISE. "Some Duncan Letters: A Memoir and a Crit-
    ical Tribute." In Light Up the Cave. New York: New Direc-
    tions, pp. 167-232.
        Slight revision of 1979.30.

13 MAUD, RALPH. "Charles Olson: Posthumous Editions and
    Studies." West Coast Review: A Quarterly Magazine of the Arts
    14, no. 3 (January 1980):27-33; 15, no. 3 (Winter):37-42.
        Provides a transcript of the last paragraph of the taped
    version of 1969.8, noting variation with the printed version, and
    adds an exchange between Olson and Duncan during Olson's 20 July
    1965 morning lecture, "Causal Mythology," at the Berkeley Poetry
    Conference. Corrects and adds some Duncan allusions in 1978.6.

14 MIDDLETON, PETER. Revelation and Revolution in the Poetry of
    Denise Levertov. London: Binnacle Press, pp. 5-7, 11, passim.

Discusses Duncan's "Answering" as a "corrective" to
Levertov's "Claritas," and comments on the relationship of the
two poets.

15 MORROW, BRADFORD, and COONEY, SEAMUS. A Bibliography of the
    Black Sparrow Press, 1966-1978. Santa Barbara, Calif.: Black
    Sparrow Press, pp. 6-7, 11, 41-42, 87-88, 93-94, passim.
        Provides a descriptive bibliography for Duncan's Epilogos,
    Christmas Present, Christmas Presence! (1967), Names of People, A
    Selection of 65 Drawings, and Tribunals: "Passages," 31-35, as
    well as listing his other contributions to Black Sparrow publica-
    tions, including essays, statements, and introductions. See
    1986.2 for the fullest bibliography on Duncan.

16 NELSON, CARY. "Between Openness and Loss: Form and Dissolu-
    tion in Robert Duncan's Aesthetic." In Our Last First Poets:
    Vision and History in Contemporary American Poetry. Urbana:
    University of Illinois Press, pp. 97-144.
        Quoting extensively from Duncan's prose, discusses his the-
    ory of open form, especially as it applies to revision. Examines
    his use of inconclusive forms and his receptiveness to an emerging
    form as opposed to conventional or preconceived forms. Also dis-
    cusses Duncan's sense of the poem as an organic, democratic field,
    a "form among forms, dismantling and reassembling its own struc-
    ture." Uses "Often I Am Permitted to Return to a Meadow," "My
    Mother Would Be a Falconress," and "The Torso: Passages, 18" to
    exemplify "Duncan's sense of form as cohering dissolution," and
    notes his "desire for that enduring but erosive center" in "Sonnet
    4," explicating all four poems.
        Comments on Duncan's themes of loss, the center, unfolding
    form, sexuality, the body, and religion. Also notes his treatment
    of America, war, violence, history, and language. Comments on his
    images of the rose and the field, as well as his technical use of
    rhyme, punctuation, and the repetition of sound and imagery.
    Examines his sense of the relationship of the poem to the nation,
    poetry as a political force, the dangers of associations in open
    form poetry, and the inseparability of "American openness and
    American malice."

17 PALMER, MICHAEL. "Autobiography, Memory, and Mechanisms of
    Concealment (Part 1 or One Part)." Hills, no. 8 (Summer),
    pp. 59-77.
        Palmer briefly mentions the biographical note that Duncan
    wrote for his Blake's Newton. Reprinted: 1985.45.

18 PAUL, SHERMAN. The Lost America of Love: Rereading Robert
    Creeley, Edward Dorn, and Robert Duncan. Baton Rouge and
    London: Louisiana State University Press, pp. 168-276, passim.

RD1981

Includes a revision of 1978.34, and occasionally quotes from unpublished sources. Examines Duncan's treatment of critics, especially New Critics, and of H.D. in his The H.D. Book. Finds The H.D. Book and his poetry assume a role in the poet's "soul-making," noting the participation they demand of the reader. Observes the treatment of love and his development as a poet in The Truth and Life of Myth (1968.12). Records H.D. and Olson's importance to Duncan, surveying the influence of Olson and Duncan upon each other. Speculates on the title of Ground Work: Before the War. Mentions Duncan's continual treatment of war, imagination, the mother figure, and childhood, and notes the role of myth and the use of correspondences as rhymes in his poetry. Occasionally relates Duncan to Carlyle, and often briefly mentions "The Venice Poem." Notes Duncan's use of periodic and aperiodic structures.

In The Opening of the Field, examines Duncan's treatment of the field, earth, Kore, childhood, love, light, and day. Also examines his use of Whitman's line, composition by field, and mythology; and the role of dance, mystery, desire, memory, and dream in the volume. Finds the work a "psychic journey," and outlines the role of return and the treatment of the meadow, reverie, and the dream of Atlantis in "Often I Am Permitted to Return to a Meadow." Provides extended and detailed treatment of "A Poem Beginning with a Line by Pindar," reviewing the treatment of art, Psyche, Eros, transformation, and the "quest for light and love." Also records the role of myth, dance, and muthos as "mother tongue, vernacular"; and details the treatment and/or echoes of W.C. Williams, Whitman, Olson, Pound, and Eliot in the poem.

In Roots and Branches, lists the potential associations of the tree metaphor. Claims the volume is a "book of survival," outlining the despair; the treatment of the lady and mother figures, love, and the cave; and the role of H.D. Also finds echoes of Creeley in the volume, and comments on "A Sequence of Poems for H.D.'s Birthday." Studies the treatment of imagination and meditation in "Apprehensions," and examines the treatment of Olson in "Variations on Two Dicta of William Blake." Notes the role of myth in "Osiris and Set." Also discusses Duncan's use of the line and collage, and comments on a few poems in The Structure of Rime sequence.

Treats Bending the Bow as a political book, cataloging the role of the primordial, love, Eros, and Dante, as well as the treatment of war, strife, earth, community, Orpheus, and Olson in the volume. Finds Duncan an American poet, and stresses Whitman's importance to Duncan in the book. Comments on many of the poems in the Passages sequence, noting the treatment of love and its relationship to other poems. Discusses the Passages sequence as a single long poem, and speculates on its title.

*19   POWER, KEVIN. "Post Modern Poetics: Four Views." Revista
       canaria de estudios ingleses, no. 2 (March), pp. 51-69.
          Presumably uses Duncan's work as an example of post-
modernism. Unavailable for annotation; listed in 1981 MLA
International Bibliography, I.7361.

                              1982

1   BEIDLER, PHILIP D. American Literature and the Experience of
      Vietnam. Athens: University of Georgia Press, p. 71.
         Briefly claims Duncan's poetry about the Vietnam War, as
that of others of his generation, was "the product of moral, philosophical, [and] ideological argument" but was only minimally
concerned with "concrete actuality."

2   BERNSTEIN, MICHAEL ANDRÉ. "Bringing It All Back Home: Deriva-
      tions and Quotations in Robert Duncan and the Poundian Tradi-
      tion." Sagetrieb: A Journal Devoted to Poets in the Pound-
      Williams Tradition 1, no. 2 (Fall):176-89.
         Continually quoting from The H.D. Book, discusses Duncan as
a derivative poet who establishes his own tradition by his choice
of influences. Compares his use of the tradition to Pound's, but
finds Duncan connects "the Poundian tradition" to "those strains
to which Pound himself was most resistant," including romanticism
and Freudianism. Comments on his "roles of poet, critic, and
translator," mentioning 1967.6 and his translations of Gérard de
Nerval. Notes Duncan's sense of permission, of the commonality of
language, and of the accidental. Also notes his ideas on "the
relationship between imagination and desire" and on "being
'called' by a certain constellation of 'masters.'" Believes
Duncan's poetry "continues--and thus renews--the modernist tradition at its most ambitious by undertaking a synthesis of heteroge-
neous 'origins' as potentially disruptive of one another as those
in Pound's own work."

3   BERTHOLF, ROBERT J[OHN]. "Robert Duncan: Blake's Contemporary
      Voice." In William Blake and the Moderns. Edited by Robert
      J[ohn] Bertholf and Annette S. Levitt. Albany: State Univer-
      sity of New York Press, pp. 92-110.
         Discusses the direct influence of Blake on Duncan and their
"spiritual affinities." Finds Duncan and Blake "claim a member-
ship in a universal poem which reveals itself . . . through the
interaction of contending powers of good and evil." Finds both
create "from the middle of a mythological reality," although
Duncan stresses that this is a "fictive version of the grand
poem." Compares and contrasts their treatment of Christ, Eros,
the self, memory, innocence, war, and freedom, as well as their
view of Dante. Also compares their political vision; their use of

myth and mythological figures; and their belief in "imaginative freedom," "visionary reality," and the value of "the tensions between contrary states." Notes Duncan's emphasis on origins and process, as well as his sense of emerging form. Comments on a number of Duncan's works, notably discussing the role of struggle and conflict in "My Mother Would Be a Falconress" and the treatment of "inner contentions" and love as a "manifestation of the eternal mind" in "Variations on Two Dicta of William Blake."

4   BROOKER, PETER. "The Lesson of Ezra Pound: An Essay in Poetry, Literary Ideology, and Politics." In Ezra Pound: Tactics for Reading. Edited by Ian F.A. Bell. Critical Studies Series. London: Vision Press; Totowa, N.J.: Barnes & Noble, pp. 9–49.
     Briefly notes Pound's influence on Duncan and Duncan's views on Pound, politics in poetry, and myth.

5   CARRUTH, HAYDEN. "Scales of the Marvelous." In Working Papers: Selected Essays and Reviews, by Hayden Carruth. Edited by Judith Weissman. Athens: University of Georgia Press, pp. 96–100.
     Slight revision of 1964.4.

6   COOK, RALPH T. The City Lights Pocket Poets Series: A Descriptive Bibliography. La Jolla, Calif.: Laurence McGilvery; San Diego, Calif.: Atticus Books, pp. 33–34.
     Provides a descriptive bibliographical entry for Duncan's Selected Poems.

7   CREELEY, ROBERT. "On the Road: Notes on Artists and Poets, 1950–1965." In Claims for Poetry. Edited by Donald Hall. Ann Arbor: University of Michigan Press, pp. 62–71.
     Slightly revised version of 1974.7.

8   DUNCAN, ROBERT. "Crisis of Spirit in the Word." Transcribed by Robert [John] Bertholf. Credences: A Journal of Twentieth-Century Poetry and Poetics 2, no. 1 (Summer):63–68.
     In a transcribed 7 February 1982 sermon in Buffalo, N.Y., Duncan comments on the role of language in his work and his sense of the word. Also notes his ideas on the word as God and on creation, and mentions reading Christian texts.

9   _____. "Ideas of the Meaning of Form." In Claims for Poetry. Edited by Donald Hall. Ann Arbor: University of Michigan Press, pp. 78–94.
     Revision of 1961.1.

10   _____. "Statement by the Author on the Following Poem." Wch Way, no. 4 (Summer), p. 5.

Duncan believes the planned printing of "Santa Cruz Propositions" by Wch Way does not attempt to capture the "articulation of
the elements" present in his typescript.

11   . Towards an Open Universe. Aquila Essays, no. 17.
Portree, Isle of Skye, Scotland: Johnston Green & Co., Aquila
Publishing, 15 pp.
Revision of 1966.10.

12 GARDNER, THOMAS MICHAEL. "'A created "I"': The Contemporary
American Long Poem." Ph.D. dissertation, University of
Wisconsin at Madison, pp. 1-6, 152-200.
Continually drawing upon 1970.7, demonstrates that Duncan's
Passages sequence, like Whitman's Song of Myself, helps create the
poet's identity, "unfold[s] the poet's nature by making it real,
lifting it to form." Notes the relation between the poet and the
community as the individual is formed within and apprehends the
"ensemble," a communal and universal, unfolding form.
Shows Duncan trying to find a communal ground with which to
identify and realizing it in "the evolving forms of man's imagination." Discusses many of the individual poems of the first twelve
sections of the Passages sequence, concentrating on "At the Loom:
Passages, 2," "The Collage: Passages, 6," "The Architecture:
Passages, 9," and "Wine: Passages, 12." Finds Duncan "extended
and developed by whatever arouses him and causes his slender theme
to participate in the enormous world surrounding him." Mentions
his use of moon and sea imagery, and comments on his treatment of
language, the body, recesses in a room, and the figure of the
loom.
In later poems from the Passages sequence, especially "The
Fire: Passages, 13," "The Currents: Passages, 16," and "Orders:
Passages, 24," discusses the "communal meanings" of the poem,
focusing on Duncan's treatment of the Vietnam War and his varying
"attempt to create an artistic structure" that will encompass both
the creative and the destructive activities of man, in which
"birth and destruction become simply two phases, two different,
contrasting elements of a larger whole." Demonstrates that Duncan
realizes "the poet must draw from the entire ensemble in order to
accomplish both his extended self-realization and to assist in the
acting out of mankind's potential."
Revised in part: 1985.28. See Dissertation Abstracts
International 43 (1983):2666-67A.

13 GÉFIN, LASZLO. Ideogram: History of a Poetic Method. Austin:
University of Texas Press; Stony Stratford, Milton Keynes:
Open University Press, pp. 99-108, 116, passim. (Published in
England as Ideogram: Modern American Poetry.)
A revised version of 1979.19.

RD1982

14   GUNN, THOM. "Homosexuality in Robert Duncan's Poetry." In The
     Occasions of Poetry: Essays in Criticism and Autobiography.
     London: Faber & Faber, pp. 118-34.
     A slight revision of 1979.22.

15   JOHNSON, MARK A[NDREW]. "Robert Duncan." In Critical Survey
     of Poetry, English Language Series. Vol. 2. Edited by Frank
     N. Magill. Englewood Cliffs, N.J.: Salem Press, pp. 897-907.
        Provides a brief biography, and discusses the sense of
     "limits, boundaries, and margins" in Duncan's life and work, not-
     ing their role as metaphors in his poetry, especially in The
     Opening of the Field, Roots and Branches, and Bending the Bow.
     Finds Duncan's art transcends conventional boundaries; feels "it
     ultimately dissolves the very restraints and boundaries he recog-
     nizes in the act of transgressing them, and it thus weds man to
     nature and to other men." Discusses a number of poems, especially
     "Often I Am Permitted to Return to a Meadow," "The Continent,"
     "Apprehensions," and the Passages sequence.

16   KOPCEWICZ, ANDREJ, and SIENICKA, MARTA. Historia literaury
     Stanów Zjednoczonych w zarysie: Wiek XX. [In Polish.]
     Warsaw: Państwowe Wydawnictwo Naukowe, pp. 189-90, passim.
        Providing an overview of his work and mentioning a number of
     his poems, comments on Duncan as a writer of process poetry and
     projective verse.

17   McCLURE, MICHAEL. Scratching the Beat Surface. San Francisco:
     North Point Press, pp. 12, passim.
        McClure occasionally comments on Duncan's influence on him,
     and describes Duncan's 1955 reading of Faust Foutu at the Six
     Gallery in San Francisco.

18   MOTTRAM, ERIC. "Pound, Merleau-Ponty, and the Phenomenology of
     Poetry." In Ezra Pound: Tactics for Reading. Edited by Ian
     F.A. Bell. Critical Studies Series. London: Vision Press;
     Totowa, N.J.: Barnes & Noble, pp. 121-47.
        Briefly notes Duncan's views on physics.

19   NICOSIA, GERALD. "'The closeness of mind': An Interview with
     Robert Duncan." Unspeakable Visions of the Individual, no. 12
     [Beat Angels issue], pp. 13-27 [the text on pp. 17 and 18 is
     transposed].
        In this July 1978 interview, Duncan provides a number of
     ·biographical details, especially about his relationship to Kerouac
     and Creeley. Comments on meeting Kerouac in 1956; reading
     Kerouac's fiction and poetry; and the role of Kerouac's sexuality
     in their relationship. Also mentions his relationship to Ginsberg
     and other Beats, as well as Rexroth, arguing against the assess-
     ment, in 1957.2, about Pierre Reverdy's influence on him. Notes

his relationship to Michael McClure, pointing to his influence on McClure. Also mentions his other reading, his homosexuality, and his refusal to take drugs.

20 PAUL, SHERMAN. So to Speak: Rereading David Antin. London: Binnacle Press, pp. 1, 7, 12, 22, 35, passim.
     Occasionally very briefly mentions Duncan's ideas and criticism as well as Antin's criticism of Duncan.

21 PETERS, ROBERT. "'Where the Bee sucks': A Meditation on Robert Duncan's 'Night Scenes.'" In The Great American Poetry Bake-Off. 2d ser. Metuchen, N.J., and London: Scarecrow Press, pp. 38-41.
     Reprint of 1980.26.

22 POWER, KEVIN. "A Conversation with Robert Duncan." Revista canaria de estudios ingleses, no. 4 (April), pp. 71-106.
     In this lengthy 1976 interview, Duncan recounts his appreciation of contemporary art in the 1950s and its influence on him, providing biographical details from the same period. Also gives an account of his first meeting with and his subsequent relationship to Jess, occasionally mentioning their work together. Parallels Letters to Jess's pasteups, and refers to Jess's drawings for A Book of Resemblances, as well as his own for A Selection of 65 Drawings. Also comments on his dislike of coherence, his lack of revision, and his following of the "vowel leadings" of language. Mentions his use of "layers of meanings," puns, syntax, the fire image, and open form, noting its relationship to field composition. Refers to the importance of dance in his work and his poetry's lack of boundaries. Surveys his sense of collage, romanticism, and the authentic.
     Duncan discusses writing a number of works, including The Opening of the Field; "The Venice Poem," noting its relationship to Pound, art, and music; Caesar's Gate, providing information concerning Jess's illustrations; and "Dante Études," commenting on the city in it. Mentions the influence of others on him, especially Whitehead, with his sense of man as an event. Also mentions the influence of Stein, H.D., and W.C. Williams, the latter two especially on Medieval Scenes. Remarks on the role of love and jealousy in "The Venice Poem," noting the sense of a "new consciousness" being born in the poem and the importance of the poem to him. Relates the intent of "Domestic Scenes," and refers to his relationship to Spicer and Olson. Rebuts Robert Michael Davidson's criticism of the personalities in The Structure of Rime sequence, probably in an early version of 1973.7 and/or 1979.14. Abridged and slightly revised: 1986.14.

RD1982

23   RASULA, JED. "Placing Pieces." Sagetrieb: A Journal Devoted
      to Poets in the Pound-H.D.-Williams Tradition 1, no. 3 [Robert
      Creeley: Special Issue] (Winter):163-69.
             In terms of composition by field, briefly notes that
      Duncan's poetry is part of a "communal practice" with other poets
      like Creeley and Olson, all of whom "bring themselves . . . to an
      articulate mutual localtiy." Reprinted: 1984.23.

24   "Reflector Interview: Robert Duncan." Reflector (Shippensburg
      State College, Pa.), pp. 49-59.
             In this interview, Duncan provides biographical details and
      comments on his poems as "imaginary constructions." Also mentions
      his multiphasic writing and his use of the vernacular, of American
      speech, as well as the role of fancy in his life and himself as a
      derivative poet. Relates that he feels as though he steals po-
      etry. Comments on imitating Stein and coming to his own voice in
      the mid-1950s. Notes the influence of Pound and W.C. Williams on
      him, and comments on writing "My Mother Would Be a Falconress"
      quickly at one sitting.

25   SHIVELY, CHARLEY [CHARLES]. "John Wieners." In "Gay Sunshine"
      Interviews. Vol. 2. Edited by Winston Leyland. San
      Francisco: Gay Sunshine Press, pp. 259-77.
             Slightly revised and abbreviated from 1973.27, with an added
      27 March 1977 interview.

26   SHURIN, AARON, and ABBOTT, STEVE. "Robert Duncan." In "Gay
      Sunshine" Interviews. Vol. 2. Edited by Winston Leyland. San
      Francisco: Gay Sunshine Press, pp. 75-94.
             Revision and abbreviation of 1979.1, dropping approximately
      one half of the interview.

                              1983

1   BOLLOBÁS, ENIKÖ. "The Grammetrical Reading of Robert
      Duncan's 'The Propositions, 2.'" Acta Litteraria Scientiarium
      Hungaricae 23, nos. 3-4:303-11.
             Provides a "grammetrical" reading--a linguistically-oriented
      explication examining the "consonance/dissonance, cooperation/
      counterpoint, coindicende/non-coincidence [sic] of prosodical and
      grammatical units"--of the second section of "The Propositions."
      Also notes the "'valences' or combinational possibilities" of
      these units. Mentions Duncan's use of sound associations, "struc-
      tural and semantic ambiguities," "lexical pairs and oppositions,"
      diction, tone, "discontinuous syntax," and "lexical connections
      between sentences." Focuses on the reciprocity and the treatment
      of love in the poem. Expanded and revised: 1986.3.

                              344

2   BOONE, BRUCE. "Robert Duncan and Gay Community: A Reflection." Ironwood 11, no. 2 [whole no. 22] [Robert Duncan: A
Special Issue] (Fall):66-82.
        Considers Duncan, Spicer, and Blaser as the Berkeley Renais-
sance and as a "gay band," noting their relations with their
teachers like Ernst Kantorowicz. Discusses Duncan's relationship
to Spicer and compares their work, noting how Duncan's poetry
changes more since he continually attempts "to redefine ego boundaries." Also compares their treatment of sex and the gay community, discovering Duncan, unlike Spicer, wished to break "down the
barriers between gay and non-gay" and see all sexuality as natural
and acceptable. Also compares them in terms of their masculinity,
and speculates on Duncan's influence on Spicer.
        Occasionally relates Duncan's anarchism to his ideas of
community, refers to his sense of writing as magic, comments on
"I Am Not Afraid," and notes the homosexuality in "The Torso:
Passages, 18." Examines the male figure in the latter poem and
elsewhere, and notes the sensual and musical qualities of these
figures. Discovers a "trauma of sexuality" in his work of the
1940s and 1950s, when he wished to treat homosexuality openly but
rarely did. Comments on his treatment of Federico García Lorca in
"Four Poems as a Night Song," noting the role of death in his
treatment of sexuality. Examines his treatment of homosexuality
in "Heavenly City, Earthly City," Caesar's Gate, Medieval Scenes,
and "The Venice Poem," especially noting a "despondency over the
possibility of gay love." Refers to Duncan's femininity in early
sexual contacts, and quotes from a yet unpublished interview with
him.

3   BURNETT, GARY. "Introduction" to "Letters on Poetry and
Poetics," by Robert Duncan. Ironwood 11, no. 2 [whole no. 22]
[Robert Duncan: A Special Issue] (Fall):96-97.
        In this introduction to 1983.10, mentions the criteria for
the inclusion of letters, and provides a few details about
Duncan's relationship to other poets in the San Francisco area in
the late 1950s, especially Spicer.

4   CARRUTH, HAYDEN. "Duncan's Dream." Ironwood 11, no. 2 [whole
no. 22] [Robert Duncan: A Special Issue] (Fall):5-8.
        Quoting from and commenting on "Passages, 36" from A
Seventeenth Century Suite, discusses Duncan's skill and power as a
poet, finding his "poetic imagination continuously evolving within
overlapping cycles of personal and social, intellectual and emotional experience."

5   COHN, JACK R., and O'DONNELL, THOMAS J. "An Interview with
Robert Duncan." In Interviews with Contemporary Writers,

2d ser., <u>1972-1982</u>. Edited by L[awrence] S[anford] Dembo.
Madison: University of Wisconsin Press, pp. 224-59.
   Reprint of 1980.5.

6   DAVIDSON, [ROBERT] MICHAEL. "Cave of Resemblances, Caves of
    Rimes: Tradition and Repetition in Robert Duncan." <u>Ironwood</u>
    11, no. 2 [whole no. 22] [Robert Duncan: A Special Issue]
    (Fall):33-45.
       Compares Duncan's theory of tradition to Eliot's and that of
    the New Criticism. Finds Duncan sees tradition in romantic terms
    as the "cooperation with and response to the open field of crea-
    tive life" as he allows a variety of sources to enter his work.
    Briefly examines his use of other texts which his poetry often
    meditates upon and transforms. Finds Duncan believes that the
    romantic poet should unlock the "potencies in common things" and,
    as though on a quest, become both "the subject and object of his
    creation."
       Considering 1954.2 and 1955.1, compares Olson and Duncan's
    sense of tradition. Comments on Duncan's "participatory act of
    reading" as in <u>The H.D. Book</u>. Also mentions his use of repeti-
    tion, personalities, and rhyme of ideas and sounds in <u>The Struc-
    ture of Rime</u> sequence. Comments on a number of individual works,
    especially "<u>The Structure of Rime</u>, I," notes his desire to seek
    origins, and quotes from one of his unpublished notebooks.

7   DUNCAN, ROBERT. "The Adventure of Whitman's line." <u>Convivio:
    A Journal of Poetics from New College of California</u>, no. 1,
    pp. 15-29.
       Commenting on reading Whitman and Whitman's sense of the
    line, Duncan notes his affiliations with Whitman in terms of their
    homosexuality, poetry, and belief in the democratic. Mentions an
    allusion to Whitman in the title of <u>The Opening of the Field</u>, and
    notes his own derivative nature as a poet. Reprinted: 1985.17.

8   _____. "Chapter 5 of Part I: <u>The H.D. Book</u>." In <u>The
    Alchemical Tradition in the Late Twentieth Century</u>. Edited by
    Richard Grossinger. Io, edited by Richard Grossinger, no. 31.
    Berkeley, Calif.: North Atlantic Books, 203-22.
       Reprint of 1964.7.

9   _____. "<u>The H.D. Book</u>: Outline and Chronology." <u>Ironwood</u> 11,
    no. 2 [whole no. 22] [Robert Duncan: A Special Issue] (Fall):
    65.
       Duncan provides a bibliography of the sections of <u>The H.D.
    Book</u> published to date, mentions his intent for further sections,
    and briefly describes writing the work.

10 _____. "Letters on Poetry and Poetics." <u>Ironwood</u> 11, no. 2
    [whole no. 22] [Robert Duncan: A Special Issue] (Fall):95-135.

In these letters to Spicer and Robin Blaser from 1956 to
1959, Duncan discusses the courses that he was planning to give in
1957 and his relationship to Spicer, Jess, and Wieners. Duncan
also comments on his current reading including Whitehead, Yeats,
George Herbert, Whitman, Igor Stravinsky, Shelley, and David
Lindsay, as well as his sense of being in the service of Poetry.
He mentions his relationship to younger poets, Spicer's Poetry as
Magic Workshop, and the first publication of Letters and of the
first seven sections of The Structure of Rime. Refers to his
alignment with Olson, Creeley, Levertov, and others; a conversation with Olson; and his sense of projective verse, field, and the
"form/content quandry." Refers to Olson's relationship to and
influence on him, and remarks on early publication plans for The
Opening of the Field.

Gives an account of writing The Opening of the Field in
general and "Crosses of Harmony and Disharmony," "A Poem Beginning
with a Line by Pindar," and "A Poem Slow Beginning" in particular.
Comments on a number of works from this volume, including The
Structure of Rime sequence, "The Performance We Wait For," "At
Christmas," and "The Question." Mentions writing, rewriting, and
publishing Faust Foutu as well as poems, noting his feelings about
revision. (The editor provides an earlier version of "Often I Am
Permitted to Return to a Meadow.") Details cutting "For the Innocence of the Act" (see 1986.2, F157 and F164) to become "Nor Is
the Past Pure." Criticizes the "lack of scope" and the "wander-
ings" in "An Essay at War," and notes that Jess sensed that some
of his recent poems were a "return" to "Heavenly City, Earthly
City."

Prior to its publication, Duncan expresses a dislike of The
New American Poetry, 1945-1960, ed. Donald M[erriam] Allen (New
York: Grove press, 1960), desiring that his work be excluded.
Mentions his correspondence with Pound, providing a portion of a
letter from Pound to him which he "incorporated" in "The Venice
Poem." Also mentions his correspondence and arguments with
Michael McClure. Occasionally provides a few biographical
details.

11   . "The Self in Postmodern Poetry." Convivio: A Journal
      of Poetics from New College of California, no. 1, pp. 129-45.
      Provides biographical details about his childhood and par-
ents, including their hermeticism and love of and belief in poetry, Duncan comments on his sense of self while growing up.
Notes the treatment of the self in his early and later poetry,
writers important to his idea of the self, including Freud and
Emerson, and the questioning of the self in the Passages sequence.
Provides allusions to Whitman and to his Aunt Alvie's Gnostic
group in "Another Animadversion." Claims one of the "underlying
currents" in his work "is the weaving of a figure unweaving, an
art unsaying what it says." Treats the role of the self in "A

Sequence of Poems for H.D.'s Birthday," providing the occasion for
a portion of the poem, "Adam's Way," and "Narrative Bridges for
'Adam's Way.'" Mentions the desire for dissolution of the self in
"And a Wisdom as Such." Admits to affinities with Jung, and mentions the lack of self will in his writing. Reprinted: 1985.17.

12   ELLINGHAM, LEWIS. "Blaser's Trail: Robin Blaser in San
      Francisco." Poetry Flash: The Bay Area's Calendar and Review,
      no. 126 (September), pp. 1, 8.
      Mentions Duncan's difficulty with Blaser's translations of
Gérard de Nerval's Les Chimères (see 1967.6) and, quoting Duncan's
"Sonnet 3," his relationship with Blaser.

13   FAAS, EKBERT. Young Robert Duncan: Portrait of the Poet as
      Homosexual in Society. Santa Barbara, Calif.: Black Sparrow
      Press, 361 pp.
      Provides a detailed biography of Duncan from 1919 to 1950.
Interviews many of Duncan's friends, acquaintances, and family
members, and quotes from unpublished sources, including Duncan's
notebooks and diaries, unpublished poems and versions of poems,
and numerous unpublished letters to and from Duncan as well as
third-party letters that discuss Duncan. Continually quotes from
published, unpublished, and/or uncollected poems to illustrate
Duncan's feelings during a period or his feelings about a person
or event. Provides biographical context for numerous poems, many
of which were written well after 1950 but that reflect upon the
period at hand. Occasionally implies the influence of Henry James
on Duncan, and details his relationship to numerous people.
      Quotes from Duncan's poetry, some unpublished, and prose
dealing with his childhood from 1918 to 1926. Describes his adoptive parents, Edwin Joseph and Minnehaha Harris Symmes, his grandmother, and a few other relatives, especially Aunt Fay. Indicates
their interest in the occult and the hermetic, and observes the
role of storytelling in the family. Theorizes on the origin of
Duncan's sense of mystery, of the hidden, of things "behind," and
uses the theories of Jacques Lacan to speculate on the development
of his sense of self. Provides biographical context, guessing at
causes and sources, for a number of poems and sections of poems.
      For the years 1927-35, considers Duncan as a student, espe-
cially as a contributor to his high school's student journal and
as an editor of his high school's newspaper, referring to other
early writing. Comments on his teachers, especially recognizing
the influence of Edna Keough, and in turn of H.D., on Duncan.
      Gives an account of Duncan as a student at the University of
California at Berkeley from 1936 to 1938. Notes his role as editor of Berkeley's Campus Review, and comments on his writings in
college, including poems for Berkeley's Occident, mentioning his
treatment of war. Indicates his realization of himself as a poet
and his relationships to students and others, especially Lillian

Fabilli, Cecily Kramer, Virginia Admiral, Mary Fabilli, and Ned C. Fahs. Examines his growing homosexuality and relationship to homosexual lovers, his role in Epitaph, and his early and later poems, especially "Ritual," designating sources and providing biographical context.

For 1939, recounts his travels to New York and elsewhere, and details his love of art museums and the theater. Examines his relationship to James Peter Cooney and his publications in the Phoenix, and provides excerpts from uncollected poems. Discusses his growing political affiliations, the influence of surrealism as well as D.H. Lawrence and T.S. Eliot on him, and his growing sense of himself as a poet. outlines his relationship to Anaïs Nin (see 1969.18), Henry Miller, Sanders Russell, and Pauline Kael, and details his publication in Grizzly and his role in Ritual.

Discusses Duncan's role-playing, and provides original versions of some poems from 1940. Notes his relationship to William Everson and Kenneth Patchen, his role in Experimental Review, and his writing on homosexuality. Refers to Duncan's encounter with his draft board.

Recounts the beating Duncan received in 1935 from a homosexual, his being homeless in New York in 1941, and his homosexual relationship to Anaïs Nin's cousin, known only as Paul, in that year. Also relates the dissolution of his friendship with Nin, his psychoanalysis, and his sexual escapades in New York. Examines his use of a diary and its role in his life. Records his relationship to Marjorie McKee, and comments on his making love to women.

Explains Duncan's change of name from Symmes to Duncan in 1942, referring to his relationship to and feeling for his adoptive mother. Recounts his period in the Army, his discharge, and his relationship to Hamilton Tyler and Sanders Russell. Also records his eventual breakup with Russell, his attending a séance, and his return to Berkeley. Mentions his writing and publishing in 1942 and uses poems to illustrate Duncan's mood during this period. Finds sources in Milton and Federico García Lorca, exploring the role of Milton in "The Years as Catches."

Chronicles Duncan's marriage to and separation from Marjorie McKee in 1943, using "Love," his short story, to illustrate their relationship. Details his job for Dell Publishing Company, and recounts his suicide attempt. Discusses his trip to Florida, his sadomasochistic homosexual affair, and his role as a "gigolo."

For 1944, examines Duncan's relationship to Dwight Macdonald and his contributions to Politics. Details John Crowe Ransom's reaction to "The Homosexual in Society" (1944.1), and Ransom's withdrawal of "An African Elegy" from slated publication in Kenyon Review, noting how Ransom's apparent Freudian interpretation of the poem found it a "homosexual advertisement" (see 1985.20). Provides Duncan's explanation of the poem as well as his sense of opposition from the New Critical literary establishment. Also considers his political views of the period, notes his reading in 1944, and recounts his life in Provincetown.

In 1945, details his relationships to his adoptive sister, Barbara Symmes; a homosexual lover, Leslie; a woman lover, Friedl; William Humphrey; and Werner Vordtriede. Also mentions his dissociation from Macdonald and his time at Smith College. Comments on his interest in painting and in the Stefan George Circle, as well as his renewed contacts with Everson and Russell. Reviews his prose of the period, provides an unpublished poem and portions of others, and outlines his life at Woodstock, New York. Notes Duncan's obsession with Pierre's mother in Melville's Pierre. Recounts his nervous breakdown in 1945 at his Aunt Fay's in Sacramento, California, providing Duncan's own unpublished account. Examines the breakdown in terms of R.D. Laing's analysis of schizophrenic family patterns.

Mentions Duncan's relationship to his adoptive mother during 1945, and recounts his life with Hamilton and Mary Tyler at Pond Farm and Treesbank as well as his relationship to Kenneth Rexroth, noting his eventual role in the San Francisco Renaissance. Specifies his selection of poems for his proposed The Years as Catches, and speculates on his view of his early work, especially that which has not been collected. Mentions his poetry and prose of the period, his feelings for View and Charles Henri Ford, his anarchism, and his role in the Libertarian Circle. Reports that he read Finnegans Wake in this period and comments on his publication in the Ark and elsewhere.

For 1946, details Duncan's affair with Richard Moore, his thoughts on love and sex, and his return to Berkeley. Examines his relationship to Josephine Miles and his affair with an unspecified woman. Provides a section of the original version of "An Apollonian Elegy" and some of Duncan's unpublished commentary on the poem. Remarks on his other poetry of the period, especially "Song ['How in the dark the cows lie down']." Depicts the meetings and Duncan's lectures on modern writers at Throckmorton Manor in Berkeley. Relates his relationship to Rasario Jimenez and his writing of "Portrait of Two Women." Comments on his treatment of love, sex, and female and mother figures in "Berkeley Poems." Describes the composition process of and the personal elements in "Heavenly City, Earthly City," finding the coda "an important turning point" for Duncan. Notes sources for his work in H.D. and Edith Sitwell, and mentions Duncan's meeting Spicer.

Chronicles Duncan's relationship to Dick Brown, James Broughton, and Madeline Gleason, as well as Spicer. Recounts the sessions, including poetry readings and "poetry as magic" sessions, at the Hearst Street, "New Athens," house in Berkeley in 1947. Commenting on the role of sex in, and giving sources from Duncan's unpublished "Notes to Medieval Scenes" (see 1986.2, F19.m), provides biographical context for Medieval Scenes. Indicates W.C. Williams's influence on the poems in Medieval Scenes and on "Domestic Scenes," noting his reaction to the latter as well as to "Heavenly City, Earthly City." Outlines Duncan's initial meetings with Olson and his correspondence with and feelings for Pound. Describes his hitchhiking trip across the country and his encounter with Pound, and briefly details his stay in New York.

For 1948, relates Duncan's return to California and his relationship to Hugh O'Neill, Muriel Rukeyser, and especially Janie O'Neill. Records his role in the delivery of and care for Janie's baby, and describes their sexual relationship, speculating on its role in "The Revenant." Details Duncan's competition for poetry awards, providing unpublished references by others for the Bender Award. Notes the events surrounding his honorable mention for the James D. Phelan Award. Details his homosexual relationship to Gerald Ackerman and the composition and biographical background of "The Venice Poem," commenting on the lack of revision; the sources, including Igor Stravinsky and Pound; and the treatment of art and rebirth. Mentions other poetry of the period, noting Pound's influence, and explains Duncan's sense of the "tone leading of vowels," including assonance, in poetry. Lists the classes Duncan took at Berkeley at this time, emphasizing his studies under Ernst Kantorowicz.

The last chapter, treating 1949 and early 1950, covers the dissolution of Duncan's relationship to Ackerman, noting Paul Goodman's part in the breakup. Also treats Duncan's role in The Berkeley Miscellany and, with Spicer and Robin Blaser, in Literary Behavior and the Writers' Conference at Berkeley. Comments on his relationship to Spicer and Jaime de Angulo and his awareness of Allen Ginsberg and other poets later associated with Black Mountain poetry, especially Charles Olson. Discusses his sense of his poetry as "a bridgehead between modernism and tradition." Also notes others' reaction to "The Venice Poem"; comments on 1949.1; provides biographical context for "A Poet's Masque"; and relates the dissolution of "the Berkeley scene."

Records his, Faas's, contacts with Duncan's natural sister, Anne Spaulding, who explained the causes of Duncan's adoption and described his natural family, especially his father, Edward Howard Duncan.

Includes reprints of 1944.1; 1949.1. See also 1984.1.

14   FINKELSTEIN, NORMAN M[ARK]. "Robert Duncan: Poet of the Law." Sagetrieb: A Journal Devoted to Poets in the Pound-H.D.- Williams Tradition 2, no. 1 (Spring):75-88.

Revision of 1980.17, emphasizing Duncan as "a poet of lawfulness," the law being "the measure, in a work of art, of appropriate response to historical exigencies, the recognition, which is itself freedom, of what must be done in the realm of necessity."

15 FREDMAN, STEPHEN [ALBERT]. Poet's Prose: The Crisis in Amer-
    ican Verse. Cambridge: Cambridge University Press, pp. 94–98,
    passim.
        In a revision of "Sentences: Three Works of American Prose
    Poetry" (Ph.D. dissertation, Stanford University, 1980), compares
    Duncan's "The Structure of Rime, I" and "The Museum" to Creeley's
    Presences (with Marisol [New York: Charles Scribner's Sons,
    1976]), finding both involved with process. Feels Duncan is more
    likely to employ "a fiction of language and textuality," and
    claims Creeley avoids the fictive to maintain "the path of
    presence."

16 GRUNDBERG, CARL; PATLER, LOUIS; and THORPE, JOHN. "Student
    Notes from Lectures by Robert Duncan in 1980–81: The Active
    Mode of Composition." Edited by Jim Thorpe. Convivio: A
    Journal of Poetics from New College of California, no. 1,
    pp. 72–94.
        Provides a consolidation of student notes taken at Duncan's
    lectures at the New College of California (San Francisco) in 1980–
    81 in which he discusses creation, the creative process, and the
    emergence of the poem. Duncan mentions the poet's immersion in
    the poem, multiphasic form, and poetics, including the use of
    syllables and the lack of revision. He also comments on his prep-
    aration to write, why he writes, the ordeal of writing, and why he
    teaches poetics.

17 HAMALIAN, LINDA. "Robert Duncan on Kenneth Rexroth."
    Conjunctions: Bi-Annual Volumes of New Writing, no. 4,
    pp. 85–95.
        In this spring 1982 interview, Duncan reminisces about his
    relationship to Rexroth from the early 1940s on. Duncan focuses
    on his similarities to Rexroth in terms of politics and mysticism
    and notes both he and Rexroth related "to history in terms of
    spiritual epochs." Comments on their roles in the San Francisco
    Renaissance, notes Rexroth's appraisal of his poetry, and mentions
    Rexroth's attempts to get him published. Does not feel that
    Rexroth had much influence on his own work, but notes his own
    "sweep of landscape," albeit rare, may owe something to Rexroth.
        Duncan also comments on his feelings about Marianne Moore,
    his reading of French poets and Rexroth, his lack of poetic deco-
    ration, and his soirees in the 1940s.

18 JOHNSON, MARK [ANDREW]. "Passages: Cross-Sections of the
    Universe." Ironwood 11, no. 2 [whole no. 22] [Robert Duncan:
    A Special Issue] (Fall):173–91.
        Discusses poems in the Passages sequence as "discrete enti-
    ties in a complex interrelated whole." Comments on the senses of
    passage in the sequence, notes the ways in which it is composed in
    field composition, and compares it to The Structure of Rime

sequence. Finds sources in Whitehead, especially his ideas of
process, order, and the "interrelatedness of all experience."
Reviews Duncan's emphasis on the present and his use of chance and
discord. Discusses his treatment of the City, the female figure,
the poet, the household, evil, community and order. In "The Architecture: Passages, 9," examines the treatment of the house and
his use of Gustave Stickley's Craftsman Homes (New York: Craftsman Publishing Co., 1909; more recently, Craftsman Homes: Architecture and Furnishing of the American Arts and Crafts Movement
[New York: Dover, 1979]). Also discusses the use of the opening
and closing matrix of words, as well as the treatment of boundaries and of the paintings of Piero de Cosimo and Hieronymus Bosch
in "The Fire: Passages, 13." Mentions the treatment of community
in "The Multiversity: Passages, 21" and the treatment of order
and poetry in "Passages, 31: The Concert (Tribunals)." Provides
a brief bibliography of the sequence (but see 1986.2).

19   . "Robert Duncan's 'momentous inconclusions.'"
Sagetrieb: A Journal Devoted to Poets in the Pound-H.D.-
Williams Tradition 2, no. 2 (Summer-Fall):71-84.
        Discusses Duncan's sense of process, discord, perfection,
and finality in terms of Whitehead's Process and Reality. Notes
the inconclusiveness and lack of closure and stasis in his work.
Also comments on his sense "of the complicated interrelatedness of
all experience" generating "the poem as a field of activity which
is entered by the poet" and the reader. Quotes from an 11
November 1977 recording of Duncan in class and from an unpublished
letter from Duncan on the polysemous nature of parts in a poem, on
his Passages sequence, and on his sense of order. Notes the ways
in which Duncan's work is and is not teleological, and compares
his ideas to Emerson's. Comments on the participatory role re-
quired of Duncan's audience.

20   KENNER, HUGH. "1680 Words on Duncan's Words." Ironwood 11,
no. 2 [whole no. 22] [Robert Duncan: A Special Issue] (Fall):
23-27.
        Noting the "ordinariness of his materials" as well as
Duncan's playfulness and ability to "run with" an idea, comments
on a section of "An Arrangement" and on a few of the scenes in "An
Essay at War." Also mentions his use of etymology and his parallels with Stein.

21   MacINTYRE, WENDY [ELIZABETH]. "Psyche, Christ, and the Poem."
Ironwood 11, no. 2 [whole no. 22] [Robert Duncan: A Special
Issue] (Fall):9-22.
        Discusses Duncan's treatment of love, Rilke, Whitman,
Pindar, Cupid as Eros, and Psyche as a Christ figure in "A Poem
Beginning with a Line by Pindar," outlining his use of Apuleius as
a source. Also comments on his treatment of Eros, Christ, fear,

RD1983

longing, opposition, struggle, despair, poetry and the coming to wholeness of self, and the universe in other poems. Notes the role of love and desire in "An Alternate Life," and details the treatment of "the co-inherence of love and death" and the Christ image in "Epilogos," examining his use of Psyche from Keats's "Ode to Psyche." Points out that Duncan gives himself over to the power of words.

22   MATTHIAS, JOHN. "Robert Duncan and David Jones: Some Affinities." *Ironwood* 11, no. 2 [whole no. 22] [Robert Duncan: A Special Issue] (Fall):140-57.
        Notes that for both Duncan and Jones art is "a gratuitous and intransitive activity which . . . implies also an element of transitivity or sign that is sacramental in its nature. . . ." Points out that Duncan was given his knowledge of the past and of hermetic lore by a "loved voice as a source," especially that of his parents, and comments on his reading and use of Celtic and Christian texts. Refers to Duncan's poetry as a poetry of enactment and his sense of man as a maker, a "homo faber," of play, art, and myth.
        Also discusses his use of his work as referential or at least "made over to the gods." Examines the importance of the hearth, the cave, and the meadow to him, and examines his treatment of Christ and of the feminine, including the muse, the goddess, the mother, and virgin figures. Observes his treatment of Kore as a restorative figure in Bending the Bow, especially in the Passages sequence.

23   MAZZARO, JEROME. "Witnessing: Robert Creeley's 'I.'" *Crazyhorse*, no. 24 (Spring), pp. 59-78.
        Briefly mentions Duncan's influence on Creeley's use of the autobiographical, on his treatment of the self.

24   MOLESWORTH, CHARLES. "Truth and Life and Robert Duncan." *Ironwood* 11, no. 2 [whole no. 22] [Robert Duncan: A Special Issue] (Fall):83-94.
        Examines Duncan's "obscurantism," modernism, symbolism, and "bifocalism." Believes his obscurantism's center is "embodied in his notion of Life as a collection of evolved and evolving forms." Finds his modernism and obscurantism are bound by his "concern with process rather than product" and his "theme of a secret self" as in "My Mother Would Be a Falconress." Notes his "allegiance to premodern modes of writing," specifically "the symbolist doctrine of correspondence," mentioning his sense of the relationship between the spiritual and physical realms.
        Discusses a section of "Narrative Bridges for 'Adam's Way,'" noting Duncan's use of the creation myth. Examines his use of metaphor, finding his "poetry is preoccupied with the maintenance

of a body of central, interrelated metaphors" that are "illustrative of each other" and "supporting some grand scheme of . . .
metaphysical truth" as in "An Interlude." Comments on his treatment of President Johnson in "Up Rising: Passages, 25." Notes
his dislike of the rational, his emphasis on poetry as autonomous,
and his treatment of dance.

25   NICOSIA, GERALD. Memory Babe: A Critical Biography of Jack
      Kerouac. New York: Grove Press, pp. 385, 529, passim.
        Briefly mentions Duncan's assessment of Kerouac's work, and
provides details of their first meeting in 1956.

26   NOEL, DANIEL C. "'Muthos is mouth': Myth as Shamanic Utter-
      ance in Postmodern American Poetry." Journal of the American
      Academy of Religion Studies 49, no. 2 [Art/Literature/Religion:
      Life on the Borders issue]:117-24.
        Using 1968.12, briefly mentions Duncan's use of myth.

27   QUARTERMAIN, PETER. "Duncan, Robert (Edward)." In American
      Writers since 1900. Edited by James Vinson and D.L.
      Kirkpatrick. St. James Reference Guide to American Literature.
      Chicago: St. James Press, pp. 181-84.
        Reprint of 1979.37.

28   RAKOSI, CARL. "A Letter to Robert Duncan." Ironwood 11, no. 2
      [whole no. 22] [Robert Duncan: A Special Issue] (Fall):134-35.
        Rakosi mentions his conversations with Duncan and notes the
quality of song in Duncan's work.

29   RASULA, JED. "Exfoliating Cosmos." Sagetrieb: A Journal
      Devoted to Poets in the Pound-H.D.-Williams Tradition 2, no. 1
      (Spring):34-71.
        Occasionally quotes from Duncan's poetry to illustrate ideas
on the "fabric of life's matter" in the cosmos.

30   REED, SABRINA. "Bounds Out of Bound: Robert Duncan's Poetics
      of Strife." M.A. thesis, Carleton University, 148 pp.
        Examines the role and treatment of strife, including war,
conflict, disruption, order, and disorder in Duncan's poetry.
Feels Duncan believes that "the poem is a carefully crafted organism" that draws inspiration from the language.
        Reviewing a number of specific poems in The Years as
Catches, finds Duncan's "early poetic persona sees himself as a
victim in a struggle over which he has no control," and mentions
the treatment of suffering, mother and women figures, love, and
the "death of the intellect." Notes his use of passive personae
who lack volition and retreat "from a hostile environment." Discusses the treatment of love and war in "A Spring Memorandum:

Fort Knox" and of the dark side of the mind and the "complex workings of the human psyche" in "An African Elegy." Examines his
treatment of the redeemer figure, Christ, and love in "Heavenly
City, Earthly City." Also notes the role of Eurydice and the
"realization that imaginative life begins in our world and not
some other, 'perfect,' existence" in the latter poem. Examines
the treatment of love, art, the creative process, painting, sound,
and "violent change and destruction," as well as the use of the
music metaphor in "The Venice Poem." Explains that Duncan presents different propositions for poetry in this poem, using the
mirror and the rose as metaphors for poetic theories from the
mimetic to the organic.

In "An Essay at War," discusses Duncan's treatment of "two
kinds of war": a coercion, which "has as its object control," and
a strife, which "deliberately breaks up established orders."
Notes the paradox between the design of the poet and the poem's
"inner directive" in the work, as well as his treatment of language, poetry, death, love, perfection, and war, including the
Korean War. Also mentions his use of the hearth images and "the
language of war to describe the poetic process." Chronicles his
treatment of the Vietnam War in other poems from the Passages
sequence. In "Passages, 26: The Soldiers," reviews the treatment
of war and coercion and the use of Ahriman. Mentions his treatment of law in other poems.

Investigates the treatment of authority and of the "poetic
craft and its relationship to its materials" in "Nel Mezzo del
Cammin di Nostra Vita." Feels Duncan is concerned with "the discord in poetry," "the interconnectedness of seemingly disparate
elements," death and resurrection, land and sea, and "disorder
existing within order" in "The Continent." Remarks on Duncan's
sense of the grand collage in the poem.

Discussing his poetics, finds Duncan's linkage of "the creative process to the myth of Kore . . . to [Sir Charles Scott]
Sherrington's concept of the cell [from Man on His Nature
(Cambridge: Cambridge University Press, 1940)] . . . stresses the
parallels between creativity in poetry and the natural life processes." Also notes Duncan's use of Darwin to propose a sense of
evolving forms and the need for strife. Reviews his use of the
dance image and his sources in Zukofsky, especially in "After
Reading Barely and Widely." Comments on the role of tensions and
contraries in "Bending the Bow," and mentions the treatment of the
jewel, cyclical changes, peace, caves, order, and harmony in "Apprehensions." Compares his poetics to Olson's projective verse,
noting Duncan's use of closed forms.

Examines Duncan's belief in an ordered universe and his
sense of rhyme as correspondence. Comments on a number of individual poems from The Structure of Rime sequence, noting the role
of open and closed forms and of order and disorder in the sequence.

In the Passages sequence, explains his sense of the interconnectedness of all things, of design in the universe, and of man as
a "separate entity" which is "part of an unfolding design." Commenting on a number of individual poems, notes the diversity of
materials in the Passages sequence, as well as the lack of sequen-
tial order and the role of memory.

31   RUDMAN, MARK. "Sometimes a Painful Existing." Ironwood 11,
     no. 2 [whole no. 22] [Robert Duncan: A Special Issue] (Fall):
     159-72.
        Comments on the lack of intention in Duncan's work, and
     mentions the role of process in and the provisional nature of his
     poetry. Examines his search for truth as in Tribunals, noting his
     treatment of the real and of war. Observing his openness to dis-
     tractions, claims Duncan is against "the tyranny of subject mat-
     ter." Believes his work is often too little grounded in the pres-
     ent and places too much weight on a "cultural hierarchy," but
     finds it memorable. Uses examples from the Passages sequence
     throughout.

32   SCHIFFER, REINHOLD. "Robert Duncan." [In Italian.] In I
     contemporanei: Novecento americano. Vol. 2. Edited by
     Elémire Zolla. Rome: Lucarini Editore, pp. 825-38.
        In a translation and expansion of 1980.29, develops the role
     of romanticism, Eros, love, emotion, and homosexuality in Duncan's
     work. Comparing him to Emerson and Whitman, notes that Duncan's
     syncretism extends to the vegetable and mineral worlds, and
     notes sources for his ideas in the Neoplatonists and Pre-
     Socratics. Discovers Manichaeism in his poetry on the Vietnam
     War, noting his treatment of evil. Comments on his sense of art
     being beyond time and on the truth or falsity of his work. Finds
     him a secular poet compared to Levertov, a religious poet. Com-
     pares his sense of composing the poem through messengers to H.D.'s
     sense of the creative process, noting Duncan's emphasis on the
     psychological.

33   STEAD, C.K. "The Swarm of Human Speech?" PN Review 10, no. 3
     [whole no. 35]:23-25.
        Criticizes Duncan at the International Poetry Festival in
     Toronto in May 1981, finding his conversation totalitarian and his
     poetry overly eloquent. Notes the imprecise diction of "Night
     Scenes," claiming Duncan's "words lack reference" due to his lack
     of observation. Comments on his argument with Levertov on polit-
     ical poetry, and compares their work on the Vietnam War, finding
     Duncan's better due to his confidence and "literariness."

34   SYLVESTER, WILLIAM. "Creeley, Duncan, Zukofsky, 1968-: Melody
     Moves the Light." Sagetrieb: A Journal Devoted to Poets in
     the Pound-H.D.-Williams Tradition 2, no. 1 (Spring):97-104.

RD1983

Notes a typical movement in Duncan's poetry: "a gaze, a
long gaze, and then a shift, the movement sometimes repeated."
Also emphasizes the activity of the perception in his poetry,
illustrating with a number of works, especially from the Passages
sequence.

35   TAGGART, JOHN. "Of the Power of the Word." Ironwood 11, no. 2
     [whole no. 22] [Robert Duncan: A Special Issue] (Fall):192-98.
     Finds Duncan a major poet whose poetic "throws everything
into question." Quoting from 1968.12, examines Duncan's sense of
the word, the power of the word, the "word's self," myth, and
Christ as the incarnate word or Logos. Mentions Duncan's acknowledgment of "silence as the final reference" through a "contrived
failure or frustration of statement" and his use of poetry as "a
ground for play."

36   WEINSTEIN, NORMAN. "Beyond 'The Egotistical Sublime': Recon-
     siderations of Identity in Language-Centered Writing." Boxcar:
     Magazine of the Arts, no. 2, pp. 48-51.
     Comments on Duncan's views of personal identity, especially
"the notion of a single unifying personality as the organizing
principle for poetry."

37   WILLBERT, DAVID. "Murther: The Hypocritic and the Poet."
     Bucknell Review 28, no. 2 [Rhetoric, Literature, and Inter-
     pretation issue]:80-94.
     Provides a hypocritical reading of "My Mother Would Be a
Falconress," demonstrating the "interface" between the critic and
the poem. Applies "close reading techniques, psychoanalytic theory, biographical information, and inference" to the poem. Notes
"ambiguous syntactic structures" and the role of myth, and discusses the treatment of sources, origins, "unity and separation," the
mother, union, childhood, and "permission and inhibition." Comments on his use of myth and treatment of the mother figure, including her relationship to language, in other poems.

38   WRIGHT, JAMES. "The Few Poets of England and America." In
     Collected Prose. Edited by Anne Wright. Ann Arbor: Univer-
     sity of Michigan Press, pp. 268-78.
     Reprint of 1961.4.

                              1984

1   ABBOTT, STEVE. Review of Young Robert Duncan: Portrait of the
     Poet as Homosexual in Society, by Ekbert Faas. Poetry Flash:
     The Bay Area's Poetry Calendar and Review, no. 134 (May), pp.
     1, 11.

In this unfavorable review article of 1983.13 corrects a number of biographical errors.

2   ALTIERI, CHARLES. "Dal pensiero simbolista all'immanenza: Il fondamento della poetica americana postmoderna." [In Italian.] Translated by Massimo Pesaresi. In Postmoderno e letteratura: Percorsi e visioni della critica in America. Edited by Peter Carravette and Paolo Spedicato. Studi Bompiani. Milan: Bompiani, pp. 123-60.
        Abridged translation of 1973.3.

3   AUPING, MICHAEL. "Jess: Paste-Ups (and Assemblies), 1951-1983." In Jess: Paste-Ups (and Assemblies), 1951-1983, by Jess [Collins] and Michael Auping. Sarasota, Fla.: John and Mabel Ringling Museum of Art, pp. 10-17.
        In this introduction to an exhibition book, mentions Duncan's influence on Jess's art and their collaborations.

4   BRESLIN, JAMES E.B. From Modern to Contemporary: American Poetry, 1945-1965. Chicago and London: University of Chicago Press, pp. 157-58, passim.
        Briefly mentions Duncan's relationship to and influence on Levertov.

5   CANTWELL, JACQUELINE. "Flashback: Re: David Levi Strauss' 'On Duncan and Zukofsky on Film,' [Poetry Flash] #135, June 1984." Poetry Flash: The Bay Area's Poetry Calendar and Review, no. 136 (July), p. 7.
        Provides a different account of Duncan's reaction to Barrett Watten than 1984.30. See also 1984.14-15, 18-19, 24-25, 27, 29; 1985.52.

6   DONOGHUE, DENIS. Connoisseurs of Chaos: Ideas of Order in Modern American Poetry. 2d ed. New York: Columbia University Press, pp. 49-50.
        Reprint of 1965.2.

7   DUNCAN, ROBERT. "The Museum." In Ground Work: Before the War. New York: New Directions Books, pp. 59-61.
        Reprint of 1972.7.

8   _____. "Preface" to "Dante Études." In Ground Work: Before the War. New York: New Directions Books, p. 94.
        Reprint of 1974.10.

9   _____. "Re Mary Butts." In The Writings and World of Mary Butts: A Conference, The University of California, Davis, February 23rd and 24th, 1984. [Davis, Calif.]: n.p., [pp. 3-4].

RD1984

Duncan briefly mentions his relationship to Seon Givens and his reading of Mary Butts.

10   . "Some Notes on Notation" to Ground Work: Before the
   War. New York: New Directions Books, [pp. ix-xi].
      In these notes, Duncan discusses his sense of silences in
   poetry "as phrases, units in the measure" and his concept of
   rhythm following from the physical, the body. Provides explanation for his notational system in Ground Work: Before the War,
   consisting chiefly of spaces, stanza breaks, punctuation, and
   margins that should be used "for the performance of the reading."

11   . "Structure of Rime, XXVII." In Ground Work: Before
   the War. New York: New Directions Books, pp. 54-55.
      Slight revision of 1969.12.

12 ELLINGHAM, LEWIS. "Chapter 5 [of The Spicer Circle in San
   Francisco, 1956-1965]: The Sunday Afternoon Meetings." Acts,
   no. 3, pp. 89-106.
      Recounts Duncan's role in the Sunday afternoon meetings of a
   poetry workshop from the fall of 1957 through spring 1958. Relies
   on published and unpublished interviews and conversations. Joanne
   Kyger remembers Duncan's reaction to her work. David Meltzer
   remembers an argument between Spicer and Duncan on rhetoric in
   poetry. Harold Dull notes a loss of energy after Duncan stopped
   attending in March 1958. George Stanley recounts Duncan's reactions to the poetry read, notes he "didn't very often disagree
   with Spicer," and recounts what he said about imitation. Also
   records the events given in 1964.5.

13 GLUCK, ROBERT. "Robert Duncan: A Vast, Nervous, Contradic-
   tory, Worldly Life." Advocate (Malibu, Calif.), no. 397
   (26 June):35-40.
      In the introduction and in comments interspersed, mentions
   Duncan's homosexuality, provides a few biographical details, and
   remarks on "The Torso: Passages, 18." In a 1984 taped interview,
   Duncan refers to his homosexual affairs in Berkeley and elsewhere,
   including his contraction of gonorrhea. Duncan also comments on
   his sense of eros, his marriage to Marjorie McKee, his reason for
   choosing a domestic life with Jess, and his decision to wait fifteen years between publishing collections.

14 GRAY, DARRELL. "Flashback: Re: Response to Ron Silliman's
   Letter in [Poetry Flash] #136, Responding to David Levi
   Strauss' 'On Duncan and Zukofsky on Film,' [Poetry Flash] #135,
   June 1984." Poetry Flash: The Bay Area's Poetry Calendar and
   Review, no. 137 (August), p. 7.

In a response to 1984.27, briefly claims to prefer to hear about Zukofsky from Duncan than from Barrett Watten. See also 1984.5, 15, 18-19, 24-25, 29-30; 1985.52.

15 GRUNDBERG, CARL. "Flashback: Re: Response to Ron Silliman's Letter in [Poetry Flash] #136, Responding to David Levi Strauss' 'On Duncan and Zukofsky on Film,' [Poetry Flash] #135, June 1984." Poetry Flash: The Bay Area's Poetry Calendar and Review, no. 138 (September), p. 9.
    In a response to 1984.27, claims Duncan's interruption of Barrett Watten on 8 December 1978 was in keeping with his theory of "returning to the poem rather than our pet theories." See also 1984.5, 14, 18-19, 24-25, 29-30; 1985.52.

16 HASS, ROBERT. "Some Notes on the San Francisco Bay Area As a Culture Region: A Memoir." In Twentieth Century Pleasures: Prose on Poetry. New York: Ecco Press, pp. 214-25.
    Very briefly mentions Duncan's interest in the Cathars.

17 HELLER, MICHAEL. "The True Epithalamium." Sagetrieb: A Journal Devoted to Poets in the Pound-H.D.-Williams Tradition 3, no. 1 (Spring):77-88.
    Provides a reading of "A Poem Beginning with a Line by Pindar" as an epithalamium, as a Pindaric ode depicting victory over trials, and as "a disquisition on love, as an investigation of love's modalities." Examines the role of myth in the poem, especially of Psyche and Venus and the separation and the return of Psyche to Cupid as "a journey to self-knowledge" toward love. Outlines Duncan's use of puns "not only of words, but of times, myths, poems, and painting." Investigates the "poetic space" of the poem, and compares Duncan's "poetic activity" to everyday life and logic. Notes the treatment of the political, love, and knowledge, as well as the role of the dance in the poem. In the last section, finds a "participatory cosmos" in which the past and present, "micro and macro dimensions, notions of individuality and generality co-exist."

18 JENKINS, JOYCE. "Some Information." Poetry Flash: The Bay Area's Poetry Calendar and Review, no. 136 (July), pp. 2-3.
    Apologizes to Barrett Watten for the "too impassioned" account of 1984.29. See also 1984.5, 14-15, 19, 24-25, 27, 30; 1985.52.

19 JOHNSTON, ALASTAIR [M.]. "Flashback: Re: Response to Ron Silliman's Letter in [Poetry Flash] #136, Responding to David Levi Strauss' 'On Duncan and Zukofsky on Film,' [Poetry Flash] #135, June 1984." Poetry Flash: The Bay Area's Poetry Calendar and Review, no. 137 (August), p. 7.

RD1984

In a response to 1984.27, briefly claims that Duncan's reminiscence of Zukofsky "is infinitely more illuminating than [Barrett] Watten's semi-logical exegesis." See also 1984.5, 14-15, 18, 24-25, 29-30; 1985.52.

20   MEACHEN, CLIVE. "Robert Duncan: 'To complete his mind.'" In *Modern American Poetry*. Edited by R.W. (Herbie) Butterfield. London: Vision Press; Totowa, N.J.: Barnes & Noble Books, pp. 204-17.
      Mentions Duncan's sense of language, the openness and inclu-siveness of his poetry, and his treatment of destruction, apoca-lypse, God, and renewal. Notes Pound's influence, and comments on Duncan's poems as "poetic events" and on Duncan as an inspired poet. Discusses the lack of linearity in his poetry and how it, with "energies of the primary imagination," can possess the reader.

21   NORRIS, KEN[NETH WAYNE]. *The Little Magazine in Canada, 1925-80: Its Role in the Development of Modernism and Post-Modernism in Canadian Poetry*. Toronto: ECW Press, pp. 108-10, 120, passim.
      Revision of 1980.25.

22   O'BRIEN, GEOFFREY. Review of *Ground Work: Before the War*. *Village Voice Literary Supplement*, no. 30 (November), p. 5.
      In this favorable review, finds Duncan out of step with the times, "a rhapsodist intent on ecstasies which those around him would rather deconstruct," but notes the musical quality and the "mysterious wholeness" of the poetry.

23   RASULA, JED. "Placing *Pieces*." In *Robert Creeley: the Poet's Workshop*. Edited by Carroll F. Terrell. The Poet's Workshop Series. Orono, Maine: University of Maine at Orono, National Poetry Foundation, pp. 163-69.
      Reprint of 1982.23.

24   RODEFER, STEPHEN. "Corrections." *Poetry Flash: The Bay Area's Poetry Calendar and Review*, no. 137 (August), p. 7.
      Revision of 1984.25. See also 1984.5, 14-15, 18-19, 27, 29-30; 1985.52.

25   _____. "Flashback: Re: David Levi Strauss' 'On Duncan and Zukofsky on Film,' [*Poetry Flash*] #135, June 1984." *Poetry Flash: The Bay Area's Poetry Calendar and Review*, no. 136 (July), p. 7.
      Provides a further account of Duncan's reaction to Barrett Watten than 1984.29. Revised: 1984.24. See also 1984.5, 14-15, 18-19, 27, 30; 1985.52.

26   SHARMA, K.K. "Poetry as an 'Exposed, Open Form': Robert
      Duncan's Poetics." Indian Journal of American Studies 14, no.
      1 (January):67-75.
            Providing no new information or original insight, para-
      phrases Duncan's prose, especially 1966.10, on the poet's link
      with the cosmos and God; on truth, music, and language in poetry;
      and on the creative process.

27   SILLIMAN, RON. "Flashback: Re: David Levi Strauss' 'On
      Duncan and Zukofsky on Film,' [Poetry Flash] #135, June 1984."
      Poetry Flash: The Bay Area's Poetry Calendar and Review, no.
      136 (July), p. 7.
            Provides a different account of Duncan's reaction to Barrett
      Watten than 1984.30. See also 1984.5, 14-15, 18-19, 24-25, 29;
      1985.52.

28   SORRENTINO, GILBERT. "Black Mountaineering." In Something
      Said. San Francisco: North Point Press, pp. 242-51.
            Reprint of 1970.18.

29   STRAUSS, DAVID LEVI. "Flashback: Re: Response to Ron
      Silliman's Letter in [Poetry Flash] #136, Responding to David
      Levi Strauss' 'On Duncan and Zukofsky on Film,' [Poetry Flash]
      #135, June 1984." Poetry Flash: The Bay Area's Poetry
      Calendar and Review, no. 137 (August), pp. 3, 7.
            Claims the attacks on Duncan in 1984.27 were "pointless and
      absurd" since Duncan's action toward Barrett Watten on 8 December
      1978 cannot be considered censorship. Also comments on Duncan's
      teaching methods at the New College of California. See also
      1984.5, 14-15, 18-19, 24-25, 30; 1985.52.

30   _____. "On Duncan and Zukofsky on Film: Traces Now and
      Then." Poetry Flash: The Bay Area's Poetry Calendar and
      Review, no. 135 (June), pp. 1, 5, 10.
            Discusses the original filming of Duncan in 1965 and 1966
      for National Educational Television's "USA: Poetry" series and
      the recent reconstruction of the film's outtakes. Also discusses
      Duncan's introduction to a showing of a Zukofsky film on 8
      December 1978 and his usurpation of the podium during Barrett
      Watten's lecture on Zukofsky. See also 1984.5, 14-15, 18-19, 24-
      25, 27, 29; 1985.52.

31   [STRAUSS, DAVID LEVI.] "Preface to Chapter 5 of Lewis
      Ellingham's Projected Book, The Spicer Circle in San Francisco,
      1956-1965." Acts, no. 3, [p. 88].
            In this preface to 1984.12, mentions the controversies be-
      tween poets in San Francisco in the late 1950s that Duncan gave
      witness to in As Testimony (1964.5).

32   WAGGONER, HYATT H[OWE]. American Poets: From the Puritans to
      the Present. Rev. ed. Baton Rouge and London: Louisiana
      State University Press, p. 600.
          Briefly notes Duncan's sense of religion and myth and his
      use of the occult. Compares him to Whitman.

33   WILLIAMSON, ALAN. Introspection and Contemporary Poetry.
      Cambridge, Mass.: Harvard University Press, pp. 9-10.
          Comments on Duncan's argument with Macha Lewis Rosenthal in
      1972.10. Briefly mentions that in Duncan's poetry "there are, as
      in psychoanalysis, no wrong turnings."

                              1985

1   BARONE, DENNIS. "Nothing but Doors: An Interview with Robert
      Kelly." Credences: A Journal of Twentieth Century Poetry and
      Poetics, n.s. 3, no. 3 (Fall):100-122.
          Kelly provides information concerning Duncan's withdrawal of
      his poetry from A Controversy of Poets: An Anthology of Contempo-
      rary American Poetry, ed. Paris Leary and Robert Kelly (Garden
      City, N.Y.: Doubleday & Co., Anchor Books, 1965).

2   BERNSTEIN, MICHAEL ANDRÉ, and HATLEN, BURTON. "Interview with
      Robert Duncan." Sagetrieb: A Journal Devoted to Poets in the
      Pound-H.D.-Williams Tradition 4, nos. 2-3 [Robert Duncan Spe-
      cial Issue] (Fall-Winter):87-135.
          In this 7 January 1985 interview, Duncan discusses publish-
      ing in Origin and the Black Mountain Review and his relationship
      to and/or sense of Olson, Creeley, Corman, Lowell, and Levertov,
      including his quarrel with Levertov. Recounts his reading over
      the years, especially of Freud, Pound, Crane, Joyce, Sitwell,
      Stein, and Homer. Gives his impressions of a number of younger
      poets, noting the ones he has made use of in his work. Discusses
      his relationship to and sense of W.C. Williams, Pound, D.H.
      Lawrence, and Zukofsky, touching upon his correspondence with
      Zukofsky. Also notes Rexroth's directions to him, and claims
      imitating Stein helped him write of his homosexuality and love.
      Remarks on the influence of Milton on his use of rhyme, and com-
      ments on Pound and Spicer's reaction to "The Venice Poem."
          Duncan considers his own use of the poetic line, finding
      sources in W.C. Williams and Eigner, especially for the Passages
      sequence. Claims his line is "tolerant of polyphony" and is,
      unlike the line of Pound and Blake, one of compromise so that
      "every phrase can be compromised by the coexistence of other
      phrases." Explains his sense of the collagist method and its use
      in Caesar's Gate, and points out his original intentions with "The
      Venice Poem" and Heavenly City, Earthly City. Notes he has not
      returned to the burlesque since Faust Foutu. Comments on the

                              364

listing in "For a Muse Meant" and writing "Dante Études" and "Passages, 35: Before the Judgment (Tribunals)." Occasionally mentions his plans for and the writing of Ground Work II: In the Dark. Considers the meaning of the subtitle of Ground Work: Before the War, referring to his necessity to write of war.

Indicates Olson called him a humanist, observing how that is so. Claims he threatened to pull out of The New American Poetry, 1945-1960, ed. Donald Merriam Allen (New York: Grove Press, 1960), if Allen did not include Larry Eigner. Provides biographical details, occasionally mentioning teaching and working on Occident. Notes his desire for strangeness in poetry; and claims he goes "to religion to find out the condition of man," not to promote a theology. Discusses his dislike of totalitarianism and his desire for a pluralism, noting conflicts with Olson, Patchen, Pound, and Stein on this.

In a prefatory note, Hatlen describes the occasion of the interview. Bernstein notes Duncan's view that modernism is a continuation of romanticism.

3   BERNSTEIN, MICHAEL ANDRÉ. "Robert Duncan: Talent and the Individual Tradition." Sagetrieb: A Journal Devoted to Poets in the Pound-H.D.-Williams Tradition 4, nos. 2-3 [Robert Duncan Special Issue] (Fall-Winter):177-90.
Believes "the tradition Duncan continues never existed before him, and its creation increasingly begins to seem like the central poem of his imagination," especially since it includes such different poets as Pound and Stevens. Examines how Duncan breaks "Poundian taboos" by emphasizing continuities between romanticism and modernism, by using iambic meters and forms distrusted by Pound as in A Seventeenth Century Suite, and by using Mallarmé as an influence. Also contrasts their poetics, "Duncan's poem-as-grand-collage and Pound's ideogram," finding basic differences in Duncan's emphasis on accident compared to intention and on the process of thinking compared to representation of thought. Believes Duncan lacks a sense of the tragic because he does not, like Pound, fail to achieve a previously conceived project.

4   BOWERING, GEORGE. Craft Slices. Ottawa, Ontario: Oberon Press, pp. 30-36, 86.
In a revision of an unlocated, previously published essay, Bowering outlines his and other young Vancouver poets' initial contacts with Duncan and Duncan's influence on their writing. Also comments on Duncan's occultism, hermeticism, and poetry against the Vietnam War.

5   BURNETT, GARY. "Robert Duncan's Ground Work." Jimmy and Lucy's House of "K," no. 3 (January), pp. 32-35.
Noting the importance of a sense of origin to Duncan, finds the idea of origin and extension in the titles of his collections,

RD1985

including Ground Work: Before the War. Also comments on his
sense of language and the role of derivations in his work.

6   BUTTERICK, GEORGE F. "'Seraphic predator.'" Brick, no. 25
     (Fall), pp. 13-16.
        Reprint of 1985.7.

7   _____. "'Seraphic predator.'" Poetry Flash: The Bay Area's
     Poetry Calendar and Review, no. 143 (February), pp. 1, 3-4.
        In a lengthy, favorable review of Duncan's Ground Work:
     Before the War, mentions Duncan's "grandiloquence of purpose," his
     use of rhyme and assonance, and his treatment of war and language,
     and speculates on the meaning of the subtitle. Comments on a
     number of poems, and discusses "Santa Cruz Propositions."
     Reprinted: 1985.6. Revised and expanded: 1985.8.

8   _____. "'Seraphic predator': A First Reading of Robert
     Duncan's Ground Work." Sagetrieb: A Journal Devoted to Poets
     in the Pound-H.D.-Williams Tradition 4, nos. 2-3 [Robert Duncan
     Special Issue] (Fall-Winter):273-83.
        In a revision and substantive expansion of 1985.7 on Ground
     Work: Before the War, comments on "The Museum," "The Missionaries
     [Passages]," and "Circulations of the Song." Detects some failed
     poems such as A Seventeenth Century Suite in which Duncan's
     "embroidered strain" becomes an end unto itself, and comments on
     his use of puns, associations, and diction.

9   CARPENTER, JOHN. "Ground Work: Before the War." In Magill's
     Literary Annual, 1985. Vol. 1. Edited by Frank N. Magill.
     Englewood Cliffs, N.J.: Salem Press, pp. 329-33.
        In Ground Work: Before the War, discusses Duncan's use of
     myth, often overshadowing the quotidian; his references to and
     sources in Pound; and his treatment of the contemporary world,
     war, and destruction, indicating an "appetite" for condemnation.
     Finds Duncan an heir of the modernists in his erudition and use of
     the archaic.

10   CARTER, STEVEN MICHAEL. "Epistemological Models Shared by
     American Projectivist Poetry and Quantum Physics." Ph.D. dis-
     sertation, University of Arizona, pp. vii-viii, 86-96, 102-18,
     129-30, 134-35, passim.
        Finding projectivist verse shares epistemological assump-
     tions with quantum physics, notes Duncan's treatment of science
     and discusses his attempt to write poetry that "'follow[s] the
     primary processes' of life." Examines his aperiodic structure,
     breaking up temporality and grammar, and his emphasis on a process
     poetics. Details his belief in the "synthesis between the poet
     and the physical cosmos," between his "personal and cosmic iden-
     tity." Discusses a number of poems as self-reflexive: "At the

Loom: Passages, 2," mentioning its treatment of poetry and the
composition process; "The Collage: Passages, 6," noting its duality and its commentary on its own language; and "Spelling: Passages, 15," mentioning it as performance, both "the dancer and the
dance." Finds parallels between Duncan and Lucretius, and comments on other poems, notably "A Poem Beginning with a Line by
Pindar" and "Chords: Passages, 14." Notes how the reader is
asked to become a "participant-observer" in Duncan's poetry. See
Dissertation Abstracts International 46 (1985):980A.

11   COHN, JACK R., and O'DONNELL, THOMAS J. "'The Poetry of Un-
      evenness': An Interview with Robert Duncan." Credences: A
      Journal of Twentieth Century Poetry and Poetics, n.s. 3, no. 2
      (Spring):91-111.
          In this interview (probably from 1976) which covers some of
      the same ground as 1980.5, Duncan discusses the complexity of his
      poetry for the reader, his sense of language, his mysticism, and
      1974.24, especially concerning a misreading of "The Multiversity:
      Passages, 21." Duncan also discusses the composition of "Up
      Rising: Passages, 25" and, especially, "Often I Am Permitted to
      Return to a Meadow," reading from earlier versions, providing
      references for the female figures, mentioning his use of the
      Zohar, and commenting on the poem's Platonism. Duncan mentions
      his distrust of a purpose or plan in composing the Passages se-
      quence and his treatment or use of others in his poetry, including
      Chancellor Edward William Strong, Adlai Ewing Stevenson (1900-
      1965), Pierre Teilhard de Chardin, Victor-Marie Hugo, and Jakob
      Böhme. Duncan also comments on his prefaces, his use of homonyms,
      and his treatment of war, lions, and doors. Mentions his sense of
      writing a book as an artistic whole.

12   DAVIDSON, [ROBERT] MICHAEL. "A Felt Architectonics of the
      Numinous: Robert Duncan's Ground Work." Sulfur: A Literary
      Tri-Quarterly of the Whole Art 4, no. 3 [misnumbered as no. 2]
      [whole no. 12]:133-39.
          In this lengthy, favorable review of Ground Work: Before
      the War, notes the printing of the volume in typescript, the cover
      illustration by Jess, and Duncan's belief that his poems give
      testimony to a greater Poetry. Discusses Duncan's treatment of
      war, noting its relationship to love as in the Passages sequence.
      Also mentions Duncan's composition of books as entities, and com-
      ments on his use of works by others in long poems, notably "Dante
      Études," discussing the rhythm and rhyme in "The Household"
      section.

13   ____. "Notes beyond the 'Notes': Wallace Stevens and Con-
      temporary Poetics." In Wallace Stevens: The Poetics of
      Modernism. Edited by Albert [J.] Gelpi. Cambridge Studies

RD1985

in American Literature and Culture, edited by Albert [J.]
Gelpi. Cambridge: Cambridge University Press, pp. 141-60.
        Briefly claims Duncan's "Often I Am Permitted to Return to a
Meadow" parallels Stevens's use of poetry to explore an "alien
landscape whose outlines are familiar but whose terms of order and
coherence remain obscure."

14   ____. "Robert Duncan." In The Beats: Literary Bohemians in
        Postwar America. Part 1, A-L. Edited by Ann Charters. Dic-
        tionary of Literary Biography, vol. 16. Detroit: Gale Re-
        search Co., Bruccoli Clark Book, pp. 169-80.
        Provides an expanded version of 1980.4's bibliography and a
brief biographical summary, echoing 1980.4. Notes Duncan's cor-
respondences with Beat poets and his relationship to Rexroth and
Jess. Comments on a number of works, especially "Passage over
Water," "The Song of the Borderguard," Caesar's Gate, Medieval
Scenes, "Apprehensions," and The Structure of Rime sequence. Also
remarks on the Passages sequence, especially "Up Rising:
Passages, 25." Mentions the musical structure of "The Venice
Poem," the sense of permission in The Opening of the Field, and
the treatment of poets and presidents in "A Poem Beginning with a
Line by Pindar." Refers to the range of styles in Roots and
Branches and the title of Bending the Bow.

15   DOYLE, CHARLES. "Duncan, Robert (Edward)." In Contemporary
        Poets. Edited by James Vinson and D.L. Kirkpatrick. 4th ed.
        New York: St. Martin's Press, pp. 210-12.
        Reprint of 1980.10 with an updated bibliography.

16   DUNCAN, ROBERT. "The Delirium of Meaning." In The Sin of the
        Book: Edmond Jabès. Edited by Eric Gould. Lincoln and
        London: University of Nebraska Press, pp. 207-26.
        Duncan mentions reading Jabès and the associations with
others he has read. Also notes that reading French is for him,
like writing poetry, a charting of a voice from beyond.

17   ____. Fictive Certainties. New York: New Directions,
        234 pp.
        Includes reprints of 1955.1; 1956.3; 1961.1; 1965.7;
1966.10; 1968.12; 1969.9; 1970.7; 1983.7, 11.

18   ____. "The H.D. Book, Book II: Chapter 6." Southern Review,
        n.s. 21, no. 1 (January):26-48.
        Duncan occasionally mentions his intention in writing The
H.D. Book and comments on his reader. The editor provides the
publication record of The H.D. Book to date.

19   ____. "H.D.'s Challenge." Poesis: A Journal of Criticism 6,
        nos. 3-4:21-34.

Duncan mentions conversations with H.D. and others, The H.D. Book and correspondences between him and H.D. Mentions the role of hermeticism in his upbringing, and notes he is frustrated with current politics and bored with hating presidents.

20 _____. "The Homosexual in Society." Jimmy and Lucy's House of "K," no. 3 (January), pp. 51–69.

Duncan adds an introduction, a postscript, and footnotes to a slightly revised version of 1944.1. In the introduction, analyzes his feelings in and for the original essay. In the postscript, notes his subsequent sense of community with artists, homosexuals, and friends.

In footnotes that were written in 1959, Duncan provides a portion of John Crowe Ransom's letter to him rejecting the previously accepted "An African Elegy" from publication in Kenyon Review; notes his search through "gnostic and cabalistic speculation for a more diverse order"; and comments on his own homosexuality. Duncan also provides a portion of the 1945 letter from an unnamed homosexual poet asking him not to publish an essay on the sexuality in his, the poet's, work.

21 _____. "'Where as giant kings we gathered': Some Letters from Robert Duncan to William Everson, 1940 and After." Edited by Lee Bartlett. Sagetrieb: A Journal Devoted to Poets in the Pound-H.D.-Williams Tradition 4, nos. 2–3 [Robert Duncan Special Issue] (Fall–Winter):137–74.

In his letters from May 1940 to June 1942, Duncan refers to his role in Ritual and Experimental Review, requesting work from Everson. Comments on his relationship to Virginia Admiral and a few others. Notes correspondence with and learning from Sanders Russell, and provides a portion of a letter to him from Russell. Mentions his reaction to Everson's work. Provides biographical details from the period about living in New York, visiting his mother in 1941, and going back to school and looking for work in 1942. Also explains his sense of being persecuted by the state and his political and religious beliefs, including beliefs in anarchism and reincarnation.

Comments on a number of his own poems, especially "The Protestants (Canto One)," "From 'Toward the Shaman,'" "We Have Forgotten Venus," "Hamlet: A Draft of the Prologue," "Persephone," and "Ritual," noting his intentions, how the poems were written, what he learned from them, and/or his plans for their publication. Explains references in "The Gestation," and provides versions, including early versions, of a few poems including "The Gestation," "Hamlet: A Draft of the Prologue" and "An African Elegy." Discusses writing as a serious responsibility and other writers as his guides. Mentions his sense of obeying his own "law of . . . individual integrity" as he becomes "lost in the Shaman when writing."

RD1985

In his 21 September 1960 letter, Duncan writes of his and
Everson's earlier correspondence and mentions Everson's reaction
to his early work. Speaks of his care "for each immediate syllable," the "tone leading of vowels," and his use of alliteration.
Also compares his own beliefs to Everson's.

In his introduction, Bartlett provides a few biographical
details concerning Duncan and Everson's correspondence. In the
appendix, Bartlett presents Duncan's 7 November 1948 letter in
support of Everson's application for a Guggenheim Fellowship.
Also provides a program for a 1 March 1959 reading by Duncan at
the Poetry Center in San Francisco, which includes a list of poems
to be read and a lengthy prose statement by Duncan in which Duncan
claims to dislike the title of a "first-rate poet"; comments on
his sense of a poet being in the service of the divine, of Poetry;
and discusses his lifelong quest for an "Other life," a spiritual
world, through poetry.

22   EIGNER, LARRY. "Postcard to Thomas Parkinson." Jimmy and
     Lucy's House of "K," no. 5 (November), p. 20.
     Noting Duncan's influence on him, Eigner expresses pleasure
that Duncan was given the National Poetry Award.

23   ELLINGHAM, LEWIS. "From The Spicer Circle: An Excerpt from
     Chapter 18: Conflicts." Jimmy and Lucy's House of "K," no. 4
     (June), pp. 61–68.
     Provides 5 June and 12 June 1962 letters from Duncan to
Spicer in which Duncan comments on reading Spicer, regrets
Spicer's "opposition" to his work and to Jess, declines an invitation to read at Katie's "Bourbon Street" bar, comments on
Ellingham, and mentions a revision of "Forced Lines" and the
completion of "A New Poem (for Jack Spicer)." In a 29 August 1962
letter to Robin Blaser, Duncan mentions a 28 August dinner reception for Spicer and the termination of their friendship. In an
interview, Duncan reminisces about this reception.
     Ellingham discusses the relationship of Duncan to Spicer in
1962, especially their dispute, mentions his own relationship to
Duncan and Duncan's distrust of him, and briefly notes Spicer's
view of Duncan's collection of art.

24   _____. "From The Spicer Circle: An Excerpt from Chapter 4:
     Territories." Jimmy and Lucy's House of "K," no. 3 (January),
     pp. 72–74.
     Describes, with the help of an interview with Duncan,
Olson's lecture at Duncan's house in February 1957, noting Olson's
relationship to Spicer. Provides biographical details.

25   ESBJORNSON, CARL DANIEL. "Hunting Duncan: Caesar's Gate and
     Robert Duncan's Poetics of Risk." Ph.D. dissertation, Univer-
     sity of Iowa, 347 pp.

370

Provides a "serial essay" on Duncan's Caesar's Gate but also comments on many poems from other volumes. Finds Duncan's poetry focused on "self-making" within "a larger continuity of things," noting Duncan's sense, then, of reissuing the book as a rereading of the self and commenting on the reader's participatory role in this reading of the self. Discusses Duncan's sense that the poet's forms for self-deception and concealment are, as in Caesar's Gate, revealing. Also discusses Duncan's sense of poetry as process, noting sources in Whitehead, and his use of a "deconstructive poetics." Mentions his sources in and parallels to Olson, Dante, Eliot, and Samuel Beckett, and notes his use of bee mythology.

Esbjornson includes an edited series of letters that he wrote to Sherman Paul from June to October 1982 in which he comments on Duncan's work, including Duncan's treatment of language and use of the net motif. Discusses "A Storm of White," emphasizing its process and treatment of "the self-creating universe." Notes Duncan's use of Dante and his treatment of love in the last poems of The Opening of the Field, especially "Out of the Black." Notes his faith in the regenerative power of the self and language, and compares his spontaneity to the spoken art of David Antin, illustrating with "Epilogos." Finds Duncan "trapped in a pattern of continual estrangement and momentary self-fulfillment," using "Cyparissus" and "Structure of Rime, XX" as examples. Occasionally mentions "The Fire: Passages, 13" in these letters and elsewhere.

Continually commenting on the prefaces to Caesar's Gate, especially 1972.10 and mentioning 1967.12, notes Duncan's choice to present the facile and pretentious posturing in the volume since the poems are ultimately a "dis-closure of his true needs as a poet." Finds Caesar's Gate "emblematic of the poet's desolation and psychic dismemberment" as the poems "enact the struggle of the duende with the creator," finding numerous sources in and correspondences to Federico García Lorca. Also mentions Duncan's sense that rhyme is an awareness of correspondences, and that the poem is "the made place of the mind." Comments on the role of hell in the volume as "an actual place of the soul's habitation," as a "psychic underworld," noting Duncan's sense of being "decentered."

In "Four Poems as a Night Song," discusses Duncan's "identification with Lorca" and the "tension between creativity and impasse." Also examines the treatment of form, the creative process, love, homosexuality, and the self entering a "psychic void" in the poem. Notes the sources in Lorca, the treatment of the city, and the role of rage in "Aurora Rose." Touches on the "artistic impasse" of "The Second Night in the Week." Mentions the treatment of love and lust and the role of self-deception in "Processionals I" and "Processionals II." Comments on the

demon lover in "An Incubus." Notes the treatment of love's relationship to bestial rage in "Tears of St. Francis" and the treatment of corrupted vision in this and in "Eyesight, I" and
"Eyesight, II," mentioning the role of the worm in the latter two
poems. In "Upon Another Shore of Hell," mentions the treatment of
Hell and the parallels to Dante.

Notes Duncan's "attempt to forget the true self by merely
imagining new beginnings" in "Bon Voyage!" Discusses the treatment of love, memory, and youth, as well as the role of statues
and the attempt to "re-situate the self" in "Goodbye to Youth."
Mentions how this poem corresponds to "Heavenly City, Earthly
City," with the latter's use of myth and treatment of love, lust,
anger, and hate. In "H.M.S. Bearskin," notes Duncan's treatment
of poetry, homosexuality, and the New York social scene, and comments on his use of satire and a persona to conceal the self.
Also mentions the role of the butterfly and worm in this poem, and
notes sources or possible sources in Mina Loy, Pound, H.D., and
Whitman.

Focuses on the visionary quality and the prophetic voice,
and notes the role of images and Peggy Linnet, and the use of the
"Eyesight" poems in "Forms within Forms." Also mentions the
treatment of survival in this poem, and finds correspondences to
the Passages sequence's treatment of evil and call for a new
humanness. In "What Is It You Have Come to Tell Me, García
Lorca?" discusses his treatment of Lorca and tradition, his use of
the bee mythos and animal images, and his treatment of homosexuality and poetry. Discusses the treatment of truth and love in "The
Voyage of the Poet into the Land of the Dead," noting the sources
in Arthur Rimbaud here as well as in "From 'A Season in Hell.'"
Comments on the latter's treatment of "unfulfilled expression" and
language. In "At Home in Eden" notes the treatment of corruption
and innocence, and in "The Conqueror's Song" notes the treatment
of rage. Also comments on the last poems and fragments in
Caesar's Gate, focusing on "See the Stone Lions cry." Discusses
the treatment of youth, despair, and desolation in "Despair in
Being Tedious," noting this poem's relationship to "Passages, 31:
The Concert (Tribunals)."

A small section is revised as 1985.26. A few brief sections
are revised: 1987.8. See Dissertation Abstracts International 46
(1985):1626A.

26 ESBJORNSON, CARL D[ANIEL]. "Tracking the Soul's Truth: Robert
    Duncan's Revisioning of the Self in Caesar's Gate." Sagetrieb:
    A Journal Devoted to Poets in the Pound-H.D.-Williams Tradition
    4, nos. 2-3 [Robert Duncan Special Issue] (Fall-Winter):257-72.
        An abridgment and revision of 1985.25, focusing on the 1972
    republication of Caesar's Gate as a rereading of the self and on
    the discussion of "H.M.S. Bearskin."

27   FINKELSTEIN, NORMAN [MARK]. "'Princely manipulations of the
     real' or 'A noise in the head of the prince': Duncan and
     Spicer on Poetic Composition." Sagetrieb: A Journal Devoted
     to Poets in the Pound-H.D.-Williams Tradition 4, nos. 2-3
     [Robert Duncan Special Issue] (Fall-Winter):209-23.
          Discusses Duncan's sense of inspiration and poetic composi-
     tion, comparing it to Spicer's. Focuses on Duncan's sense of
     form, order, and coherence which complements his "Utopian sense of
     openness and possibility" and his use of open form. Feels his
     best work, such as "Circulations of the Song," "implicitly tran-
     scends the open/closed dichotomy." Comments on his sense of
     futurity and mentions the lack of a distinct border between his
     separate poems and volumes. Finds this lack of separation due to
     his sense of a poem as a part of a greater "Poetry" or "grand
     collage," noting the difficulty the New Critical approach has with
     Duncan's poetry.

28   GARDNER, THOMAS [MICHAEL]. "'Where we are': A Reading of
     Passages, 1-12." Sagetrieb: A Journal Devoted to Poets in the
     Pound-H.D.-Williams Tradition 4, nos. 2-3 [Robert Duncan Spe-
     cial Issue] (Fall-Winter):285-306.
          In a fairly extensive revision of part of 1982.12, provides
     a fuller discussion of "Tribal Memories: Passages, 1" and "As in
     the Old Days: Passages, 8."

29   GUNN, THOM. "Homosexuality in Robert Duncan's Poetry." In The
     Occasions of Poetry: Essays in Criticism and Autobiography.
     Expanded ed. San Francisco: North Point Press, pp. 118-34.
          Slight revision of 1979.22.

30   HAMILTON, R.S. "After Strange Gods: Robert Duncan Reading
     Ezra Pound and H.D." Sagetrieb: A Journal Devoted to Poets in
     the Pound-H.D.-Williams Tradition 4, nos. 2-3 [Robert Duncan
     Special Issue] (Fall-Winter):225-40.
          Discusses Duncan's treatment of Pound in The H.D. Book, and
     compares the two. Observes Duncan's affinities with the early
     Pound of The Spirit of Romance and the late Pound of The Pisan
     Cantos, the less authoritarian Pound whose "language outstrips the
     intended meaning." Compares their sense of language, finding
     Duncan emphasizes an autonomous language that can "function as
     Muse," whereas Pound desires an objective language. Also outlines
     their different beliefs concerning Eros, reason, law, love, and
     hate. Finds Duncan locates Hell within the individual, "recog-
     nizes that suffering and pain are an integral part of love," and
     notes the identical nature of the genders and of love and hate,
     whereas Pound locates disruptive forces beyond the individual and
     treats love and hate as dissimilar. Uses a number of sections
     from Duncan's poetry to illustrate.

RD1985

Also notes Duncan's treatment of H.D. in The H.D. Book,
noting her influence on him. Finds them similar in terms of their
dualism, theosophical and Freudian orientations, and views on
language.

31 IRBY, KENNETH. Review of Ground Work: Before the War.
Conjunctions: Bi-Annual Volumes of New Writing, no. 7,
pp. 261–67.
In this lengthy, favorable review, focuses on the structure
of the book, the sequencing of the poems—commenting on many in
the first fifty pages—and the despair of the volume. Finds this
despair and the theme of war always present in Duncan's work, but
claims "Ground Work: Before the War moves . . . from despair and
war to clarion affirmation of Love," but a love "tinged with the
dark."
Feels the volume is "an enactment of a self . . . in all its
complexity" and contradictions, in "texture and counter-texture,"
"strife and eros," "female and male," etc. Finds Duncan "at the
height of his technical power," especially as seen in his use of
the long line and the "remarkable counterpoint of voices and
texts," as in "Santa Cruz Propositions."
Believes that there is yet "no serious extended study of
Duncan's work," and feels even his heirs, as the L=A=N=G=U=A=G=E
poets, have not yet carried their "differences into print." Discusses the title and typology of the book and Duncan's need for
fifteen years between collections.

32 JOHNSON, RONALD. "The Fertile Ground." Jimmy and Lucy's House
of "K," no. 3 (January), pp. 28–32.
In a favorable review of Ground Work: Before the War, mentions Duncan's typographic notation and a number of poems, especially A Seventeenth Century Suite and "Dante Études." Finds the
volume a continuation of Duncan's earlier poetry, and comments on
the subtitle.

33 [JOHNSTON, ALASTAIR M.] A Bibliography of the White Rabbit
Press. Berkeley, Calif.: Poltroon Press in association with
Anacapa Books, pp. 9–12, 17, 20–21, 25, 31–34, 42–43, 49, 54,
85–88, passim.
Provides a bibliographical description of Duncan's books
done by White Rabbit Press: Faust Foutu: A Comic Mask, Act One
of Four Acts; As Testimony: The Poem and the Scene; The Sweetness
and Greatness of Dante's "Divine Comedy": Lecture Given October
27th, 1965 at the Dominican College of San Rafael; and The Cat and
the Blackbird. Also notes Duncan's participation with the press
and Graham Mackintosh, including Duncan's illustration for books
of others. Provides biographical details concerning Duncan's
relationship to and possible influence on Spicer, and relates an

incident concerning a reading by David Meltzer in the late 1950s at Joe Dunn's house.

Also briefly outlines the errors occurring in Duncan's books due to printers.

34 KAMENETZ, RODGER. "Realms of Being: An Interview with Robert Duncan." Southern Review, n.s. 21, no. 1 (January):5-25.

In this 1984 interview, Duncan mentions reading the Kabbalah, Whitman, Gershom Gerard Scholem, and the Zohar, noting the latter's role in Letters. Mentions his use of the Kabbalah and Finnegans Wake and his fascination with father and Adam figures, as in Letters and The Opening of the Field. Notes the role of John Adams in "The Law I Love Is Major Mover" and "Jacob as the deceiver" elsewhere. Comments on his sense of words, law, language, mistake, and examines the relationship between his art and life. Provides his sense of wrestling with syntax or riding a line during the creative process as in The Structure of Rime sequence, noting the role of rhyme in this sequence. Gives biographical details, notably about his parents' religion and his visit to Paris in 1963.

In his introduction and elsewhere, Kamenetz provides the occasion for the interview and Duncan's participation in the Gathering of Poets program at Louisiana State University in 1984. Mentions being in a poetry workshop with Duncan in 1973, what Duncan taught him about Jewish texts, and Duncan's illness that began in 1984. Briefly notes Duncan's use of "Jewish mystical themes" and the Jacob figure in The Structure of Rime sequence.

35 KELLY, ROBERT. Note to the Reader of "Lations: A Suite for Robert Duncan." Sagetrieb: A Journal Devoted to Poets in the Pound-H.D.-Williams Tradition 4, nos. 2-3 [Robert Duncan Special Issue] (Fall-Winter):25.

Kelly mentions his reaction to Duncan's October 1982 seminar at Bard College and writing "Lations: A Suite for Robert Duncan" from "the contexts of [Duncan's] talk."

36 KITAJ, R.B. "After Duncan." Conjunctions: Bi-Annual Volumes of New Writing, no. 8, pp. 19-21.

Kitaj reminisces about Duncan's visit to Paris when Duncan stayed with him and posed for drawings. Describes Duncan's French, and mentions their topics of conversation.

37 KOSTELANETZ, RICHARD. "Poet's Prose." American Book Review 7, no. 3 (March-April):13-14.

In a review of Claims for Poetry, ed. Donald Hall (Ann Arbor: University of Michigan Press, 1982), dislikes "the apparent assumption that the Poet . . . is permitted to deprecate what he does not know" in Duncan's "Ideas of the Meaning of Form" (originally 1961.1).

RD1985

38   KRONICK, JOSEPH G. "Robert Duncan and the Truth that Lies in
     Myth." Sagetrieb: A Journal Devoted to Poets in the Pound-
     H.D.-Williams Tradition 4, nos. 2-3 [Robert Duncan Special
     Issue] (Fall-Winter):191-207.
          Examines Duncan's theory of myth, outlining its relationship
     to his ideas of language, especially the "everlasting Sentence,"
     the grand collage, memory, and the poet as derivative. Compares
     Duncan to Olson and Jung who both placed "man in the center rather
     in the universe as an open field," and notes Duncan's rejection of
     Jungian archetypes. Compares Freud and Duncan especially in their
     emphasis on the everyday, the trivial, and the literal, commenting
     on the lack of distinction between the literal and the figurative
     in Duncan's work. Also considers Duncan's treatment of memory and
     mother figures, including Mnemosyne and the Great Mother, and
     their relationship to language. Claims Duncan believes "the
     mythic origin is an event in language." Examines his sources in
     Whitman, W.C. Williams, and Pound, pointing out references to the
     latter in "At the Loom: Passages, 2." Also comments on "At
     Christmas" and on his use of dance and measure metaphors as in
     "Often I Am Permitted to Return to a Meadow."

39   LEIDER, EMILY. "National Poetry Award to Robert Duncan." San
     Francisco Review of Book 10, nos. 2-3 (Fall-Winter):5.
          Describing the ceremonies at which the National Poetry Award
     was presented to Duncan, in absentia, relates the cause for the
     creation of the award. (A copy of the award is included on pp.
     [353-56] of Sagetrieb: A Journal Devoted to Poets in the Pound-
     H.D.-Williams Tradition 4, nos. 2-3 [Robert Duncan Special Issue]
     [Fall-Winter 1985].)

40   McCLURE, MICHAEL. "The Glade." Sagetrieb: A Journal Devoted
     to Poets in the Pound-H.D.-Williams Tradition 4, nos. 2-3
     [Robert Duncan Special Issue] (Fall-Winter):17-20.
          McClure mentions visiting Duncan, noting Duncan encouraged
     his own reading of Heidegger. Finds Duncan's poetry, like
     Heidegger's thinking, physical, realizing the Being of language.
     Comments on the role of The Structure of Rime sequence in The
     Opening of the Field, mentions listening to Duncan read Letters in
     the 1950s, and relates Duncan's comments on his own Rare Angel.

41   ____. "In Interview." Conjunctions: Bi-Annual Volumes of
     New Writing, no. 7, pp. 69-86.
          In this interview, Duncan mentions his high blood pressure,
     his avoidance of "a program that would govern" a poem, and his
     sense that Ground Work: Before the War is neither sequential or
     simultaneous, discussing the role of chronology and simultaneity
     in his work. Comments on the creative process, including his
     sense of "indwelling" in his work while writing. Mentions struc-
     turalism frees his "poetry of any sense of being literary," and

comments on his reading of Troubadour poets and French poets including Jabès and Baudelaire. Relates his role in the ordering of
The New American Poetry, 1945-1960, ed. Donald Merriam Allen (New
York: Grove Press, 1960), and his role in the Poetics program at
the New College of California. Notes his purpose for not publishing a collection of poetry for fifteen years. Comments on titling
Ground Work: Before the War and Ground Work II: In the Dark, and
claims he rarely deliberately uses biological references in a
poem.
  McClure comments on the organic quality of Duncan's work
compared to the structural foundation of Pound's.

42 [MURRAY, TIMOTHY, et al.]. A Guide to the Modern Literary
    Manuscripts Collection in the Special Collections of the
    Washington University Libraries. St. Louis: Washington
    University Libraries, pp. 37-38, passim.
      Describes Duncan's papers in Washington University Librar-
    ies, including manuscript material and letters. Also lists let-
    ters by Duncan in others' papers.

43 O[LNEY] J[AMES]. "Editorial Note." Southern Review, n.s. 21,
    no. 1 (January):1-3.
      Mentions Duncan's withdrawal of "'Eidolon of the Aion'" from
    the Southern Review, and comments on Duncan's teaching and health.
    Provides a letter from Duncan on the context of "After a Long
    Illness."

44 OPPEN, GEORGE. "An Adequate Vision: A George Oppen Daybook."
    Ironwood 13, no. 2 [whole no. 26] [George Oppen: A Special
    Issue] (Fall):5-31.
      Oppen briefly mentions Duncan, contrasting his own use of
    familiar materials to Duncan's use of the unfamiliar, mentioning
    Duncan's scope, and comparing Duncan to Jung.

45 PALMER, MICHAEL. "Autobiography, Memory and Mechanisms of
    Concealment (Part 1 or One Part)." In Writing/Talks. Edited
    by Bob Perelman. Poetics of the New. Carbondale: Southern
    Illinois University Press, pp. 207-29.
      Reprint of 1981.17.

46 PARKINSON, THOMAS. "The National Poetry Award." Sagetrieb: A
    Journal Devoted to Poets in the Pound-H.D.-Williams Tradition
    4, nos. 2-3 [Robert Duncan Special Issue] (Fall-Winter):309-21.
      Comments on the reception of Ground Work: Before the War
    and Duncan's receipt of the National Poetry Award (a copy of the
    award is included on pp. [353-56] of this issue of Sagetrieb).
    Includes responses by fifty-four poets (pp. 311-21) on "the nature
    and importance of Duncan's poetry." A few, including Wendell
    Berry and William Everson, reminisce about their relationship to

RD1985

Duncan. Others, including Creeley, Rachel Blau DuPlessis, Thomas
Meyer, and Michael Palmer, mention Duncan's influence on them.
Jack Micheline and Carol Jane Bangs mention hearing Duncan read
his own poetry.

47   _____. "Robert Duncan's Ground Work." Southern Review, n.s.
      21, no. 1 (January):52-62.
      In an introduction to Ground Work: Before the War, notes
influences on Duncan, his relationship to modernism, and his sense
of mystery and the accidental. Discusses him as a postmodernist
and a derivative poet. Notes his allusions, his use of the serial
poem, and his typewriter notations. Compares Robert Southwell's
"The Burning Babe" to Duncan's "From Robert Southwell's 'The Burning Babe.'"

48   PERLOFF, MARJORIE [G.]. "The Contemporary of Our Grand-
      children: Pound's Influence." In Ezra Pound among the Poets.
      Edited by George Bornstein. Chicago: University of Chicago
      Press, pp. 195-229.
      Notes the influence of Pound's rhythms on Duncan, and men-
tions Duncan's "own characteristic rhythm," scanning a number of
lines from "A Poem Beginning with a Line by Pindar."

49   RUDMAN, MARK. "'The right chaos, the right vagueness.'" New
      York Times Book Review, 4 August, pp. 13-14.
      In a favorable review of Ground Work: Before the War, notes
Duncan's complexity, sense of tradition and integration, and use
of the long poem.

50   SCHELLING, ANDREW. "Of Maps, Castelli, Warplanes, and Divers
      Other Things That Come 'Before the War.'" Jimmy and Lucy's
      House of "K," no. 3 (January), pp. 40-51.
      Details the importance of Dante and Marco Polo to Duncan's
work, including Caesar's Gate, and compares his work to theirs.
Notes his pluralism, war poetry, and sense of language. Also
mentions his use of history, his typographical notation, and his
difficulties with printers. Especially comments on "Passages, 35:
Before the Judgment (Tribunals)."

51   SILLIMAN, RON. "Waves of Meaning." American Book Review 7,
      no. 6 (September-October):10-12, 23.
      In a favorable review of Duncan's Ground Work: Before the
War, comments on his language and theosophy, as well as the volume's sense of timelessness and its emphasis on the "[o]neness at
the heart of all that is matter, and all that is not." Mentions
the treatment of death and the role of the individual, sound, and
silence in the volume. Notes the importance of "Dante Études" and
A Seventeenth Century Suite to the work, especially commenting on

"From Robert Southwell's 'The Burning Babe'" and "['"A pretty Babe"--that burning Babe']."

52 SLOAN, DE VILLO. "'Crude mechanical access' or 'Crude personism': A Chronicle of One San Francisco Bay Area Poetry War." Sagetrieb: A Journal Devoted to Poets in the Pound-H.D.-Williams Tradition 4, nos. 2-3 [Robert Duncan Special Issue] (Fall-Winter):241-54.
     Compares the L=A=N=G=U=A=G=E poets with the "mainstream poetic avant-garde," represented by Robert Duncan and others, in terms of the inheritance of postmodernism. Feels the basic argument focuses on a political "definition of SELF" opposed to a humanistic personism, associated with Duncan. Quotes from and discusses 1984.30, detailing the subsequent arguments in Poetry Flash, especially 1984.27 and 1984.29. See also 1984.5, 14-15, 18-19, 24-25.

53 von HALLBERG, ROBERT. American Poetry and Culture, 1945-1980. Cambridge, Mass.: Harvard University Press, pp. 143-44, passim.
     Briefly mentions Duncan's indictment of political leaders in his poetry of the 1960s.

54 WEISS, THEODORE. "Theodore Weiss." In Contemporary Authors: Autobiography Series. Vol. 2. Edited by Adele Sarkissian. Detroit: Gale Research Co., pp. 425-50.
     Provides details of a Bard College reading by Duncan in the early 1950s, and finds Duncan a "prodigious talker."

55 WESLING, DONALD. "The Prosodies of Free Verse." In The New Poetries: Poetic Form since Coleridge and Wordsworth. Lewisburg, Pa.: Bucknell University Press; London and Toronto: Associated University Presses, pp. 145-71.
     Revision of 1971.21.

1986

1 BARTLETT, LEE. Talking Poetry: Conversations in the Workshop with Contemporary Poets. Albuquerque: University of New Mexico Press, pp. 75-77, 253-54.
     A number of poets briefly mention Duncan. In their discussions, William Everson comments on his relationship to Duncan, providing a few biographical details, and Diane Wakoski mentions Duncan reading in Buffalo, New York, in the early 1980s.

2 BERTHOLF, ROBERT J[OHN]. Robert Duncan: A Descriptive Bibliography. Santa Rosa, Calif.: Black Sparrow Press, 491 pp.
     A full, detailed, and illustrated descriptive bibliography of books, proof copies, pamphlets, and broadsides, as well as

RD1986

contributions to books and periodicals by Duncan. Also descriptively lists program notes for readings, book blurbs, drawings, Christmas cards, notes for classes and readings, and other publications by Duncan, as well as interviews with Duncan, his letters, proof papers, manuscripts and notebooks, translations into foreign languages, records, and tapes. Also includes secondary items: reviews, articles, books, sections of books, theses, dissertations, and newspaper notices about Duncan, including notices in college-affiliated newspapers, as well as photographs of Duncan and "musical settings" of his work. Provides photographs of Duncan's books, including pages from privately published materials and expurgated and unexpurgated versions of "The Venice Poem."

A number of the sections of notes on individual titles are miniature essays that provide numerous biographical details and quote from advertisements, booksellers' catalogs, and prefatory material from scarce and rare editions. These notes also list variants and provide sections from unpublished letters by Duncan and others concerning the composition, revision, and publication history of individual works and Duncan's relationship to publishers, printers, and others. The titles with lengthy sections of notes include Heavenly City, Earthly City, Fragments of a Disordered Devotion, Faust Foutu, Caesar's Gate: Poems, 1949–1950, Letters, The Opening of the Field, The Years as Catches: First Poems, 1939–1946, A Book of Resemblances: Poems, 1950–1953, and Bending the Bow. The fullest bibliography on Duncan to date.

3 BOLLOBÁS, ENIKO. Tradition and Innovation in American Free Verse: Whitman to Duncan. Budapest: Akadémiai Kiadó, pp. 44, 277–78, 286–307.
    In an expansion and revision of 1983.1, combines some ideas of Duncan on poetics with those of other postmodern poets to create "postulates of grammetrics," which are then applied to the second section of "The Propositions."

4 _____. "Versions of the Whole Earth Catalog: On the Poetry of Robert Duncan and Edward Dorn." In High and Low in American Culture. Edited by Charlotte Kretzoi. Budapest: L. Eötvös University, Department of English, pp. 39–53.
    Mentions Duncan's sense of poetry's "moral commitment" to increase man's awareness, and examines his "attempts at recapturing the lost wholeness of the universe," relating this to his political themes and his attempts "to discover the immanent meanings of the universe." Comments on his treatment of power, law, order, nature, and beginnings.

5 CREELEY, ROBERT. "Preface" to Robert Duncan: A Descriptive Bibliography, by Robert J[ohn] Bertholf. Santa Rosa, Calif.: Black Sparrow Press, 9–10.

Deems Duncan "that poet of my generation who brought the communal world of [poetry] forward again." Mentions his wide-ranging artistic affiliations, and relates him to Whitman.

6   DUNCAN, ROBERT. "['Robert Duncan reading from his poetry and talking about the impact of Romanticism on his poetry']." Edited and transcribed by Gail Kirgis and Norman Weinstein. In When Poetry Really Began, It Practically Included Everything: Selections from Poetry Readings and Talks at the Boise Gallery of Art, 1984-1985. Edited by Gail Kirgis and Norman Weinstein. N.p., pp. 129-49.
       In this transcription from a 12 June 1985 reading with commentary, Duncan briefly mentions the romanticism, rhymes, rhythms, and syntax of his work. Also notes the figure in "Ancient Questions," the sources for "Achilles' Song" and "Circulations of the Song," and the lineation and use of caesurae in "The Torn Cloth." Also mentions others poets as his models and the influence of Stein.

7   ELLINGHAM, LEWIS. "The Death of Jack Spicer." Ironwood 14, no. 2 [whole no. 28] [Listening for the Invisible: Dickinson/ Spicer issue]:152-64.
       Provides biographical details of Duncan's relationship to Spicer in August 1965 when Spicer was dying and after.

8   GARDNER, THOMAS [MICHAEL]. Review of Ground Work: Before the War. American Poetry 3, no. 2 (Winter):90-95.
       In this highly favorable review, notes that Duncan, like Whitman, identifies the self with the "world as an evolving whole." Finds he is "prodded" to "imagine a greater whole" because the "'discord' of our involvement" in the Vietnam War destroys "the old order." Notes also that Duncan evokes presences who provide him direction such as Herbert in the sixth section, "George Herbert, 'Jordan' (I)," of A Seventeenth Century Suite.

9   GELPI, ALBERT [J.]. "Re-Membering the Mother: A Reading of H.D.'s Trilogy." In H.D.: Woman and Poet. Edited by Michael King. Man and Poet Series. Orono, Maine: University of Maine at Orono, National Poetry Foundation, pp. 173-90.
       Briefly notes Duncan's sense of the poet being his "own mother and child" since the "poet and the poem are both mother and child of the other."

10   HATLEN, BURTON. "Interview with Carl Rakosi." Sagetrieb: A Journal Devoted to Poets in the Pound-H.D.-Williams Tradition 5, no. 2 (Fall):95-123.
       In a 6 January 1985 interview, Rakosi briefly mentions his affinity with Duncan, and notes Duncan's mysticism is not religious but a "mysticism of the imagination."

RD1986

11 LEVERTOV, DENISE. "A Memoir and a Critical Tribute." In
    Contemporary Poets. Edited by Harold Bloom. Modern Critical
    Views. New York: Chelsea House Publishers, pp. 57-83.
        Reprint of 1979.30.

12 MATHIS, MARY S., and KING, MICHAEL. "An Annotated Bibliography
    of Works about H.D." In H.D.: Woman and Poet. Edited by
    Michael King. Man and Poet Series. Orono, Maine: University
    of Maine at Orono, National Poetry Foundation, pp. 393-511.
        Annotates eight sections of The H.D. Book.

13 PAUL, SHERMAN. In Search of the Primitive: Reading David
    Antin, Jerome Rothenberg, and Gary Snyder. Baton Rouge and
    London: Louisiana State University Press, pp. 48, 76, 83, 95,
    173, 204, 289-90, 297-98, passim.
        Occasionally compares Duncan to Antin, Rothenberg, and
    Snyder. Comments on Duncan's sense of myth and his relationship
    to Snyder and Rothenberg, which Rothenberg terms "supportive" in
    his response to the chapter on him.

14 POWER, KEVIN. "A Conversation with Robert Duncan about Poetry
    and Painting: Interview at Robert Duncan's Home in San
    Francisco, 1976." Line: A Journal of Contemporary Writing at
    Its Modernist Sources, nos. 7-8, pp. 23-55.
        Reprinted, with slight revisions, from 1982.22.

15 SILBERG, RICHARD. "The Far West." Poetry Flash: The Bay
    Area's Poetry Calendar and Review, no. 159 (June), pp. 1, 3-6.
        In an article edited from March and April 1986 interviews
    with Robert Hawley, Hawley comments on Duncan's publications with
    Oyez and his own relationship to Duncan as an editor and as a
    friend.

1987

1   BRESLIN, PAUL. The Psycho-Political Muse: American Poetry
    since the Fifties. Chicago and London: University of Chicago
    Press, pp. 205-10, passim.
        Notes Duncan's treatment of Levertov in "Santa Cruz Proposi-
    tions." Mentions the relationship of his political poetry against
    the Vietnam War to his religious ideas, "stripped of doctrine," of
    a grand design. Examines his treatment of the relationship of war
    to poetry in "Passages, 26: The Soldiers" and elsewhere. Finds
    his treatment of war "lose[s] sight of experience" and, ironically
    for a nonconventional poet, adheres to the doctrines of the New
    Left.

2   BROWN, NORMAN O. "Cleveland State University Poetry Center
     Jubilation of Poets Panel, 'Homage to Robert Duncan,' October
     23, 1986." Sulfur: A Literary Tri-Quarterly of the Whole Art
     7, no. 1 [whole no. 19] (Spring):11-23.
          Quotes from and briefly comments on a number of Duncan's
     poems and prose works, and provides a few reminiscences.

3   BUTLING, PAULINE [formerly Pauline Wah]. "Play and Carnival in
     the Formation of a Postmodern Poetics: A Study of Robert
     Duncan, Phyllis Webb, and bp Nichol." Ph.D. dissertation,
     State University of New York at Buffalo, pp. 1-5, 19-33, 63-76,
     passim.
          Discusses Duncan's study of the modernism in the 1940s,
     especially Pound, but outlines differences due to his "investiga-
     tion of forms and processes which did not demand a centre or an
     overall plan" including those of Stein, Olson, and open field
     poetics. Examines Duncan's play with sound and meaning "to draw
     attention to the words themselves, to 'force a new sense of inter-
     rupted movement,' and to open up a multiplicity of meaning."
     Notes his emphasis on "the physicality of language" and the dis-
     ruptive. Comments on his development of a postmodern aesthetic
     and influence on Webb; occasionally compares his development to
     that of Webb and Nichol.
          In The Opening of the Field, which reflects the "disorder,
     discontinuity, and contradiction . . . of a pluralistic, multi-
     phasic world," mentions the influence of Whitehead and Duncan's
     sense of a "multiphasic personality." Also comments on his use of
     field poetics, of play, and of "an interactive process" created by
     "forms and techniques that generate presence." Remarks on the
     role of the meadow as a center, as in modernism, in "Often I Am
     Permitted to Return to a Meadow," but also notes the role of flux
     and process. Points to the treatment of process in "A Poem Begin-
     ning with a Line by Pindar," and finds the poem resists "'meanings
     below the surface' directing attention instead to the interplay of
     elements." Notes the treatment of control, the role of language,
     the plurality and play of meanings in The Structure of Rime se-
     quence, using the "Structure of Rime, XVII" as an example.
          Claims Duncan follows "the play of sound in a poem," as in
     "Roots and Branches," and attends "to the interaction of particles
     [sounds, ideas, and associations] in the expanding field of the
     poem." Also comments on his use of circular form and collage
     form, as in the Passages sequence, which uses "correspondence or
     recurrence" as an "organizing principle." Notes how Duncan also
     "allows for discontinuity and disjunction," and remarks on his
     treatment of Eros as the "truth and meaning of an experience."
          Finds Ground Work: Before the War generally less explora-
     tory and processional than earlier volumes. Records the treatment
     of "reunion with the Beloved" in "Achilles' Song" and throughout
     the volume, speculating that he has lately circled "'back' to re-

embrace earlier themes." Occasionally quotes from unpublished lectures by Duncan from July 1963 at the Vancouver Poetry Conference. In one section, Duncan mentions beginning The Opening of the Field with the intention of "breaking the commands laid down for the Modernist."

4   DUNCAN, ROBERT. Ground Work II: In the Dark. New York: New Directions, pp. 20-21, 30, 74.
    Includes reprints of 1979.15, 16b; 1981.9.

5   _____. Note to "Three Letters from Jack Spicer's Correspondence with Duncan." Acts: A Journal of New Writing, no. 6 [A Book of Correspondences for Jack Spicer issue, edited by David Levi Strauss and Benjamin Hollander], pp. 5-6, 9-10.
    In these 1974 notes preceding Spicer's letters to him (see 1987.15), Duncan provides some biographical information, mainly from the late 1940s, including his relationship to Spicer, Jaime de Angulo, Robert Louis Benson, Robin Blaser, Hugh O'Neill, and Gerald Ackerman. Duncan also mentions the composition of "The Venice Poem" and Spicer's rejection of it.

6   _____. Preface to "Two Sets of Tens: Derived from Confucian Analects." In Ground Work II: In the Dark. New York: New Directions, p. 55.
    Notes his correspondence with Pound, mentions his study with Peter Boodberg at the University of California at Berkeley, and comments on writing "Two Sets of Tens." Original version not located.

·7 _____. "A Reading of Thirty Things." In Robert Creeley's Life and Work: A Sense of Increment. Edited by John Wilson. Under Discussion, edited by Donald Hall. Ann Arbor: University of Michigan Press, pp. 301-9.
    Reprint of 1978.15.

8   ESBJORNSON, CARL D[ANIEL]. "Mastering the Rime: Strife in Robert Duncan's Poetry." North Dakota Quarterly 55, no. 4 [Some Others: Contemporary American Poetry issue] (Fall): 74-88.
    Finding he "adopts a Heraclitean creative-destructive mythos," discusses the role of strife in Duncan's work as both a destructive and a "formative principle." Comments on the treatment of love, hate, and the community as well as the relationship between language and strife in his work. Also mentions the role of loss, naming, wordplay, and estrangement. Notes the role of strife and the treatment of self-deceit in Caesar's Gate, and the treatment of the Vietnam War, community, law, and loss and the use of the Atlantean dream in the Passages sequence. Comments on The

Structure of Rime sequence and Duncan's sense of oral performance,
finding Duncan's poetry is a "communal art."
A few, brief sections, revised from 1985.25.

9   HARRIS, MARY EMMA. The Arts at Black Mountain College.
     Cambridge, Mass., and London: M.I.T. Press, pp. 202, 204, 212-
     13, passim.
        Comments on Duncan's role at Black Mountain College and his
     collaborations with Robert Huss on plays at Black Mountain and San
     Francisco: The Origins of Old Son (unpublished play) and Medea at
     Kolchis. Occasionally briefly quotes from unpublished letters by
     and an interview with Duncan.

10   OLSON, CHARLES, and CREELEY, ROBERT. Charles Olson and Robert
     Creeley: The Complete Correspondence. Vol. 7. Edited by
     George F. Butterick. Santa Rosa, Calif.: Black Sparrow Press,
     pp. 50, 169-70, 184, 193.
        In their correspondence from 25 July to 4 October 1951,
     Creeley and Olson occasionally and briefly mention Duncan.

11   _____. Charles Olson and Robert Creeley: The Complete Cor-
     respondence. Vol. 8. Edited by George F. Butterick. Santa
     Rosa, Calif.: Black Sparrow Press, pp. 103, 149-50, 169, 185-
     86, 209-11, 246, passim.
        In their correspondence from 4 October to 28 December 1951,
     Olson and Creeley occasionally comment on Duncan, noting "Africa
     Revisited" and "The Song of the Borderguard."

12   PERKINS, DAVID. A History of Modern Poetry: Modernism and
     After. Cambridge, Mass., and London: Harvard University Press,
     Belknap Press, pp. 486-97, 515-27, passim.
        Notes the influence of W.C. Williams and Pound on Duncan and
     Olson's open poetics, including their emphasis on spontaneity.
     Also notes Duncan's desire "to emulate life in its process" and to
     reflect the unpredictability of nature by using dissimilar ele-
     ments in his work, commenting on his use of the serial poem. Also
     notes his use of "esoteric cults and myths," and often compares
     him to Keats. In the Passages sequence, comments on the sense
     that the poems belong to a greater whole and on their diversity
     and continuity. Focuses on Duncan's use of painting and word
     lists in "The Fire: Passages, 13," and provides a reading of "The
     Currents: Passages, 16."

13   SILLIMAN, RON. "'My vocabulary did this to me.'" Acts: A
     Journal of New Writing, no. 6 [A Book of Correspondences for
     Jack Spicer issue, edited by David Levi Strauss and Benjamin
     Hollander], pp. 67-71.
        Contrasts Spicer's sense of language to Duncan's.

RD1987

14   SPICER, JACK. "Selected Letters from the Spicer/Duncan Cor-
      respondence." Acts: A Journal of New Writing, no. 6 [A Book
      of Correspondences for Jack Spicer issue, edited by David Levi
      Strauss and Benjamin Hollander], pp. 13-30.
         In these letters from October 1950 through 1964, Spicer
      provides details of his relationship to Duncan and comments on a
      few of Duncan's poems.

15   _____. "Three Letters from Jack Spicer's Correspondence with
      Robert Duncan." Acts: A Journal of New Writing, no. 6 [A Book
      of Correspondences for Jack Spicer issue, edited by David Levi
      Strauss and Benjamin Hollander], pp. 5-12.
         In the letter from April 1947 (p. 7), Spicer briefly com-
      ments on "Ode for Dick Brown.

Index to the Works of Creeley

Index to the Works of Dorn

Index to the Works of Duncan

Heavenly City, Earthly
City, 1948.1, 3;
1978.36; 1985.2;
1986.2
"H.M.S. Bearskin,"
1972.10; 1979.1, 22;
1980.1; 1985.25-26
"Homage and Lament for
Ezra Pound in
Captivity, May 12,
1944," 1974.33;
1977.11
"Hommage to The Brothers
Grimm," 1969.24;
1977.11. See also:
"Strawberries under
the Snow."
"Homosexual in Society,
The," 1944.1; 1983.13;
1985.20
"Horus," 1969.15. See
also: "The Chimeras
of Gérard de Nerval."
"Household, The,"
1985.12. See also:
"Dante Études."
"Human Communion Traces,
The," 1956.2

"I Am Not Afraid," 1983.2
"['I must wake up into
the morning world'],"
1972.10. See also:
"A Sequence of Poems
for H.D.'s Birthday."
"Imaginary War Elegy,
An," 1966.8; 1977.11
"Imitations of Gertrude
Stein, 1953-1955," a
section in
Derivations: Selected
Poems, 1950-1956,
1979.41. See also:
Derivations: Selected
Poems, 1950-1956,
Writing Writing: A
Composition Book for
Madison, 1953: Stein
Imitations.

"Inbinding, The" 1980.32.
See also: "Another
Animadversion," "The
inbinding mirrors a
process returning to
roots of first
feeling."
"inbinding mirrors a ⹁
process returning to
roots of first
feeling, The,"
1972.25. See also:
"Another
Animadversion," "The
Inbinding."
"Incubus, An," 1985.25
"Ingmar Bergman's Seventh
Seal," 1968.16;
1972.25; 1977.11
"Interlude, An," 1983.24
"In the Place of a
Passage 22," 1972.25;
1977.11; 1979.39;
1980.32
"['It is deep going from
here']," 1981.11

"Keeping the Rhyme,"
1967.1; 1972.15, 20
"King Haydn of Miami
Beach," 1966.6

"Language for Poetry, A,"
1974.33
"Law, The," 1965.10;
1966.9; 1971.6;
1972.15, 25; 1976.17;
1978.40
"Law I Love Is Major
Mover, The," 1974.28;
1978.24; 1985.34
"Letter, A," 1980.5
Letters: Poems, 1953-
1956, 1958.2; 1959.1;
1960.2; 1966.15;
1967.1; 1968.11;
1969.24; 1971.10;
1972.10; 1974.19, 30;
1976.22; 1977.11;

1979.5; 1980.4-5, 27;
1982.22; 1983.10;
1985.34; 1986.2
"Letters for Denise
Levertov: An a Muse
Meant," 1969.2. See
also: "For a Muse
Meant."
"Light: Passages, 28,
The," 1980.5
"Light Song," 1968.2
"Love" (short story),
1983.13

"Maiden, The," 1974.33
"Masterbation: For the
Innocence of the Act."
See: "For the
Innocence of the Act,"
"Nor Is the Past
Pure."
Medea at Kolchis: The
Maiden Head, 1965.4;
1968.31; 1972.2;
1977.11; 1987.9
Medieval Scenes, 1964.1;
1966.15; 1967.1;
1968.2, 3b; 1973.7;
1974.19; 1976.22;
1977.11; 1978.3, 7,
14, 24; 1979.20;
1980.1, 16; 1982.22;
1983.2, 13; 1985.14
"Missionaries [Passages],
The," 1985.8
"Moira's Cathedral,"
1972.18
"Mother to Whom I Have
Come Home," 1977.25
"Moving the Moving Image:
Passages, 17," 1975.9
"Multiversity: Passages,
21, The," 1965.3;
1972.25; 1975.19;
1983.18; 1985.11
"Museum, The," 1973.11;
1983.15; 1985.8
"My Mother Would Be a
Falconress," 1964.6;

1966.7; 1968.7;
1971.3; 1972.15;
1977.11, 25; 1979.2,
22, 40; 1980.1, 4;
1981.16; 1982.3, 24;
1983.24, 37

Names of People, 1971.7;
1977.11; 1981.15
"Narration for Adam's
Way." See:
"Narrative Bridges for
Adam's Way."
"Narrative Bridges for
Adam's Way," 1983.11,
24
"Natural Doctrine, The,"
1972.25
"Nel Mezzo del Cammin di
Nostra Vita," 1971.6;
1972.25; 1978.40;
1983.30
"New Poem (for Jack
Spicer), A," 1972.25;
1979.22; 1985.23
"Night Scenes," 1976.31;
1977.11; 1978.40;
1979.33-34; 1980.26;
1983.33
"Nor Is the Past Pure,"
1971.6; 1972.25;
1983.10. See also:
"For the Innocence of
the Act."
"Notes on Poetics
Regarding Olson's
Maximus," 1966.1
"Now the Record Now
Record," 1971.6

Ode and Arcadia, An,
1974.6
"Ode for Dick Brown,"
1974.6; 1977.11;
1987.15
"Often I Am Permitted to
Return to a Meadow,"
1966.15; 1967.3,

12; 1971.4, 6; 1972.
15, 22, 25; 1973.23;
1974.3-4, 28, 33;
1975.19-20; 1977.11;
1978.8, 34; 1979.14;
1980.4-5, 16; 1981.16,
18; 1982.15; 1983.10;
1985.11, 13, 38;
1987.3

Opening of the Field,
The, 1960.6; 1961.2;
1962.2, 5; 1963.1-2;
1965.2; 1969.16;
1972.10, 25; 1973.7;
1974.28, 33; 1975.19;
1976.14, 17, 22, 24-
25; 1977.2a, 11;
1979.14, 22, 30;
1980.3-5, 21, 27, 32;
1981.18; 1982.15, 22;
1983.7, 10; 1985.14,
25, 34, 40; 1986.2;
1987.3

"Orchards," 1977.2a

"Orders: Passages, 24,"
1972.25; 1979.39;
1980.5, 23; 1982.12

Origins of Old Son, The
(unpublished play),
1987.9

"Osiris and Set,"
1972.25; 1981.18

"Out of the Black,"
1985.25

"Over There," 1972.11;
1973.7

"Owl Is an Only Bird of
Poetry, An," 1974.30;
1980.3-4

"Passage over Water,"
1975.19; 1985.14

Passages, 1964.10;
1968.1, 6, 18; 1970.8,
10; 1971.3-4, 7, 15,
18; 1972.25; 1973.18;
1974.17-18, 33;
1975.4, 7, 19, 21;
1976.14, 17, 22, 25;

1977.2a, 5, 10-11;
1979.10, 32, 38-39;
1980.4, 17, 21, 23,
27; 1981.15, 18;
1982.12, 15; 1983.11,
18-19, 22, 30-31, 34;
1985.2, 11-12, 14, 25;
1987.3, 8, 12. See
also: Tribunals:
"Passages," 31-35.

Passages et Structures,
1978.39

"Passages, 1." See:
"Tribal Memories:
Passages, 1."

"Passages, 2." See: "At
the Loom: Passages,
2."

"Passages, 6." See:
"The Collage:
Passages, 6."

"Passages, 8." See: "As
in the Old Days:
Passages, 8."

"Passages, 9." See:
"The Architecture:
Passages, 9."

"Passages, 10." See:
"These Past Years:
Passages, 10."

"Passages, 11." See:
"Shadows: Passages,
11."

"Passages, 12." See:
"Wine: Passages, 12."

"Passages, 13." See:
"The Fire: Passages,
13."

"Passages, 14." See:
"Chords: Passages,
14."

"Passages, 15." See:
"Spelling: Passages,
15."

"Passages, 16." See:
"The Currents:
Passages, 16."

"Passages, 17." See: "Moving the Moving Image: Passages, 17."

"Passages, 18." See: "The Torso: Passages, 18."

"Passages, 19." See: "The Earth: Passages, 19."

"Passages, 21." See: "The Multiversity: Passages, 21."

"Passages, 22." See: "In the Place of a Passage 22."

"Passages, 23: Benefice," 1975.19; 1979.39; 1980.4, 27

"Passages, 24." See: "Orders: Passages, 24."

"Passages, 25." See: "Up Rising: Passages, 25."

"Passages, 26: The Soldiers," 1967.5; 1969.25; 1971.4, 6; 1972.18, 25; 1977.1, 6; 1979.39; 1980.24; 1983.30; 1987.1

"Passages, 27." See: "Transgressing the Real: Passages, 27."

"Passages, 28." See: "The Light: Passages, 28."

"Passages, 29." See: "Eye of God: Passages, 29."

"Passages, 30: Stage Directions," 1972.25

"Passages, 31: The Concert (Tribunals)," 1971.11; 1972.22; 1976.20; 1977.11; 1983.18; 1985.25. See also: Tribunals: "Passages," 31-35.

"Passages, 32: [Ancient Reveries and Declamations] (Tribunals)," 1970.11; 1977.6; 1980.23. See also: Tribunals: "Passages," 31-35.

"Passages, 34: The Feast (Tribunals)," 1970.8; 1977.6. See also: Tribunals: "Passages," 31-35.

"Passages, 35: Before the Judgment (Tribunals)," 1972.15; 1985.2, 50. See also: Tribunals: "Passages," 31-35.

"Passages, 36," 1983.4. See also: "A Seventeenth Century Suite in Homage to the Metaphysical Genius in English Poetry."

"Passages, 37: O," 1980.4

Passages without numbers. See: "The Missionaries [Passages]."

"Performance We Wait For, The," 1983.10

"Persephone," 1977.11; 1985.21

Play Time, Pseudo Stein: From the Laboratory Records: Notebook, 1953, 1969.10; 1980.16

"Poem Beginning with a Line by Pindar, A," 1963.3; 1964.1, 5; 1966.1, 10, 15; 1967.1, 12; 1968.2, 12, 14, 24; 1969.19; 1970.13, 22; 1971.6, 21; 1972.3, 18, 25; 1973.5, 23; 1974.30; 1975.19; 1976.3, 10, 14, 24; 1977.11, 25;

"Sequence of Poems for
    H.D.'s Birthday, A,"
    1967.12; 1972.10, 25;
    1977.11; 1978.40;
    1979.34; 1981.18;
    1983.11. See also:
    "Dream Data," "['I
    must wake up into the
    morning world']."
"Set of Romantic Hymns,
    A," 1966.3; 1979.34;
    1980.21
Sets of Syllables, Sets
    of Words, Sets of
    Lines, Sets of Poems
    Addressing: Veil,
    Turbine, Cord, & Bird.
    See: Veil, Turbine,
    Cord, & Bird.
"Seventeenth Century Suite
    in Homage to the Meta-
    physical Genius in
    English Poetry, A,"
    1973.12; 1975.7;
    1977.11; 1979.31;
    1983.4; 1985.3, 8, 32,
    51; 1986.8. See also:
    "From Robert
    Southwell's 'The
    Burning Babe'";
    "George Herbert,
    'Jordan' (I)";
    "Passages, 36";
    "['"pretty Babe"--that
    burning Babe, "A"']."
"Shadows: Passages, 11,"
    1967.5
"Shelley's 'Arethusa' Set
    to New Measures,"
    1970.17
"Shrine to Ameinias, A,"
    1977.11
"Sleeping All Night,"
    1977.11
"Song ['How in the dark
    the cows lie down'],"
    1983.13

"Song of the Borderguard,
    The," 1977.11; 1980.4;
    1985.14; 1987.11
"Song of the Old Order,
    A," 1971.6
"Sonneries of the Rose
    Cross," 1972.25
"Sonnet 1," 1965.10;
    1976.10. See also:
    "Sonnets."
"Sonnet 3," 1983.12. See
    also: "Sonnets."
"Sonnet 4," 1981.16. See
    also: "Sonnets."
"Sonnets," 1968.6;
    1979.22. See also
    "5th Sonnet," "Sonnet
    1," "Sonnet 3,"
    "Sonnet 4."
"Spelling: Passages,
    15," 1977.11; 1985.10
"Spring Memorandum: Fort
    Knox, A," 1975.19;
    1977.11; 1983.30
"Storm of White, A,"
    1966.10; 1977.2a;
    1985.25
"Strains of Sight,"
    1970.17
"Strawberries under the
    Snow," 1969.24. See
    also "Hommage to The
    Brothers Grimm."
Structure of Rime, The,
    1962.1; 1967.1;
    1969.9; 1972.15, 25;
    1973.7; 1974.13, 33;
    1975.19; 1976.22;
    1977.5, 11; 1979.10,
    19; 1980.4, 17, 21;
    1981.2, 18; 1982.22;
    1983.6, 10, 18, 30;
    1985.14, 34, 40;
    1987.3, 8
"Structure of Rime, I,
    The," 1976.22; 1983.6,
    15
"Structure of Rime, II,
    The," 1962.1

"Two Presentations,"
1963.5; 1972.15, 25;
1975.19; 1977.11;
1979.34. See also:
"Two Messages."
"Two Sets of Ten:
Derived from Confucian
Analects," 1987.6

"Under Ground," 1972.25
unpublished drama. See:
The Origins of Old
Son.
unpublished novel,
1978.21
unpublished poetry,
1980.3; 1983.13. See
also: "A Pre Preface
for James on His
Sixtieth Birthday, 10
Nov. 1973."
"Up Rising: Passages,
25," 1968.31; 1969.9;
1970.11; 1972.13, 18,
25; 1977.11; 1978.24;
1979.39; 1980.24;
1983.24; 1985.11, 14
"Upon Another Shore of
Hell," 1985.25

"Variations on Two Dicta
of William Blake,"
1967.6; 1973.7;
1980.21; 1981.18;
1982.3
"Variations upon Phrases
from Milton's The
Reason of Church
Government, 1977.11
Veil, Turbine, Cord, &
Bird, 1979.16b;
1980.33. Used for:
Sets of Syllables,
Sets of Words, Sets of
Lines, Sets of Poems
Addressing: Veil,
Turbine, Cord, & Bird.
"Venice Poem, The"
1966.15; 1967.1;

1968.3b, 12; 1970.9,
14, 22; 1972.10;
1973.7; 1974.7, 22,
29-30; 1975.3, 19, 21;
1976.22, 25; 1977.11;
1979.1; 1980.4, 16,
30; 1981.18; 1982.22;
1983.2, 10, 13, 30;
1985.2, 14; 1986.2;
1987.5
Venice Poem, The, 1976.30
"Voyage of the Poet into
the Land of the Dead,
The," 1985.25

"Waste, The Room, The
Discarded Timbers,
The," 1980.1. See
also: "Four Poems as
a Night Song."
"We Have Forgotten
Venus," 1985.21
"What Do I Know of the
Old Lore?" 1972.25
"What Happened:
Prelude," 1979.34
"What Is It You Have Come
to Tell Me, García
Lorca?" 1972.4;
1985.25
"What the Sonnet Means
the Sonnet Means,"
1979.16b
"Wine" (the broadside
version of "Wine:
Passages, 12"),
1976.16
"Wine: Passages, 12,"
1971.4; 1982.12. See
also: "Wine."
Writing Writing: A
Composition Book for
Madison, 1953: Stein
Imitations, 1966.8;
1973.2; 1979.41. See
also: "Imitations of
Gertrude Stein, 1953-
1955."

"Years as Catches, The,"
    1979.40; 1980.30;
    1983.13
Years as Catches, The,
    1966.6; 1967.11;
    1968.31; 1971.16;
    1976.17; 1977.11;
    1978.7; 1983.13, 30;
    1986.2
"Yes, As a Look Springs
    to Its Face ['as
    earth, light and grass
    illustrate the
    meadow,']," 1972.25

Author and Subject Index

Abălută, C., RC1974.11;
ED1974.5; RD1974.21
Abbott, Keith, RC1986.1
Abbott, Steve, RD1979.1;
1980.1; 1982.26;
1984.1
absence, RC1972.2; 1979.1;
1982.31; RD1973.7.
See also: loss,
presence.
abstract, the,
RC1975.21; 1977.23.
See also: the
concrete.
abstract expressionism,
RC1981.15; 1987.18.
See also: action
painters, artists,
Willem de Kooning,
Philip Guston, Franz
Kline, New York
painters, Jackson
Pollock.
abstraction, RC1960.2;
1966.4; 1969.15;
1973.29, 33, 42;
1977.14; 1978.4, 72;
1980.36; 1983.15, 33;
1984.1; ED1985.3;
RD1978.2. See also:
the concrete,
generalization, the
mental, technique.
abstract nouns, RC1977.23.
See also: word use.
absurd, the, RD1974.33
abyss, the, RC1972.2. See
also: the void.
academia, ED1985.7
academic poetry, RC1978.5.
See also: literary
establishment, the
New Criticism.
academic poets, RC1974.23;
ED1985.7; RD1971.5;
1974.30. See also:
literary
establishment,

literary movements.
acceptance, RC1980.27;
1981.17; 1984.1, 26;
RD1974.33; 1980.26
accidental, the, RC1974.26;
RD1979.30; 1979.38;
1982.2; 1985.3, 34,
47. See also: chance,
coincidence, errors,
interruptions,
unpredictability.
accuracy, RC1983.26. See
also: precision.
Achilles, RD1971.4. See
also: mythological
figures.
Ackerman, Gerald, RD1979.1;
1983.13; 1987.5
acquisition, ED1978.18;
1981.11. See also:
expropriation,
wealth.
acting, RD1965.4
action, RC1962.1; 1968.10;
1971.21; 1972.2;
1973.2; 1981.2. See
also: movement,
passivity.
action painters, RC1981.30;
RD1974.7. See also:
abstract
expressionism,
artists, Franz Kline,
Jackson Pollock,
painters.
action painting, RC1967.20;
1969.9; 1982.47. See
also: painting.
activity, poetry as,
RC1974.21; 1975.18;
1976.19; 1978.61, 63,
67; 1979.4; 1981.13,
15; 1984.1, 10, 31;
1985.15; RD1968.13;
1969.24; 1983.34. See
also: creative
process.
actual, the, RD1976.14. See

415

also: attention.
Alexander, Floyce,
    RC1982.44
Alexander, Jim, RD1970.20
Alexander, Michael RC1966.2
Alexander the Great,
    RD1972.10. See also:
    leaders, war.
alienation, RC1963.18;
    1972.2; 1978.42;
    RD1971.4. See also:
    estrangement,
    isolation,
    separation,
    withdrawl.
all, the, RC1984.1. See
    also: the One.
Allan, Tony, RC1973.39
allegorical, the,
    RC1980.37; ED1970.4;
    1978.9; 1985.4;
    RD1976.3
allegory, ED1977.9; 1980.4;
    1981.5; 1985.1. See
    also: symbols, genre.
Allen, Donald Merriam,
    RC1965.8, 17, 22;
    1970.14; 1973.1, 7,
    18, 39, 47; 1974.20;
    1979.11, 15, 26;
    1980.1; 1983.25;
    1984.42; ED1970.1;
    1971.5; 1973.4;
    1974.9; 1975.5;
    1978.4; 1979.3;
    1980.3, 5-6;
    RD1960.3, 5; 1965.11;
    1969.8; 1970.4;
    1973.1, 10; 1978.13;
    1979.13; 1980.9, 18,
    31; 1985.41. See
    also: The New
    American Poetry,
    1945-1960.
Allen, Don Cameron
    RD1968.24
Allen, Gay Wilson, RC1965.1
alliteration, RD1973.7;
    1976.20; 1985.21. See
    also: consonance,
    technique.

allusions, RC1970.8;
    1972.3; 1975.18;
    1977.9-10, 13;
    1978.9, 63; 1980.30;
    1981.15; 1982.42;
    1986.7; 1987.18;
    ED1978.3; 1980.7, 10,
    13; 1981.15;
    RD1967.5; 1968.2;
    1969.1, 23; 1970.10;
    1973.7; 1975.3, 21;
    1976.10, 14; 1977.1,
    11, 25; 1978.6;
    1979.2, 20, 26;
    1980.4, 6, 19, 28,
    30; 1981.13;
    1983.6-7, 11; 1985.9,
    38, 47. See also:
    classical allusions,
    identifications,
    literary allusions,
    technique.
Alpert, Barry, RC1980.1;
    ED1972.1-2; 1977.2;
    RD1973.2; 1974.2;
    1975.1; 1976.2
alphabet, RD1969.5
alternatives, RC1978.27
Altieri, Charles, RC1972.2;
    1973.2; 1974.1;
    1978.3-4; 1979.1;
    1984.2-3; RD1973.3;
    1976.3; 1979.3-4;
    1984.2
Altoon, John, RC1981.9. See
    also: artists.
Alvie, Aunt. Use: Aunt
    Alvie.
ambiguity, RC1962.1;
    1967.4; 1968.1;
    1972.2; 1978.35, 62;
    1980.23; 1981.15, 17;
    ED1966.3; 1977.9;
    1983.1; RD1973.7;
    1977.6; 1983.1. See
    also: technique,
    vagueness.
America, ED1970.5; 1977.9;
    1980.7; 1981.11;
    1983.1; 1984.1;
    RD1975.21; 1979.26;

417

1969.13; 1975.5-6;
1977.6, 11; 1983.2,
10, 12-13; 1985.23;
1987.5. See also:
Canadian poets, San
Francisco poets.
Blazek, Douglas, RC1972.5
Blevins, Richard, RD1974.5
Bliss, Donald Thayer,
RD1964.5
blood, RD1979.1. See also:
the body.
blood imagery, RD1972.10.
See also: imagery.
blood pressure, RD1985.41.
See also: health.
Bloom, Harold, RD1986.11
Bluford, Ken, RD1975.7
Bly, Robert, RC1959.1;
1968.6; 1976.18;
1980.16; RD1976.13;
1978.24; 1980.15. See
also: surrealists.
Boardway, Stephen,
RC1984.27
boat, the. See: the ark;
the Wynken, Blynken,
and Nod boat.
body, the, RC1969.2;
1973.29; 1976.26;
1977.14; 1980.18;
1981.15; 1982.32;
1984.1, 10; RD1967.1;
1969.1; 1977.11, 15;
1978.35; 1979.33;
1981.16; 1982.12. See
also: blood, flesh, the
head, the heart,
organism, the physical,
the soul, the spirit.
body, relationship to
poetry, RC1976.24;
RD1966.1; 1970.22;
1973.23; 1979.8;
1980.21; 1984.10;
1985.40. See also:
breath line, the
physicality of
language, projective
verse.
Böhme, Jakob, RD1972.15;

1985.11. See also:
mysticism.
Bolinas, California,
RC1973.3; 1973.14;
1974.27; 1986.1
Bollobás, Enikő, ED1986.2;
RD1983.1; 1986.3-4
Boodberg, Peter, RD1987.6
book of God. See: the world
as the book of God.
Boone, Bruce, RD1983.2. See
also: San Francisco
poets.
boredom, RC1975.19
Bornstein, George,
RD1977.9; 1985.48
Bosch, Hieronymus,
RD1977.9; 1983.18.
See also artists,
painting.
Boston, Massachusetts,
RC1974.7; 1980.26;
1980.27; 1987.10
boundaries, RC1978.63;
RD1969.17; 1973.7;
1977.2a; 1982.15, 22;
1983.2, 18. See also:
limits, margins,
thresholds,
transgression.
boundlessness, RD1979.31.
See also: the
infinite.
bow, the, RD1975.27
Bowen, C., RC1970.5. See
also: Harrison-Ford,
Carl.
Bowering, George, RC1971.2;
1983.25; 1985.2;
RD1964.3; 1971.1;
1976.6, 18; 1978.2;
1985.4. See also:
Canadian poets, Tish,
Vancouver poets.
Bowman, Sylvia E.,
RC1967.25; RD1967.14
Brabner, Wendy, RC1981.2
Bradford, James, RC1969.12
Brakhage, Stan, RC1972.18;
1978.8; 1981.2;
1982.4; ED1974.8;

RD1963.2; 1970.2;
1971.2; 1977.26. See
also: film, <u>Two:</u>
<u>Creeley McClure</u>.
branches, RD1971.6. See
also: the plant, the
tree.
Brautigan, Richard,
RC1971.1; 1974.26;
1986.1. See also: San
Francisco poets.
breath, the, RD1972.22
breath line, the,
RC1974.14; 1975.21;
1978.29, 42;
RD1976.17. See also:
body, relationship to
poetry; line,
end-stopped;
lineation; the
physicality of
language, projective
verse.
Breslin, James E.B.,
RD1984.4
Breslin, Paul, RC1980.2;
ED1980.1; RD1987.1
Bresson, Robert, RC1984.26;
1984.35. See also:
film.
brevity, RC1962.10. See
also: concision.
Brien, Dolores Elise,
RC1969.2; RD1969.1;
1975.8
British, the, ED1972.1. See
also: England.
British poets, RC1973.39;
1982.40. See also:
W.H. Auden, the
Augustans, William
Blake, Basil Bunting,
Robert Browning,
George Gordon Byron,
Thomas Campion, Bob
Cobbing, Samuel
Taylor Coleridge,
John Donne, the
eighteenth century,
T.S. Eliot,
Elizabethan poetry,

Thom Gunn, George
Herbert, Irish
writers, David Jones,
Ben Jonson, John
Keats, Philip Larkin,
D.H. Lawrence,
metaphysical poets,
John Milton,
Pre-Raphaelite poets,
Sir Walter Raleigh,
Tom Raworth,
renaissance poetry,
William Shakespeare,
Percy Bysshe Shelley,
Robert Southwell,
Nathaniel Tarn, Dylan
Thomas, Charles
Tomlinson, William
Wordsworth.
British writers. See: the
Augustans, Thomas
Carlyle, Samuel
Johnson, Rudyard
Kipling, D.H.
Lawrence.
Brockport, New York,
RC1973.34
Bromige, David, RC1963.4;
ED1976.2; RD1973.2;
1975.9; 1980.2
Bromwich, David, RC1977.3
Bronfman, Larry, RC1985.3
Bronk, William, RC1978.44
Brooker, Peter, RD1982.4
Brotherston, Gordon,
ED1968.2; 1977.7;
1981.10
Broughton, James, RD1980.3;
1983.13. See also:
film, San Francisco
poets.
Broughton, Orion, RD1980.3
Brower, Reuben A.,
RC1971.23; ED1971.7;
RD1971.21
Brown, Dick, RD1974.6;
1983.13
Brown, Harvey, RD1979.32
Brown, Norman O.,
RD1971.10; 1987.2
Brown, Slater, RC1954.4;

cooperation, RD1983.1
Corbett, William, RD1978.8
Corman, Cid, RC1951.2-3;
1953.1; 1954.1;
1960.3; 1962.4;
1963.17; 1966.26;
1968.4, 18; 1969.7;
1970.4, 12, 29;
1971.16; 1973.5-6,
15, 36-38; 1975.4,
8-9, 15-16; 1976.22;
1978.13; 1980.27;
1981.22; 1982.8, 35;
1983.5, 30; 1985.7,
15; 1987.10, 11;
RD1968.22; 1985.2.
See also: Black
Mountain poets,
Origin.
corporate, the, ED1985.4.
See also: power.
correspondence (letters),
RC1951.2-3; 1954.4;
1961.3; 1962.12;
1963.6, 20; 1965.4-5,
26; 1966.7-8, 17, 30;
1968.6, 18, 26;
1970.29; 1971.16-17;
1972.8, 16, 18;
1973.4, 15-16, 26,
38; 1974.23; 1975.20;
1976.22; 1977.6;
1978.9, 17, 36, 41,
52, 60, 65; 1979.21;
1980.4, 26-27;
1981.2, 11, 15, 20,
22-23, 27; 1982.35,
37, 43; 1983.2, 13,
20, 29-30; 1984.13,
15, 17; 1985.14-15;
1986.10; 1987.2-3, 8,
10-11, 16, 20;
ED1972.7; 1975.7;
1978.3; 1980.2;
1981.11, 15; 1983.3;
1985.3; RD1954.1;
1956.1; 1958.1;
1962.3; 1964.5, 8,
18; 1967.6; 1968.22;
1970.9, 20; 1972.16,
25; 1973.27;

1974.14-15, 17, 19,
30, 34; 1975.5, 16,
22; 1976.16, 20, 22;
1977.6; 1978.6, 21,
24, 32; 1979.30, 39;
1980.30-31; 1983.3,
10, 13, 19; 1985.2,
20-21, 23, 42-43;
1986.2; 1987.3, 5-6,
9-11, 14-15
Corrington, John William,
RC1963.5
corruption, RD1972.25;
1985.25. See also:
evil.
COSMEP Conference, in
Buffalo, New York
(1970), RC1972.20
cosmic, the, RD1979.16a;
1980.17, 29
cosmic identity, RD1971.4.
See also: identity.
cosmic processes, RD1968.2;
1972.22. See also:
process.
cosmology, RD1980.21. See
also: Gnostic
cosmology, religion.
cosmos, the, RD1966.3;
1971.4; 1972.15, 18;
1974.23; 1975.21;
1976.3; 1977.11;
1979.31; 1983.29;
1984.17, 26; 1985.10.
See also: space, the
universe.
Costello, James Thomas,
ED1983.1
counterpoint, RD1983.1;
1985.31. See also:
music, technique.
couplet, the, RC1976.3. See
also: stanzaic
patterns, technique.
courtly love, RC1978.42.
See also: love.
cowboy, the, ED1969.3;
1980.7; 1981.1, 11
cowboy figure, the,
ED1980.3; 1983.1. See
also: the drifter

1981.18; 1982.3;
1985.25, 50
dark, the, RD1971.6;
1979.40; 1985.31. See
also: the light, the
night.
darkness, RC1971.15;
1978.39; RD1967.1;
1972.18; 1979.1
Darras, Jacques, RD1981.5
Dartmouth's library,
RC1980.27
Darwin, Charles Robert,
RD1975.21; 1980.5;
1983.30. See also:
evolution.
Davey, Frankland Wilmot,
RC1965.11; 1968.10;
1976.16; RD1965.1;
1967.4; 1968.2;
1970.5; 1974.8;
1975.12; 1976.8-9;
1977.21. See also:
Canadian poets, Tish,
Vancouver poets.
David Haselwood Books,
RD1976.16
David, Jack, RD1978.2
Davidson, Robert Michael,
RC1973.21; 1977.9;
1978.27; 1980.13;
1981.10-11; 1983.7;
1985.9; ED1978.8, 10;
1980.4; 1981.4-5;
1985.1, 10; RD1973.7;
1976.10, 1978.26;
1979.14; 1981.6-7;
1982.22; 1983.6;
1985.12-14
Davie, Donald, ED1965.1;
1967.3; 1970.2-3;
1972.4; 1977.2;
1979.4-5
Davies, Alan, RC1974.6
Davison, Peter, RC1962.6
Dawson, Dave, RC1963.9;
RD1963.3. See also:
Canadian poets, Tish,
Vancouver poets.
Dawson, Fielding,
RC1967.13; 1973.22;

ED1974.3
day, the, RD1981.18. See
also: the light, the
night.
Day, Frank, RC1980.14
Deane, Peter, RC1963.10
de Angulo, Jaime, RD1979.9;
1983.13; 1987.5
death, RC1968.2; 1969.2;
1970.21; 1975.18;
1977.10; 1978.63;
1980.21; 1984.1;
ED1980.10; 1983.1;
1987.2; RD1967.7;
1968.26; 1972.25;
1973.7; 1975.19;
1978.24; 1979.16b,
31; 1980.21; 1983.2,
21, 30; 1985.51. See
also: dying,
mortality, suicide.
decision, RC1978.27;
ED1984.1; RD1972.22.
See also: choice,
judgment.
decomposition, RD1974.33
deconstructive poetics,
RD1985.25. See also:
Jacques Derrida,
poetics.
decoration, RD1983.17. See
also: ornamentation.
decreation, RC1980.32;
RD1976.3. See also:
creation,
disintegration.
dedication, RC1978.32. See
also: the
devoltional.
deep image, the, RC1986.11.
See also: image,
imagery, surrealism.
Defanti, Charles, RC1978.28
deferrals, RC1985.17
defiance, RC1981.17;
RD1979.22. See also:
struggle.
deficiency, ED1968.3. See
also: loss.
definition, RC1968.10;
1978.50; 1982.6;

1983.26. See also: description, self-definition.
Deguy, Michel, RC1968.12. See also: French writers.
de Kooning, Willem, RC1978.63. See also: abstract expressionism, artists, painters.
Dell Publishing Co., RD1983.13
De Loach, Allen, RC1972.20; 1981.7
Dembo, Lawrence Sanford, RC1972.15; 1983.8; ED1983.5; RD1966.3; 1972.25; 1983.5
democracy, ED1980.16; RD1970.7. See also: political systems.
democratic, the, RD1983.7
demon lover, the, RD1985.25. See also: mythological figures.
demonic, the, RD1944.1; 1956.4; 1969.9. See also: Satan.
DeMott, Robert J., RD1975.4; 1979.26
denotative, the, RC1973.29; RD1979.41. See also: language.
Dent, Peter, RC1983.28
de Planchard, Etienne, RC1975.7; ED1975.3
depression, RC1981.4. See also: despair, despondent.
depth, RD1963.2
derivative, the, RD1959.1; 1969.4; 1976.17; 1979.31, 34; 38; 1980.22-23; 1982.2, 24; 1983.6-7; 1985.5, 12, 38, 47. See also: imitation, parody.
derivative poet, Duncan as a, RD1969.1; 1974.33
Derrida, Jacques,

RC1982.31; RD1976.25. See also: deconstructive poetics, French writers.
Descartes, René. See: the Cartesian.
descent, RC1977.10
description, RC1964.1, 5; 1972.2; 1973.29; 1978.42; 1984.23; ED1981.3, 5; 1983.1. See also: definition, the mimetic.
descriptive, the, RC1976.30; 1981.15; ED1979.4
descriptive language: RC1976.30; ED1979.4. See also: language, prescriptive language.
desertion, 1968.10. See also: escape, isolation, renunciation, separation, withdrawal.
design, RD1976.3; 1983.30. See also: intention, pattern, purpose, the teleological.
desire, RC1972.2; 1974.17; 1978.4, 42; RD1978.39; 1980.17; 1981.18; 1982.2; 1983.21. See also: longing, love.
desolation, RD1985.25. See also: loss, the wasteland.
despair, RC1973.45; 1974.13; 1978.42; 1982.40; RD1981.18; 1983.21; 1985.25, 31. See also: depression, weeping.
despairing husband, the, RC1979.2. See also: marriage.
despondent, RC1971.20. See

444

divine law, RD1972.25. See also: the law.

divine order, RD1966.10. See also: order.

divorce, RC1977.10; 1978.42. See also: disaffection, marriage, relationships.

doctrine, RD1987.1. See also: dogmatic.

Dodsworth, Martin, ED1970.2

Dogan, Adele, RC1987.10

dogmatic, the, ED1984.1. See also: the didactic, doctrine.

dogmatism, RD1968.23; 1971.1

Doherty, Thomas, ED1983.2

domestic, the, RC1955.1; 1969.2; 1973.34; 1974.23; ED1961.4; RD1977.11; 1980.23, 1984.13. See also: the hearth, marriage.

domestication, RD1979.1

domesticity, RC1978.39

Donadio, Stephen, RC1966.13

Donkers, Jan, RC1966.6

Donne, John, RD1976.17. See also: British poets.

Donoghue, Denis, RD1965.2; 1970.6; 1984.6

Doolittle, Hilda. Use: H.D.

doom, RD1975.21. See also: apocalypse.

doors, RD1985.11. See also: house.

Dorfman, Elsa, RC1974.7

Dorn, Edward, RC1970.17; 1972.1; 1975.7; 1978.57; 1980.1-2, 15, 36; 1981.24; 1983.27; 1986.2; RD1965.3; 1978.26; 1980.9. See also: Black Mountain poets.

Dorn, Edward, works of. See Works of Edward Dorn index.

Dorn, Jennifer Dunbar, ED1972.6; 1983.3.

Used for: Jennifer Dunbar. See also: biographical information, wife.

Dorn, Louise Abercrombie, ED1974.4; 1978.8; 1983.1. See also: biographical information, family, mother, parents.

Dorsey, Willie, ED1981.11; 1983.1. See also: American Indian, Shoshoni Indians.

Dostoevskiĭ, Fedor Mikhailovich, RC1968.17; 1980.26-27

double vision, RD1967.16; 1978.35. See also: bifocalism, cross-eyed, the eye, vision.

doubt, RC1964.2; 1984.18. See also: belief, skepticism, uncertainty.

Doyle, Charles, RD1980.10; 1985.15

draft board, the, RD1983.13. See also: the Army.

drama, RC1968.17; 1973.23; ED1974.8; RD1969.9; 1970.3; 1976.4; 1987.9. See also: genre, performance of drama, the theater.

dramatic, the, RC1980.23; ED1978.8-9

dramatic narrative, ED1980.7. See also: narrative, genre.

Draves, Cornelia P., RC1973.23; 1974.8; 1987.5

drawing (verb), RD1971.1; 1974.30

drawings, RC1982.35; ED1983.1; RD1972.16; 1977.11; 1982.22; 1985.36; 1986.2. See

1981.24; 1982.18, 34,
39; 1983.9, 13;
1985.1, 10, 16. See
also: Black Mountain
poets, Epitaph,
Experimental Review,
Ritual, San Francisco
poets.
Duncan, Robert, works of.
See Works of Robert
Duncan index.
Dunn, Joe, RD1985.33
Dunn, Steve, RC1971.8
Duplessis, Rachel Blau,
RD1985.46
duration, RC1987.4
Durgnat Raymond, ED1970.4
Dutch, RC1966.6
dying, RC1981.1. See also:
death.
Dyke, E.F., ED1978.7

eagle, the, RD1969.9. See
also: animals, birds.
earth, the, ED1985.4;
RD1969.1; 1981.18.
See also: the
elemental, the
environment,
geography, mother
earth, the sun, the
world.
ease, RC1977.16
Eastlake, William, RC1983.6
Eastman, Julie, RC1981.9
Easy, Peter, RC1980.28
eccentric, the, ED1983.1
Eckman, Frederick,
RC1956.2; 1980.3;
RD1956.4. See also:
Golden Goose.
eclecticism, ED1961.4;
RD1971.3
economics, RC1984.10;
ED1977.6, 9; 1980.7;
1981.5, 11; 1983.1;
1987.3. See also:
commercialism, greed,
mercantilism,
political poetry,
poverty, trade,

wealth.
ecstasies, RD1984.22
ecstasy, RD1962.1. See
also: joy, rapture.
Edelberg, Cynthia Dubin,
RC1977.10;
1978.33-34; 1979.17;
1982.19; 1984.42
Eden, RD1977.9, 11;
1979.34. See also:
Adam figure,
Christian mythology,
creation, Eve, the
fall, garden,
paradise.
Edenic, the, RD1976.17
editor, work as, RC1969.7;
1970.32, 35; 1973.38;
1974.1; 1976.22;
1981.22; 1982.20;
1983.11, 25, 32;
1984.17; RD1965.9.
See also:
biographical
information, little
magazines,
publishers.
education, RC1985.12;
RD1974.1
egalitarianism, RD1979.26.
See also: elitism,
equality, political
systems.
Eggins, Heather, RC1981.12
ego, the, RC1968.10;
1970.22; 1972.3;
1973.12, 22; 1975.11;
1976.33; 1978.63;
1979.2; 1982.32;
1984.11; ED1960.2;
1974.3; 1978.7;
1980.4, 10; 1981.8,
13; 1985.1;
RD1972.18; 1975.19;
1977.11; 1979.10. See
also: "I," the id,
the identity, the
personal, the self.
egocentricity, RC1978.35
egoist, in Creeley's "I
Know a Man,"

Evans, Paul J.D., RD1975.19
evasion, RD1974.33
Eve, RD1966.2. See also:
    Adam figure, Eden,
    Christian figures,
    mythological figures.
event, RC1973.2; ED1983.10;
    RD1974.26; 1979.38;
    1980.17; 1982.22
Everson, Landis, RD1975.5
Everson, William,
    RD1971.14; 1974.15;
    1977.3; 1980.14;
    1983.13; 1985.21, 46;
    1986.1. Used for:
    Brother Antoninus.
    See also: San
    Francisco poets.
everyday, the, RD1984.17;
    1985.38. See also:
    the familiar, the
    local, the mundane,
    the quotidian; the
    trivial.
evil, ED1974.8; 1977.4;
    1978.11; RD1965.12;
    1971.4; 1972.18;
    1979.26, 39; 1980.24;
    1982.3; 1983.18, 32;
    1985.25. See also:
    corruption, the good,
    hell, morality,
    Satan, sin.
evolution, RD1972.15;
    1976.3; 1978.16. See
    also: Charles Robert
    Darwin, genetics.
evolving form, RC1977.2;
    RD1972.15; 1975.4;
    1976.3; 1977.2a;
    1983.24, 30. See
    also: conventional
    form, emerging form,
    form.
excluded third, the,
    ED1978.7. See also:
    logic.
exclusion, RC1966.20. See
    also: isolation,
    separation.
exhaustion, RD1979.31

existence, RC1978.35
existential, the, RC1984.26
existentialism, RC1973.34;
    1978.35, 63; 1980.14,
    28; 1984.33. See
    also: philosophy.
existential writers,
    RC1978.36. See also:
    Samuel Beckett,
    Albert Camus.
expansionism, RD1975.21
expectations, RC1981.15;
    RD1976.24. See also:
    intention.
experience, RC1972.21-22;
    1973.28, 29; 1974.29;
    1978.27, 44, 64, 67;
    1980.23, 32; 1981.30;
    1982.28; 1984.19, 37;
    1987.6; RD1964.1;
    1966.15; 1967.1. See
    also: innocence;
    life; participation
    in experience,
    treatment of;
    reality; reification.
experiential, the, ED1972.2
experimental, the,
    RC1982.45. See also:
    innovation,
    invention.
experimentalism, RC1982.28,
    47; 1983.15;
    RD1969.21; 1977.10;
    1979.27. See also:
    avant-garde.
experimental lyric, the,
    RC1980.28. See also:
    the lyric.
Experimental Review,
    RD1983.13; 1985.21.
    See also: Virginia
    Admiral, Robert
    Duncan, Sanders
    Russell.
experimentation, RD1961.2;
    1974.33; 1977.2a
explication, RC1954.1;
    1964.7; 1966.19;
    1967.2; 1968.1, 21,
    23; 1971.13; 1973.5;

1977.2; 1978.4, 29,
53, 69-70, 72;
1979.23; 1980.18;
1981.24; 1982.1;
1983.33; 1985.13;
ED1974.3; 1981.13;
RD1970.17; 1971.3, 6;
1974.28; 1980.26;
1981.16; 1983.1. See
also: New Criticism.
exploration, ED1981.15. See
also: John Ledyard,
Álvar Núñez Cabeza de
Vaca, Marco Polo.
explorative, the,
RC1980.13. See also:
discovery.
exposure, RC1975.18
expression, RC1978.27;
ED1985.3; RD1985.25.
See also: voice.
expropriation, ED1983.1.
See also:
acquisition.
extension, RD1985.5
exterior, the, RC1983.26;
ED1981.11. See also:
the interior, the
world.
exteriority, RD1980.17. See
also: interiority.
external, the, RC1975.18;
ED1972.2; 1983.1;
1985.4; 1987.2. See
also: the internal,
the outer, the world.
eye, the, RC1972.9;
1978.42, 53, 67;
1980.27; 1984.39, 40;
ED1983.1. See also:
bifocalism,
cross-eyed, double
vision, sight.

Faas, Ekbert, RC1976.18;
1977.11; 1978.35-38;
1980.16-17; 1983.11;
1984.17; RD1976.13;
1977.4; 1978.21-25;
1980.15-16; 1983.13;
1984.1

Fabilli, Lillian, RD1966.4;
1983.13
Fabilli, Mary, RD1960.3;
1983.13
fables, RC1962.1. See also:
Buddhist fable,
fiction, genre, myth.
fabulous, the, RC1980.18
facile, the, ED1985.3;
RD1985.25
factuality, RD1979.8. See
also: actuality, the
empirical,
objectivity, truth.
Fahs, Ned C., RD1983.13
failure, RC1969.2; 1971.13;
1976.34; RD1983.35.
See also: loss.
Fairchild, Hoxie Neale,
RD1968.15
fairies, RD1979.20. See
also: mythological
figures.
fairy figures, RD1977.11
fairy tales, RD1964.7;
1977.11. See also:
myth, nursery rhymes.
faith, RD1980.24. See also:
belief.
Falck, Colin, 1967.15
fall, the, RD1971.6. See
also: Eden.
familiar, the, RC1978.36.
See also: the
everyday, the
quotidian, the
unfamiliar.
family, the, RC1973.23, 32;
1976.9; 1980.26;
1984.39-40;
RD1974.22; 1977.11;
1983.13. See also:
Aunt Bernice, Aunt
Fay, biographical
information,
children, Ann
Creeley, David
Creeley, Genevieve
Jules Creeley, Helen
Creeley, Oscar Slate
Creeley, Penelope

femininity, RD1969.1;
1974.33; 1977.11;
1983.2
Fenollosa, Ernest
Francisco, **RC**1987.10
Ferrini, Vincent,
RC1962.14; 1973.4,
16; 1980.27; 1987.10
fertility, RD1979.22
Ficino, Marsilio,
RC1973.34; RD1972.15.
See also:
philosophers.
fiction, RC1968.18;
1973.29, 38; 1975.5;
1976.25, 33;
1978.35-36; 1981.22;
1982.28, 37; 1984.14;
1986.10. See also:
fables, fantasy,
genre, myth, the
novel, prose, the
short story.
fictional, the, ED1980.8
fictive, the, RC1963.8;
1980.18; RD1982.3;
1983.15
fictive self, the,
RD1973.7; 1975.3-4.
See also: the
persona, the self.
fictive voice, the,
ED1974.1; 1980.7;
RD1974.4. See also:
voice.
fictive world, the,
RD1979.8. See also:
the world.
field, the, RC1978.39;
ED1978.11; 1983.1;
1985.4; RD1968.15;
1970.17; 1973.7, 23;
1974.3, 33; 1975.4;
1977.11; 1979.14, 39;
1980.5, 16; 1981.10,
16; 1981.18. See
also: landforms, the
meadow, the open
field.
field composition,
RC1968.10; 1970.22;

1971.21; 1973.26;
1978.4, 32, 39, 42,
63; 1980.22, 27;
1982.39; RD1966.15;
1967.1; 1969.6;
1971.1; 1972.15, 21,
25; 1973.25; 1974.33;
1976.17, 20, 27;
1977.16; 1978.24;
1979.14, 19, 26;
1980.16-17, 21;
1981.2, 10, 16, 18;
1982.22-23; 1983.10,
18-19; 1987.3. See
also: Black Mountain
poetry, collage
method, conventional
form, ensemblism,
Charles Olson, open
poetry, organic
poetry, the poetic
field, projective
verse,
proprioception.
field poetics, RD1979.4
fifteen years between
collections (Duncan).
See: publication of
collection.
fights, RC1968.26; 1983.27;
1985.3. See also:
argument, beating of
Duncan by homosexual,
disaffection,
struggle.
figurative, the, RD1985.38.
See also: the
literal.
figures. See: the female
figure, historical figures,
male figures,
mythological figures.
figures, variety of, in
Dorn's *Slinger*,
ED1972.1; 1974.1;
1980.7; 1981.5;
1985.1. See also:
characterization,
characters,
personalities,
voices.

1986.6; RD1983.13.
See also:
biographical
information,
neighbors,
relationships.
friendship, RC1965.14;
1969.2; 1978.53;
1984.18; RD1985.23.
See also:
companionship.
frivolous, the, ED1972.4.
See also: the
trivial.
Frost, Robert, RC1967.27;
1984.20. See also:
New England
tradition.
frustration, RD1983.35
fulfillment, RC1972.2. See
also:
self-fulfillment.
function, ED1985.3
function words, RC1977.23.
See also: word use.
Funk, Robert W., RD1968.20
Furth, Pauline, RD1979.18
fury, RD1979.22. See also:
rage, wrath.
futility, RC1967.4;
1978.42; RD1972.25.
See also:
helplessness, hope.
future, the, ED1985.3;
RD1968.20. See also:
the past, the
present, time.

Galassi, Jonathan,
RD1973.18
gaps, RD1980.6. See also:
junctures.
ganjha. See: marijuana.
García Lorca, Federico,
RC1980.18; RD1966.6;
1972.10; 1974.5;
1976.14, 17; 1977.11;
1983.2, 13; 1985.25.
See also: duende,
surrealism.
garden, the, RC1971.21;

RD1974.3; 1979.34.
See also: Eden, the
plant.
gardener, the, RD1971.6
Gardner, Thomas Michael,
RD1982.12; 1985.28;
1986.8
Gassire, figure in Duncan's
Passages sequence,
RD1979.39; 1980.23.
See also:
characterization.
Gathering of Poets at
Louisiana State
University (1984),
RD1985.34
gay community, the,
RD1983.2. See also:
community, cult,
homosexuality.
Geddes, Gary, RC1973.17
Géfin, Laszlo, RC1979.19;
1982.21; RD1979.19;
1982.13
Gelpi, Albert J., RC1984.3;
1985.9; RD1967.7;
1985.13; 1986.9
gender, RD1985.30. See
also: the female, the
male.
gender codes, RC1985.17
generality, RD1984.17
generalization, RC1968.2;
1973.29; 1981.15;
ED1985.3. See also:
abstraction, the
mental, technique.
genesis, RD1975.4. See
also: beginnings,
creation.
genetics, ED1987.2. See
also: evolution.
genre, RC1982.31. See also:
allegory, antilyric,
autobiography,
comedy, concrete
poetry, drama,
dramatic narrative,
the epic, epigrams,
epithalaium, erotica,
essays, fables, fairy

16-20; ED1972.5;
RD1982.7, 9; 1985.37;
1987.7
Haller, Robert A., RC1982.4
Halter, Peter, RC1982.23
Hamalian, Linda, RD1983.17
Hamburger, Michael,
RC1970.22; RD1970.12
Hamilton, R.S., RD1985.30
Hammond, John Greer,
RC1964.7; 1973.29;
1975.12; RD1973.19
Hammond, Mac, ED1984.2
Handbook of American
Indians North of
Mexico. See:
Frederick W. Hodge,
Handbook of American
Indians North of
Mexico.
Hardy, Thomas, RC1979.28;
1984.26, 35
harmony, RC1984.1;
RD1969.19; 1972.18;
1976.20; 1977.9, 11;
1983.23, 30. See
also: discord,
dissonance, music,
polyphony.
Harris, Daniel A.,
RC1963.16
Harris, Mary Emma,
RC1987.8; RD1987.9
Harrison, Ford Carl,
RC1970.5; RD1970.13
Harrison, Jane, RD1972.15
Harrison, Jim, RD1968.18
Harrison, Lou, RD1972.13;
1979.23. See also:
composers.
Harryman, Carla, RC1985.11
Harsanyi, N., RD1974.33
Harte, Barbara, RC1969.5;
RD1969.3
Harvard, RC1968.17; 1971.1;
1973.9, 13, 23, 32,
38; 1976.22; 1978.26;
1979.9; 1984.15;
1984.42. See also:
The Wake.
Haskell, Dennis, RD1977.8

Hass, Robert, RC1984.21-22;
RD1984.16
hate, RC1978.39; RD1985.25,
30; 1987.8. See also:
anger, emotion, love,
rage, self-hatred,
the vindictive,
wrath.
Hatlen, Burton, RC1985.1;
RD1979.24; 1985.2;
1986.10
Havelock, Eric, RC1983.26
Haven, Richard, RD1977.9
Hawkes, John, RC1984.42;
1987.11
Hawley, Robert, RD1986.15
Hawthorne, Nathaniel,
RC1969.2. See also:
New England
tradition.
Hayes, Frederick Philip,
RC1978.23, 42;
RD1978.27
Hayman, Ronald, RD1970.14
Hazel, Robert, ED1962.2
H.D., RC1971.2; RD1966.4;
1968.5, 9; 1969.5;
1972.15, 25; 1973.4;
1974.23, 31; 1975.21;
1976.17, 25; 1977.11;
1980.16; 1981.18;
1982.22; 1983.13, 32;
1985.2, 19, 25, 30.
Used for: Hilda
Doolittle. See also:
The H.D. Book (in the
Works of Robert
Duncan index),
modernism.
head, the, RC1973.29. See
also: the body.
health, RD1985.43. See
also: biographical
information, blood
pressure, illness.
Hearst Street house in
Berkeley. Use: "New
Athens."
heart, the, RC1973.29. See
also: the body.
hearth, the, RD1979.14;

465

medium, the poet as; messangers, role in creative process; the muse.

instinctive, the, RD1972.25. See also: the intuitive.

instinctual, the, RD1971.6

insufficiency, RC1977.16

insulation, ED1983.1

insult, use of, ED1985.3. See also: the rhetorical, style.

integration, RC1984.1; ED1980.10; RD1976.25; 1985.49

intellect, the, RC1977.10; 1983.26; ED1985.3; RD1972.19; 1983.30. See also: the mental.

intellection, RC1973.34; 1984.1, 25

intellection, poetry as, ED1978.11. See also: creative process.

intellectual, the, ED1970.4; 1985.3

intellectualization, RC1972.21-22; 1978.48. See also: the mind, thought.

intellectuals, ED1981.15

intelligence, the, RD1968.31

intensity, RC1968.26; 1982.47. See also: style.

intention, RC1951.1; 1954.3; 1964.4; 1966.14; 1967.11-12; 1968.10, 27; 1970.15; 1971.8; 1973.8; 1974.21, 23; 1978.42, 67; 1980.23, 26; 1982.32; 1984.1; ED1968.2; RD1953.1; 1962.1; 1964.17; 1968.13; 1970.12; 1972.19, 22; 1974.30; 1976.22; 1978.18; 1979.19, 30; 1980.5,

11, 27; 1982.22; 1983.11, 30-31; 1985.2-3, 11, 18, 21, 30, 41; 1987.3. See also: creative process; design; discovery; emerging form; expectations; improvisation; preconception, role of; purpose.

interaction, RD1982.3; 1987.3

interconnectedness, RD1978.40; 1980.23; 1983.30. See also: interrelatedness.

interior, the, RC1983.26; ED1981.11. See also: the exterior.

interior monologue, the, RC1980.28. See also: style.

interiority, RC1975.10; 1983.26; ED1983.1; RD1980.17. See also: exteriority.

internal, the, ED1972.2; 1983.1. See also: the external, the inner.

internalization, RC1970.3

international, the, ED1977.6

International Poetry Festival in Toronto (1981), RD1983.33. See also: Canada.

interrelatedness, RD1980.29; 1983.18-19. See also: interconnectedness, the multiphasic.

interrogative, the, RC1980.18. See also: the conjectural, the propositional, the question, the rhetorical.

interruptions, RC1984.37; RD1964.17. See also: the accidental,

Manus, character in Creeley's The Island, RC1969.7. See also: characterization.

manuscripts, RC1967.26; 1973.38; 1976.2; 1978.17; 1980.5; 1982.33; 1983.2; 1987.11; ED1976.1; 1980.2; RD1976.1; 1978.3, 20; 1980.4-5, 33; 1985.14, 42; 1986.2. See also: biographical information, illuminated manuscripts, notebooks, the typescript.

Many, the, ED1980.10. See also: the One, personalities, plurality.

maps, RD1974.17. See also: geography, location.

March on the Pentagon (1967), RD1968.6. See also: biographical information, politics, protest, Vietnam War.

Marcus, Steven, RC1952.2

Marge, character in Creeley's The Island, RC1976.34. See also: characterization.

margins, RD1982.15; 1984.10. See also: boundaries, limits, thresholds.

Mariani, Paul Louis, RC1978.52; 1981.20; 1984.24

Marie, Odile, RD1978.35

marijuana, RC1968.1, 26; 1978.47; 1982.35. See also: drugs.

Marisol, RC1976.20; 1978.25, 63; 1980.18; 1983.13; 1984.38. See also: artists, sculpture.

Marisol. See: Jose Ramon Medina, Marisol.

Marks, Saul, RD1974.17. See also: printers.

Marlatt, Daphne, RC1983.25; RD1972.17. See also: Canadian poets.

Marovitz, Sanford E., RD1975.4

Marowski, Daniel G., RC1986.9

marriage, RC1964.9; 1967.2, 4; 1968.2; 1969.2; 1972.2; 1973.38; 1976.15, 34; 1977.10; 1978.42, 53, 65; 1979.2-3; 1981.2; 1982.15, 19; 1984.18; RD1977.11; 1983.13. See also: the despairing husband, divorce, the domestic, husband, monogamy, relationships, wife.

Martien, Norman, ED1971.4

Martin, John, RD1974.17. See also: Black Sparrow Press.

Martin, Robert Kessler, RD1978.31; 1979.33

Martz, Louis L., RC1969.15

Marx, Karl, RC1973.35; RD1971.1; 1980.24

Marxist approach, RC1974.12

masculine, the, RD1977.11. See also: man.

masculinity, RD1969.1; 1983.2. See also: chauvinism.

mask, the, RD1979.1

Maslow, Ellen, RC1966.20

Massachusetts. See: Boston; Gloucester; Harvard; West Acton; WMEX.

Master of Rime figure, the, in Duncan's The Structure of Rime sequence, RD1972.15; 1977.11. See also:

characterization.
mastery, RD1979.34. See
also: craftsmanship,
power.
material, the, RD1980.17.
See also: the object,
the physical.
materiality, RD1975.20
Matheson, William,
RC1978.17
Mathis, Mary S., RD1986.12
matrix, the, RD1980.32
matters, RD1976.24
Matthias, John, RD1983.22
Matthiessen, F.O.,
RC1973.13
Matuz, Roger, RC1986.9
Maud, Ralph, RC1966.23;
1970.28; 1975.17;
1978.58-59; ED1981.9;
RD1966.12; 1970.15;
1975.22; 1978.32-33;
1979.32; 1981.13
Mazzaro, Jerome, RC1970.27;
1973.27, 34; 1980.24;
1983.26; RD1983.23
Mazzocco, Robert, RD1965.10
Meachen, Clive, RD1984.20
meadow, the, RD1971.6;
1972.15, 22; 1974.4;
1977.11; 1980.4-5,
32; 1981.18; 1983.22;
1987.3. See also: the
field, landforms.
meaning, RC1969.2; 1978.12;
1980.14; 1982.31;
ED1977.8; 1983.1;
1987.3; RD1964.5;
1974.30; 1977.2a;
1980.29; 1982.12;
1987.3. See also:
coherence,
communication,
referentiality,
signification,
themes, truth.
meanings, layers of,
RD1982.22. See also:
the multiphasic, the
polysemous.
measure, RC1962.14;

1963.13; 1964.4;
1966.15; 1968.16;
1972.17; 1973.19;
1974.17; 1978.25, 52,
67; 1980.18, 32;
1982.2, 32; 1983.26;
1984.1, 10-11;
1987.9; RD1972.25;
1973.6; 1984.10;
1985.38. See also:
distance; locate, to;
meter; proportion;
the relational;
scale; scansion;
size.
media, the, ED1978.6. See
also: film, movies,
popular culture, the
radio, television.
mediation, RD1977.11
medieval, the, RD1964.17;
1971.3; 1974.33. See
also: the past, the
Renaissance.
Medina, José Ramon,
Marisol, RC1983.13
meditation, ED1966.4;
RD1981.18. See also:
observation, thought.
medium, the poet as,
RD1970.19; 1978.24.
See also: creative
process; guides of
the poet;
inspiration;
messengers, role in
creative process; the
muse; Poetry, in the
service of;
visitations.
mediumistic, the, RD1979.31
melodic, the, RD1966.15
melodic form, RD1972.15.
See also: form,
musical forms,
structure.
melody, RC1966.14; 1983.24;
RD1966.10; 1978.24;
1979.1, 34. See also:
music.
melos, RD1979.34

Mnemosyne, RD1979.39;
1985.38. See also:
the muse,
mythological figures,
memory.
Model of the Brain. See:
John Zachary Young,
Model of the Brain.
Modern American Poetry
Conference at
Polytechnic of
Central London
(1973), RD1973.26.
See also: England.
modern poets, RD1975.19
modernism, RC1978.4, 44;
1981.15; 1984.5;
1987.9; RD1957.2;
1974.32; 1978.10;
1979.36; 1980.17, 27;
1982.2; 1983.13, 24;
1985.2-3, 9, 47;
1987.3. See also:
Basil Bunting, Hart
Crane, e.e. cummings,
T.S. Eliot, Ford
Madox Ford, H.D., The
H.D. Book (in the
Works of Robert
Duncan index), James
Joyce, Franz Kafka,
D.H. Lawrence,
literary movements,
Henry Miller,
Marianne Moore, Anaïs
Nin, George Oppen,
postmodernism, Ezra
Pound, Carl Rakosi,
Gertrude Stein,
Wallace Stevens,
William Carlos
Williams, William
Butler Yeats, Louis
Zukofsky.
modernist poetry,
RD1980.17. See also:
postmodernist poetry.
modernist tradition, the,
RD1982.2. See also:
tradition.
modifiers, RC1977.23. See

also: word use.
Molesworth, Charles,
RC1984.26; RD1983.24
moment, the, RC1978.39. See
also: time.
momentary, the, RC1963.4;
1983.16
momentous, the, ED1969.3
Monett, Missouri, RC1968.23
money, RC1981.22; 1982.35;
1985.15. See also:
poverty, wealth.
Monk, Thelonious,
RC1984.35. See also:
composers, jazz,
musicians.
monogamy, RC1984.18. See
also: marriage.
Monsieur Teste, character
in Valéry's Monsieur
Teste, RC1977.10;
1983.26.
montage, use of, RD1972.15.
See also: collage
method, technique.
Montana, ED1974.8
moon, the, RC1972.18;
ED1985.4; RD1977.11;
1982.12. See also:
stars.
Moon, Samuel, RC1966.21;
1978.53
Moore, Marianne, RC1976.22;
1980.28; ED1975.7;
RD1967.16; 1983.17.
See also: modernism.
Moore, Richard, RC1978.54;
ED1978.12; RD1983.13
moralism, RC1970.5
morality, RC1960.2;
1967.16; 1970.3;
1978.27; 1980.18;
ED1985.10; 1986.2.
See also: the
ethical, evil, the
good, immorality.
Moramarco, Fred, RC1987.9
Morgan, Edwin, RC1976.28
Morgan, Stuart, RD1976.24
Morice, David, RC1980.10.
See also:

1978.32; 1981.18;
1982.47; RD1966.3,
15; 1971.4; 1972.11;
1973.7; 1974.29-30;
1975.4, 9; 1976.14;
1977.11; 1979.23, 39;
1981.7; 1982.22;
1983.30; 1984.26. See
also: avant-garde
music, composers,
contemporary music,
counterpoint, the
dance, dissonance,
harmony, jazz, the
lyre, melody,
musicians, the piano,
the rhapsodic,
romantic music, song.
musical, the, RC1984.31;
RD1961.4; 1975.4;
1977.11; 1979.23;
1980.10; 1983.2;
1984.22
musical forms, use of,
RD1976.22; 1978.7.
See also: form,
melodic form, sonota
form, structure,
symphonic form.
musicality, RC1973.26;
RD1969.24
musical phrase, the,
RD1972.15. See also:
the phrase.
musical structure, the,
RD1979.34; 1985.14.
See also: form,
structure.
musical version of
Creeley's poetry.
See: Steve Swallow,
Home.
musical version of Duncan's
"Up Rising: Passages,
25." See: "Peace
Piece Two: 'Passages,
25' by Robert
Duncan."
musicians, RC1973.27;
1978.55; 1982.40. See
also: composers,

Thelonious Monk,
music, Charlie
Parker.
mutability, RC1967.4. See
also: change.
mutation, ED1981.15;
1985.4; 1987.2. See
also: transformation.
muthos, RD1981.18. See
also: myth.
mystery, RC1979.4;
RD1972.15; 1979.11,
30; 1981.18; 1983.13;
1985.47. See also:
the enigmatic, the
occult.
mystical, the, RC1978.42;
RD1944.1; 1972.15;
1974.4; 1975.4;
1985.34. See also:
the visionary.
mysticism, RD1959.1;
1962.2; 1966.3;
1967.12; 1969.16, 25;
1970.1; 1971.19;
1973.17; 1979.33, 37;
1983.17; 1985.11;
1986.10. See also:
William Blake, Jakob
Böhme, Gershom
Gerhard Scholem.
myth, RC1971.21; 1973.29;
1976.19; 1980.22;
ED1980.10; 1983.1;
RD1958.2; 1963.2;
1966.8; 1967.1, 7;
1968.12-14, 20;
1969.1, 16; 1970.1,
22; 1971.4, 6;
1972.3, 7, 15, 25;
1973.22; 1975.1, 4-5,
19, 21; 1976.3-4, 17,
22; 1977.11, 16;
1978.16, 40; 1979.1,
10-11, 34, 38-39;
1980.17, 21, 24, 27,
32; 1981.18;
1982.3-4; 1983.22,
24, 35, 37; 1984.11,
17, 32; 1985.9, 25,
38; 1986.13; 1987.12.

the story, technique.
narrative, the, RC1980.18,
27; 1982.40; 1985.17;
ED1980.7; 1981.5;
1982.4; RD1969.6. See
also: dramatic
narrative, plot.
narrative codes, ED1982.4
narrative frame, RC1982.19.
See also: framing.
narrative line, the,
ED1971.7
narrative poetry, ED1972.1;
1974.8. See also:
genre.
narrative time, RC1970.21.
See also: linearity.
narrative voice, the,
ED1965.1. See also:
point of view, voice.
narrator, the, RC1966.21;
1968.2; 1978.35;
1980.9; 1982.35
nation, the, RD1968.24;
1981.16. See also:
America, empire, the
state.
National Educational
Television,
RC1978.54; ED1978.12;
RD1984.30. See also:
television.
nationalism, RD1975.21. See
also: America.
National Poetry Award, the,
RD1985.22, 39, 46.
See also: poetry
awards.
natural, the, RC1978.39;
1982.19; RD1971.4;
1977.9; 1983.30. See
also: the organic.
natural order, the,
RD1966.10; 1970.6.
See also: order.
nature, RC1972.2; 1973.29;
1974.23; 1976.19;
1982.19; 1983.26;
1985.19; 1987.6;
ED1967.2; RD1969.19;
1971.6; 1973.3;

1976.3; 1978.40;
1979.34; 1982.15;
1986.4. See also: the
organic, the
teleological.
Navero, William, RC1974.19;
1978.55; ED1974.7;
RD1974.26
necessity, RD1983.14
necessity, figure in
Duncan's "Santa Cruz
Propositions,"
RD1978.16. See also:
characterization.
negation, RC1983.14;
ED1978.7. See also:
nullity.
negative, the, RC1983.1
negativity, ED1985.4
Neidhardt, Jane E.,
RC1986.9
neighbors, RC1980.27;
1981.22. See also:
biographical
information, friends.
Nelson, Cary, RD1981.16
Nelson, Rudolph Lorens,
RD1969.17; 1971.15
Nemerov, Howard, RC1966.14;
1973.24; RD1966.10;
1973.15
neologisms, RC1977.23. See
also: word use.
Neoplatonism, RD1969.1;
1972.15; 1974.23;
1983.32. See also:
the ideal,
philosophy,
Platonism.
Nerval, Gérard de,
RD1967.6; 1969.13,
15; 1970.11; 1971.6;
1977.6, 25; 1982.2;
1983.12. See also:
French writers.
nervous breakdown,
RD1983.13. See also:
biographical
information, illness,
psychology.
net, the, RD1977.2a;

1985.25. See also:
tapestry.
N.E.T. Use: National
Educational
Television.
neurosis, RC1978.36. See
also: illness,
obsession,
psychology.
New American Poetry,
1945-1960, The
(1960), RC1961.4;
RD1961.4; 1971.5;
1974.12; 1983.10;
1985.2, 41. See also:
Donald Merriam Allen,
anthologies.
"New Athens" (2029 Hearst
Street, Berkeley,
California),
RD1983.13. See also:
biographical
information, house.
New College of California,
the, RD1983.16;
1984.29; 1985.41
New Criticism, the,
RC1966.7; 1974.23;
1978.44, 66-67;
1983.31; RD1974.30;
1981.18; 1983.6, 13;
1985.27. See also:
academic poetry, T.S.
Eliot, explication,
literary
establishment, the
objective
correlative, John
Crowe Ransom.
New Directions in Prose and
Poetry, no. 13
(1951), RC1952.2;
1985.15; 1987.10. See
also: James Laughlin,
little magazines.
New England, ED1971.3. See
also: America.
New England tradition, the,
RC1978.39. See also:
American poetry,
American tradition,

Emily Dickinson,
Ralph Waldo Emerson,
Robert Frost,
Nathaniel Hawthorne,
Herman Melville,
Henry David Thoreau,
tradition, Walt
Whitman.
New Hampshire, RC1968.26;
1972.14; 1973.32, 38;
1978.26, 67; 1983.30;
1987.10-11. See also:
Dartmouth's library,
Holderness School,
Littleton.
new left, the, RD1987.1.
See also: politics.
New Mexico, RC1976.9;
1982.9. See also:
Albuquerque, Santa
Fe.
New Mexico Highlands
University RC1970.7
New Mexico Quarterly,
RC1987.11. See also:
little magazines.
Newton, J.M., ED1966.4
New Writing in the U.S.A.
(1976), RC1983.25.
See also:
anthologies.
New York City, New York,
RC1967.13; 1982.35;
ED1961.2; 1981.7;
RD1983.13; 1985.21,
25
New York painters,
RC1974.23. See also:
abstract
expressionists,
painters.
New York poets. See:
American poetry, John
Ashbery, Imamu Amiri
Baraka, Carol Bergé,
Bill Berkson, Diane
di Prima, Kenneth
Koch, Gerard Malanga,
Frank O'Hara, Ed
Sanders, Anne
Waldman.

New York State: See: Bard
College, Brockport,
Buffalo, Contemporary
Voices in the Arts,
COSMEP Conference,
State University of
New York at Buffalo,
WBAI, Woodstock.
New York State Council on
the Arts, RC1967.7
New Zealand, RC1976.10;
1983.31; RD1977.2b.
See also: the
University of
Auckland, the world.
Nichol, bp, RC1983.25;
RD1987.3. See also:
Canadian poets.
Nicosia, Gerald, RC1982.34;
1983.27; RD1982.19;
1983.25
Niedecker, Lorine,
RC1983.28
Nietzsche, Friedrich
Wilhelm, RC1980.18;
RD1979.33. See also:
philosophers.
Nietzschean humor,
ED1983.6. See also:
humor.
night, the, RD1979.34. See
also: the dark, the
day.
Nin, Anaïs, RD1969.18;
1972.10; 1977.11;
1978.21; 1979.17;
1983.13. See also:
disaffection with
Duncan, modernism.
nobility, RD1974.33. See
also: dignity.
Noël, Bernard, RD1978.35.
See also: French
writers.
Noel, Daniel C., RD1983.26
nomadic, the, ED1978.11.
See also: the
wanderer.
nonhuman, the, RD1966.1.
See also: the human.
nonlinear, the, RD1968.18.

See also: linearity.
nonsense, RC1962.1;
ED1981.15. See also:
the rational.
nonsense literature,
ED1981.15. See also:
dadaism.
Norris, Kenneth Wayne,
RC1980.25; 1984.28;
RD1976.18; 1977.12;
1980.25; 1984.21
North Carolina. See: Black
Mountain College.
Northeast Harbor, Maine,
RC1973.14
Norwegian, RC1974.27
notation, RC1975.10;
RD1968.6; 1970.8;
1974.17; 1981.6;
1982.10; 1984.10;
1985.32, 47, 50. See
also: performance,
relationship to
poetry; spacing;
typewriter;
typography.
notebooks, RC1981.13;
1982.33; ED1978.6, 8;
RD1971.10; 1972.10;
1973.7; 1978.21;
1979.14; 1980.5;
1983.6, 13; 1986.2.
See also: diary;
journal, Creeley's
personal;
manuscripts.
nothingness, RC1972.2;
1973.34. See also:
emptiness, nullity,
the void, zero.
nouns, RC1977.23. See also:
proper nouns, word
use.
novel, the, RC1951.1;
1973.39; 1981.22. See
also: fiction, genre,
prose, the short
story.
Novik, Geraldine Mary,
RC1972.23; 1973.9-10,
36-38; 1979.26;

RD1973.24

nullity, RC1962.1. See
also: negation,
nothingness, void,
zero.

numbering of Duncan's
Passages sequence,
RD1964.10

numbers, relationship to
structure. Use:
numerical structure.

numbers, sense of,
RC1973.19; 1978.36;
RD1972.18. See also:
zero.

numbers, treatment of,
RC1977.10; 1978.42

numbers, use of, RC1971.21;
1972.2; 1976.28;
1978.42; 1981.13;
1984.38; RD1981.9.
See also: five, zero.

numen, the, RD1968.13. See
also: the divine, the
numinous.

numerical structure,
RC1976.7; 1978.62;
1984.38; 1986.12. See
also: quantity,
relationship to
structure; structure;
triadic structure.

numinous, the, RC1980.18;
RD1968.2; 1975.4;
1977.2a; 1980.29. See
also: the divine, the
numen.

Núñez Cabeza de Vaca,
Álvar, ED1980.7. See
also: exploration.

Nurmi, Ruth, RD1975.3

nurse voice, the,
RD1977.11. See also:
voice.

nursery animals, RD1977.11.
See also: animals.

nursery rhymes, RD1977.11.
See also: fairy
tales; the Wynken,
Blynken, and Nod
boat.

Oates, Joyce Carol,
RC1976.29

obedience, RD1966.3-4, 15;
1972.18; 1976.3, 20;
1979.34; 1980.6. See
also: the law;
permission; Poetry,
in the service of.

Oberg, Arthur, RC1972.24;
1977.16; 1978.56

Obermeyer, Ray, ED1972.1.
See also: artists.

object, the, RC1972.2;
1973.2; 1984.1;
RD1978.40; 1980.17;
1983.6. See also: the
material, the subject.

objectification, RC1972.25;
1980.22; 1982.32;
1983.26; 1984.18;
RD1972.22. See also:
projective verse,
proprioception,
reification.

objective, the, RC1970.1;
1974.23; 1978.50;
1980.22, 27; 1983.26;
1984.1; ED1981.5;
RD1966.1; 1980.27.
See also: the
empirical, the outer,
the physical,
reality, the
subjective, the
world.

objective correlative, the,
RC1978.50. See also:
T.S. Eliot; the New
Criticism.

objectivism, RC1970.34;
1978.4; 1980.22;
1984.1; RD1979.8

objectivity, RC1973.34;
1977.11; 1980.26;
1982.32; 1984.1;
ED1984.1. See also:
factuality,
subjectivity.

objects, RC1968.10;
1974.17; 1978.7, 29;
1984.10; 1987.6;

Rahv, Philip, RC1966.13
railroad, the, ED1980.7;
    1981.11. See also:
    aircraft, the
    automobile.
Rajnath, RC1984.31
Rakosi, Carl, RD1983.28;
    1986.10. See also:
    modernism.
Raleigh, Sir Walter,
    RD1977.11. See also:
    British poets.
random, the, RC1962.8;
    1981.15. See also:
    chance.
Random House, RC1981.22
Ransom, John Crowe,
    RC1980.27; 1981.22;
    RD1979.27; 1980.5;
    RD1983.13; 1985.20.
    See also: <u>Kenyon
    Review</u>, the New
    Criticism.
rapture, RD1980.21. See
    also: ecstasy.
Rasula, Jed, RC1982.39;
    1984.32; RD1979.38;
    1982.23; 1983.29;
    1984.23. See also:
    L=A=N=G=U=A=G=E
    poets.
ratiocinative, the,
    ED1980.4. See also:
    reason, thought.
rational, the, RC1973.29;
    1977.10; RD1969.1;
    1972.22; 1973.19;
    1983.24. See also:
    irrational, nonsense,
    reason.
rationalism. See:
    antirationalism.
rationality, RD1961.1
Raworth, Tom, RC1966.8;
    ED1986.4. See also:
    British poets.
Ray, David, ED1970.5;
    1975.6; 1980.12;
    1985.6; RD1975.23
reader, the, RC1977.2;
    ED1986.2; RD1980.27.

See also: audience.
reader, the ideal,
    RD1972.10. See also:
    audience, the ideal.
reader participation. Use:
    participation of
    reader.
reading (the poets'
    personal reading),
    RC1968.17; 1971.7-8;
    1972.8, 10; 1973.8,
    23; 1976.15; 1978.19,
    63, 67; 1979.8, 12;
    1980.12, 27, 31;
    1981.22; 1984.14, 15,
    42; 1986.6; 1987.3,
    10-11; ED1964.1;
    1972.5; 1978.8;
    1979.9; 1980.16;
    RD1963.4; 1964.5, 7;
    1965.7; 1966.8;
    1968.5, 12, 19;
    1969.5-6, 8-9, 11;
    1971.1, 10; 1974.2,
    19; 1975.17; 1977.11;
    1978.15, 40;
    1979.16a, 20;
    1980.14, 27; 1982.8,
    19; 1983.6-7, 10, 13,
    17, 22; 1985.2, 16.
    See also:
    biographical
    information,
    influence on subject
    authors.
reading, treatment of,
    RD1980.27
reading poetry aloud. Use:
    poetry reading.
real, the, RC1980.22;
    RD1976.14; 1977.11;
    1983.31. See also:
    the actual, the
    authentic, the ideal,
    the unreal.
reality, RC1962.1; 1968.10;
    1976.34; 1978.44;
    1979.19; 1981.13;
    1984.31; ED1978.7, 9;
    1980.11; RD1978.5.
    See also: the

21
romantic poets, RC1979.17;
RD1955.1. See also:
William Blake, George
Gordon Byron, Samuel
Taylor Coleridge,
E.T.A. Hoffman, John
Keats, the poet,
Percy Bysshe Shelley,
William Wordsworth.
romantic tradition, the,
RC1981.2. See also:
tradition
rooms, RC1968.2; RD1977.11;
1982.12. See also:
house, treatment of
the.
rootlessness, RC1981.12.
See also: the
wanderer.
roots, RD1971.6. See also:
the plant, the tree.
rose, the, RD1973.7;
1981.16; 1983.30. See
also: flower imagery.
Rose, Bob, ED1976.5
Rosenmeier, Henrik,
RD1978.37
Rosenthal, Macha Lewis,
RC1958.1; 1963.18;
1964.10; 1967.23;
1973.42; 1975.18;
RD1959.1; 1967.12;
1970.17; 1972.10;
1984.33
Ross, Jean W., ED1980.16
Rothenberg, Jerome,
RC1962.12; 1981.27;
1986.11; ED1986.3;
RD1986.13
Roumanian. Use: Rumanian.
Rousseau, Henri, RD1975.3.
See also: artists,
painters.
Rowell, Henry T., RD1968.24
Rudman, Mark, RD1983.31;
1985.49
Rukeyser, Muriel, RD1948.3;
1983.13
Rumaker, Michael,
RC1978.65; RD1974.19;

1978.38. See also:
Black Mountain
writers.
Rumanian, RC1974.11, 26;
ED1974.5; RD1974.21,
33
Rupert, character in Dorn's
Slinger, ED1985.4.
See also:
characterization,
Howard Hughes,
Robart.
Ruppert, Jim, RC1985.19
rural, the, RD1977.9. See
also: the city, farm
life.
Russell, Sanders, RD1960.3;
1966.6; 1975.19;
1983.13; 1985.21. See
also: <u>Experimental
Review</u>.

sacramental, the,
RD1983.22. See also:
religious.
Sacramento, California,
RD1983.13
sacred, the, RD1975.4. See
also: religion.
sadism, RD1972.15. See
also: cruelty, pain.
sadomasochism, RD1983.13.
See also: pain, sex.
Salt Lake City, Utah,
ED1962.1
salvation, RD1976.14. See
also: Christ,
redemption, religion,
resurrection.
San Francisco, California,
RC1968.17, 26;
1979.17; ED1975.3;
RD1970.3; 1971.8;
1972.2; 1978.22, 38;
1980.5; 1984.12, 31;
1987.9. See also:
Poetry Center of San
Francisco.
San Francisco literary
scene, RC1975.7;
ED1980.16; RD1964.17;

self-consciousness,
RC1978.61; 1981.15;
1983.26; 1984.26;
ED1980.4; 1981.5;
1983.1; RD1977.2a.
See also:
consciousness.
self-creation, RD1970.6;
1973.25; 1975.4;
1981.18; 1982.12. See
also: creation.
self-creation, poetry as,
RD1973.25. See also:
creative process.
self-criticism, RD1979.30.
See also: criticism.
self-deception, RD1985.25;
1987.8
self-definition, RC1970.27;
1978.73; RD1985.25.
See also: definition.
self-destructiveness,
RC1973.47. See also:
the destructive,
suicide.
self-evaluation, ED1985.3
self-examination, RC1962.1,
4; 1964.2; 1967.23;
1970.19; 1971.21;
1975.18
self-fulfillment,
RD1985.25. See also:
fulfillment.
self-hatred, RC1969.2. See
also: hate.
self-identity, RC1968.10;
1982.32; 1987.6. See
also: identity.
self-indulgence, RC1973.44;
RD1980.21
self-involvement,
RC1970.20; RD1969.25.
See also:
introversion,
narcissism.
self-knowledge, RD1984.17.
See also: knowledge.
self-parody, RC1968.15;
1978.4. See also:
imitation, parody.
self-realization,

RD1977.2a; 1982.12
self-reflection, RC1987.6.
See also:
introspection, the
reflective.
self-reflexive, the,
RC1978.70; RD1977.2a.
See also: the
reflexive.
self-revelation, RC1978.2.
See also: nakedness,
revelation.
senses, treatment of the,
RC1982.32. See also:
the aural, the
sensory, sight.
sensibility, RD1975.7
sensory, the, RC1976.34.
See also: the senses.
sensual, the, RC1981.15;
RD1967.1; 1976.14;
1983.2. See also: the
erotic, the physical,
the spiritual.
sentence, the, RD1972.15;
1976.3; 1985.38. See
also: the conjectural
sentence, the phrase,
syntax.
Sentence, the, figure in
Duncan's The
Structure of Rime
sequence, RD1972.25,
1985.38. See also:
characterization, the
law.
"sentence," use of the
word, RD1980.5. See
also: word use.
sentences, use of,
RC1980.18; 1983.15;
1985.15. See also:
technique.
sentimental, the, RC1984.1;
ED1981.15; RD1967.12;
1972.10. See also:
emotion.
sentimentality, ED1981.15
separateness, RC1977.23.
See also: isolation.
separation, RC1972.2;

the William Carlos
Williams
Commemorative
Centennial
Conference.
University of Wales at
Aberystwyth, the,
RD1973.14
University of Wisconsin at
Madison, the ED1986.4
unpoetic, the, RD1979.26.
See also: the
antilyric.
unpredictability,
RD1987.12. See also:
accidental.
unreal, the, RD1977.11. See
also: the real, the
surreal.
"USA: Poetry" series for
National Educational
Television,
RC1978.54; ED1978.12;
RD1984.30. See also:
television.
Utah. See: Salt Lake City.
utopian, the, RD1985.27.
See also: city, the
ideal.
utterance, RC1966.21. See
also: the spoken.

vagueness, RC1965.2;
1968.22. See also:
ambiguity.
Valéry, Paul-Ambroise,
RC1977.10; 1979.14;
1983.26; 1987.11. See
also: French writers.
Vallejo, César. See: César
Vallejo, Selected Poems, in
the Works of Edward
Dorn index.
value, RC1972.2; 1978.7,
44; 1987.9; RD1973.3.
See also: importance,
significance.
Vance, Eugene, RD1964.17
Vancouver, British
Columbia, RC1971.1;
1974.25; 1976.26;

1978.67; 1983.25;
RD1968.2; 1970.5, 19;
1974.32; 1975.12;
1976.6; 1980.25. See
also: Canada.
Vancouver Poetry Conference
(1963), RC1963.9;
1964.2-6; 1966.24;
1968.5; 1975.3-17;
1982.45; RD1963.3;
1964.1, 14-15;
1966.13; 1968.2;
1975.11, 22; 1987.3.
Used for: Vancouver
Poetry Festival. See
also: Canada.
Vancouver Poetry Festival.
Use: Vancouver Poetry
Conference.
Vancouver poets, RC1972.21;
1974.25; 1976.31;
1980.25; 1985.2;
RD1972.19; 1974.32;
1976.18; 1985.4. See
also: George
Bowering, Canadian
poets, Frankland
Wilmot Davey, Dave
Dawson, Brian
Fawcett, Stan Persky,
Tish, Frederic Wah.
Van Gogh, Vincent,
ED1976.3. See also:
artists, painters.
Varela, Willie, RD1977.26
Vas Dias, Robert, RC1968.23
vatic, RD1979.34. See also:
the bardic, the
prophetic voice, the
shaman, the
visionary.
vegetable, the, RD1983.32.
See also: the plant.
vegetative, the, RD1971.6.
See also: the
organic.
vegetative myths, RD1971.6;
1977.11. See also:
myth.
Venus, RD1984.17. See also:
the female figure,

mythological figures.
verbs, RC1977.23. See also:
  word use.
Verheggen, Jean-Pierre,
  RD1978.35
vernacular, the, RC1952.3;
  1959.4; 1963.4;
  1964.16; 1968.16;
  1971.21; 1974.23;
  1980.23; 1981.15;
  ED1979.4; 1979.11;
  RD1970.7; 1979.26;
  1981.18; 1982.24. See
  also: American
  speech, diction, the
  colloquial, common
  language, the
  idiomatic, slang,
  word choice.
Vernon, John, RC1978.70;
  1979.29
victims, ED1977.9. See
  also: political
  poetry, the poor,
  social criticism.
Victoria, ED1980.7. See
  also: American
  Indian.
victory, RD1984.17. See
  also: struggle.
Vietnam War, the,
  RC1973.39; ED1983.2;
  1985.1; RD1968.2, 6,
  26; 1969.14, 16, 25;
  1971.15; 1972.18, 25;
  1975.7, 21; 1977.9,
  11; 1978.26; 1979.30;
  1980.21, 23; 1982.1,
  12; 1983.30, 32-33;
  1985.4; 1986.8;
  1987.1, 8. See also:
  Cao Dai cult,
  political poetry,
  politics, protest,
  war.
View, RD1983.13. See also:
  Charles Henri Ford,
  little magazines.
Villa Grove, Illinois,
  ED1978.4
Vincent, Sybil Korff,

RC1977.23
vindictive, the, ED1983.6.
  See also: hate.
Vinson, James, RC1970.9;
  1975.1; 1980.6;
  1983.3; 1985.5;
  ED1970.5; 1975.6;
  1980.12; 1985.6;
  RD1970.21; 1975.23;
  1979.37; 1980.10;
  1983.27; 1985.15
violence, RC1960.2; 1962.1;
  1969.16; 1981.2;
  RD1953.1; 1981.16.
  See also: cruelty,
  destruction,
  struggle, war,
  weapons.
virgin figure, the,
  RD1983.22. See also:
  female figures.
virtuosity, RD1967.12. See
  also: craftsmanship.
visible, the, RC1966.4. See
  also: sight.
vision, ED1983.1; RD1963.1;
  1964.13; 1967.1;
  1968.31; 1971.6;
  1972.25; 1976.24;
  1977.11; 1985.25. See
  also: double vision,
  revelation, sight.
visionary, the, RD1962.1;
  1969.16; 1982.3;
  1985.25. See also:
  the bardic, the poet
  as prophet, the
  prophetic voice, the
  mystical, the shaman,
  the vatic.
visionary exegesis,
  RD1980.27. See also:
  ta'wil.
visionary poetry, RD1970.11
visionary poets, the,
  RD1975.4
visitations, RD1980.5. See
  also: dreams; guides
  of the poet; medium,
  poet as; messengers,
  role in creative

Wales. See: the University
of Wales at
Aberystwyth, the
world.
Walker, Jayne L., RD1979.41
walking, RC1968.2; 1969.3.
See also: driving,
stumbling.
wanderer, the, RC1975.18;
ED1981.11. See also:
the drifter figure,
male figures, the
nomadic, the
outsider,
rootlessness, the
searcher figure, the
stranger, travel.
war, ED1981.5; RD1971.6;
1972.18; 1975.19, 21;
1976.14; 1977.6, 11,
14; 1979.10, 39;
1980.1, 4, 23;
1981.16, 18; 1982.3;
1983.13, 30-31;
1985.2, 7, 9, 12, 31;
1987.1. See also:
Alexander the Great,
Korean War, peace,
political poetry,
religious war myth,
strife, struggle, the
Vietnam War,
violence, World War
II.
Ward, Geoffrey, ED1976.9;
1977.8
Waring, Richard, RC1981.29
war poetry, RD1979.39;
1985.50. See also:
genre, political
poetry, protest.
Warren, Kenneth, RC1980.36;
ED1980.14
Washington, D.C. See:
College of Preachers,
the March on the
Pentagon.
Washington State, ED1972.7
Washington University (St.
Louis, Missouri),
RC1973.38; 1982.33

Washington University
Libraries (St. Louis,
Missouri), RC1967.26;
1985.14; RD1967.15;
1985.42
wastage, RD1973.7
wasteland, the, RD1977.11.
See also: desolation.
water, RC1967.4; 1971.21;
1978.42, 61; 1984.18.
See also: the
elemental, the
fountain, weeping,
wetness.
Watten, Barrett, RC1973.49;
1985.24; RD1980.2;
1984.5, 14-15, 18-19,
25, 27, 29-30. See
also: L=A=N=G=U=A=G=E
poets.
WBAI, radio station in New
York, RC1963.17;
ED1963.2. See also:
radio.
Wch Way, RD1982.10. See
also: little
magazines.
"we," ED1980.10. See also:
"I," pronouns,
"them," "you."
weakness, RC1987.9
wealth, ED1987.2. See also:
acquisition,
economics, money,
opulence, poverty,
power, profit.
weapons. See: the bow, the
revolver.
Weatherhead, Andrew
Kingsley, RC1967.27;
RD1967.16; 1975.27
weaving, RD1976.22;
1977.2a; 1983.11. See
also: the loom,
tapestry.
Webb, Jon Edgar, RC1963.20
Webb, Marilyn, ED1978.6;
RD1978.18
Webb, Phyllis, RD1987.3.
See also: Canadian
poets.

Weber, Alfred, RC1971.15
Weber, Robert Charles,
    RD1972.25; 1978.43
weeping, RD1968.13. See
    also: despair, water,
    wetness.
Weil, James L., RC1963.21
Weinberger, Eliot, ED1984.3
Weinstein, Norman,
    RD1983.36; 1986.6
Weiss, Renée, RD1975.18
Weiss, Theodore, RD1975.18;
    1985.54
Weissman, Judith, RD1982.5
Welch, Lew, RC1976.8;
    RD1971.14; 1980.31.
    See also: San
    Francisco poets.
Wellman, Don, RC1981.29
Wells, Merle W., ED1967.5
Wesling, Donald, RC1965.25;
    1971.23; 1985.25;
    ED1965.5; 1971.7;
    1977.9; 1980.15;
    1984.4; 1985.1-4,
    9-12; RD1971.21;
    1985.55
West, the ED1970.2; 1974.1,
    8, 13; 1980.3, 7;
    1981.1, 5, 13, 15;
    1982.1; 1984.2. See
    also: America.
West Acton, Massachusetts,
    RC1973.32
western, the, ED1978.8;
    1985.4. See also:
    genre, horse opera.
western culture, ED1983.1-2
western hero, the,
    ED1985.4. See also:
    the cowboy figure,
    the hero, male
    figures.
western tradition, the,
    RD1976.13. See also:
    tradition.
wetness, RC1978.11. See
    also: dryness, water.
Whalen, Philip, RC1975.17;
    1978.58; RD1975.22;
    1978.32. See also:

San Francisco poets.
Wheale, Nigel, ED1979.10-11
Wheaton, Walter Bruce,
    RC1980.37; RD1980.32
White, Derryll, ED1976.5
White, Tom. Use: Joel
    Oppenheimer.
White, William, RC1973.10,
    37
Whitebird, J., RC1978.24
white culture, the,
    ED1966.2; 1977.6;
    1980.7; 1983.1;
    1985.2. See also:
    American culture,
    American Indian,
    culture, political
    poetry.
white goddess, the,
    RD1976.15. See also:
    female figures, the
    goddess, Robert
    Graves, mythological
    figures.
Whitehead, Alfred North,
    RC1978.36, 40;
    1983.26; ED1980.10;
    1983.1; RD1960.3;
    1965.10; 1972.15;
    1973.7; 1974.19;
    1976.3; 1977.25;
    1978.24; 1979.8;
    1980.5, 23; 1982.22;
    1983.10, 18-19;
    1985.25; 1987.3. See
    also: philosophers,
    process.
Whiteman, Bruce, RC1981.28
White Rabbit Press,
    RD1985.33
Whitman, Walt, RC1968.24;
    1969.2; 1973.13;
    1976.25; 1978.61, 67;
    1982.47; 1983.26;
    1984.33; ED1968.4;
    1981.11; 1983.1;
    RD1965.2; 1968.19,
    24; 1969.1; 1970.7;
    1971.1, 6; 1972.22;
    1973.5, 7, 25, 28;
    1975.7; 1976.31;

1978.26, 36, 53, 56, 67; 1980.26; 1983.22; 1985.4, 15; 1987.3, 10; ED1960.1; 1963.2; 1974.8; 1978.13; 1986.4; RD1949.1; 1966.8; 1967.3; 1968.14, 19; 1969.18; 1972.10; 1973.25; 1974.22; 1978.24; 1979.1, 30; 1980.5; 1983.2, 10, 16; 1985.11, 21, 41. See also: creative process.

writing, treatment of, RC1984.33, 37; RD1963.6; 1977.11. See also: creative process, treatment of; poetry, treatment of; reading, treatment of.

writing block, RC1976.15; 1981.7; 1982.40; 1984.17

writing habits, RC1964.6; 1968.5, 17, 26; 1973.23; 1976.3; 1978.63; 1981.13; ED1978.8; RD1980.5. See also: typewriter, use of the.

WTIC, radio station in Hartford, RD1964.17. See also: radio.

Wyman, Carl, character in Dorn's *By the Sound*, ED1972.1. See also: characterization.

Wynken, Blynken, and Nod boat, the, RD1977.11. See also: nursery rhymes.

Yates, Peter, RC1959.6
Yeats, William Butler, RC1984.15; RD1977.25; 1983.10. See also: modernism.
Yip, Wai-Lim, RC1974.29
"you," use of the word,

RC1982.2. See also: "I," others, pronouns, "them," "we."
Young, John Zachary, *Model of the Brain*, ED1974.8
youth, RC1984.1; RD1977.11; 1985.25. See also: adolescence, age, childhood.

Zabriskie, Philip T., RD1968.20
Zavatsky, Bill, ED1976.10
zen, RC1973.28
zero, RC1978.36. See also: nothingness, nullity, numbers, void.
Zinnes, Harriet, RD1969.25
Zins, Céline, RC1972.11
Zlinger. Use: Slinger.
Zohar, the, RD1956.2; 1971.10; 1972.15; 1974.23; 1985.11, 34. See also: the Judaic, the Kabbalah, Gershom Gerhard Scholem.
Zolla, Elémire, RC1983.16; RD1983.32
Zukofsky, Celia, RC1980.31
Zukofsky, Louis, RC1958.2; 1965.24; 1966.2; 1969.1; 1971.2, 21; 1973.13, 23, 35; 1974.23; 1977.1, 10; 1978.15, 67; 1980.22, 31; 1982.47; 1984.1, 17; 1987.20; RD1956.3; 1964.17-18; 1969.8; 1971.1; 1973.7; 1974.30; 1977.11; 1978.10; 1979.24; 1980.21; 1983.30; 1984.14, 19, 30; 1985.2. See also: modernism
Zverev, Aleksei, RC1976.36; RD1976.31
Zweig, Paul, RD1968.31
Zwicky, Fay, RD1979.42